# Building on a Common Foundation

# Building on a Common Foundation

The Baptist Union of Scotland, 1869–2019

Brian R. Talbot

Foreword by David W. Bebbington

PICKWICK *Publications* • Eugene, Oregon

BUILDING ON A COMMON FOUNDATION
The Baptist Union of Scotland, 1869–2019

Copyright © 2021 Brian R. Talbot. All rights reserved. Except for brief quotations in critical publications or reviews, no part of this book may be reproduced in any manner without prior written permission from the publisher. Write: Permissions, Wipf and Stock Publishers, 199 W. 8th Ave., Suite 3, Eugene, OR 97401.

Pickwick Publications
An Imprint of Wipf and Stock Publishers
199 W. 8th Ave., Suite 3
Eugene, OR 97401

www.wipfandstock.com

PAPERBACK ISBN: 978–1-7252–9867–5

HARDCOVER ISBN: 978–1-7252–9868–2

EBOOK ISBN: 978–1-7252–9869–9

Cataloguing-in-Publication data:

Names: Talbot, Brian R., author. | Bebbington, David W., foreword writer.

Title: Building on a common foundation: the Baptist Union of Scotland, 1869–2019/Brian R. Talbot, with a foreword by David W. Bebbington.

Description: Eugene, OR: Pickwick Publications, 2021 | Includes bibliographical references and index

Identifiers: ISBN 978–1-7252–9867–5 (paperback) | ISBN 978–1-7252–9868–2 (hardcover) | ISBN 978–1-7252–9869–9 (ebook)

Subjects: LCSH: Baptist Union of Scotland | Baptists—Scotland—History | Baptists—History

Classification: BX6322.S36 T35 2021 (print) | BX6322.S36 (ebook)

Typeset by Anthony R. Cross.                Manufactured in the U.S.A.

To
David W. Bebbington,
whose personal encouragement, lectures
and numerous writings have inspired
the writing of this book.

# Contents

*Foreword by David W. Bebbington* | **ix**
*Acknowledgements* | **xi**
*Abbreviations* | **xiii**

1. Introduction | **1**

2. A Time to Advance, 1869–1889 | **19**

3. Branching Out with Confidence, 1890–1914 | **50**

4. The Valley of the Shadow: Scottish Baptists and the First World War | **85**

5. The Inter-War Years: Maintaining the Well-Trodden Paths, 1919–1939 | **117**

6. 'The Struggle for Spiritual Values': Scottish Baptists and the Second World War | **152**

7. Adjusting to a Changing World, 1945–1960 | **180**

8. Christian Witness in an Age of Religious Crisis: The 1960s and 1970s | **211**

9. Shoots of Recovery: The Baptist Union of Scotland, 1980–1994 | **245**

10. Changing Times: An Era of Transition, 1994–2009 | **278**

11. An Invitation to a Journey, 2009–2019 | **313**

12. Conclusions | **348**

*Bibliography* | **371**
*General Index* | **397**

# Foreword

How can we best do good to our fellow human beings? The question was asked by James Culross, who soon afterwards became minister of Adelaide Place Baptist Church, Glasgow, in his little book *The Home at Bethany* (1876). Contemporaries, he pointed out, might recommend their favourite policies, but according to Culross the suggested remedies were inadequate to transform those who had been degraded by sin. So people needed to be brought to Christ. 'You must tell them the old Gospel', declared Culross, 'which in times past has stirred all that is deepest in human hearts, and produced a new creation, and which is still the power of God unto salvation'. There was no substitute for 'Christ the Son of God and the Son of Man, Christ the Gift of the Father's love, Christ the Propitiation for sin, Christ the Mediator between God and men, Christ the Lord of the universe whom we are to worship and obey'.[1] This powerfully felt message was the central teaching of Culross, a distinguished late nineteenth-century Scottish Baptist.

James Culross, who had been made a Doctor of Divinity by his old university, St Andrews, in 1867, published a number of biblical expositions and popular biographies, all – like *The Home at Bethany* – dwelling on devotional themes. He had been brought up in a village near Blairgowrie, attending the Secession Presbyterian Church with its firm Calvinist beliefs, but at university had been drawn to Baptist convictions under the ministry of Francis Johnston, who preached on revivalist Arminian lines. Beginning a ministry at Stirling in 1850, Culross managed to synthesise the two theological styles, valuing confessions of faith but not replacing the Bible by a dogmatic system. He placed an emphasis not on controversy but on spirituality. Accordingly he was one of the prime movers in the Scottish Baptist Association which was set up in 1856 to draw together Baptists of varying doctrinal positions so as to strengthen weaker churches and prepare young men for the ministry. These objectives remained imperatives for Culross as he went on to serve in a London church (1871–78), at Adelaide Place (1878–83) and as principal of Bristol Baptist College, the oldest ministerial training institution in the denomination (1883–96). Before these later stages of his career and while still at Stirling, he was briefly the tutor for ministerial students under the aegis of the newly formed Baptist Union of Scotland (1869–71). With his zeal for the gospel, his devotional priority and his willingness to co-operate with others, James Culross embodied the spirit of the Baptist Union at its foundation and for much of its history.

When the Union was formed in 1869, as this book shows, its first aim was home missionary work. The task of spreading the gospel in Scotland had been

---

[1] James Culross, *The Home at Bethany: Its Joys, its Sorrows and its Divine Guest* (London: Religious Tract Society, 1876), pp. 118, 119.

a prominent feature of Baptist life since the preaching tours of Robert and James Haldane in the 1790s and remained a large part of the Union's work into the twenty-first century. The second aim, creating a common fund for giving financial aid to its member churches and encouraging the creation of new congregations, was largely transferred on the financial side to other agencies, but strategic church planting was a major concern during many phases of the Union's history. Although the third aim, the provision of theological education for ministerial candidates, became the work of the Baptist Theological College of Scotland from 1894, the Union continued to co-operate with the college in ministerial training. The fourth aim, assembling information about the state of the denomination and fostering co-operation between the associated churches, was fulfilled in a great variety of ways over the years, expanding into social action and inter-church relations. The Union was to a large extent successful in bringing Baptists together. With a consistent concern for detailed evidence and a strong sense of the social and ecclesiastical context, Brian Talbot explains in this book the development of the Union together with its member churches over the hundred and fifty years of its existence. His analysis goes a long way towards demonstrating that throughout the period, as James Culross put it, 'the old Gospel . . . stirred all that is deepest in human hearts'.

David W. Bebbington
Professor of History, University of Stirling
*July 2019*

# Acknowledgements

I am very grateful to many individuals who in a variety of ways provided assistance to me in the preparation for and the writing of this book. I am thankful to the staff of the Baptist Union of Scotland for their encouragement on my many visits to Speirs Wharf to work in the Baptist Union history archive over the last five years. The largest proportion of the primary source documents used in this study is stored in that collection of Scottish Baptist historical records. I am grateful also for their assistance to the librarians at the Mitchell Library and at the University of Glasgow; the librarians at New College Library and the National Library in Edinburgh; and the librarian and archivist at the Angus Library, Regent's Park College, Oxford. I have also valued the assistance with materials and other support in my research from Neil Allison and Anthony R. Cross. I also appreciate all those individuals in different Scottish Baptist congregations who assisted with enquiries about their churches and who in a number of cases provided documents used in this study. I especially want to thank Douglas Hutcheon, Bill Slack and Alan Donaldson for providing written reflections on their time of service with the Baptist Union of Scotland that were particularly helpful as I wrote the last three chapters. In the course of writing this book I have given earlier drafts of book chapters as presentations at a number of conferences and especially at the Scottish Baptist History Project. I have greatly appreciated the feedback received from those present. In particular, I am deeply grateful to Derek Murray, David Bebbington and Ian Balfour who have read draft chapters of this book. These contributions have significantly helped to improve the work, though the author is solely responsible for any remaining errors in the text I am also appreciative of conversations with Jim Purves and Martin Hodson about this work, particularly about the writing of the more recent history of the Baptist Union of Scotland, and to our General Director Alan Donaldson for inviting me in 2014 to write this book, on the occasion of the 150th anniversary of the Baptist Union in 2019. I am also very thankful for the encouragement of Michael Haykin, during this and other writing projects, and Wipf and Stock's generous agreement for us to produce an earlier printing of this book by the Baptist Union of Scotland in time for the 150th anniversary of the founding of the Union.

I am also particularly appreciative of the support of my wife Kathryn in allowing me the time to work on this and other historical publications in recent years and the encouragement from our children Helen, Benjamin and Rachel as the project progressed. In addition, I want to thank my parents Herbert and Elizabeth Talbot for their keen interest in and support for my work. They have modelled for me both a consistent example in the home in my earlier years, together with exemplary Christian service in the local Baptist congregation where they have worshipped and worked over many years.

# Abbreviations

| | |
|---|---|
| ABTS | Arab Baptist Theological Seminary |
| ACTS | Action of Churches Together in Scotland |
| ATL | Advent Testimony League |
| BBC | British Broadcasting Corporation |
| BCC | British Council of Churches |
| BHMS | Baptist Home Missionary Society for Scotland |
| BMS | Baptist Missionary Society |
| BTCS | Baptist Theological College of Scotland |
| BUGB | Baptist Union of Great Britain |
| BUGBI | Baptist Union of Great Britain and Ireland |
| BUSY | Baptist Union of Scotland Youth |
| BUW | Baptist Union of Wales |
| BWA | Baptist World Alliance |
| BWL | Baptist Women's League |
| BZM | Baptist Zenana Mission |
| BUS | Baptist Union of Scotland |
| CARE | Christian Action Research Education |
| CE | Christian Endeavour |
| CIM | China Inland Mission |
| CMD | Continuing Ministry Development |
| CPD | Continuing Professional Development |
| DICR | Doctrine and Inter-Church Relations Committee |
| ELBA | Edinburgh and Lothians Baptist Association |
| EBF | European Baptist Federation |
| EBFBC | Evangelical Baptist Fellowship Bible College |
| FBB | Fellowship of British Baptists |
| GBA | Glasgow Baptist Association |
| IMB | International Mission Board |
| ICRTG | Inter Church Relations Task Group |
| JCC | Joint Consultative Committee |
| MAF | Missionary Aviation Fellowship |
| NBA | Northern Baptist Association |
| NHS | National Health Service |
| SACBA | Stirling and Clackmannanshire Baptist Association |
| SAM | Servants Aloft Ministries |
| SBA | Scottish Baptist Association |
| SBC | Southern Baptist Convention |
| SBLPA | Scottish Baptist Lay Preachers' Association |
| *SBM* | *Scottish Baptist Magazine* |
| SBTAS | Scottish Baptist Total Abstinence Society |
| SCC | Scottish Churches Council |

| | |
|---|---|
| WA | Women's Auxiliary to the Baptist Union |
| WCC | World Council of Churches |
| WEC | Worldwide Evangelisation Crusade |
| WIN | Witness, Involvement, Now |
| WW2 | World War Two |
| YMCA | Young Men's Christian Association |
| YPF | Young People's Fellowship |
| YWAM | Youth With A Mission |

CHAPTER 1

# Introduction

The religious climate, in which Baptists for the first time had sought to plant churches in Scotland, during the mid-seventeenth century, was anything but favourable towards this new initiative.[1] The Protestant Reformation under John Knox and his colleagues had inclined the majority of the population to accept a Presbyterian form of the Christian Church. By 1560 The Reformed Kirk was established in Scotland.[2] However, it is probable that it gained the support of the majority of the people only in the 1570s or at the latest by the 1580s, once they had become convinced that a Roman Catholic restoration was not going to happen.[3] It was, though, not until 1689 that a Presbyterian religious settlement, rather than an Episcopalian one, was finally confirmed in Scotland.[4] Presbyterian Scotland, however, was less than enthusiastic about the emergence of individuals holding beliefs associated with Baptist principles and practices. The basis for such jaundiced opinions being held owed more to the perception of some radical elements in the Continental Reformation, rather than a serious theological critique of mainstream Baptist theological views. For example, John Knox in his letter from Dieppe, France, 'To His Brethren in Scotland', dated 27 October 1557, condemns a number of opinions he termed heretical, including 'the rottin heresies of Arius and Pelagius'. He drew attention to their denial of the eternal Sonship of Jesus and Reformed teaching on Divine foreknowledge and election. In summary, he

---

[1] A detailed study of Baptists in Scotland prior to 1765 is Brian R. Talbot, 'Confronting the Powers': Baptists in Scotland prior to 1765', in Anthony R. Cross and John H.Y. Briggs (eds), *Freedom and the Powers: Perspectives from Baptist History* (Didcot: The Baptist Historical Society, 2014), pp. 35–64.

[2] A. Ryrie, *The Origins of the Scottish Reformation* (Manchester: Manchester University Press, 2006), p. 192.

[3] M. Lynch, 'John Knox, Minister of Edinburgh and Commissioner of the Kirk' in R.A. Mason (ed.), *John Knox and the British Reformations* (Aldershot: Ashgate, 1998), pp. 262–263. G. Donaldson, *The Scottish Reformation* (Cambridge: Cambridge University Press, 1960), pp. 203–224. I.B. Cowan, *The Scottish Reformation* (London: Weidenfeld and Nicolson, 1982), pp. 115–138.

[4] J.H.S. Burleigh, *A Church History of Scotland* (London: Oxford University Press, 1960), p. 153.

wrote: 'The rest of thair opinionis, maist horribill and absurd'. A footnote attached to this sentence noted that: 'The persons here alluded to, went under the general name of Anabaptists.'[5] The 1560 *Scots Confession*, Article XXIII 'To Whom Sacraments Apperteine' affirmed the appropriateness of infant baptism, prior to condemning the views of those who held to believers' baptism. 'And so we damne the error of the Anabaptists, who denies baptisme to apperteine to children, before they have come to faith and understanding.'[6] By associating all the minor sects and churches of the Radical Reformation together, Knox provides a blanket condemnation of them all, using the template of Reformed doctrine and Presbyterian ecclesiology as the basis on which to assess their claims. His approach would set a pattern that would be followed by other Scottish Presbyterians in the seventeenth and eighteenth centuries.

An example of a leading Presbyterian clergyman who followed this pattern was Robert Baillie (1599–1662). He was appointed Professor of Divinity in 1642 and later Principal (1660) of the University of Glasgow until his death in 1662.[7] Baillie was a Scottish commissioner at the Westminster Assembly. This gathering of church leaders was appointed to reform liturgy, discipline and government in the Church of England and to promote unity with other Reformed Churches in Scotland and Continental Europe.[8] He wrote his well-known book, *Anabaptism, The True Fountain of Independency, Antinomy, Brownisme & Familisme and the most of the other Errours, which, for the time doe trouble the Church of England,* in London in 1647. Baillie's forceful language and vivid prose was intended to inoculate Scottish Christians against having any sympathy for the ideas proposed by these alternative expressions of the Christian faith. Baillie was, though, normally one of the more conciliatory figures of his age, for example, concerning the differences between Episcopalianism and Presbyterianism,[9] but proponents of 'gathered churches' outside a parish system would never find favour with him.[10] His book

---

[5] D. Laing (ed.), *The Works of John Knox* (Edinburgh: Printed for the Bannatyne Club, 1855), Volume 4, pp. 269–270.

[6] *Scots Confession 1560 and Negative Confession 1581* (Edinburgh: Church of Scotland, 1937), p. 93.

[7] J.D. Douglas, 'Baillie, Robert (1599–1662)', in N.M. de S. Cameron (ed.), *Dictionary of Scottish Church History and Theology* (Edinburgh: T. & T. Clark, 1993), p. 51.

[8] S.B. Ferguson, 'Westminster Assembly and Documents', in Cameron (ed.), *Scottish Church History and Theology*, pp. 862–864.

[9] W. Makey, *The Church of the Covenants 1637–1651* (Edinburgh: John Donald, 2003), pp. 51–52, 92.

[10] Baillie's opposition to 'Anabaptists' and other Christian groups that he was convinced were growing in numbers at an alarming rate was a regular theme in his

*Anabaptism* was written specifically for the leading figures in the Scottish Church, rather than the ordinary people in Scotland, because the Church of Scotland General Assembly had put in place a strict censorship policy in December 1638. Strict controls on religious books printed in the country ensured that all works intended for publication had to obtain the approval of the clerk of the assembly and advocate for the Kirk, Sir Archibald Johnston of Warriston.[11] In August 1643 the General Assembly had ordered ministers 'especially . . . upon the coasts', to 'search for all books tending to separation'. All such works and their distributors were to be referred to local presbyteries to 'hinder the dispersing thereof'.[12] By 1647 as a result of the increasing debates between Independents and Presbyterians, the General Assembly passed an Act to prohibit the printing, importing or distribution of literature 'maintaining Independencie or Separation, and from all Antinomian, Anabaptisticall, and other erroneous books and papers.'[13] The reason for these increasingly strict measures was the serious alarm raised by the Scottish Commissioners to the Westminster Assembly, in the light of what they had witnessed in London. They were intended to prevent 'the errours [which] . . . have (in our neighbour kingdome of England) spread as a gangraen' from causing similar distress in Scotland.[14] In the 1640s such literature was intended to prevent the start of a Baptist witness in Scotland, but in the following decade there would be a significant change of the religious environment that would allow for Baptist pioneers to begin a work in this country.

The legacy of hostility towards Baptists and other smaller Christian Churches in Scotland was part of the battling for control of the Scottish Church by Roman Catholic, Episcopalian and Presbyterian Churches that had sought supremacy in the nation's ecclesiastical affairs. The deliberate confusion of more moderate and mainstream Calvinistic (Particular) or Arminian (General) Baptists in the United Kingdom with Continental

---

correspondence with colleagues in Scotland. See D. Laing (ed.), *The Letters and Journals of Robert Baillie A.M.* (3 Vols; Edinburgh: Robert Ogle, 1842); for example, Vol. 2, pp. 117 (Dec. 1643), 157 (March 1644), 169 (April 1644), p. 191 (June 1644), p.215 (August 1644); Vol. 3, p. 289 (1655).

[11] T. Pitcairn (ed.), *Acts of the General Assembly of the Church of Scotland 1638–1842* (Edinburgh: The Edinburgh Printing and Publishing Company, 1843), p. 30.

[12] Pitcairn (ed.), *Acts of the General Assembly,* pp. 75–76. This injunction was repeated in 1647, which presumably meant it had not been enforced adequately in previous years, p. 160.

[13] Pitcairn (ed.) *Acts of the General Assembly,* p. 160.

[14] Pitcairn (ed.) *Acts of the General Assembly,* p. 160.

Anabaptists[15] was not only an issue in the seventeenth and eighteenth centuries, but, remarkably, a few examples can be found as late as the nineteenth century as well. For example, Sydney Smith, a High Church Episcopalian from Edinburgh, wrote a series of articles on 'Indian Missions' for the *Edinburgh Review* in 1808. In his April 1808 contribution, he wrote at length about the Baptist Missionary Society (BMS) and its work in India, but insisted on referring to the 'Anabaptist Society for Missions' and 'Anabaptist missionaries'[16] and ridiculing their 'pernicious and extravagant' theological convictions.[17] In context, he was particularly criticizing their promotion of believers' baptism and teaching that the 'Great Commission' of Matthew 28:18–20 was a duty incumbent upon Christians in every generation. Smith was not the only individual at that time to use such language with reference to Baptists. The last known usage in writing of 'Anabaptist' as a term of abuse against Baptists in Scotland was by Coll MacColl, a Roman Catholic clergyman. He was a convert to that Church from a Church of Scotland background on the island of Tiree. His father and grandfather had been parish ministers. Coll MacColl made reference to Baptists in a letter to Roman Catholic Bishop Andrew Scott in Greenock on 10 July 1838. In this context, he was deeply unhappy that the Proprietor of Lochalsh in the Western Highlands of Scotland was distributing copies of a new translation of the New Testament in the local community. He informed the Bishop that he had advised his parishioners to either

> send them back or burn them for tho they will not lose their Religion by the many errors of that Translation . . . yet they will inevitably acquire the Twang and Cant of the Baptists and Anabaptists of the Highlands, much owing to that half HibernoScotian translation, particularly of the New Testament.[18]

The examples above were exceptions to the changing perceptions of Baptists in Scotland that became increasingly accepting of their presence in the country in the second half of the eighteenth century. Certainly as the nineteenth

---

[15] See Toivo Pilli, 'Anabaptists', in J.H.Y. Briggs (ed.), *A Dictionary of European Baptist Life and Thought* (Milton Keynes: Paternoster, 2009), pp. 10–11; and F.L. Cross and E.A. Livingstone (eds), *The Oxford Dictionary of the Christian Church* (2nd ed.; London: Oxford University Press, 1974), pp. 47–48.

[16] Sydney Smith, 'Indian Missions', *Edinburgh Review*, Vol. 12, April 1808 (Edinburgh: Archibald Constable, 1808), pp. 158, 162.

[17] Smith, 'Indian Missions', *Edinburgh Review*, April 1808, p. 180.

[18] Scottish Catholic Archives, Oban Letters 1/25/6. Rev. Coll MacColl, Morar, to Bishop Andrew Scott, Greenock, 10 July 1838. See also Alasdair Roberts, 'Coll MacColl (1787–1842): Son of the manse and Highland priest', *West Highland Notes and Queries*, 3, 26 (October 2014), pp. 13–23. I am grateful to Alasdair Roberts for drawing my attention to this reference and supplying this information.

century progressed there was a broader toleration and acceptance of a wider range of interpretations of the Christian faith.[19] By the time of the launch of the 1869 Baptist Union of Scotland, its members and adherents were viewed by other Evangelical Protestants as fellow travellers advocating similar Christian convictions.

The first Baptist churches in Scotland began in the 1650s, in the Commonwealth era, at a time when greater religious freedom allowed both Arminian and Calvinistic Baptists associated with the New Model Army the opportunity to spread their Baptist convictions in a previously inhospitable religious environment.[20] After a few short years of prosperity, the restrictions of former years were re-imposed in the late 1650s by the Government. The public witness of Baptists in Scotland ceased[21] until the founding of the church in Keiss by William Sinclair in 1750[22] and the re-emergence of Baptists in the Central Belt of Scotland in 1765.[23] It was, then, from that

---

[19] The welcome presence of Scottish Baptist representatives at the formation of the Evangelical Alliance in 1846 was confirmation of their embrace by paedobaptist Reformed Evangelicals at that time. One of those Baptists present, James Haldane, had earlier recorded his impressions of moves to launch this body in June 1845. See Alexander Haldane, *Robert and James Alexander Haldane* (Edinburgh: Banner of Truth Trust, 1990 [1853]), pp. 658–659.

[20] Talbot, '"Confronting the Powers": Baptists in Scotland prior to 1765', pp. 35–64; See also the wider background of that era in Scott Spurlock, *Cromwell and Scotland: Conquest and Religion 1650–1660* (Edinburgh, John Donald, 2007). Matthew Bingham has questioned the use of the term 'Baptist' in the seventeenth century, as anachronistic usage. Matthew Bingham, *Orthodox Radicals* (Oxford: Oxford University Press, 2019), pp. 8–11. In Scotland, although the label 'Anabaptist' was most commonly used by opponents, it is still fair to use the term 'Baptist' as a less inadequate alternative term, although it is accepted that the individuals in question would not fit neatly with the generic Baptist label used today. However, given the diversity in the world Baptist family at the present time it would still be necessary to provide qualifying statements to explain how, for example, Baptists in the former Soviet Republic of Georgia who adopted the clerical vestments and liturgical style of the state Orthodox Church and Independent Baptists in the USA could both still self-identify as 'Baptists'.

[21] Spurlock, *Cromwell in Scotland*, pp. 173, 184–197; however, there were examples of individual Baptists living in Scotland between 1660 and 1765, see Talbot, '"Confronting the Powers': Baptists in Scotland prior to 1765', pp. 59–64.

[22] Christine Lumsden, *A Rich Inheritance: Sir William Sinclair and Keiss Baptist Church* (Didcot: Baptist Historical Society, 2013).

[23] Brian R. Talbot, *Search for a Common Identity: The Origins of the Baptist Union of Scotland, 1800–1870* (Carlisle: Paternoster Press, 2003), pp. 29–72; see also Derek B. Murray, 'The Scotch Baptist Tradition in Great Britain', *Baptist Quarterly*, 33.4 (1989), pp. 186–198.

point in time, that the evidence clearly shows the continuous history of Baptist churches in Scotland.

The vast majority of Baptist congregations founded in the remaining years of the eighteenth century were of the Scotch Baptist tradition. At the end of that century, there were around 400 members and 1000 adherents in their churches.[24] Their name was chosen to distinguish them from 'two classes of Baptists in England, known as the General or Arminian and Particular or Calvinistic Baptists . . . they differ materially from both bodies above named in their views of the Gospel, and especially in regard to church order.[25] In addition to a plurality of elders in church leadership, this body was recognised as being more rigorous than other Baptist traditions in the exercise of church discipline with respect to its members. However, one of the most distinctive features of their churches was an attempt to follow as closely as possible to the pattern of life found within the Early Church. William Jones, one of their key leaders in London explained their position:

> They also hold it their indispensable duty to follow entirely the pattern of the primitive apostolic churches, as recorded in the New Testament, and to attend to all the directions given to them, which they consider to be inseparably connected with genuine love to the truth, and steadfastness and liveliness in the faith and hope of the gospel . . .[26]

In practice, they sought unanimity when making decisions or changing the way they operated, but as the number of their congregations grew throughout mainland Britain it became ever more difficult to maintain this approach to corporate decision making and led in time to some damaging splits in their ranks. However, there was a degree of flexibility in certain issues, for example, concerning their willingness to cooperate in supporting the overseas mission work of English Particular Baptists through the BMS.[27] After the first two decades of the nineteenth century, the majority of Scotch Baptists began to work more closely with other branches of the Baptist family in Scotland, especially in the work of home evangelisation.

---

[24] John Rippon (ed.), *The Baptist Annual Register* (London: Dilly, Button & Thomas, 1795), Vol. 2, pp. 373–374.

[25] Patrick Wilson, *The Origins and Progress of the Scotch Baptist Churches from their rise in 1765 to 1834* (Edinburgh: A. Fullarton, 1844), p. 3; J. Everson, 'The Scotch Baptist Churches', *The Christian Advocate and Scotch Baptist Repository*, 1.1 (March, 1849), p. 1.

[26] William Jones, 'A Compendious Account of the Principles and Practices of the Scottish Baptists', *The Theological Repository*, 4.23 (April, 1808), pp. 199–200.

[27] Rippon (ed.), *Baptist Annual Register*, 1795, Vol. 2, pp. 379–380.

A second network of Baptists in Scotland began in the 1790s. Members of this tradition were known as 'English' Baptists, that is, they followed the pattern of English Particular Baptist Churches in operating with a pastor and deacons' model of leadership. They had a stronger focus than the Scotch Baptists on evangelism. They experienced greater numerical growth, in both churches and membership figures, in the first few decades of the nineteenth century. This was the most efficiently organised network of Baptist churches. They utilised their limited financial resources effectively for home evangelisation, and were equally committed to work overseas. They were very committed to supporting theological education for prospective pastors, and prior to the formation of a theological institution in Scotland, sent students to train at Horton Baptist College, Bradford.[28] It was from their ranks that the vision of a Baptist Union of Scotland emerged and the most effective promoters of this cause were 'English' Baptists. The first President of the 1869 Union was Jonathan Watson, an 'English' Baptist who had consistently advocated for this cause since the late 1820s. It is clear that they were encouraged by the growing and effective witness of Particular Baptists in England whom they viewed as a sister denomination. The future pattern of church governance, approach to evangelism and commitment to the Baptist Union in the vast majority of Baptist churches in Scotland owed most to the understanding of Baptist identity articulated by the 'English' Baptists and modelled so effectively by their main leaders George Barclay of Irvine and Christopher Anderson in Edinburgh.[29]

A third family of churches then associated with Independency, (later known as Congregational Churches), under the leadership of Robert and James Alexander Haldane, came to adopt a Baptist view of the ordinance of Baptism and seceded from their former ecclesiastical family between 1808 and 1810. Many of these individuals had begun their faith journey in the Church of Scotland, but had felt obliged to leave the parish system due to pressures from the Moderate majority in the General Assembly who disapproved of their zeal for home evangelisation through the work of the Society for the Propagation of the Gospel at Home in the 1790s. There was also significant dependence on the financial resources of Robert Haldane, not only for funding theological training and church-planting initiatives, but also for some pastors' stipends and major contributions towards the cost of erecting suitable premises for some of the newly founded congregations. In a context of financial dependency, there was undoubtedly unspoken pressure to conform to the newer ideas that Robert Haldane in particular adopted in the first decade

---

[28] In the period 1806 to 1837 they sent twenty-two men to Horton Baptist College. *Northern Baptist Education Society Reports*, 1805–1805 to 1837–1838. See also for more details Talbot, *Search for a Common Identity*, pp. 147–150.

[29] 'English Baptists', in Talbot, *Search for a Common Identity*, pp. 115–152, 310.

of the nineteenth century that included believers' baptism, but also a range of other theological convictions about church governance. The Haldanes were also more committed to a generic form of conservative Evangelicalism that was seen in the effective work of Robert Haldane in Geneva and later in France, together with James' support for the work of the newly formed Evangelical Alliance in the 1840s.[30] Their followers, many of whom were very conscious of the need for collective funds to support not only home evangelisation, but also to aid struggling churches, were much more committed to the idea of forming a Baptist Union of Scotland.[31]

All three groups had their own mission agencies engaging in outreach work in Scotland in the second decade of the nineteenth century. However, financial struggles and recognition that pooling their resources would strengthen their collective witness caused each agency to reconsider its position in the 1820s. It led to the formation of the Baptist Home Missionary Society for Scotland (BHMS) in 1827.[32] The new agency prospered, quickly increasing the number of agents employed and the quantity of work accomplished. Up to 1827, there had been very limited interest in uniting Baptists in Scotland. However, that year was a turning point, as for the first time Scottish Baptists began to recognise that it was possible that they might accomplish more in spreading the good news of the Christian gospel together than separately. Commitment to the work of the BHMS in its home mission endeavours was at the heart of the Scottish Baptist collective identity from the late 1820s. Overwhelmingly, representatives of the different Baptist networks in the country were supportive of its work, even when some of them were less than convinced of the need for a Baptist Union. Although the Home Mission would later merge with the Union in the twentieth century, due to changing circumstances, it certainly united Scottish Baptists in the nineteenth century.[33]

The second major development that year was the founding of the first Baptist Union of Scotland, because of pioneering efforts to reach this goal by five members of Charlotte Chapel, Edinburgh, with the full support of their pastor Christopher Anderson. The early success of the united Home Mission

---

[30] Talbot, *Search for a Common Identity*, p. 89; James Haldane had been at the June 1845 meeting in Edinburgh to promote the formation of the Evangelical Alliance, but was not, though, one of the Scottish Baptist delegates at the follow up meeting in Glasgow on 5 August 1845. William Innes, Robert Kettle, Alex McLeod and James Paterson were the four Scottish Baptists present. See, *Free Church Magazine*, January to December, 1845, Vol. 2, (Edinburgh: John Johnstone, 1845), pp. 313–314.

[31] 'Haldaneite Baptists', in Talbot, *Search for a Common Identity*, pp. 73–114.

[32] 'The Baptist Home Missionary Society: A Substitute Union, 1827–1868?' in Talbot, *Search for a Common Identity*, pp. 153–159.

[33] Details of the ongoing work through this mission agency are given in 'Baptist Home Missionary Society: A Substitute Union, 1827–1868?' pp. 153–190.

pointed to the probable wisdom of taking this second step of united witness. Forty-five per cent of the Baptist churches in Scotland became members of the new body, including members of all three existing networks of Baptist churches. This step, however, was more difficult to accomplish successfully because the Scotch Baptist Churches had a much more rigid structure and found it extremely difficult to agree to any changes in working practices. They were also much more particular than the other two groups in watching over the theological convictions of the men who preached in their pulpits. This Union would founder by 1830, primarily over the difficulties caused by one congregation in the new Union, on one occasion, having a visiting preacher who had been suspected of holding Arminian tendencies. Although the issue was resolved, it highlighted the fact that members of the new union had different undeclared expectations for how it would operate in practice.[34]

Although to the great disappointment of many of the participants, the first attempt at arranging a collective witness had failed, it did not take away the need that many in its ranks had felt for such a body. This was particularly the case by the small Perthshire Baptist congregations that had depended up the financial support they had received from the Haldane brothers in earlier years. These churches were the prime movers behind the launch of the Scottish Baptist Association (SBA) that existed between 1835 and 1842. Unfortunately, the larger Baptist churches in Scotland, with few exceptions, chose to remain outside this body and it struggled to continue its work. There was a lack of visionary leadership in the SBA at that time to articulate clearly enough the reasons why a collective witness was important for Baptist

The situation changed in 1842 when a young Baptist minister called Francis Johnston joined the SBA and was appointed as its Secretary. He drew up a clear statement of what this agency stood for and articulated a clear vision for evangelism, church-planting and the mutual support of the churches, together with the necessity of providing theological education for prospective ministers. Johnston proposed changing the name of this body from the SBA, to return to the earlier 'Baptist Union of Scotland'. The inspirational leadership offered by Johnson in the early 1840s, and his associated vision for mission, resulted in a steady trickle of additional Baptist congregations in Scotland affiliating with the new Baptist Union of Scotland (BUS). Johnston had a particular passion for urban church-planting, where the majority of the unreached population of Scotland lived. He was convinced that the Baptists in Scotland had been too focused on evangelistic work in the Highlands and Islands and remoter communities of Scotland, at the expense of the towns and cities of the country. Johnston persuaded many colleagues that the BHMS would take care of these traditional areas of mission and the new Union, by contrast, would focus on the under-churched urban communities. The clarity

---

[34] 'The Attempts to Form a Baptist Union of Scotland', 1827–1842, in Talbot, '*Search for a Common Identity*', pp. 191–212, 354–357.

of his vision and the charisma with which he promoted it led to high expectations of future growth of both Baptist witness in Scotland, together with the effective ministry of the Baptist Union.[35]

Unfortunately, in the later 1840s Johnson was convinced that the Union would be more effective in its evangelistic work if it adopted exclusively Arminian doctrinal convictions and he set about revising the constitution of this body to reflect his new-found convictions. The imposition of a new doctrinal test on 1 January 1850 was a disaster. The Baptist Union collapsed as the vast majority of the pastors and churches did not agree with his theological changes. Johnson resigned from his post and it was an extremely difficult time for Baptists in Scotland.[36] However, a small group of Baptists, mostly from the Hope Street Baptist Church in Glasgow, but with others from Stirling Baptist Church, started to rebuild relationships between the pastors in the mid-1850s. They gradually increased the scope of their endeavours as their efforts met with increasing success. By the 1860s, collective meetings in Glasgow and Edinburgh brought together an increasing proportion of Scottish Baptist leaders, especially in the Central Belt of Scotland. The trust that had built up between them then allowed the question of re-forming a Union of Churches to be considered once again. The experience of London Baptists in forming a practical Union to accomplish common purposes was the model for their operations. That network of Baptists had included strong Calvinists like Charles Spurgeon, militant Arminians like William Landels, and mainstream conservative Evangelicals like William Brock. It was a model that equally suited Scottish Baptists. They had common objectives in church-planting and evangelism; supporting struggling churches and providing theological education for young men training for pastoral ministry. The new proposed structure would also make it difficult for the kind of ideological takeover that had happened in the later years of the previous Baptist Union.[37] Therefore, on the threshold of 1869, there was real confidence that it was the right time to form a new Union of Baptist churches that could succeed and prosper in the years to come.

*Building on a Common Foundation* seeks to give an overview of the first century and a half of the life of this body. It would be impossible to give a complete account of the life and activities of all branches of the Union. Therefore, the intention was to give, in chronological order, an account of the collective witness of Scottish Baptists over these years that included both an

---

[35] 'The Third Attempt to Form a Baptist Union of Scotland, 1843–1856', in Talbot, *Search for a Common Identity*, pp. 229–239.

[36] See for details, 'Third Attempt to Form a Baptist Union of Scotland, 1843–1856', pp. 240–276.

[37] 'The Genesis of the 1869 Baptist Union', in Talbot, *Search for a Common Identity*, pp. 277–317.

*Introduction* 11

outline of some of the major developments, but also some illustrations of particular forms of work with examples from the life of local churches in different parts of the country. It should be clear that there was no golden era of church growth, when all was straightforward, or times when the wider society was so unreceptive to the Christian message that there were no examples of numerical growth or other encouraging developments in this family of churches. In the more recent years in the twenty-first century, when printed sources were less available, assistance from local churches in providing information about their work has been greatly appreciated. The inclusion of some churches as examples in particular chapters was intended to illustrate the kinds of developments taking place at that time and could equally have been represented by the use of other examples. It is always necessary to be selective in the choice of examples used. On occasions, there was an intention to seek geographical representation of causes from different parts of the country; at other times, information was more readily accessible in printed sources about particular congregations; it is hoped that the choices made are seen as a fair presentation of the work and witness of Baptist churches in Scotland over these years.

There have been short histories written of many Baptist congregations in Scotland, together with a range of scholarly articles or other booklets written on particular aspects of the collective witness of Scottish Baptists. The first attempt to write a major history of Scottish Baptists took place in the 1920s under the editorship of George Yuille. *A History of Baptists in Scotland* was published in 1926.[38] It was a major accomplishment at the time, and it continues to serve as a valuable source of information for future historians. A detailed examination of this work, however, reveals that there were significant gaps in the record on certain topics, but that was usually because the written documents required had either not been produced, or more often had been lost. A second history of the denomination was produced in 1969, for the centenary of the Baptist Union, by Derek Murray, entitled: *The First Hundred Years*.[39] It is an excellent short account of key people and events in the first hundred years of the present Baptist Union. In the 1980s, it was felt that the time was right for a new history of Baptists in Scotland. The Scottish Baptist History Project was formed at that time as a way in which information could be shared and papers delivered, in preparation for the writing of *The Baptists in Scotland: A History* (1988), edited by David Bebbington.[40] There were

---

[38] George Yuille (ed.), *History of the Baptists in Scotland* (Glasgow: Baptist Union of Scotland, 1926).

[39] Derek B. Murray, *The First Hundred Years: The Baptist Union of Scotland* (Glasgow: Baptist Union of Scotland, 1969).

[40] David W. Bebbington (ed.), *The Baptists in Scotland: A History* (Glasgow: Baptist Union of Scotland, 1988).

introductory chapters that covered overviews of Baptist witness over the past four centuries, and then, the majority of the book contained thorough detailed regional histories of Baptist witness in Scotland. A particular strength of this book is that it provides information on the continuing witness of Baptist churches in the years since the Yuille book was written; as well as more accurate and detailed accounts of some of the earlier work by these congregations. *Search for a Common Identity: The Origins of the Baptist Union of Scotland, 1800–1870* (2003), the companion volume to this study, was focused on a more detailed study of earlier attempts by Scottish Baptists to form a collective witness, as well as an investigation into the distinctive convictions of the different groups of Baptists that existed in Scotland prior to the attempts to form a Union of churches. In 2014, a series of studies by different authors, in *A Distinctive People*, edited by Brian Talbot, explored some aspects of the collective witness of Baptists in Scotland over the twentieth century.[41] It was an opportunity to look at a number of areas of work over a complete century. The above studies have advanced our knowledge of the heritage of Scottish Baptists over recent centuries. However, it is clear that there are still many areas where further work needs to be done.

The second chapter of this book will explore the early years of this Baptist Union between 1869 and 1889. It will first outline the aims and objectives of this new organisation which were clear and practical. In the second half of the nineteenth century Scottish Churches placed a greater focus on the tasks to which they were committed, with a lesser emphasis on commitment to a detailed doctrinal statement of theological convictions. The wider society was rapidly changing, with an increasing proportion of the population living in densely packed urban areas. It was inevitable that the churches would seek to establish a presence in these areas, seeking to meet both spiritual and practical needs of the local communities.

Chapter two will also explore how successful were the attempts at urban evangelism and church-planting in particular. It will draw attention to the number of baptisms and the membership statistics for these years. However, it was not an easy time for churches in certain parts of the country. Some of the factors that caused these difficulties will be raised. It is clear that local social and economic circumstances played a significant part in determining the prospects for each particular congregation. These Scottish Baptist churches attempted to work with people of all ages. How successful were they in reaching, for example, children and young people at this time? What initiatives were taken to reach people who would not consider attending Sunday services at some of the remarkably impressive new church buildings erected during these years? Scottish Baptists although fully committed to home evangelisation were equally convinced of the importance of work

---

[41] Brian R. Talbot (ed.), *A Distinctive People: A Thematic Study of Aspects of the Witness of Baptists in the Twentieth Century* (Milton Keynes: Paternoster, 2014).

Introduction 13

overseas. This chapter will highlight aspects of the overseas ministries supported by Baptists in Scotland. It will also draw attention to a key project led by a Baptist deacon, William Quarrier, who demonstrated the application of his faith in everyday life. It was a good example of a strong and growing commitment to social action, with a visionary leader like Quarrier highlighting the social inequalities in their midst; in his case, in particular, focussing on the needs of children forced to live on the streets of the cities of Scotland. It will also provide a clear overview of whether growth or decline took place during the first two decades of the work of the churches in fellowship within the Baptist Union of Scotland.

In the approximately two decades prior to the First World War, a number of the smaller families of churches in Scotland saw increases in their numbers, for example, the Christian Brethren, Methodists, and the Salvation Army. Chapter three will examine whether Scottish Baptists saw further numerical growth like these other smaller networks of churches or whether in the early twentieth century there were some of the first signs of decline in attendances at Sunday services. A variety of examples from local churches will allow a clear picture to emerge of growth or decline in particular local communities. Where growth has taken place or been maintained an attempt will be made to explain key reasons for these developments. This was the era when women gained a higher profile both in churches and in the wider society. Chapter three will also look at the work of Jessie Yuille and her attempts to promote the formation of Women's Auxiliaries in every Baptist congregation. It will also focus on the growing importance of the Temperance movement and on the input given to the promotion of its cause by the Scottish Churches. Scottish Baptists, after years of relying on tutors working in the most basic of conditions, gained not one but two theological colleges in this era. There will be a brief discussion on the work of both the smaller Baptist Bible College in Dunoon and the continuing Baptist Theological College of Scotland, founded in 1894. It will explain what changed at that time that led to the establishment of these institutions. In the 150 years of the Baptist Union's history, this was the era of the most serious divergence in understanding of biblical and theological issues within this family of churches, with the majority retaining conservative Evangelical views, but there were other colleagues holding to broader more liberal theological convictions. Did these differences have a major impact on their collective witness? Modern communications and travel opportunities were much greater at this time. How did these developments impact relations with the wider Baptist family in Europe as well as in other parts of the world? In the decade leading up to the World Missionary Conference in Edinburgh in 1910, Scottish Churches, in proportion to their numbers, sent overseas as many missionaries as any other country in the world. Did Scottish Baptists share the enthusiasm for this work in line with Christians in other denominations? What impact did the rapid rise in the numbers of new Faith Missions have on the allegiances of Scottish

Baptists at that time? Taking the year 1911 to illustrate the choices being made within local Baptist churches in Scotland, it will be clear to see how many of the newer mission agencies had attracted support from congregations historically committed to supporting the BMS. The dark clouds of war overshadowed Europe in 1914. In terms of its own work, how satisfied could Scottish Baptists affiliated to the Baptist Union of Scotland be at that time? Did they have credible expectations of future progress in their work or were signs of decline evident in their ranks?

The First World War has been a prominent subject for historical studies of the first quarter of the twentieth century. Chapter four will explore the attitudes of Scottish Baptists on the threshold of this conflict and also how they viewed its progress prior to the cessation of hostilities in 1918. Did Scottish Baptists make a distinction between the German national leaders and ordinary people in Germany when they spoke or wrote about the war? The example of one Baptist minister in Scotland will be used to illustrate the impact of this war on an individual who was probably representative of many other people, in terms of the toll the war effort took on his health. Walter Mursell, minister of Thomas Coates Memorial Church in Paisley, was though unusual in terms of the detailed written record we possess of the sermons he preached at the beginning and end of the war, together with two volumes of poetry composed at the same time as his sermon series. However, these written records provide a window into that world and enable us to see how the war was viewed at the time by an acute contemporary observer. What reasons did Scottish Baptists give as a justification for supporting the war effort? Did any articulate the views of a conscientious objector? At the end of the war, how did Scottish Baptists articulate their convictions about the future in the light of the difficult experiences so many people had faced? This chapter will attempt to convey their convictions about what was experienced between 1914 and 1918.

The war years were undoubtedly difficult for the families whose loved ones were serving away for extended periods of time. As time went on and the number of individuals seriously injured or killed rose to unprecedented levels, the numbers of homes and communities affected naturally grew year by year. Was the Baptist Union of Scotland able to make a difference to assist congregations impacted by the war? How successful were Scottish Baptist congregations at reintegrating service personnel into their ranks when they returned after up to four years away on active service? The 1920s and 1930s were difficult years with so many people suffering serious hardship as a result of traumas experienced during the war or through the economic problems experienced at that time. Were Scottish Baptist churches able to motivate their members to continue their dedicated service during these years? Did their numbers increase or decrease between 1869 and 1919 when fifty years of Union life were acknowledged? How did this distinctive social context impact Scottish Baptists as they sought to continue their work in the post war years?

*Introduction* 15

George Yuille retired from his key leadership role within the Baptist Union in 1919 after an incredible thirty-nine years of service. His wife had since their marriage twenty-five years earlier also contributed significantly. Attention will be drawn to some of the things they accomplished. The city of Glasgow will be the area used to illustrate the success or otherwise of the outreach strategy of the Baptist Union at that time. Scotland had changed in so many ways since the formation of the BHMS in 1827. Its work had continued in parallel to that of the Evangelism Committee of the Baptist Union over a number of decades. However, a decision was taken to explore the merger of the Home Mission and the Union in 1932. The factors that led to this decision will be explored. A particular blessing, from a Christian point of view, in the Inter-War years, was the spiritual awakening in North East Scotland. Many churches in coastal communities were greatly encouraged with the entrance of new converts into their congregations during the 1920s. Did this religious Revival affect Baptist churches? If it did, was it only those causes based in communities associated with the fishing industry or were the effects of the Revival being experienced in other places as well? Scottish Baptists had been characterised by being outward-looking during the life of the Baptist Union. In the war effort, soldiers had learned to work very closely together without distinguishing between people, for example, with respect to their denominational affiliation. How closely did Scottish Baptists work in the 1920s and 1930s with both fellow Baptists in Europe and other Churches in Scotland? In the later 1930s, as the shadow of another World War loomed, how motivated were Scottish Baptists to maintain their missional priorities? There was no doubt relief at the ending of the war in 1945, but in the light of the inevitable apprehension about what might happen if there was another major war in 1939, how did this affect church and Sunday School attendances at that time. The 1930s in particular were a decade of growing uncertainty about what might happen on the international stage. This chapter gives an account of the work of one of the smaller networks of churches in Scotland at this crucial time in the nation's history.

As World War Two began there were calls for fortitude both within and outside the Christian Churches in order to overcome the serious challenges posed by Nazi Germany. Pacifism had been a cause advocated by many British citizens in the 1920s and 1930s. How influential was this movement in Baptist ranks? Were there sufficient numbers to influence the perspectives of national leaders? In the later years of World War One, it was clear that with hindsight that ill-feeling towards the German Government had spread to a broader animosity towards the German people as a whole. How did church leaders like James Scott, the Baptist Union Secretary, get on in their determination to ensure that this mistake was not made in Scotland during the Second World War? Did the war effort change priorities in the life of local Baptist congregations or did they continue with regular services and activities as before the war? In the later years of the war, by which time it was clear that the Allied Forces were going to be successful in defeating the German military machine, how did Christian leaders suggest the peace could be won as effectively as the war? Also, after such great sacrifices had been made once again for the nation by ordinary working people from both at home and the Empire countries, what changes needed to be made to the social fabric of society to ensure a better quality of living was available for all citizens? In 1945, Scottish Baptist congregations appeared to be in good heart, looking forward with optimism concerning their future prospects. However, there was recognition that there was a need for both spiritual renewal within congregations as well as a great deal of hard work to be done, if the churches were to have a significant impact on fellow citizens in the coming years.

There was a real sense of optimism about the future in Britain once hostilities were concluded in 1945. How did the Churches in Scotland view that time? What initiatives did they promote in the light of their convictions about the future? For a number of decades there had been a steady and serious decline in the number of children and young people affiliated to any church in Scotland; this chapter will consider the responses of some of the churches as they attempted to reverse the decline. What kind of home mission strategies did they put in place to build bridges with people who had chosen not to go to church? How successful were they in bringing people closer to putting their trust in God? Were Baptist churches inclined to co-operate closely with one another in evangelistic campaigns in those years? The most prominent, sustained, outreach venture in the early 1950s was the Tell Scotland movement in the Church of Scotland. Under its auspices there was remarkable enthusiasm for a wide variety of forms of outreach based in local parish settings. There were large numbers of both adults and children who joined or who were restored to active participation in the life of their local parish church. In some communities these outreach initiatives were run on an ecumenical basis, so Baptists and other Scottish Christians were able to work alongside Church of Scotland colleagues. The mission event that had greatest prominence in the 1950s was the All Scotland Billy Graham Crusade, based in Glasgow in 1955. It is clear that the prominence of the Christian message in the public square at that time was truly remarkable, with saturation coverage in the print media and broadcast services on the radio, together with the Good Friday service where Billy Graham preached to around thirty million viewers live on national television. Unfortunately, the decision to invite Billy Graham to Scotland divided the Tell Scotland leadership team and feelings were so strong that the movement never regained its former momentum in later years. What was the impact of this mission on Scotland in the 1950? How did the split between Presbyterians over the suitability of Billy Graham as a missioner in Scotland impact their work in the years that followed? Did Baptist churches gain numerically from the Graham visit? It must not be forgotten that in the years 1945 to 1960 there were numerous other evangelistic ventures and many church-extension projects organised by the Scottish Churches. How successful were they? Were there good examples of churches that were planted at that time that continued in future years? Examples will be given of new Baptist causes planted. How would the church members active in 1959 have viewed that decade? Would they have seen the years post World War Two as successful or not – from a Christian point of view?

The 1960s and 1970s have been described by a number of scholars as a time of 'religious crisis'. There is no doubt that overall numbers of people attending church for Sunday worship did fall in this era, but was there also any good news for churches at that time? Did any churches that were both creative and committed to sharing their faith effectively within the context of their local communities see significant growth? Andrew MacRae was the new General Secretary in post. He was younger than the previous holders of this office. However, he was a man with a big vision for the churches and had real confidence that church growth could be a reality for many congregations. He argued that if churches adapted the way they operated and were also willing to work very hard for a sustained time, over a number of years, then there should be evidence of the success of their efforts in leading people to faith in Jesus Christ. Another important question from that time is this: Were the churches able to stem the tide of departures of younger people from their activities? How successful was Andrew MacRae in his determination to raise the profile of Scottish Baptists within the European Baptist Federation (EBF)? Did Peter Barber, his successor, maintain the momentum in outreach activities at home as well as a range of other forms of service in EBF in particular? Scottish Baptists had since 1948 held increasingly polarised views over the ecumenical movement. A proportion sincerely saw the post-World War Two developments as a sign to commit further to this cause, whereas others were equally adamant that it was not the right way to go. How did local churches respond when decisions reached at Annual Assemblies did not go their way? Another issue that began to be discussed at that time was the appropriateness of churches having the option to call a woman as a Minister. In the 1960s there was a renewed focus on social reforms in society. What impact did this have on Scottish Baptists? Were there any church-based social projects begun at that time that were inspired by these developments?

In the 1980s and early 1990s there were shoots of genuine recovery and a reward for intensive efforts in home missionary work. This chapter will highlight the perspectives of key national leaders at the start of these years, and then examine the reasons why there was so much success in church-planting and other forms of effective evangelism. There were many outreach initiatives pioneered at that time, some within this network of congregations and others joint ventures of churches from different traditions working collaboratively in particular geographical locations. It will seek to explain why the influence of events that took place during these years had the greatest impact of any mission supported by Scottish Baptists during the twentieth century. There was continuity with the strong focus on work in Europe. Scottish Baptists would play a full part in EBF activities under the leadership of Peter Barber. This chapter will discuss the key areas of service in which Scottish Baptists contributed to the wider Baptist cause in Europe. There was also a first in the Union's history when it hosted the 1988 Baptist World Alliance (BWA) Youth Conference in Glasgow in 1988. It will also consider the level of commitment by members of these churches to service overseas in the last decade of the century and discuss the two major debates at Annual Assemblies over women in the ministry and inter-church relations. Had attitudes changed on these subjects since previous national debates in Scottish Baptist ranks? The social outworking of the Christian faith continued to be a major priority for Scottish Baptists. Two examples of this principle will be used to illustrate the contribution made to the wider society by members of this family of churches.

Chapters ten and eleven covering the time period 1994 to 2019 are clearly periods of transition. Many of the older ways of relating within the Union, and some aspects of work carried out through local churches were changed with a view to seeking to become more effective in living out the faith at a time when enthusiasm had noticeably diminished for using familiar patterns of outreach work that had been so effective in earlier years. These chapters will look at the changes made and their impact on some examples of local churches in different parts of Scotland. It is clear that in some areas of collective Baptist witness the changes made have been effective and reversed previous decline. However, there are others where this was definitely not the case. Although some forms of Christian ministry had been less open to Scottish Christians in recent years, the changing nature of others has provided opportunities which Scottish Baptists have taken, for example, in various forms of chaplaincy provision. On the two issues that had long polarised opinions in Baptist ranks in Scotland, the place for women in ministry and inter-church relations, decisions were taken during these years that have had broad acceptance and led to greater harmony at Annual Assemblies. It appears that Scottish Baptists although facing major challenges, like other Christian Churches in an increasingly secular society, have a sense of purpose and a confidence that in building on a common foundation they have genuine hope for future success in reaching fellow Scots in the twenty-first century with the Christian Gospel.

CHAPTER 2

# A Time to Advance, 1869–1889

### The Journey to the Baptist Union

The formation of the present Baptist Union of Scotland in October 1869 was a cause for rejoicing in Scottish Baptist ranks. However, it had been a long and difficult road for those committed to this path to persuade sufficient of their colleagues that this was the right way to go.[1] An unhealthy level of attachment to an 'independence mind-set' had prevented appropriate co-operation between local congregations in Scotland. William Tulloch, secretary of the new Baptist Union of Scotland, in his speech at the Annual Assembly, 20 October 1869, declared that the current efforts to form a union of churches had taken place at various times over the past thirty years.[2] In fact, the efforts to form a union of churches had gone back as far as 1827 when the initial efforts were led by a group of men in membership with Charlotte Baptist Chapel in Edinburgh. Within a mere two months nearly half of the Baptist churches in Scotland had committed themselves to this new venture, but sadly the prominent Scotch Baptist contingent used to a requirement of unanimity in their own ranks had some of their number unwilling to accept that other Baptist congregations might have slightly different theological convictions or practices, which led to the demise of this body within approximately three years. A second attempt at union between 1835 and 1842 was largely an association of smaller Baptist causes mainly in Highland Perthshire who relied on outside assistance to continue their work, but the absence of the larger churches and their ministers ensured that little progress was made.[3] A third launch of a collective Baptist witness in 1843 that survived into the 1850s began with much promise under a visionary leader Francis Johnston. At its height thirty-eight Baptist churches were identified with it,[4] but an inflexible leadership style combined with a demand by Johnston for radical theological

---

[1] Baptists in England were also reluctant to commit wholeheartedly to a Union in the nineteenth century. See J.H.Y. Briggs, *The English Baptists of the Nineteenth Century* (Didcot: Baptist Historical Society, 1994), pp. 214–219.

[2] *First Report of the Baptist Union of Scotland* (Edinburgh: John Lindsay, 1869), p. 6.

[3] The details of these first two attempts at a united Baptist witness are given in Talbot, *Search for a Common Identity*, pp. 191–228, 354–359.

[4] Talbot, *Search for a Common Identity*, pp. 360–361.

changes to the doctrinal basis for union ensured this union would not succeed.[5] Other Baptist leaders would need time to rebuild relationships in their collective ranks before another attempt to re-form a union of churches.[6] However, after more than a decade of working increasingly closer together, a critical mass of fifty-one Scottish Baptist congregations committed themselves to the newly constituted Baptist Union of Scotland in 1869,[7] a body that has continued to the present day. The previous attempts to form a union of churches may not have succeeded, but the need for such a body became increasingly obvious as the nineteenth century progressed. Its success in the years that followed vindicated the perseverance of the pioneers who worked to this end, prior to 1869.

### The Aims and Objectives of the Baptist Union of Scotland

The new Baptist Union had a minimalist approach to a common doctrinal statement in which it was stated that the new body 'shall consist of Churches and Individuals holding Evangelical doctrines, as distinguished from Rationalism and Socinianism on the one hand, and from Ritualism and Romish error on the other.'[8] There were those in the ranks, like the first Baptist Union President Jonathan Watson, minister of Dublin Street Baptist Church, Edinburgh, who would have preferred a Confession of Faith to which members subscribed but who recognised such a position was 'unpopular at present'.[9] Although further comments on this subject will be made in the next chapter, it is sufficient here to state that this statement was retained until a new constitution was drawn up in 1908 in which the current Declaration of

---

[5] Talbot, *Search for a Common Identity*, pp. 229–276 for more details.

[6] Talbot, *Search for a Common Identity*, pp. 277–317 for more details. Two of these leaders also spent time with Francis Johnston helping him come to recognise his doctrinal error concerning the work of the Holy Spirit and his need to engage in a more conciliatory manner with Baptist colleagues. A fuller account of this engagement and Johnston's theology is found in B.R. Talbot, 'Competing Voices: Contrasting Approaches to the Development of a Distinctive Evangelical Identity amongst Baptists in Nineteenth-Century Scotland', in Mark Smith (ed.), *British Evangelical Identities Past and Present*. Volume 1 (Milton Keynes: Paternoster, 2008), pp. 61–73; and B.R. Talbot, '"Preserved from Erroneous Views?": The Contribution of Francis Johnston as a Baptist Voice in the Scottish Evangelical Debate, in the mid-Nineteenth Century, on the Work of the Holy Spirit', in Dyfed Wyn Roberts (ed.), *Revival, Renewal And The Holy Spirit* (Milton Keynes: Paternoster, 2009), pp. 95–106.

[7] Talbot, *Search for a Common Identity*, pp. 366–367.

[8] *First Report of the Baptist Union of Scotland*, p. 4.

[9] Jonathan Watson, Presidential Address: 'Ecclesiastical Liberty, Equality and Fraternity', *First Report of the Baptist Union of Scotland*, p. 8.

Principle was adopted. It has remained the only doctrinal statement binding on churches and ministers in the Baptist Union of Scotland.[10] It was assumed that those joining this new initiative knew and upheld all the former convictions and decidedly stood firm against the latter positions. The emphasis in the Constitution and Rules of the new body was decidedly on the practical objects of the new union. There were four main objects of which the first concerned a commitment to engage in home missionary work in Scotland. The second was the establishment of a common fund to enable financially disadvantaged congregations to be aided in their work, together with resources to encourage the planting of new congregations. The third aim was to support the provision of theological education for young men preparing for the work of Christian ministry. The fourth aim was to disseminate information between the churches concerning their progress in the work of the gospel and to promote 'brotherly co-operation' between member churches in carrying out agreed objectives. Here were very clear guidelines for the work of member churches on which they all agreed and provided a solid basis on which to work together. This was not unique to Baptists, but part of a pattern seen across the different networks of Protestant Churches in this era.

The confidence they had in the Christian gospel and the enthusiasm with which they desired to spread it across their home nation was very high at that time. This sense of passion and clear convictions is very much in evidence in the Presidential Address given at the 1872 Baptist Union Assembly. It was a challenge to greater commitment to outreach activities not least because compared to some other denominations many Scottish Baptists had previously placed evangelism too low on their list of priorities thus hindering potential church growth. Now the opportunities for advancement were clear. In the Union there had been nearly 20% growth in the number of affiliated congregations, from fifty-one to sixty churches in the first three years alone of the new body.[11] Delegates were called to 'visit every town in Scotland and not to rest till we see planted thriving, fruitful churches of truly converted souls . . .' They were also asked to invest in good theological education training future ministers, together with raising adequate finance to pay pastors a fair stipend and to build a fund to assist them when 'laid aside through age or infirmity'.[12] The final challenge to that Assembly was a call for the Baptist Union to commit itself 'to blow a trumpet clear and loud, giving no uncertain sound' to Total Abstinence from intoxicating drinks.[13] This commitment

---

[10] Derek Murray, *The First Hundred Years: The Baptist Union of Scotland* (Glasgow: Baptist Union of Scotland, 1969), p. 37.

[11] *Fourth Annual Report of the Baptist Union of Scotland* (Edinburgh: John Lindsay, 1872), pp. 20, 29–31.

[12] *Fourth Annual Report of the Baptist Union of Scotland*, pp. 23–24.

[13] *Fourth Annual Report of the Baptist Union of Scotland*, p. 26.

urged was both a challenge to a personal lifestyle choice together with a request to seek parliamentary action to advance this cause across the nation.[14] Scottish Baptists were increasingly seeking to promote a holistic gospel of both a healthy lifestyle and evangelistic endeavour. This was an approach held in common with many other Christian Churches in Scotland in the mid-to-late nineteenth century.

## A Time of Rapid Changes in Scotland

Scotland had changed rapidly in the Victorian period. There had been steady population growth throughout the nineteenth century from a total of 1,608,420 in 1801 to 2,888,742 in 1851 and up to 4,474,103 by 1901, an increase of 2,865,683 people in only one hundred years.[15] However, what must also be noted was the high rate of emigration from Scotland, whether to England or overseas. Between 1861 and 1901 just under half a million Scots went abroad, with the peak emigration decade being the 1880s, during which 41 per cent of the natural increase in population, 218,274 people, left the country.[16] Within the country there was a major redistribution of the population with the eastern lowlands centred on Edinburgh increasing from 785,814 to 1,400,675 between 1841 and 1901, and the western lowlands where Glasgow was the biggest urban centre increased from 628,528 to 1,976,640 in the same time period.[17] This rapid expansion of these cities in both acreage and population required a whole new infrastructure of tramways, piped water, gas lights and sewers. In addition, the rapid expansion of major factories, for example, in Glasgow, Tennants at St Rollox producing bleaching powder for textiles and William Dixon's, one of the largest producers of iron and coal with sites in Govan, various locations in Lanarkshire and some further afield, together with growing ship-building and engineering works provided employment for large numbers of workers; but while some citizens prospered, an alarming number in the city barely survived living in appalling conditions. This was a major challenge for both government agencies and the voluntary sector such as the churches to address. Edinburgh, by contrast, although facing its own social and economic challenges, engaged in a building programme in the nineteenth century that was deeply impressive and grand in scale with, for example, the remodelling of St Giles Cathedral and the

---

[14] For more details see 'The Significance of the Temperance Movement', in Talbot, *Search for a Common Identity*, pp. 240–246.

[15] James Gray Kyd (ed.), *Scottish Population Statistics* (Edinburgh: Scottish Academic Press, 1975), p. xvii.

[16] Sydney and Olive Checkland, *Industry and Ethos: Scotland 1832–1914* (London: Edward Arnold, 1984), p. 13.

[17] Checkland, *Industry and Ethos*, p. 13.

erection of New College, together with the reshaping of the Castle and its Esplanade and the landscaping of Holyrood Park; and the extension of residential areas beyond the imposing buildings of the Edinburgh New Town amongst other developments. Dundee had also grown rapidly with the expansion of the Power-loom weaving facilities at Dens Works run by the Baxter family together with the Cox family's vast Camperdown works producing jute in Lochee, which attracted significant numbers of Irish immigrant workers to the city. Aberdeen had a more mixed economy based on a range of industries that included fishing and shipbuilding whereas some smaller urban centres concentrated primarily in the production of one product, for example, fine table linen (Dunfermline) and floor coverings (Kirkcaldy). The Borders region was known, for example, for its tweed in Selkirk and stocking knitting in Hawick. It was, though, not just the big cities that were growing in population many major burghs had also seen significant growth in this era.[18] However, rural areas in the north and south of the country by contrast had suffered increasing depopulation, especially of younger people in search of employment. In one industry, agriculture, for example, the rural economy had seen large-scale changes, during which the number of male workers employed in this field had more than halved between 1851 and 1901, falling from around 25% of the workforce to 11% in the early twentieth century.[19] In this time of significant changes it was inevitable that like the rest of society the Christian Church would be required to adjust its work to the changing environment in which it operated. Areas of rapid population growth had potential for increases in the size of congregations and communities that had potential for new church-planting efforts. However, by contrast, in areas from which there was significant migration to other parts of the country or significant emigration overseas there was a significant likelihood of reduced congregations or even in the worst cases a potential threat of closure.

## A Focus on the Priority of Urban Evangelism

There was a concerted effort to engage both in extensive evangelistic endeavours in the urban centres of Scotland, together with a more focused approach to planting new congregations in areas where a Baptist witness had

---

[18] R.J. Morris, 'Urbanisation and Scotland', in W. Hamish Fraser and R.J. Morris (eds), *People and Society in Scotland: Volume II, 1830–1914* (Edinburgh: John Donald, 1990), pp. 73–81.

[19] R.H. Campbell and T.M. Devine, 'The Rural Experience', in Fraser and Morris (eds), *People and Society in Scotland: Volume II, 1830–1914*, p. 46. More details of these changes are given on pp. 46–72. Agnes Mure Mackenzie, *Scotland in Modern Times 1720–1939* (London: W.R. Chambers, 1941), p. 157, claimed that the proportion of the Scottish workforce on the land had fallen from 31% in 1801 to as low as 4.5% in 1901, an even greater fall in rural employment levels.

been absent. This understanding of the priority of urban mission had been recognised by the then General Secretary of the Baptist Union Francis Johnston as early as 1843. Johnston determined that the Baptist Union of Scotland needed to prioritise the most populous urban locations for its evangelistic efforts and become more strategic in planning the locations it chose.[20] This emphasis would be continued in the newly formed Baptist Union in 1869. There was recognition that financial resources were limited so creativity was essential in implementing this strategy. In 1870 arrangement were made for ministers with strong evangelistic gifts to go in pairs for up to a fortnight to a 'populous and destitute localities to labour and preach, both outdoors and within doors'...Brethren Maclean of Greenock and Crouch of Paisley visited Dunbartonshire; Brethren Wills of Dundee and McLellan of Cupar spent a fortnight in Aberdeenshire; and Brethren Brown of Perth and Lennie of Leith, . . . laboured in Dundee.'[21] In addition to planting new causes in places like Wishaw.[22] the Union also provided resources to strengthen weak congregations in areas of increasing population such as Hawick, Leith and Falkirk.[23] As early as 1872 great encouragement was received in the progress of these new initiatives; it was noted that in the last three years more progress had been made in church extension than in the previous eight to ten years with four new churches founded through united constructive efforts in well-populated communities that had the best prospects for establishing strong churches in the coming years.[24] However, there was also an acknowledgement that other causes were struggling. A conference to address this problem was held in Hope Street Baptist Church, Glasgow, in October 1873 under the chairmanship of retiring Union President Francis Johnston.[25] Honesty in facing the challenges that underlay these difficulties and a willingness to work together to resolve them was a good basis on which to develop their collective witness. Scottish Baptists also worked with other denominations in evangelistic outreach. It had happened previously in the 1859–60 Revival prior

---

[20] F. Johnston, *An Inquiry into the means of advancing the Baptist Denomination in Scotland*, 1843, pp. 6–12.

[21] *Second Annual Report of the Baptist Union of Scotland* (Edinburgh: John Lindsay, 1870), pp. 10–11.

[22] *Wishaw Baptist Church: Rooted and Built up in Christ Jesus 1871–1971* (privately printed for the church, 1971), pp. 7–8.

[23] *Third Annual Report of the Baptist Union of Scotland* (Edinburgh: John Lindsay, 1871), pp. 10–13.

[24] *Fourth Annual Report of the Baptist Union of Scotland*, pp. 9–10.

[25] *Fifth Annual Report of the Baptist Union of Scotland* (Edinburgh: John Lindsay, 1873), pp. 30–38.

to the start of the 1869 Union,[26] and was particularly true of the D.L. Moody and Ira D. Sankey campaigns, whose ministry in Scotland in the 1870s introduced a simpler less doctrinal form of preaching by Moody,[27] combined with the use of new hymns with catchy tunes by Sankey that were eventually published as *Sacred Songs and Solos*. The fact that this title when issued was one of the best-selling books in the Victorian era revealed how popular their mission work had been with church-going people.[28] Their visit also gave renewed impetus to evangelistic work in Scotland by the Churches.[29] Scottish Baptist Churches reported an increase in baptisms in 1875 with the large Dublin Street and Rose Street congregations in Edinburgh baptising forty-six and thirty-two candidates respectively, but smaller causes in Forfar and Burray, Orkney saw forty-seven and twenty-four baptisms. The biggest impact was in the Arbroath Church where the twenty-eight admissions by baptism doubled the membership of the church.[30] The majority of converts were from the fringe of supporting congregations, especially Presbyterian Churches, and of more respectable working-class and middle-class backgrounds. Some critics objected that it had not touched the poorest section of society.[31] but no approach to outreach activities will command universal assent. There was no attempt to hide the fact that 'the great bulk of those converted to God in Scotland during the Moody and Sankey revival were church members.'[32]

The shoots of new life were beginning to spring up across the country which was particularly satisfying to William Tulloch the Union Secretary in

---

[26] Brian R. Talbot, "A larger outpouring of the Spirit of God": British Baptists and the "1859 Revival", with a particular focus on Scotland', in W. Pitts (ed.), *Baptists and Revival* (Mercer University Press, 2018). It certainly stimulated greater evangelistic efforts and closer ties of union amongst Baptist churches in England during and after this revival. Briggs, *English Baptists of the Nineteenth Century*, p. 300.

[27] A book length study of Moody's theological convictions is Stanley N. Gundry, *Love Them In: The Life and Theology of D.L. Moody* (Grand Rapids: Baker, 1976).

[28] W.R. Moody, *The Life of Dwight L. Moody* (London: Morgan & Scott, n.p. [1904]), pp. 156–158. Andrew L. Drummond & James Bulloch, *The Church in Late-Victorian Scotland, 1874–1900* (Edinburgh: St Andrew Press, 1978), pp. 9–12; James F. Findlay, Jr. *Dwight L. Moody: American Evangelist 1837–1899* (Chicago: University of Chicago Press, 1969), pp. 153–163.

[29] *SBM*, 12.1 (January 1886), p. 16.

[30] Murray, *First Hundred Years*, p. 60.

[31] J. MacPherson, *Revival and Revival-Work: A Record of the Labours of D.L. Moody & Ira D. Sankey* (London: Morgan and Scott, n.d. [1876?]), p. 293.

[32] *Tenth Annual Report of the Baptist Union of Scotland* (Glasgow: Baptist Union of Scotland, 1878), p. 36.

his October 1874 annual Report. He reported that the net growth that year amounted to an average of eleven members per congregation with in excess of 780 baptized believers and five newly affiliated churches joining the Baptist Union. In addition to cottage and kitchen meetings, the sixty-eight member churches had 130 preaching stations.[33] Scottish Baptists were united and committed to the new Union and its efforts. This early progress confirmed the wisdom of this course of action.

### An Example of One of the Newly-Planted Churches

Although the overall picture was one of progress it is helpful to illustrate from one new work some of the reasons that encouraged growth and obstacles that hindered it. Broughty Ferry Baptist Church was formed in November 1876. It was an era of growing prosperity in the neighbouring city of Dundee in the jute and engineering industries. The new railway links to the city enabled easier travel to and from work. As a result a significant number of owners and managers within these businesses sought to live in homes in Broughty Ferry.[34] It was a growing community. The original 230 residents in 1800 had become 3,500 by the 1861 census, 5,700 in 1871 and 7,400 in 1881 and reaching 10,000 people by 1900.[35] Although there were church attenders living in Broughty Ferry, the first Established Church mission station, St Aidans, did not begin until 1826, becoming a recognised Parish Church in 1863. During the 1840s the Free Church, the United Presbyterians and the Episcopalians had established congregations, followed by the first Congregationalist cause in 1860. The launch of a Baptist witness was, therefore, part of the wider growth of Christian Churches in the village that reached a total of twelve churches in 1911.[36] There was also a committed core of founder members. These included James Simpson who was the first pastor from 1876 to 1882. He led the fund-raising efforts that enabled them to erect their own building and stayed until the new congregation was established in its newly built premises.[37] John

---

[33] *Sixth Annual Report of the Baptist Union of Scotland* (Edinburgh: John Lindsay, 1874), pp.9–10.

[34] Nancy Davey, 'Broughty Ferry before 1913' in Hugh M. Begg, Chris Davey & Nancy Davey, *The Memory of Broughty Ferry* (Dundee: The Authors, 2013), pp. 1–15.

[35] Nancy Davey and John Perkins, *Broughty Ferry Village to Suburb* (Dundee: Dundee City Council, 1976), p. 2.

[36] Ramsay G. Small, *Broughty Ferry Baptist Church: The First Hundred Years* (privately printed for the church, 1976), pp. 1–3. Nancy Davey, 'The Churches of Broughty Ferry', in Begg, Davey and Davey, *Memory of Broughty Ferry*, pp. 21–28.

[37] *Broughty Ferry Baptist Church Jubilee Souvenir 1876–1927* (privately printed for the church, 1927), n.p.

Gibson and his wife, whose home 'The Grove' was used initially for baptismal services, were Baptists who had moved to Broughty Ferry from Cupar. He was a merchant in Dundee.[38] Members of the Cummings family were also prominent with Miss Elizabeth Cummings donating the ground on which the church was built and later in her will left her adjacent home to be used as a manse, together with Mr and Mrs William Murray, ironmonger and plumber, who were committed members for over forty years.[39] In addition, there were key supporters of this work in other Baptist churches. Trustees of the church when the building was erected in 1881 had included Robert Anderson, an influential member of the Long Wynd Baptist Church, Dundee, and a jute-mill owner in the city who was active in supporting new causes, together with William Tulloch Jr, a merchant in Glasgow.[40] Financial assistance from the Baptist Union was also important in the early years. However, this congregation struggled to grow numerically in the early years, reaching only sixty-six members by the end of the century whereas another new Baptist Church in Dundee at Lochee had received 119 members by that date.[41] The founding pastor suggested that the main reasons for the slow rate of growth were the high proportion of local people already attached to another church in Broughty Ferry, together with many Baptists living locally who chose to worship in larger sister causes in the city.[42] The church was established, but would remain relatively small in the next few decades.

## The First Decade of the New Baptist Union

The growth of the Baptist Union of Scotland over the first decade of its existence can be seen very easily by comparing the statistics since its formation in 1869. There was, though, no room for complacency as the Union secretary William Tulloch made plan in his 1868 annual report. He wrote:

---

[38] John Gibson, the church secretary and deacon died in February 1886. All thirty baptisms conducted during the first pastorate of James Simpson were conducted in his home. *Eighteenth Annual Report of the Baptist Union of Scotland*, 1886, p. 22.

[39] George Yuille (ed.), *History of the Baptists in Scotland* (Glasgow: Baptist Union of Scotland, 1926), p. 159.

[40] Small, *Broughty Ferry Baptist Church*, p. 5.

[41] *The Scottish Baptist Yearbook 1900* (Glasgow: William Asher, 1900), pp. 145–146. The claim of Nancy Davy, 'Churches of Broughty Ferry', p. 26, that the total congregation was only twenty people is too small as the membership figure was up to thirty by the end of the first year in 1877. *Ninth Annual Report of the Baptist Union of Scotland* (Edinburgh: John Lindsay, 1877), p. 35.

[42] James Simpson, 'Broughty Ferry', in *Ninth Annual Report of the Baptist Union of Scotland*, p. 16. *Tenth Annual Report of the Baptist Union of Scotland*, pp. 15–16.

> The addition of three or four hundred to the membership of our churches, or of one or two new churches to the Union's Roll in a year, is a rate of increase which is altogether inadequate.... Greater earnestness in the work of Church Extension, is, therefore, indispensable for the progress of the denomination, and for the more effective discharge of our mission in the world.[43]

At the launch of the Baptist Union there were fifty-one churches with 3,794 members. Twenty-eight of the churches had Sunday Schools with 2,467 children in attendance. Sixteen of the congregations had Bible classes with 695 young people attending them. It was a time of growth in the ranks with 363 new members added in 1869.[44] A decade later in 1879 there were now eighty churches; a growth of twenty-nine congregations in only ten years which is a remarkable degree of progress. There were many remarkable stories of effective witnessing for the faith, but few that could compare to the impact of Thomas Whitson Lister of Leslie who was converted as a twelve-year-old in 1873 and immediately began witnessing to his school friends, some of whom were converted. His mother, almost certainly his role-model, was also a gifted evangelist who had led many women who worked in the nearby spinning and bleaching mills to faith in Jesus Christ. His first evangelistic meetings for other teenagers were held under a bridge in Leslie where they were 'free from interruptions. Later they were transferred to his mother's kitchen. The numbers of converts grew and home meetings were established in 'the neighbouring villages of Walkerton, Balbirnie Square and Woodside.' By 1880 this bank trainee was offered a permanent post in the Govan branch of the Union Bank. However, a meeting on 10 June 1880 of the converts and other friends in Leslie decided to form a church and invite Lister, aged nineteen to be the pastor of the new cause. His brother John, an architect, supervised the erection of a church building in 1884.[45] Baptismal statistics of Baptist congregations were now being collected by the national body and 690 candidates were immersed upon profession of faith that year. The total number of members in Union-affiliated causes had now risen from 3,794 to 8,666, an increase of 517 on the previous year, and 4,872 more than in 1869. The churches in the Baptist Union also erected twenty-four new church buildings that could accommodate over 10,000 people at a cost of £59,435, of which £48,785 had already been paid off by 1878. In the tenth year of its work alone, new premises were opened in Greenock, Kelso, Irvine, Fraserburgh,

---

[43] *The Tenth Annual Report of the Baptist Union of Scotland* (Glasgow: Baptist Union of Scotland, 1878), p. 20.

[44] *First Report of the Baptist Union of Scotland* (Edinburgh: John Lindsay, 1869), pp. 22–23; 'Annual Report of the Baptist Union of Scotland', *The Twenty-First Annual Report of the Baptist Union of Scotland 1888–1889* (Glasgow: Baptist Union of Scotland, 1889), pp. 23–24.

[45] Yuille (ed.), *History of the Baptists in Scotland*, pp. 152–153.

Peterhead, Pitlochry, Stroma and Colonsay. If the funding provided by the late Robert Haldane was excluded, the sums raised for new premises in this decade exceeded the total obtained in Baptist ranks in all previous generations of its witness in Scotland. Yet there were still sufficient resources to double the ordinary income of the Union over this decade, without taking account of money donated to Baptist causes overseas.[46] It was a most impressive achievement in such a short timescale.

It was, though, a mixed picture. Twenty-three congregations had declined in membership and ten reported the same figures as the previous year. Difficult economic circumstances had been reported as the cause of a significant movement of unemployed workers to other places in search of new jobs.[47] However, forty-seven declared a clear increase since 1878, with four of the five fastest growing churches reporting more than thirty converts baptised and added to the membership and the other recorded an increase of fifty-seven added to the church.[48] The overall picture was one of growth, but local circumstances did have a significant impact on the progress of these congregations.

There were sixty-eight congregations reporting the work of Sunday Schools, up from twenty-eight; and the number of pupils had risen sharply to 7,162 under the care of 907 teachers. Bible classes were now found in forty-seven congregations and 1906 young people in attendance. In addition to work in the main premises of a local congregation, data was also now collected on the number of cottage meetings and preaching stations under the supervision of these local congregations. A total of 188 were reported in 1879, an average of more than two per affiliated congregation.[49] In a single decade after the commitment to work together in fellowship in the Baptist Union of Scotland and work collaboratively in communities across the country the evidence of its success is abundantly clear. There was a clear significant increase in the number of congregations, membership totals, work amongst children and young people and the launching of new outreach activities in the districts around existing congregations.

---

[46] *Tenth Annual Report of the Baptist Union of Scotland*, pp. 9–12.

[47] *The Eleventh Annual Report of the Baptist Union of Scotland* (Glasgow: Baptist Union of Scotland, 1879), pp. 12–13.

[48] *The Eleventh Annual Report of the Baptist Union of Scotland* (Glasgow: Baptist Union of Scotland, 1879), pp. 12–13.

[49] *Eleventh Annual Report of the Baptist Union of Scotland*, 1879, pp. 12–13, 46–48; *Twenty-First Annual Report of the Baptist Union of Scotland 1888–1889*, pp. 23–24.

## Baptist Home Mission

It is also important to remember that there had been much effective evangelistic work taking place throughout the nineteenth century through the Baptist Home Missionary Society for Scotland (BHMS).[50] One third of the founding churches were in Home mission territory.[51] Although modest in total, its income was fairly steady during this period with significant support from English Baptist churches. In 1868, for example, £606 was raised from individuals and churches in Scotland and an impressive £424 from supporters south of the border, with legacies and other modest income streams resulting in a total income of £1,543.6.5.[52] In 1898 English supporters had contributed just under £583, compared to £1,762 raised in Scottish Baptist churches, including £759 in mission congregations, out of a total of £2,490.12.10.[53] The strength of ongoing support for the work of the BHMS in Scotland in different parts of the United Kingdom was part of the reasons for its retention of a separate identity to the Baptist Union until well into the twentieth century. Its work was primarily located in the more rural, Highland and Island communities, together with initiatives in a smaller number of communities in other regions of Scotland. Around the time of the launch of the Baptist Union the BHMS was responsible for twenty-six mission stations and twenty-five home missionaries.[54] The fact that the number of mission stations and workers had declined to twenty mission-stations and positions for nineteen home missionaries by 1898[55] indicated almost certainly two things. First of all, some spheres of service on the mainland had been incorporated as regular churches within the life of the Baptist Union of Scotland, for example, Kilmarnock Baptist Church, and secondly, a much greater priority of investment of Union resources was now focussed on the larger towns and cities of Scotland. In the far north in Shetland three were three home missionaries covering five congregations in Spiggie, Dunrossness, Burra, Semblester and Sandsting and in Orkney another three workers responsible

---

[50] For more details see 'The Baptist Home Missionary Society: A Substitute Union, 1827–1868?' in Talbot, *Search for a Common Identity*, pp. 153–190.

[51] Murray, *First Hundred Years*, p. 83.

[52] *Report of the Baptist Home Missionary Society for Scotland*, 1868, pp. 23–37.

[53] *Report of the Baptist Home Missionary Society for Scotland*, 1899, n.p.

[54] This report is the nearest surviving one to the years covered in this chapter. *Report of the Baptist Home Missionary Society for Scotland chiefly for The Highlands and Islands* (Edinburgh: D.R. Collie & Son, 1868), p. 22.

[55] *Report of the Baptist Home Missionary Society for Scotland* (Glasgow: William Asher, 1899), p. 4. This report is the first one available from the era of the present Baptist Union of Scotland. Information about some other home mission congregations is provided in Murray, *First Hundred Years*, pp. 83–90.

for its ministries in Kirkwall, Eday and Burray. In Caithness two home missionaries served at Keiss and Mey, with a similar pattern in Morayshire at Branderburgh and Forres. Perthshire throughout the nineteenth century had been a major focus for home mission work and in the late 1860s five colleagues were engaged to carry out its work in Glenlyon, Blair Atholl, Tullymet, Crieff and Blairgowrie. Off the west coast of Scotland, home missionaries served in Uig on Skye, Tobermory and Ross on Mull, Bowmore covering Islay and Colonsay, and Lismore, with responsibilities there also for Appin and the surrounding district and on Tiree. The BHMS also had responsibility for the churches in Lochgilphead in Argyllshire, Tullibody in Clackmannanshire and Kilmarnock in Ayrshire.[56] Although the greater focus and energy for new work rested in the Union's urban initiatives, there were also a smaller number of fresh ventures carried out by the Home Mission. In 1868 there were three new workers appointed to serve at home mission-stations. These examples will illustrate some different obstacles and opportunities faced by Scottish Baptists at that time. First of all, J. Munro Campbell was stationed at Branderburgh, a fishing community in Morayshire, six miles from Elgin. This community and neighbouring Lossiemouth had a population of approximately 3,000 inhabitants. Branderburgh and Lossiemouth would combine to become a police burgh in 1890. It was an attractive location for new work since the new Morayshire railway had opened in August 1852, the first railway line north of Aberdeen, although it initially only provided a service from Lossiemouth to Elgin.[57] Campbell provided effective leadership to the small Baptist congregation there and it grew in numbers to the extent that the BHMS committee were expecting that it would soon become entirely self-supporting, as well as erect much larger and more suitable premises for its work. The minister reported that within a few months of his arrival in August 1867 the hall was comfortably filled on Sunday mornings and in the evening many people had to stand as between 250 and 300 people typically attended. He was encouraged by the growth in the Sunday School over the following year and noted that in his Bible class there were usually between thirty and forty young people present. In less than a year twenty-six additions had been made to the membership roll.[58] This work was a particularly promising development for the Home Mission.

The second appointment had been to a small congregation in Forres that had been launched nine years earlier. James Scott from the Pastor's College in

---

[56]*Report of the Baptist Home Missionary Society for Scotland chiefly for The Highlands and Islands* (Edinburgh: D.R. Collie & Son, 1868), p. 23.

[57] The railway was amalgamated with the Great North of Scotland railway in 1881. This route was closed in 1966 and has become a trail for walkers. http://www.heritagepaths.co.uk/pathdetails.php?path=288 accessed 26 January 2018.

[58] *Report of the Baptist Home Missionary Society for Scotland*, 1868, pp. 11–12.

London was settled as the first full-time pastor of that cause.[59] Baptists in that community had found it harder to attract new attenders, possibly due to stronger established congregations of other denominations, together with the remarkable progress of the Free Church of Scotland, a body that from the 1840s had attracted many former Presbyterian adherents who had been attending Baptist congregations due to the absence of an Evangelical Presbyterian ministry in their locality. It is also probable that the absence of a settled minister had hindered their prospects as well. Under Scott's ministry the morning congregation gradually increased and the evening meetings were crowded. It was standard in Scottish Protestant Churches in the Victorian era to have higher congregations at evening services. Congregations in Baptist causes followed the same pattern as other Scottish Churches. Scott had also overseen the establishment of a Sunday School whose average attendance was thirty-one pupils per week. He concluded: 'Being a stranger at Forres, I have not had that free access to the people one could have wished, but I trust the longer I remain among them, I may be the more successful.'[60] His downbeat report must not be misunderstood. His congregation was consistently growing in numbers, but simply not as fast as he had hoped.

The third work that existed only in embryo prior to the appointment of David Young as minister had a much more difficult task to establish a permanent witness in Blairgowrie. There were as few as ten members who formed the church when Young, the former United Presbyterian minister at Kinclaven, Perthshire, was appointed to this post. In the first eight months, over the time of a Scottish winter, he had increased the congregation to fifteen people. This was a welcome accomplishment when, in addition to no halls in the town being available during the week, even the one hired for Sundays had a major drawback. 'The hall we meet in being intensely cold; nothing but warm love for the Lord, the Redeemer, and burning zeal for his glory, can induce hearers of the Word to worship with us then.'[61] Another difficulty was that a number of his small membership had a significant distance to walk to church – up to ten miles. Then, Young reported, 'At first there was an impression on many minds that a Baptist minister would teach heresy, and that of the darkest and deadliest complexion; but this impression, I have good reason for believing, has been entirely effaced.'[62] Another discouraging factor was that some able and prominent citizens of the town privately claimed to be

---

[59] Students of the college led by C.H. Spurgeon had been placed in Baptist churches in Scotland since 1859 and had been effective evangelists and pastors as well as key supporters of the Baptist Union of Scotland. See Talbot, *Search for a Common Identity*, pp. 300–307.

[60] *Report of the Baptist Home Missionary Society for Scotland*, 1868, p. 13.

[61] *Report of the Baptist Home Missionary Society for Scotland*, 1868, pp. 13–14.

[62] *Report of the Baptist Home Missionary Society for Scotland*, 1868, pp. 14.

Baptists, but seemed happy to remain in paedo-baptist churches, even in some cases allowing their children to receive infant baptism. Worst of all, Young in the BHMS report indicated that he had received notice that the inadequate hall in which they met would soon become unavailable as it was being sold and converted into a dwelling-house. On top of these issues he noted that a number of interested people had declined to join the church because Young had only been sent for a trial period of one year by the BHMS to Blairgowrie. They wanted a guarantee that the church would continue beyond the year before they would commit to join it. In the event it struggled on prior to closure in 1880.[63] However, there was one encouragement – Sunday evening congregations were described by this minister as: 'usually very large and attentive audiences, composed, chiefly, of the more intelligent and godly of Blairgowrie.'[64] Even in an era of vigorous church growth not every attempt to found a new congregation would succeed. In Blairgowrie there were simply too many factors that hindered growth to enable this cause to become established in that community.

By contrast, there was plenty of scope for fresh ventures being initiated in the more heavily populated communities by the Baptist Union. Although some Scottish Baptists were keen to keep the two evangelistic agencies separate, there were others who clearly would have preferred a merger in order to combine their efforts. For example, William Tulloch, President of the Baptist Union in 1882, declared in his presidential address: 'if however the Society [BHMS] and the Union had combined in this work . . . and [if they] had the sympathy and hearty co-operation of the pastors and churches, who can calculate the amount of good that might have been accomplished?'[65] Prior to this statement, Tulloch had drawn attention to the outreach work the Baptist Union had carried out, in addition to the BHMS activities, between 1869 and 1882.

There is no part of Union work on which I look back with greater satisfaction than the evangelistic and church extension work. Nor any I think in which the Union has been so successful. Not to speak of my own labours and the labours of our summer evangelistic deputies, I regard the formation of the Govan, Wishaw, Irvine, Broughty Ferry, and [Ward Road] Dundee Churches and the fostering into self-sustentation of these and the Arbroath,

---

[63] Yuille (ed.), *History of the Baptists in Scotland*, p. 276.

[64] *Report of the Baptist Home Missionary Society for Scotland*, 1868, pp. 14.

[65] William Tulloch, 'President's Address', *The Fourteenth Annual Report of the Baptist Union of Scotland* (Glasgow; Baptist Union of Scotland, 1882), pp. 47–48. Tulloch would have been aware that the Home and Irish Missions of the Baptist Union of Great Britain and Ireland had merged in 1878, prior to amalgamating with the Union in 1882. See Briggs, *English Baptists of the Nineteenth Century*, p. 299.

Rothesay, Elgin, St Andrews and Leith Churches as the best thing the Union has done.'[66]

These initiatives had happened informally under the general auspices of the Baptist Union but it was not until November 1889 that a group of leading Scottish Baptists met to form the Evangelistic Committee of the Baptist Union of Scotland. The remit given by the Baptist Union Council was to: 'arrange evangelistic meetings in suitable centres of population and to assist Baptist churches in evangelistic efforts. That the committee have power to nominate for election by the Council one or more evangelists, should funds be subscribed for that purpose . . . .'[67] Even at its inception there was a significant overlap in membership between the Home Mission and the Evangelism committees. Regrettably no copies of home mission annual reports have survived between 1869 and 1898, however a comparison between the names listed on the 1898 BHMS committee and that of the earlier 1889 Evangelism committee reveals that ten of the thirteen members of the latter agency were also identified with the home mission, including prominent Edinburgh Civil servant Percival Waugh, the secretary of the Home Mission and an elder at Bristo Place Baptist Church in Edinburgh.[68] At this early stage in the life of the Baptist Union it was the first step to the institutional control of Baptist home mission work under the Union's auspices.

## The Wider Picture

Although the underlying picture of church growth looked encouraging for Scottish Baptists there were significant local variations, for example, in 1880. In some locations churches lost high numbers of members seeking work at a time of economic depression; out of eighty one churches there twenty-seven that recorded decreases in membership that was in large measure due to individuals having to move to obtain employment. Three of the smallest churches closed that year at Eyemouth, Crieff and Blairgowrie. However, the overall total was higher due to the increases of between fifteen and thirty-five new members in thirty-six other congregations, together with the successful launch of three new congregations in Leslie, Fife, Canning Street, Calton, in Glasgow and on the island of Stroma. Work amongst children and young people was particularly encouraging with Sunday School numbers up from the previous year by 611 pupils to 7,162 and Bible class numbers increased by 209 to 1,906 attendees.[69] By 1874 it appeared that there was a growing expectation

---

[66] Tulloch, 'President's Address', 1882, p. 47.

[67] *The Twenty-Second Annual Report of the Baptist Union of Scotland 1889–90* (Glasgow: Baptist Union of Scotland, 1890), p. 42.

[68] *Twenty-Second Annual Report*, 1890, p. 42.

[69] *Twelfth Annual Report of the Baptist Union of Scotland*, 1880, p. 11.

of further growth in the Union. That year the landmark figure of ninety affiliated congregations was reached for the first time with three new causes at Dunoon, Dalkeith and Crieff received into fellowship. Baptismal figures were very healthy with an average of more than seven per affiliated church that year. There were only twelve congregations that had no additions to membership by baptism and the same number whose membership total deceased, a figure down from nineteen churches the previous year. It is significant that the majority of these struggling causes were based in rural rather than urban locations.[70] The decision of the Baptist Union to prioritise church-planting in the larger towns and cities was vindicated by this sustained growth in its witness.

After a second decade of work the overall picture was one of further advancement with an increase of eight more congregations in fellowship with the Baptist Union of Scotland, up from eighty-one in 1879 to eighty-nine in 1889. Baptismal figures were also high with 795 carried out that year. The Baptist Union compiled its statistics in 1889 from the seventy-nine churches that gave full returns on data and assumed the same figures for the ten who did not reply. This decision at a time of steady annual growth would imply that there was potential for a slight under-reporting of the total figures. Membership of affiliated churches was given as 11,543, an increase of 3,034 over the decade. Sunday Schools had increased from sixty-eight to eighty with 10,220 children in attendance, an increase of 3,058. Bible classes were also more numerous in Baptist ranks now up from forty-seven to fifty-five, with 2,825 young people, that is 919 more than in 1879. In addition, there were 155 preaching stations and cottage meetings. It was not a uniformly positive picture. Extensive growth in some churches more than compensated for the decline in thirty-one congregations which between then had lost 261 members in the previous year as a result of roll revisions or emigration, or in two cases by the loss of a significant number of members for other unstated reasons. Seven further churches had reported the same number of members. However, overall it had been a time to advance in Scottish Baptist ranks between 1869 and 1889. Of the thirty-eight additional congregations in fellowship with the Baptist Union at the end of this period, the majority, thirty-one were new causes that had been planted since the formation of this Baptist Union and, in addition, thirty-seven church buildings had been erected or acquired over these years.[71] It can be fairly assumed that Baptists in Scotland entered the last decade of the nineteenth century in good heart.

---

[70] *Sixteenth Annual Report of the Baptist Union of Scotland*, 1884, p. 13.

[71] *The Twenty-First Annual Report of the Baptist Union of Scotland 1888–1889* (Glasgow: Baptist Union of Scotland, 1889), pp. 23–24.

## Ministerial Education

The need for good theological training for Baptist pastoral ministry had been recognised as one of the pressing needs for the newly founded Baptist Union to address. However, between 1869 and 1894, when the Scottish Baptist Theological College was established, there were more conflicts and tensions surrounding this subject than any other faced by Scottish Baptists in their collective witness. Prior to the formation of the Baptist Union there had been a number of different approaches taken. The Haldane brothers had organised seminary classes in Grantown-on-Spey for several years in the 1820s under Lachlan Mackintosh. He trained up to twenty men in this way.[72] An obvious route to take in the earlier nineteenth century had been to send students for training to English Baptists Colleges, first at Bristol and then Horton Baptist College, Bradford. Between 1806 and 1843, for example, Scottish Baptists had sent thirty-three men to train at Horton College.[73] It had seemed particularly promising when the Baptist Academical Society had been established in 1837 to oversee the training of potential ministers using English Baptist theological colleges, but this body ceased to exist within a few years because of the limited success of their endeavours. Of the first thirty students sent south of the border to prepare for pastoral ministry only six had returned to pastor churches in Scotland.[74] It was evident that a new approach had to be taken within Scotland. Francis Johnston, the secretary of the newly created Baptist Union formed in 1843, in his *The Circular Letter of the Baptist Union* that year placed theological education very high on his agenda. He had noted that there were many colleagues dissatisfied with the current state of affairs and had established committees in Glasgow and Edinburgh some years previously to attempt to find a solution to this difficulty. In summary, Johnston made this proposal: 'We anxiously desire that the Edinburgh and Glasgow brethren, and all the churches, would combine to raise a Baptist Theological Institution in Scotland.'[75] It took until 1846 for this new body to be launched. There were eighteen men trained under its auspices by Johnston and other part-time lecturers in the decade to 1856. However, there were two issues that seriously hindered its operations. First of all, support from the churches was limited to those associated with Johnston already in the Baptist

---

[72] Yuille (ed.), *History of the Baptists in Scotland*, p. 251. For more details see Talbot, *Search for a Common Identity*, pp. 106–110, 215–220.

[73] *Northern Baptist Educational Society Reports* (*NBES*), 1806–1806 to 1842–1843. The names of the first twenty-two are given in Talbot, *Search for a Common Identity*, Appendix 2, p. 345.

[74] Yuille (ed.), *History of the Baptists in Scotland*, p. 251.

[75] Francis Johnston, *An Inquiry into the means of advancing the Baptist Denomination in Scotland* (1843), pp. 10–11.

Union, and even amongst some of these colleagues serious concerns were raised about some of the theological opinions he had adopted in more recent years.[76] It was inevitable in the light of these limitations on commitment to this new body that in the ten years of its existence there was a serious struggle to raise sufficient finance to maintain its operations.[77] However, the desire to see good theological education provided for men training for pastoral ministry was undiminished. In the period 1856 to 1869 James Patterson, minister of Hope Street Baptist Church, Glasgow, was appointed the sole tutor for ministerial students and twenty-two individuals were prepared for service in classes conducted in the premises of this church. Most notably these included George Yuille from Irvine who later became secretary of the Union and Duncan Macgregor, later minister of Dunoon Baptist Church and the founder of a theological college associated with that congregation.[78] It was, though, recognised that a fresh start was required when the present Baptist Union was formed in 1869.

At its first assembly in October 1869 James Culross, minister of Stirling Baptist Church and the newly appointed tutor of ministerial students, who had succeeded James Paterson in this post, made a powerful speech on the subject of 'Ministerial Education in Scotland'. His call for a new approach to this subject was heeded by the delegates. On a motion proposed by Oliver Flett, minister of Storie Street Baptist Church, Paisley, and seconded by James Haig, minister of Whyte's Causeway Baptist Church, Kirkcaldy, a unanimous decision was attained to appoint a sub-committee on ministerial education to provide proposals for the way forward. By December of that year it came to the following conclusions. First of all, candidates for pastoral ministry should undertake a general course in the Department of Arts in a Scottish University as well as studies in Hebrew, alongside education in theological subjects under the direction of a tutor during the months of August and September. The latter shorter courses should cover the fields of biblical criticism, systematic theology, homiletics, apologetics, church history and elocution.[79] It appeared to be an encouraging start to this area of collective

---

[76] A letter published in an English Baptist periodical confirmed the decline in support for the Theological Institution due to Johnston promoting controversial theological views. *The Primitive Church Magazine*, New Series, 6.3 (March 1849), pp. 91–92.

[77] For more details see Talbot, *Search for a Common Identity*, pp. 246–247, 267–274.

[78] On this era of Scottish Baptist theological education see Derek B. Murray, *Scottish Baptist College Centenary History 1894–1994* (Glasgow: Scottish Baptist College, 1994), pp. 4–5; and Talbot, *Search for a Common Identity*, p. 312–316.

[79] Appendix two of the *First Report of the Baptist Union of Scotland*, 1869, p. 25. A fuller account of their recommendations is given in the *Second Report of the Baptist Union of Scotland* (Edinburgh: John Lindsay, 1871), p. 25.

witness, but Dr Culross accepted a call to a London pastorate and his last service as a tutor prior to his departure was in 1871. Hugh Anderson, minister of Bratton Baptist Church, Wiltshire, and nephew of Christopher Anderson, founding pastor of Charlotte Baptist Chapel, Edinburgh, was appointed to serve as tutor in his place, but died suddenly before he could even commence his post.[80] It was not surprising that with all the sudden changes and the inability to plan too far ahead in its work that there was reported to be 'not a little unsettledness and consequent weakness came to be associated with the carrying on of the work.'[81] Over the next decade there were broadly three viewpoints put forward regarding the work of theological education. The first view was the appointment of a sole tutor who was to be freed from the responsibilities of pastoral ministry to concentrate on this work. A second opinion was to send the men to existing Presbyterian Colleges or their Baptist equivalents in England. The third and more progressive idea was to set up a fully equipped and adequately endowed Scottish Baptist College with a mix of full and part-time staff.[82] Scottish Baptists were not of one mind regarding the approach to take on this subject. The unsettlement caused by the removal of tutors within quick succession in the early years of the Union led to serious concern about the way forward.

However, it must not be forgotten that there were a good number of candidates who had come forward for theological training. It is helpful to remember the variety of spheres of service in which they would engage in future years. For example, from the start of this Baptist Union to 1882 forty-four men had come forward and commenced training, of which forty were either in ministry or engaged in studies in the latter year. Two men Donald Grant and George Watt had died and William Dunnet and Charles Donald had chosen not to proceed along the ministry pathway. Five men had chosen to serve overseas. George Durno and Alexander Grant had gone to Canada, Charles Brown to Montego Bay in Jamaica and Alexander Young to Cuttack in India, together with John Anderson who was serving in Spezzia, Italy. Two men had moved to take up charges in England, James Douglas in Falmouth and Jervis Shanks in Redruth. Of those remaining in Scotland there was one individual Lachlan McPherson who had been appointed as a hospital chaplain at the Western Infirmary in Glasgow, though no details have been found so far about it.[83] It is probable that he was the first Scottish Baptist minister to be

---

[80] *Fourth Report of the Baptist Union of Scotland* (Edinburgh: John Lindsay, 1872), pp.13–15.

[81] *Fifth Report of the Baptist Union of Scotland* (Edinburgh: John Lindsay, 1873), p. 20.

[82] Yuille (ed.), *History of the Baptists in Scotland*, pp. 254. Murray, *First Hundred Years*, pp. 71–74.

[83] *Fourteenth Annual Report of the Baptist Union of Scotland*, 1882, p. 25.

appointed a hospital chaplain in Scotland. In the midst of the challenges of working out a system for appropriate training in Scottish Baptist ranks it is important not to forget those who were trained effectively and engaged in fruitful Christian service.

No-one could deny, though, that this problem of the structure needed to be resolved and fairly quickly as it was probable that it was not unconnected to the limited number of candidates putting their names forward in recent years. Howard Bowser made a spirited appeal to progress this issue in the April 1875 *Scottish Baptist Magazine* (*SBM*).[84] This Glasgow Baptist set out a convincing case for the formation of a theological college to train Ministers, but there were still enough other colleagues who were yet to be convinced. There had been some modest encouragements, for example, in 1876 when five candidates were accepted that year for ministerial training, the largest number per annum since the 1869 Union had begun,[85] but this was still a less than adequate number in a context of great need for trained Ministers. At the October 1879 Baptist Assembly, the secretary William Tulloch drew attention to a concern about the shortage of trained ministers, with an immediate need of twelve individuals to fill vacant charges. There was also a recognition that others were required on a locum basis to fill in temporarily for 'men temporarily laid aside by hard labour'. It was further proposed that a sanatorium for overworked ministers and missionaries would be greatly welcomed and he sought a benefactor to provide the funding for such a venture. There was, though, another difficulty acknowledged that the Union was seeking to address. A number of churches had called ministers without any reference to advice on their suitability from the Baptist Union and in some cases had made unsuitable appointments which had hindered their growth. Churches were asked to take greater care and not rely on written testimonials as to a candidate's suitability for their congregation.[86] Accounts have been given in detail elsewhere of the disagreements over a number of years concerning whether to continue with the tutor-led basis of theological education or move to the founding of a college, particularly between Oliver Flett who favoured the establishment of a college and William Landels who opposed it with vigour, preferring to retain the older approach.[87] It came to a head in 1893 when as a result of severe underfunding of the existing form of training that

---

[84] *Scottish Baptist Magazine*, 1.4 (1 April 1875), pp. 49–52.

[85] *Eighth Report of the Baptist Union of Scotland* (Edinburgh: John Lindsay, 1876), p. 21.

[86] *Eleventh Annual Report of the Baptist Union of Scotland*, 1879, p. 13.

[87] Murray, *Scottish Baptist College*, pp. 5–11; Yuille (ed.), *History of the Baptists in Scotland*, pp. 254–257; Murray, *First Hundred Years*, pp. 72-75; for example, *SBM*, 11.3 (March 1885), pp. 64–66; 12.1 (January 1886), pp. 15–16; 12.2 (February 1886), pp. 47–51; 12.6 (June 1886), pp. 160–166, 170–171.

the Education Committee drew up the following motion: 'That in the interests of the Baptist denomination in Scotland it is advisable to promote the formation of a Society affiliated to, but separate in organisation from, the Union, for the special education of young men considered suitable for the Christian Ministry.'[88] Negotiations were engaged and it was recognised that the best way forward was through the formation of the Baptist Theological College of Scotland. The launch date for that body was 25 September 1894.[89] A new chapter in the collective witness of Scottish Baptists would begin under its auspices.

## Mission Work Outside of Scotland

It is important to set the Scottish Baptist contribution to overseas mission within the wider context of remarkable growth of the Protestant missionary movement in the nineteenth century.[90] It had been Archibald McLean, an Edinburgh Baptist minister, as early as December 1795, who had the honour of being the first Scottish Protestant clergyman since the Reformation to argue that the Great Commission of Jesus in taking the Gospel to the world was a duty to be taken seriously by Scottish Christians.[91] By the following year Evangelicals in different denominations were making a similar proclamation, inspired by the work of William Carey and his BMS colleagues in India.[92] From a handful of Scottish missionaries overseas prior to the 1830s, at which time it was estimated that the total had risen to around thirty individuals, of which six were Scottish Baptists, and up to 100 by 1850.[93] At the start of the

---

[88] *Twenty-Fifth Annual Report of the Baptist Union of Scotland* (Glasgow: Baptist Union of Scotland, 1893), p. 19.

[89] *The Baptist Theological College of Scotland Jubilee 1894–1944* (Glasgow: private publishing, 1944), p. 3.

[90] A fuller account of this work is given in B.R. Talbot, 'Spreading the Good News from Scotland: Scottish Baptists and Overseas Mission in the first three decades of the Twentieth Century', in Anthony R. Cross, Peter J. Morden and Ian. M. Randall (eds), *Pathways and Patterns in History* (London: Spurgeon's College and the Baptist Historical Society, 2015), pp. 145–171.

[91] Archibald McLean, *The Promise that all Nations shall be brought into Subjection to Christ* (Edinburgh: J. Guthrie, 1796).

[92] Brian Talbot, '"Rousing the Attention of Christians": Scottish Baptists and the Baptist Missionary Society prior to the Twentieth Century', in J.H.Y. Briggs and A.R. Cross (eds), *Baptists and the World: Renewing the Vision* (Vol. 8; Oxford: Centre for Baptist History and Heritage Studies, Regent's Park College, 2011), pp. 53–60.

[93] Figures taken from the *New Edinburgh Almanac*, cited by E. Breitenbach, *Empire and Scottish Society: The Impact of Foreign Missions at Home c1790-c.1914* (Edinburgh: Edinburgh University Press, 2009), p. 57. Details of Baptist missionaries see Talbot,

twentieth century, including missionaries' wives, the Church of Scotland was supporting 115 men and women in the mission field,[94] and the United Free Church of Scotland an impressive total of 406.[95] In the National Church this was approximately equivalent to one missionary for every twelve congregations. By contrast the United Free Church had the equivalent of one missionary for every four of its churches. All of the serving missionaries in the former Free Church of Scotland had chosen to affiliate with the new body comprised of the United Presbyterian Church and the vast majority of the Free Church of Scotland. The latter body continued but its foreign mission work would have to commence afresh with new staff and fresh opportunities for service. W. Roundsfell Brown, Convenor of its Foreign Missions Committee, reported to the 1901 enduring Free Church Assembly the following statement: 'In the circumstances of the Church, the Committee finds itself for the moment not in actual touch with any mission. The United Free Church has been enriched, and we impoverished on many points: on none more than on this. All the Foreign Missionaries have preferred to attach themselves to the larger denomination.'[96] Even a small denomination like the Baptist Union of Scotland had commissioned fifty-one members for overseas service with its own mission agency the BMS,[97] even apart from an unknown number of those serving under the auspices of other usually non-denominational bodies, prior to 1900. On the threshold of the twentieth century Scottish Christians expected the continued growth in the numbers and success of their overseas workers in spreading the good news from Scotland.

Scottish Baptists in the nineteenth century were primarily committed to the work of their denominational agency. A Glasgow auxiliary society to the BMS had been founded as early as 1819 and later an Ayr auxiliary to the

---

'Rousing the Attention of Christians' and M. McVicar, *A Great Adventure Scotland and the BMS* (Glasgow: Baptist Union of Scotland, 1992), p. 14.

[94] *Report of the Schemes of the Church of Scotland* (Edinburgh: William Blackwood, 1900), pp. 80–81.

[95] *United Free Church of Scotland Report to the General Assembly of the United Free Church of Scotland 1901* (Edinburgh: T. & A. Constable, 1901), No. XXX *Report of Committee on Statistics*, pp. 2–4.

[96] W. Rounsfell Brown, 'Report of the Foreign Missions Committee', *Principal Acts of the General Assembly of the Free Church of Scotland 1901* (Edinburgh: William Nimmo, 1901), p. 371. See also W.D. Graham, 'Beyond the Borders of Scotland: The Church's Missionary Enterprise', in C. Graham (ed.), *Crown Him Lord of All: Essays on the Life and Witness of The Free Church of Scotland* (Edinburgh: The Knox Press, 1993), pp. 101–102.

[97] McVicar, *Great Adventure*, pp. 70–83.

Orissa (General Baptist) Mission[98] had been formed in 1869. When the 1869 Baptist Union was constituted it sought to ascertain the level of giving to overseas work and asked the affiliated churches in its second year to declare the amounts being donated to the BMS. A small Baptist church in Lochgilphead, for example, had contributed £20 and two of the larger causes, Hope Street (later, Adelaide Place) in Glasgow and Dublin Street in Edinburgh had given £279 and £265 respectively that year. Organised auxiliaries of the BMS were formed, with the first constituted in Glasgow in January 1881 in Adelaide Place Baptist Church, under the chairmanship of Howard Bowser. A Foreign Missions Committee of the BUS was constituted on 22 November 1898 under the chairmanship of Thomas Martin. Its remit was to foster greater interest in overseas mission and organise deputation tours of BMS personnel in Scotland.[99]

One particular aspect of its contribution to this work was the support given to the Baptist Zenana Mission (BZM). It had been formed in London in 1867 out of recognition that the only way to make contact with women living in segregated women's quarters of Hindu and Muslim homes (Zenanas) in India was to create a specialist women's agency to accomplish this work.[100] The first Zenana missionary was Mrs Elizabeth Sale.[101] When she and her husband retired to Helensburgh in 1874 it stimulated significant interest in this work. Scottish auxiliaries to the Zenana mission were formed first in Edinburgh in autumn 1875 with Mrs Hugh Rose as secretary and Mrs Walcott as Treasurer and then in Adelaide Place Baptist Church, Glasgow in September 1877 where Mrs Alexander Rose was appointed secretary and Mrs Allan Macdiarmid the treasurer.[102] The two bodies agreed to co-operate as the Scottish auxiliary to the BZM in 1881 and extend their spheres of influence by changing their respective names to the Eastern and Western divisions. In the later nineteenth century women were beginning to take their rightful place in leading initiatives in both churches and increasingly in the wider society.[103] Scottish Baptist women were reflecting this change.

---

[98] Brian Stanley, *The History of the Baptist Missionary Society* (Edinburgh: T. & T. Clark, 1992), pp. 162–168.

[99] Yuille (ed.), *History of the Baptists in Scotland*, pp. 263–264.

[100] McVicar, *Great Adventure*, p. 9.

[101] More details of her work is given in Olive Mary Coats, 'Elizabeth Sale: A Pioneer Among Women', in A.S. Clement (ed.), *Great Baptist Women* (London: Carey Kingsgate Press, 1955), pp. 56–63; and Stanley, *History of the Baptist Missionary Society*, pp. 228–230. See also Talbot, 'Rousing the Attention of Christians', pp. 62–64.

[102] McVicar, *Great Adventure*, p. 3.

[103] Susan Mumm, 'Women and philanthropic cultures', in Sue Morgan and Jacqueline de Vries (eds), *Women, Gender and Religious Cultures in Britain, 1800–1940*

Another field of particular interest to Scottish Baptists was the developing Baptist mission work in Continental Europe. In the 1870s two sons of William Landels settled in Italy. In 1875 the second son W.K. Landels was appointed by BMS to work in Naples, where premises were erected in 1881 after successful fundraising efforts by William Landels. In 1877 the older son John was appointed to work in the Italian mission. After short terms of service in Rome and Naples, he settled in Genoa where he planted a church that continued after his death from typhoid in 1879.[104] On two occasions representatives of this outreach work addressed the Scottish Baptist Annual Assembly.[105] The Baptist witness in Bohemia, now part of the Czech Republic, was also strongly promoted in Scotland. Here there was a personal link with Henry Novotny, now a Baptist minister, but formerly a Presbyterian, whose training for pastoral work had included time at the Free Church of Scotland College in Edinburgh. Novotny, while serving as a Free Reformed minister in Prague had become convinced of the need for believers' baptism and in 1885 had become a Baptist.[106] In the 1880s a Ladies' Auxiliary was formed in both Edinburgh and Glasgow to aid the Bohemian Baptist Mission.[107] His itinerant labours, prior to his death in 1912, had led to the planting of more than thirty churches. Scottish Baptist churches were the principal source of external finance for Baptist work in Bohemia.[108] Novotny's tours of Scotland were promoted in the *SBM*, as were the reports of the

---

(Abingdon: Routledge, 2010), pp. 54–71. Jocelyn Murray, 'Gender Attitudes and the Contribution of Women', in John Wolffe (ed.), *Evangelical Faith and Public Zeal: Evangelicals and Society in Britain 1780–1980* (London: SPCK, 1995), pp. 97–116. David W. Bebbington (ed.), *The Dominance of Evangelicalism* (Leicester: IVP, 2005), pp. 206–212.

[104] Stanley, *History of the Baptist Missionary Society*, pp. 220–222. Oliver Flett, 'Baptist Missions in Italy', *SBM*, 1.9 (September 1875), pp. 135–138. 'Italy, Naples', *SBM* 3.9, (September 1877), pp. 142–143. 'Our Italian Missions', *SBM*, 4.7 (July 1878), pp. 97–101; *SBM* 6.5 (May 1880), p. 78;

[105] Murray, *First Hundred Years*, p. 77.

[106] Brian Talbot, 'Blest be the Tie that Binds: Scottish Baptists and their Relationships with Other Churches 1900–1945', in Talbot (ed.), *Distinctive People*, pp. 89–90.

[107] Yuille (ed.), *History of the Baptists in Scotland*, pp. 267–268

[108] Chas T. Byford, *Peasants and Prophets: Baptist Pioneers in Russia and South Eastern Europe* (London: The Kingsgate Press, 1911), pp. 15–25. J. Novotny, *The Baptist Romance in the Heart of Europe: The Life and Times of Henry Novotny* (East Orange, New Jersey: Czechoslovak Baptist Convention in America and Canada, 1939), pp. 126–127.

progress of his labours at home.[109] After his death the work was led by his son Joseph, also a Baptist minister, who maintained the link with their Scottish supporters.[110] Scottish Baptists also supported the Grande Ligne Mission in Quebec, not least because its travelling representative in the UK was Joshua Denovan, formerly a Baptist pastor from Glasgow.[111] It was part of a wider interest in Baptist work in Canada.[112] A call was made in 1875 in the *SBM* for a Foreign Missions Committee of the Baptist Union, but this appeal would go unheeded for another three decades.[113] Scottish Baptists in the first two decades of the Baptist Union were seriously interested in Christian work outside the boundaries of their country, though in similar fashion to Christians in other traditions in Scotland their primary allegiance was to the work of their denominational agency.

## Social Action

In the nineteenth century, Evangelical Christians across the United Kingdom were engaged in an increasing range of social ministries in an attempt to alleviate the desperate poverty and suffering of a growing underclass in many of the larger urban communities. Scottish Baptists played their part alongside other churches in a growing commitment to this aspect of ministry in local communities.[114] The range of issues covered was much wider than traditional areas of concern such as personal morality. There were issues like Education in which all the Scottish Churches had taken a special interest over the years, but now major changes had occurred with the passing of the Education (Scotland) Act in 1872. Churches were concerned that this Act would lead to a growing secularisation of public education, but with one third of Scottish

---

[109] *SBM*, 27.10, (October 1901), p. 172; 28.1, (January 1902), p. 11; See also the notices of details of his death, 38.2, (February 1912), p. 24; 38.3, (March 1912), p. 52.

[110] Talbot, 'Blest be the Tie that Binds', pp. 89–90.

[111] 'Grande Ligne Mission', *SBM* 3.9 (September 1877), p. 142; 4.5 (May 1878), p. 76.

[112] For example, 'Sketches of Canadian Baptist Churches', *SBM*, 4.1 (January 1878), pp. 6–7; 4.2 (February 1878), pp. 27–29; 4.3 (March 1878), pp. 40–42;

[113] *SBM*, 1.6, (June 1875), pp. 85–88.

[114] The literature on this subject is vast. Some examples include: Brian Dickey, "Going about and doing good': Evangelicals and Poverty c.1815–1870', in Wolffe (ed.), *Evangelical Faith and Public Zeal*, pp. 38–58. Kathleen Heasman, *Evangelicals in Actions: An Appraisal of their Social Work* (London: Geoffrey Bles, 1962). Gertrude Himmelfarb, *Poverty and Compassion: The Moral Imagination of Late Victorians* (New York: Vintage Books, 1991); Stewart J. Brown, *Providence and Empire 1815–1914* (Harlow: Pearson, 2008), pp. 353–355.

children attending no school and a third of school buildings in a dreadful state, it was inevitable that a new approach was necessary and for the Government to take action to remedy this situation. The Churches no longer had direct control over the schools, but Presbyterian Churches did retain significant control over Teacher-training in the late nineteenth century. During the last three decades of this century Teacher-training was the principal permanent function of the Church of Scotland's General Assembly's Education Committee.[115] To take another example, housing; a census in 1861 revealed that 34% of Scottish houses had only one room and a further 37% had only two rooms. There had only been a modest improvement half a century later.[116] There were an increasing proportion of Christians in this era convinced that something needed to be done.[117] William Blaikie, minister of Pilrig Free Church, Edinburgh, together with his colleague James Begg, Minister of Newington Free Church, Edinburgh, campaigned for better housing for working people and saw significant new developments in the provision of larger and more suitable homes available to rent at a fair price between the 1840s and 1890s in that city, although the supply was still considerably less than the demands for it.[118] One of the most obvious issues that needed attention was the problem of children living on the streets of major cities with very little, if anything, being done to address this pressing need prior to the intervention of a Baptist businessman from Glasgow named William Quarrier.[119] It was an age of individuals, like Blaikie, Begg and Quarrier seeking to rouse their fellow citizens to address the growing social

---

[115] The Church of Scotland Committee on Education, *Centenary of Education (Scotland) Act, 1872* (Edinburgh: William Blackwood & Sons, 1972), pp. 2–4. See also Checkland, *Philanthropy in Victorian Scotland*, pp. 104–131, and Stewart Mechie, *The Church and Scottish Social Development 1780–1870* (Oxford: Oxford University Press, 1960), pp. 146–153.

[116] T.C. Smout, *A Century of the Scottish People, 1830–1950* (London: Fontana, 1987), pp. 33, 44, 50.

[117] Donald C. Smith, *Passive Obedience and Prophetic Protest: Social Criticism in the Scottish Church 1830–1945* (Bern: Peter Lang, 1987), pp. 245–290.

[118] A.C. Cheyne, *The Transforming of the Kirk* (Edinburgh: St Andrews Press, 1983), pp. 119–122. Mechie, *Church and Scottish Social Development 1780–1870*, pp. 119–135. Olive Checkland, *Philanthropy in Victorian Scotland* (Edinburgh: John Donald, 1980), pp. 290–296. T.M. Devine, *The Scottish Nation 1700–2000* (London: Penguin, 1999), pp. 364–366.

[119] Brian Talbot, 'William Quarrier: Philanthropist and Social Reformer', *Records of the Scottish Church History Society*, 39, (2009), pp. 89–129.

inequalities in their midst. The work of William Quarrier[120] will illustrate what could be accomplished in addressing particular social problems.

As a child growing up he experienced the hardship of deep poverty, memories that stayed with him throughout his life. One particular memory had shaped his future life. In 1872 he wrote:

> Thirty-five years ago, when a boy about eight years of age, I stood in The High Street of Glasgow, barefooted, bareheaded, cold and hungry, having tasted no food for a day and a-half, and, as I gazed at each passer-by, wondering why they did not help such as I, a thought passed through my mind that I would not do as they, when I would get the means to help others . . . .[121]

His mother and her young children had moved from Greenock to Govan following the early death of his father after contracting cholera while in Quebec around 1832, which necessitated her looking for work to provide for the family. Conditions in the Wynds of Glasgow were increasing desperate for the thousands of people looking for both homes and employment. A Government official J.C. Symons gave this description of Govan at the time the Quarrier family were living there:

> This quarter consists of a labyrinth of lanes, out of which numberless entrances lead into small courts, each with a reeking dunghill in the centre. Revolting as was the outside appearance of these places, I was little prepared for the filth and destitution within. In some of these lodging-houses (visited at night) we found a whole lair of human beings littered along the floor, sometimes fifteen or twenty, some clothed and some naked, men, women and children, huddled promiscuously together. Their bed consisted of a layer of musty straw intermixed with rags. There was generally no furniture in these places.[122]

Here Mrs Quarrier obtained home-based employment from a Glasgow warehouse, supplying the finishing touches to manufactured articles of clothing, alongside many other women in similar circumstances.[123] William

---

[120] Quarrier was first a member of Blackfriars Street Baptist Church, Glasgow, a congregation later known as John Knox Street Baptist Church; later he transferred his membership to Hope Street Baptist Church, later known as Adelaide Place Baptist Church when that congregation moved to its current site in Glasgow.

[121] William Quarrier, *A Narrative of Facts relative to Work done for Christ in connection with the Orphan and Destitute Children's Emigration Homes, Glasgow*, (Glasgow: George Gallie, 1872), p. 3.

[122] J.C. Symonds, cited with no details, A. Magnusson, *The Village A History of Quarrier's*, (Bridge of Weir: Quarrier's Homes, 1984), p. 5.

[123] J. Urquhart, *The Life Story of William Quarrier* (London: S.W. Partridge, n.d. [1901?]), p. 12.

and his elder sister Agnes joined their mother in spending very long hours sewing clothes, with William delegated to carry work to and from the warehouse. It was a grim childhood, but alarmingly common amongst working class families of his day.

What did William Quarrier accomplish in his concerns for street children? He first advertised his proposed venture in 1871. He had been assisting boys by setting up a shoe-shine brigade, a newspaper brigade and a parcel brigade to deliver mail, all successful ventures. The need for a night shelter quickly became apparent, but significant extra funding was required. A former church building, Dovehill Church, centrally located near Gallowgate, had the upper floor available to rent from the City Improvements Trust. By 1870 funds were available to open this shelter. In 1870 3,397 boys took up the three nights' accommodation allowed to each one, together with good food for the duration of their stay and in the process confirmed the great need for more permanent homes for them.[124] Quarrier then gained sufficient funding to secure premises at 10 Renfrew Lane, Glasgow, a fairly modest property, was obtained that same year. It had been an empty warehouse, but the erection of a kitchen, the garnishing of the bare walls with brightly coloured Scripture texts and the addition of all necessary furniture ensured that the premises were equipped for the children that began to fill its rooms in November 1871.[125] Within a year it was too small so a decision to vacate it and obtain larger premises was made. A spacious old mansion, Cessnock House in Govan Road, Glasgow, was secured for housing boys and 93 Renfield Street, Glasgow for girls. In order to consolidate the facilities the girls' home moved to new premises in Govan Road near the boys' accommodation, prior to the settlement in Glasgow in the larger City Orphan Home in James Morrison Street in April 1876.[126] Further Glasgow properties followed, but the major development came with the purchase of a farm at Bridge of Weir which became known as The Orphan Homes of Scotland, a remarkable village which by the time of his death consisted of sixty four buildings, including thirty-eight large cottages for orphan children, 'Oswald Home' for invalid girls, 'Elim' home for invalid boys, 'James Arthur' a training ship on land, and a poultry Farm Home for boys, together with assorted buildings that included a Church, Schoolhouse, Laundry and Blacksmith's Shop and accommodation for some staff. In his later years he had ventured into addressing medical needs focussing on two types of medical needs. The first was to treat patients suffering from tuberculosis. He erected a Consumption Sanatorium that comprised of seven buildings. His final initiative was to provide a building erected to cater for

---

[124] Gammie, *William Quarrier*, 4th ed., pp. 84–85.

[125] Gammie, *William Quarrier*, 4th ed., pp. 84–86, 91.

[126] Quarrier, *Narrative of Fact*, 1876, p. 4.

children who had epilepsy.[127] *The North British Daily Mail*, a paper sympathetic to his cause concluded in September 1878 that: 'The fact remains that to Mr Quarrier belongs the credit of having, to all intents and purposes, made the only practical attempt to grapple with and successfully solve the great social problem of what to do with the gutter children.[128] It was a remarkably successful venture.

If only a smaller number of Scottish Christians were directly involved in this project, then the opposite would be true of the most prominent Evangelical social campaign, against the 'evils of drink' through the temperance movement. George Barclay, minister of Irvine Baptist Church had published a sermon advocating this cause as early as 1832. Within a decade a growing number of Baptist ministers, lay-leaders and churches had joined colleagues from other denominations to promote this cause.[129] From the more conservative and theologically Reformed Hope Street congregation in Glasgow, James Patterson the minister exerted a powerful influence as the editor of the Scottish Temperance League's early journals, *The Scottish Temperance Review*, and *The Scottish Review*,[130] and Robert Kettle, from the same congregation was one of the most prominent advocates of this cause in the first two decades of this movement.[131] Equally, William Landels who was one of the most fervent advocates of Arminian theological convictions was also a passionate promoter of temperance, particularly in his Cupar ministry.[132] Scottish Baptists across the Calvinist–Arminian theological divide who had struggled in earlier years to work together in evangelistic projects had easily found a common cause in promoting reform on this social issue. The *Jubilee Number* report on Scottish Baptist support for this cause came to the following conclusions about the level of support for its principles in this Scottish denomination. 'There is no lack of leaders, abstainers abounded in

---

[127] A. Gammie, *A Romance of Faith: The Story of the Orphan Homes of Scotland And The Founder* (Glasgow: Pickering and Inglis, 1937), pp. 157–158.

[128] *North British Daily Mail*, 18 September, 1878, quoted in full in Quarrier, *Narrative of Facts*, 1878, pp. 26–27.

[129] A list of Baptist ministers, lay-leaders and churches committed to this cause before 1842 is given in Appendix 5 of Talbot, *Search for a Common Identity*, pp. 362–363.

[130] *Adelaide Place Baptist Church 1829–1929* (Glasgow; Adelaide Place Baptist Church, 1929), p. 11.

[131] P.T. Winskill, *The Temperance Movement and its Workers* (4 Vols; Glasgow: Blackie & Son Ltd, 1893), Vol.2, p. 74. For more details on Baptist commitment to this cause before 1869, see Talbot, *Search for a Common Identity*, pp. 240–246.

[132] T.D. Landels, *William Landels D.D.* (London: Cassel and Company, 1900), pp. 202–203.

the churches, the temperance feeling was marked.'[133] Scottish Baptists were in line with the growing convictions of many Scottish Protestants in the second half of the nineteenth century. The link between piety and temperance was increasingly strong.[134] A series of motions in favour of this cause were presented at the Annual Assembly from 1876 including one 'calling on the churches to devise means to end the prevalent vice' which was adopted unanimously in 1879.

A milestone in Baptist Union support for temperance work took place during the 1881 Baptist Assembly in Edinburgh. The Union President William Grant took the chair of a meeting set up to form 'a Total Abstinence Society in connection with the Union.'[135] The Scottish Baptist Total Abstinence Society (SBTS) was inaugurated on 25 October 1881.[136] Local branches of this agency were then formed around the country, for example, at Long Wynd Baptist Church, Dundee, in December that year.[137] Temperance was a key cause that increasingly united Scottish Baptists as they entered the last decade of the nineteenth century.

The first two decades of the life of the Baptist Union of Scotland formed in 1869 had been most encouraging in almost every area of its work. The number of ministers, churches and outreach activities were all substantially higher than when it began. Their commitment to social causes as part of a holistic approach to ministry was increasingly recognised as essential issues to address if credibility was to be maintained with the wider society. All concerned would have viewed these decades as a time of significant advance within their ranks.

---

[133] *Special Jubilee Number 1881–1931 and Annual Report 1930–31* (Glasgow: Baptist Union of Scotland Temperance Committee, 1931), pp. 2–3.

[134] Checkland, 'Piety and Temperance', in Checkland, *Philanthropy in Victorian Scotland*, pp. 90–101.

[135] *Thirteenth Annual Report of the Baptist Union of Scotland*, 1881, p. 8.

[136] 'Scottish Baptist Total Abstinence Society', *SBM*, 7.12 (December 1881), pp. 193–194.

[137] 'Dundee Scottish Baptist Total Abstinence Society', *SBM*, 8.1 (January 1882), p. 15.

CHAPTER 3

# Branching out with Confidence, 1890–1914

## A Time of Encouragement

The last quarter of the nineteenth century was a time of both creative new forms of outreach amongst the Christian Churches in the United Kingdom, together with significant growth in some forms of ministry as well as in numerical terms in the ranks of some of the smaller Evangelical denominations in Scotland such as the Brethren[1] and Salvation Army[2] as well as Scottish Baptists.[3] Methodists in Scotland too saw an increase in their ranks at this time, but growth had taken place at a much slower rate, in part due to their stricter membership requirements compared with most other churches.[4] The continued growth in the numbers of members and churches within BUS affiliated congregations was most encouraging in these years prior to the First World War. The 1890s was the decade in which the rate of increase in membership reached its highest point during the first fifty years of the present Baptist Union with no fewer than twenty-six new congregations

---

[1] Neil T.R. Dickson, *Brethren in Scotland 1838–2000* (Carlisle: Paternoster Press, 2002), pp. 78–133.

[2] David Armitstead, *The Army of Alba: A History of the Salvation Army in Scotland, 1879–2004* (London: The Salvation Army, n.d. [2017]), pp. 14–99. An editorial comment in the *SBM*, 20.8 (August 1894), p. 219, declared that: 'The Salvation Army is a great success.'

[3] It must not be forgotten that a significant section of the Scottish population had no church connection. In 1891, statistician Robert Howie calculated that more than 1,517,000 Scots were in this category. Robert Howie, *The Churches and the Churchless in Scotland* (Glasgow: David Bryce & Son, 1893), p. 119. Even the large Presbyterian denominations were aware that their growth in membership had not kept pace with the increase in population in Scotland, unlikely the rapidly increasing numbers of Roman Catholics, largely due to Irish immigration. Douglas M. Murray, *Rebuilding the Kirk: Presbyterian Reunion in Scotland 1909–1929* (Edinburgh: Scottish Academic Press, 2000), pp. 6–7.

[4] Margaret Batty, *Scotland's Methodists 1750–2000* (Edinburgh: John Donald, 2010), p. 109. See also the explanation for slower growth between 1850 and 1870, pp. 101–102.

formed.⁵ The annual statistics for 1890 actually presented quite a mixed picture, despite the overall continued growth in numbers. Out of the ninety-two congregations, admissions to membership by baptism were up on the previous year from 795 to 908. The total increase in membership on the previous year in forty-six churches was 601, but twenty-six others recorded a decrease of 223 between them, and fourteen registered no change. The total membership of affiliated churches was up from 11,543 to 11,846. Sunday School attendances may be steady, but at the same time there was a decrease of fifty-one pupils and fourteen classes across the churches with respect to young people of Bible-class age. In the reports from aided congregations there was a similarly mixed picture. The church at Helensburgh was delighted with a net increase of thirteen members and the one at Crieff by five; but by contrast the congregation in Hamilton were discouraged after a year of diminishing numbers. In similar fashion at Peterhead Baptist Church economic difficulties in the wider community had hindered their work. They reported that 'three families had gone abroad and the bad state of trade has affected the finances of the church', but some fund-raising efforts had allowed them to balance the books. Pitlochry and Broughty Ferry congregations reported healthy financial circumstances over the previous year, despite the former loosing younger members moving to larger cities for work. Motherwell Baptist Church declared that their financial health had never been better, as a result of greater commitment of existing members, rather than new members coming in. The George Street congregation in Aberdeen had carried out two very intensive and successful evangelistic campaigns during the year which resulted in forty-two new members added after baptism and nineteen others upon profession of faith; after deducting those members who were no longer in the church, there was a net increase that year of thirty-nine members, and a total of 254.⁶ The underlying numerical trend nationally was clearly upwards, but local circumstances had a far greater impact on the life of any particular congregation. For example, Pitlochry Baptist Church might have been able to recruit a greater number of new local people to offset the regular loss of younger people to the bigger cities of Scotland, but the economic downturn around Peterhead had required people that cause could ill-afford to lose to move elsewhere for work. Strong leadership and intensive evangelistic campaigns had produced excellent responses in the George Street congregation in Aberdeen, whereas Motherwell Baptist Church had consolidated its work as a result of greater commitment from existing members. Overall, it was a time of significant encouragement.

---

⁵ A.T. Richardson, 'The Later Advance: 1850–1925', in Yuille (ed.), *History of the Baptists in Scotland*, p. 87.

⁶ All this data comes from *Twenty-Second Annual Report of the Baptist Union of Scotland* (Glasgow: Baptist Union of Scotland, 1890), pp. 22–26.

This pattern of a mixed picture of growth and decline was consistent in the years up to the First World War. The headline figures look most encouraging. At the October 1913 Baptist Assembly the annual report indicated that the number of churches in the Union had risen from ninety-two to 137. The overall membership was up from 11,846 to 20,527, with admissions by baptism up to 1,073 from 908 in 1890. However, consistently over the years there had been many congregations decreasing in membership as well as others who were favoured with numerical growth. It was surprising that the overall total continued to increase when more than fifty congregations registered a decline in any given year. For example, in 1908, fifty-seven churches had an increase while fifty-four had a decrease. By 1913, the figures were fifty-eight to fifty-six, with only two more congregations seeing numerical growth than those that had declined. Fifteen others had seen no change over the previous year. The underlying picture of local church life was clearly more complex than might have been expected if only religious factors were taken into account. Social and economic factors played a greater role than might have been expected in determining the growth or decline of any one particular local congregation.

There was more encouraging news over young people's work and from some of the evangelistic outreach activities of local churches. Sunday Schools had increased from 152 in 1908 to 160 in 1913. The numbers attending had also increased from 18,039 to 19,552. Bible classes had also prospered increasing in number from seventy-four to eighty-seven and the number attending up from 4,260 to 4,754.[7] The Motherwell Church had reached their highest membership total in its history at 308, after adding seventy-eight new members that year, sixty-eight by baptism. During evangelistic missions held over thirty-seven days by the Baptist Union Field Secretary, D. Merrick Walker, congregations at Bellshill, Paisley and Irvine saw around forty professions of faith in Jesus Christ.[8] The Ayr church had grown slowly, and though it had difficulty attracting children to the Sunday School, a home visitation scheme was planned to boost its numbers. The sand services it organised on the beach were very popular. They were aided by the warm weather and large crowds attended their open-air services at the band stand on July Sunday evenings. Largo Baptist Church in Fife was also encouraged by the numbers of children attending its open-air work on the sands. In Dumfries after some internal difficulties the church had been reconstituted in June 1913 and within the first five months had gained more than fifty members. The Vale of Leven Church had grown from forty to 106 members in only two years and had been particularly encouraged to see around twenty young men and women profess faith in Christ during a November 1913

---

[7] 'Annual Report', *Scottish Baptist Yearbook 1914*, p. 56.

[8] 'Field Secretary's Seventh Annual Report', *Scottish Baptist Yearbook 1914*, p. 85.

mission led by Edinburgh evangelist A.Y. McGregor.[9] However, other causes reported very different circumstances that year. Peterhead Baptist Church struggled to run its ministries due to the number of members and adherents away for longer than usual at sea in the fishing industry and the Port Glasgow congregation lost so many members by removal from the district that it was grateful to have survived; both causes expressed deep appreciation for the support of the Baptist Union during a difficult year.[10] Overall, on the threshold of World War One Scottish Baptists had much to be encouraged about concerning the growth in their ranks. Over just two decades there had been steady and consistent growth in a significant minority of the churches that had more than compensated for those that had seen numerical decline.[11]

### Regional Associations

One of the catalysts for further growth in Baptist ranks came about through the formation of regional associations. The tone of optimism in the benefits of working together was evident in the annual report of the Union in 1876. In the first seven years of the Baptist Union four new regional bodies were formed. First of all that year the Northern Association which comprises the Baptist churches of Caithness, Orkney and Shetland was formed[12] and then by the Ministerial Association of Perthshire, Stirlingshire and Fifeshire; it was followed by the formation of the Aberdeen, Banff, Moray and Inverness Association together with the Glasgow Association. 'So much for the happy influence of the Baptist Union of Scotland in drawing the churches of the denomination closer together, and teaching them to work in harmony.'[13] In 1894 the Leslie Baptist Church brought other congregations in Fife together

---

[9] More details about A.Y. McGregor are given in Tom Lennie, *Glory in the Glen: A History of Evangelical Revivals in Scotland 1880–1940* (Fearn: Christian Focus, 2009), pp. 85–88, 119–120, 131n154, 143, 214. McGregor was a member of the Argyle Place United Free Church in Edinburgh where his father was an elder and treasurer. He was a baptised believer and trained for his work at the Moody Bible Institute in Chicago. He conducted many missions in Scottish Baptist congregations, not least in his 1911 meetings in Peterhead Baptist Church where around 300 people professed conversion during the campaign (Lennie, *Glory in the Glen*, pp. 85 and 214.

[10] The Ayr to Port Glasgow examples are taken from the 'Annual Report', *Scottish Baptist Yearbook* 1914, pp. 58–63.

[11] All data in this paragraph comes from the *Scottish Baptist Yearbook* (Glasgow: Baptist Union of Scotland, 1914), pp. 56–64.

[12] J.S Fisher, 'The North East', in D.W. Bebbington (ed.), *The Baptists in Scotland: A History* (Glasgow: Baptist Union of Scotland, 1988), p. 270.

[13] 'Report', *Eighth Annual Report of the Baptist Union of Scotland* (Glasgow: Baptist Union of Scotland, 1876), p. 9.

to set up a regional association which became known as the Fifeshire and Clackmannanshire Association. In partnership with the Baptist Union of Scotland its evangelistic work resulted in the formation of new causes at Pathhead in Kirkcaldy (1900), Pittenweem in 1902; Bowhill in 1904; Inverkeithing in 1905; Lochgelly and Buckhaven in 1909 and Rosyth in 1920,[14] together with Banton (1903),[15] Larbert (1904) and Bo'ness (1909), in the Stirling and Clackmannanshire area of the Association.[16] Although not all new church-plants in this region were successful, a work launched in Grangemouth in 1894 struggled throughout its existence prior to its closure in 1911.[17] Edinburgh and Lothians Baptist Association, founded in 1894, had been responsible for the planting of new causes at Abbeyhill in 1895 and Gorgie in 1908.[18] In Edinburgh, successful church plants at this time took root in the areas of new housing and numerical growth such as South Leith Baptist Church in 1891, Morningside Baptist Church in 1894 and Portobello Baptist Church that had begun with missions in the 1880s and was finally constituted in 1897.[19] One regional body, though, found it difficult to establish itself. In Tayside a District Committee of the Baptist Union was formed in 1892 with some Baptist Union assistance. It soon became known as the Angus and Perthshire District Association, though it struggled to accomplish the evangelistic goals it had sought to achieve.[20] Co-operative efforts undoubtedly were significant in this church growth, but good leadership and often factors like rapid population growth in new housing areas were also important in successful church-planting initiatives.

It is helpful to take a closer look at one association to highlight some particular factors at work. The Stirling and Clackmannanshire Baptist

---

[14] John Wishart, 'History of Fife Baptist Association', in *Fife Baptist Association: "75 Years Old"* (Anstruther: C.S. Russell & Sons, 1970), n.p. See also S.D. Henry, 'Fife', in Bebbington (ed.), *Baptists in Scotland*, pp. 224–225.

[15] Information on the start of Banton Baptist Church is given in *SBM*, 31.11 (November 1905), p. 209.

[16] Brian R. Talbot, *A Brief History of Central Baptist Association 1909–2002* (Glasgow: Baptist Union of Scotland, 2002), p. 3.

[17] Stirling and Clackmannanshire Baptist Association Minute Book, May 1909 to August 1963, 25 March and 15 April 1911 entries, n.p. This MS is in the Scottish Baptist History Archive in Glasgow.

[18] Christine Lumsden, *A Century of Association: 100 Years of Baptists in Edinburgh and Lothians* (Edinburgh: Strathfleet), 1995, p. 3. Yuille (ed.), *History of the Baptists in Scotland*, p. 242.

[19] J.R. Barclay, 'Edinburgh and Lothians', in Bebbington (ed.) *Baptists in Scotland*, pp.101–102.

[20] Jack Quinn, 'Tayside', in Bebbington (ed.) *Baptists in Scotland*, p. 248

Association was founded in 1909. The key individual here was George Yuille, minister of Stirling Baptist Church and part-time Secretary of the Baptist Union. In January 1893 the Stirling Church had received an invitation to join the Fifeshire Association, but Yuille persuaded his congregation to wait until a local association could be formed. He made contact with each of the local Baptist causes and would in time persuade all but Banton to associate. Why did it take so long? A Deacons' Meeting minute in the Stirling Church gave the reason. Yuille explained that it was 'on account of the Alva Church being unwilling to join. The proposal was still to be kept in view'.[21] The Alva Church was the most outward looking and evangelistically successful Baptist cause in the district, planting short-lived congregations in Dunblane and Callander in 1890, though they had both closed by 1902; it supported William Wright's work in founding Denny Baptist Church in 1891,[22] together with commissioning and funding two of its members, a Mr and Mrs Potter to engage in pioneer church-planting in Natal, South Africa, until their work became self-supporting, together with the Tillicoultry church-plant founded in 1893 that was also successful.[23] It was a remarkable achievement for a church of only fifty-seven members.[24] However, this Alva congregation felt no need for wider fellowship as it was self-sufficient in its work, until its numbers like the Tillicoultry congregation were significantly reduced in the first couple of decades of the twentieth century. It is likely that co-operating more closely with fellow Baptists then became a more attractive proposition. Another factor that possibly contributed to this decision was the change of pastor, with John Miller replacing D.W. Laing in 1906.[25] Here a visionary leader called George Yuille persuaded his colleagues of the benefits of association for fellowship, evangelism and more effectively promoting Baptist

---

[21] Deacons' Meeting Minute Book, 5 February 1883 to 24 November 1902, Stirling Baptist Church, p. 92. The MS is deposited in Stirling Archive.

[22] For more details on William Wright and this congregation see A.D. Gillies, *Pastor William Wright* (Denny: private publication, 1927), pp.18-21; and *Denny Baptist Church 1891–1991* (Denny: For the Church, 1991).

[23] Talbot, *Brief History of Central Baptist Association*, p. 4; See also R.M. Armstrong, *A Brief History of Alva Baptist Church 1882–1982* (private publication, 1982); and 'Alva Baptist Church' in Yuille (ed.), *History of the Baptists in Scotland*, pp. 225-226.

[24] R.A. Barclay, *The Story of Alva Baptist Church 1882–1952* (private publication, 1952), pp. 4-6.

[25] *Tillicoultry Baptist Church: Centenary 1893–1992* (Tillicoultry: Clackmannan District Libraries, 1993), p. 5; and Brian R. Talbot, 'Alva Baptist Church 126th Anniversary Celebrations: The Witness of Alva Baptist Church in its Community and as part of the wider Baptist witness in Central Scotland', unpublished historical lecture, 2009, pp. 5-7.

convictions in the district. It took a time of economic hardship to persuade the Alva congregation of the merits of association, with the Banton cause still insisting on its strict independence. However, the majority of Baptist churches in Stirling and Clackmannanshire were persuaded of the benefits of backing this initiative at its launch in 1909. Regional Associations would become a valuable part of the collective Baptist witness in Scotland throughout the twentieth century.

## Doctrinal Developments

The Scottish Baptist Association established in 1856 had been led by James Paterson, minister of Hope Street [Adelaide Place] Baptist Church, Glasgow, and other men who held mainly to the older orthodox Calvinistic Baptist views, as their statement of faith revealed.[26] However, the purpose of Baptist union in their minds was for practical ends, like the London Baptist Association formed in 1865.[27] As a result, in the 1860s men of overtly Arminian views such as Francis Johnston were welcomed into the Association, prior to the formation of the present Baptist Union of Scotland in 1869. It is clear that from 1869 onwards the doctrinal emphasis is on 'Evangelical' beliefs rather than the more traditional Calvinistic theological understanding. At the turn of the century, in 1899, a much more liberal ethos was dominant amongst Scottish Baptists. The 'Distinctive Principles of the Baptists', produced by a group of West of Scotland Baptist ministers at this time, reveals an openness to new theological ideas and an insistence on freedom to travel down untried doctrinal paths.[28] This document 'Distinctive Principles', however, was never adopted as an official document of the Baptist Union of Scotland despite its inclusion in the yearbook from 1899 to 1933. In theological matters the majority of Baptists in Scotland held to more conservative views than many in some other Scottish denominations. The decision of the United Free Church in its General Assembly of 1901 to clear

---

[26] Talbot, *Search for a Common Identity*, pp. 279–280, 289.

[27] For details of the significance of this body and its influence on Scottish Baptists, see Talbot, *Search for a Common Identity*, pp. 300–307. The standard history of this association is W. Charles Johnson, *Encounter in London: The Story of the London Baptist Association 1865–1965* (London: Carey Kingsgate Press, 1965).

[28] Examples of these more liberal sympathies included Walter Mursell, Minister of Thomas Coats Memorial Church, Paisley. See his 'The Spirit of Discernment' sermon in Walter A. Mursell, *The Waggon and the Star* (Paisley: Alexander Gardner, 1903), pp. 157–158; and D. Witton Jenkin's 1894 Presidential Address, 'Baptists and the New Reformation', *The Twenty-Sixth Annual Report of the Baptist Union of Scotland 1893–1894* (Glasgow: Baptist Union of Scotland, 1894), pp. 78–86. Murray's assessment of this trend is a good summary, *First Hundred Years*, pp. 56–57.

George Adam Smith of heresy over his 'advanced' theological views,[29] for example, was described as an action of 'well-meaning but weak-kneed ecclesiastics', in a lengthy and blunt article in the *SBM* that sought to expose the folly of such behaviour. It concluded with an appeal for repentance. 'The critics like the prodigal have gone into a far country, and let us hope they will speedily repent and return to their Father's house'.[30] By contrast, the September issue of the same periodical made reference to a model Christian scholar, in an 'In Memoriam' to Joseph Angus, former Principal of Regent's Park Baptist College, London. 'Dr Angus was too wise a man to be dazzled by the will-o'-the-wisps of criticism like those that have so abundantly been imported from Germany.[31] A Scottish example of a fine Conservative Evangelical scholar, in contrast to Smith, according to the *SBM*, was Baptist minister John Urquhart, whose pamphlet the 'Case for the Higher Criticism: Is there anything in it?', a reply to the views of Smith, was warmly commended.[32] There was a move led by Thomas Martin, minister of Adelaide Place Baptist Church, Glasgow, to produce a constitution for the Baptist Union of Scotland that was much closer to that of the Baptist Union of Great Britain and Ireland (BUGBI). A subcommittee of the BUS Council was appointed to work on this issue in 1907. It concluded its work with the successful acceptance of the new constitution and the associated 'Declaration of Principle' at the Annual Assembly of the Baptist Union of Scotland in October 1908.[33] This new statement of Baptist convictions was a more conservative Evangelical document compared with the broader theological sympathies evident in the 'Distinctive Principles' document of the previous

---

[29] R.A. Riesen, 'Smith, George Adam (1856–1942)', in Cameron (ed.), *Scottish Church History & Theology*, p. 780. Details of the case are given in George M. Reith, *Reminiscences of the United Free Church General Assembly (1900–1929)* (Edinburgh: Moray Press, 1933), pp. 28-31. Also see Kenneth B.E. Roxburgh, 'Your Word is Truth: Theological Developments among Twentieth-Century Scottish Baptists', in Talbot (ed.), *A Distinctive People*, pp. 128–130.

[30] 'The "Higher Critics" and the Bible', *SBM*, 28.8 (August 1902), pp. 135–236,

[31] In Memoriam 'The Rev. Principal Angus D.D.', *SBM*, 28.9 (September 1902), p. 152. A similar high respect for Angus was accorded amongst Baptists in England at this time. R.E. Cooper, *From Stepney to St Giles: The Story of Regent's Park College 1810–1960*, (London: Carey Kingsgate Press, 1960), p. 65.

[32] *SBM*, 29.3 (March 1903), p. 39. See also J. Urquhart, *The Inspiration and Accuracy of Holy Scripture*, (Glasgow: Pickering and Inglis, n.d.), and J.M. Gordon, 'The Later Nineteenth Century', in Bebbington (ed.), *Baptists in Scotland*, pp. 55–56.

[33] See Murray, *First Hundred Years*, pp. 79–80. For details on the history of the Declaration of Principle in BUGBI see R. Kidd (ed.), *Something to Declare: A Study of the Declaration of Principle of the Baptist Union of Great Britain* (Oxford: Whitley Publications, 1996), pp. 19–23.

decade. It was, therefore, no surprise that it commanded a wider acceptance in Scottish Baptist ranks and has been retained to the present day.

## Women's Work

On Tuesday 20 October 1908 Jessie Yuille, wife of the Secretary of the Baptist Union George Yuille, presented a motion to the Annual Assembly of this body with a recommendation that the women in Scottish Baptist congregations be organised as a distinctive women's organisation within the Baptist Union.[34] This proposal was referred to the Baptist Union Council and resulted in a motion presented to the Annual Assembly the following year on 19 October 1909. 'That this meeting cordially approves of the formation of the Women's Auxiliary to the Baptist Union of Scotland, adopts the Constitution already approved by the Union, and earnestly commends its objects to the co-operation of the churches'.[35] It was a call for Baptist women (1) to organise for the spread of evangelical truth (2) to assist the Baptist Union in promoting any scheme for the advance of the denomination in Scotland, (3) to appoint and support Deaconesses, and (4) to organise Women's Work in the churches.[36] It was not the first organisation run by women in Scottish Baptist churches. That honour belonged to the Auxiliaries to the Baptist Zenana Mission formed in Edinburgh in 1875 and Glasgow in 1877 to promote the work initiated in India by Elizabeth Sale and Marianne Lewis.[37] It is noteworthy that Jessie Yuille had been the secretary of the West of Scotland auxiliary for nineteen years and had built up a network of likeminded women prior to launching the Women's Auxiliary (WA).[38] What is less well known is that she had formed her own women's meeting in Stirling Baptist Church as early as January 1906,[39] and had organised a meeting in Aberdeen in 1908 to outline her vision for future women's work in Baptist churches in Scotland.[40] In addition, the Baptist Women's League (BWL) had been launched in England also in 1908 in the Baptist Union of Great Britain and Ireland under the guidance of John Howard Shakespeare, the secretary of that Union together with Mrs C.S. Rose, the gifted organising secretary of

---

[34] 'Annual Session of the Union', *Scottish Baptist Yearbook 1909*, p. 17.

[35] 'Annual Session of the Union', *Scottish Baptist Yearbook 1910*, p. 19.

[36] Yuille (ed.), History of the Baptists in Scotland, p. 245.

[37] Stanley, *Baptist Missionary Society 1792–1992*, pp. 150, 229.

[38] Olive Mary Coats, *'After Twenty-One Years': Women's Auxiliary To The Baptist Union of Scotland 1909–1930* (private printing, 1930), p. 3.

[39] *Stirling Journal*, January 1908, p.1.

[40] In Memoriam, 'Mrs Jessie Yuille', *SBM* 51.4 (April 1925), pp. 47–48.

that new body.[41] Therefore, prior to her speech at the Scottish Baptist Assembly in 1908 Jessie Yuille had experienced a working model of a Baptist women's organisation to commend to the assembled delegates, as well as knowledge of a growing interest in women's work elsewhere in the United Kingdom.

In the first year of its operations eighteen branches of the WA were formed, a number that grew steadily over its first decade of existence, with twenty-eight affiliated branches of this national agency formed by October 1912 and sixty by 1920. In fulfilment of the first aim local groups were encouraged to meet regularly for prayer and consideration of the spiritual needs of their district. Within two years systematic visitation of their districts was undertaken by some WA women distributing a little magazine entitled *Good Words*, edited by a Baptist minister named E.B. Woods. It was a periodical aimed for the unchurched. Ten thousand copies were distributed monthly until this form of outreach was suspended in 1920 due to the increasing financial cost of printing this periodical. The effective administrative skills displayed through this work resulted in the Baptist Union asking the WA to take over its own work in distributing tracts and Baptist literature. After the Woods left Scotland, the ladies distributed copies of *The Monthly Messenger* edited by John Climie. The WA in 1912 helped to build the 'Pearl Hut' at Lerwick to assist in the Baptist Union's Mission to Fisher Girls, a work conducted by Miss Jane Henderson, the deaconess in Stirling Baptist Church. In May 1913 Jessie Yuille asked Henderson to become the WA deaconess from the following September with the Lerwick Mission being taken over by the WA.[42] The new deaconess spent the rest of that year helping to organise women's work among the churches, engaging in special missions and home visitation. Another initiative that the WA embraced was the commitment to raise a quarter of the £30,000 the Baptist Union of Scotland sought to raise from February 1914 through its Settlement and Sustentation Fund. The purpose of that scheme was to provide financial aid for struggling churches and to augment the modest stipends of Baptist Ministers. Scottish Baptists would give generously to this fund. The WA had obtained promises for half of its share of the target as early as August 1914[43] revealing a level of generosity that was matched elsewhere in Scottish Baptist ranks. The target was raised to £50,000 and by the time the fund closed in 1920 the sum of

---

[41] Randall, *English Baptists of the Twentieth Century*, pp. 75, 85.

[42] Further details of the life and work of Jane Henderson is found in B.R. Talbot, *Standing on the Rock: A History of Stirling Baptist Church 1805–2005* (Stirling: Stirling Baptist Church, 2005), p. 58; and C. Lumsden, 'Her Children Arise and Call Her Blessed: The place of women in Scottish Baptist Life', in Talbot, *A Distinctive People*, pp. 66–71.

[43] Coats, *'After Twenty-One Years'*, pp. 4–5.

£52,000 had been given for its work.[44] WA members had given in total £12,500 in response to this appeal.[45] There was no doubt that the WA was firmly established both in many local churches as well as more generally in Scottish Baptist ranks by the time the First World War began in the autumn of 1914.

### Youth and Children's Work

In 1889 it was recorded in the returns from the ninety-two churches in the Baptist Union of Scotland, that there were eighty-two Sunday Schools organised by Union affiliated congregations with 1,155 teachers and 10,576 pupils.[46] By 1914 the number of Sunday Schools had more than doubled to 162 with 2,778 teachers and 19,838 enrolled children, with an average attendance of 15,619.[47] This rate of progress was significantly higher than the larger more established denominations.[48] By 1890 the number of Baptist churches with no Sunday School work had dropped from nine in 1889 to only six that year. It was an encouragement to note that the number of children in Sunday School had gone up to 10,935, with an increased number of teachers as well, up to 1,223 on the rolls. In addition, there were five more Bible classes and sixty-six more young people present than in the previous year.[49] Although, there had been a fall in the number of over fifteens attending down from 1,218 to 1,096, together with only ninety-eight of them becoming church members compared to 126 the previous year.[50] On the threshold of World

---

[44] Murray, *First Hundred Years*, p. 92.

[45] I. Watson, Secretary, '"Tenth Annual Report" The Women's Auxiliary', *Scottish Baptist Yearbook 1920*, p. 62.

[46] *The Twenty-Second Annual Report of the Baptist Union of Scotland 1889–1890* (Glasgow: Baptist Union of Scotland, 1890), p. 39. Sunday Schools across the United Kingdom encompassed a wide variety of activities beyond religious education by the late nineteenth century. One of the most remarkable examples comes from Harborough Congregational Church Sunday School in Leicestershire. It included a Young Men's Institute, a Young Men's Bible Class, a gymnasium, a debating a society, a Band of Hope, a Christian Endeavour Society, football and cricket clubs and a sick fund. K.D.M. Snell and Paul S. Ell, *Rival Jerusalems: The Geography of Victorian Religion* (Cambridge: Cambridge University Press, 2000), p. 282.

[47] 'Sunday School Report', *Scottish Baptist Yearbook 1915* (Glasgow: Baptist Union of Scotland, 1915), p. 130.

[48] Michael Lynch, *Scotland A New History* (London: Pimlico, 1992), p. 403.

[49] '*The Twenty-Third Annual Report of the Baptist Union of Scotland 1889–1890*, p. 26.

[50] *The Twenty-Third Annual Report of the Baptist Union of Scotland 1890–1891*, p. 46.

War One there had been only a modest improvement in the retention rate of these older young people. It was reported that the numbers of young adults in the churches over fifteen years of age in 1914 was stated as 1,592, but of this number only 380 had become church members, of which 150 had done so in the previous year.[51] Scottish Baptists in common with other Christian denominations set up a range of new meetings and activities to strengthen their ties with young adults. Kelso Baptist Church, for example, set up a Young Worshipper League, and a mid-week winter meeting for children in Kelso that was successful in attracting young people who were outside of the orbit of any local congregation.[52] Although there were some encouragements noted above, it is equally clear that there were challenges to be addressed particularly with respect to retaining the allegiance of older young people.

The best-known organisation used by Scottish Baptists to disciple young Christians was the Christian Endeavour (CE) movement. It was started in the USA by Francis Clark in 1881 as a means of strengthening the faith of young new believers.[53] The first society was formed in Scotland in 1887 in Dundee, but that group lasted only short time. The first continuing CE body in Scotland was formed at Crown Terrace Baptist Church, Aberdeen, in 1891. Other churches also adopted CE in Scotland leading to a Scottish Convention in Glasgow as early as 1895.[54] It had spread rapidly throughout the country. It was an interdenominational movement embraced across Protestant Churches. By 1895, for example, there were 795 CE Societies affiliated to Baptist churches in the United Kingdom, a total that had grown to 1,640 by the time of the World Convention of Christian Endeavour in London in July 1900.[55] In 1901, for example, St Andrews Baptist Church reported that 'The work in connection with the Endeavour Society is heartily taken up and the membership well maintained . . . it is very encouraging to see the deep interest taken in spiritual things by a few of our senior scholars.' Forfar Baptist Church had started a CE Society in February 1901 and declared; 'this meeting has been well attended, and much interest taken in the various branches.' Largo Baptist Church although not reporting new growth was delighted to have retained existing attendees at various meetings including 'the pastor's Bible

---

[51] 'Sunday School Report', *Scottish Baptist Yearbook 1915*, p. 130.

[52] *Scottish Baptist Yearbook 1914*, p. 60.

[53] W. Knight Chaplin, *Francis E. Clark*, (London: The British Christian Endeavour Union, 1920), pp. 24–36.

[54] W. Knight Chaplin and M. Jennie Street, *Fifty Years of Christian Endeavour 1881–1931* (London: The British Christian Endeavour Union, 1938), pp. 32–36.

[55] W. Knight Chaplin and M. Jennie Street (eds), *"Advance Endeavour!" Souvenir Report of the World's Convention of Christian Endeavour, London 1900* (Wilmore, Kentucky: First Fruits Press, 2016 [Original ed. 1900]), p. 122.

Class, and the Christian Endeavour Society [that] have been maintained as in former years.'⁵⁶ By autumn 1905 there were CE Societies in sixty-four Scottish Baptist congregations with sixty-three senior and twenty-two junior comprising of 3,630 individuals with an average weekly attendance of 2,169. 1442 Endeavourers were members of their churches and 283 joined the Church during the year.⁵⁷ After rapid initial growth numbers plateaued in the years immediately prior to World War One,⁵⁸ but it was evident that an effective form of Christian discipleship for older young people had been found that would enable a greater proportion of youth to continue as active participants in these particular local churches. It was clear, though, that more work was needed to be done to ensure many other young people soon to enter the world of work or going on to higher education would commit themselves to active involvement in a local congregation in the years to come. The overall numbers were still up, but there was no room for complacency.

It was a real cause for concern across the churches that some fresh approaches were required to build ties with many young people outside the church and to maintain active participation by others as they entered adult life. One successful method was to use sports as a means of building friendships with young people by the churches in the late nineteenth century.⁵⁹ It was one of a number of creative methods used by churches in that era. Another venture was the vision of William Smith, who had noted the formation of the YMCA in 1844 as a holistic Christian organisation to reach and retain young men in their late teens and early twenties within the orbit of the Christian Churches.⁶⁰ As early as 1874 he had formed a Young Men's Society modelled closely to the YMCA at the College Free Church in the West End of Glasgow. However, Smith had noted that many boys had already left Sunday Schools in their early teenage years and his motivation for founding his new youth organisation was to bridge this gap in provision.⁶¹ He launched 'The Boys' Brigade' in 1883 to address the growing problem of increasingly

---

⁵⁶ All three examples were taken from the *Scottish Baptist Yearbook 1902*, pp. 85–87.

⁵⁷ 'Scottish Baptist Christian Endeavour Report', *Scottish Baptist Yearbook 1906*, p. 103.

⁵⁸ 'Scottish Baptist Christian Endeavour Report', *Scottish Baptist Yearbook 1914*, pp. 134–135; *Scottish Baptist Yearbook 1915*, pp. 140–141.

⁵⁹ Hugh McLeod, 'Sport and the English Sunday School, 1869–1939', in Stephen Orchard and John H.Y. Briggs (eds), *The Sunday School Movement* (Milton Keynes: Paternoster, 2007), pp. 109–123.

⁶⁰ Clyde Binfield, *George Williams and the Y.M.C.A.: A Study in Victorian social attitudes* (London: Heinemann, 1973).

⁶¹ John Springhall, *Sure and Steadfast: A History of the Boys' Brigade 1883–1983* (Glasgow: Collins, 1983), pp. 22–23.

disinterested older working-class boys in Sunday Schools. His vision of an organisation that combined 'Drill and Discipline' would produce order, obedience and self-respect as in the British Army, but it could in this new organisation be combined with games, gymnastics and other sports as well as hymns and prayers.[62] On 4 October 1883 the boys of the North Woodside Mission Sabbath School of the Free Church of Scotland were invited to join 'The Boys' Brigade' led by a Captain brought up in the Church of Scotland and two lieutenants, John and James Hill, who became clergymen in the Church of England. From the original fifty-nine boys who signed up to that first company, within twenty years more than 12,000 boys were committed to this new youth organisation.[63] By October 1885 there were fifteen companies in Scotland, three in Edinburgh and Twelve in Glasgow.[64] The 3rd Glasgow Company had been founded at the St Clair Street Mission of Adelaide Place Baptist Church. However, the mother church's Deacons' Court refused to allow its continuance as they refused to sanction the continuance of 'anything that tends to foster a warlike spirit in boys'.[65] Baptist churches did host Boys' Brigade Companies in the United Kingdom but less so in Scotland than in its stronghold of the north of England.[66] It is possible that this Glasgow Baptist cause was representative of others that were not enthused by uniformed organisations.[67] However, Baptists like other Scottish Christians were

---

[62] Donald M. McFarlan, *First For Boys: The Story of the Boys' Brigade 1883–1983* (Glasgow; Collins, 1983), pp. 11–16.

[63] F.P. Gibbon, *William A. Smith of The Boys' Brigade* (Glasgow: Collins, 1934, pp. 38, 42–46.

[64] The 76th Company of the Boys' Brigade was formed in the Partick Mission of Hillhead Baptist Church on 24 September 1887. Anne Semple, *Hillhead Baptist Church 1883–1983* (Glasgow: Hillhead Baptist Church 1983), p. 24. Bridgeton Baptist Church also had a company, but the date of the foundation is unknown, *SBM* 50.4 (April 1924), p. 50, as did Victoria Place Baptist Church, Glasgow, *SBM* 53.6 (June 1927), p. 91.

[65] Deacons' Court Minutes, 3 June and 1 July, 1885, records held in Adelaide Place Baptist Church. See also Springhall, *Sure and Steadfast*, p. 41.

[66] Springhall, *Sure and Steadfast*, p. 126.

[67] This church was not an isolated example. Alex Dodds, of Marshall Street Baptist Church, Edinburgh, stated that his church chose to establish a Scout Troop instead. 'We are not militarists. We do not even go in for military drill', *SBM*, 52.6 (June 1926), p. 76. Although, other churches were happy to have both Scouts and Boys' Brigade Companies in their ranks, for example, Leven Baptist Church, Fife. See *SBM* 52.7 (July 1926), p. 95; and South Leith Baptist Church, Edinburgh, had amongst its affiliated organisations Brownies and Girl Guides as well as the Boys' Brigade Company, *SBM* 54.3 (March 1928), p. 34.

committed to finding innovative ways of promoting their faith to children and young adults in the years preceding the First World War.

## Temperance

There were many social issues that Scottish Baptists had concerns about in these years, but there would have been little doubt that for the majority of them the problem of drunkenness and its consequences would have been amongst the most pressing issues to address.[68] However, other denominations were quicker to form temperance committees, including the Free Church of Scotland and the United Presbyterian Church in 1847 and the Church of Scotland in 1848.[69] It is probable that the greater autonomy of Baptist congregations had contributed to the delay in forming a collective Baptist agency to promote this cause.[70] Alexander Wylie, then a Glasgow Baptist minister, was the first to propose that Scottish Baptists form a society to address this issue at the 1876 Annual Assembly. This issue was raised each year until in 1879 the Assembly unanimously agreed to the formation of the Scottish Baptist Total Abstinence Society (SBTAS), an agency that was formally inaugurated on 25 October 1881. The wording of the pledge was clear: 'I agree to abstain from all intoxicating drinks as a beverage and to promote the practice of Abstinence in the Community'. The earliest roll of members contained 135 names of which approximately forty were ministers,[71] and a high proportion of those training for pastoral ministry were also advocates of this cause. Many Scottish Baptists would have agreed with a statement of David Lloyd-George in 1907 in which he declared that alcohol: 'bred more poverty, disease, crime and vice than any single cause in the land and was responsible for a great mass of festering degradation.' J.W. Horsley, a prison chaplain stated that he viewed crime as 'condensed alcohol.' Another correspondent to the SBTAS in 1907 wrote that the: 'cursed traffic [of alcohol] ruins more souls in a week than the preaching of the gospel rescues in

---

[68] An excellent overview of this movement in Scottish churches in this era is provided by N.D. Denny, 'Temperance and the Scottish Churches, 1870–1914', *Records of the Scottish Church History Society,* Vol. XXIII, Part 2, 1988, pp. 217–239.

[69] Denny, 'Temperance and the Scottish Churches, 1870–1914', pp. 223–224.

[70] As suggested by Denny, 'Temperance and the Scottish Churches, 1870–1914', p. 229.

[71] There does seem some confusion as to the exact number of subscribing Baptist Ministers in 1881. For example, *Baptist Union of Scotland Temperance Committee Special Jubilee Number 1881–1931* lists 'thirty-five out of seventy' on p. 10, though 'forty' on p. 5. John S. Bone, 'The Scottish Baptist Total Abstinence Society', in *The Scottish Temperance Annual,* 1901, p. 67, stated that the number of Ministers listed was '43'.

a year ...'[72] These sentiments would have been commonly held in Scottish Baptist ranks at the start of the twentieth century. However, they were not downcast, but very confident in the future success of their cause. As early as 1901, John S. Bone, a Baptist temperance advocate, took great satisfaction in recording that: 'It is believed that there are not more than six non-abstaining Baptist ministers in Scotland [in 1901].... The Society [SBTAS] is also entitled to much credit for the fact that almost every church in the Union now celebrates the Communion with unfermented wine.'[73] Lists of ministers advocating temperance principles and churches using unfermented wine at communion were published in the *Scottish Baptist Yearbook* up to World War One, by which time the vast majority of Baptist ministers and congregations were supportive of this cause.[74] In fact, by the end of the nineteenth century almost every Baptist congregation was using unfermented wine at communion.[75] Out of a printed list of 112 churches, only Dublin Street Baptist Church, Edinburgh, was reported to be offering both fermented and unfermented wine by 1898.[76] Scottish Baptists, in line with other mainstream Churches in Scotland were active in political representations supporting the tightening of licences in, for example, the Forbes Mackenzie Act of 1853. Seventy Baptist congregations sent petitions supporting the unsuccessful Local Options Bill,[77] an attempt by the Liberal Government in 1894 to provide opportunities for local communities to restrict the sale of alcohol in their communities. However, by 1914 morale was high as the new Temperance (Scotland) Act came into force, restricting opening hours of

[72] These three quotations are found in 'The Scottish Baptist Total Abstinence Society Twenty-Seventh Annual Report 1907–1908', *Scottish Baptist Yearbook 1909*, pp. 270–271.

[73] Bone, 'Scottish Baptist Total Abstinence Society', p. 67.

[74] *Baptist Union of Scotland Temperance Committee Special Jubilee Number 1881–1931*, pp. 10–11.

[75] Murray, *First hundred Years*, p. 68.

[76] 'The Scottish Baptist Total Abstinence Society Seventeenth Annual Report 1897–1898', *Scottish Baptist Yearbook 1899*, Appendix C, pp. 14–15. It is more accurate to state that at least two churches made the change later. Hillhead Baptist Church continued offering fermented wine at communion until at least 1913. Thomas Coats Memorial Church, Paisley, was the last to conform on this matter only changing to unfermented wine in April 1953 at the request of new minister William Grant. See Chapter five, page 147, n145 for more details. This point was confirmed by a conversation with Robert and Eleanor McIntyre, long-standing members at Coats Memorial Church, on 10 September 2018. See also Derek Murray, 'Be Not Conformed but Transformed: Scottish Baptists and Social Action', in Talbot (ed.), *Distinctive People*, p. 233.

[77] Yuille (ed.), *History of the Baptists in Scotland*, p. 247.

Public Houses and granting an opportunity for local ratepayers to vote on this subject in 1920.[78] The SBTAS took satisfaction that one of its Vice Presidents Sir John Mills McCallum, a soap manufacturer and the Liberal M.P. for Paisley, and a deacon of Thomas Coats Memorial Church, Paisley, 'had a prominent share in promoting in parliament the Temperance (Scotland) Act, 1913'.[79] This was one of the highpoints of this cause on the threshold of the First World War.

From the 1870s there was a significant shift to prioritise advocacy of this cause amongst young people because education was seen as crucial in changing attitudes in the country. The organisation that was particularly influential in this work was the 'Band of Hope'. It was founded by Jabez Tunnicliffe, a Baptist minister in Leeds, who was profoundly affected in June 1847 by a conversation with a former member of his church's Sunday School, who was dying as a result of alcohol consumption. The young man challenged the minister 'to warn young men against the first glass'. A series of meetings led eventually to the founding of this juvenile temperance society on 4 October 1847, with the objective of teaching children the importance and principles of sobriety and teetotalism.[80] When the SBTAS was formed in 1881, the Band of Hope was still a small organisation. However, this movement had grown dramatically over the following years with a rise to 570 branches in 1887 and 700 by 1908.[81] Amongst Scottish Baptists it was reported that there were seventy-five Baptist congregations having a Band of Hope by April 1898.[82] In addition, the first chairman of the Band of Hope Union in Glasgow was William Quarrier, the Baptist figurehead of the Orphan Homes at Bridge of Weir, who had witnessed at first hand the devastating consequences of drunkenness in the families of many of the children he had rescued. Educating the young on this subject was a priority for Quarrier. Band of Hope provided activities for children up to sixteen years. Out of this organisation came the idea for Crusaders to take care of young people too old for the Band of Hope,

---

[78] The Scottish Baptist Total Abstinence Society Thirty-Third Annual Report 1914', *Scottish Baptist Yearbook 1915*, p. 6.

[79] *Baptist Union of Scotland Temperance Committee Special Jubilee Number 1881–1931*, p. 6. See also D.W. Bebbington, 'Baptist Members of Parliament in the Twentieth Century', *Baptist Quarterly*, 31.6 (April 1986), p. 270.

[80] Frederic Smith (ed.), *The Jubilee of the Band of Hope Movement* (London: United Kingdom Band of Hope Union, 1897), pp. 44–48.

[81] Lynch, *Scotland: A History*, p. 403.

[82] 'Scottish Baptist Total Abstinence Society Seventeenth Annual Report 1897–1898', Appendix C, pp. 8–13.

but too young for adult temperance societies. It would prove a great success.[83] Temperance Committees had also developed as part of another Christian youth movement, CE at this time.[84] It is difficult more than a century later for many people to appreciate both the passion for and the success of this cause in Scotland in the decades prior to World War One.[85] However, it is clear that in partnership with other measures to alleviate poverty and improve the lives of people in many of the poorer communities in Scotland the Temperance movement made a significant contribution to the progress that undoubtedly was made at that time.

## Theological Education

A new step was taken by Scottish Baptists with the launch of the Baptist Theological College of Scotland (BTCS) in September 1894. The first President of this new institution was Professor Joseph Coats,[86] who held the Chair of Pathology in Glasgow University. The wider Coats family were firmly committed to the college and its work and alongside other leading laypeople like Howard Bowser, a partner in D.Y. Stewart & Co, cast-iron pipe manufacturers,[87] put it on a sound financial footing with an endowment fund that had grown to £5,000 by 1906. The family of the late Thomas Coats would later donate a further gift of £17,000, in honour of his commitment to Baptist Theological education, in 1913, which increased the Endowment Fund to a respectable £22,400 and ensured the college now had a solid financial foundation for its work.[88] It is important to acknowledge that there was much debate over the appointment of the first tutors and the Baptist Union's commitment to handing over this area of its work without knowing the names of the tutors in advance. One correspondent to the *SBM* in April 1893 had written: 'It would be a terrible mistake if it should go back into the

---

[83] David Strachan, *Scottish Band of Hope Union Diamond Jubilee Brochure* (Glasgow 1931), cited by E. King, *Scotland Sober and Free: The Temperance Movement, 1829-1979* (Glasgow: Glasgow Museums and Art Galleries, 1979), p. 13.

[84] *Baptist Union of Scotland Temperance Committee Special Jubilee Number 1881-1931*, pp. 6–7.

[85] 'Scotland Back in the Day: Spirited Souls led the fight to defeat the demon drink', *The National*, 12 April 2016.

[86] His death in 1899 was a heavy blow to the young college. See 'The Late Professor Joseph Coats', *SBM*, 25.2 (February 1899), pp. 21–23.

[87] Bowser also died in 1899. 'The Late Mr Howard Bowser, J.P.', *SBM*, 25.10 (October 1899), pp. 163–166.

[88] *Baptist Theological College of Scotland Jubilee 1894-1944*, pp. 6–7; Yuille, *History of Baptists in Scotland*, p. 257; Murray, *First Hundred Years*, p. 75.

hands of the men in whom the churches have not confidence and I think a sad blow to the evangelical of the churches in this land.'[89] Another anonymous correspondent suggested it might lead to other small colleges being founded, 'like that already existing down the Clyde, receiving men whose application the Union has declined.'[90] It is clear that there are echoes of the Downgrade Controversy that had begun amongst English Baptists in 1887 primarily over the emergence of liberal theological convictions in their midst, but also secondarily over related concerns about the nature of theological education on offer in the various English denominational colleges.[91] Meetings were held between representatives of the Baptist Union and of the new Baptist College to address this issue. Jervis Coats, Minister of Govan Baptist Church, Glasgow, handled Biblical Criticism and Exegesis; Alexander Wylie of Marshall Street Baptist Church, Edinburgh, was appointed to lecture in Biblical and Systematic Theology, together with Thomas Martin, Minister of Adelaide Place Baptist Church, Glasgow, in Homiletics, General Pastoral Work, together with Baptist History and Principles. John McLellan, the former minister of Cupar Baptist Church who had resigned his pastorate in 1888 to become the full-time tutor,[92] directing the educational work of the Baptist Union in the years immediately prior to 1894, was invited to lecture in Apologetics and Church History. There is no doubt that he had expected to be offered the lectureship on Systematic Theology and the hesitant recommendation of the Baptist Union for the launch of this college made this point very clear that he was not alone in this expectation.

> The sub-committee arrived at this recommendation with considerable hesitation, but had Mr McLellan been appointed to the Lectureship on Systematic Theology this hesitation would not have been experienced. They are in hopes that even yet some method of securing Mr McLellan's services to the denomination in the special department which he has undertaken for so many years with such distinguished success may be accomplished.[93]

---

[89] 'Correspondence', *SBM*, 19.4 (April 1893), pp.104–105; See also *SBM* 19.5 (May 1893), pp. 131–132; 19.6 (June 1893), p. 160; 19.7 (July 1893), p. 193.

[90] 'Correspondence', *SBM*, 19.8 (August 1893), pp. 219–220.

[91] Murray, *Scottish Baptist College*, p. 12. See also Ernest A. Payne, *The Baptist Union A Short History* (London: Carey Kingsgate Press, 1958), pp. 127–143; Briggs, *English Baptists of the Nineteenth Century*, pp. 79–80; 175–188; Patricia Stallings Kruppa, *C.H. Spurgeon: A Preachers Progress* (Abingdon: Routledge, 2017 [first published in 1982]), pp. 404–444; Mark Hopkins, *Nonconformity's Romantic Generation* (Milton Keynes: Paternoster, 2004), pp. 125–166, 193–248.

[92] Yuille, *History of Baptists in Scotland*, p. 126.

[93] *The Twenty-Seventh Annual Report of the Baptist Union of Scotland 1894–1895* (Glasgow: Baptist Union of Scotland, 1895), p. 37. A motion passed unanimously at

Unfortunately, with hindsight it does appear that the College representatives made an unwise choice that upset not only this individual colleague, but also others in the wider Baptist family and would ensure that personal differences that had existed between a number of leaders over this subject of theological education would persist longer than they might otherwise have done.[94] The perspective offered in the *SBM* confirms this interpretation of this predicament. 'We cannot but think that an invaluable opportunity of uniting the denomination on this subject of education has been lost, and that a tactical blunder has been committed as regards the interests of the college itself'.[95] It is possible that they would have argued that in offering McLellan a post at all was a fair offer to the former Baptist Union tutor. McLellan chose to reject the subjects offered and these courses were then divided between the other three tutors for the next two decades, until there were sufficient financial resources to appoint a fourth lecturer to the staff team. However, there was an additional colleague, P.J. Rollo, minister of John Knox Street Baptist Church, Glasgow, who served as the Convenor of the Board of Studies and oversaw the devotional and social side of college life for approximately thirty years.[96] It was a step forward that this fresh start in Baptist theological education had begun in Scotland, but it would take a number of years before it was a firmly established institution in this particular constituency.

Another reason why some Scottish Baptists might have been less committed to this institution was the fact that it was not the only theological institution operated by Scottish Baptists. In 1893 the minister of Dunoon Baptist Church, Duncan Macgregor founded the Dunoon Baptist College as an independent body for the training of evangelists and missionaries.[97] It had a strong revivalist and holiness emphasis in the theological teaching of that institution. Macgregor had trained for Baptist ministry under James Paterson in Glasgow, prior to serving in America in a Chicago Baptist Church.[98] He then returned to Scotland in 1885 to become minister of Dunoon Baptist Church until his retirement from it twenty-four years later in 1909, in order to

---

the Baptist Union Council on 23 October 1895 highlighted McLellan's suitability for such a post, ibid, pp. 15–16. See also *SBM*, 21.3 (March 1895), p. 77.

[94] See *SBM* 20.8 (October 1894), 'Notes', p. 276.

[95] *SBM*, 21.4 April 1895), p. 101.

[96] *Baptist Theological College of Scotland Jubilee 1894–1944*, pp. 5–6.

[97] McGregor and Jervis Coats were friends and preached for each other. I am grateful to Derek Murray for highlighting this information. See Murray, *Scottish Baptist College Centenary History 1894–1994*, p. 12.

[98] D.E. Meek, 'Macgregor, Duncan (?-1915)' in N.M. de S. Cameron (*et al* eds), *Dictionary of Scottish Church History and Theology* (Edinburgh: T & T. Clark, 1993), pp. 514–515.

work full-time in the College which closed after his death in 1915.[99] However, it is clear that its graduates served not only overseas but also as home missionaries and pastors within Scottish Baptist churches. Ministerial students trained in Dunoon included its first student Peter Fleming, who later was called to Duncan Street Baptist Church, Edinburgh,[100] William Crozier who went to George Street, Paisley,[101] T.S. Metrustry who was called to Irvine Baptist Church;[102] Alex Black who was appointed pastor of Old Cumnock Baptist Church in 1899,[103] followed by Thomas Jones in that church from the same college in 1900 after his predecessor's resignation and Robert White who was called as pastor of South Leith Baptist Church, Edinburgh, until 1911.[104] A more prominent former student at Dunoon was Thomas McQuiston who gave years of distinguished service as an evangelist and minister in Baptist Union ranks.[105] However, the best known individual associated with the college was Oswald Chambers (1874–1917). He was the fourth son of Hannah and Clarence Chambers, the latter was minister of Crown Terrace Baptist Church, Aberdeen between 1866 and 1877.[106] Chambers entered the Dunoon College to train for the pastoral ministry in 1897, but was retained as a member of staff teaching Logic, Moral Philosophy and Psychology between 1898 and 1906. His Bible teaching ministry was increasingly valued making trips overseas to Japan and America in 1906–1907. After a short itinerant ministry working primarily with the League of Prayer, Chambers became the first Principal of the Clapham Common Bible

---

[99] Yuille, *History of Baptists in Scotland*, p. 279; Murray, *First Hundred Years*, p. 90; D.E. Meek, 'The Highlands', in Bebbington (ed.), *Baptists in Scotland: A History*, p. 292.

[100] *Twenty-Seventh Annual Report of the Baptist Union of Scotland 1894–1895*, 1895, p. 30. Yuille, *History of Baptists in Scotland*, p. 280.

[101] *Twenty-Eighth Annual Report of the Baptist Union of Scotland 1895–1896*, 1896, p. 29.

[102] *Twenty-Ninth Annual Report of the Baptist Union of Scotland 1896–1897*, 1897, p. 31.

[103] *Scottish Baptist Yearbook 1899* (Glasgow: Baptist Union of Scotland, 1899), p. 59.

[104] *Scottish Baptist Yearbook 1900* (Glasgow: Baptist Union of Scotland, 1900), p. 67. Yuille, *History of Baptists in Scotland*, p. 133.

[105] Murray, *First Hundred Years*, p. 90; McQuiston also produced several works including most prominently *Church Evangelism* (London: Kingsgate Press, 1926).

[106] *Oswald Chambers His Life and Work* (London: Marshall, Morgan and Scott, 1959), p. 13. Franklin Chambers in this book puts his father's move to a Baptist ministry in Stoke in 1879, but this is unlikely to be accurate. See Yuille, *History of Baptists in Scotland*, pp. 89–90.

Training College, London, in 1911. He enlisted to serve with the YMCA in Egypt in 1915 and died there in 1917. His many posthumously published writings were originally given as practical talks to students and soldiers.[107] The Dunoon College may have been established on very limited resources, but it made a small but significant contribution to Scottish Baptist theological education prior to its cessation in 1915. It is also important to note that there was also another interdenominational Bible College, founded after the Moody and Sankey campaigns in Scotland, the Bible Training Institution in Glasgow. The first two known Scottish Baptist pastors trained under its auspices commenced their ministries in 1897. James Mackay who was called as pastor by Oban Baptist Church and Joseph Kemp who settled that year in Kelso Baptist Church.[108] After too many years with inadequate facilities for theological education the scene was significantly transformed by the start of the twentieth century.

## Overseas Mission

The Baptist Union of Scotland established a Foreign Mission Committee in 1909. This new body later that year launched an enquiry into the level of interest in and support for overseas missionary work within the churches of the denomination.[109] Out of 139 churches invited to complete the 'Schedule of Inquiry', 125 of them completed the form, together with three others who sent in the required information in a different format. Therefore, the published report is a most helpful guide to the commitment of Scottish Baptist Churches to this aspect of Christian service. There were four BMS-related monthly missionary periodicals taken by the churches, the *Missionary Herald*, *Wonderlands*, *Zenana Magazine* and *Medical Missionary*, as well as two other free BMS publications, the *Quarterly for General Readers* together with the *Quarterly for Juvenile Readers*. Out of a membership of 14,744, Scottish Baptists in 106 congregations took 8,391 monthly magazines. The younger children's periodical *Wonderlands* was taken in fifty congregations by 3.051 individuals out of a total of 7,488 Sunday School children. Although only fifty, mainly larger congregations took the 850 subscribed copies of the

---

[107] J. Taylor, 'Chambers, Oswald (1874–1917)' in Cameron (*et al* eds), *Dictionary of Scottish Church History and Theology*, p. 161. For more details see *Oswald Chambers His Life and Work* and D. McCasland, *Oswald Chambers Abandoned to God* (Grand Rapids: Discovery House Publishers, 1993).

[108] *Twenty-Ninth Annual Report of the Baptist Union of Scotland 1896–1897*, 1897, p. 31.

[109] 'Foreign Mission Committee Report', *Scottish Baptist Yearbook 1911* (Glasgow: Baptist Union of Scotland, 1911), pp. 152–161. All information unless indicated to the contrary in this section comes from this report.

Women's *Zenana Magazine*. No further data was available regarding the 1,554 subscriptions to the *Medical Missionary*. It does seem remarkable that in addition to these four monthly subscribed publications there were free quarterly periodicals for adults and children respectively offered by the BMS. However, only seventeen Baptist congregations in Scotland obtained copies of these additional sources of information on Baptist overseas mission work and twenty-eight obtained none of the above publications. It is clear that many Scottish Baptist congregations were committed supporters of BMS and eager to receive its printed reports, although, one in five for unknown reasons appeared to have limited interest in its work or possibly in any form of mission outside of their native land.

BMS was also good at providing speakers to congregations who wished to receive more detailed presentations on its activities. There were 104 churches that annually had a BMS missionary or other representative speak in their congregation. Sixty-one had speakers from the Baptist Zenana Mission give updates on their work, together with fifty who welcomed Medical Auxiliary agents to meetings each year, of which thirty-seven congregations welcomed representatives of all three Baptist agencies on an annual basis. What is remarkable is that twenty-eight churches indicated that if BMS could supply them then even more speakers such a development would be warmly welcomed. It was also clear that many Scottish Baptist causes had specific individuals called to promote or collect for this work in their local context. Fifty-five had appointed a missionary secretary and treasurer, of which twenty had formed a missionary committee; twenty-four had created mission study committees and more than twenty had young people's missionary auxiliaries established. There was a range of ways that collections were obtained for this work. The Bible classes in some churches set targets for the year; other churches nominated a specific Sunday in the month for 'retiring collections' for missionary work. Some churches provided members with missionary boxes, small cardboard boxes for personal contributions to be added at home. A few congregations retained the older practice of appointed collectors who visited members in turn at home at regular intervals to obtain contributions. Other churches gave out envelopes that were returned with contributions on a monthly basis; in addition, there were churches that held annual sales of goods. The funds raised were donated to the designated missionary society. Dissemination of information about various forms of missionary service by personnel who were serving overseas was a significant part of the promotion of BMS-related work. In the same way local congregations utilised a wide range of means to raise funds for its work.

However, Baptists like Christians of other major Protestant denominations in Britain in the late nineteenth and early twentieth centuries were unable to raise sufficient funds to cover the significantly increased costs of their expanding ministries overseas and their mission agencies had some difficult choices to make.[110] British Baptists had raised a respectable £114,670 in 1892, the centenary year of the commencement of the Baptist Missionary Society's work. When the size of their constituency is taken into account and the lack of many wealthy donors, in comparison with some of the other denominations, it was a welcome increase in funding for the society's work. The office bearers stated: 'the sum of £100,000 contemplated has not only been obtained, but considerably exceeded.'[111] This was an encouraging response, but it was not a representative one. In too many years expenditure exceeded income. In Scotland in particular, the figures for Church of Scotland's overseas work grew significantly, in particular in the last quarter of the nineteenth century. The Church of Scotland set aside £10,117 in 1879 for overseas work. This total had risen to £50,691 by the end of the century in 1899;[112] £56,114 by 1911[113] and £67,889 by 1919.[114] Although it must be noted that this funding came from a small number of individuals and a minority of parishes. It appears that only approximately one-third of its parishes were seriously committed to supporting its overseas work.[115] The financial giving of the United Free Church at home for its overseas mission projects had reached £109,645 as early as 1901[116], but was only £84,698 in 1910 and relied on legacies to balance the books. It was a cause of real concern to their Foreign Mission Committee.[117] These Churches had other sources of funding for overseas work as well, but the statistics cited above give good comparative figures for the two largest Presbyterian denominations in the early part of the twentieth century. BMS, the agency supported by Scottish Baptists, after the encouragements of funds raised in 1892, saw its regular income drop in the following year leaving a deficit of £15,874 in 1893 alone.

---

[110] Talbot, 'Spreading the Good News from Scotland', pp. 148–151.

[111] J.B. Myers (ed.), *The Centenary Celebrations of the Baptist Missionary Society 1892-1893* (London: The Baptist Missionary Society, 1893), pp. vi, 721.

[112] *Report of the Schemes of the Church of Scotland for the Year 1900* (Edinburgh: William Blackwood and Sons, 1900), pp. 82–83.

[113] *Report of the Schemes of the Church of Scotland for the Year 1911* (Edinburgh: William Blackwood and Sons, 1911), pp. 88–89.

[114] *Report of the Schemes of the Church of Scotland for the Year 1919* (Edinburgh: William Blackwood and Sons, 1919), pp. 60–61.

[115] Andrew C. Ross, 'Scottish missionary concern 1874–1914', *Scottish Historical Review*, Vol.51, No.151 (1972), pp. 69–70.

[116] 'Report of Committee on Statistics', No. XXX, *Reports to the General Assembly of the United Free Church of Scotland 1901* (Edinburgh: T. & A. Constable, 1901), p. 8.

[117] 'Eleventh Report on Foreign Missions', *Reports to the General Assembly of the United Free Church of Scotland 1911* (Edinburgh: T. & A. Constable, 1911), pp. 5–6.

£46,000 of the funds raised in the centenary appeal had to be used to erase the accumulated debts of the early 1890s. The highest annual income figures attained occurred in 1897–1898 when £78,546 was raised, but it was still some way short of the stated goal of £100,000.[118] Great opportunities for overseas work had been grasped by the different churches, but all without exception struggled to find the financial resources to pay for all the projects to which they were committed. Tough choices would soon have to be made.

Scottish Baptists did not only support BMS. There were seven other Baptist agencies that received funds from these congregations. They were: the Baptist Industrial Mission of Scotland,[119] the Baptist Pioneer Mission, the Bohemian Mission, the Canadian North-West Mission, the German Baptist Mission, the Grande Ligne Mission in Quebec and the Spezzia Mission in Italy. Outside of Baptist agencies there were sixteen non-denominational bodies that received support. These were the China Inland Mission; the Southern Morocco Mission; Paraguay Mission; Poona and India Village Mission; Regions Beyond Missionary Union, Central Africa Mission, Ceylon and India General Mission; Mildmay Jewish Mission; Mission to Lepers; Help for Brazil; South Africa General Mission; North Africa Mission; San Pedro Mission, Angola Mission and the Waldensian Mission.[120] The era of only supporting a denominational overseas mission agency was drawing to a close. During the twentieth century, despite the greater financial constraints on churches, the number of specialist non-denominational bodies seeking support from the churches would steadily increase. With a limited pot of money on which to draw greater creativity was required to accomplish the goals and objectives of most overseas missionary societies.

## Ties with Other Baptists

It was not surprising that Scottish Baptists had a high regard for their ties with the Baptist Union of Great Britain and Ireland (BUGBI). However, they

---

[118] *BMS Annual Report*, 1892–3, pp. 3–4, 92–93; 1893–94, pp. 93–94; 1894–95, p. 98; 1897–98, p. 120, cited by B. Stanley, *The History of the Baptist Missionary Society 1792–1992*, (Edinburgh: T. & T. Clark, 1992), pp. 226–227.

[119] For a brief history of this mission see Ernest Gray, *A Short History of the Baptist Industrial Mission of Scotland in Nyasaland, 1895–1930* (Cambridge: Churches of Christ Historical Society, 1987). For a more detailed study see Kenneth Coulter, 'The context of the Baptist Industrial Mission of Scotland to Nyasaland', M.Th. thesis, University of Aberdeen, 1989.

[120] 'Foreign Mission Committee Report', *Scottish Baptist Yearbook 1911*, pp. 160–161. For more details on support for these other non-denominational agencies by Scottish Baptists, see Talbot, 'Spreading the Good News from Scotland', pp. 162–171.

did not want to be merged into the larger body as a regional association.¹²¹ At their annual Assembly in 1872 BUGBI leaders had simply assumed that the Scottish Union was affiliated to the larger organisation, rather than established as a separate denomination. The 1872 BUGBI Assembly motion declared: That the Union recognises the Baptist Unions of Wales and Scotland as affiliated

> to the Baptist Union of Great Britain and Ireland, and resolves that the Chairman, Secretary and Treasurer of each of these Unions be entitled, ex officio, to seats on the Committee of this Union.¹²²

This assumption irritated the independent-minded Scots. The 1872 Scottish Assembly ensured that this false perception was graciously corrected. The minute, dated October 24, 1872, stated:

> The Session whilst grateful for and most desirous to reciprocate the practical courtesy of the Baptist Union of Great Britain and Ireland is doubtful of the propriety of affiliation with the larger society.¹²³

The Scots did not wish their friendship to be taken for granted and wished to work together as equal partners. The motion was followed up by the BUS Executive Committee in July 1873. They were determined to ensure that 'our relation to that Union should be more clearly defined'. The secretary was instructed to inform BUGBI that they ought to consider changing 'the name of the larger Union' to 'The Baptist Union of England and Wales.'¹²⁴ The younger body was grateful for assistance from their British colleagues, but had a strong sense of their distinct identity in the last quarter of the nineteenth century. However, it is probable that one of the greatest means of strengthening ties between these two bodies was the regular movement of ministers between churches in England and Scotland. On the occasion of the transfer of a minister from Scotland, a letter was sent commending him to the

---

¹²¹ Details of this discussion are given in B.R. Talbot, 'Blessed be the tie that binds', in Brian R. Talbot (ed.), *A Distinctive People* (Milton Keynes: Paternoster, 2014), pp. 82–83.

¹²² BUGBI, Committee Meeting, 21 November, 1871; Annual Session, 22 April, 1872, MS in Angus Library, Regent's Park College, Oxford; *Baptist Handbook*, (London: Yates and Alexander, 1873), p. 41.

¹²³ Annual Session, 24 October, 1872, Baptist Union of Scotland Minute Book, 1869–1880, n.p. MS in the Historical Archive of the Baptist Union of Scotland, Baptist House, Glasgow, (as are all BUS Minute Books).

¹²⁴ Executive Committee of BUS, Minutes, 8 July, 1887, BUS Minute Book, 1869–1880, n.p.

relevant Baptist Association.[125] A similar procedure was followed when an English minister moved to Scotland.[126] Ownership of the link between BUGBI and BUS had to be in the hands of the ordinary members. The acceptance of a steady transfer of ministers between English and Scottish Union churches implied that the ties between them in the first decade of the twentieth century were increasing in strength.

This assertion of the autonomy of the smaller body was continued in the twentieth century. The consistent references to BUGBI as the 'English Union',[127] with the exception of formal citations from documents, had arisen as a result of the larger body assuming that the BUS was a branch of its own operations. The Scotch Baptists in particular, though largely identified with the BUS, were less than happy at the prospect of unduly close ties with BUGBI, when at the same time they had retained their affection for Scotch brethren outside of Scotland in the United Kingdom, and did not want to see a weakening of that relationship.[128] The particular focus of their grievance, on that occasion, was over plans for a scheme of Ministerial Recognition.[129] The Baptist Union of Scotland was interested in participating in the scheme established by BUGBI, but sought a number of changes in its regulations prior to recommending the proposals to its own constituency. There was a determination to retain control over the accreditation of its own ministers and to avoid being swallowed up by a numerically larger body. The areas of concern included the need for the examiners of Scottish candidates for accreditation to be independent of BUGBI[130] and the need for a BUS representative on the British Union's committee setting the examination papers for ministers seeking recognition.[131] At the Annual Assembly in October 1908 as part of the series of changes to the constitution and practices

---

[125] BUS Council, 8 September, 1914, a letter to the Northern Baptist Association, BUS Minute Book, 1906–1915, n.p.

[126] BUS Council, 25 February, 1931, letters from London Baptist Association and the North East district of the Lancashire and Cheshire Association, commending English ministers moving to Scotland, BUS minute Book, 1927–1931, pp. 592–595.

[127] BUS Council, 23 October, 1923, BUS Minute Book, 1915–1926, p. 530, is a representative example.

[128] BUS Council, 30 October, 1901, BUS Minute Book, 1896–1906, n.p.

[129] Details of this scheme are given in P. Shepherd, *The Making of a Modern Denomination: John Howard Shakespeare and the English Baptists 1898–1924* (Carlisle: Paternoster, 2001), pp. 53–91; and Ian M. Randall, *The English Baptists of the Twentieth Century* (Didcot: Baptist Historical Society, 2005), pp. 64–71.

[130] BUS General Committee, 12 May, 1903, BUS Minute Book, 1896–1906, n.p.

[131] BUS General Committee, 9 February, 1904, BUS Minute Book, 1896–1906, n.p.

by which the Union operated, a decision was made to change the Ministerial Recognition Scheme currently in operation to the existing scheme used by BUGB, as that would make it easier for Ministers to move across the border with England for settlement in churches.[132] Eventually general agreement was reached over the operation of a joint Ministerial Recognition Scheme, even though the Scots continued to refer to it as 'the new scheme of the English Union'. Adam Nimmo, Convener of the Scottish Ministerial Recognition Committee, believed that despite its deficiencies this common approach to accrediting ministers would 'promote unity and facilitate ministerial transfers between England and Scotland.'[133] He persuaded the BUS Council that 'we should utilise the impulse of the larger movement in order to strengthen our position in Scotland'.[134] The Annual Assembly that year, October 1912, also accepted his advocacy of this cause.[135] Preservation of a distinctive Scottish identity within a British Baptist context was a prominent theme in the first quarter of the twentieth century.

It was not surprising that the overwhelming number of references to other British Baptists in the minutes of the BUS committees and in the pages of the *SBM* concerned the largest of the British Baptist Unions. There were, though, some references to the bodies in Wales and Ireland. The Baptist Union of Wales received the least attention, with only a handful of references and these mainly to the movement of ministers between Scotland and Wales,[136] but there was also an article in 1906 on the impact of the Welsh Revival on the statistics of the Baptist churches in that land.[137] The attention given to Irish Baptists was mainly restricted to reports on the Annual Assembly of the Baptist Union of Ireland in the SBM,[138] though an article in 1910, with favourable comments, reported protests by Irish Baptists to their South African colleagues over a proposed ecumenical venture, in which the Baptist Union of South Africa was intending to participate.[139] It must be assumed

---

[132] *Scottish Baptist Yearbook 1909* (Glasgow: Baptist Union of Scotland, 1909), p. 24. See also Murray, *First Hundred Years*, p. 81.

[133] BUS Ministerial Recognition Committee, 23 January, 1912, BUS Minute Book, 1906–1915, n.p.

[134] BUS Council, 13 February, 1912, BUS Minute Book, 1906–1915, n.p.

[135] BUS Annual Assembly, 24 October, 1912, BUS Minute Book, 1906–1915, n.p.

[136] BUS Council, 6 May, 1924, BUS Minute Book, 1915–1926, p. 642. BUS Council, 21 February, 1928, BUS Minute Book, 1926–1931, p. 172.

[137] *Scottish Baptist Magazine* (*SBM*), January 1906, p. 3.

[138] *SBM*, August 1910, pp. 124–125; July 1933, p. 6, are examples.

[139] *SBM*, August 1910, p. 125; September 1910, pp. 140–141.

that, though all the references to these two sister Unions were favourable, their affairs were not prominent in the list of priorities of Scottish Baptists.

It was natural that the impact of the Baptist movement in Europe would also be of great interest to Scottish Baptists. The first significant article on European Baptists published in the BUS magazine in the twentieth century, appeared in 1905 and was a survey of the impact of Baptist witness in different parts of the world. It drew attention to a number of countries in Europe where progress was encouraging, especially Germany, Italy and Russia, but also mentioned other places like Norway where persecution of Baptists had led many families to take the decision to emigrate to America.[140] The first European Baptist Congress in Berlin during 1908 was promoted earlier that year in the *SBM*.[141] Future Congresses were also brought to the attention of Scottish Baptists. The second gathering in Stockholm, in 1913, for example, received noticeably more space in the *SBM* than the first in Berlin, indicating the growing importance of the Baptist cause in Europe to their colleagues in Scotland, despite the fact that no Scot had been invited to give a major address on this occasion.[142]

Transatlantic relationships were also greatly valued by this Scottish denomination. The regular news items and comments gleaned from America showed the respect in which the larger Baptist bodies in that country were held. It is probable that copies of *The Baptist Argus*, later called *The Baptist World*,[143] a Southern Baptist publication, were read by the editor of the *SBM*, as there were a number of occasions on which a recent issue of that American periodical was discussed. In February 1904, for example, there were comments in an *SBM* article on one entitled 'Baptist World Outlook', produced in America as recently as January that year. The editor of the Scottish magazine was delighted to pass on evidence of rapid church growth in many parts of the world, but less happy for Scottish Baptists to be described as 'a feeble folk', on the grounds that numerical growth for Scottish Baptist churches was modest. He was convinced that a more upbeat comment on his own denomination's progress was merited.[144] On a regular basis the Baptist numerical statistics

---

[140] *SBM*, February 1905, p. 21–22.

[141] *SBM*, April 1908, p. 50. Reports of their contributions are given in J.H. Rushbrooke (ed.), *First European Baptist Congress* (London: Baptist Union Publications Department, 1908), pp. 29, 75–79.

[142] *SBM*, April 1913, p. 58; August 1913, pp. 143–144; September 1913, pp. 158–159. See also B. Green, *Crossing the Boundaries: A History of the European Baptist Federation*, (Didcot: Baptist Historical Society, 1999), pp. 3–4.

[143] F.T. Lord, *Baptist World Fellowship: A Short History of the Baptist World Alliance*, (London: Carey Kingsgate Press, 1955), p. 2.

[144] *SBM*, February 1904, pp. 21–22; See also May 1904, p. 82; August 1916, p. 60.

from America were brought to the attention of his readers, with the probable intention of encouraging them by the greater numerical growth in sister churches in the USA.[145] Many Baptists in Scotland, though, were probably even more closely linked to their Canadian colleagues, due to a greater proportion of Scots choosing to emigrate to Canada rather than the USA when they moved to North America. Even in the pages of the *SBM*, for example, in April 1907, information is given of the warm welcome awaiting Scottish Baptist families who wished to emigrate to Canada. Hard-working men will be remunerated with 'wages [that] are the very highest that I suppose are paid in any country', and a certain Charles Brodie of Aberdeen 'is in a position to give [letters of] introduction' for such desirable young people.[146] This article followed one in December 1905 commending those Scottish Baptists who had accepted the challenge of life in Canada. Interest in Baptist work in that country was further stimulated by the visit of Rev. A.J. Vining, a representative of Canadian Baptist Churches, who was apparently 'making a deep impression' in the Scottish congregations he had visited in 1905. It was also important to note that, in addition to the American Baptist periodical mentioned earlier, the editor of the *SBM* also received a regular copy of the *Canadian Baptist*. It is unlikely that more than a handful of Scottish Baptists obtained this periodical. However, regular information from Canada was obtained with a view to seeing 'a deeper interest in the Canadian enterprise awakened at home.'[147] When this kind of information was combined with regular news from Scottish Baptist ministers who had moved to Canada, for example, the Rev. Edward Stobo in Quebec, then it is clear that this link across the Atlantic was strong. News was, however, a two-way process, as Stobo made plain in his lengthy letter. 'For over thirty years I have been kept in touch with Scottish brethren, and largely through the magazine reaching me once a month.'[148] In addition, a regular movement of Baptist ministers from their homeland to Canada ensured that the personal interest of many Baptists in Scotland remained strong.[149] Strong personal ties to individuals in North America ensured that consciousness of a shared commitment to the same ecclesiastical convictions had grown over recent decades.

---

[145] For example: *SBM*, July 1904, pp. 123–124; July 1905, p. 119; April 1908, p. 50.

[146] *SBM*, April 1907, p. 70.

[147] *SBM*, December 1905, p. 214; See also August 1939, p. 6, for a further reference to the *Canadian Baptist*, implying that the same editorial policy was in place over the longer term.

[148] *SBM*, June 1903, pp. 105–106.

[149] For example: *SBM*, Rev. W.G. Taylor, Keiss to Canada, September 1906, p. 158; Rev. John Elder, Scarfskerry to Canada, September 1908, p. 134.

The evidence from the *SBM* in the earlier years of the twentieth century is clear in stating that ties with North American Baptists dominated articles about the international Baptist scene in this monthly magazine, however, it was not an exclusive interest in one part of the world. Baptists in Central and South America also received some attention, with several reports on the work in Chile,[150] and two reports about Brazil. The first story related to BMS plans to consider sending pioneer missionaries to work in the Amazon valley.[151] Close kinship was also felt with Baptists in Australia and New Zealand. Once again the emigration of Scottish Baptists provides the basis for building a relationship to sister churches in these countries. Albert Bean moved from Kelvinside Baptist Church, Glasgow, to accept a pastorate in Tasmania in 1904,[152] closely followed by George Menzies who moved from Arbroath to Freemantle Baptist Church, Western Australia.[153] Menzies was also helpful in providing reports of Baptist progress in Western Australia for the *SBM*.[154] James Mursell, who left Dublin Street Baptist Church, Edinburgh, in 1905, for a temporary pastorate at Flinders Street Baptist Church, Adelaide, South Australia, was called to that Baptist congregation on a permanent basis in 1907.[155] William Allen was another Baptist minister leaving Arbroath for Australia, in his case accepting a call to Mount Morgan Baptist Church, Queensland, in 1908.[156] Some pastors served for a limited time in Australia before returning to Scotland. One example of this phenomenon was Peter Fleming who left Duncan Street Baptist Church, Edinburgh, in 1908, to replace James Mursell in Adelaide, before returning to Scotland in 1922 to become the pastor of Dublin Street Baptist Church, Edinburgh, after distinguished service amongst Australian Baptists for 14 years.[157] References to New Zealand in this Scottish periodical were significantly less than to its larger neighbour. It is most likely that this is due to fewer Scottish Baptist ministers choosing to emigrate to that country. William Hay moved from Grantown-on-Spey to Dunedin in 1904 and reported back to Scotland a few years later on the progress of his work.[158] He was replaced in Grantown by

---

[150] *SBM*, April 1904, p. 75; November 1909, p. 225; March 1914, p. 34.

[151] *SBM*, February 1908, p. 18.

[152] *SBM*, February 1904, p. 22.

[153] *SBM*, October 1904, p. 203.

[154] *SBM*, May 1905, p. 82; January 1908, pp. 7–8.

[155] *SBM*, December 1907, pp. 213–214.

[156] *SBM*, December 1908, p. 190.

[157] *SBM*, February 1922, p. 13.

[158] *SBM*, September 1904, p. 163; May 1908, p. 77.

James Ings, who ironically had also been serving a Baptist congregation in New Zealand.[159] It is also important to note the enthusiasm amongst Scottish Baptists for the newly launched Baptist World Alliance. Minutes of the BUS Council, for 25 October 1905 record that 'the General Committee take the steps necessary for associating this Union with the Alliance. . . . The Resolution was heartily adopted'.[160] The measure of support by Scottish Baptists for this organisation can be seen in the fact that between 1900 and 1945 there were more items published in the *SBM* with reference to this external agency than to any other Baptist body. There were detailed articles encouraging people to attend BWA Congresses and also reports from those people who had attended as delegates.[161] Better communication and transport links ensured that Baptists like the other major Christian World Communions had formed an international organisation to unite their various national bodies. Scottish Baptists embraced the new opportunities for fellowship with their colleagues overseas.

### Fellowship with Other Christian Churches

The key event that had a major impact on ecumenical relations between Protestant Churches in the early twentieth century was the World Missionary Conference held during 1910 in Edinburgh.[162] The Baptist Union of Scotland wholeheartedly welcomed this event taking place in Edinburgh.[163] Baptists, however, were critical of the concessions made by the conference organisers to Anglo-Catholic bishops Charles Gore of Birmingham and Edward Talbot of Southwark, who, together with H.H. Montgomery of the Society for the Propagation of the Gospel had insisted that the conference could not consider Protestant missions in Roman Catholic or Orthodox areas, for example, in Europe and South America. The Wesleyan Missionary Society and the China Inland Mission also strongly criticised this decision.[164] Two representatives of

---

[159] *SBM*, July, 1903, p. 115.

[160] BUS Council, 25 October 1905, BUS Minute Book, 1896–1906, n.p.

[161] For example, *SBM*, August 1905, pp. 133–134, 136–140; April 1911, pp. 54–55; June 1911, p. 91; August 1911, pp. 121–129; Fuller details of BWA Congresses are found in the volumes published after each event and in Lord, *Baptist World Fellowship: A Short History of the Baptist World Alliance*.

[162] The standard history of this gathering is Brian Stanley, *The World Missionary Conference, Edinburgh 1910* (Grand Rapids: Eerdmans, 2009).

[163] BUS Council, 10 May, 1910, Baptist Union of Scotland Minute Book, 1906–1915, n.p.; *SBM*, 36.6 (June 1910), pp. 86–87.

[164] Correspondence between Talbot, Gore and J.H. Oldham, the conference secretary, is in the Oldham papers (Box 1, Folder 2), New College, Edinburgh. See also Oldham to Mott, 21 May, 1909, Oldham Papers, (Box 1, Folder 3). Both

Scottish Baptists were included in the BMS delegation.¹⁶⁵ Thomas Martin was minister of Adelaide Place Baptist Church, Glasgow, a lecturer at the Baptist Theological College of Scotland and a former President of the Baptist Union of Scotland.¹⁶⁶ William Nicholson was joint-pastor of Bristo Baptist Church, Edinburgh, with William Grant and was to become a future secretary of the Baptist Union of Scotland.¹⁶⁷ It was Nicholson who wrote the Conference report for the *SBM*.¹⁶⁸ It is evident that relationships with other Scottish Protestant denominations were also harmonious on an individual basis, as well as in formal ecumenical bodies. The twentieth century has been described as 'the century of ecumenism'.¹⁶⁹ This statement appears to be an accurate description of ecclesiastical relationships in Scotland in this period. 1900 saw the merger of the United Presbyterian Church with the majority of the Free Church of Scotland to form the United Free Church. This new body was eventually to merge with the Church of Scotland in 1929 producing a denomination which contained the vast majority of all the Presbyterians in Scotland.¹⁷⁰ Although Scottish Baptists were not involved in these unions there were regular updates in the *SBM* of plans for a merger between the Church of Scotland and United Free denominations. Editorial comments in

---

references cited by Brian Stanley, in his 'Edinburgh 1910 and the Oikumene', in Anthony Cross (ed.), *Ecumenism and History* (Paternoster Press, 2002), pp. 97–99. K. Clements, *Faith on the Frontier A Life of J.H. Oldham*, (Edinburgh: T. & T. Clark, 1999), pp. 73–99, provides much helpful material on this conference.

¹⁶⁵ World Missionary Conference, 1910, *Volume IX: The History and Records of the Conference*, (Edinburgh and London, n.d.), p. 41.

¹⁶⁶ *SBM*, 44.8, (August 1918), pp. 116–124, gives details of his life and work.

¹⁶⁷ *SBM*, 46.6, (June 1920), pp. 68–69, offers a helpful summary of his Christian service.

¹⁶⁸ *SBM*, 36.7, (July 1910), pp. 115–117. See also *SBM*, 36.7 (July 1910, p. 107; 36.12, (December 1910), p. 199; and especially 37.1, (January 1911), p. 2, for additional items about this gathering.

¹⁶⁹ T.W. Moyes, 'Scottish Baptist Relations with the Church of Scotland in the Twentieth Century', *Baptist Quarterly*, 33.4 (October 1989), p. 174. There are several examples of church unions in the United Kingdom and overseas given in J.R. Fleming, *The Story of Church Union in Scotland*, (London: James Clarke & Co., 1929), pp. 51–52.

¹⁷⁰ J. Kirk, 'Presbyterianism', in Cameron (ed.), *Scottish Church History & Theology*, p. 675. Fissiparous tendencies had not been totally eradicated from Presbyterian ranks. In 1893 the Free Church of Scotland had split with a significant proportion of its Gaelic-speaking Highlanders forming the Free Presbyterian Church of Scotland. See J.L. MacLeod, *The Second Disruption*, (East Linton: Tuckwell Press, 2000), for more details.

June 1907 on a plan to unite all Protestant Churches into one National Church set out a critical appraisal of current merger proposals noting that union on the basis of the lowest common denominators would not produce a church that resembled New Testament principles.[171] There was, however, encouragement to the Presbyterian bodies to unite as their differences were minor, in comparison to that which they held in common.[172] This encouragement was notably absent when potential merger talks were opened between the Church of Scotland and the Episcopal Church.[173] Here points of principle were deemed to be at stake that could not be overlooked. Unity was the goal for relationships between Christian Churches, but not uniformity. This understanding of Christian union was the message proclaimed consistently by the vast majority of Scottish Baptists.

In the period from 1890 to 1914 Scottish Baptists had experienced remarkable growth not only in numbers of people and congregations in their ranks, but also in the range of work and service they were performing in their local communities. The new regional associations across the country were strengthening ties between their churches and enabling more effective work in church-planting and support for struggling causes to take place. The launch of the WA and its effective work, together with the growing innovative ventures amongst children and young people provided real optimism for the future of Baptist witness in Scotland. There was also a greater interest in seeking to address social issues to alleviate the hardship faced by many people. The most prominent cause in which this Christian constituency adopted at that time was Temperance. It had the overwhelming backing of Ministers and church members alike, in line with many other Christian denominations. Past disputes over the form of theological education for potential pastors was largely settled, with the vast majority valuing the training provided by theological colleges, in particular the new Baptist Theological College. Commitment to work overseas, especially but not exclusively through the BMS, was strong, but Baptist mission agencies like those of other denominations were facing serious financial challenges to cover the costs of their work. Fundraising initiatives simply could not match the rapidly increasing costs of providing services on the mission field, such as health and education. However, growing confidence in their own work and witness enabled Scottish Baptists to form increasingly strong ties with fellow Baptists and Christians of other traditions both in the United Kingdom and overseas

---

[171] *SBM*, 33.6 (June 1907), pp. 101–102.

[172] *SBM*, 35.7 (July 1909), p. 129; 36.7 (July 1910), pp. 105–106; 38.5 (May 1912), pp. 77–78, are examples regarding Church of Scotland – United Free Church discussions.

[173] *SBM*, 58.7 (July 1932), p. 103.

in these years. It was fair to say that between 1890 and 1914 Scottish Baptists were branching out with confidence.

CHAPTER 4

# The Valley of the Shadow:
# Scottish Baptists and the First World War[1]

There is no doubt that the events of World War One had an extraordinary impact on the citizens of the countries who participated in it. Debates about the causes of the war and the complexity of the events themselves has generated a vast literature and there is still a lively discussion about which country or countries should bear the greater responsibility for what took place with little chance of agreement in the scholarly literature.[2] At a time when the European nations were publicly at least committed to Christian principles and convictions,[3] however generously that might have been interpreted, it is important to reflect on the views stated in the public domain by church leaders and the contribution they made in shaping the convictions of church-goers and possibly having some impact on the opinions of other people in their local communities. The focus of this study is primarily centred on one Scottish Christian tradition, and the views expressed within its ranks concerning this war.

### Scottish Baptists prior to July 1914

In the years immediately prior to the start of the war the *SBM*, the monthly periodical of this constituency, gave no indication either of the forthcoming war or any expectation that such a conflict was likely to erupt in the near

---

[1] An earlier version of this chapter was published as Brian R. Talbot, 'Scottish Baptists and the First World War', in Larry J. Kreitzer (ed.), *'Step Into Your Place: The First World War and Baptist Life and Thought* (Centre for Baptist History and Heritage Studies Volume 9; Oxford: Regent's Park College, 2014), pp. 40-69. This material is used here with permission granted by Dr Kreitzer.

[2] For example, Max Hastings, *Catastrophe: Europe goes to war 1914* (London: William Collins, 2013), pp. xviii-xxii. Sean McMeekin, *July 1914: Countdown to War* (London: Icon Books, 2013), pp. 383–405. Martin Gilbert, *A History of the Twentieth Century: Volume One 1900–1933* (London: Harper Collins, 1997), pp. 312–316.

[3] M. Snape, 'The Great War', in H. McLeod (ed), *The Cambridge History of Christianity: World Christianities c.1914–2000* (Cambridge: Cambridge University Press, 2006), p. 139.

future. The *SBM* although it disproportionately represented the voices of ministers and national Baptist figures, nevertheless its articles usually were representative of the majority opinions in this constituency. Scottish Baptists had every reason to be encouraged in the second decade of the twentieth century with continued growth in numbers, which was not true of all Protestant denominations. There was no triumphalism about this state of affairs. An article in the February 1912 issue of the *SBM*, for example, entitled 'Christian Statistics Home and Foreign', while pleased at the growth of the Christian Church in India, noted the decline in numbers in recent years of English and Welsh Nonconformists, together with a recognition that high levels of emigration of Baptists and others from Scotland ensured that there were no grounds for complacency if the advance in the homeland was to continue.[4] The tone of the magazine was normally measured and thoughtful across its range of topics, for example, in an article entitled 'Japan and Christianity' that reported the views of the Japanese Government published by that body in a remarkable circular that expressed positive sentiments about all the major world religions and the contribution they could make in reinforcing the moral fibre of the nation and strengthening ties between the nations of the world. There was only a hint in the article that this aspirational document was not entirely convincing in its presentation.[5] The picture presented in the *SBM* in the years leading up to 1914 was of a quiet confidence in the future labours of its Baptist constituency in Scotland, together with no apparent sense of alarm at any major potential conflict in Europe.

However, there were some hints that all was not well in Continental Europe. Concerns about matters in the Balkans, in particular about the behaviour of the 'Unspeakable Turk' had ensured that the possibility of a European war could not be ruled out. Prayer for peace in this region was required:

> ... and such prayer should surely be followed up by eager and persistent efforts to combat on the one hand the militarism and on the other the jealousy and panic fear of other nations and their activities, which are at work like fevers in the blood of the European peoples.[6]

These concerns, though, were general in nature and it does not appear that the writer of those words was expecting a Continental war that might involve the United Kingdom. The April 1913 issue of the *SBM* had an article looking forward to the summer and forthcoming holidays. In it readers were urged to consider attending the second European Congress of the Baptist World

---

[4] *Scottish Baptist Magazine* (*SBM*), 38.2 (February 1912), p. 23.

[5] *SBM*, 38.4 (April 1912), p. 63.

[6] *SBM*, 39.1 (January 1913), p. 2.

Alliance, due to be held in Stockholm, Sweden, in July that year.[7] The article spoke warmly of the privilege some of their number had in attending the first European Baptist Congress in Berlin in 1908 where two Scots, Peter Campbell J.P. of Perth and J.T. Forbes of Glasgow, had been amongst the list of speakers.[8] This gathering in Germany, itself the firstfruits of the success of the first Baptist World Alliance Congress in London in 1905,[9] had attracted around eighteen hundred delegates from all over Europe, with one third of the delegates from the United Kingdom. Peter Campbell, the Baptist Union of Scotland President, in his speech made reference to concerns about militaristic sentiments in some unspecified quarters. 'We are all subjects of Jesus Christ, the Prince of Peace. We long that international peace should be preserved. We abhor the brutality and horrors of war. We mourn that such enormous sums are spent in time of peace on preparations for war.'[10] The message was clear that though our countries may have some differences of views, what we have in common is much greater. This opinion did not change in Scottish Baptist ranks in the years prior to July 1914.

The biggest concern in July 1914 was of a potential civil war between Republicans in the south and Ulster Unionists in the north of Ireland.

> The possibilities are terrible. No Christian man can peacefully contemplate them. Politicians on both sides may speak jauntily of the 'rivers of red blood' that will flow, but the man of God sees in it all the love of strife and the workings of undisciplined hearts.... Civil War in Ireland will mean misery and shame unthinkable. The present position is a call to prayer and humiliation.[11]

Leaders of the Free Church of Scotland were also concerned about the situation in Ireland, but appeared to be most concerned that their Ulster brethren risked facing 'the Lord's wrath' at this time because in a gathering to oppose 'Romish rule in Ireland' they 'permitted themselves to sing [Roman Catholic John Henry] Newman's 'Lead Kindly Light'.[12] Certain members of the British Government, including the Foreign Secretary Sir Edward Gray,

---

[7] *SBM*, 39.4 (April 1913), p. 58.

[8] *SBM*, 34.4 (April 1908), p. 50. Reports of their contributions are given in J.H. Rushbrooke (ed.), *First European Baptist Congress* (London: Baptist Union Publications Department, 1908), pp. 29, 75–79.

[9] Rushbrooke (ed.) *First European Baptist Congress*, p. 43. Details of the 1905 gathering are found in *The Baptist World Congress, London July 11–19, 1905* (London: Baptist Union Publication Department, 1905).

[10] Rushbrooke (ed.) *First European Baptist Congress*, p. 29.

[11] *SBM*, 40.7 (July 1914), p. 106.

[12] *The Monthly Record of the Free Church of Scotland*, 14.5 (May 1914), p. 66.

also thought a civil war in Ireland had been a real possibility in the summer of 1914.[13] Scottish Baptists were not alone in their concerns over the situation in Ireland.[14] However, it is remarkable that only weeks before the First World War began that the editor of this Baptist periodical was concerned primarily about a potential war not on the European mainland, but in Ireland.

In the same issue of this periodical there was a short article reflecting on the changes in naval warfare. It was noted that the Dreadnoughts, the large vessels that had been central to the military strategy of the Royal Navy in previous years were no longer the deterrent they had previously been. Instead, aircraft and submarines were replacing them. The writer appeared to imply that the possession of the new technology available to Western Governments might have a significant deterrent effect against war between countries possessing aircraft and submarines. The article concluded with these considered comments:

> We can look with satisfaction upon anything that makes war unlikely either on sea or land, but would much rather the cessation from fear sprung from the diminution of jealousy and the increase of good will than in the mere increase of effectiveness in the implementation of destruction.[15]

It was not only citizens that had doubts about whether Britain could defeat Germany in a naval encounter at that time. Winston Churchill was reported to have commented in the late summer of 1914 that Admiral Jellicoe could 'lose the war in an afternoon' if the German High Seas Fleet had defeated the Royal Navy in a battle in the North Sea.[16] Scottish Baptists were not alone in recognising a delicate balance of military power in Europe in 1914. The monthly issues of the *SBM* in the years immediately prior to the start of World War One give no indication that a major war involving the United Kingdom was either desired or expected.

---

[13] Gray's House of Commons speech of 3 August 1914 included these words: 'the one bright spot in the very dreadful situation is Ireland', Hastings, *Catastrophe*, p. 96.

[14] Further evidence in support of this viewpoint is given in Keith Robbins, *England, Ireland, Scotland, Wales The Christian Church 1900–2000* (Oxford: Oxford University Press, 2008), p. 105; John Wolffe, *God and Greater Britain: Religion and National Life in Britain and Ireland 1843–1945* (London: Routledge, 1994), p. 234; and Stewart J. Brown, *Providence and Empire*, Harlow: Pearson Educational Limited, 2008), pp. 450–452.

[15] *SBM*, *40*.7 (July 1914), p. 106.

[16] Andrew Roberts, *A History of the English-speaking Peoples since 1900* (London: Weidenfeld and Nicolson, 2006), p. 89.

## Scottish Baptists and the Declaration of War

After war had been declared on Germany and her allies the office-bearers of the Baptist Union of Scotland wrote a letter to their family of churches offering some immediate thoughts on this situation. In its opening paragraph, the letter included these words: '. . . in view of the most lamentable war into which so many of the nations of Europe, ourselves among the rest, have been so suddenly plunged.'[17] The tone was clear that this was an unexpected and unwelcome development.[18] Sympathies were expressed with those who would inevitably suffer the consequences of war, both civilians as well as service personnel. There was no pleasure in contemplating the prospects of war. There was a careful but clear statement of confidence in the British government in the action which it had taken. '[C]onfident by the knowledge that our statesmen all through the crisis have laboured so strenuously to secure peace and have only declared war when it seemed that peace could no longer be honourably maintained.'[19] What action did they recommend to all the members of Scottish Baptist congregations?

> We would fervently urge a continuation of those prayers which have been rising day and night from our churches and homes with such passionate earnestness since the war cloud began to gather in the sky, If we cannot any long pray that war may be averted, let us plead that the mercy of God may be shown to all who are engaged in the conflict; that wisdom may be given to our rulers in their unexpected responsibility; that the end may come speedily and may be somehow for the glory of God and the good of the nations.[20]

It was a responsible, measured and appropriate response from the leaders of this Christian body.

There are plenty of reasons why this was the case, but the strongest was the deep sense of sadness at the strain this war would put on the very real friendships Scottish Baptists had enjoyed with their German colleagues.

---

[17] *SBM*, 40.9 (September 1914), p. 137.

[18] It is probable that a large proportion of the population was less than enthusiastic about the declaration of war with Germany. See C. Pennell, *A Kingdom United: Popular Responses to the Outbreak of the First World War in Britain and Ireland* (Oxford: Oxford University Press, 2012), p. 4. Scholars who appeared to accept the myth of mass enthusiasm for the war include: Arthur Marwick, *The Deluge: British Society and the First World War* (London: Macmillan, 1965), p. 309; Kalevi J. Holsti, *Peace and war: armed conflicts and international order 1648–1989* (Cambridge: Cambridge University Press, 1991), p. 164; and W.J. Reader, *At Duty's Call: A Study in Obsolete Patriotism* (Manchester: Manchester University Press, 1988), p. 104.

[19] *SBM*, 40.9 (September 1914), p. 137.

[20] *SBM*, 40.9 (September 1914), p. 137.

Scottish Baptists in the late nineteenth and early twentieth Centuries were most enthusiastic about maintaining and strengthening ties with fellow Baptists both throughout the British Empire, together with colleagues in Continental Europe and the United States of America. There were many articles in the *SBM* about the witness of co-religionists in other countries. The first major one in the twentieth century was found in the February 1905 issue of this periodical, it focused mainly on Baptist work in Germany, Russia and Italy, but mentioned a range of other countries as well.[21] It was characteristic of representatives of this constituency to feel a deep sorrow for the plight of German Baptists and the strains it would put on their mission work. In a short piece entitled 'War and Missions', Sir George Macalpine was reported as expressing these sentiments about them: 'Whatever may be our opinion of the aristocratic and military party in Germany, those of us who know the leaders of the missionary enterprise in that great empire regard them with an affection to which war can make no difference.'[22] The writer of the piece, the editor of the *SBM*, offered his own fulsome praise for German colleagues. 'The German Baptist community is one of the sweetest flowers which grows on German soil, and British Baptists will have no holier work than to pray for the German Churches, and to help in the saving of their missionary work from extinction.'[23] In the spirit of impartiality, the editor immediately followed this article by a short one on Russian Baptists and their contribution to their own country by the establishment of three hospitals in their native land 'at Kieff, Odessa and St Petersburg.' He declared: 'Our Brethren are not slow to prove their loyalty by Christian-like acts, and seem to be among the first to recognise the claims of Christian love – and Christian forgiveness.'[24] However, it was ties with German Baptists that were especially cherished. These representative comments which undoubtedly were accepted in this constituency highlighted the wider context in which Scottish Baptists viewed the prospects of a war with Germany.

The strongest evidence of these ties was individual friendships. The editor of the *SBM*, A.T. Walker, minister of Ward Road Baptist Church, Dundee, for example, had spent his summer holiday that year in Hamburg. He provided a fairly lengthy article describing his experience of meeting German Baptists in the city at such a difficult time when Germany had already declared war with Russia, but not yet with Britain. He visited Claus Peters, pastor of the largest Baptist church in the city on Sunday afternoon 2 August 1914 and made this observation.

---

[21] *SBM*, 31.2 (February 1905), pp. 21–22. See Chapter three, pp. 74–81.

[22] *SBM*, 40.9 (September 1914), pp. 138–139.

[23] *SBM*, 40.9 (September 1914), p. 139.

[24] *SBM*, 40.9 (September 1914), p. 139.

> There was not a sign of any bitterness against the British, neither in the pastor's household, nor anywhere else. War between Britain and Germany had not then been declared, and the feeling may now have changed, but certain it is that previous to the 4th August, amongst the humbler and unofficial classes I came into contact with, I never heard an unkind word against Britain.[25]

This is a remarkable testimony on the eve of war and an important contemporary eyewitness observation in this German city. On the same day Walker attended both services at a Baptist church near to the Christliches Hospice where he had obtained lodgings. In the second, an evening service, communion was central to that act of worship. This Scottish visitor was asked to bring greetings, interpreted by the pastor, and then urged upon his return home to pray for brothers and sisters in Christ in Germany. His conclusions at the end of his visit were clear. 'These German Baptists are a splendid people. It costs them something to remain loyal to their faith and practise. ... Let us keep our German brothers and sisters in mind and remember them in our prayers.'[26] Walker's experience was not unique. In the same issue of the *SBM* A. Grant Gibb, minister of Gilcomston Park Baptist Church, Aberdeen, since 1903,[27] reported on his vacation in both Belgium and the Rhineland. His account was very similar. 'Had any fellow traveller ventured to predict that these fair and peaceful scenes would shortly be the theatre of a European war, one would almost have questioned his sanity.'[28] It is not difficult to sense the shock and disbelief that war had broken out between two countries that appeared to have so much in common.

The experience of Scottish Baptists was very similar to that of their colleagues in the Baptist Union of Great Britain. Its leaders prior to August 1914 had been strongly opposed to any thought of war with Germany.[29] Charles Brown, President of the Baptist Union of Great Britain (BUGB), had represented this position clearly in his address to the 1908 European Baptist Congress in Berlin.

> I can assure you that it is our desire that complete peace should continue between Germany and England, and I may say that there is no nation in Europe with which we as Christians are more closely connected than with Germany. We

---

[25] *SBM*, 40.9 (September 1914), p. 147.

[26] *SBM*, 40.9 (September 1914), p. 147–148.

[27] Yuille (ed.), *History of the Baptists in Scotland*, p. 90, gives details of Gibb's powerful and effective ministry.

[28] *SBM*, 40.9 (September 1914), p. 149.

[29] Keith W. Clements, 'Baptists and the Outbreak of the First World War', *Baptist Quarterly*, Vol. XXVI, No.2 (April 1975), p. 77.

love your family life and your true Protestant faith, and we hope that the bonds of friendship may never be broken.[30]

The same sentiments were expressed in the address from English Baptist minister and Baptist World Alliance President John Clifford.

> We are committed to the extermination of war and of the spirit that breeds it, and the flagitious newspaper methods on which it thrives. War is directly opposed to the spirit and teaching of Christ. He is the Prince of Peace. His kingdom is the kingdom of peace and this Baptist Brotherhood is pledged in His name, and in every land to fight against the Spirit of militarism. And whilst nations are everywhere preparing armies and navies, inventing and multiplying new engines of slaughter, we must by prayer and speech and example do our utmost to secure peace on earth and goodwill amongst men.[31]

In a Congress that also had a section entitled: 'Baptists and Universal Peace',[32] the groundwork was laid for strong ties between the Baptists of these respective countries in the years that followed.

English Baptist leaders such as John Clifford and John Henry Rushbrooke played a prominent part in the Anglo-German Churches' peace movement in the years that followed with exchange visits to the respective countries a regular feature of the pre-war years. Details of the various meetings and publications are given elsewhere,[33] but the pattern of both continuing and deepening friendship with German colleagues was the norm.[34] This was confirmed by a leader article in the 9 January 1914 issue of the *Baptist Times* which went into great detail about Anglo-German relations in recent months and explained why there are no grounds to fear a possible war with Germany.[35] Baptists in England like their colleagues in Scotland would be stunned at the unfolding of events in the second half of 1914.

---

[30] Rushbrooke (ed.) *First European Baptist Congress*, p. 25.

[31] Rushbrooke (ed.) *First European Baptist Congress*, p. 51.

[32] Rushbrooke (ed.) *First European Baptist Congress*, pp. 134–141.

[33] Ernest A. Payne, *James Henry Rushbrooke 1870–1947 A Baptist Greatheart* (London: Carey Kingsgate Press, 1954), pp. 26–33. Bernard Green, *Tomorrow's Man A Biography of John Henry Rushbrooke* (Didcot: Baptist Historical Society, 1997), pp. 60–67.

[34] David W. Bebbington, *The Nonconformist Conscience* (London: George Allen &Unwin, 1982), pp. 125–126.

[35] Clements, 'Baptists and the Outbreak of the First World War', pp. 81–82.

Other Protestant Churches in Scotland were equally dismayed by the prospects of war with Germany in 1914.[36] A report to the General Assembly of the United Free Church of Scotland stated that it 'came with shock of great surprise'.[37] Ties with Germany were strong due to relationships established between church leaders in the two countries. A significant number of Scottish Presbyterian ministers had spent some time in German theological institutions. For example, John and Donald Baillie had many German friends 'the result of idyllic summer semesters spent in the Universities of Heidelberg, Jena and Marburg',[38] and James Denney had treasured memories as a postgraduate student of a summer spent studying in Germany. It was in the light of that experience that it was natural for him to support an Assembly motion that suggested that the United Kingdom 'should seek peace with Germany, because of most countries in the world, the Germans were close of kin with ourselves, and they had a large interest in common in the spiritual interest of mankind.'[39] Scottish Baptists like other Scottish Christians were unprepared for the military conflict that would last for the next four long years.

There was a clear consensus in Scottish Baptist ranks that the war was not sought by the United Kingdom. In a miscellaneous article in the October 1914 issue of the *SBM* the editor penned these words:

> In one of our religious papers a correspondence is taking place as to the attitude of the churches and the ministry in time of war. It is necessary to discriminate. We certainly did not rush into this war in any jocund spirit. The voices are very few that say we were not forced into it. But it lies very heavy on the hearts of Christian men and Christian ministers.[40]

Thomas Coats Memorial Baptist Church, Paisley, was a representative example. When World War One began some members of Walter Mursell's congregation wished him to avoid any mention of the war in the Sunday

---

[36] This was a common feeling across the churches and a significant part of British society. See A.J. Hoover, *God, Germany and Britain in the Great War* (New York: Praeger, 1989), pp. 19–20.

[37] 'Report of the Committee on Presbyterian Chaplains in the Army and the Navy', in *Report to the General Assembly of the United Free Church of Scotland*, Report No. XXII (Edinburgh: T. & A. Constable, 1915), p. 1.

[38] George Newlands, 'John Baillie and Friends, in Germany and at War', in Stewart J. Brown and George Newlands (eds), *Scottish Christianity in the Modern World* (Edinburgh: T. & T. Clark, 2000), pp. 133–152; the quotation is from p. 135.

[39] *United Free Church Assembly Papers*, 1913, p. 298; cited by James M. Gordon, *James Denney (1856–1917) An Intellectual and Contextual Biography* (Carlisle: Paternoster, 2006), p. 196.

[40] *SBM*, 40.10 (October 1914), p. 154.

worship services. This was a particular request to refrain from allowing the events in Europe to influence the topics and approaches to his preaching plans during those years. It was a request he felt unable to heed as the unfolding events demanded comment and reflection to give guidance and encouragement to the people of God as they faced those difficult days together.[41] This view was shared by other Scottish Churches also. A unanimously adopted resolution of the Free Church of Scotland Assembly on 26 August 1914 stated:

> the circumstances of the country were indeed very serious. None of them could recall any circumstances to which the present could be compared with any propriety. They had had wars within the recollection of some of them, but not one which bore so threatening an aspect to this country.... There was one aspect that was encouraging. That was, that the war was not one of their seeking and in that connection it was just.[42]

Certainly, the tone of this lengthy resolution was sober and reflective, and far from displaying enthusiasm for the forthcoming war. The Church of Scotland likewise echoed the same spirit.

> It is a wholesome feature of the struggle into which France and her allies have been plunged this year that in no place has there been thoughtless and noisy excitement. The gravity of the issues, the inevitable suffering and misery and anxiety which must be faced, sobered all men. Not unworthily have our people met the most solemn crisis of their history. Such a mood is worthy of Christian men.[43]

The consistency of tone by these and other churches in the weeks that followed the declaration of war with Germany was clear and measured, but also calm and supportive of the decision of the British Government to resist what they viewed as an unsought war. In fact, the responses of the various churches highlighted were in line with the majority of people in the United Kingdom.[44] Only once other options were exhausted did they support the war effort.

---

[41] Walter A. Mursell, *The Bruising of Belgium and other sermons during war time* (Paisley: Alexander Gardner, 1915), p. 5. Mursell was wrongly identified as a Church of Scotland Minister by Michael Lynch, *Scotland A New History* (London: Pimlico, 1992), p. 422.

[42] *The Monthly Record of the Free Church of Scotland*, 14.9 (September 1914), p. 163.

[43] *Life and Work*, 36.9 (September 1914), p. 258.

[44] The myths of the enthusiasm of the French and German populations for war has also been debunked in more recent scholarship, see Pennell, *A Kingdom United*, pp. 4–5.

However, feelings towards Germany, even German Baptists, had begun to change by the time of the annual Scottish Baptist Assembly that year. A motion expressing sympathy for German Baptists, proposed by a pastor, J. Bell Johnston, was withdrawn due to lack of support in favour of one more general in its scope. The implications of this decision were remarked on by the editor of the *SBM*. 'We must be prepared for misunderstanding and even ill-will on the part of our German brethren. Truth will filter through to them very slowly, if ever, but we can always remember them in our prayers.'[45] However, Grant Gibb, whose own sympathies towards the German Baptists had been made clear, nevertheless recognised that very quickly attitudes had changed towards Germany amongst his fellow citizens, some of whose attitudes had 'doubtless become one of bitterness.'[46] English Baptists too, or at least some of them, were also quick to change the tone of their attitude to the war. Within ten days of the declaration of war an article in the *Baptist Times* declared that all along the German Government had been preparing for war.[47] It was followed in the next issue by a lengthy article on 'Christian patriotism' in which an attempt was made to justify the duty of a Christian to support the state in a time of warfare.[48] It made no reference to the current war, but no reader could fail to make the association. Already the ground was being laid to justify British Baptists giving their full support to the war efforts of the state.

## Scottish Baptists and the Grounds for Supporting this War Effort

On what grounds did the vast majority of Scottish Baptists support the war? There were a number of articles and comments that appeared in the *SBM* during the war years, but the most clear and articulate presentation of the case for war came in a sermon of a prominent minister Thomas Martin, published in the October 1917 issue of this periodical. The author gave six reasons why he was convinced the war was just. First of all, 'it is a conflict against the rule of brute force', a war for which he alleged Germany had been preparing for the last forty years, and behind it all was an intention 'to dominate the whole world'.[49] In these comments there appeared to be a lack of awareness of how the rest of the world might view Britain's intentions concerning its maintenance of a vast empire around the world, even if the criticism of Germany was accurate. No reference either was given to the Boer War and the serious ethical questions a tiny minority of British Christians and others

---

[45] *SBM*, 40.11 (November 1914), p. 170.

[46] *SBM*, 40.9 (September 1914), p. 149.

[47] *Baptist Times*, 14 August 1914, p. 641.

[48] *Baptist Times*, 21 August 1914, pp. 653–654.

[49] T.H. Martin, 'A Review of the War', *SBM*, 43.10 (October 1917), p. 147.

raised over the conduct of the British armed forces during that conflict.[50] The second reason raised by Martin was that 'It was a conflict on behalf of the rights of the smaller and weaker nationalities'. He cited the example of Germany seizing Schleswig Holstein from Denmark in 1864; 'a considerable slice of Austria in 1866' and in 1870 two provinces from France, as a pattern of inappropriate conduct which raised serious concerns about Germany's intentions in this war.[51] Although the assignation of Archduke Franz Ferdinand, the heir to the throne of the Austro-Hungarian Empire on 28 June 1914 in Sarajevo was the initial cause of the First World War, it was the invasion of Belgium by Germany, thus violating its neutrality that ensured the inevitability of war.[52] The third reason was that 'it was a conflict on behalf of honourable conduct in international affairs'. International laws had been put in place to set boundaries for the actions of individual nations. By implication, the author explained, Germany was out of line with the standards expected from honourable nations.[53] The fourth reason was that 'it is a conflict of moral ideals . . . a struggle between Thor the God of War and Christ the Prince of Peace'.[54] The fifth reason was that 'it was a conflict for world peace'. Martin cited as evidence attempts to bring about a League of Nations that would enable the Powers to 'keep the peace among themselves'.[55] Finally he declared that this conflict 'has been a test of our national character'. Martin was under no illusions that in 1914 the outcome of the war was uncertain; the case for resisting German aggression against Belgium may have been right, he argued,

---

[50] English Baptist John Clifford was a prominent clerical critic of the Boer War. Charles T. Bateman, *John Clifford Free Church Leader and Preacher* (London: National Council of the Evangelical Free Churches, 1904), pp. 192–193. See especially G. Cuthbertson, 'Pricking the 'nonconformist conscience': religion against the South African War' in D. Lowry (ed.), *The South African War reappraised* (Manchester: Manchester University Press, 2000), pp. 169–187, but also Paula M. Krebs, *Gender, Race, and the Writing of Empire: Public Discourse and the Boer War* (Cambridge: Cambridge University Press, 1999), pp. 32–54.

[51] Martin, 'Review of the War', *SBM*, 43.10 (October 1917), p. 147.

[52] The Treaty of London in 1839 guaranteeing Belgium's neutrality was signed by Britain, France, Austria, the German Federation (led by Prussia), Russia and the Netherlands. Violation of this treaty was the principal cited reason for the inevitability of this war. See for example, Hastings, *Catastrophe*, pp. 85–96; Reader, *At Duty's Call*, p. 104. Although other historians believe botched British diplomacy, in failing to make clear to the Germans the consequences of invading Belgium, in the first few days of August 1914, were more significant. See McMeekin, *July 1914*, pp. 401–404.

[53] Martin, 'Review of the War', *SBM*, 43.10 (October 1917), p. 148.

[54] Martin, 'Review of the War', *SBM*, 43.10 (October 1917), p. 148.

[55] Martin, 'Review of the War', *SBM*, 43.10 (October 1917), p. 148.

but this did not guarantee that right would ultimately prevail.[56] Martin's address was a clear and consistent presentation of his convictions with the last point in particular pointing to an attempt to make some kind of sense out of all the suffering and death that would impact Western society for many years.

How did other Scottish Baptists make sense of the war effort? It is appropriate to look at some representative examples. There is no doubt that the general conviction was that the war was just. Joseph Burns, minister of Motherwell Baptist Church, and President of the Baptist Union in 1914–1915, in his Presidential address in the autumn of 1914, included these comments: 'Yet, though we do not believe in War, we feel that the rightness of our cause justifies the action of the British nation at this time. . . . It is evident that the enemy is out for plunder; we are out for justice.'[57] How did he interpret God allowing this war to take place? 'During the many years of peace we have as a Nation enjoyed, luxury and pleasure have very largely taken the place of piety. If these years of peace had been devoted to the pursuit of higher things, many of our national vices would not be so prevalent, Let us pray that our beloved land will come out of this titanic struggle as 'gold tried in the fire, seven times purified.'[58] It was clear that Burns believed that the United Kingdom's people had fallen short of God's standards. However, Germany's shortcomings were greater. It was through the message of the cross of Jesus alone that people would be able to put the suffering and sacrifices of the next few years into a meaningful context.[59]

W.T. Oldrieve, the Baptist Union President that followed Burns, declared: 'Many of us detest war, but now we feel that we would count it an honour to make any sacrifice we can to aid the overthrow of Powers which have oppressed weaker nations with brute force on a subverted principle so opposed to the Christian ideal.'[60] Oldrieve thanked the churches for the willingness of so many men to volunteer to serve. He was aware already of at least 2,500 men serving in the forces, with many more continuing to come forward as the war progressed.[61] Here was a sober and solemn reminder that victory would cost dearly but no other course was open to Scottish Baptists at this time. Walter

---

[56] Martin, 'Review of the War', *SBM*, 43.10 (October 1917), p. 148–149. Although McMeekin, *July 1914*, pp. 404–405, presents evidence that in July and August 1914 the German Government seriously doubted that it could win the war.

[57] Joseph Burns, 'Presidential Address', Autumn 1914, *Scottish Baptist Yearbook* (Glasgow: John Cossar, 1915), p. 30.

[58] Burns, 'Presidential Address', Autumn 1914, p. 30.

[59] Burns, 'Presidential Address', Autumn 1914, pp. 40–41.

[60] W.T. Oldrieve, 'Presidential Address: The Church in Emergency', Autumn 1915, *Scottish Baptist Yearbook*, 1916, p. 25.

[61] Oldrieve, 'Presidential Address: The Church in Emergency', p. 25.

Richards, the President in 1916–1917, in a wide-ranging address acknowledged that 'anxious and broken hearts are every day becoming more numerous . . . .'[62] as the numbers of dead and wounded continued to rise. His main emphasis was on challenging myths that he believed were gaining in popularity as the war progress. These included, claims that the war had erased social classes; that the war would diminish the effectiveness of the churches' witness; that the day of denominationalism was over to be replaced by (for Nonconformists) 'a federation of the churches'. In each case Richards challenged these proposed changes in British society. The war would have its impact but Jesus Christ would always be the same and the gospel message also would continue to change lives through the efforts of those 'with a passionate love for Jesus'.[63] Jervis Coats, Principal of the Scottish Baptist College, was President in 1917–1918. His address entitled: 'Vision' – 'Atmosphere' made only a brief reference to the war. He acknowledged the awfulness of war, but said equally that it could be described as a 'moral and even sacred necessity.' He made a passing reference to the rightness of redressing the wrongs done to 'small nations'. However, he made plain his conviction that: 'War is a thing of horror, but there may be worse things than war. It is worse to lose one's soul, and the soul of Britain would have been lost, if we had not come to the rescue of those principles of good faith and humanity which make life worth living.'[64] Therefore, although Germany had made some tentative peace proposals, Coats was insistent that if we 'accept a peace "made in Germany", we may look out for another and more terrible war within a limited number of years.' He was insistent on an unqualified surrender from Germany to ensure that such a war could not happen again.[65] His fear that a second world war with Germany was not out of the question would prove unfortunately to be well-grounded. Coates who became editor of the *SBM* at the end of 1916[66] took a much firmer line than his predecessors in that post. In his editorial comments in January 1917 he was insistent that as well as securing our own freedom as a nation, the allied forces must have a 'determination to promote and maintain the independence and security of small nations'. This task would be difficult to achieve, but the war must be continued until this was accomplished.[67] The

---

[62] Walter Richards, 'Presidential Address' Autumn 1916, *Scottish Baptist Yearbook*, 1917, p. 27.

[63] Richards, 'Presidential Address' Autumn 1916, pp. 28–42.

[64] Jervis Coats, '"Vision" – "Atmosphere"', Presidential Address Autumn 1917, *Scottish Baptist Yearbook*, 1918, p. 26.

[65] Jervis Coats, '"Vision" – "Atmosphere"', Presidential Address Autumn 1917, pp. 26–27.

[66] *SBM*, 42.12 (December 1916), p. 182.

[67] *SBM*, 43.1 (January 1917), p. 18.

final war-time Presidential address was given by R.E. Glendening, entitled: 'The Church and the New Age'. His focus was on what kind of moral principles will shape and direct European society once hostilities are concluded. 'The issue is not so much a question of politics, or of nations as of intrinsic righteousness; whether a nation is to make its conscience, or conscience the nation.'[68] Glendening was convinced that Germany's leaders had departed from their Christian ethical foundations, but Britain too had room for improvement. Also significant were his perceptive comments concerning 'the men of the east', those from the empire who sacrificed for the cause. 'They can never more be put back into the old conditions existing prior to the war'.[69] Core Christian principles and practices don't change, but their application must in a world that has in some respects irrevocably changed. These addresses whose themes were replicated in other shorter pieces present a well-reasoned and thoughtful contribution to interpreting the times through which western European nations were living.

## The Particular Plight of Belgium

There was, though, one issue that particularly galvanised Scottish Baptist support for the war effort, namely the ill-treatment of Belgium by the Germans. One Scottish Baptist minister in particular, Walter Mursell, preached some particularly influential sermons in the first year of the war that resonated with the righteous anger felt in this constituency. The sermon whose title was used for the wider collection was preached on Sunday 15 November 1914 entitled: 'The Bruising of Belgium'. It was based on the text of Luke 4:18: 'To set at liberty them that are bruised'. The passion of Mursell leaps off the page as his manuscript is read:

> No people since history began has ever been so bruised as Belgium. That one word – 'Belgium' is enough to justify our entry into this war, enough to rouse the chivalry of our people, enough to determine us to fight to such a finish that tyranny will never again be able to create or grasp such an opportunity again.[70]

Mursell painted a picture of complete devastation of a once fertile prosperous country now in ruins, towns and villages destroyed; its fields trampled upon and its buildings ruined; its treasures looted and its magnificent buildings heaps of rouble. Its people of all classes where they can have fled and Belgium

---

[68] R.E. Glendening, 'The Church and the New Age', Presidential Address Autumn 1918, *Scottish Baptist Yearbook*, 1919, p. 25.

[69] Glendening, 'The Church and the New Age', Presidential Address Autumn 1918, pp. 28–29.

[70] Mursell, 'The Bruising of Belgium', *Bruising of Belgium and Other Sermons during War Time*, p. 24.

has become like 'the Jews ... an entire nation of refugees.'[71] The preacher then turned to Matthew 25:31–46, words that speak of the duty of Christians to treat their brothers and sisters in Christ as if Jesus were the person in need. However, Mursell applied these words to the people of Belgium.

> I do not hesitate to say, with these quoted words before me, that Belgium is Christ to us today – Christ clothed in modern garb, Christ embodied and represented in the unspeakable need of his hunted brethren ... Christ a refugee, holding out imploring hands for help in desperate extremity ....[72]

Mursell acknowledged that it was a heavy burden to bear, but when Belgium was liberated and its people restored to their land, we shall 'see the face of a Shining One, and it will be revealed to us that we have done some humble service to him who was himself bruised for our iniquities, who bore our sins and carried our sorrows.'[73] These convictions were behind his other wartime messages as well. In another sermon 'The Martyrdom of Motherhood' he made reference to the sacrifice of Christian missionaries in Africa in the cause of spreading the good news of Jesus. It 'is as true as God to say that our sons are laying down their lives for the redemption of Europe ... that is what we steadfastly believe in regard to this present time.'[74] For whom is this sacrifice being made primarily? 'Belgium is the sufficient answer to any carping critic or doubtful-minded citizen'.[75] The popularity of Mursell's sermons in part was due to his capturing what most Scots felt about the injustice of the treatment of the people of Belgium. It is noteworthy that the Irish and the Welsh were also outraged by what had happened to Belgium.[76] An editorial note in the *SBM* in December 1914 expressed it this way: 'War is always cruel, but we cannot conceive a British Army on its way to Berlin leaving behind it such tears of blood and anguish as the Germans have scattered broadcast over Belgium.'[77] The centrality of the suffering of the Belgians was key to galvanising support for the war in Scottish Baptists ranks.

Were the concerns of Scottish Baptists regarding Belgium viewed in a similar way by their English colleagues? English Free Churchmen prior to the German invasion of Belgium were working earnestly to build ties with church leaders across Europe. As late as the first week in August 1914, for example,

---

[71] Mursell, 'Bruising of Belgium', pp. 24–27.

[72] Mursell, 'Bruising of Belgium', pp. 29–30.

[73] Mursell, 'Bruising of Belgium', pp. 31–32.

[74] Mursell, 'The Martyrdom of Motherhood', in *Bruising of Belgium*, p. 40.

[75] Mursell, 'The Martyrdom of Motherhood', p. 40.

[76] Wolffe, *God and Greater Britain*, p. 234.

[77] *SBM*, 40.12 (December 2014), p. 190.

English Baptists John Clifford and J.H. Rushbrooke were amongst the British delegation at the World Council of Churches gathering in Constance, Switzerland, working in vain to oppose the expected war. There had been a possibility as late as Tuesday 4 August that year that Britain might take a neutral position over the war and seek to lead settlement talks but the events in Belgium had torpedoed those hopes.[78] The Nonconformist periodical *The British Weekly* on 6 August changed its line from opposition to support for a war with Germany over both Belgium and the secret mobilisation plans of Germany for war over the last month. It had been an agonising choice for its editor William Robertson Nicoll.[79] John Clifford, in an evening sermon in his home church Westbourne Park Baptist Church, London, on 16 August 1914 explained his position in the light of the evidence of German brutality. 'I hate war with the whole of my being. It is anti-Christian, wicked, devilish, diabolical. Yet when I looked into the situation and weighed the whole of the evidence, I could not see that our Government had taken a wrong step.'[80] Neither could the vast majority of his fellow English Baptists together with a similar proportion of other Free Churchmen.[81]

The turning point in Free Church opinion was settled at a Free Church National Council meeting in the City Temple in London on 10 November 1914. David Lloyd-George was the key speaker who in his own dramatic style explained his departure from his former pacifist position to support for this war. The response of the gathering was overwhelmingly favourable to his cause. On the night, the minister of that charge R.J. Campbell proposed support and John Clifford was the seconder of the motion.[82] From that point onwards the Free Churches overwhelmingly backed the war efforts.[83] The

---

[78] Stephen Koss, *Nonconformity in Modern British Politics* (London: B.T. Batsford, 1975), pp. 126–129.

[79] Keith A. Ives, *Voice of Nonconformity: William Robertson Nicoll and the British Weekly* (Cambridge: The Lutterworth Press, 2011), pp. 230–231. Koss, *Nonconformity in Modern British Politics*, pp. 130–131.

[80] H. Edgar Bonsall & Edwin H. Robertson, *The Dream of an Ideal City Westbourne Park 1877–1977* (York: The Ebor Press, 1978), pp. 102–103. The full sermon text was printed in the *Christian World Pulpit*, 26 August 1914.

[81] Clements, 'Baptists and the Outbreak of the First World War', pp. 86–88. Clergymen across all the churches were horrified by the details of German atrocities. Hoover, *God, Germany and Britain in the Great War*, p. 22.

[82] Keith Robbins, *The Abolition of War: The Peace Movement in Britain 1914–1919* (Cardiff: University of Wales Press, 1976), p. 32.

[83] E.K.H. Jordan, *Free Church Unity: History of the Free Church Council Movement 1896–1941* (London: Lutterworth Press, 1956), pp. 140–141. Alan Ruston, 'Protestant Nonconformist Attitudes towards the First World War', in Alan P.F. Sell and Anthony R. Cross (eds), *Protestant Nonconformity in the Twentieth Century*

dramatic change of stance over the previous four months could not be overstated. No longer were Free Churchmen outsiders, they were committed to the national cause.

Looking back to the start of the war, in November 1914 an anonymous English Baptist wrote words that many people in this constituency could have identified with.

> I was once, alas! A peaceful civilian . . . schooled in the old Liberal belief that war was impossible, that to launch a Dreadnought was as absurd as throwing £2 million into the sea. As a Nonconformist I stood for independence and freedom. How many times from public platforms have I exhorted the working classes to regard every German as a brother? Now I am paying for it all. The bugle has sounded, and after a few months under canvas I emerge a disappointed Liberal, and with no feelings of brotherhood against the Kaiser. However, I am still a strong Baptist![84]

It would take years to process the full implications of these changes both in Scottish as well as English Baptist ranks.

How did other Scottish denominations view the German violations of Belgian neutrality? *Life and Work*, the Church of Scotland periodical contained a number of references to this issue. 'A big price is paid for loyalty to a contract; but it is not grudged. Not Belgium only, but the whole world is taught that a self-respecting nation regards its word as its bond.'[85] A lengthy article in January 1915 entitled: 'The Stricken People of Belgium' explained the suffering of the Belgians and drew attention to the growing number of Belgian refugees arriving in Scotland. The article's author, W. McConachie, reminded his readers that Belgium was 'the immediate cause of our taking an active part in the war; justice, fair play and national honour were all bound up with our making her quarrel our own.'[86] The United Free Church of Scotland had a special 'Diet of the General Assembly in relation to the War' in 1915 at which three speakers sought to bring God's word to their denomination at that time. Sir Alex Simpson in his talk 'The Enemy', highlighting how far Germany had gone astray, made reference to a letter written by prominent

---

(Carlisle: Paternoster Press, 2003), pp. 243–245. Bebbington, *Nonconformist Conscience*, p. 126 stated that for Nonconformists in the autumn of 1914 'The Great War became a Crusade'.

[84] *Baptist Times*, 27 November 1914, p. 869.

[85] *Life and Work*, December 1914, p. 357.

[86] *Life and Work*, January 1915, pp. 15–16. A financial appeal to assist Belgian refugees was made in an article in the November 1915 issue of *Life and Work*, p.337. The October 1917 issue of *Life and Work* reviewed Arnold Toynbee's new book, *The German Terror in Belgium*, p. 155. German atrocities in that country would not be forgotten.

German Christian academics and theologians in defence of the invasion of Belgium; the implication was clear this was a moral battle that had to be won by the allied forces. Germany had lost its moral compass.[87] James Denney, another speaker at that gathering had already raised this issue in one of his most well-known war sermons, 'War and the Fear of God', preached on 21 January 1915. The fear of God was lacking in Germany he explained. The 'ruthless devastation of Belgium by the Germans is a sombre confirmation of the lesson. It is reinforced by the official report of the French Commission, with its verified record of rape, arson, murder and pillage.'[88] Denney went on to state: 'These barbarous misdeeds must be punished, but not with the wild justice of revenge, not by doing in Germany the very things which we condemn in Belgium and France.'[89] In other words although this war with Germany was just and must be prosecuted with all our might, it must be conducted in a manner consistent with Christian convictions. In a similar fashion the Free Church of Scotland laid the blame for the war squarely at the feet of Germany and its leaders who were 'responsible for these Belgian outrages and those dastardly feats of mine-laying at sea.'[90] Various articles in this periodical emphasised that German Higher Criticism had undermined the authority of the Bible and consequently allowed those influenced by it to carry out unspeakable atrocities in Belgium and elsewhere.[91] The consistency of the arguments of each of these churches showed that German misconduct with respect to Belgium was a key catalyst in convincing their members that the First World War was a just and necessary fight that had to be fought and won.

## Other Causes of Outrage against Germany

There were a small number of actions of the German military that caused particular outrage during the war years. In the midst of the madness in Belgium the destruction of the library at Louvain and the beautiful cathedral at Rheims that could have no possible military significance, for example, had

---

[87] Sir Alex. R. Simpson 'The Enemy', one of three sections of a larger article 'The Church, The Nation, and the War', *The Record of the Home and Foreign Mission Work of the United Free Church of Scotland*, 15.7 (July 1915), pp. 286–288.

[88] James Denney, 'War and the Fear of God', January 21, 1915, in James Denney, *War and the Fear of God* (London: Hodder & Stoughton, 1916), pp. 27–28.

[89] Denney 'War and the Fear of God', p. 28.

[90] *The Monthly Record of the Free Church of Scotland* 14.10 (October 1914), p. 182.

[91] *Monthly Record of the Free Church of Scotland* 14.10 (October 1914), pp. 181–182; 'The War and Some of its lessons' 15.4 (April 1915), pp. 55–56 and the 'Sad Moral Condition of Germany', 16.6 (June 1916), pp. 102–103 also make the same points.

raised questions in some minds as to whether Germany had a conscience left at all![92] However, as concrete evidence of further atrocities in France and Belgium was revealed to the general public support for the war effort was further strengthened.[93] The sinking of the Lusitania provoked outrage from the Prime Minister of the United Kingdom downwards. The editor of the *SBM* highlighted how British naval vessels had saved the lives of German naval men in the sea, but no attempts were known of the German navy reciprocating. There was real anger at the sinking of this vessel but the editor regretted the decision of the British Government to allow Allied Forces to use chemical weapons in response to German gas attacks. In taking such a decision 'we are sinking down together' ... (he continued) ... 'Christian men are accepting now, and even approving, methods which, nine months ago would have filled them with horror. Such is progressive barbarity.[94] This Baptist minister admitted that: 'it is difficult to repress feelings of vindictiveness and demands for vengeance'.[95] A new low was reached with the execution of a British nurse Edith Cavell, on the grounds that she was assisting allied fugitives to escape from German forces. 'The death of Nurse Cavell has caused a shock of horror and indignation almost equalling that caused by the sinking of the Lusitania.'[96] Feelings of revenge were running high in certain parts of Scotland that led to riots in some communities against German civilians living there and causing damage to their properties. However, it is unclear why riots took place in some places but not others.[97] The *SBM* editor expressed his regret at the decision to bomb defenceless cities and non-military populations. He concluded: 'We went into the war with clear consciences and we would come out of it with clean hands. ... We will win through yet, without the necessity of murdering helpless women and children in cold blood.'[98] Here is a determined attempt to retain the moral high ground in the midst of increased carnage and the erasing of moral boundaries. Other Scottish Churches give similar responses to these outrages. The tone of anger was real, for example, as the Free Church *Record* reported

---

[92] Hoover, *God, Germany & Britain in the Great War*, p. 22.

[93] See the editorial comments on the International Commissions' reports from France and Belgium, *SBM*, 41.3 (March 1915), pp. 33–34.

[94] 'Progressive Barbarites', *SBM*, 41.6 (June 1915), p. 82.

[95] SBM, 41.7 (July 1915), p. 98.

[96] *SBM*, 41.11 (November 1915), p. 162.

[97] Catriona M.M. Macdonald, 'May 1915: Race, Riot and Representations of War', in Catriona M.M. Macdonald and E.W. McFarland (eds), *Scotland and the Great War* (East Linton: Tuckwell Press, 1999), pp. 145–171.

[98] *SBM*, 41.11 (November 1915), p. 162.

the loss of the Lusitania. 'It will be a good relief when this bully of Europe, this godless militant nation is ground to powder, like Napoleon 100 years ago, and Nebuchadnezzar many centuries earlier.'[99] However, behind the visible acts of evil is a spiritual battle, as Church of Scotland readers were reminded in the April 1915 issue of *Life and Work*. Therefore, it is right and proper to pray for victory. 'There should be no timidity, no half-hearted hesitation, in this matter. We believe the Allies are fighting for a righteous cause – for the sanctity of treaties, for the preservation of little nationalities, for the defence of humanity against the reign of force and cruelty and terrorism.'[100] In the face of evil, these denominational periodicals reminded us, there must be a resolute determination to stand firm against it. There should be careful thought as to how the Allied Forces respond to atrocities. They were clear in indicating that if we respond in like manner then we are no better than the Germans. However, God will grant victory in time to those whose consciences are clear with respect to their conduct.

## Making Sense of the War

In Scotland as a whole there had been a wholesale commitment by its people to playing their part for King and Country. There had been a huge number of volunteers who came forward to enlist within the first couple of months and approximately forty per cent of all professional men had signed up within the first two years of the war. Working class men were also keen to play their part. In total around one-third of a million Scots had enlisted voluntarily, prior to the introduction of conscription in January 1916.[101] Many ministers uttered strong messages in support of the war. James Denney uttered these memorable words at the 1915 United Free Church General Assembly: 'If a Christian cannot take sides in this war and strike with every atom of his energy, then a Christian is a being that, so far as this world is concerned, has committed moral suicide.'[102] William Tulloch, from Hillhead Baptist Church, Glasgow, wrote an irate letter to the *Baptist Times* annoyed at the weak tone of the Baptist Union of Great Britain manifesto on the war. He pointed to the much stronger and clearer response from Scottish Baptists. His own congregation had not waited for volunteers to be sought to sign up, already 120 had already enlisted, including all but one of the male Sunday School

---

[99] *The Monthly Record of the Free Church of Scotland*, 15.7 (July 1915), p. 118.

[100] *Life and Work*, 37.4 (April 1915), p. 100.

[101] Richard Finlay, *Modern Scotland 1914–2000* (London: Profile Books, 2004), pp. 3–7.

[102] Cited in Augustus Muir, *John White* (London: Hodder & Stoughton, 1958), p. 338.

teachers.[103] Scottish Baptists like fellow Christians in the other Scottish denominations had willingly served in the ranks in 1914.

Christians from the different churches in Scotland may have been hesitant about going to war in the first place, but once a decision had been reached that it was a just and necessary war they had given it their full and energetic support. The main Presbyterian denominations highlighted the number of 'sons of the manse' who had volunteered for military service. In the first year alone an estimated 450 men, ninety per cent of Church of Scotland ministers' sons had signed up,[104] likewise 'rather more than ninety-one per cent' of those from United Free Church families had made the same commitment.[105] Scottish Baptists had also signed up in significant numbers. In a discussion on 'Church Problems in War Time' at the Baptist Union of Scotland Assembly in October 1915, the Convener of the Committee of Social Service remarked on the impact felt in the work of the churches as a result of 'between 4,000 and 5,000 men associated with churches and congregations' being away on active service.[106] This total included approximately 2,500 members of Scottish Baptist Churches, one in nine of the total membership of Baptist Union causes that year.[107] Eight Scottish Baptist ministers had been appointed as Forces Chaplains and a further twenty-three had served with the YMCA.[108] There had been genuine disappointment at the introduction of conscription in 1916. 'We are sensible of a feeling of regret that such a fine record shall be broken for the sake of bringing in a few thousands, whose addition to the effectiveness of the army may be almost negligible.'[109] The rights of conscientious objectors not to engage in military service had to be respected, and regrets were expressed at the harsh treatment meted out to some of them at tribunals.[110] However, the editor of the *SBM* expressed surprise at the

---

[103] *Baptist Times*, 2 October 1914, p. 736.

[104] *Reports on the schemes of the Church of Scotland*, 1915, p. 535; cited by Stewart J. Brown, "A Solemn Purification by Fire': Responses to the Great War in the Scottish Presbyterian Churches 1914–1919', *Journal of Ecclesiastical History*, 45.1 (January 1994), p. 84.

[105] George M. Reith, *Reminiscences of the United Free Church General Assembly 1900–1929* (Edinburgh: The Moray Press, 1929), p. 165.

[106] *SBM*, 41.11 (November 1915), p. 172.

[107] Oldrieve, 'Presidential Address: The Church in Emergency', p. 25.

[108] S.D. Henry, 'Scottish Baptists and the First World War', *Baptist Quarterly*, 21.2 (April 1985), p. 63.

[109] *SBM*, 42.3 (March 1916), p. 33.

[110] 'Conscience Again', *SBM*, 42.7 (July 1916), p. 98. More recent scholarship has identified that a greater number of people held this minority viewpoint, but it was still

limited number of people claiming this status. 'The remarkable thing is not that the pleas of a conscientious objection to fighting are so many, but that relatively they are so few.[111] However, although accepting their right to express this point of view was not the same as being convinced by it. 'Whilst not wishing to judge any man, we believe it is a tender conscience and a love of righteousness and liberty which have driven the choicest of our sons and brothers to take their place in the King's forces.'[112] There was one, and only one, Scottish Baptist conscientious objector who challenged this conviction. This anonymous contributor was angry and passionate in his letter to the editor A.T. Walker.

> What drivel! Coming from a source that should be authoritative. What utter, abominable drivel. It is no wonder our church is in such a low condition when ostensible heads and teachers pour forth from their carnal hearts statements diametrically opposed to the teaching of the Word of Truth . . . .[113]

The editor was careful and considered in his response: 'We would tranquilize our pugnacious brother by assuring him that the paragraph quoted is quite innocuous'.[114] No other known voices were raised in this cause in Scottish Baptist ranks. English Baptists too resigned themselves to accepting conscription and other restrictions on personal liberty with barely a whimper. The *Baptist Times* made these comments: 'We distrust Conscription, but we dread a German victory still more . . . .'[115] 'Whether . . . it was necessary to abandon the voluntary principle for compulsion, it is not for us to say. We have not the means of judgement.'[116] The virtual silence from Nonconformists at this departure from their principle of the liberty of conscience ensured that the impact of the 'Nonconformist Conscience' in British public life had drawn to a close. The price of acceptance by the establishment was the loss of significant features of their historic identity.[117]

---

a small minority of the population. Scottish Brethren preacher Hunter Beattie published a series of sermons advocating this perspective entitled: *The Christian and War* (Glasgow: Hunter Beattie, n.d. [1916]). He indicated that his views were held by a much cricitised minority in Brethren ranks, 'Preface', pp. 7–8.

[111] 'Conscience', *SBM*, 42.4 (April 1916), pp. 50–51.

[112] Conscience', *SBM*, 42.4 (April 1916), p. 51.

[113] 'Correspondence', *SBM*, 42.5 (May 1916), pp. 75–76.

[114] *SBM*, 42.5 (May 1916), p. 76.

[115] *Baptist Times*, 14 January 1916, p. 18.

[116] *Baptist Times*, 2 June 1916, p. 339.

[117] This point is noted by Michael R. Watts, *The Dissenters from the Reformation to the French Revolution* (Oxford: Clarendon Press, 1978), Vol.1, pp. 3–5. Clements,

This war had produced a scale of death and injuries greater than had been experienced in the United Kingdom for many generations. There were 745,000 British dead according to the parliamentary return of 1921. At the time the official estimate of Scottish deaths was around 74,000, but the National War Memorial White paper of 1920 produced a more likely figure of 100,000 Scottish deaths, thirteen per cent of the total. Scotland had lost five per cent of its male population, nearly double the British average.[118] In total, Scottish Baptists had lost at least 500 killed from their congregations, with, for example, the large Hillhead Baptist Church alone losing fifty-five from their congregation, Thomas Coats Memorial Church, Paisley twenty-three, with the smaller causes at Fraserburgh and Anstruther loosing ten and eleven members respectively.[119] In addition, eighty-one received special honours. No wonder the *SBM* comment after listing these awards exhibited real pride in what these individuals had accomplished.

> This is a splendid and heart-burning record. It represents a series of brave deeds and heroic self-abnegation, of which we as a denomination may well be proud. It represents too, many hearts which are sad and sore at the loss of dear ones who will never cheer their lot again in this world, and also the loss to the churches of fresh young lives which might have been of such inestimable aid to them in their life and work.[120]

A great price had been paid by Scottish Baptists, alongside their fellow citizens through the war years. It is difficult to grasp the extent of the trauma many people endured during and after the war years.[121] An example will be

---

'Baptists and the Outbreak of the First World War', pp. 89–91 states that leading English Baptists John Clifford and J.H. Shakespeare had recognised the significance of the price Nonconformists would pay for their stance during the war. See also Ruston, 'Protestant Nonconformist Attitudes to the First World War', pp. 262–263 on this important subject.

[118] Christopher Harvie, *No Gods and Precious Few Heroes* (Edinburgh: Edinburgh University Press, 1993), p. 24. Richard Finlay, 'The Turbulent Century', in Jenny Wormald (ed.), *Scotland A History* (Oxford: Oxford University Press, 2005), p. 244.

[119] Memorial Service for those who died on active service, Sunday morning 15 April, 1919, Minute Book of the Congregation of Baptists meeting in Thomas Coats Memorial Church Paisley, Vol.III,14 July 1913–28 March, 1948, p. 59 and Henry, 'Scottish Baptists and the First World War', p. 63.

[120] *SBM*, 45.5 (May 1919), p. 60.

[121] Some people in Britain turned to Spiritualism as a way of coming to terms with the loss of their family member or friends. See for example, 'The Church of England and spiritualism', in Georgina Byrne, *Modern Spiritualism and the Church of England, 1850–1939* (Woodbridge: Boydell Press, 2010), pp. 144–177; and Jay Winter, *Sites of*

given of how one man was affected by the war both at its commencement and its close.

### Rev Walter Mursell of Paisley[122]

Walter Mursell admitted: 'I was one of those who at first thought it was the duty of our nation to maintain neutrality . . . .'[123] However, in this his first sermon preached after the declaration of war on 6 September 1914, he explained: that he had changed his mind and that he now was convinced of 'the justice of our cause. We are fighting for our life as a nation; but we are doing more than that – we are fighting for civilisation and humanity against the most monstrous military tyranny and arrogant autocracy that the world has ever known'.[124] He sought to assure his congregation that in the mysterious permissive will of God out of evil the divine purpose will be fulfilled. Our calling is intercessory prayer, to plead for God's will to be done as Jesus did in Gethsemane the night before his crucifixion. Mursell was convinced that: 'Out of such sacrifice and supreme surrender there will spring a regenerated Europe, a continent ruled 'not by might, nor by power, but by my Spirit, saith the Lord of hosts.'[125] The sermons delivered in the first few weeks of the war by this Scottish Baptist pastor contained no stirring rhetoric about the glories of war. On the contrary, a very solemn and sober recognition of what lay ahead was aptly articulated to his congregation.[126] In his undated sermon 'The Courage of Duty' the author highlighted the sacrifice of a young soldier of the Royal Irish Regiment who gave his life to save his colleagues. The cost of standing for our principles will be high. 'Such a time of heart-searching is with us now; and if we use such a time humbly and wisely, waiting upon God for light and strength, good will come out of this evil and

---

*Memory, Sites of Mourning* (Cambridge: Cambridge University Press, 2014), pp. 54–77.

[122] A fuller account of this minister's wartime service is given in Brian R. Talbot, *The 'Fellowship of Trial': Religious Rhetoric in World War One: The Sermons and Poetry of Revd Walter Mursell* (J.H. Shakespeare Memorial Paper 1917; Helensburgh: United Board History Project, 2017).

[123] 'Intercession During Wartime', 6 September 1914, in Mursell, *Bruising of Belgium*, p. 12.

[124] 'Intercession During Wartime', pp. 12–13.

[125] 'Intercession During Wartime', pp. 13–19.

[126] There were church leaders enthusiastic about the war in August 1914 (see, for example, Hoover, *God, Germany, And Britain in The Great War*, pp. 115–116), but others like Mursell had a perception that this war though just would exact a heavy price before it was concluded.

blessing out of the curse of war; and the lessons learned in the stern school of suffering are not likely to be thrown away.'[127] Already in 1914 Mursell is acutely aware of the death toll caused by the war. His volume of published poetry, *Afterthoughts,* provides insights into his thinking that year. 'In the Silent Room' is a representative example of his wrestling with the meaning and significance of death but it concludes with a reference to John 14 and life beyond the grave.[128] Mursell has no doubts about life beyond the grave, but in his poem 'Hereafter' admits that he cannot connect with images of 'gates of pearl and streets of gold, of saints who walk there clothed in spotless white ... and waving palms which in their hands they hold.' He concludes: 'I am not moved by such high state as this; not home would such a city be to me; to live and learn and love would be more bliss in some fair land where I would ever be reminded of the Earth from whence I came but with no vestige of its sin and shame.'[129] The war was only in its early stages but the lives of civilians who had never seen the carnage on the battlefield had begun to change as well as those serving 'God and Country' in the line of fire. Soldiers at the Front as the war progressed increasingly 'wanted faith without dressing, Christ without myth and experience without dogma'.[130] Many too on the home front would articulate similar sentiments. Returning soldiers would view life differently once the war had ended, but civilians too had been changed by what they had experienced. For Walter Mursell this process of change had already begun in the autumn of 1914. His poem 'Strife' was an attempt to make sense of the pain that he had both experienced and observed, with the recognition that 'the summit I fain would greet is not reached in a day',[131] though it is doubtful that he or any of his contemporaries imagined the war would last for four long years.

---

[127] 'The Courage of Duty', an undated sermon, in Mursell, *Bruising of Belgium*, pp. 85–94.

[128] 'In The Silent Room', Mursell, *Afterthoughts* (Paisley: Alexander Gardner 1914), pp. 69–71.

[129] 'Hereafter', Mursell, *Afterthoughts*, p. 72.

[130] N.E. Allison, *The Clash of Empires 1914–1939*, The Official History of the United Board Revised Volume One (Norfolk: The United Navy, Army and Air Force Board, revised edition 2014), pp. 88–89.

[131] 'Strife', Mursell, *Afterthoughts*, pp. 47–48. Someone else who would be articulating similar sentiments was Charles Allan, a Church of Scotland Minister in Greenock, whose son George died with his best friend on 17 May 1915 at Richebourg. His December 1914 sermon, 'Where God comes in' was an attempt to make sense of what was happening in the war. 'VI 'Where God comes in', in Charles Allan, *The Beautiful Thing That Has Happened To Our Boys And Other Messages In War Time* (Greenock: James McKelvie & Sons, 1915), pp. 69–78.

How did Mursell view the approaching end of the war and the years that would follow? His volume of sermons *Ports in a Storm*, preached in 1918 but published in 1919, contain his considered reflections in the later stages of the war and its immediate aftermath. On 18 February 1918 'The Heart of the Gospel' sermon was based on I Peter 1:21 *So that your faith and hope might be in God.* It was an exhortatory message urging his hearers to gain or retain a right view of a loving Father and His Son in the midst of their own trials. Once more he mentioned the agonies of Jesus in Gethsemane as the demonstration of costliness of obedience to the Father allowing his hearers to connect their struggles and trials with the greater ones of one who would lay down his life for us.[132] His thoughts in 1918 also turned to the possibilities of the future. In his 'The Maker of Men' sermon based on Matthew 4:19, Mursell wished to highlight the transformation possible in a human being when they have dedicated their lives to God. His examples included missionaries James Chalmers and John G. Paton together with social reformers Thomas Barnardo and William Quarrier. He saw in them models of hope to inspire his congregation to make a difference in their generation.[133] Mursell constantly urged his hearers to grasp opportunities presented to them.[134] His sermon 'False Pretexts' in April 1918 was a good example. The future path before you may be difficult, but it is no excuse for not embracing it. Once more Jesus' example in Gethsemane of accepting the Father's plan for his life is seen as a model for Christian manliness. His congregation was left with this challenge: '... you who have to make up your mind to stern decisions and to face up to situations that strain the sinews of the soul – dwell much in the garden of Gethsemane.'[135] A fool is hesitant, unwilling to get on with the tasks before him. The message to be heeded was this: 'Do *something*. Decide one way or another; but don't go on drifting, dreaming postponing . . . .'[136] The Christian man who would play a useful role in the post war years needed to have 'something big about him', something 'rugged' and something 'solid' but also something 'sweet and gracious'. It was a wholehearted

---

[132] 'The Heart of the Gospel', 10 February 1918, in Walter A. Mursell, *Ports In The Storm* (Paisley: Alexander Gardner, 1919), pp. 217–227.

[133] 'The Maker of Men', 10 March 1918, in Mursell, *Ports In The Storm*, pp. 251–260.

[134] It has to be remembered that in the First World War, the home front mattered almost as much as the battle front. See David Reynolds, *The Long Shadow: The Great War And the Twentieth Century* (London: Simon & Schuster, 2013), pp. 430–431.

[135] 'False Pretexts', 28 April 1918, in Mursell, *Ports In The Storm*, pp. 135–145.

[136] 'Mistaken Perspective', 19 May 1918, in Mursell, *Ports In The Storm*, pp. 125–132.

dedication to Christian service that was required.[137] 'The vast upheaval of the last four years has broken up all our cherished ideas, and made a break with the past that can never be bridged over.'[138] How did Mursell view the future for the Christian Church? He stated that the Church needed to be: 'A Hospitable Church – a Church receptive to new ideas, fresh plans and purposes, fresh adaptations and applications.' He looked forward to a new day when more generous and open-minded theological convictions were proclaimed.

In his second volume of poetry *Echoes of Strife*, published in 1919 it is clear that there was a heavy cost for his wartime service. This volume was dedicated to Joseph Callan, a colleague in the YMCA who had been very supportive of him during his time in France in 1916. A number of the poems were written in France during Mursell's time there in either autumn 1916 or early 1919. The opening poem '1914' expresses his shock at the commencement of the war. 'No one saw the creeping cloud, till the day of thunder came.'[139] 'A Soldier's Heart' asks the powerful question:' What are we fighting for?' It challenges simplistic answers that trip off the tongue and concludes that home and families are the most significant reason for answering the call to fight.[140] A number of the poems reflect the hardship the soldiers' experience regarding variable quality of food for meals;[141] 'Nightmare', 'The Shadow', 'The Footstep' and 'The Voice' reflect on the difficulty of getting to sleep after experiencing some of the horrors of war, possibly based on Mursell's own experience of life in France.[142] 'To Stanley Millar' was a tribute to a longtime friend who died in Flanders.[143] Mursell in his prose writings gives few clues about his inner feelings concerning the war. He did enjoy the comradeship experienced in serving with the YMCA in France and indicated that he would willingly have done another tour of duty. In his poem 'Rouen: a Contrasted

---

[137] 'A Man's Character', 30 June 1918, in Mursell, *Ports In The Storm*, pp. 13–23.

[138] 'More Stately Mansions', 3 November 1918, in Mursell, *Ports In The Storm*, pp. 67–76.

[139] '1914', in Walter A. Mursell, *Echoes of Strife*, (Paisley: J. And R. Parlane, 1919), p. 9.

[140] 'A Soldier's Heart', in Mursell, *Echoes of Strife*, p. 10; this was a common question asked during the war and a subject addressed by different authors. For example, 'What are we fighting for' in G.A. Studdert Kennedy, *Rough Rhymes of a Padre* (London: Forgotten Books, 2015 [1918]), pp. 97–99.

[141] 'ODE: On A Distant Prospect of A Square Meal', in Mursell, *Echoes of Strife*, pp. 22–25.

[142] 'Nightmare', 'The Shadow', 'The Footstep', 'The Voice', in Mursell, *Echoes of Strife*, pp. 30–31, 50–52.

[143] 'To Stanley Millar', in Mursell, *Echoes of Strife*, p. 13.

Picture', he pictured a place so scarred by warfare, but contrasted that bleak scenery with the treasured memories of men with whom he had served. In the midst of details of memories of life at the Front, Mursell makes this upbeat comment:

> To the fellows who beat the Huns;
> I'd return for them
> To the old Y.M.;
> Whatever befall,
> I'd answer the call, –
> Ah! How I'll remember it all![144]

However, in some of the poems in this book there is a hint of the emotional suffering he experienced like so many others at that time. His poem 'Regrets' expresses a longing to recapture his childhood when all was so innocent and lovely. Verse two recounts his current state of mind.

> If I could have the dream once more
> That made my heart so light,
> I should not feel so sad and sore
> Nor weep alone at night.[145]

An even more solemn poem was 'ACELDAMA: Flanders 1918'. This poem is worth quoting in full to allow the solemnity of its message to be experienced.

> Earth is broken like a toy,
> Shattered are the dreams of youth,
> Gone the days of hope and joy,
> Desolate the House of Truth.
>
> God has turned away His face,
> Men have made a field of blood,
> Terror reigns with iron mace,
> Thunder rolls across the mud.
>
> Prayer is strangled in its birth,
> Stifled with the poison breath;
> Hopeless now of peace on earth,
> We have learned to welcome death.

---

[144] 'ROUEN: A Contrasted Picture', in Mursell, *Echoes of Strife*, pp. 14–15.

[145] 'Regrets', in Mursell, *Echoes of Strife*, p. 35.

> Old in heart, yet young in years,
> All my friends have left my side;
> Nothing now but unshed tears, -
> Would to God that I had died.[146]

The solemnity of these words is so clear and hint at a cost that would never be forgotten. His poem 'PEACE: November 11th, 1918' conveys a sense of great relief that the war is over, but also that his heart struggled to express too much happiness at its conclusion. The pain experienced by so many people, including Mursell himself, was too deep to allow him to move on too easily to focus on what lay ahead in the post-war era. *Echoes of Strife* is the volume Mursell penned in the war era that enables us to see something of the emotional impact he experienced at that time and it serves as a backdrop to his emotional struggles after the war was concluded. Millions of other people, including many Scottish Baptists, were equally affected by their war service. The next two decades were unquestionably overshadowed by the impact of World War One.

## Planning for the Future

But were there outstanding issues to address or new concerns to face in the post war years? The biggest issue over which the churches in unison campaigned unceasingly during the war years was Temperance.[147] Prohibition for the duration of the war was their simple request –without it they argued the effectiveness of the war effort will be diminished. The April 1915 issue of the *SBM* stated: 'The drink trade comes second only to German militarism in the thoroughness of its preparations and the ramifications of its interests. . . . It would rather see Britain "free, than sober". Unless something is done, and that quickly, it will soon be neither free nor sober.'[148] They did have some successes in this campaign, but they were modest and post-war hopes to see Scotland 'dry' like America would be dashed. Scottish Christians across the denominations recognised that the social inequalities in their country had to

---

[146] 'ACELDAMA Flanders 1918', in Mursell, *Echoes of Strife*, p. 11. Charles Sorley, 'When you see millions of the mouthless dead' in Hilda D. Spear, *Remembering We Forget: A Background Study to the Poetry of the First World War* (London: Davis Pointer, 1979), p. 21, conveys a similar powerful testimony to the horrors of this war.

[147] See for example, 'The War and Temperance', *The Record of the Home and Foreign Mission Work of the United Free Church of Scotland* 15.4 (April 1915), pp. 143–144; 'Temperance and the War', *Life and Work*, 38 (1916), May 1916, p. 123; *Monthly Record of the Free Church of Scotland*, 14.6 (June 1914), pp. 93–94.

[148] *SBM* 41.4 (April 1915), pp. 49, 54–55. See also Yuille (ed.), *History of the Baptists in Scotland*, pp. 246–247, and Bebbington (ed.), *Baptists in Scotland*, p. 80 for a summary of the achievements and limitations of its Temperance work.

be addressed in the post war years. The rise of secular socialist agencies was greatly feared by some Christians,[149] but the criticisms of injustice they raised had to be addressed.[150] Wage inequality was a scandal that had to be addressed.[151] Women had to be given their rights and treated with the respect they deserved,[152] the welfare of children had to become a higher priority[153] and the Churches had to recognise a society changed by the war that wanted to hear a message that was relevant to its needs or attendances would continue to decline in many places of worship.[154] In the December 1918 issue of the *SBM*, the editor Jervis Coats, challenged his readers: 'The church may need to review her mission and revise her message, giving this generation a new interpretation of the divine will. The new age must not be a repetition of the old with its tendency to identify progress with material prosperity.'[155] What must the church proclaim at this time? Coats highlighted the doctrine of the cross that had 'received a wonderful justification in the war. . . . The new age will also demand a new emphasis on the doctrine of immortality. The bitterness of the war has made that vital.'[156] The rise in interest in spiritualism

---

[149] 'A serious menace to the religion and morals of our time arises from the growing prevalence of the Socialist movement', *Monthly Record of the Free Church of Scotland*, 14.6 (June 1914), pp. 94–95.

[150] See Donald C. Smith, *Passive Obedience and Prophetic Protest Social Criticism in the Scottish Church 1830–1945* (Bern: Peter Lang, 1987), pp. 327–362.

[151] James Denney raised this point in a private letter to his friend Robertson Nicoll, dated 27 June 1914, in *Letters of Principal James Denney to W. Robertson Nicoll 1893–1917* (London: Hodder and Stoughton, 1920), pp. 238–239. Some people were doing well financially out of the war, but others less so; *SBM*, 42.8 (August 1916), p. 113; 43.2 (February 1917), p. 18.

[152] *SBM*, 44.5 (April 1918), p. 51.

[153] One wartime sermon that addressed this issue included these words: 'It is more dangerous to be a child in the slums of London or Glasgow than to be a soldier in the trenches of Flanders', Peter C. Matheson, 'Scottish War Sermons 1914–1919', *Records of the Scottish Church History Society*, Vol. XVII (1972), p. 213.

[154] *SBM*, 43.7 (July 1917), p. 98. Anglican former padre G. Studdert Kennedy recognised this sense of disillusionment in the experience of many people in Britain after the war. His book of sermons, *Lies* (London: Hodder and Stoughton, 1919), was written to counter this phenomenon and replace it with hope and the Christian Gospel.

[155] *SBM*, 44.12 (December 1918), p. 181.

[156] *SBM*, 44.12 (December 1918), p. 181.

that had come about through the loss of so many young people undoubtedly lay behind this point made by Coats.[157] In conclusion, he wrote:

> The substratum of our whole life is loyalty . . . to Christ. The spirit of obedience to high command should win for us the approval of our men, when they return, if we can show them that our teaching and practice and life accord with the commands of the Saviour King.[158]

Scottish Baptists had entered the war years in good heart, though conscious of the challenges which lay ahead. Their responses to the new situation which faced them in the autumn of 1914 was in line with statements and actions of the Baptists in England, and also very similar to the responses from the other mainstream Scottish Churches. Their continued numerical growth in the decade that followed the cessation of hostilities in 1918 was a clear statement that the message they were proclaiming resonated clearly with a small but increasing section of the Scottish population.

---

[157] One of the best studies of this subject is Winter, *Sites of Memory, Sites of Mourning*, pp. 54–77.

[158] *SBM*, 44.12 (December 1918), p. 181.

CHAPTER 5

# The Inter-War Years: Maintaining the Well-Trodden Paths, 1919–1939

## Baptists and Other Churches in Scotland at the End of the War

Scottish Baptist churches like those of other denominations had struggled through the war years with diminished manpower and reduced financial resources. A Baptist Union survey of member congregations received reports from 101 of them indicating that at least 4,305 men from those churches had been serving in the Forces. Twenty-eight pastors had aided the war effort with seven appointed as Army Chaplains and the others working under the auspices of the YMCA or the Soldiers Christian Association. It was, therefore, no surprise that at the end of the war there were twenty-five congregations with pastoral vacancies, but a source of encouragement that despite the upheaval of recent years, membership figures had continued to increase, a modest increase of 141 in 1918. Once again it was not a uniform picture, because although seventy-six churches had increased in membership, forty-one had declined and thirteen recorded the same total as the previous year.[1] Twenty-five churches had received financial grants from the Baptist Union to aid their work in November 1918. It was a significant investment from shared funds to support sister churches. The sense of solidarity between member churches was strong as they entered the post-war years.[2] R.E. Glendening, in his October 1918 Presidential address 'The Church and the New Age', provided a stimulating challenge to the churches to recognise how the world had changed and to seize the new opportunities that had been presented. He highlighted the 'breaking down of privilege' which included the recognition of the rights of women and a new understanding of the significance of the children in our midst. Our perspective on work overseas must also change he declared. There needed to be a greater sense of partnership 'The men of the east have stood side by side as comrades and equals with men of the west in this terrific struggle, shared in a common sacrifice, moved by the same great ideals of liberty and right.'[3] He also

---

[1] *Scottish Baptist Yearbook 1919*, p. 37.

[2] *Scottish Baptist Yearbook 1919*, pp. 42–45.

[3] R.E. Glendening, 'The Church and the New Age', *Scottish Baptist Yearbook 1919*, pp. 28–29.

highlighted failings of the Churches in Scotland prior to the war. These included:

> Different standards of ethics were tolerated. . . . Big industrial combinations were not expected to follow the rules governing one-man businesses. Her voice was silent on many of the great social questions affecting the general life of the nation. Absorbed with the personal, civic righteousness had small place in her programme. She was so insistent on the spiritual, as to be largely out of touch with the social and actual. Her moral leadership was flouted because she seemed to have no message for the daily life and needs of the people.[4]

It is clear that the emphases of the Churches picked up by many people in the wider society were out of line with some of their greatest priorities. In the next decade, for example, it has been argued that the larger Presbyterian Churches were so focused on their plans for union, completed in 1929, that they raised hardly any prophetic voices against social injustice and offered little of a social vision going forward.[5] This perception on the part of some was not entirely fair because there was significant cooperation between the Churches in the post war years to address some of the outstanding social evils. It had built on the more serious attention to social issues in the churches over the previous two decades.[6] Collaboration in this kind of work, including the special congresses of the Church of Scotland and United Free Church dealing with the moral, spiritual and social implications of the war, and the ecumenical gathering of representatives of nine Protestant denominations to address the subject of industrial reconstruction, showed that the Churches did endeavour to play their part in the rebuilding of social structures between the two world wars.[7] But the extent of the hardship and increasing unemployment amongst the skilled working classes in Scotland in the post-war years was greater than many in the Establishment had realised, not just the Churches.[8] However, it is fair to acknowledge that the largely middle-class led major Presbyterian Churches appeared out of touch with the suffering of many working-class people, in the first three decades of the twentieth century, who increasingly turned to more secular socialist political organisations to articulate their

---

[4] Glendening, 'The Church and the New Age', p. 30.

[5] Stewart J. Brown, 'Reform, Reconstruction, Reaction: The Social Vision of Scottish Presbyterianism c.1830-c.1930', *Scottish Journal of Theology*, Vol.44, (1991), p. 489.

[6] Cheyne, *Transforming of the Kirk*, pp. 148–153.

[7] Smith, *Passive Obedience and Prophetic Protest*, pp. 356–372. Devine, *Scottish Nation 1700–2000*, pp. 382–383.

[8] Smout, *Century of the Scottish People*, pp. 114–116.

concerns,⁹ not least during the General Strike of 1926 and related labour disputes.¹⁰

William Adamson M.P. had warned the October 1919 Baptist Union Annual Assembly of the seriousness of the situation. '[L]abour was no longer content to acquiesce in the system by which industry is conducted for the benefit of the few and which involved the servitude and exploitation of the mass of the people.'¹¹ He reminded fellow delegates that during the First World War the workers had been promised major improvements in their standards of living at its conclusion. The ensuing debate revealed strong sympathies with the aspirations of the workers, but Labour leaders were also asked to support moves for increased economic productivity, the abolition of the drink trade and the development of individual responsibility both to God and our fellow man.¹² This message was echoed by P.T. Thomson, M.A., a London Baptist minister. In his address he challenged the assembled delegates to make their voices heard on the major issues of the day if they wished to be seen as presenting a message of relevance to the wider society. He gave the example of a recent railway workers strike and challenged those present – if anyone could enlighten him as to the views of the Archbishop of Canterbury or the Free Church leaders on this subject. Thomson informed the Assembly that the Pope had uttered a vague speech on the subject that was full of platitudes, but the silence from Protestant Churchman was worse. He declared: 'The moral of these grievous facts is that the Church, faced with moral issues, national and international, has no message. . . . The masses outside have somehow come to believe that we can be counted upon not to do or say anything that means anything.'¹³ These words were not entirely fair because the issue for many Scottish Baptists was not a lack of opinions on contemporary social issues, but a reluctance to take sides on questions viewed as political. Scottish Baptists, though, were still confident that if the Churches played their part, the future was still promising for extending God's kingdom. However, Glendening had already warned the Baptist Assembly in October

---

⁹ Tony Dickson (ed.), *Scottish Capitalism: Class, State and Nation from before the Union to the Present* (London: Lawrence & Wishart, 1980), pp. 272–278. Devine, *Scottish Nation*, pp. 383–384. William Ferguson, *Scotland 1689 to the Present* (Edinburgh: Mercat Press, 1965), p. 379. Callum Brown, *Religion and Society in Scotland since 1707* (Edinburgh: Edinburgh University Press, 1997), pp. 139–142.

¹⁰ Smith, *Passive Obedience and Prophetic Protest*, pp. 366–368.; and Brown, 'Reform, Reconstruction, Reaction', pp. 507–517. Lynch, *Scotland*, pp. 424–428.

¹¹ *Scottish Baptist Yearbook 1920*, pp. xxxii–xxxiii.

¹² *Scottish Baptist Yearbook 1920*, p. xxxiii.

¹³ P.T. Thomson, in The Home Mission Public Meeting, Baptist Union of Scotland Assembly, October 1919, *Scottish Baptist Yearbook*, 1920, pp. xlii–xliii.

1918 that church members returning from the war would come back 'enlarged in outlook. . . . The Churches must make ready to meet them, be prepared for great sacrifices to attain the supreme end and bring in the Kingdom of God on earth. . . . The Church will not get with ease after the war what came with difficulty before it.'[14] Scottish Baptists did rise to the challenge as their numbers continued to increase throughout the 1920s.

The Jubilee Assembly of October 1919 had been an occasion for quiet satisfaction in Scottish Baptist ranks at the steady progress made by affiliated congregations over the previous fifty years. In 1869 there had been only fifty-one churches with 3,688 members. Now there were 140 churches with 21,346 members. There were no grounds for complacency because although fifty churches were increasing in numbers, sixty-four others had seen numerical decline, compared with forty-one in 1918, and the total figures of reporting churches that year were slightly down on the previous year. A large contribution to this figure was caused by the roll revision carried out by only four churches that revealed a loss of 122 members. A new cause at Larkhall had affiliated to the Union, though the Jedburgh Baptist Church had closed. Sunday School numbers had held up well during the war years, but Bible Class attendances had seen a significant fall during the war years, although there was a modest upturn in the months after the end of the war in 1918.[15] George Yuille, in his last address as Baptist Union Secretary, provided a memorable address as he reflected on the changes in Scottish Baptists ranks over the previous half-century. He reminded his colleagues that this current union was not the first attempted by Scottish Baptists, but the spirit of independence and more rigid doctrinal views on a variety of issues had kept many Baptists apart prior to 1869. Yuille explained that a common commitment to home and overseas mission work had been a catalyst for the formation of the current Baptist Union. He listed some important individuals, lay-people as well as Ministers, who had contributed to the formation of the Baptist Union. He admitted that the struggles over Ministerial Education in Scotland was a battle between 'the ideal and the practical' approaches to this subject. However, this issue was now settled in Baptist ranks. Yuille was pleased to note that the first act of the 1869 Baptist Union was to form a Ministers' Provident Fund that had grown and was now paying out £40 per annum to retired Ministers and their wives and £20 per annum to widows. He was delighted to outline the growth of Sabbath Schools from seventy-eight in 1869 to 156 in 1919 and from 8,000 children and 967 teachers to over 18,000 children and 2,179 teachers. The commitment to evangelism and church-planting had borne fruit with twenty new causes planted as a result of the work of Baptist Union Evangelistic and Church-Extension Committee; sixty

---

[14] Glendenning, 'The Church and the New Age', pp. 35–36.

[15] *Scottish Baptist Yearbook*, 1920, pp. 34, 37–38.

others were formed under the direction of other Scottish Baptists and ninety-six places of worship had been built in the last fifty years. Interest in and commitment to overseas mission had also grown steadily over recent decades, in line with developments amongst other Scottish denominations.[16] His message was abundantly clear that Scottish Baptists had a lot to be grateful for as they reviewed their recent progress. It was a fitting time for Yuille's retirement after thirty-nine years as Union Secretary. He had been ably assisted by his wife Jessie who had been working closely with him over the last twenty-five years.[17]

## A Focus on Glasgow

The changing social context for Christian witness in the 1920s and 1930s is most clearly illustrated by developments in the city of Glasgow. Since the formation of the Baptist Union in 1869 the most encouraging growth had been in Glasgow and the West of Scotland where the fourteen churches in 1869 had become fifty-three.[18] In the city of Glasgow alone by the start of the First World War twenty-seven churches and five missions had been established resulting in a presence in most areas of the city, together with missions established in the poorest working-class neighbourhoods of the city.[19] However, the trauma caused by the casualty rates from the war that deprived churches of many gifted young people and rising materialism in the general population caused a significant weakening of receptivity to the gospel and diminished the zeal of many to engage in evangelistic work in the inter-war years. Hillhead Baptist Church was a remarkable exception to this trend with more than 250 members added during the ministry of Dr John MacBeath (1929–1942). He was a charismatic preacher and a regular contributor to the Keswick Convention who attracted very large crowds to Sunday evening services at Hillhead. This congregation was also very keen to participate in the inter-church evangelistic campaigns of this era, including the 1931 'Glasgow West End Campaign' aimed exclusively at the eighteen to thirty-five year-old age group; the Lionel Fletcher Mission of 1933; and the nationwide 'Recall to Religion Mission' in 1938.[20] The pattern of life in the

---

[16] George Yuille, 'The Jubilee of the Union', *Scottish Baptist Yearbook 1920*, pp. xlvii-lii.

[17] Dr Coats, 'Resolution to Assembly', *Scottish Baptist Yearbook 1920*, p. 24.

[18] *Scottish Baptist Yearbook*, 1920, p. li.

[19] D.R. Watts, 'Glasgow and Dunbartonshire', in Bebbington (ed.), *Baptists in Scotland*, 1988, p. 175.

[20] Semple, *At Work in the World: Hillhead Baptist Church 1883–1983*, p. 10; Watts, 'Glasgow and Dunbartonshire', p. 177.

majority of the congregations, however, was very different with restricted budgets limiting the extent of mission activities and making it hard to maintain premises and pay stipends of ministers. This would result in a plateauing of membership in Baptist churches in the city throughout this period with losses in the inner city due to redistribution of people to the better housing in the suburbs only compensated for by the planting and growth of new causes in the suburbs. The growing churches tended to be in areas of population growth like Springburn and Whiteinch. The ministry of Hugh Mackenzie (1919–1922) was particularly encouraging for the Springburn congregation. Within four months of his arrival in May 1919 the attendances had surged with evening services up from thirty to one hundred attendees and the prayer meeting up from twelve to forty-five. In the next twelve months the membership had risen from seventy-nine to 105, together with Sunday morning attendances averaging 200 people.[21] Whiteinch Baptist Church in 1924 baptised fifty candidates and received a remarkable fifty-six individuals into membership, together with a further twenty-seven new members in 1925. The membership total that year of 204 was the highest in its history.[22] However, there was much excellent work still going on in less promising locations and significant numbers of people were being impacted by the churches.

A few examples from Glasgow churches will illustrate some aspects of their outreach activities. Four months prior to its constitution as Hermon Baptist Church in June 1920, a gifted evangelist called Duncan McNeil was appointed as the pastor to this congregation. His powerful ministry not only gave the church a clear vision for its ecclesial identity, but its focus on outreach activities during his three-year ministry, enabled the work to grow significantly.[23] For example, the Christmas concert of Hermon Baptist Church on 1 December 1922 attracted a remarkable 900 people who heard the pastor express heartfelt thanks to God for their spiritual and financial progress over the previous three years, together with the 'excellent musical programme' arranged for that evening by the church choir.[24] This was an attendance more than eight times their church membership figure that year. The annual Sunday School social of the Bridgeton Baptist Church in February 1924 was attended by 650 boys and their friends, who enjoyed a programme prepared by the church Boys' Brigade Company and the Sunday

---

[21] Edward W. Burrows, *Change at Springburn: A Centenary History of Springburn Baptist Church 1892–1992* (Glasgow: Campsie Litho, 1992), pp. 42–44.

[22] *SBM*, 50.11 (November 1924), p. 146; 51.11 (November 1925), p. 155; Watts, 'Glasgow and Dunbartonshire', p. 176.

[23] Yuille, *History of Baptists in Scotland*, p. 176.

[24] *SBM*, 49.2 (February 1923), p. 26.

School Primary Class.²⁵ Partick Baptist Church began as a mission of the Hillhead Church with eighteen members in 1899 and was constituted as independent Baptist church in 1904 with 200 members. Premises were erected with assistance both from the mother church, Glasgow Baptist Association and the Baptist Twentieth Century Fund, with evening congregations in the 1920s larger than their premises could accommodate, with a membership of 400 in 1925, together with the largest Sunday School in the Partick and Hillhead Sunday School Union.²⁶ Harper Memorial Church in Govan was remarkably creative and successful in attracting the attention of unchurched people. One example will illustrate the pioneering spirit of church members encouraged to carry out their independent evangelistic endeavours. The April 1923 issue of the *SBM* contained a brief account of two members, Mrs Sawers in her 70s and Miss Sawers commissioned for their 'Emmanuel Gospel Caravan' ministry that had a vision of reaching people 'in the out-of-the-way places'. They had engaged in some preaching tours of rural Stirlingshire in summer 1922 and now were planning to focus on rural Ayrshire in 1923. What is even more remarkable was that Mrs Sawyers had spent many earlier years travelling around rural Scotland on foot carrying out her work.²⁷ Innovative outreach activities did achieve some successes, but it was becoming noticeably harder to engage the interest of many in the wider population in the post-war years.

It was in the new suburban areas that were the focus of most new ventures in the 1920s. Examples included the new works in Cathcart and Mosspark. Members of Queens Park Baptist Church assisted by the Glasgow Baptist Association gave attention to the growing population of Cathcart and Muirend areas of the city and formed a church in Cathcart in 1923 meeting in the Couper Institute. Services had begun in September 1923 and it was constituted with forty members in December that year. This total had increased to seventy by the time its own premises had been erected two years later, in 1925,²⁸ on ground purchased in Merrylee Road with funds contributed from the Baptist Union Twentieth Century Fund, with Thomas Stewart the Secretary of the Baptist Union interim Minister for the first three years of its work.²⁹ A vision for a church-plant in Mosspark area of the city in 1924 was a joint venture between the Baptist Union Joint Church Extension Committee and the Glasgow Baptist Association (GBA). The catalyst for this

---

²⁵ *SBM*, 50.4 (April 1924), p. 50.

²⁶ Yuille, *History of Baptists in Scotland*, p. 183.

²⁷ *SBM*, 49.4 (April 1923), p. 54.

²⁸ *SBM* 51.11 (November 1925), p. 138; Yuille, *History of Baptists in Scotland*, p. 173.

²⁹ Watts, 'Glasgow and Dunbartonshire', p. 177.

initiative was the move by several Baptist families into Glasgow Corporation housing in Mosspark who had begun meeting in a house and sought assistance to develop this witness. They also used local halls and a school until the church was opened in 1925.[30] Loans for the building and grant-aid towards paying the Minister's stipend were provided by the Baptist Union and the GBA raised funds to pay off the debt on the building.[31] The work flourished in Mosspark. At the Annual Meeting on 19 January 1927 favourable reports were received from the Sunday School concerning the work amongst its 130 children; the Band of Hope with its 160 regular attendees, Christian Endeavour, Bible Class, Young Worshipper League, Home and Foreign Missions Committees and the Women's Auxiliary.[32] The rate of growth had slowed in the 1920s, but creative outreach and new church-planting initiatives allowed the overall figures to continue on an upward trajectory.

## Home Mission

In the post war years the social context in which BHMS workers were serving had changed significantly as a result of many former service personnel returning home 'with new ideas and large expectations'. Although there were some young people more open to discuss with them about the Christian faith, others had 'a profound indifference to spiritual things which is difficult to combat and remove. The new heaven and new earth are being sought for in an improvement in material surroundings and in the quest for pleasure and amusement.'[33] However, the picture was not all bleak as the vast majority of church members returned safely after the 1914–1918 war. The regular church activities were resumed or strengthened by returning personnel and the offerings in the Mission Churches were increasing, attaining a record high in 1926, which was necessary as the General Strike in England had 'interfered with the (BHMS) Travelling Agents' visitation there' and resulting in much smaller financial donations for home evangelisation work in Scotland. It was also encouraging that there were four Gaelic-speaking students in training for pastoral ministry in the Western Highlands and Islands where congregations

---

[30] *SBM* 51.11 (November 1925), pp. 138, 152.

[31] *SBM* 50.5 (May 1924), p. 62; Stewart Crabb, *A History of Mosspark Baptist Church* (Glasgow: private printing, 1974), pp. 3–5; Watts, 'Glasgow and Dunbartonshire', p. 177.

[32] *SBM* 53.3 (March 1927), p. 37.

[33] 'Report of the Baptist Home Missionary Society for Scotland 1919', *Scottish Baptist Yearbook* (Glasgow: John Cossar, 1920), p. 8.

required a minister who could preach in their native language.[34] Scottish Baptist Evangelist Thomas McQuiston noted that: 'the year 1926 has been one of the most fruitful in the history of our evangelistic enterprise' with reports of conversions in missions in the following Baptist churches: George Square and Orangefield, Greenock; Gourock, Port Glasgow, Helensburgh, Millport, Dunoon and Johnstone. Hermon Baptist Church, Glasgow, which had suffered a serious loss of members to other causes, regained its previous numerical strength after a six week mission.[35] Even though it had been a successful year in Scottish Baptist home mission, key leaders in the Baptist Union were of the opinion that even more effective work could be carried out by the merger of the BHMS with the Union's Church Extension and Evangelism Committee. At a time of sustained growth, not decline, the Union and the BHMS entered negotiations to discuss their future partnership in mission in Scotland.[36]

The initial response of the BHMS in October 1927 to the merger proposals from the Union was a negative one, although the door to further discussions was not closed. In any case the home mission was dependent on a significant degree of financial support from the Sustentation Fund of the Baptist Union; the substantial sum of £747 had been given in that financial year alone.[37] The case for amalgamating the two bodies was strong. By 1928 of the forty-eight members of the Home Mission committee no fewer than forty-five served on the Baptist Union Council. The pastors of the aided Home Mission Stations required Union recognition and could be eligible for the Union Provident Fund. Also, the long summer missionary tours had all but ceased and BHMS workers increasingly had pastoral ministries in a settled location like Baptist colleagues in the lowlands. Opposition to the merger was not due to disagreement with the above facts rather it was a concern that work in the smaller more remote communities would take a lesser priority than had been the case for the previous century of BHMS work.[38] Thomas Stewart,

---

[34] 'Report of the Baptist Home Missionary Society for Scotland 1926', *Scottish Baptist Yearbook* (Glasgow: Baptist Union of Scotland, 1927), pp. 6–7.

[35] T.A. McQuiston, 'The Evangelist's Report for 1926', *Scottish Baptist Yearbook*, 1927, pp. 142–143; Similar sentiments were expressed in the 1929 Evangelistic Committee report, *Scottish Baptist Yearbook 1930*, p. 119

[36] 'Report of the Baptist Home Missionary Society for Scotland 1926', p. 7; 'Home Mission' in the Sustentation Executive Report, 31 May 1926, 'Baptist Union of Scotland Minute Book 1926–1931, pp. 17–18.

[37] 'Report of the Baptist Home Missionary Society for Scotland 1927', *Scottish Baptist Yearbook 1928*, p. 7.

[38] 'Report of the Joint Committee appointed by the Assembly of the Baptist Union of Scotland and the Annual Meeting of the Baptist Home Missionary Society for

secretary of the Baptist Union, frustrated by the delay in considering these issues sent a stronger letter to the BHMS annual meeting in October 1928. He wished them to appoint representatives to meet with a group convened by the annual Assembly of the Union to discuss the merger of the two bodies, the position of the BHMS with respect to Union funding and 'to do this without delay so as to bring definite proposals on these matters before the Annual Meetings next year'. The home mission accepted these proposals and appointed representatives for the negotiations.[39] The catalyst for the Union proposals had been the reflection upon the Scottish Churches' Council report on the general religious situation in Scotland at the October 1927 Baptist Union Assembly. Those present agreed to set up a Commission of Enquiry with a wide-ranging remit to look at every aspect of outreach work in Baptist churches over the last seven years; to consider the detailed statistical returns submitted by the churches; to draw attention to places in towns and cities where church extension may be possible; to consider the present distribution of resources in workers and finance, in relation to population and need; to cover existing work in agricultural districts exploring whether itinerant evangelists might be better suited to ministry in those areas, together with a smaller number of settled pastors in those rural locations; and how Baptists could join with other Evangelical Churches in extending the Christian faith in Scotland.[40] This was an extremely thorough study which revealed some clear patterns on which action needed to be taken.

In the period 1920 to 1927 Baptist Churches in Scotland had grown numerically by 5% on average, but Home Mission Churches decreased in size by the same percentage. Sunday School attendance in Baptist Churches grew by 3% in this time period, however Home Church Sunday Schools saw a fall of 15% in the number of scholars. This particular figure though corresponded with other data from the Highlands which indicated that significant numbers of younger people were leaving the Highlands in the 1920s, according to this Baptist Commission Report. Another part of the study covered financial investment in home mission work. In that seven-year period the Baptist Union had invested over £20,000 in grants to the churches, of which approximately £13,438 had gone to Union Churches and £6,874 to Home Mission ones. However, the BHMS had also made grants to each of the churches under its care of just over £8,000. Home Mission congregations per annum were receiving nearly £15,000 in total. The Commission also found

---

Scotland', *Scottish Baptist Yearbook 1929*, p. 2 [of this Report]. Murray, *First Hundred Years*, pp. 83–85.

[39]'Report of the Baptist Home Missionary Society for Scotland 1928', *Scottish Baptist Yearbook 1929*, pp. 4–5.

[40]'Report of Commission of Enquiry 1927–1929', *Scottish Baptist Yearbook 1930*, p. 1 [of this Report].

that the cost of living in the 1920s was 'decidedly lower' in the Highlands and Islands of Scotland. They also pointed to the need for fairness in distributing resources to the churches in proportion to the population they sought to reach with the Christian Gospel. In this connection they drew attention to the fact that of the twenty-one Baptist Churches in areas with a population of less than 2,000 people, seventeen were Home Mission supported causes. It was also reported that eleven of the aided churches under the auspices of the Baptist Union, in urban areas in lowland Scotland, became wholly self-supporting during these years and recorded an increase in membership of 1,012, proving the soundness of this investment, whereas the potential for numerical growth in the areas where Home Mission causes were located was extremely limited.[41] In Appendix D the report considered the needs and possibilities for church extension in the larger towns and cities.

> While not overlooking the needs and claims of the smaller towns, we are of the opinion that Church Extension should follow the movements of the population in our large cities, keeping in view the various town-planning schemes in progress and in prospect at the present time.[42]

The authors of the report named Barrhead, Montrose, Musselburgh, Saltcoats and Stevenston as five examples of towns with a population of over 10,000 people but without a Baptist Church. In this section of the study there is the clearest declaration that Scottish Baptist Home Mission ought to place a far greater priority on work in the larger urban areas. It was noted that the Church of Scotland, the United Free Church, Congregationalists and the Brethren all had extensive work going on in rural areas of Scotland, in addition to the work of independent agencies such as the Faith Mission and the West Coast Mission in the 1920s.[43] If the Baptists reduced their financial input in evangelism in rural locations where all these other churches were active it might make little difference. However, there were too many larger urban centres in Scotland that had a shortage of Christian churches and ministers. It was time for more creative approaches to ministry in the countryside. Possibly the Methodist approach of joining churches in a circuit with one minister and a team of lay-preachers might be the key. In conclusion it stated the Baptist Union needed to streamline its management of home mission work by bringing all the committees dealing with it into the Baptist Union and directly responsible to the annual Assembly.[44]

---

[41] 'Report of Commission of Enquiry 1927–1929', pp. 15–20.

[42] 'Report of Commission of Enquiry 1927–1929', p. 20.

[43] 'Report of Commission of Enquiry 1927–1929', p. 23. Information on the work of the interdenominational West Coast Mission can be found in F.D. Bardgett, *Devoted Service Rendered* (Edinburgh: St Andrews Press, 2002), pp, 191–199

[44] 'Report of Commission of Enquiry 1927–1929', pp. 20–22.

The Joint Committee of members from the Baptist Union and Home Mission that met in Glasgow in October 1929 unanimously recommended the union of the two bodies from the Baptist Union Assembly meetings in October 1930. Their report highlighted a number of issues. It was clear that there was no longer a clear geographical boundary separating their spheres of operations, both organisations were engaged in similar work around the country which led to an ineffective bureaucratic structure for communication with two sets of officials duplicating each other's efforts. Pastors of former Home Mission charges who had become unemployed had been ineligible for assistance from the Baptist Union. This was something that had to be addressed by Scottish Baptists. The dual system of financing work was ineffective. The Joint Committee claimed that a merger was likely to result in an increase in funds to aided causes, as happened when the three Scottish Baptist home mission agencies had merged in 1827.[45] Although the figures from the financial year 1931 to 1932 did not support their expectations as donations from Scottish churches and individuals for the BHMS actually fell though English subscriptions increased slightly.[46] It is unknown but possible that the explanation for the Scottish figures was due to confusion over whether the Baptist Union of Scotland was obtaining funds from other sources to fund some of the home mission work. The Joint Committee were also convinced that there was no major legal obstacle to transferring ownership of BHMS properties to the Baptist Union.[47] On all but the latter legal point their arguments were broadly accepted. The outstanding legal issues were resolved through the assistance of Mr J Robertson Christie, K.C., an eminent authority on legal ecclesiastical issues.[48] The date of completion of the merger was 21 October 1931.[49] One chapter in Scottish Baptist Home Mission had come to an end, but equally a new one was beginning with expectations of greater evangelistic advances to come.

Fears on the part of some BHMS supporters that the Union might show less enthusiasm for mission in more remote parts of the country was seen to be misplaced in the 1930s. Following the amalgamation of the two bodies there were a series of outreach initiatives developed in those years. The Evangelistic

---

[45] Talbot, *Search for a Common Identity*, pp. 161–165.

[46] 'Report of the Baptist Home Missionary Society for Scotland 1931–32', *Scottish Baptist Yearbook 1932*, p. 10 [of the Report].

[47] 'Report of the Joint Committee', 2 October 1929, pp. 5–6.

[48] 'Home Mission – Report of Joint Commission', *Scottish Baptist Yearbook 1931*, pp. 118–120, 187–188; 'Report of the Baptist Home Missionary Society for Scotland 1930–31', *Scottish Baptist Yearbook 1931*, pp. 5–16 [of the Report].

[49] 'Report of the Baptist Home Missionary Society for Scotland 1931–32', *Scottish Baptist Yearbook 1932*, pp. 4–5.

Committee of the Union proposed that a campaign be held in every Baptist church over the winter of 1932–33. Beginning with an intensive two-week mission shortly after the October 1932 Annual Assembly each local church was asked to form a Prayer Fellowship for Revival with at least one weeknight service per month set apart for prayer for this purpose in the church. In addition, it was suggested that home groups and family networks should also focus on this theme. Regional Associations should have quarterly conferences with speakers preaching on evangelism or revival or related themes. Each local church and association was asked to arrange services of dedication for this work. The slogan for the mission was 'Every Member a Missionary'; words taken from the motto of Gerhard Oncken, the famous German Baptist leader of the nineteenth century. In addition each church was asked to issue a quarterly four-pages bulletin setting out the aims, plans and progress of this initiative and each minister in the denomination had been invited to a conference on 'the work of soul-wining' in May 1933.[50] This appeal was heeded by Scottish Baptists as almost 'all our churches are making plans for aggressive evangelistic effort'.[51] No less than five hundred conversions, for example, were reported in 1933 following three missions in the churches at Irvine, Wishaw and Tiree.[52] Former BHMS churches had also risen to the challenge. A report on the work in the Western Highlands by BHMS travelling secretary James Reid in the summer of 1932 declared: 'to call my visit a pleasure would be putting it mildly. It was infinitely more than a pleasure it was an inspiration! . . . to see such crowded meetings and to hear of conversions taking place and baptisms following,' though it was also reported that 'in several places the fishing industry has failed, markets have collapsed and the value of live stock has depreciated'.[53] The year, 1932, had been a transition not only for the BHMS but also for the Evangelistic Committee because its convener for the past five years, Baptist minister John Shearer, retired from its work on health grounds. In addition, the Union Evangelist Thomas McQuiston also stepped down from his post as Baptist Union Evangelist in order to accept the pastorate of Cambridge Street Baptist Church, Glasgow.[54] The new era for home mission work in Scotland had begun with great expectations of further spiritual and numerical growth in Baptist ranks.

---

[50] 'Proposed Evangelistic Campaign', *Scottish Baptist Yearbook 1932*, pp. 131–132.

[51] 'Evangelistic Committee', *Scottish Baptist Yearbook 1933*, p. 166.

[52] 'Evangelistic Committee', *Scottish Baptist Yearbook 1934*, p. 166.

[53] 'Baptist Home Missionary Society for Scotland Annual Report 1932–33', *Scottish Baptist Yearbook 1933*, p. 182.

[54] 'Evangelistic Committee', *Scottish Baptist Yearbook 1932*, pp. 158–159.

The outreach work of the denomination was aided by a variety of means in addition to the work of its ordained ministers. In 1934, for example, the Baptist Theological College of Scotland (now the Scottish Baptist College) students conducted missions in Victoria Place and John Street Baptist Churches in Glasgow and led a beach mission at Portobello, Edinburgh, for the whole of July 1937.[55] A different type of contribution was made in 1934 through the influence of the Oxford Group Movement. 'Several of our ministers and churches testify to a quickening of life and enduement of power with the Holy Spirit as a direct result of contact with the movement'.[56] A surprising number of financial donations for the work of Baptist home mission came from individuals in membership with other Christian churches in Scotland. Financial gifts from English Baptist churches were also encouraging to the travelling secretary of the home mission whose deputation work in 1936 to foster this support took him as far south as Southampton and included conducting a mission and a baptismal service for sixteen candidates in a Baptist Church in Nottingham.[57] A number of Scottish Baptist churches adopted the Scottish Churches' Council plan for simultaneous national evangelism that consisted of dedication, visitation, campaigning and shepherding, a scheme heartily commended by the Evangelistic Committee of the Union.[58] This Committee was also proposing to inaugurate a denominational outreach campaign 'immediately on the conclusion of the Simultaneous Campaign'.[59] Baptists alongside other Scottish denominations heeded the 'Recall to Religion' message of the Archbishop of Canterbury, together with Nonconformist Churches in England, and willingly co-operated with other Churches in outreach activities in the open air in parks and at the entrances of public works, at Trades Union meetings and in cinemas, a series of initiatives that appeared to have some degree of success.[60] However, all the success in outreach initiatives was overshadowed by a gradual decrease in subscriptions to home mission work by Scottish Baptist Churches since the merger of the BHMS with the Baptist Union. As a result of expenditure greatly exceeding income James Reid had to step down as travelling secretary

---

[55] 'Evangelistic Committee Annual Report', *Scottish Baptist Yearbook 1935*, p. 177; 'Evangelistic Committee', *Scottish Baptist Yearbook 1938*, p. 174.

[56] 'Evangelistic Committee Annual Report', *Scottish Baptist Yearbook 1935*, p. 177.

[57] James Reid, 'Travelling Secretary's Report', *Scottish Baptist Yearbook 1937*, pp. 225–226.

[58] *Scottish Baptist Yearbook 1937*, pp. 119, 171.

[59] 'Evangelistic Committee', *Scottish Baptist Yearbook 1938*, p. 174.

[60] *Scottish Baptist Yearbook 1938*, p. 168; *1939*, p. 184; *1940*, p. 182; *1941*, p. 174.

in 1937 with no-one appointed to take his place.[61] Scottish Baptists were not reducing their commitment to home mission work instead they saw it increasingly as one aspect of the collective work of Baptist Union affiliated churches, rather than the distinctive role of the Home Mission.

### Revival in North East Scotland

In Lowestoft in Suffolk in Spring 1921 a remarkable revival began under the ministry of Douglas Brown, the Minister of London Road Baptist Church. By October that year it spread to Yarmouth where several thousand Scottish young people who worked in the fishing industry had arrived to assist in the gutting, pickling and barrel packing of herring. It had been one of the most difficult years in the industry. Not only had the British Government revoked existing subsidies for the Scottish herring industry, but a flourishing continental market for their produce had diminished, and this together with bad weather and poor yields that year had led many to fear for their livelihoods.[62] However, many analyses of this revival fail to note that economic considerations were only a secondary not a primary factor in this phenomenon. Revival services were already taking place in Lowestoft before the arrival of the Scottish workers under the influence of the Advent Testimony League (ATL), an agency that was promoting a particular premillennial Christian understanding of the future. Likewise, The Pilgrim Preachers in Wick and others associated with the ATL, as well as the Christian Brethren, were actively promoting a message that highlighted expectations of revival in communities that had a history of periodic religious revivals. In fact, the Brethren churches had emerged out of the 1859-60 revival, so memories of that time of awakening would have been retained in these communities.[63] Social and economic factors alone would not have produced a conducive setting for revivals otherwise this religious phenomenon would have been experienced more widely in the economically challenging

---

[61] 'Annual Report of the Home Missionary Society', *Scottish Baptist Yearbook 1938*, p. 228.

[62] John Lowe Duthie, 'The Fishermen's Religious Revival', *History Today* 33 (1983), p. 27, cited by Donald E. Meek, 'Fishers of Men: The 1921 Religious Revival- Its Causes, Context and Transmission', *Scottish Bulletin of Evangelical Theology* 17.1 (Spring 1999), pp. 40-43; See also Jackie Ritchie, *Floods upon the dry ground: God working among fisherfolk* (Peterhead: Peterhead Offset, 1983), pp. 14-37; Lennie, *Glory in the Glen: History of Evangelical Revivals in Scotland 1880-1940*, pp. 224-225; together with Stanley C. Griffin, *A Forgotten Revival East Anglia and NE Scotland - 1921* (Bromley: Day One, 1992).

[63] Meek, 'Fishers of Men', pp. 44-46. The Brethren Churches in Scotland did benefit significantly from this revival see Dickson, *Brethren in Scotland 1838-2000*, pp. 188-191.

times experienced in Scotland in the 1920s. Douglas Brown and Scottish lay-preacher Jock Troop preached many evangelistic sermons to the underemployed workers in Yarmouth. A month later, the Scottish workers returned to their ports on the East coast of Scotland in Lothian, Fife, Aberdeenshire and as far north as Wick and Lerwick.[64] Religious factors in a cultural context of experience of earlier revivals undoubtedly were the major influence here, though other factors were also contributory influences on what took place.

A few examples will be given of this remarkable phenomenon. The economic situation in Fraserburgh that year was one of the worst in its history with chronic unemployment and a third of the house rents remained unpaid.[65] There was no doubt that many local people had more time available to participate in the services than might have been the case in more economically prosperous times. However, expectations of revival based on past experiences of it was a more plausible explanation of people attending the meetings in droves; initially in the Baptist Church, later in the larger Congregational Church when the first venue became too small to accommodate those who wished to attend. The congregations were overwhelmingly male, the majority in the twenty-five to thirty age range, and most had served in the Navy or were currently fishermen. Moody and Sankey hymns were sung with gusto. There were a hundred converts in the first week of Troup's mission with around 400 in total during the five-week campaign. The majority of the converts were young men and women aged between sixteen and twenty-six and almost all were connected to the fishing industry.[66] A large proportion of the converts became members of the Baptist and Congregational Churches in Fraserburgh.[67] In Wick both the Baptist Church and the Salvation Army were the centres of the revival. It was believed that three hundred people, mostly young people associated with the fishing community, had made professions of faith. In a town of 9,000 people the revival had a profound impact with the cinemas and dance halls deserted and few customers visiting the public houses.[68] Peterhead Baptist Church also experienced crowded congregations

---

[64] Duthie, 'Fishermen's Religious Revival', *History Today* 33 (1983), p. 27, cited by Meek, 'Fishers of Men, pp. 40–43; See also Ritchie, *Floods upon the dry ground*, pp. 14–37; Lennie, *Glory in the Glen*, pp. 224–225.

[65] *Fraserburgh Herald*, 3 January 1922, p. 3; cited by Lennie, *Glory in the Glen*, p. 225.

[66] 'The Religious Revival Among Scottish Fisher Folk', *SBM*, 48.2, (February 1922), pp. 15–17; See also *Bright Words*, 1922, p. 5; cited by Lennie, *Glory in the Glen*, p. 229.

[67] Ritchie, *Floods upon the dry ground*, pp. 57–63.

[68] 'Revival in the North', *SBM*, 48.1, (January 1922), p. 3; 'The Religious Revival Among Scottish Fisher Folk', *SBM*, 48.2, (February 1922), pp. 17–18; also in *The*

for Gospel services with thirty-one adults together with some children who made professions of faith. In this case nearly all of them were already associated with the congregation.[69] Samuel Conway, Minister of Hopeman Baptist Church reported united services amongst the churches in the village for the evangelistic meetings and stated that 140 had professed faith on top of seventy who had earlier been converted in Yarmouth. 'The whole place is transformed, and praise of God is heard in the streets far into the night. The people are crowding to the churches. Thus, though the herring fishing has been a failure and many of the boats are home in debt there is joy and great thankfulness among the people.'[70] There was no doubt that the major revival influences were felt in the east coast fishing communities, but there is ample evidence of other churches and communities being influenced by this revival in other parts of the country. Anstruther and Pittenweem Baptist Churches, fishing communities in Fife, saw more than sixty and seventy-six professions of faith respectively,[71] Stirling Baptist Church had thirty-seven[72] and other church affected included Paisley Road, Victoria Place and Cambridge Street Baptist Churches in Glasgow, together with Cambuslang Baptist Church.[73] However, there were also factors that contributed to its containment, not least influential Christian leaders, like Graham Scroggie, minister of Charlotte Baptist Chapel, Edinburgh, who called for a moderation in the emotional tone of addresses by revival preachers like Douglas Brown.[74]

## Relationships with other Baptist Churches

Scottish Baptists sought to play their part in rebuilding ties with Baptists in Germany after World War One. There was a particular attempt to build relationships between young people in the United Kingdom with others in

---

*Christian Herald*, 5 January 1922, cited by George Mitchel, *Revival Man: The Jock Troup Story* (Fearn: Christian Focus, 2002), pp. 65–67.

[69] Revival in the North', *SBM*, 48.1, (January 1922), p. 3; Mitchel, *Revival Man*, p. 63.

[70] 'Revival in the North', *SBM*, 48.1, (January 1922), p. 3.

[71] 'The Religious Revival Among Scottish Fisher Folk', *SBM*, 48.2, (February 1922), p. 18;

[72] *SBM*, 48.5, (May 1922), p. 54;

[73] 'Revival in the North', *SBM*, 48.2, February 1922), pp. 13, 25; 48.3; (March 1922), p. 45. See also Mitchel, *Revival Man*, pp. 69–81.

[74] W. Graham Scroggie, 'Edinburgh and Revival', *SBM* 48.5 (May 1922), pp. 60–61; Meek, 'Fishers of Men', pp. 49–54. Ian L.S. Balfour, *Revival in Rose Street: Charlotte Baptist Chapel Edinburgh, 1808–2008* (Edinburgh: Rutherford House, 2008), p. 217.

mainland Europe. 'Fellowship Tours' were organised in 1934, for example, in order that:

> Young Baptists of different lands may discuss the new nationalisms -the British and Germans may, without heat or bitterness, speak about war guilt and Hitlerism. . . . From such fellowship arises such mutual respect and affection that War between them would seem to be madness.[75]

The Baptist Union of Scotland had also put aside money for the support of Baptist mission work in Europe, for example, in 1937 a figure of £200 was made available.[76] Scottish Baptists participated in the Second Young Baptist International Congress in Zurich in 1937, including A.A. Wilson, minister of Hawick Baptist Church, on the organising committee, who also chaired the first morning session of the conference, and Dr J.N. Tennent, who gave a short speech on behalf of Baptists in Scotland at the event.[77] The European Committee of the Union also kept colleagues aware of the changing situation in mainland Europe. The November Baptist Union Council in 1939, at the advent of the Second World War, was urged by members of this committee to remember in prayer, in particular, their Baptist colleagues in Europe.[78] It is evident that links between Scottish and European Baptists were not only maintained but increasing in the twentieth century. This pattern may be due in part to better communications and transport, but also in large measure to a growing desire for fellowship with fellow Baptists living on the same continent.

The majority of references to Baptist work in Europe, in Scottish Baptist literature and minutes of this period, however, referred to events in particular countries. Russia and Romania received the greatest attention, with more than twenty articles about the former and fourteen concerning the latter. The principal reason for the dominance of these countries was due to the regular waves of persecution that were visited upon Baptists and other Evangelical Christian bodies. Oppression of Russian Baptists had begun under the regime of the Czars.[79] Its extent usually depended on the local officials in any given part of the Russian Empire. In theory religious liberty for dissenters from Orthodoxy had been guaranteed after 1905, but the picture was somewhat

---

[75] *SBM*, 60.4, (April 1934), p. 2.

[76] Annual Meeting of BUS Nominees Ltd, 30 November, 1937, BUS Minute Book, 1935–1939, p. 455.

[77] *'Christ Our Life' Addresses given and Resolutions passed at the Second Young Baptist International Congress, Zurich 1937* (London: Youth Committee of the Baptist World Alliance, 1937), pp. xi, xix, 51.

[78] BUS Council, 29 November, 1939, BUS Minute Book, 1939–1942, p. 122.

[79] Green, *Tomorrow's Man*, pp. 153–154.

different in practice.[80] The affliction of these Christians increased greatly with a famine that was brought to the attention of Scottish Baptists in February 1922. An open letter signed by the leaders of the 'Baptist Union of All Russia', P.V. Pavloff, M. Timoshenko and W.G. Pavloff, painted an appalling picture of mass starvation in their homeland.[81] British Baptists, led by J.H. Rushbrooke, the Baptist World Alliance (BWA) Commissioner for Europe, rallied to the cause, providing enough food for 'a Baptist Relief Train'. Most of the Scottish Baptist Churches took collections to assist this effort.[82] At the end of March 1922 Rushbrooke was able to welcome the relief train into Moscow. It would provide food for over 12,000 people until the next harvest. Aid appeals to Baptists in other parts of Europe and North America also produced large quantities of food supplies.[83] In addition to the stories of hardship from Russia there were also some good news reported such as the union of the two Baptist denominations in that country in 1944,[84] and the encouraging evidence of religious freedom in the immediate post-war period. Scottish Baptists would have been delighted to read statements such as these from their Soviet brothers: 'We do most gratefully report that we are now enjoying a measure of freedom unknown by Baptists in all the years of our witness in Russia.'[85] This information came from a group of Christians who had been almost totally cut off from the outside world since their last period of repression from 1928 to 1943.[86] Baptists in Scotland, in line with fellow Baptists in Europe, and some further afield, were grateful for opportunities to stand alongside their Russian colleagues in very practical ways.

Romanian Baptists also suffered severe persecution at the hands of their Government at the instigation of the Orthodox Church. This problem was at its most severe in the 1930s when, in spite of all their claims to be in favour of promoting religious tolerance, Archbishop Colan was the Minister of Cults

---

[80] Byford, *Peasants and Prophets: Baptist Pioneers in Russia and South Eastern Europe*, pp. 82–87.

[81] *SBM*, 48.2, (February 1922), p. 14.

[82] *SBM*, 48.3, (March 1922), p. 30.

[83] Green, *Tomorrow's Man*, pp. 93–94.

[84] *SBM*, 70.4, (April 1944), p. 2.

[85] *SBM*, 73.1, (January 1947), p. 2. Caution must be expressed regarding the accuracy of this claim. No doubt the level of persecution had decreased, but by the mid-1940s the Government had imposed new restrictions on churches placing limitations on forms of worship and forcing baptistic churches to operate as one denomination. 'Baptists and Evangelical Christians in the USSR (1919–1991), in A.W. Wardin, *Baptists Around The World: A Comprehensive Handbook* (Nashville: Broadman and Holman, 1995), p. 216.

[86] Green, *Tomorrow's Man*, pp. 156–157.

and the Patriarch of the Orthodox Church was the Prime Minister.⁸⁷ This oppression culminated in the notorious 1938 decree enforcing the closure of all the approximately 1600 Baptist Churches in Romania, a policy enforced for over five months.⁸⁸ Baptist protests at this infringement of basic religious and civil liberties had some impact on the Romanian Government, especially when presented in person in Romania by J.H. Rushbrooke.⁸⁹ James Hair, writing in the *SBM*, left no doubt about the strength of feeling in his own constituency about this appalling situation. 'There is a striking similarity between their actions and that of the Nazi Government in Germany, although the Romanians in their treatment of those outside the State Church have out-Heroded Herod!'⁹⁰ Hair's remarks were put in a more succinct manner in the open letter sent to the Romanian ambassador in London on behalf of the BUS Council in September 1938. Scottish Baptists also sent a copy to the BWA to encourage them also to continue to work hard to resolve this difficult situation.⁹¹ There were two ministers, George Yuille (Glasgow) and Alex Wylie (Edinburgh), who passed on the news of the work in what became Czechoslovakia, in the first three decades of the twentieth century, and two laymen, W.M. Urquhart S.S.C. of Edinburgh and Frank Ramsay from Glasgow, who coordinated the collection of finance to fund the work in that country.⁹² It was no surprise, for example, when the political and social crisis in Czechoslovakia reached its height in 1939, due to Nazi German pressures, that Scottish Baptist Churches took up collections to alleviate the hardship being faced by their fellow Baptists.⁹³ It is certain that the spiritual and emotional ties for this group of Christians in Scotland were as great, if not greater, with their Czechoslovak brethren than with any other comparable Baptist body in Europe.⁹⁴ It was recognised that pressure from many bodies was required to bring about the necessary resolution to these problems. Baptists in Scotland had played a full part, both as a member of the BWA and

---

⁸⁷ *SBM*, 64.3, (March 1938), p. 4.

⁸⁸ Decizie [Law] No.26, 208, cited by Green, *Tomorrow's Man*, p. 152. The BWA letter of protest at this Decizie is printed in the *SBM*, October 1938, p. 16.

⁸⁹ *SBM*, 61.11, (November 1935), p. 2; 64.5, (May 1938), p. 7, are examples.

⁹⁰ *SBM*, 65.1, (January 1939), p. 5.

⁹¹ BUS Council Resolution to the Romanian Ambassador, London, BUS Minute Book, 1935-1939, pp. 632-633.

⁹² *SBM*, 37.5, (May 1911), pp. 76-77; [The gap was due to the war in Europe] 45.7, (July 1919), p. 78; 46.3, (March 1920), pp. 28-29; 48.9, (September 1922), p. 106; 50.9, (September 1924), p. 109;

⁹³ *SBM*, 65.3, (March 1939), p. 21.

⁹⁴ *SBM*, 46.8, (August 1920), p. 101.

as an independent Union in seeking to do all they could during the Inter-War years.

## Overseas Mission

In the twentieth century there had been a pattern of steady growth in numbers of missionaries employed by the different Scottish Protestant denominations. Overall from the United Kingdom there were approximately 10,000 Christian missionaries serving overseas by 1900, the greater proportion of course on behalf of the numerically larger English churches.[95] In the Church of Scotland from a baseline figure of 115 missionaries engaged in 1899–1900[96] this total grew to 170 in 1910–1911[97] and as high as 190 in 1924–1925.[98] To see the extent of the growth of this work in their ranks they had progressed from employing the equivalent of one missionary for every twelve congregations in 1899–1900 to more than one for every eight by 1924–1925. The United Free Church in 1900–1901 had 406 serving missionaries;[99] a total that reached 506 in 1910–1911[100] and a highpoint of 630 in 1924–1925.[101] In the same time period, the UFC had increased from the equivalent of one missionary for every four congregations to just over one for every two congregations by 1924–1925. In the case of both bodies this was indisputable proof of a great commitment to the cause of world mission.[102] Amongst the smaller denominations the Congregational Union of Scotland had thirty missionaries employed overseas in 1920–1921, reaching the highest total of thirty-eight in

---

[95] A. Porter, 'An Overview, 1700–1914', in N. Etherington (ed.), *Missions and Empire* (Oxford: Oxford University Press, 2005), p. 40.

[96] *Reports of the Schemes of the Church of Scotland for the Year 1900*, p. 82.

[97] *Reports of the Schemes of the Church of Scotland for the Year 1911*, p. 88.

[98] *Reports of the Schemes of the Church of Scotland for the Year 1925* Edinburgh: William Blackwood, 1925), pp. 175–177.

[99] 'Report of Committee on Statistics', No. XXX, *Reports to the General Assembly of the United Free Church of Scotland 1901*, p. 8.

[100] 'Eleventh Report on Foreign Missions', *Reports to the General Assembly of the United Free Church of Scotland 1911*, p. 13.

[101] 'Twenty-Sixth Report on Foreign Mission', *Reports to the General Assembly of the United Free Church of Scotland 1926*, p. 90.

[102] Hilary Carey has pointed out what she considered the 'tragic waste of resources' of the different Presbyterian bodies duplicating 'India Missions', 'Colonial Missions and for the Conversion of the Jews'. Hilary M. Carey, *God's Empire: Religion and Colonialism in the British World, c.1801–1908* (Cambridge: Cambridge University Press, 2011), p. 239.

1925–1926; this was growth from the equivalent of one missionary for between every five or six churches in 1920–1921 to one for between every four or five congregations in 1925–1926.[103] The Free Church of Scotland had rebuilt a missionary presence overseas with two supported agents in 1910–1911, a minister named A. Dewar in South Africa, and Miss Elizabeth McLeod in India;[104] a decade later a strong work was established with the school in Lima, Peru,[105] with up to nine individuals supported by 1925–1926.[106] BMS also experienced significant growth in the number of personnel it employed between 1900–1901 and 1921–22. In the former year it employed 311 people rising to a remarkable 515 two decades later.[107] It is no surprise that this agency struggled to raise the necessary finance to support so many agents in the field. A significant contribution to the increase was the growing medical work under its auspices. The rising cost of medical missions was greater than the home constituency could afford at that time.[108] By 1932–33 BMS missionaries were reduced in number to 397. Changing circumstances such as rising nationalism in India in the wider population, together with the anti-foreigner movement in China in 1927[109] ensured that BMS staffing levels of missionaries would not attain again the heights of the 1920s.[110] This

---

[103] I am grateful to Revd Dr W.D. McNaughton in May 2014 for assistance with the figures from the then Congregational Union of Scotland and his willingness to discuss the contributions made by the Scottish Congregationalists to overseas mission in the early twentieth century.

[104] *The Principal Acts of the General Assembly of the Free Church of Scotland*, 1901, p. 371. Fuller details of the missionaries who served in India from this denomination are given in Anne M. Urquhart, *Near India's Heart* (Edinburgh; Knox Press, 1990), pp. 51–70.

[105] *The Principal Acts of the General Assembly of the Free Church of Scotland* (Edinburgh: William Nimmo, 1911), pp. 582–583. Details of the work in Peru are given in *Free Church of Scotland Missionary Enterprise South Africa, India, Peru 1900–1949* (Edinburgh: Free Church of Scotland, 1949), pp. 45–71; and John M. Macpherson, *At The Roots of a Nation: The Story of San Andres School in Lima, Peru* ((Edinburgh: Knox Press,1993).

[106] *The Principal Acts of the General Assembly of the Free Church of Scotland* (Edinburgh: William Nimmo, 1926), pp. 257–258.

[107] H/96–7, BMS Details of Missionary Staff 1900–1949, cited by Stanley, *Baptist Missionary Society*, p. 383.

[108] Stanley, *Baptist Missionary Society*, p. 383.

[109] Liu Yi, 'From Christian Aliens to Chinese Citizens: The National Identity of Chinese Christians in the Twentieth Century,' *Studies in World Christianity*, 16.2 (2010), pp. 147–152.

[110] Stanley, *Baptist Missionary Society*, p. 385.

phenomenon was common amongst the Protestant mission agencies at that time. The Church of Scotland alarmed by the continuing large deficits in its overseas mission budgets appointed a Survey Committee to review the situation at its 1932 General Assembly. There was a reluctant decision to call for a £10,000 cut in expenditure overseas, together with an urgent plea for an additional £10,000 to be raised annually. The financial challenge was not quite as bad as first stated because of the growing number of staff vacancies on the field, but this was only a temporary aid to their cause. Inevitably, less work would be accomplished going forward unless replacements were found. An awareness of the need for financial cuts occurred at the same time as a drop in applications for work overseas. It is probable that there is some connection between them. Difficult choices needed to be made concerning its priorities in overseas work by the National Church in the 1930s.[111] Scottish Baptists had undertaken a detailed survey of the overseas workers supported by their churches in 1925. This detailed report published in 1926,[112] which although incomplete and inaccurate in places, is an invaluable guide to the prominence of overseas evangelistic work amongst this branch of the Scottish Christian family. This brief survey of a range of Protestant Churches in Scotland has shown that the numbers of missionaries engaged in overseas service continued to grow in the first three decades of the twentieth century, as had been the case throughout the previous century. It was in the 1930s that the first reductions were made in staffing levels. Claims that missionary activity declined after the First World War[113] are not sustained by the evidence available from the major Protestant Churches in Scotland in the 1920s. The numerical high point may have been reached in this decade, but it would be nearer the middle of the century before a substantial drop in the numbers of serving missionaries was experienced.

In the nineteenth century Scottish Baptists primarily gave their finances for missionary work to the Baptist Missionary Society, with whom the vast majority of Scottish Baptist overseas missionaries had served. However, this situation changed with the formation of a growing number of other mission agencies seeking the support of the wider Christian community, especially during the later decades of that century. As a result, by the time of the Baptist Union survey in 1925 looking at the missionaries serving overseas from

---

[111] *A Survey and A Call: The Report of the Foreign Mission Committee to the General Assembly of 1935* (Edinburgh: Wm Blackwood & Sons, 1935), pp. 37–40, 45–48. By contrast, the over optimistic expectations for the 1930s onwards by J.H. Morrison, *The Scottish Churches' Work Abroad* (Edinburgh: T. & T. Clark, 1927), pp. 223–235, was shown to be unwarranted.

[112] Yuille (ed.), *Baptists in Scotland*, pp. 290–295.

[113] Contra R.J. Finlay, 'Missions Overseas', in M. Lynch (ed.), *Oxford Companion to Scottish History* (Oxford: Oxford University Press, 2007), pp. 424–425.

Scottish Baptist congregations, it was clear that the range of mission agencies and fields of service had multiplied as the twentieth century had progressed. It must be acknowledged that the figures stated here are provisional due to the incomplete nature of the data. Although Yuille's work is an excellent basis on which to build a more complete picture of Scottish Baptist missionaries working overseas, it is clear that there were significant gaps in the data recorded in that account. The total number of men and women recorded in the 1925 survey came to 207; a total that had risen to 215, as a result of McVicar's more accurate recording of Scottish Baptist personnel serving with BMS from 149 congregations.[114] A more detailed examination for this study of the limited data available on the majority of Scottish Baptists serving with other mission agencies in this time period has revised the total number of those working overseas upwards to 260 individuals. It is possible that the number of BMS affiliated missionaries omitted from the Yuille list may be as high as eighteen Scots, of which eight came from other Scottish denominations and ten from Scottish Baptist causes. However, there were also twenty-nine men and women named by Yuille who had completed their service in the twentieth century with BMS before 1925. The tentative number of Scottish Baptists who may have been serving overseas as missionaries in 1925–1926 is eighty-nine with BMS and the China Inland Mission (CIM), together with fifty-two named persons on Yuille's list now retired. Of the remaining 119 individuals it is probable that the majority were in active service at this time with a variety of other mission agencies. The accurate BMS and CIM data, when combined with the less certain knowledge of some of the work of smaller mission agencies, allows us to determine that these encouraging statistics point to a family of churches seriously committed to the work of overseas mission. It is very likely that the overwhelming majority of Baptist congregations in Scotland were committed to carrying out the Great Commission of Jesus by spreading the good news of the Christian message overseas through their appointed representatives.

### Relations with Other Scottish Churches

The Missionary Congress of Scottish Churches that took place in Glasgow in October 1922 was a development from the 1910 World Missionary Conference. Its aims were clear:

> bringing the whole congregational life of the country face to face with the opportunity and urgency of world-wide service. The basis of the Congress is the

---

[114] 'Scottish Baptists in the Mission Field', in Yuille (ed.), *Baptists in Scotland*, pp. 290–295. *The Baptist Handbook for* 1926 (London: Baptist Union Publications Department, 1926), p. 168. McVicar, *Great Adventure*, pp. 70–83.

conviction that Christ is the need of the world, and that the present condition of the nations makes the need for the Gospel of Christ more insistent than ever.[115]

John MacBeath, the conference secretary,[116] who had resigned his pastorate at Cambuslang in order to prepare properly for this mission gathering,[117] and had undertaken the task of promoting this conference through the *SBM* was convinced that this 'occasion would be a landmark in the history of the Scottish Churches and their missions overseas'. There were seventy-five Scottish Baptists registered as official delegates, a significant number of representatives from a small denomination. MacBeath was convinced that a people with vision who prayed hard for God to be at work in the world would see that 'the churches shall be full of increase and all lands shall see the glory of the Lord'.[118] One of the follow-up events to this gathering was a major mission week in Aberdeen in which all the Protestant churches participated. 'The campaign from Monday, 30 October, to Sunday 12 November, succeeded in arousing interest in Aberdeen as no religious effort has done for the past decade. ... All the churches ... co-operated in the enterprise, thus affording a superb demonstration of the unity that lies deeper than their differences.'[119] MacBeath, in his summary of the two-year missionary campaign in Scotland, sought to underline the uniqueness of its successes.

> It was the first effort in which all the Reformed Churches united together. There were no precarious negotiations concerning union – there was rather the impulse of a great task that could best be done together. The Campaign has created a new spirit of fraternity throughout the churches which will do much to facilitate common service in the future.[120]

This event underlined the benefits of co-operation in mission and led to other forms of united action. Here the principle of unity for mission first of all, followed by other forms of united action, was a pathway travelled by a number of Scottish Christian bodies during the nineteenth and twentieth centuries.[121]

---

[115] *SBM*, 48.3 (March 1922, pp. 32–33).

[116] *SBM*, 48.11 (November 1922), p. 125.

[117] *SBM*, 48.11 (November 1922), p. 138.

[118] *SBM*, 48.8 (August 1922), p. 92. MacBeath echoed similar sentiments in a final article before the conference in the same periodical, 48.10 (October 1922), pp. 115–116.

[119] *SBM*, 48.12 (December 1922), p. 147.

[120] J. MacBeath, 'The Close of the Missionary Campaign', *SBM*, 49.6 (June 1923), pp. 75–76.

[121] One example here will suffice: Scottish Baptists established the Baptist Home Missionary Society for Scotland in 1827, following the merger of three separate

One major development that came from this ecumenical progress was the creation of the Scottish Churches Council (SCC), formed in 1924, bringing together representatives of the Church of Scotland, the United Free Church, the Episcopal Church of Scotland, the Congregational Union of Scotland, the Baptist Union of Scotland and the Original Secession Churches. The purpose of this body was to enable these Scottish Christians to engage in concerted action on questions of national importance.[122] Proposals for this new body were discussed at the May BUS Council meeting in 1923. The fact that the discussions centred on who the six Baptist members of the one-hundred-member SCC should be, gave a clear indication of the support of Scottish Baptists for this cause.[123] There was, however, one matter of concern to Scottish Baptists, raised in 1926, with reference to the SCC. It had been feared that Unitarians might be invited to join this new body, but assurances from the secretary of the SCC confirmed that such fears were unfounded.[124] The key issue for Scottish Baptists, with respect to ecumenical co-operation in their homeland was mission. It is not surprising that the following comments were received after the SCC report at the November BUS Council in 1929: 'it was agreed to express appreciation of the Council's [SCC] report, especially the section dealing with the Home Mission situation'.[125] There was general satisfaction with the work of this ecumenical body in the years prior to World War Two.

## Theological Education

The acceptance of the provision of theological education in the Baptist Theological College in Glasgow for those training for Baptist pastoral ministry in Scotland had been accepted by the majority of Scottish Baptists prior to the First World War. However, the troubling case of Eric Roberts,

---

mission agencies, but it took several attempts to form a union of churches prior to the establishment of a union of Baptist churches in Scotland. See Talbot, *Search for a Common Identity*, for further details. W.D. McNaughton, *Early Congregational Independency in the Highlands and Islands and North-East of Scotland*, (Tiree: Trustees of Ruaig Congregational Church, 2003), provides similar information with respect to Scottish Congregationalists.

[122] D.B. Forrester, 'Ecumenical Movement', in Cameron (ed.), *Dictionary of Scottish Church History and Theology*, pp. 273–274.

[123] BUS Council, 8 May 1923, Baptist Union of Scotland Minute Book, 1915–1926, pp. 573–574.

[124] BUS Council, 2 February 1926, Baptist Union of Scotland Minute Book, 1915–1926, p. 770.

[125] BUS Council, 26 November 1929, Baptist Union of Scotland Minute Book, 1926–1931, p. 387.

Minister of Grantown-on-Spey Baptist Church, caused some of the earlier tensions to re-emerge within this family of churches. Roberts had admitted in a letter to M.E. Aubrey. Secretary of the Baptist Union of Great Britain, dated 18 April 1931, that since his student days he had followed the creed of his former Philosophy Professor at Glasgow University, Henry Jones, and had always denied the Deity of Jesus and entertained misgivings about 'the doctrinal questions involved in the Declaration of Principle', though, he stated that he had been careful in his public pronouncements to avoid causing offence to other Christians.[126] However, Roberts had subsequently written a letter that was published in the *Christian World* on 4 February 1932 highlighting his 'Modernist' theological convictions. The Office Bearers of the Baptist Union were convinced that the letter 'clearly gave expression of views concerning the person of Christ which were not in keeping with the distinctive principles of the Baptist denomination'.[127] It was followed by a heterodox sermon preached at a united Easter Sunday 1932 evening service in his town and later the same year by a letter in the *Strathspey Herald* denying that the Bible is 'the word of God'.[128] The Baptist Union Council was sufficiently concerned to set up a special committee comprising the Office-bearers and six other members to investigate Robert's doctrinal views.[129] A report to the September 1932 Council was clear in stating that: 'the minister concerned had advanced Non-Trinitarian or Unitarian views, the Council strongly protested against such doctrines, and decided to ask the minister to consider whether ... he could honourably continue as a minister of a Baptist Church.'[130] There was gracious and fair discussion of Roberts' views over two days of assembly, Tuesday 18 and Wednesday 19 October 1932, but delegates were convinced that the Grantown-on-Spey Minister had articulated convictions contrary to those held by accredited ministers of the Union and in a second motion re-affirmed their belief in the Deity and Lordship of Jesus

---

[126] E.J. Roberts, to M.E. Aubrey, 18 April, 1931, copy retained in BUGB Minute Book, Angus Library, Regent's Park College, Oxford.

[127] BUS Office-bearers' Meeting, 2 November 1931, p. 751; BUS Council, 29 March 1932, Baptist Union of Scotland Minute Book 1932–October 1935, pp. 45–47.

[128] *Strathspey Herald*, 6 May 1932. See also Digest of Minutes of the Baptist Union of Scotland Assembly, 19 October 1932, *Scottish Baptist Yearbook 1933*, p. 126. The fullest account of his life and theological views is given in Kenneth B.E. Roxburgh, 'Eric Roberts and Orthodoxy among Scottish Baptists', *Baptist Quarterly* 39.2 (April 2001), pp. 80–95.

[129] BUS Council Minutes, 25 May 1932, *Scottish Baptist Yearbook 1933*, p. 105.

[130] BUS Council Minutes, 21 September 1932, *Scottish Baptist Yearbook 1933*, p. 105.

Christ.[131] Attempts to persuade Roberts to return to orthodox convictions over the next year were unsuccessful and by 272 votes to 73 Assembly delegates voted to remove him from the list of accredited ministers, together with a second vote to remove the 'Distinctive Principles of the Baptists' statement from the *Scottish Baptist Yearbook*, a form of words that Roberts had claimed gave him the liberty to hold his convictions.[132] The high number of votes against his removal was not an indication that other colleagues shared his opinions, rather that they were unhappy with the manner of his removal.[133] This Grantown clergyman was the only one removed from the list of accredited Baptist Ministers for heretical convictions during the first 150 year history of this family of churches.

Over the next decade concerns over the theological soundness of the Baptist College were articulated, in large measure due to the reluctance of its Principal and a minority of other Scottish Baptists to vote at Assembly to remove Roberts from the list of accredited ministers.[134] Up to this time many Baptist theological students had been content to affiliate with the Student Christian Movement, but by the 1930s adverts in the *SBM* highlighted an alternative conservative theological body, the increasingly prominent Inter-Varsity Fellowship.[135] The most prominent critic of the Baptist College was John Shearer, Minister of Rattray Street Baptist Church, Dundee (1921–1941). There had already been a notice of motion submitted at the 1930 Baptist Union Assembly by Percival Waugh of Bristo Baptist Church, Edinburgh, calling for the College and the denominational periodical, the *Scottish Baptist Magazine*, to become departments of the Union. The latter request did take place a short time later, but negotiations over Union representation on the Baptist College committee spread out over a number of years, with a decision to appoint six representatives elected by open ballot at assembly was concluded at the 1937 assembly. Another source of unease was

---

[131] BUS Assembly, Digest of Minutes, Tuesday 18 and Wednesday 19 October, 1932, *Scottish Baptist Yearbook 1933*, pp. 124–127.

[132] BUS Assembly, Digest of Minutes, Tuesday 24 and Wednesday 25 October, 1933, *Scottish Baptist Yearbook 1934*, pp. 128–130, 140

[133] Roxburgh, 'Eric Roberts and Orthodoxy among Scottish Baptists', p. 89; Kenneth B.E. Roxburgh, 'Your Word is Truth: Theological Developments among Twentieth-Century Scottish Baptists', in Talbot (ed.), *Distinctive People*, pp. 140–142.

[134] A full discussion of this debate is given in Kenneth B.E. Roxburgh, 'The Fundamentalist Controversy Concerning the Baptist Theological College of Scotland', *Baptist History and Heritage*, Vol.36, Nos 1–2 (Winter/Spring 2001), pp. 251–272.

[135] Adverts for SCM, for example, *SBM*, 60.9 (September 1934), p. 18; and for IVF, 59.8 (August 1933), p. 14; 62.12 (December 1936), p. 22; In the latter advert it was stated that: 'The Evangelical Union tries to save the Christian student from losing his keenness by creating an atmosphere where his zeal is maintained . . . .'

concern over the number of men who had left pastorates to join the Church of Scotland. A Commission of Enquiry, set up in 1939 and reporting back two years later, revealed a variety of causes including financial strains caused by low Baptist stipends and the absence of security in pastorates, as well as a smaller proportion due to a change in theological outlook.[136] Tensions rose further when Shearer produced a series of pamphlets attacking 'the modernism' that had arisen from the college. The Dundee Minister was supported by some colleagues, including Sidlow Baxter, Minister of Charlotte Chapel, Edinburgh, who published material from these pamphlets in the June and July 1944 issues of *The Chapel Record*.[137] However, the angry tone of Shearer in the 1940s did not help his case and even strong supporters such as Sidlow Baxter,[138] failed to support the later new Evangelical Baptist Fellowship Bible College launched in Glasgow in 1949. The Baptist Theological College would weather the storm in the post-war years as the new theological institution failed to attract sufficient support. Many people had some concerns, but insufficient to set up a rival institution. In the year of its Jubilee in 1944 annual assembly delegates offered their sincere congratulations for its work and the place this institution occupied in the life of the denomination.[139]

## Social Issues

### *Temperance*[140]

The Temperance battle was one in which Scottish Baptists were keen to engage. On 23 October 1918 at the Annual Assembly Alexander Bremner proposed: 'That this Assembly of the Baptist Union of Scotland most respectfully approaches His Majesty's Government asking for the Prohibition of the Traffic in Intoxicants; being convinced that Public Opinion on Scotland is in favour of such a measure . . . .'[141] Assembly adopted this motion. It was followed by a second from the same Minister: 'That the Assembly

---

[136] Murray, *Scottish Baptist College Centenary History 1894–1994*, pp. 23–24.

[137] Roxburgh, 'The Fundamentalist Controversy Concerning the Baptist Theological College of Scotland', pp. 259–268; Murray, *Scottish Baptist College Centenary History 1894–1994*, p. 25; and Brian R. Talbot, 'A Clear and Certain Sound: The Ministry of John Shearer, 1913–1921', in Talbot, *Standing on the Rock: A History of Stirling Baptist Church 1805–2005*, pp. 74–77.

[138] See Balfour, *Revival in Rose Street*, pp. 266–267 for more details on this subject.

[139] *Scottish Baptist Yearbook 1945*, pp. 52–53.

[140] A fuller study of this subject is planned for publication in the near future, Brian R. Talbot, 'Scottish Baptists and Temperance 1829–1929', in William L. Pitts Jr. (ed.), *Baptists, Gospel and Culture* (Macon, GA: Mercer University Press) forthcoming.

[141] *Scottish Baptist Yearbook 1919*, p. 23.

earnestly urges all Baptist congregations to at once begin to organise and educate, so as to be able to take full advantage of the provisions of the Temperance (Scotland) Act, 1920, for clearing communities of the Traffic in Drink.' It was adopted.[142] Morale already high was boosted by the votes in Norway and the United States of America to adopt prohibition by 1920.[143] Expectations for a similar result in Scotland had seemed quite reasonable in the light of this news, but advocates of this cause would soon be disappointed. In Dundee, for example, there were three polls at three-year intervals in the 1920s. The first poll campaign in November 1920 saw the Christian community split on the issue. Despite the General Assembly of the Church of Scotland promoting the *No Licence* campaign some local parish ministers were demonstrating in favour of 'an Honest Christian Dram and the citizens right to have one', claiming that only ten per cent of the attendees of the General Assembly who voted for prohibition were teetotallers. Edward Scrymgeour, a prominent Temperance campaigner who would famously oust Winston Churchill from the Dundee seat at the 1923 election on a Temperance manifesto was suitably outraged by their actions. The result was 36,452 for *No Change* and 15,491 for *No Licence*, a majority of 20,961. (The later votes had a similar result with the majority reduced to 16,037 in 1923 and 17,556 in 1926) The Town Council had voted itself dry in January 1920, but not enough citizens shared their convictions. However, the unconfirmed reports that the *No Change* campaign in the city had spent approximately £50,000 on their campaign compared to the *No Licence* team's £1,100 indicated they had held genuine fears of a different result at the polls, at least in 1920.[144] The momentum in the political campaigns for temperance reforms had dissipated by the end of the 1920s. Temperance convictions were still firmly upheld in Baptist and other Protestant churches and amongst many people in the Middle Classes, but they never commanded a sufficient majority in Scotland for prohibition to be adopted.

---

[142] *Scottish Baptist Yearbook 1919*, p. 23. It was sent to all the affiliated churches requesting their active involvement in support of this cause. The vast majority were strong supporters of this cause. However, this was not necessarily true of all. For example, this Assembly motion appears to have been presented at one Baptist church as simply information to note and there is no evident to indicate any discussion followed the presentation. It is likely that Thomas Coats Memorial Church's members had mixed views on this matter. 'Church Meeting', 29 October 1919, 'Minute Book of the Congregation of Baptists meeting in the Thomas Coats Memorial Church, Paisley', Volume III, 14 July 1913–28 March, 1948, pp. 65–66.

[143] 'The Scottish Baptist Total Abstinence Society Thirty-Eighth Annual Report 1919', p. 3, in the *Scottish Baptist Yearbook 1920*.

[144] 'Wet or Dry' in David Phillips, *The Hungry Thirties: Dundee Between the Wars* (Dundee: David Winter & Son, 1981), pp. 37–39.

The use of alcohol in the wine used at communion had largely ceased in Scottish Baptist Churches by the end of the nineteenth century,[145] but the movement from using a common cup took a longer period of time to change. The Scottish Baptist Individual Cup Communion Association launched a campaign on Sunday October 6, 1907, distributing 5,000 leaflets in aid of their cause in Baptist churches in Glasgow advocating the adoption of 'the hygenic individual cup'.[146] It is probable that this proposal was strongly resisted in many congregations at first because it is likely that this change took place in the majority of Scottish Baptist congregations in the 1920s. There were some early adopters of this new practice, for example, Queen's Park Baptist Church, Glasgow, made the change in 1910 and Leslie Baptist Church shortly prior to World War One. Other congregations in the years shortly after the war, for example, George Street Baptist Church, Paisley, 'after 1918' and Cambuslang Baptist Church in 1920.[147] Charlotte Chapel in Edinburgh adopted this practice in November 1922.[148] In Maxwelltown Baptist Church, Dundee, for example, they were introduced as a special feature of the Church Semi-Jubilee Celebrations on Sunday 16 December, 1923.[149] In Helensburgh Baptist Church the change was introduced in the early 1920s with the option of the common cup retained for those who

---

[145] See chapter three, pp. 64–67; Thomas Coats Memorial Church, Paisley, was most reluctant to make this change. It was only due to the insistence of the new minister William Grant that a vote took place. He had threatened to resign shortly after taking up his post, on finding out that fermented wine was served at communion. At his first deacons' meeting on 30 October 1952, he indicated that he was 'shocked' by this finding. Deacons' Meeting, 30 October, 1952, in Thomas Coats Memorial Church (Baptist), Paisley, Deacons' Minute-Book, January 1947 to July 1955, n.p.; At a heated Church Meeting on 21 January, 1953, a vote on this subject was tied with the pastor's resignation still a real possibility. A fresh vote at the next Church Meeting on 8 April 1953 supported Grant's position by 106 votes to 67. Thomas Coats Memorial Church, Minute Book Volume IV, 14 July 1948 to 29 March 1973, pp. 86–90. I am grateful to Derek Murray for drawing my attention to the significance of William Grant in this decision.

[146] *Christian World* 51, no. 2,636 (10 October, 1907), p. 12.

[147] This information comes from a survey of Scottish Baptist church life 1918–1939, conducted by David Edwards in 1977–1978. Unless another source is given, the dates for particular congregations in this paragraph come from this survey. There were only a relatively small number of returns, but it is invaluable about the life of these particular congregations. I am grateful to Dr Ian Balfour for providing copies of these returns and of his paper 'Congregational Life in Twelve Central Belt Baptist Churches, 1918 to 1939', presented at the Scottish Baptist History Project, Stirling, 27 April 2019.

[148] Balfour, *Revival in Rose Street*, p. 184.

[149] *SBM*, 50.1 (January 1924), p. 9.

preferred it, but by 1925 the church minutes record that everyone preferred the individual cups.¹⁵⁰ In Broughty Ferry Baptist Church the change occurred in 1928 against the wishes of the deacons who had hoped to retain both the individual and the common cup.¹⁵¹ Ayr Baptist Church made the change in the late 1920s; Partick Baptist Church between 1928 and 1929; New Prestwick Baptist Church in 1930 and Clydebank Baptist Church around 1932; There was an advertisement each month in the *SBM* from 1929 to 1935 which stated: '**Danger at the Communion Table** Doctors and Public Health Officers pronounce the use of the Common Cup as liable to convey Infectious Diseases' and urged reads to obtain individual cups from a Birmingham supplier of individual cups. The advert changed in 1935 to '**Safety at the Communion Table**' with the same warning from Doctors and Public Health Officers.¹⁵² Not every Baptist church was willing to go along with the change at that time. Keiss Baptist Church in Caithness, for example, was committed to retaining the common cup in 1925,¹⁵³ and Harper Memorial Baptist Church, Glasgow, was still using a common cup as late as 1950. In time Scottish Baptist Churches changed from a common cup to individual glasses at communion, almost certainly on health grounds. For many congregations there was a clear reluctance to make the change but eventually it became standard practice in the communion services.

## War and Peace

The Baptist Union President's New Year message in January 1919 spoke of 'entrancing hope and thrilling opportunity' now that World War One was finally concluded. However, there was equally concern about the impact of the war on soldiers now returning to civilian life. 'How will they return? What will they find when they return?'¹⁵⁴ The *SBM* editor in the same issue called for the permanent liberation of the German colonies and expressed real concern that the spirit of German militarism had not gone away and warned against the possibility of World War Two with Germany.¹⁵⁵ The following issue of this periodical reflected on the 1919 peace conference in Paris intended to

---

[150] Kenneth McNeish, *A History of Helensburgh Baptist Church 1881–1998* (Helensburgh: For the church, 1998), 14.

[151] Small, *Broughty Ferry Baptist Church: The First Hundred Years*, p. 12.

[152] Reference to these adverts is given in Balfour, 'Congregational Life in Twelve Central Belt Churches, 1918 to 1939', p. 7.

[153] *SBM*, 51.3 (March 1925), p. 39.

[154] *SBM*, 45.1 (January 1919), p. 1.

[155] *SBM*, 45.1 (January 1919), pp. 2–3; 45.3; (March 1919), p. 26; 45.7 (July 1919), pp. 73–74.

bring an end to the conflict. There were many questions raised about this process and a reminder of how difficult it is to produce a lasting and just settlement, combined with a warning that the agreement concluded would have a lasting positive or negative impact on the years to come.[156] In the February 1920 issue of the *SBM* an editorial comment noted that: 'peace is still far away and seems to be getting more distant as time goes on.'[157] A couple of months later the same columnist declared: 'the future is dark and uncertain.'[158] Plans for a League of Nations to prevent future wars were welcomed, but in contrast to the enthusiasm of some for this new body, the editor of the *SBM* had severe doubts about it accomplishing very much.[159] The opinions expressed about the then current political situation in this periodical appear remarkably perceptive with hindsight. The annual two-minute silence on the eleventh hour of 11 November, first observed in 1919 was welcomed as an appropriate commemoration of World War One.[160] It was clear that though the desire for peace and reconciliation was strong in this Christian constituency there were serious doubts in the years immediately after the war about the stability of the agreement between the major powers.

In the 1920s there was a greater focus in this periodical on domestic issues, particularly the economic difficulties and related industrial disputes,[161] but there was also a more hopeful note sounded about international relations. It was not all plain sailing. A decision not to offer Germany a permanent seat on the League of Nations Council was lambasted as a 'tragedy',[162] while the reversal of that decision and the admission of Germany to that body with a permanent seat was welcomed 'as the greatest single step which has been taken since the foundation of the League towards securing European peace; and …makes war between Britain, France and Germany, if not impossible, more unlikely than it has ever been.'[163] A motion enthusiastically adopted by delegates at the October 1927 Baptist Union Assembly included these words: 'That this assembly rejoices in the progress that is being made in the elimination of the War Spirit and the creation of a Will to Peace.' This

---

[156] *SBM*, 45.2 (February 1919), pp. 13–14.

[157] *SBM*, 46.2 (February 1920), p. 13.

[158] *SBM*, 46.4 (April 1920), p. 37.

[159] *SBM*, 45.4 (April 1919), p. 38; 45.5 (May 1919), p. 49;

[160] *SBM*, 45.12 (December 1919), pp. 141–142.

[161] For example, 'The Great Strike', *SBM*, 52.6 (June 1926), p. 69; 'Coal Dispute', *SBM*, 52.7 (July 1926), p. 86; 'The Coal Deadlock', *SBM*, 52.8 (August 1926), p. 97; 'The Coal Dispute', *SBM*, 52.9 (September 1926), p. 109.

[162] *SBM*, 52.4 (April 1926), p. 45.

[163] 'The League of Nations', *SBM*, 52.10 (October 1926), p. 121.

lengthy motion drew attention to constructive steps being taken by respective governments in working towards a sustainable peace between them and urged churches to play their part in support of these initiatives.[164] It did appear that a decade on from the cessation of hostilities the nations of Europe had turned a corner in the direction of more constructive relations between them.

However, in the 1930s, in the years leading up to the war, there were obvious signs of increased anxiety. There was anger at the ill-treatment of Jews in Germany. A motion passed at the May 1933 Baptist Union Council declared: '... their indignation at the persecution of the Jews in Germany, their dismay at the actions of governments in denying freedom and the full rights of citizenship to well-disposed subjects on the grounds of race or religion or political beliefs ....'[165] Although, in a message for younger readers of the SBM in 1934, Douglas Stewart sought to assure them that the majority of German people wanted peace and social justice as much as anyone in this country. He did, however, highlight pressure from the great armament firms whose profits and business was much more lucrative in times of war, and who had no real desire for peace.[166] The Baptist Union Council unanimously accepted a motion presented at its February 1937 meeting, expressing a clear concern about 'the fateful rise in armaments'.[167] A clear anti-war message had been consistently presented by Scottish Baptists during this decade, and stated, for example, in the notes for Bible Class leaders in the November 1935 issue of the *SBM*.[168] It was, though, clear in 1938 that a change of tone was evident in this periodical. The German annexation of Austria was strongly condemned,[169] and the same country's seizure of the Sudatenland in Czechoslovakia was accepted with resignation.[170] But there was still fulsome praise for Prime Minister Neville Chamberlain's attempts to maintain peace in

---

[164] Thursday 27 October 1927, Baptist Union of Scotland Assembly, *Scottish Baptist Yearbook 1928*, p. 121.

[165] Social Service Committee Motion, BUS Council, *SBM*, 59.7 (July 1933), p. 14. See for more details on this subject, Lee B. Spitzer, 'The Nazi Persecution of the Jews and Scottish Baptist Indignation', *Baptist Theologies* 9.2 (2017).

[166] Douglas Stewart, 'Youth and War', *SBM*, 60.10 (October 1934), p. 9; Alan Storkey, *War or Peace?* (Cambridge: Christian Studies Press, 2015), highlights the significant contribution towards the rearming of Europe and the promotion of Fascism by major armament companies in the years leading to World War Two, pp. 220-391.

[167] BUS Council, 24 February 1937. *SBM*, 63.3 (March 1937), P. 10.

[168] E.O. Hopkins, 'Must We Have War?', *SBM*, 61.11 (November 1935), p. 12.

[169] 'The Rape of Austria' *SBM*, 64.4 (April 1938), pp. 1–2.

[170] 'The Outlook', *SBM*, 64.11 (November 1938), pp. 1–2.

Europe – even if he was ultimately unsuccessful.[171] A consistent commitment to a peaceful resolution of difficulties had been maintained by Scottish Baptists in the 1930s, although towards the end of 1938 they recognised that they were now living under the 'shadow of war'.[172]

Scottish Baptists had navigated through the difficult inter-war years with a confidence in the gospel they were proclaiming which was reflected in the continued growth in their numbers for the majority of these two decades. There had been particular progress in the greater Glasgow area, but not exclusively so and significant encouragement had been received as a result of the numbers converted through the religious revival that took place primarily in the North East of Scotland. The Home Mission work of the Union was now consolidated as a branch of the national body, and the commitment to overseas service was still strong throughout these years. Relations with fellow Baptists and with other churches in Scotland were strengthened, though tensions over theological education had arisen in large measure as a result of the Eric Roberts case. There had been genuine disappointment as a result of the Temperance referendum defeats, but it did not stop Scottish Baptists offering contributions on a variety of social issues during these years. There was, though, a consistency in the approach presented to issues of war and peace. Their fears over the 1919 terms of settlement of the First World War as the basis of future peace were justified, but support for the British Government's efforts to maintain peace were unwavering. However, like many fellow citizens who shared these convictions, hopes of avoiding another major war would be dashed.

---

[171] 'The Outlook', *SBM*, 64.8 (August 1938), p. 1. A Social Services Committee resolution at the October 1938 Baptist Union Assembly declared its thankfulness war had been averted, recognising 'how much the country owes to the earnest and unrelaxing efforts of the British Prime Minister in the saving of the Peace', *SBM*, 64.11 (November 1938), p. 18.

[172] 'The Shadow of War' 64.10 (October 1938), pp. 1–2.

CHAPTER 6

# 'The Struggle for Spiritual Values'[1]: Scottish Baptists and the Second World War[2]

In the post-war years very few people indeed considered it likely that there would be another world war within a generation of the conclusion of the 1914–1918 conflict.[3] The trauma inflicted by what took place during those years ensured that there was a real determination that it would not happen again. It is really important to grasp how deeply such a conviction was held by the majority of the population, not just the churches.[4] As late as October 1938, James Maxton, MP for Bridgeton and a former 'Red Clydesider', rose in the House of Commons to commend Prime Minister Neville Chamberlain for the agreements made with Hitler at Bad Godesburg and Munich over the fate of Sudetan Germans in Czechoslovakia. He thanked the Prime Minister for doing 'something that the mass of common people of the country wanted done.'[5] However, with hindsight it is clear that the harshness and vindictiveness of the terms of the Treaty of Versailles, the peace treaty that concluded hostilities between Germany and the Allied Powers, ensured that the conditions were in place that could be exploited in later years by Adolf

---

[1] Rev. Alexander Clark, Resolution on behalf of the Social Services Committee, adopted at the Baptist Union of Scotland Council, 20 September, 1939; *Scottish Baptist Yearbook 1940*, p. 126.

[2] An earlier version of this chapter was published as Brian R. Talbot, 'The Struggle for spiritual values: Scottish Baptists and the Second World War' in *Perichoresis*, The Theological Studies Journal of Emmanuel University, Romania, Volume 16, Issue 4 (2018), pp. 73-94. Permission to reuse this material was granted by the journal editor, Corneliu C. Simut.

[3] Robbins, *England, Ireland, Scotland Wales: The Christian Church 1900–2000* (Oxford: Oxford University Press), p. 279.

[4] Alan Wilkinson, *Dissent or Conform? War, Peace and the English Churches 1900–1945* (London: SCM, 1986), pp. 85–90.

[5] Quoted in Trevor Royle, *A Time of Tyrants: Scotland and the Second World War* (Edinburgh: Birlinn, 2011), p. 9.

Hitler and his National Socialists,[6] although it was the Great Depression in 1929 and the economically challenging times that followed in the early 1930s that provided the conditions in which the Nazis rose to power in Germany.[7] Many voices recognised that military solutions to conflict were less than adequate. There had to be a better way to resolve differences between the nations. 'Nothing but a potentially vast moral and spiritual reformation of global proportions could possibly be honoured by antagonisms so venomous and contradictory in character, and so world-wide in scope.'[8] The individual just cited was a supporter of the influential Moral Rearmament movement, but his judgement was similar to that of many other people who were not affiliated to that particular cause. Another war was unthinkable and no step must be neglected that could prevent it. This paper attempts to look at the response of one Scottish denomination, the Baptist Union of Scotland and its response to the Second World War.

### On the Threshold of the Second World War

A good example of the mood in this constituency was given in 'The Outlook' an editorial article in the January 1939 issue of the *SBM*. The author, James Hair, Minister of Bristo Baptist Church, Edinburgh, recognised that there had been some difficult times in the previous year but urged a spirit of fortitude upon its readers. He highlighted an example of this spirit in the media.

> During the week of tension in September one of our newspapers persisted, day in day out, despite all appearances to the contrary, in declaring that there would be no war, and urged its readers to be of good courage. Not always have we deemed that journal a wise and reliable guide; but on that occasion we relished its optimism and thanked God for its message.[9]

In addition, the author commended the Prime Minister Neville Chamberlain for the path he had taken. He 'keeps to his chosen path with a pertinacity that

---

[6] A.J. Hoover, *God, Britain and Hitler in World War II: The View of the British Clergy, 1939–1945* (Westport: Praeger, 1999), pp. 3–4.

[7] James Holland, *The War in the West A New History, Volume 1: Germany Ascendant 1939–1941* (London: Bantam Press, 2015), p. 15. There were a minority of people, especially those of pacifist convictions who were dismayed by the terms imposed at Versailles at the time and feared for future. Robbins, *Abolition of War: The Peace Movement in Britain 1914–1919*, pp. 179–181.

[8] A senior Army officer quoted in Frank N.D. Buchman, *Remaking the World: The Speeches of Frank N.D. Buchman* (London: Blandford Press, 1947), p. xxvii.

[9] 'The Outlook', *SBM*, 65.1 (January 1939), p. 3.

is beyond praise. So long as he is in power, we can rest assured that the last possibility of maintaining peace will be explored.'[10] This stance was not taken in ignorance of what was happening to Jewish people in Germany. Scottish Baptists had become, like other Scottish Churches,[11] increasingly critical of the actions of the German Government, with real fears as to what might happen in the next few years. Although some Jews had been able to emigrate to other countries, many more were unable to find a destination to take them. It was not only Germany that was increasingly unwelcoming to the Jewish people, but Germany was by far the worst oppressor and the cause of this crisis.[12] What might be the way forward? J. Allan Wright, minister of Knightswood Baptist Church, Glasgow, was convinced that moral and spiritual rearmament was the key. He cited the Queen of the Netherlands and H.W. (Bunny) Austin,[13] of tennis fame, as promoters of this cause. He reminded readers of this Scottish periodical that the next Baptist youth conference would be looking at this subject as a fruitful way forward and also quoted a letter from several individuals last Armistice Day, in *The Times* newspaper that articulated so clearly his own perspective.

> The choice is moral rearmament or national decay. Moral rearmament must be the foundation of national life, as it must be of any world settlement. The miracle of God's Living Spirit can break the power of pride and selfishness, of lust and fear and hatred; for spiritual power is the greatest force in the world.[14]

Scots too shared these convictions, he argued, citing a letter by several prominent Scotsmen in the Edinburgh newspaper, *The Scotsman*, last St

---

[10] 'The Outlook', *SBM*, 65.1 (January 1939), p. 3. The judgement of the editor of the Baptist Times was very clear even after war had begun that Neville Chamberlain's course of action had been carried out with 'a good conscience', 'Mr Chamberlain', *Baptist Times*, 10 October, 1940, p. 590. This was a commonly held view in the churches and wider society. Hoover, *God, Britain and Hitler in World War II*, pp. 86–87.

[11] English Baptists held a similar view. See J.H. Rushbrooke, 'The Jews: What Can We Do? *Baptist Times*, 2 February, 1939, p. 90. The most detailed study of Scottish Baptist attitudes to the plight of the Jews is given in Spitzer, 'The Nazi Persecution of the Jews and Scottish Baptist Indignation', pp. 68–84.

[12] 'The Outlook', *SBM*, 65.1 (January 1939), p. 5; 'The Crime of being a Jew in Germany', *SBM*, 65.1 (January 1939), p. 16.

[13] Austin was a member of the Moral Re-Armament movement. I appreciate David Bebbington highlighting this point. See also D.W. Bebbington, 'The Oxford Group Movement between the Wars', in W.J. Shiels and Diana Wood (eds), *Voluntary Religion* (Oxford: Basil Blackwell, 1986), pp. 495–507.

[14] J. Allan Wright, 'Moral and Spiritual Rearmament', *SBM*, 65.3 (March 1939), pp. 7–8.

Andrews Day. They advocated 'the call of an enterprise greater by far than the crossing of continents and launching of mighty ships. Moral and Spiritual Rearmament calls forth that strength of character which has always been Scotland's greatest wealth. The voice of God must become the will of the people.'[15] It is important to grasp how people viewed the crisis unfolding around them in the 1930s prior to war, without the perspective of hindsight. What was abundantly clear was that Scottish Baptists in line with the wider constituency were very supportive of every attempt by the Government to maintain the peace and avoid the start of another World War. A call for a moral reformation at home was the priority in the nation at that time.

William C. Charteris, a distinguished former WW1 chaplain and now minister of Stirling Baptist Church,[16] had also articulated clearly the message consistently proclaimed in Scottish Baptists ranks in a motion he proposed to the 1938 Baptist Union Assembly in Edinburgh on Thursday October 27.

> The Assembly of the Baptist Union of Scotland, met in Edinburgh, expresses its thankfulness to Almighty God that war has been averted.
>
> The members recognise how much the country owes to the earnest and unrelaxing efforts of the British Prime Minister in the saving of the Peace.
>
> They have marked with satisfaction the universal dread of war, and the consensus of opinion among the common people all over the world in favour of the settlement of international difference by agreement.
>
> While insisting that no abiding settlement can be reached save on the basis of righteousness . . . .[17]

It is important to note that two amendments to this motion were rejected. The first in particular was significant as two ministers Campbell Dovey (Crieff Baptist Church) and R.W. Aitken (Kirkintilloch Baptist Church), wanted to delate the paragraph commending Neville Chamberlain for the decisions he had made. It was a first hint in Scottish Baptist ranks that a stronger line against the actions of the German Government needed to be taken.

A further example of Scottish Baptist opinions on the eve of the war comes from the 1938 Baptist Union Presidential address delivered by W. Holms Coats, the Principal of the Scottish Baptist Theological College. It was a very

---

[15] Wright, 'Moral and Spiritual Rearmament', p. 8.

[16] 'Endure hardness as a good soldier of Jesus Christ: The Ministry of William C. Charteris O.B.E. M.C. 1921-39', in Talbot, *Standing on the Rock*, pp. 91-108.

[17] W.C. Charteris, motion, Baptist Union of Scotland Assembly, Thursday October 27, 1938, *Scottish Baptist Yearbook* (*SBY*) *1939*, pp. 165-166. Mainstream American church leaders took a similar line to their colleagues in the UK, see Gerald L. Sittser, *A Cautious Patriotism: The American Churches and the Second World War* Chapel Hill: The University of North Carolina Press, 1997, pp. 16-26.

frank and sobering address as Coats shared his assessment of the world situation at that time. 'Amid all our relief at being delivered from the nightmare of war, we cannot disguise from ourselves that that deliverance was effected by yielding to a show of naked and brutal force such as the world has seldom witnessed.'[18] He admitted that 'we have all sinned' in allowing these events to take place. 'The present situation is disheartening and terrifying enough. But from another point of view, it is full of hope. For it does not, as is often said, demonstrate the failure of Christianity, but rather its vindication.'[19] The Scottish Churches had demonstrated a similar conviction of the need for a return to Christian principles in the nation. In the winters of 1937 and 1938 Scottish Baptists had co-operated fully in the 'Recall to Religion Campaign',[20] which appeared to have had an encouraging response.[21] In his Seventieth Annual Report in October 1938 the Baptist Union Secretary came to the following conclusions about the need of the nation at that time. 'It is recognised on all hands that there is a clamant need for a re-emphasis on spiritual values.'[22] It can be suggested in summary that Scottish Baptists were aware of what was going on in the world during the 1930s, but like fellow Christians in other denominations, there was a strong determination to explore every possible avenue for peace to avoid if at all possible another world war.

A similar sober assessment of the situation was noted amongst other British Baptists. The 5 January 1939 issue of *The Baptist Times* contained this statement by the editor, after reflecting on Neville Chamberlain's return from Germany in 1938 after coming to an agreement with Hitler over the fate of Czechoslovakia.

> We were not afraid of war, there was no cowardice or sense of inferiority, but a deep seriousness. If the nation went into conflict, it would be with open eyes and some understanding of the horrors that must lie ahead. Anyone who talks of the glory of war ought to be put under restraint, either as a lunatic or a traitor to

---

[18] Rev. Principal W. Homs Coats, 'The Church's Task' Presidential Address 1938, *SBY*, 1939, p. 168.

[19] Homs Coats, 'The Church's Task', pp. 168–169.

[20] Details of what happened in the 'Recall to Religion' campaigns is given in Frank Bardgett, *Scotland's Evangelist D.P. Thomson* (Haddington: The Handsel Press, 2010), pp.152–157. One Baptist Church that participated in this campaign was Adelaide Place Baptist Church, Glasgow. John Stewart, *Adelaide Place Baptist Church During World War II* (Glasgow: Adelaide Place Baptist Church, 1983), p. 1.

[21] Innovative interdenominational evangelistic initiatives continued during the war. For example, Robert F. Chisholm, 'Victory Through The Cross: The Challenge of the Glasgow Evangelistic Campaign.' *Life and Work*, Vol. XV, May 1944, pp. 72–73.

[22] '70th Annual Report By The Union Secretary', *SBY*, 1939, p. 184.

humanity. Occasions might arise when a war of defence would be unavoidable, but pray God such occasions may not come. I give God thanks for our statesmen and for all who have sought peace and have helped to maintain it.[23]

Welsh Baptist Gwilym Davies, in the same issue of this periodical, despite acknowledging the difficulties in Europe in 1938, wrote:

> The year 1938 was not all bad. Who can ever forget the thrill when the news came that Mr Chamberlain had wrested an extension of the armistice of 1918? And who can estimate what promise for the future may be centred in the undoubted fact that millions of people in Germany and in Italy shrank from the horror of another European War?[24]

It is likely that although concerns about Germany's actions towards other countries had increased as the 1930s progressed, the majority of British Baptists were hopeful that a full-scale war might be avoided, even as late as the early months of 1939.[25]

One factor that ought to be mentioned was the strength of the pacifist movement amongst both British Christians and the wider society.[26] In the early 1930s pacifists had developed a growing confidence that disarmament was achievable and that the League of Nations might be able to police international agreements and bring 'moral sanctions' on nations that stepped out of line.[27] Attempts to form pacifist groups within British denominations began when W.H. Auden sent out letters to the clergy of the major

---

[23] 'Alone With My Memories', *Baptist Times*, 5 January, 1939, p. 1.

[24] Gwilym Davies, 'Enter 1939!' *Baptist Times*, 5 January, 1939, p. 9.

[25] For example, see Arthur Porritt, 'Hitler in Reasonable Mood', *Baptist Times*, 6 April, 1939, p. 267. 'Desperate But Not Hopeless', *Baptist Times*, 4 May, 1939, p. 1.

[26] Some brief comments on Baptist pacifism in the 1920s and 1930s is given in Ian M. Randall, 'Baptists and the First World War: The Place of Pacifism', in Kreitzer (ed.), *Step Into Your Place*, pp.36–39. The Pacifist movement was equally strong amongst Protestant clergy in the USA as well between the two world wars. See Kenneth Scott Latourette, 'Christianity and the Peace Movement', in Rufus M. Jones (ed.) *The Church, the Gospel and War* (London: Harper Brothers, 1948), pp. 103–104.

[27] Martin Ceadel, *Pacifism in Britain 1914–1945: The Defining Of A Faith* (Oxford: Clarendon Press, 1980), p. 87. However, there were some voices in the Church of Scotland, as early as the General Assembly of 1933, who argued that the nation might need to go to war against Germany again, in defence of a righteous cause. Stewart J. Brown, 'The Social Ideal of the Church of Scotland During the 1930s', in Andrew R. Morton (ed.) *God's Will in a Time of Crisis: A Colloquium Celebrating the 50th Anniversary of The Baillie Commission* (Edinburgh: Centre for Theology and Public Issues, The University of Edinburgh, 1994), p. 24.

denominations in 1929 commending the pacifist 'Congregational Covenant'.[28] By 1931 an attempt was made to form a Baptist Ministers Peace Group. It took until 8 December, 1932 for a committee promoting this cause to meet at Baptist Church House in London. They undertook to get two peace sermons published in the *Christian World Pulpit* periodical the following year, and then to distribute 1,000 copies of this issue at the Baptist Union of Great Britain and Ireland Assembly in Glasgow in April 1933. The level of interest was high as 400 ministers attended a session for this cause at the 1934 Assembly. By 1937 up to 448 Baptist ministers and lay-people in the UK had formally associated with this cause. In the minutes of the January 1938 meeting six Scottish Baptist ministers were listed as members: Robert Black (Kilmarnock); Peter Cowie (Airdrie); Alexander Law (Uddingston); J. McGuiness (Girvan); Reginald Waddelow (Adelaide Place, Glasgow) and F.R. Scofield (Dennistoun, Glasgow).[29] There were likely to be other Scottish Baptist ministers who were supportive of this position. In the March 1938 issue of the *SBM*, for example, there is a reference to the Baptist Pacifist Fellowship with the names of the two contact people for whom readers interested in this topic could contact. They were Stanley Andrews, Minister of Cathcart Baptist Church and John McKendrick, Minister of South Leith Baptist Church.[30] Once the war began significantly less detail was recorded of members, but membership continued to rise up to the end of 1942.[31] Although the majority of Scottish Baptists did not identify with this position, there was a greater determination to support the liberty of conscience for those who did. It was a surprise when Neville Chamberlain announced the introduction of conscription in peace time in the House of Commons on 26 April, 1939, however, both his speech and the opposition comments were dignified and restrained. The responses amongst the churches were similarly subdued as most people recognised that difficult times were ahead.[32] R.B. Hannen wrote an article in the June 1939 issue of the *SBM* reminding Scottish Baptists that it was our Baptist forbears who were the first to articulate clearly the full

---

[28] 'The Baptist Pacifist Fellowship, Minute Book 1933–9 Sept 1946', Angus Library, Regent's Park College, Oxford. There are no page numbers for entries.

[29] 'The Baptist Pacifist Fellowship (printed) List of Members, 31 December, 1936, gives a full list of names at that time, Angus Library, Regent's Park College, Oxford.

[30] 'Baptist Pacifist Fellowship', *SBM*, 64.3 (March 1938), p. 11.

[31] 'Annual Committee Report', 15 February, 1943, Baptist Pacifist Fellowship, Minute Book 1933- 9 Sept 1946, n.p., listed 1276 men and 628 women in the fellowship, including 270 Baptist ministers. The Anglican Pacifist Fellowship had 1,500 members by September 1939 and the Methodist Peace Fellowship had 3,500 members at that time. All the Pacifist Societies had rapid growth in membership in the late 1930s. Ceadel, *Pacifism in Britain*, p. 210.

[32] 'The Outlook', *SBM*, 65.6 (June 1939), p. 1.

doctrine of liberty of conscience.³³ The Cupar Baptist Church minister concluded with these words:

> If a man cannot see his way to take part in a war, or have anything to do with the military machine after he has given the matter every consideration and intelligently consulted his conscience, then every Baptist worthy of the traditions of his denomination, ought to recognise and respect that man's right to make that stand. ... We must at all costs maintain the principle of liberty of conscience.³⁴

Hannan, as a representative Scottish Baptist, was one of many convinced that maintaining our spiritual values was absolutely essential even in difficult circumstances.

## The Declaration of War

It was not a surprise when Prime Minister Neville Chamberlain issued his ultimatum to Germany in a radio broadcast on Sunday 3 September, 1939. The invasion of Poland by Hitler two days previously was the final straw which led to this course of action. Sidlow Baxter, minister of Charlotte Baptist Chapel, Edinburgh, made this comment:

> We ourselves deplore war even as the extreme resort, but we are at one with all our fellow-Britishers in believing that our cause is righteous. The war was thrust upon us ... ample facts have accumulated before us to expose Hitler's hypocrisy and his blame for the newly broken out conflict. The fact remains, therefore, that in this war we are without doubt championing right and truth against a brutal system of oppression which threatens our very civilisation.³⁵

---

³³ For more details on the history of this conviction see Anthony R. Cross, 'Christ Jesus ... exalted ... farre aboue all principalities and powers': Baptist Attitudes to Monarchy, Country, and Magistracy, 1609–1644', in Anthony R. Cross and John H.Y. Briggs (ed.), *Freedom and the Powers: Perspectives from Baptist History* (Didcot: Baptist Historical Society, (2014), pp. 3–22.

³⁴ R.B. Hannen, 'Liberty of Conscience', *SBM*, 65.6 (June 1939), pp. 3–4.

³⁵ Sidlow Baxter, *The Record*, 1939, pp. 177, 193, quoted by Balfour, *Revival in Rose Street*, p. 251. The editorial article in the 7 September issue of the BUGBI periodical the *Baptist Times* issued similar sentiments. 'In all our Country's long history Britain has not entered upon war with a conscience more at ease or a conviction more clear of a righteous cause.' 'The Church in Time of War', *Baptist Times*, 7 September, 1939, p. 677. See also the comments of the BUGB Secretary M.E. Aubrey, 'Baptists And this War', *Baptist Times*, 5 October, 1939, p.m739. The editor of the *Baptist Times* John C. Carlile also set out clearly why the war was being fought in a response to an American critic. *Baptist Times*, 4 January, 1940, p. 9. Carlile's obituary was published in the *Baptist Times*, 21 August, 1941, p. 407.

Henry Turner, minister of John Knox Street Baptist Church, Glasgow, while regretting the necessity of the war, noted his thankfulness, that 'our statesmen did all that was in their power to prevent war'.[36] The Baptist Union Council met on 20 September, 1939. The major item of business was a motion presented by Alexander Clark, minister of Viewfield Baptist Church, Dunfermline, on behalf of the Social Services Committee, which was subsequently adopted by the Council. The motion expressed 'its profound sorrow at the outbreak of war' and its sympathies to the Polish nation for what they had to endure.

> It marks with thanksgiving the unity, solemnity and self-dedication with which the British Commonwealth of Nations has entered the struggle for spiritual values, without which civilisation must perish. It offers unceasing prayer that these values may not be lost sight of during the war or in the making of peace, but that righteousness, mercy and peace may characterise the nation in all its actions.[37]

The motion was taken to the Annual Assembly on 25 October, 1939, and carried with thirteen dissentients.[38] No reason was given for the few that voted against the motion, but it is possible it was an expression of pacifist sympathies. In the 1930s pacifist convictions had been particularly influential in Free Church ranks,[39] though out of 16,500 conscientious objectors registered during the war only seventy-three were Baptists.[40] David Hicks, one of those who held to this position, later reflected on it.

> I grew up in the aftermath of the First World War and the memory of that awful slaughter cast a long dark shadow. … It seemed obvious to me and to many others that if only everyone refused to fight then wars would cease; and this surely was what the teaching of Jesus required? … The Revd Dick Shepherd of St Martins-in-the-Field had founded the Peace Pledge Union in the thirties and I was one of many who signed it. The rise of Hitler could surely

---

[36] Henry Turner, 'Glasgow Baptist Association Report', *Scottish Baptist Yearbook 1940*, p. 115.

[37] *Scottish Baptist Yearbook 1940*, p. 126.

[38] *Scottish Baptist Yearbook 1940*, pp. 159–160.

[39] M. Snape, *God and the British Soldier: Religion and the British Army in the First and Second World Wars* (Abington: Routledge, 2005), p. 85.

[40] Balfour, *Revival in Rose Street*, p. 251. A more detailed study of this topic is Ann Kramer, *Conscientious Objectors of The Second World War* (Barnsley: Pen & Sword Publishers, 2013).

best be met – so it rather naively seemed to me at the time – by spreading the Gospel of Pacifism in Germany.[41]

However, as the Second World War progressed even some committed pacifists had a change of mind and joined the Armed Forces. A representative Baptist example was William Speirs, who had been convinced of the case for pacifism in his school years. He had registered as a Conscientious Objector while at New College, Edinburgh. He joined the Forces as a Baptist Chaplain in 1942. It was a hard decision to make but the bombing of the free city of Rotterdam by the German Armed Forces was decisive. He spoke later of suffering 'a conflict of conscience as if in a sense (he) was denying Christ'.[42] However, the horrors perpetrated by the Nazi regime were such that many pacifists such as Speirs were convicted that opposition to it was the lesser evil.

The official responses to the war declaration in Scottish Baptist ranks had been measured, though clear.[43] The editorial article, 'The Outlook', in the *SBM*, accepted that the Government had no choice under the circumstances. However, 'pacifist and non-pacifist alike agree that the ultimate aim of all Christian people must be to keep the Christian values[44] alive even during this frightful time, so that they may be the dominant influence in the peace that must be made someday.'[45] James Scott, Secretary of the Baptist Union, in his own reflections noted that: 'Doubtless there are economic causes underlying all wars, but we are convinced that the main causes are of a moral nature. Greed, selfishness, lust of power, racial hatred and pride, are among the root causes of war.'[46] The same issue of this periodical contained a sermon

---

[41] Dr David Hicks, 'Memoirs of World War Two', unpublished document, 2008, in the possession of Neil E. Allison, quoted in Neil E. Allison, 'Fighting the Good Fight: Changing Attitudes to War', in Talbot (ed.) *Distinctive People*, p. 193.

[42] Letter of William Speirs to Neil E. Allison, 18 March 1997, quoted in Neil E. Allison, *The Scottish Thistle: Rev. Dr William (Bill) Speirs* (Dereham: private publication, 2013), pp. 10–11.

[43] This was in line with the pronouncements of the Church of Scotland and other Scottish Churches. See Smith, *Passive Obedience and Prophetic Protest*, p. 373.

[44] There was a broad consensus about the distinctiveness of this war. For example, historian J.M. Roberts stated: 'the war of 1939–45 in Europe remains a moral struggle in a way, perhaps, in which no other great war has ever been.' J.M. Roberts, *Twentieth Century: The History of the World 1901–2000* (London: Viking, 1999), p. 430.

[45] 'The Outlook', *SBM*, 65.10 (October 1939), p. 1.

[46] James Scott, 'Church House Echoes: The Church in War Time', *SBM*, 65.10 (October 1939), p. 6. Details of Scott's life and an assessment of his accomplishments are given in Edward Burrows, 'Without a vision the people perish: The distinctive contribution to Scottish Baptist life by key leaders of the Baptist Union', in Talbot (ed.), *Distinctive People*, pp. 7–9.

preached by R.J. Smithson on 10 September, 1939. It was a stirring call to courage to stand for their principles. At its heart this war, Smithson claimed, was a conflict between Christianity and Nazism, but not between ordinary British people and Germans. His hearers were urged not to hate or bear ill-will towards ordinary German people. The mistake of doing so by many in the previous war should not be repeated.[47] However, 'It is plainly evident that the vast majority of Christian people feel that they go into this conflict with a clear conscience, and that it is God's work to which they have put their hands. In the last analysis the battle is not ours: it is God's.[48] The BUGBI Council acknowledged that 'the British Government after the invasion of Poland could have avoided war only by disastrous moral surrender.'[49] The editor of *Life and Work*, the Church of Scotland periodical wrote: 'Never in the history of the world has a war been entered on in a less warlike spirit.'[50] In similar fashion, Scottish Baptists broadly welcomed Neville Chamberlain's Allied war aims, commending him for stating: 'No gains at the expense of Germany: no vindictiveness towards Germany: and a renewed system of collective security.'[51] These comments reveal a quiet confidence that God would bring the nation through this testing time, but they had to retain their spiritual values in how they conducted themselves during the war and in the planning for the peace that would follow.

---

[47] This view was widely held amongst British Church leaders. See Andrew Chandler, 'The Second World War in Europe', in Hugh Macleod (ed.), *Christianity: World Christianities c.1914- c.2000* (Cambridge: Cambridge University Press, 2006), p. 265. American Church leaders were also much more careful to speak in considered tones about the war and many denominations declined to give an official blessing to the war. Norman V. Hope, 'The American Church and the Present World War', *Life and Work*, Vol. XIV, March 1943, pp. 37–38.

[48] R.J. Smithson. "The Battle is not Yours, but God's', *SBM*, 65.10 (October 1939), pp. 4–5.

[49] 'The Baptist Union and the Present Situation', *Baptist Times*, 21 March, 1940, p. 184.

[50] George Carstairs, 'The Church in War-Time', *Life and Work*, Vol. X New Series, October 1939, pp. 406–407. Church of Scotland preaching was very different in this war compared to WW1. 'The Church is a humbler Church today. We feel the personal shame and horror of this war as we did not do twenty-five years ago.' George B. Burnet, 'The Church in War-Time', *Life and Work*, Vol. XI, June 1940, pp. 185–186.

[51] 'The Outlook', *SBM*, 65.11 (November 1939), p. 1.

## Scottish Baptists Making Sense of the War

The war was now going ahead, but how did Scottish Baptists attempt to make sense of what was taking place? The war was undoubtedly a test of their convictions – would they stand true to them: 'truth, righteousness, peace, loyalty and love'? In his 1941 Seventy-third Annual Report the Union Secretary was convinced that at this point in the war 'the devotion of our people has never wavered.'[52] This is not surprising as this relatively small Christian denomination had attracted many dedicated hard-working Christian men and women to its ranks. However, the issue here was in understanding the significance of the conflict in which European nations were once again engaged. It appeared that there was a consensus amongst British Church leaders from the Archbishop of Canterbury downwards that 'war is the judgement of God'.[53] Minister of Marshall Street Baptist Church, Edinburgh, and former distinguished padre from World War One, T.N. Tattersall,[54] wholeheartedly agreed with this diagnosis. He added: 'A moral law runs through the world: whatsoever a nation soweth, that shall the people also reap.'[55] However, Tattersall warned against advancing simplistic notions as to why the war was happening. The reasons advanced in common conversation just as much as those sounded on the lips of religious leaders may be part of the truth, but are far from the whole explanation.[56] Life on the front line in the previous war ensured that simplistic solutions would not find favour with Tattersall. Whatever views were put forward by local ministers not all would agree. R.W. Waddelow, one of the strongest pacifists amongst Scottish Baptist clergy, admitted that one or two of his congregation in Adelaide Place Baptist Church, Glasgow, had left the church unhappy at the 'politics in the pulpit'.[57] W. Harold Parsons, the lay President of Angus and Perthshire Baptist Association told assembled delegates at their summer conference in 1940 that he found the present situation more comfortable than it had been a year earlier. 'As a nation we are in this awful conflict with clean hands, and if

---

[52] '73rd Annual Report by the Union Secretary', *SBY*, 1942, p. 172.

[53] Quoted in T.N. Tattersall D.S.O., 'War and the Judgement of God', *SBM*, 66.1 (January 1940), p. 4.

[54] See the references to Tattersall in Allison, *Clash of Empires 1914–1939: The Official History of the United Board Volume One* (Norfolk, revised ed. 2014).

[55] Tattersall, 'War and the Judgement of God', p. 4.

[56] Tattersall, 'War and the Judgement of God', pp. 4–6.

[57] R.W. Waddelow, 'Youth and the War', *SBM*, 66.2 (February 1940), pp. 4–5. However, there were people who came back to church after time away in the light of the efforts of Neville Chamberlain to avoid war and the more considered tone of Church leaders during the war. A Man in the Pew, 'What I owe to the Church', *Life and Work*, Vol. 12 new series, January 1941, pp. 31–32.

we had stood aside our neutrality would have been a crime.'[58] It is likely this more robust approach to supporting the war effort resonated better with the majority of people in the congregations, but there was certainly no joy at the prospects of what lay before them. Alexander Clark, vice-President of the Baptist Union called the war an 'Optimistic Tragedy', quoting the words of theologian Hugh R. Mackintosh. He used the stories of the testing of Abraham and Isaac on Mount Moriah in Genesis 22 and the offering of Jesus by God the Father in John 3:16 to illustrate how good can come out of apparently tragic situations.[59] Yet in his Presidential Address given six months later in October 1940, Clark underlined just how serious the problems had become which needed to be addressed. He highlighted the extremist political ideologies dominant in Russia, Italy and Germany, but recognised that a deeper problem still had to be overcome. 'The spiritual foundations of Western civilisation have been undermined. There is need for radical transformation, for a spiritual, moral and mental energy to make all things new.'[60] In other words our struggle for the retention or restoration of spiritual values at the centre of our national life would determine whether the war had been won or lost in our nation.

It was to be expected that Baptists and other Scottish and other British Christians would express a desire for a national day of prayer. William Whyte, minister of Portobello Baptist Church, Edinburgh, on behalf of the Evangelism Committee, at the quarterly meeting of the Baptist Union Council on 28 Feb 1940, called for 'His Majesty the King, to appoint a National Day of Repentance for our shortcomings, and of prayer to Almighty God for a just and righteous peace, in which the Houses of Parliament would participate.'[61] The Union Secretary later the same year in his annual report explained why the priority of prayer in this situation must be upheld.

> One thing is clear. The war is not a mere clashing of rival powers but a conflict between good and evil, for Germany has challenged those great principles which the Christian Church has cherished for generations and for which our forefathers shed their blood – the principles of freedom, righteousness, truth and peace. That being so, we must resort to prayer and continue in prayer; spiritual

---

[58] 'Angus and Perthshire Baptist Association' report, *Scottish Baptist Yearbook*, 1941, pp. 109–110. The same words were used by J.C. Carlile in a Baptist Times editorial article, 'When Neutrality is a Crime', *Baptist Times*, 4 April, 1940, pp. 209–210.

[59] Alexander Clark, 'The War –Optimistic Tragedy', *SBM*, 66.3 (March 1940), pp. 4–5.

[60] Alexander Clark, 'The Church and the New Order' Presidential Address October 1940, *SBY*, 1941, pp. 154–164.

[61] 'The Outlook', *SBM*, 66.4 (April 1940), p. 11.

evil can only be defeated by spiritual power. . . . Prayer is the great secret of spiritual power.[62]

Scottish Baptists did not see a contradiction between declaring the priority of prayer and also in expecting the Government to do what it could to win the war. Or as it was expressed in the pages of the *SBM*: 'Trust in God and re-armament are no contradiction, unless "Give us this day our daily bread" is an encouragement to idleness. . . . Prayer will keep our motives pure, deliver us from fear and the spirit of revenge that fear breeds and enable God to give us a victory that will be His not ours.'[63] As news filtered out about the impact of Nazi ideology in German-dominated territories and that of Communism in Russian domains, it was not difficult to argue as some did that this was a war to defend 'Christian civilisation', as opposed to godless ones.[64] However, there was still care needed as to how we pray for victory, according to W. Holms Coats. He had highlighted a dispute within Church of Scotland ranks where some had rightly taken issue with colleagues over their inaccurate portrayal of the Allies as entirely innocent and the Nazis the opposite in this conflict. By contrast:

> As Christians we must acknowledge very humbly and penitently that we have had our share as a nation in the widespread materialism, secularism, selfishness, cowardice, opportunism, political irresponsibility, lack of social conscience that are the deeper causes of the present dreadful state of things in Europe. To acknowledge this is not weakness but strength. We believe that the cause of Christian civilisation would be put back by generations by a victory for Germany, therefore we pray for courage and strength to win the war.[65]

There was both clarity and a consistency in the Scottish Baptist understanding of World War II.[66] However, it was a vision shared very widely in the broader Christian constituency. It would be an interpretation of events with which they could live very comfortably after this war, unlike the revisionary interpretations that began after 1918.

---

[62] '72nd Annual Report' by the Union Secretary, *Scottish Baptist Yearbook 1941*, p. 170.

[63] 'The Outlook', *SBM*, 66.6 (June 1940), p. 2,

[64] 'Is this a war for Christian Civilisation?' *SBM*, 66.6 (June 1940), p. 7.

[65] W. Holms Coats, 'Praying for Victory', *SBM*, 66.8 (August 1940), p. 2.

[66] There was a quiet satisfaction in Scottish Baptist ranks after the war that its Padres and others had spoken and acted much more consistently as Christians in this conflict than in WW1. *SBM*, 72.8 (August 1946), p. 1.

## Changing Attitudes during the War

Scottish Baptists attempted to see what positive benefits arise could from this situation which their Government had tried so hard to avoid. W. Holms Coats, as early as the October 1939 Baptist Union Assembly, made these comments in a speech on behalf of the Office-bearers of the Baptist Union.

> The situation offers an opportunity of recalling our people and the nation to the abiding virtues and the things which cannot be shaken; to faith in Divine providence, judgement and mercy; to consecration, self-surrender and sacrifice; to the sustaining power of Christian faith in the hour of crisis and suffering.[67]

It was an acknowledgement that though difficult times lay ahead there was an opportunity to reassess priorities and to gain a clearer sense of moral focus in the coming years.

There were, though, two key themes that were particularly prominent in the messages and addresses from both Baptist and other Church leaders in Scotland during the war years. The first and most expected was a renewed call for greater personal renewal[68] and evangelistic efforts. This had already begun in the years immediately preceding the war, already mentioned in the 'Recall to Religion' campaign in 1937 and 1938, but was sustained in the years that followed. Alexander Clark, in his Presidential address of October 1940 declared: 'Fearless proclamation of the Gospel is the Church's best answer to the assertion that: "religion is opiate"' by those who have no time for Jesus Christ. Clark urged his hearers to make 'a highway for our God into home and school, into the slums and suburbs of our cities, into Stock Exchange, market place and factory, into the Houses of Parliament, and wherever the fate and fortune of men, women and children are being decided . . . .'[69] John Noble, Burgh Chamberlain, Peterhead, and lay-President of the Northern Association, delivered his Presidential address on 12 November, 1941, on the subject of: 'The Emphasis of Conversion'. Noble was pointedly reminding his hearers that desirable improvements in social and economic conditions in the country would only be beneficial if there were 'new men' transformed by the Spirit of God. 'They could not have Christian principles unless they first had Christian men.'[70] The other speaker at that event, John MacBeath, minister of Inverness Baptist Church, reinforced the same point in his address entitled: 'The Peril of God-forgetfulness'.[71] Scottish Baptist congregations were

---

[67] 'Message to the Churches', *SBM*, 65.11 (November 1939), p. 3.

[68] For example, 'The Five Years Plan' that included a stronger emphasis on Bible Study and Prayer, had begun in 1941, *SBM*, 67.9 (September 1941), pp. 2–3.

[69] Clark, 'The Church and the New Order', *Scottish Baptist Yearbook 1941*, p. 159.

[70] *Scottish Baptist Yearbook 1942*, p. 118.

[71] *Scottish Baptist Yearbook 1942*, p. 118.

making every effort to take the opportunities they had for evangelism at this time. In the winter of 1940, it was noted that Baptist churches were almost the only ones open for evangelistic 'gospel services'. In the early war years, a number of churches had tried open-air Sunday Schools with 'considerable encouragement'. Others tried open-air services in the back courts of tenement blocks or public places that are popular for socialising in public. In Princes Street Gardens in Edinburgh, churches of different denominations joined for open air services that attracted audiences varying from two to three thousand people at a time. Others held seaside services in Ayr, Dunoon, Kinghorn, and Portobello with reported professions of faith from both children and adults.[72] The convenor of the Evangelistic Committee, William Whyte, attributed the increased evangelistic activity to an invitation from the Baptist World Alliance Congress in Atlanta in 1939 to member Unions and Conventions 'wherever it is possible, our Conventions and Unions should lay plans for an organised advance in evangelism. Your Committee and Council have answered the call, and a campaign committee has been appointed representative of the whole life and activity of our Union.'[73] Scottish Baptists had been consistently committed to organised outreach initiatives during the war years.

The year 1942 in the 'Five Years Campaign' was highlighted in the Baptist Union as a year in which a significant emphasis on preparation for and the active participation in personal evangelistic efforts by church members.[74] Members of the Baptist Union Evangelistic Committee were visiting local congregations promoting three forms of evangelism: 'specialised evangelism' – with reference to work by people called to serve as 'evangelists'; 'pastoral evangelism', by which they understood evangelistic sermons by local pastors and 'personal evangelism' – the work of all church members.[75] Thomas A. McQuiston, Minister of Cambridge Street Baptist Church, Glasgow, in his 1942 Presidential Address declared: 'To become static is to perish; to evangelise is imperative. . . . The lack of a militant evangelism is responsible for the multiplicity of quack and counterfeit substitutes. We plead for personal evangelism, pastoral evangelism, church evangelism, inter-church evangelism,

---

[72] 'Evangelistic Committee', *Scottish Baptist Yearbook 1941*, p. 174.

[73] 'Evangelistic Committee', *Scottish Baptist Yearbook 1941*, p. 174. Details of this congress are given in J.H. Rushbrooke (ed.), *Sixth Baptist World Congress, Atlanta, Georgia, USA, July 22–28, 1939* (Atlanta: Baptist World Alliance, 1939). The motto of the Atlanta Congress was 'None but changed people can change the world.' J.H. Rushbrooke, 'Baptist World Alliance Sunday 4 February', *Baptist Times*, 25 January, 1940, p. 60.

[74] William W. Wilson, 'The Evangelistic Campaign', *SBM*, 68.2 (February 1942), p. 4. An update on the proposed work in year four (of five) in this campaign is given in Matthew F. Wright, 'The Five-Year Campaign', *SBM*, 70.4 (April 1944), p. 2.

[75] William A. Ashby, 'The Evangelistic Campaign', *SBM*, 68.3 (March 1942), p. 3.

and ecumenical evangelism.'[76] The Baptist Union Secretary James Scott noted that some of the churches were seeing encouraging responses to this increased focus on outreach. One city church saw conversions at its winter Sunday evening services; another church in a provincial town experienced the joy of a record ten candidates professing faith at a baptism service; other congregations reported encouraging interactions with members of the Armed Forces stationed in their area.[77] The following year, in October 1943, James Scott reported that although active membership figures for Union congregations was down by 400 compared with the previous year, Sunday School numbers were up by 400 in the same time period.[78] In addition, by creative new approaches other churches increased their numbers of evening services by, for example, having 'youth services' or 'women's services'. Other signs of renewal were increases in attendances at some church prayer meetings and the early repayment of building debts by other Baptist congregations.[79] Scottish Baptists had seen a slight drop in membership figures in the years immediately prior to World War Two, but this fall accelerated during the war years with a drop from 23,024 members in 1940 to 21,121 reported in 1945.[80] The work of the churches was undoubtedly hindered by conscription, requisitioning of

---

[76] T.A. McQuiston, 'The Leadership of the Church', Presidential Address Oct 1942, *Scottish Baptist Yearbook 1943*, p. 58.

[77] '74th Annual Report by the Secretary', *Scottish Baptist Yearbook*, 1943, p. 67. Innovative evangelistic approaches in secular venues were also reported amongst English Churches during the war. 'Christian Commando', *Baptist Times*, 9 August, 1945, pp. 1–2. The Christian Commandos were a Methodist organised programme designed to appeal to 'the man in the street', mainly inspired by Colin Roberts and the 'World Methodist Year of Evangelism' – see Rupert Davies, A. Raymond George and Gordon Rupp (eds), *A History of the Methodist Church in Great Britain* (Vol. 3; London: Epworth Press, 1983), p. 383; and Colin A. Roberts (ed.), *These Christian Commando Campaigns* (London: Epworth Press, 1945).

[78] *Scottish Baptist Yearbook 1944*, p. 46. The growth in Sunday School numbers was common in the mainstream Protestant Churches in Scotland in the 1940s and into the 1950s. The Congregational Churches saw their highest figures in 1956, the Episcopal Church in 1953 and the United Free Church in 1955. I am grateful to Kenneth Roxburgh for access to an as yet unpublished paper 'The Mission of the Church in Scotland 1940–1960', p. 36, for this information. The Church of Scotland, for example, saw a 41% increase in numbers between 1941 and 1956. Brown, *Religion and Society in Scotland since 1707*, p. 160.

[79] '75th Annual Report by the Secretary', *Scottish Baptist Yearbook 1944*, pp. 46, 66.

[80] David Hunt, *Reflections on Our Past: A Statistical Look at Baptists in Scotland 1892–1997* (Hamilton: Hamilton Baptist Church, 1997), 'Appendix 2: Table of Annual Statistics', n.p. A discussion of the significance of these statistics is found in 'Baptist Statistics', *SBM*, 70.3 (March 1944), pp. 1–2.

buildings and transfers of members to work in England during the war,[81] together with the deaths of some members in the Forces and the significant civilian losses in the blitzed Clyde area,[82] but the enthusiasm for sharing their faith was still clearly a significant priority at that time.

The second prominent emphasis that was particularly in evidence in the years prior to and during the war was the moves to greater unity between the Christian Churches.[83] In the years following World War One the Churches realised the benefits of working more closely with one another. There were both Communist and Fascist ideologies flourishing as well as social and economic challenges throughout Europe which presented a challenge the Churches which they were convinced were better faced in a stronger partnership with each other. This pattern seen in different European countries was clearly in evidence in Scotland. The Scottish Churches Council began in 1924[84] and Scottish Baptists sent delegates to SCC meetings until that body's demise in 1948.[85] Relationships between Scottish Protestant Churches were increasingly warm in the interwar years and this spirit continued into the 1940s. At the Baptist Union of Scotland Annual Assembly in October 1940 George Kirk, a Minister from Glasgow and representative to the Assembly from the Congregational Union of Scotland, offered greetings that included these words on this subject:

> ... emphasising there were many things in common between his denomination and our own. In view of the big problems presently confronting the Church and which would confront the Church after the war, he stressed the need for a greater degree of unity amongst the different denominations. The Church ought

---

[81] Balfour, 'The Twentieth Century since 1914', in Bebbington (ed.), *Baptists in Scotland*, p. 68.

[82] Murray, *First Hundred Years*, p. 105.

[83] Some English Ministers in Baptist, Congregationalist, Methodist and Presbyterian Churches called for the formation of 'A United Free Church of England'. *SBM*, 67.10 (October 1941), pp. 3-4. 'Free Church Union', *Baptist Times*, 11 September, 1941, p. 444.

[84] *Scottish Baptist Yearbook 1924*, p. 86; D.B. Forrester, 'Ecumenical Movement', in Cameron (ed.), *Dictionary of Scottish Church History and Theology*, 273-274. For more details on this subject see Brian R. Talbot, 'Fellowship in the Gospel: Scottish Baptists and their Relationships with other Christian Churches', *Evangelical Quarterly* Vol. 78, No.4, (October 2006).

[85] Murray, *First Hundred Years*, p. 103. See also Brian R. Talbot, 'Baptists and Other Christian Churches in the First Half of the Twentieth Century', in David W. Bebbington and Martin Sutherland (eds), *Interfaces: Baptists and Others* (Milton Keynes: Paternoster, 2013), pp. 161-162, 169-176.

to be leading public opinion, but could not do so unless she spoke with a united voice.[86]

This was a common conviction. At the very same Assembly the Moderator of the General Assembly of the Church of Scotland, the Right Rev. J.R. Forgan, in his greetings to assembled delegates 'emphasised the need for greater unity in the church'.[87] In introducing the Moderator to the Assembly the Baptist Union President Alexander Clark reported that the Church of Scotland had taken the initiative in requesting that there should be reciprocal visits to the respective assemblies by representatives of these two denominations, and in his own Presidential address that year heartily commended this ecumenical initiative towards the Baptist Union of Scotland and wished God's blessing on their future partnership with the National Kirk.[88] A similar warm commendation of the closer ties with other Scottish Churches came from Thomas McQuiston in his Presidential address in October 1942:

> The Church may be all the better for diversity in unity. The call for the outward unification of Christendom is in the air around us and we welcome the movement. We are keen and eager for the closest and heartiest co-operation with our brethren of other churches; but always on New Testament terms.[89]

Scottish Baptists had been enthusiastic about working with other Baptists since the present Union was formed in 1869,[90] but closer co-operation with other Christian Churches was also now seen as a priority. The success of the Scottish Churches Council discussed earlier, was the reason why Scottish Baptists were to reject a Continuing United Free Church proposal for the establishment of a Free Church Council in Scotland.[91] The closest affinity was felt towards the Congregational Union of Scotland with whom Assembly

---

[86] 'Visit of Representative of the Congregational Union of Scotland', Baptist Union Assembly 29 October, 1940, *Scottish Baptist Yearbook 1941*, pp. 141–142.

[87] Baptist Union Assembly 29 October, 1940, *Scottish Baptist Yearbook 1941*, p. 142.

[88] Baptist Union Assembly October 1940, *Scottish Baptist Yearbook 1941*, pp. 142, 162. A warm welcome for the visit of Adam Farquhar, Baptist Union of Scotland President, to the Church of Scotland Assembly in May 1940, the first such welcome to a Scottish Baptist representative, was reported in *SBM*, June 1940, p. 6.

[89] Thomas A. McQuiston, 'Presidential Address', October 1942, *Scottish Baptist Yearbook 1943*, p. 59.

[90] For more details see Talbot, 'Blest be the tie that binds', in Talbot (ed.), *Distinctive People*, pp. 80–98.

[91] BUS Council, 25 May, 1943, Baptist Union of Scotland Minute Book, 1942–1945, 245.

delegates had been routinely exchanged. A similar offer was made to the Churches of Christ in Scotland, but in their reply they indicated that there was no separate annual meeting for their connexion in Scotland. There was, therefore, no need to exchange representatives with this small group of Scottish Christians.[92] The 1940s was a decade in which Scottish Baptists had felt sufficiently secure in their own identity to seek to build better relationships with most other Scottish Christians. The narrow insularity of some earlier years appeared to have been abandoned as out of step with the needs of the mid-twentieth century.[93] However, the fears that had diminished were still held by a significant proportion of the constituency and the potential for their reawakening would become clearer in the post-war era. There were some limits to the extent of formal unity with other churches. In 1939 BUS Office-bearers, for example, 'after careful consideration they decided not to recommend affiliation with the proposed World Council of Churches. It was felt the Baptist position would be sufficiently represented by the Baptist Union of Great Britain and Ireland (BUGBI)'[94] on the grounds that as Scottish Baptists had 'little hope of sending a representative' to meetings there was little point in a formal affiliation.[95] At this stage of the debate Scottish Baptists were broadly in agreement with one another, though underlying differences of opinions on ecumenical relations would reappear in the post-war years.

The special relationship with the Scottish Congregationalists had been enhanced by some common grievances. One particular issue, which will serve as an example, had been the lack of Baptist and Congregationalist chaplains in

---

[92] BUS Council, 26 February, 1946, Baptist Union of Scotland Minute Book, 1945-1950, 59.

[93] James Hair who represented Scottish Baptists at the inaugural meetings of the British Council of Churches presented a cautious but favourable report of proceedings. James Hair, 'Inaugural Meetings of the British Council of Churches', *SBM*, 68.12 (December 1942), pp. 4–5. It was a perspective commonly found amongst Scottish Baptists at that time. See, for example', William L. McAslan, 'The Church and Readjustment' *SBM*, 71.1 (January 1945), p. 4; He declared: 'Modern conditions call for closer co-operation between the denominations.'

[94] 'BUS Council', 31 May, 1939, *Scottish Baptist Yearbook 1940*, p. 124. The strength of the concerns of congregations such as Charlotte Baptist Chapel in Edinburgh was probably significant in this decision. See Balfour, *Revival in Rose Street*, pp. 302–305; The BUGBI Council declared its support for this inter-church initiative with greater confidence than their BUS colleagues. 'The World Council of Churches' & 'The Ecumenical Movement', *Baptist Times*, 4 May, 1939, p. 344.

[95] BUS Council, 25 May, 1938, Baptist Union of Scotland Minute Book, 1935–1939, 556; BUS Office-bearers.

20 April, 1939, Baptist Union of Scotland Minute Book, 1935–1939, pp. 773–774.

the Armed Forces during the First World War. Part of the reported difficulty was due to incorrect listing of a soldier's denominational allegiance by a recruiting sergeant when enlisted, as it was too often assumed that an individual was Anglican, if English, and Presbyterian, if Scottish. As a result very few soldiers were listed as associated with other denominations, thus weakening their case for appointed chaplains.[96] The first Scottish Baptist Army Chaplain had been appointed in 1914.[97] Success in this matter was rightly attributed to the United Army and Navy Board. This body comprising Baptists, Congregationalists, Primitive and United Methodists enabled these denominations to join together to ensure a fair representation of their men were placed in post in the British Army and Navy.[98] It was not a battle won overnight as problems had persisted in the Navy into 1918.[99] Great improvements in relationships between the churches by the 1940s ensured that by the Second World War there was a better allocation of chaplaincy posts.[100] An article in the *SBM*, in December 1941, described how chaplains of different denominations were working harmoniously together.[101] Other joint ventures included an ordination training course in Jerusalem for United Board candidates for ministry in the Middle East.[102] A refresher course for Anglican and Free Church chaplains was held in Brussels in May 1945,[103] and a joint series of membership preparation classes was run by chaplains jointly for Baptist, Congregationalist and Methodist service personnel working in Germany in December 1945.[104] Scottish Baptist padre William Speirs was

---

[96] *SBM*, 40.10 (October 1914), 154; 43.2 (February 1917), p. 22.

[97] *SBM*, 40.10 (October 1914), p. 158.

[98] *SBM*, 41.8 (August 1915), pp. 118–119. A standard history of this work is F.C. Spurr, *Some Chaplains in Khaki*, (London: Baptist Union of Great Britain and Ireland, 1916). A more recent study on the most prominent Scottish Baptist army chaplain, is N. Allison, 'Shakespeare's Man at the Front The Rev. William Cramb Charteris O.B.E., MC.,' *Baptist Quarterly*, 41.4 (October 2005), pp. 224–235. See also David Stowe, 'Rethinking 10/West Yorks at Fricourt', *Standto! The Journal of the Western Front Association* (August/September 2008), pp. 39–47. This article presents the context in which Charteris served. He is mentioned on p. 40. The standard history of the United Board is Allison, *Clash of Empires 1914–1939*.

[99] *SBM*, 44.4 (April 1918), p. 58.

[100] Fuller details of this progress are found in Neil E. Allison, *The Clash of Ideologies 1939–1950: The Official History of the United Board Volume Two* (Norfolk: United Navy, Army and Air Force Board, revised ed. 2015).

[101] *SBM*, 67.12 (December 1941), p. 5.

[102] *SBM*, 71.3 (March 1945), p. 2.

[103] *SBM*, 71.5 (May 1945), p. 2.

[104] *SBM*, 71.12 (December 1945), p. 2.

also invited in 1946 to supervise theological training for German chaplains in Italy.[105] Chaplaincy work in the Armed Forces was another sphere of Christian service in which Scottish Baptists recognised their need to work with other Christian Churches. Ecumenical relations in the middle of the twentieth century between Scottish Churches appeared to be in a healthy state. Scottish Baptists had recognised that they could work not only with traditional friends such as the Congregationalists, but also other Protestant denominations in their native land. Barriers between churches that had once seemed insurmountable were removed to enable a healthier ecumenism to take its place, but this ecumenism was a 'tender plant' whose continued growth was far from certain, at least amongst the Baptist constituency in Scotland.

## The Post War Settlement

There was a wide ranging recognition that although the Allied Forces had won the military aspects of the First World War, yet there had been too little attention paid to the peace settlement that followed after it.[106] As a result there was a determination that things needed to be very different for both churches and the state once the Second World War was concluded.[107] The editorial article in the March 1940 *SBM* devoted some space to considering what was required to achieve lasting peace in Europe.[108] In addition to the military defeat of Germany, the author argued that Germany needed to see she had more to gain by living in co-operation with her neighbours than by domination of them. The peace treaty must not leave Germany with a legitimate sense of grievances otherwise it will only lead to another conflict at a later date. 'Let the German nation be heartily welcomed into a comprehensive plan for economic reconstruction, disarmament and peace in Europe under democratic leadership and there is hope.'[109] It was a vision commonly shared at the time and was broadly in line with the post war settlement. In the following issue of the *SBM* there was a brief discussion of

---

[105] *SBM*, 72.8 (August 1946), p. 2.

[106] American Churches also paid great attention to this subject – see Sittser, *Cautious Patriotism*, pp. 223–249.

[107] For example, see an address by the President of the Glasgow Baptist Association at this organisation's 1944 Annual Meeting. M'Aslan, 'Church and Readjustment', *SBM*, 71.1 (January 1945), p. 4.

[108] A detailed discussion of what we were fighting for and what we might hope for the future in British society is given in 'Britain, 1940 and 'Christian Civilisation', in Keith Robbins, *History, Religion and Identity in Modern Britain* (London: The Hambledon Press, 1993), pp. 195–213.

[109] 'The Outlook', *SBM*, 66.3 (March 1940), p. 1.

various peace proposals on which the war might potentially be ended. In particular, the editor W. Holms Coats highlighted the similar proposals of President Roosevelt of the USA and the Pope, compared to those potentially on offer from Hitler's Germany. Although approving President Roosevelt's statement: 'We seek a moral basis for peace' and the same sentiments expressed in other words in the Vatican document, he argued that the Allied leadership could not trust the Nazi leadership to honour any potential settlement. A new type of leadership was required in Germany to build that nation's future.[110] In addition, he commended another document published by representatives of American Churches that denounced those who claimed the war was about 'rival imperialisms'. Anyone taking such a view, he argued, was suffering from 'moral blindness'.[111] The German Fuehrer had advocated a Nazi 'New Order in Europe'. It was felt that some statesmen in Britain had failed in response to articulate clearly enough that what was required was 'a Christian order, based on the freedom of nations to determine their own destinies in co-operation with all men of good will.'[112] The consistent advocacy of the importance of moral and spiritual values was something he and other Church leaders saw as distinctive in their advocacy of the Allied cause in contrast to their absence in discussions of war aims and objectives in Germany.[113]

---

[110] 'The Outlook', SBM, 66.4 (April 1940), pp. 1–2. This point was reinforced in 'The Outlook', SBM, 67.1 (January 1941), p. 3. British Churches presented their own manifesto for peace, based on the five points of the Pope's Peace suggestions, highlighted in a letter to *The Times*, signed by the leaders of three branches of the Church, the Anglican, Nonconformist and Roman Catholic. SBM, 67.2 (February 1941), p. 14. The one Baptist criticism of these proposals by J.H. Rushbrooke was that there was no reference to the need for religious liberty. W. Holms Coats affirmed the necessity of this additional point being added to the manifesto for peace. 'The "Sword of the Spirit" Campaign', SBM, 67.6 (June 1941), p. 3.

[111] 'The Outlook', SBM, 66.4 (April 1940), p. 2.

[112] 'The Outlook', SBM, 66.9 (September 1940), p. 1.

[113] An example of another reminder of these principles is given in 'The Outlook', SBM, 67.9 (September 1941), p. 1. An example of Allied Forces living these high moral principles was seen when the crew of 'The Rodney' met to pray with their chaplain for the families of the German sailors lost in the sinking of The Bismark. W. Holms Coats, 'Praying for the Enemy', SBM, 67.11 (November 1941), p. 2. An example of Continental European countries holding similar standards is seen in the decision of legal bodies in Poland, Russia, Czechoslovakia and Holland to prepare for trials of Nazi war criminals after hostilities are concluded rather than allowing such individuals to be killed on the streets by angry crowds during the war. SBM, 68.2 (February 1942), p. 1. The documents produced by the Federal Council of Churches in America and the Churches' Peace Aims Group in the UK concerning how 'to establish a just and lasting peace' showed remarkable similarities. They were agreed that: Above all else is needed the recognition of clear moral standards which the

This forward thinking not only concerned international relations and how they would be addressed in the post-war years, but also a significant amount of time was spent on reflecting on the kind of changes that were required in the United Kingdom to make our own society a much fairer one for all our citizens. It was commonly agreed that in 1919 not only had there been a failure to deal with the root causes of the war, but also a similar failure to address the serious problems of unemployment in both the United Kingdom and Germany. Better future prospects needed to be available for the whole of society.[114] Other Scottish Churches too were giving careful consideration to the future needs of the nation. For example, the Church of Scotland's establishment of the Baillie Commission, 1941–1945, under the chairmanship of John Baillie, produced some visionary reports that showed a real understanding of contemporary social and economic issues and marked a clear change of direction in the thinking of that denomination. It wholeheartedly welcomed the Beveridge report with its vision of comprehensive social welfare schemes and a national health service.[115] William McInnes, Minister of Renfrew Baptist Church, was very clear that the Church in both its local and national context needed to demonstrate more clearly the relevance of the Christian message to a contemporary society that he claimed often viewed it as irrelevant.[116] Scottish Baptists were well aware from the experience of the years immediately following the First World War that it was far from easy to attract former service personnel back to the churches once they had returned to civilian life.[117] One document that was particularly insightful with a Christian vision for the post-war years was Anglican Archbishop William

---

nations and the citizens accept.' 'The Churches' Peace Aims', *SBM* 69.9 (September 1943), p. 2.

[114] 'The Two Scourges', *SBM*, 67.1 (January 1941), p. 2.

[115] William F. Storrar, 'Liberating the Kirk: The Enduring Legacy of the Baillie Commission', in Morton (ed.), *God's Will in a Time of Crisis*, pp. 60–72; Smith, *Passive Obedience and Prophetic Protest*, pp. 373–381.

[116] William McInnes, 'The Church Must Count for More', *SBM*, 66.9 (September 1940), p. 8. Many other Christians made the same point. 'The plain fact is that organised Christianity is ignored by many high minded and enthusiastic reformers of our day. This is the point we have to start from. It is useless to complain about it.' 'Building a Better Britain', *Baptist Times*, 21 January, 1943, p. 1.

[117] 'Kodak', 'Denominational Snapshots', *SBM*, 71.1 (January 1945), p. 8. This pessimistic perspective was supported by Pte R.I. Hutcheson, 'The Returning Soldier', *Life and Work*, Vol. XVI New Series, May 1945, p. 70; A more optimistic view of their return to the churches was taken by T.B. Stewart Thomson, late Deputy Assistant Chaplain-General, 'The Return of the Soldier', *Life and Work*, Vol. XV, August 1944, pp. 117–118.

Temple's *Christianity and Social Order* published in 1942.[118] It was a strong commendation of greater social justice and fairness in post-war Britain. It was in tune with the thinking of many Christians including Scottish Baptists at that time.[119] Thomas Coats in his Baptist Union Presidential Address in October 1943 made a reference to both these subjects, but indicated that the spiritual issues were the most significant ones to be addressed. He stated:

> We welcome the Atlantic Charter with its four freedoms,[120] the Beveridge Report,[121] and its remedies for many of our social ills, and gladly support those

---

[118] William Temple, *Christianity and Social Order* (London: Penguin Books, 1942) It was reviewed very favourably by James Hair, alongside an equally favourable review by Alexander Clark of a publication from the 'Commission of the Churches' entitled: *Social Justice and Economic Reconstruction*. 'Significant Booklets', *SBM*, 68.7 (July 1942), p. 5. For more detailed comments on the significance of Temple's contribution, see Hoover, *God, Britain and Hitler in World War II*, pp. 126–130.

[119] The Churches were also in line with some of the more progressive thinkers concerning post-war reconstruction in the wider society. A. Hastings, 'British Churches in the War and Post-War Reconstruction', in Morton (ed.) *God's Will in a Time of Crisis*, p. 8.

[120] The Atlantic Charter document was drawn up by President Theodore Roosevelt of the USA and British Prime Minister Winston Churchill and issued on 14 August, 1941. At a meeting on 1 January, 1942, in Washington D.C., twenty-six nations signed a declaration in which they stated their support for the Atlantic Charter's objectives. The charter presented a vision for the future after the war in which basic human freedoms were respected; no territorial gains would be sought by the victorious powers and sovereign rights and self-government restored for those nations who had been forcibly deprived of them. For more details see Andrew Roberts, *The Storm of War: A New History of the Second World War* (London: Allen Lane, 2009), pp. 130–131; and Roberts, *Twentieth Century*, pp. 421–422, 429–430, 466.

[121] The Beveridge Report *Social Insurance and Allied Services* provided a comprehensive blueprint for post-war welfare policy. The report showed how poverty might be abolished through a comprehensive and integrated scheme of social insurance; a national health service would be created and mass unemployment that had blighted the lives of many people in the inter-war years would not be allowed to reoccur. See Peter Clarke, *Hope and Glory: Britain 1900–2000* (London: Penguin Books, revised ed. 2004), pp. 213–214, 221–224, 255, 302–303. This report of Sir William Beveridge was described as 'This masterly plan' by the editor of the *SBM*. However, the goals would not be easily accomplished. 'All our problems boil down to the moral problem of achieving a peace aim which will command the same energy, devotion and sacrifice as war has done.' 'The Outlook', *SBM*, 69.1 (January 1943), p. 2. See also 'The Outlook', *SBM*, 69.3 (March 1943), p. 1, for similar cautious comments on the Beveridge Report. It was welcomed in a similar manner in the Church of Scotland. See Lewis L.L. Cameron, 'Is Social Security Enough?' *Life and Work*, Vol. XIV New Series, January 1943, pp. 8–9; April 1943, pp. 49, 61–62.

measures which have for their object the uplift of the people and the drawing together of all nations in the spirit of brotherhood. Important and necessary as all these measures may be, we must not allow them to obscure the spiritual issues that face us today.[122]

Coats' point was that the most important changes required in society were spiritual.[123] The nation needed to gain a complete and unwavering faith in God; give loyalty to Jesus Christ and recognise the transformative power of the cross of Jesus Christ. His successor as Union President, J.T. Stark, Minister of Victoria Place Baptist Church, Paisley, gave a stirring address at his induction to office. He gave a challenge to the assembled delegates concerning the years that lay ahead of them.

> Five years' experience of a second world war has surely given us an unprecedented ray from the Lamp of Sacrifice. There has never been salvation of any sort, temporal or spiritual, without sacrifice. The great head of the Church is the Only Saviour of men because He appeared 'to put away sin by the sacrifice of Himself'. A generation of youth baptized by fire in the holocaust of war, will return to us in a mood and mind moulded to appreciate the meaning of the Cross of Christ. Let them then not find us unprepared, but ready to match their sacrifices with ours. We shall not win them for Christ and His Church while we engage in theological controversy, but only as we present the Lord of All Good Life who once died that they might live.[124]

In other words, the churches to which servicemen and women returned needed to demonstrate a wholehearted commitment to the principles they proclaimed or risk being viewed as a people lacking credibility in the eyes of many who had risked their lives for their country during the war.[125] One initiative Scottish Baptists focused on was the establishment of Men's Fellowship groups in an attempt to replicate the close ties former servicemen would have had in the years spent in the Forces. The Women's Auxiliary had been seen to work well for women, but there had been no equivalent organisation for men. It aimed to provide not only spiritual input but also

---

[122] Thomas Coats, 'Presidential Address', October 1943, *Scottish Baptist Yearbook 1944*, p. 57.

[123] The same point was made by the BUGB President Sydney G. Morris in his Presidential address 'The Church Faces the Future' in May 1943, *Baptist Times*, 6 May, 1943, p. 9.

[124] J.T. Stark, 'The Church and These Tremendous Times', *Scottish Baptist Yearbook 1945*, p. 61.

[125] 'I'm Troubled About the Future', an article by an anonymous frontline BUGBI padre concerning the men returning home after the war. *Baptist Times*, 9 September, 1943, p. 6.

outdoor activities men could do together.[126] A 1946 Church of Scotland report on Evangelism illustrated the depth of the problem. There was 'far more cynicism, bitterness and sense of frustration in young people returning from the services than their parents ever knew in 1919. Many of them have lost even the willingness to believe in anything.'[127] A Free Church of Scotland report the previous year had concluded: '. . . that religious fervour, which had been on the wane for half a century, has reached its nadir . . . attendance at Sunday School and Bible Classes is now the exception rather than the rule'.[128] The tone of Scottish Baptist reflections were more positive, but that had reflected the sustained numerical growth in their constituency up to 1935, in contrast to the decline in the more numerous Presbyterian ranks in the twentieth century.

Yet it was not just the churches that needed to take spiritual values seriously, for the wider society and its Government to prosper also needed to do so. James Scott, General Secretary of the Baptist Union, made this very clear in his 1944 annual report. He commended the Government for their advance planning for housing needs, for their preparation for European reconstruction and the reestablishment of trading relationships disputed by the war, but this still left the most important issues unaddressed.

> The supreme values are moral and spiritual, and must be put in the forefront of any scheme of reconstruction if our civilisation is to survive. No society is worthy of the name unless it is based upon the teaching of our Lord Jesus Christ. If the new civilisation is not sustained and directed by a spiritual unity, the sacrifices of the past five years will largely have been in vain.[129]

Scott's assessment of the situation facing the Union and its churches was sober but also realistic. There had been great disruption of the work of the churches due to the war and the membership losses which had begun in the late 1930s were not entirely due to the recent conflict. In 1945 the rate of decline in membership had reduced, but the numbers of baptisms, Sunday School children and teachers had increased. There were signs of optimism for the

---

[126] *SBM*, 71.6, June 1945 pp. 4–5; 71.9, Sept 1945, pp. 3–4; 71.12, Dec 1945 p. 2, reported that a Men's Fellowship had started in many churches.

[127] *Into All the World: A Statement on Evangelism by the Church of Scotland* (Glasgow, 1946), p. 55. For more details on the significance of this report and the work that followed see Peter Bisset, *The Kirk and Her Scotland* (Edinburgh: The Handsel Press, n.d.), pp. 7–14.

[128] *Free Church Monthly Record*, December 1945, pp. 188–189.

[129] 'Annual Report by the Secretary', *Scottish Baptist Yearbook 1945*, p. 66.

future, but he warned it was conditional upon 'an intensification of spiritual life in the churches'.[130]

---

[130] 'Annual Report by the Secretary', 23 October 1945, *Scottish Baptist Yearbook 1946*, p. 57.

CHAPTER 7

# Adjusting to a Changing World, 1945–1960

### The End of World War Two

A sigh of relief was undoubtedly offered by many to know that a second world war in half a century was finally over. Broughty Ferry Baptist Church members, for example, expressed their satisfaction with the news that that the vestry, kitchen and hall windows no longer needed to be painted black in conformity with black-out regulations, and the voluntary fire watch on the church premises was no longer required, but indicated that celebrations were muted by the reality that so many people had died before the peace agreement was reached. Memories of the late 1940s highlighted the continuing rationing of various goods in the shops, but on a more positive note referred to developments in technology that enabled many people to own 'transistors' and experience the latest sounds in popular music. On the international stage, members recalled that the event that stood out was the declaration of Israel as an independent state in 1948.[1] In the church the death of the Minister R.F. Conway on 9 October, 1947, during Sunday morning worship, came at a time when congregational numbers were low and no deacons' or Church meeting had been held for more than three years. It would take some years for numbers to pick up after the war.[2] This was not uncommon, but was a familiar pattern in other Baptist churches as well.

What was to be different about this new era in Scottish religious history? The first post-war assembly of the Church of Scotland, for example, discussed whether women could be elders in the Kirk, but a common mind was not reached and the matter was sent to kirk sessions to consider.[3] Melville

---

[1] Alex Rodger, Donald Stewart & Ruth Witherow, *Broughty Ferry Baptist Church 1876–1976 "These Tremendous Years"*, unpublished manuscript, 1976, n.p., a copy held by the author of this book. I am grateful to Mrs Daphne Gibson for a copy of this manuscript.

[2] *"These Tremendous Years"*, n.p., and Ramsay G. Small, *Broughty Ferry Baptist Church The First Hundred Years*, private publication, 1976, p. 18. Rev. R.F Conway', *Scottish Baptist Yearbook*, 1948, p. 120.

[3] Kenneth Roy, *The Invisible Spirit: A Life of Post-War Scotland 1945–75* (Edinburgh: Birlinn, 2014, 2nd ed.), pp. 14–15. It is doubtful whether many congregations would have been in favour of a change on this matter. Montrose Old Parish Church, for example, called a meeting to discuss and vote in the light of the

Dinwiddie, the BBC's Scottish regional director announced plans for a new Scottish Home service, and not too surprisingly for an ordained Church of Scotland minister stated that a weekly Christian service would be one of the highlights of the new schedule, alongside a wide variety of new Scottish cultural features.[4] It was, though, very clear by the middle of the twentieth century that the churches had to work much harder to retain connections with an increasing proportion of the population of Scotland, including its young people. There had also been a serious decline in the number of candidates coming forward to serve in Baptist pastoral ministry. It was not a recent development but had been an issue of increasing concern to date since 1930.[5] The annual statistics produced by the Baptist Union bore testimony to this fact. Baptist membership figures had increased to a high of 23,310 in 1935, but had declined to 21,121 by 1945. This figure was no surprise when baptismal statistics were compared from the 1920s to 1940s. In 1922 there had been 1,444 believers' baptisms in Union causes, a total reduced to 570 per annum in 1939 and merely 375 in 1941. An increase to 519 baptisms in 1945[6] could not hide the underlying difficulties that Scottish Baptists would face in their outreach work in the second half of the twentieth century. Enthusiastic and creative mission initiatives had undoubtedly brought some successes but the spiritual climate in Scotland was less favourable to Christian witness than it had been earlier in the century.

### The Challenge of Retaining Members, Especially Younger People

Even in its own ranks more nominal members of the Christian Churches were increasingly attracted to leisure pursuits on Sundays, such as golf or hiking, that were made much easier by the increasing numbers of cars on the roads. In addition, the attractions of radio and television were more appealing to others than religious services in churches, even when the BBC in London was led by a son of the manse, John Reith, and in Scotland by Melville Dinwiddie from

---

General Assembly discussions. The resulting vote was 71 members against women being called as elders with only three in favour. It would be 1972 before the first women elders were appointed in that church. Dorothy Morrison & Isobel Reynolds, *Changed Days in Montrose: The Recollections of members and friends of Montrose Old Kirk 1900–1999* (Montrose: The Open Door Committee of the Church, 2000), p. 15. However on 26 May 1966 the General Assembly of the Church of Scotland voted in favour of this change. 'Elders!', *SBM*, 92.8 (August 1966), p. 5.

[4] Roy, *Invisible Spirit*, p. 15.

[5] 'The Outlook', *SBM*, 86.2 (February 1960), p. 2.

[6] Appendix 2: Table of Annual Statistics, in D. Hunt, *Reflections on Our Past A Statistical Look at Baptists in Scotland 1892–1997*, (Hamilton: Hamilton Baptist Church, 1997), n.p.

1933–1957.⁷ After the Second World War it was claimed that in many churches those attending were largely confined to the middle-aged and elderly,⁸ with the majority drawn from the middle-classes, disproportionate to the population as a whole. Overall attendance figures were at their lowest levels in the twentieth century during and immediately after the war, prior to a degree of recovery by the 1950s, but still at a level much lower than the beginning of the century.⁹ Baptist Union President John McKendrick reflecting on his year preaching in various affiliated congregations in 1959, expressed concern at the growing absence of men, proportionate to the number of women, in Sunday worship services.¹⁰ This struggle to retain particularly younger members of the congregation can be illustrated by the experience of one of the larger congregations, Stirling Baptist Church, during the pastorate of John Wrigley.¹¹ At the deacons' meeting in September 1943 a letter was read from Dr Fraser, a member of this body, drawing attention to the need to form a 'Young People's Fellowship Organisation' (YPF) in the church. The author, in adding to the contents of his letter, explained that he was concerned about the possibility of 'our young people slipping away from our care and attention through being compelled to join a youth organisation or movement of one kind or another [outside the church]'.¹² Part of the problem was that a majority of young people in Stirling had no link with any church organisation, youth club or activity. According to Father Kenneth Cox, Roman Catholic priest in Stirling, 60% of young people had no link with any church. He, together with other people in the town, had decided to set up the Thistle Club for young people, later called Open Doors, but hoped that it would only attract 'unattached Stirling youth'.¹³ The town's young people were so keen on this venture that an upper limit of 1,000 fourteen to twenty-five year olds was fixed for each Sunday evening.¹⁴ It is very likely that this was

---

⁷ R.D. Kernohan, 'Postscript: The Kirk since 1929', in John Buchan, *The Kirk in Scotland* (Dunbar; Labarum Publications Ltd, 1985), pp. 139–140. The BBC then was explicitly favourable to Christianity. For example, see 'Radio Evangelism', in Melville Dinwiddie, *Religion by Radio* (London: George Allen & Unwin, 1968), pp. 92–103.

⁸ C. Stewart Black, *The Scottish Church* (Glasgow: William Maclellan, 1952), p. 257.

⁹ Black, *Scottish Church*, p. 258.

¹⁰ John McKendrick, 'The President Summing Up', *SBM*, 85.10 (October 1959), p. 5.

¹¹ Talbot, *Standing on the Rock*, pp. 110–127.

¹² Stirling Baptist Church, Deacons' Minute Book, 2 June 1937 to 9 September 1947, 14 September 1943, p. 170.

¹³ *Stirling Journal*, 18 March 1948, p. 5.

¹⁴ *Stirling Journal*, 1 July 1948, p. 4.

modelled on the 'Open Door' youth project launched by the Church of Scotland Presbytery of Glasgow in the winter of 1945–1946, as a means of attracting and retaining younger people within its churches. Attendances at the venue chosen exceeded 1,000 per night in the 1946–1947 Session, with hundreds turned away for lack of space. The costs of the events were underwritten by the Presbytery until November 1948 when funding pressures led to the cessation of this work.[15] The typical evening's programme included community hymn-singing led by an orchestra and epilogues by prominent Glasgow ministers. On some evenings travel films of Scotland were shown, prior to a closing religious service; on other occasions sessions included 'brains trusts' or 'quiz contests'. Tea and sandwiches were served each evening events took place. By autumn 1947, at the start of the third year of this ministry, forty other 'Open Doors' had been launched in other urban centres across Scotland.[16] This Stirling venture did not start until the following year in 1948. However, the fact that the churches were agreed that there was a problem to address did lead to some significant attempts to turn around this situation.

Youth rallies became a major feature of the lives of a significant number of Baptist young people. In Glasgow, youth rallies at Adelaide Place Baptist Church were organised as a follow-up to the All Scotland Crusade with Billy Graham. The Glasgow Baptist Association organised the first two in 1955, but they were so successful a committee was set up to continue them.[17] Edinburgh had a Baptist Students Association that met in in the 1950s in the home of Dr and Mrs Fraser, members of Bristo Baptist Church, and later in Bristo Baptist Church hall. It had begun in 1921 but had mixed fortunes in some years though it appeared to be functioning well in the 1950s.[18] It also held regular youth rallies from at least the winter of 1958–1959.[19] The Baptist Union also had a youth committee that organised conferences that attracted young people mostly from the region where events were held, but a smaller number travelled from other locations.[20] Donald McCallum became convenor

---

[15] John Highet, *The Churches in Scotland To-Day* (Glasgow: Jackson Son & Company, 1950), pp. 95–98.

[16] Highet, *Churches in Scotland To-Day*, p. 95.

[17] James Murdoch, Secretary, 'Baptist Youth Rallies', 82.4, *SBM*, (April 1956), p. 9. See also 'Youth Rally', 81.11 (November 1955), p. 9.

[18] Edinburgh Baptist Students' Association, 81.10, (October 1955), p. 13; 82.10, *SBM*, (October 1956), p. 2. I am grateful to Dr Derek Murray for information on this Association. It continued until the 1980s.

[19] 'Accent on Youth', *SBM*, 84.2 (February 1958), p. 12.

[20] See George L. McNeill, 'Accent on Youth', *SBM*, 83.1 (January 1957), p. 7; and 'Baptist Young People's Conference' Dunoon September 23-26, *SBM*, 81.11 (November 1955), p. 17.

of the Young People's Committee in January 1959.[21] He organised a series of youth rallies first in Stirling[22] and then in other locations in Scotland that were a great success with good numbers of young people attending.[23] It is possible that the majority of young people attending these rallies were already associated with Baptist churches, but retention of people of whatever age is just as important as attracting additional new members.

As early as 1940 there had been signs that serious thinking was taking place as a matter of urgency within the Baptist Union of Scotland because of the decline in attendance at church by young people, especially amongst teenage boys. The Young People's Committee of the Union produced a report entitled: 'The Problem of our Boys Between the Ages of 12 and 18'. The research they had commissioned found that an increasing number of young people had no association at all with any Sunday School. There was no significant change by 1947, as W.D. Macgregor, Convener of the Sunday School Committee of the Union, recorded in his annual report, pointing to the 'alarmingly large number of children outside the influence of Church and Sunday School.'[24] Total numbers attending Sunday Schools had fallen from 51% of school-age children in 1911 to 30.8% in 1945, a fall of over 121,000 between 1938 and 1941 alone. However, concerted efforts post-WW2 by the churches saw modest increases for the next eleven years up to the high point of 35%, 325,200 children, in 1956.[25] The number of young people aged twelve to fourteen who were leaving the church was also growing at an alarming rate. The root problem the committee found was a lack of time spent by the churches in inculcating the habit of church attendance amongst the younger children, combined with the inconvenience of the Sunday School being held at the same time as the morning service. Even more surprising apparently was the fact that many church members and parents did not grasp the seriousness of the situation. The primary weakness, though, according to the committee, was 'our failure to persuade our young people to register a decision for Jesus Christ before the age of 12 is reached'. A four-point remedy was suggested for alleviating this growing problem. First of all, there was a need to make greater

---

[21] Donald McCallum, 'Accent on Youth', *SBM*, 85.1 (January 1959), p. 12.

[22] Donald McCallum, 'Accent on Youth', *SBM*, 85.4 (April 1959), p. 10. The same issue of the *SBM* highlighted the flourishing programme of youth rallies in Glasgow and Edinburgh in 1959, pp. 10–11. The report on the 30 May 1959 youth rally in Stirling is given in *SBM*, 85.9 (September 1959), p. 6.

[23] 'Assembly Youth Rally "Pack-Out"', *SBM*, 85.12 (December 1959), pp. 3–4.

[24] W.D. MacGregor, 'Sunday School', *Scottish Baptist Yearbook 1948*, p. 132.

[25] John Sutherland, *Godly Upbringing: A Survey of Sunday Schools and Bible Classes in the Church of Scotland* (Edinburgh: Church of Scotland Youth Committee, 1960), pp. 17–22.

efforts in making contact with children that had no current involvement in church or Sunday School. A survey of the local community would identify which families had no links with a local church. Secondly, teachers should aim to spend some time with the children in their class during the week so that a friendship was developed that went beyond a teacher-pupil relationship in a formal learning environment. Thirdly given that point two would not be possible for many teachers, the establishment of youth organisations in the church would be essential to strengthen contacts with young people, especially teenage boys. Fourthly young people should be encouraged to become members at a much younger age with a view to bridging the gap between the youth and the church.[26] The report admitted that the difficulties were complex and that there was no simple solution to getting young people back into the churches.

The current received wisdom is that church and Sunday School membership, together with attendance in the churches, was high and largely maintained until the mid-1950s, then especially in the 1960s a catastrophic decline set in which still shows no sign of bottoming out.[27] On paper this viewpoint appears to be substantiated by the figures claimed by the churches. Given that roll revision was uncommon in the Established Church, however, it is likely that although attendances were less frequent, the reality on the ground was not reflected in written records. Scottish Baptists, for example, kept much more accurate accounts of those actually attending and provide therefore more reliable statistics. Even in its flagship youth organisation, Christian Endeavour, the figures for 1938 to 1939, reported in 1940, make for sober reading. The number of CE societies was down by 6.7% and the number of members declined by 6.8% in this twelve-month period. The secretary of the Scottish Baptist CE Union Philip Pont remarked that 'the decrease is serious' and urged greater efforts to reverse the decline in the following year.[28] In the decade from 1949 to 1959, for example, the fourteen CE societies in the Scottish Borders had declined to only three, though there was some growth in other areas of the country. Abel Rees reported from the

---

[26] 'The Problem of our Boys Between the Ages of 12 and 18 Report by the Young People's Committee', *Scottish Baptist Year-Book 1940*, pp. 206–207.

[27] C. Brown, *The Death of Christian Britain: Understanding Secularisation 1800–2000* (Abingdon: Routledge, 2009, 2nd ed.), p. 170. See also Callum G. Brown, 'Religion and Secularisation'. in A. Dickson & J.H. Treble (eds), *People and Society in Scotland, Volume III, 1914–2000* (Edinburgh: John Donald, 1992), pp. 48–76. Other scholars would suggest that the decline was more gradual and was in evidence post World War One. See Harvie, *No Gods and Precious Few Heroes*, pp. 82–84; with a peak figure of church membership in proportion to population as early as 1905. See also Devine, *Scottish Nation 1700–2000*, p. 368.

[28] *Scottish Baptist Yearbook 1940*, p. 194.

Baptist CE Union meeting at the October 1959 Baptist Union Assembly that 'Today ministers are finding that the youth fellowship does not meet the needs of the church . . .' and acknowledged that CE had also faced its struggles in recent years.[29] Boys' Brigade numbers were also lower, with some companies finding it very difficult to continue their work, for example, the one associated with Queen's Park Baptist Church, Glasgow that had been formed in 1932 but closed in 1961.[30] Although overall the increase in involvement in church-based youth organisations over the first half of the twentieth century did enable a significant number of families who had weaker ties to the churches to remain in contact with them,[31] it could not disguise the weakening grip of the churches on the lives of a growing proportion of Scottish people by the time of the Second World War. The situation in Scottish Baptist churches then and in the post-war years was almost certainly little different from that in other mainstream churches,[32] the only difference being that as their records were more carefully monitored than those of larger denominations, attempts at resolving the challenges could be sought at an earlier stage.

## Home Evangelism

It was recognised across the Scottish Protestant Churches that greater efforts were required to engage with local communities to gain or regain the allegiance of many people in Scotland in the middle of the twentieth century. In the decade after World War Two evangelistic initiatives of various kinds would be carried out by these Churches on a scale which in extent and variety was at least as great as in any previous era in Scottish history.[33] The Roman Catholic Church too brought in special mission teams to quicken the spiritual vitality of existing congregational members as well as priests from the English-based Catholic Missionary Society to promote the faith to the wider community and reported 'many conversions to Catholicism' through their work.[34] Major Interdenominational Evangelical agencies such as the Faith Mission had record numbers on their two year training course in 1959–1960.

---

[29] Abel J. Rees, 'Baptist C.E. Union', *SBM*, 85.11 (November 1959), p. 5.

[30] William W. Murray, *Queen's Park Baptist Church 1878–1978* (Glasgow: Queen's Park Baptist Church, 1978), p. 71.

[31] Brown, *Religion and Society in Scotland Since 1707*, pp. 147–152

[32] 'The Church Of The New Age', *British Weekly* article reprinted in *SBM*, 86.12 (December 1960), pp. 17–18.

[33] John Highet, *The Scottish Churches: A Review of Their State 400 years after the Reformation* (London: Skeffington, 1960), p. 70.

[34] Highet, *Scottish Churches*, pp. 71–72.

The Scottish branch of the Worldwide Evangelisation Crusade (WEC) utilised ministers from various churches, including from the Baptist Union, alongside their own staff, to train workers in various forms of evangelistic ministry including open air work and home visitation. The Scottish Evangelistic Council and the Scottish Colportage Society focussed on door-to-door outreach, visiting over 40,000 homes in 1958 and in total had conducted over one million home visits between 1930 and 1960.[35] However, the largest proportion of outreach ventures was initiated through the mainstream Protestant Churches. Many of these initiatives were inter-church ventures depending on local circumstances. What is clear is that real enthusiasm was demonstrated in them as Scottish Christians communicated their understanding of the Christian Gospel to the wider community.

Scottish Baptists, although they were members of one of the smaller denominations, were committed to this work. A key leader was Walter Main, who was inducted as the new Convener of the Evangelistic Committee at the October 1946 Annual Assembly. Under his leadership those assembled agreed that: 'a special and distinctive message defining Evangelism should be given by the issue of the booklet, *Evangelism – A Spirit*, and by the verbal delivery of this message up and down the country, at church services, Association conferences, and other specially convened meetings.'[36] Main also reminded delegates that members of his committee would be looking for requests from their churches to assist them with evangelistic projects. Plans were also in hand to revive seaside missions, a form of outreach that had not been used for some years.[37] In 1951 teams of young people based in local church halls conducted seaside missions in Troon, Prestwick and Ayr, with Broughty Ferry added in 1952.[38] Scottish Baptists enthusiastically supported the Edinburgh Churches Campaign of 1947 and its equivalent Glasgow Churches Campaign of 1950 that were referred to at the time as 'Commandos Campaigns'.[39] They consisted of teams of ministers and lay-people paying short visits to offices, factories, canteens, youth clubs, dance halls, cinemas, football matches and pubs, as well as the more familiar visits to schools, colleges and hospitals. In a limited time on unfamiliar territory there was an attempt in simple terms to convey the truth of the Christian gospel to people unfamiliar with church

---

[35] Highet, *Scottish Churches*, pp. 71–73.

[36] Walter Main, 'Evangelistic', *Scottish Baptist Yearbook 1948*, pp. 116, 127.

[37] Main, 'Evangelistic', p, 127.

[38] 'Baptist Advance- Evangelise or Perish', *SBM*, 78.8 (August 1952), p. 4.

[39] Edward Campbell, 'Evangelistic', *Scottish Baptist Yearbook 1951*, p. 136. 'Commando' style campaigns were first used by Methodist Church in England, prior to their use in Scotland in the post-war years. Roberts, *These Christian Commando Campaigns*, pp. 7, 13; Bardgett, *Scotland's Evangelist D P. Thomson*, p. 198.

followed by discussion of the message presented. In Glasgow the team also used street plays and played films in a mobile cinema to promote their message. The reception in these community settings was described as friendly and welcoming, but team members were also increasingly aware that many hearers had raised serious questions about the place of the Church in contemporary society.[40] One good long-term outcome of these missions was the appointment of industrial chaplains, with thirty-one requested by factories following the Glasgow 1950 campaign, alongside modest increases in church attendances in some Glasgow congregations.[41] Queen's Park Baptist Church during the pastorate of Cyril Squires in the 1940s held their Sunday evening services in the nearby Queen's Park in the form of a 'Question Time' session in which the minister attempted to answer questions posed by members of the congregation. In 1947 there was competition as two political parties, the Socialist Party of Great Britain and the Communist Party, set up nearby stands and hosted their own events on Sunday evenings. However, the meeting led by the Baptist pastor had much larger crowds from 300 to 500 attending on any given night that summer. Squires reported that the clear increase in growth of nineteen members, together with increased Sunday morning congregations had come through this work.[42] The Church of Scotland Presbytery of Glasgow had chosen to hold open air evangelistic services in three of Glasgow's parks, the Botanic Gardens, Springburn Park and Tollcross Park, in the summers of 1945 to 1948. All were well attended with the Springburn Park meetings each attracting around 1,400 people.[43] Interdenominational open-air evangelistic work in Scotland was a common feature in the post war years. In Uddingston, for example, in summer and autumn 1947 and spring 1948, Baptist, Congregational, Episcopal and Church of the Nazarene ministers co-operated and stood together in the face of heckling from Communists and some members of 'the smaller religious sects'. Attendances outdoors were much larger with the unchurched apparently happy to attend, but similar meetings in religious buildings drew much smaller attendances of around seventy to eighty people mainly from the

---

[40] Highet, *Churches in Scotland To-Day*, pp. 90–93; Highet, *Scottish Churches*, pp. 82–83; Bardgett, *Scotland's Evangelist D P. Thomson*, pp. 198–200.

[41] John Highet, 'The Glasgow Churches' Campaign, 1950', in J. Cunnison and J.B.S Gilfillan (eds), *The City of Glasgow: The Third Statistical Account of Scotland* (Glasgow: Collins, 1958), p. 738. For more details on the appointment of industrial chaplains, see *The Church At Work* (Edinburgh: Church of Scotland, 1948), p. 13; and Highet, *Churches in Scotland To-Day*, pp. 99–101.

[42] Highet, *Churches in Scotland To-Day*, pp. 87–88.

[43] 'Clericus', *Glasgow Evening News*, 15 May, 1948, cited by Highet, *Churches in Scotland To-Day*, p. 89.

local churches.[44] In Paisley the Mid-Century Campaign of 1950–51 saw over 1,000 members of fifty Protestant Churches in the town, including Baptist Churches engage in a one year visitation programme to contact the nearly 100,000 residents. Growth in confidence in the gospel and strengthening of ties of fellowship between the participating church members were its lasting legacy, alongside increased congregations and the restoration of lapsed members of local churches.[45] Scottish Churches in the post-war years were confident in their expectations of gaining a hearing for the gospel from the wider community. These examples above show that on occasions this conviction was justified.

The Baptist Advance Campaign of 1951–52 did not produce any spectacular results. It was, though, reported that: 'the mood of drift and *laissez faire* would seem to have gone, having been superseded by a new sense of urgency and a quickened desire to serve Christ in the service of man.'[46] It included an action plan, for example, of the Stirling and Clackmananshire Baptist Association, led by its ministers for a year of retreats, prayer gatherings and sustained evangelistic effort in the churches from 4 November to 2 December 1952. One week of the mission was devoted to two of the eight churches, paired in four groups, culminating in a communion service in Stirling Baptist Church on 6 December 1952. It was suggested there was an evident spiritual quickening and the shared activity had brought the churches closer together.[47] In Glasgow, a good example of a congregation that sought to continue in this style of evangelism was Adelaide Place Baptist Church. Under its inspirational minister George Young it launched another outreach scheme the following year, to build on what had already been accomplished in its locality. Year one of the new scheme was preparation in Bible study and prayer, a preliminary survey of the area and the production of literature. In the autumn of 1953 forty volunteers from the church visited over two weeks all the houses in the immediate neighbourhood. Of the thousand homes visited, one third had no church connection, one third were Roman Catholics and

---

[44] Highet, *Churches in Scotland To-Day*, p. 88.

[45] Campbell, 'Evangelistic', *Scottish Baptist Yearbook 1951*, p. 136. D.P. Thomson, *Harnessing The Lay Forces of the Church* (Glasgow: Private Publication, 1955), pp. 6–9. More details are given in D P. Thomson (ed.), *We Saw The Church in Action: The Press and the BBC Report on those Visitation Campaigns 1947 to 1954* (Crieff: D.P. Thomson, 1954), pp.14–22.

[46] '82nd Annual Report by The Secretary', *Scottish Baptist Yearbook 1952*, p. 128; *SBM*, 78.1 (January 1952), p. 9.

[47] This initiative featured in the English periodical *The Baptist Times*, 24 January 1952, p. 1; 'Stirlingshire and Clackmannanshire District Association Baptist Advance Campaign', *SBM*, 78.4 (April 1952, p. 14; Talbot, *Brief History of Central Baptist Association, 1909–2002*, p. 24.

slightly more than a third were connected with other Churches. George Young in assessing the results of all this work was pleased that the church now had a card index with information on all the householders in the area and was delighted with the wonderful comradeship between the volunteers, but acknowledged that not a single adult came to church as a result of the visitation and only a handful of additional children joined the Sunday School. He realised that this visitation programme needed to be sustained to bear fruit in future years. In Adelaide Place the initial work of visitation in 1953 was repeated half yearly into 1956 together with twenty adults going out onto Sauchiehall Street, near the church premises, prior to each Sunday evening service to invite unchurched people to attend it. As a result of these two regular activities over more than three years there was a steady trickle of visitors to services, with more than fifty new children in the Sunday School and over a hundred new members added to the church.[48] Another denominational outreach initiative was the three-year Crusade of Visitation Evangelism. There were 120 Baptist churches that joined together in this venture between 1956 and 1959. There were 148 door-to-door visitation programmes undertaken that resulted in 116 new church members, 112 adherents, 506 new Sunday School scholars and additions to other church organisations. Young in his capacity of Evangelism Convenor of the Baptist Union noted that: 'These results, though moderate, were encouraging.'[49] There was a determination to seek to have a greater impact on the nation through evangelistic work across the Scottish Churches in the post-war years. Individual denominational mission work was important, but working together with likeminded Protestant Churches was viewed as being likely to bring about a greater impact on the wider community.

The most effective home mission activities in the post war years in Scotland took place under the inspirational leadership of Church of Scotland ministers D.P. Thomson and Tom Allan. It would come to be known as the *Tell Scotland* movement. Its immediate origins came from the BBC Scotland Radio Missions of 1950 and 1952, organised by Ronnie Falconer, Religious Broadcasting Organiser for the BBC in Scotland who brought a series of key individuals together to form a team that were ably supported by representatives of mainstream Protestant denominations, including the Baptist Union of Scotland to 'challenge the careless, bring back the lapsed and strengthen the faithful.'[50] Edward Campbell, the next Convenor of the Evangelism Committee of the Baptist Union was the Scottish Baptist

---

[48] Highet, *Scottish Churches*, pp. 85–86

[49] George A. Young, 'Where do we go from here? *SBM*, 85.10 (October 1959), p. 6.

[50] R.H.W Falconer, *Success and Failure of a RADIO MISSION* (London: SCM, 1951), pp. 12–20.

representative on the Steering Committee of *Tell Scotland*.⁵¹ Campbell wrote: 'Baptists have an important part to play in this movement. By co-operating locally with other bodies of the reformed faith they will find scope for their evangelistic zeal. . . . For some social conditions will take pre-eminence over the saving of souls but for Baptists 'conversion' must be at the centre.'⁵² Campbell's comments hint at tensions within the movement caused by the breadth of theological opinions within its ranks. A second antecedent of *Tell Scotland* was the Message of Friendship mission in 1933–34 organised by George Macleod, minister of Govan Old Parish Church, Glasgow, from which several 'Iona Missions' replicating this style took place in parishes associated with his Iona movement. Its central emphasis was that the congregation itself should be the evangelising agent in its parish, rather than utilising an evangelist from outside the area to lead a mission in the parish.⁵³ This Govan mission was extremely successful with 120 new members joining the church on Palm Sunday 1934, evening weeknight services attracted up to 500 people and the church membership had increased by over 300 in six months. Over 200 children joined the Sunday School, 100 lapsed members were restored, together with 220 individuals who signed up for a ten-week course of instruction in the Christian faith, of whom 200 made professions of faith; and over eighty came forward for 'adult baptism'.⁵⁴ MacLeod was the promotor of the stronger social vision, but did not exclude evangelistic proclamation. However, Scottish Baptists were more comfortable with the third antecedent of *Tell Scotland*, the visitation campaigns of Tom Allan and D.P. Thomson. A campaign of visitation evangelism was first attempted in the parish of North Kelvinside in Glasgow and was staffed by members of the Seaside Mission team of the Church of Scotland, comprising fifty men and women, including five ministers, twelve divinity students and thirteen other Arts students, together with some of the elders and Sunday School teachers of Tom Allan's local congregation.⁵⁵ In approximately two weeks they had visited the vast majority of the nearly 2,000 homes. The remarkable results that followed included a doubling of Sunday-School attendance, adding sixty

---

⁵¹ Frank Bardgett, 'The *Tell Scotland* Movement: failure and success' *Scottish Church History Society Records*, Vol. 38 (2008), p. 110, n.22.

⁵² Edward Campbell, 'Tell Scotland', *SBM*, 80.1 (January 1954), p. 6.

⁵³ Bardgett, 'The *Tell Scotland* Movement', p. 107, n.11.

⁵⁴ Ronald Ferguson, *George MacLeod Founder of the Iona Community* (London: Collins, 1990), pp. 115–118.

⁵⁵ An excellent recent study of Tom Allan's ministry is Alexander Forsyth, *Mission by the People: Re-Discovering the Dynamic Missiology of Tom Allan and His Scottish Contemporaries* (Eugene, Oregon: Pickwick Publications, 2017). See pp. 19–28 for analysis of this particular mission.

women to the membership of the Women's Guild, record numbers were attending Sunday services and seventy of the new attendees had requested church membership. Within two years the congregation had doubled in size and in five and a half years more than 800 new members were added to the roll.[56] A year later in autumn 1948 a similar campaign was run at St Mary's Parish in Motherwell. Ian Doyle, the Church of Scotland minister, was assisted by colleagues in churches of other denominations in this venture. People in the parish were visited in their homes, places of work such as schools, hospital and the burgh slaughterhouse, and even entertainment venues such as the greyhound track, and between films in the New Cinema.[57] The success of this outreach activity focusing on the utilisation of Christian lay-people carrying out mission as the Church's ongoing task in homes, workplaces and leisure facilities, under the auspices of *Tell Scotland* in the post war years was truly remarkable. It has been described as 'perhaps the most important movement of mission that Scotland had seen in the course of the century.[58] It encouraged the various churches to launch their own distinctive and creative evangelistic strategies. However, *Tell Scotland* is probably best known today for its sponsorship of the 1955 Billy Graham Crusade.

### All Scotland – Billy Graham Crusade Glasgow 1955

The crusade began on 21 March and concluded on 30 April 1955, six weeks later, with 830,670 attending either the evening meetings in the Kelvin Hall, or the closing services in Ibrox Stadium and Hampden Park; In addition, 217,700 were present at thirty-seven relay meetings held in other parts of Scotland and a further 136,990 people attended events at which Graham or members of his team spoke during these weeks. In total 1,185,360 were present and there were 26,457 enquirers after these meetings.[59] The closing rally at Hampden Park had approximately 100,000 in attendance, the largest congregation ever to assemble in Scotland's history.[60] Graham also addressed open air meetings in Tynecastle Stadium in Edinburgh, Pittodrie Stadium in Aberdeen and in Inverness. More specialist meeting were held for National Service men in Redford Barracks in Edinburgh, for university students at the MacEwan Hall in Edinburgh University, Barlinnie Prison in Glasgow and

---

[56] Thomson (ed.), *We Saw The Church in Action*, pp. 1–2; Fuller details are given in Tom Allan, *The Face of My Parish* (London: SCM, 1953). pp. 23–37.

[57] Thomson (ed.), *We Saw The Church in Action*, pp. 4–5.

[58] It has been described as 'perhaps the most important movement of mission that Scotland had seen in the course of the century'. Bisset, *Kirk And Her Scotland*, pp. 8–9.

[59] Tom Allan (ed.), *Crusade in Scotland* (Glasgow: Pickering and Inglis, 1955), pp. 8, 22

[60] Allan (ed.), *Crusade in Scotland*, p. 15.

John Brown Shipbuilders in Clydebank, and by courtesy of the Director of Education with the co-operation of head-teachers ten thousand Glasgow schoolchildren were given permission to attend a special meeting in the city to listen to Billy Graham.[61] This crusade had the advantage of the favourable publicity generated by the Harringay Crusade in London the previous year. It ensured Billy Graham was no longer an unknown American preacher in the eyes of the British media. It had been a major success packing the 12,000 arena for almost all the meetings from 1 March to 22 May, 1954, with many future church leaders in England tracing their conversions or decision to enter Christian ministry to the Harringay Crusade. A large majority of those recorded as enquirers, around 90% specified a church with which they had some connection, but few could answer basic questions about the nominated church. It would, though, be fair to say only a very small minority had no link at all to any place of worship.[62] A major innovation had been relaying Graham's message to theatres, rented halls and churches to 430 venues in 175 towns and cities across England, Scotland, Wales and Ireland. At the final day of the 1954 Harringay Crusade in Wembley Stadium 185,000 people attended, bring the total attendance for the meetings to over two million people.[63] Newspaper coverage, especially in Scotland over the winter 1954 into 1955 was more extensive than any other religious news 'for a generation'.[64] The meetings had the full support of the Scottish Religious Broadcasting network with its programmes in March and April 1955 intended to prepare the way for his meetings.[65] With the greatest success being the national United Kingdom broadcast of the Good Friday service, the first live TV Broadcast service on the BBC with an audience of around thirty million people watching it.[66] No-one could have denied that the Christian religion was centre-stage in the life of the nation during these two crusades.

The relay meetings in other locations also saw a response to the gospel proclaimed through Billy Graham with 3,448 enquirers.[67] For example, young people taken to the Inverness relay meetings by members of Buckie Baptist

---

[61] Allan (ed.), *Crusade in Scotland*, pp. 15–19.

[62] Frank Colquhoun, *Harringay Story: A Detailed account of the Greater London Crusade 1954* (London: Hodder & Stoughton, 1955), pp. 232–240.

[63] Andrew Finstuen, Anne Blue & Grant Wacker (eds), *Billy Graham American Pilgrim* (New York: Oxford University Press, 2017), pp. 85–87.

[64] Allan (ed.), *Crusade in Scotland*, pp. 44–45.

[65] Allan (ed.), *Crusade in Scotland*, pp. 102–103 gives the details.

[66] George Burnham, *Billy Graham: A Mission Accomplished* (London: Marshall, Morgan and Scott, 1955), pp. 36–38.

[67] Allan (ed.), *Crusade in Scotland*, pp. 22–23.

Church professed faith in Jesus and subsequently were enthusiastic open-air proclaimers of the Christian faith on the streets of Buckie on Sunday early evenings prior to the Gospel services where Alex Barr, the influential Baptist pastor proclaimed with great enthusiasm the importance of following Jesus, teaching 'the three R's- Man's Ruin, God's Remedy and Man's Responsibility'.[68] On some Sundays he allowed the Christian Endeavour society in the church to take services and three of these young men later entered pastoral ministry and a fourth became a full-time evangelist in Brethren circles.[69] Official statistics of the major crusade meetings would not have any record of these benefits to local congregations, but it does explain why more evangelical congregations that prioritised outreach work both retained a greater proportion of those allocated to them, who had come forward at Billy Graham events, and then saw others join churches through their subsequent witness.

However, it is important to assess the significance of the Glasgow Crusade, in particular upon that city. What was its impact in the years that followed? The church attendance figures for the seven Protestant denominations surveyed showed a three-Sunday average of 56,503 in 1954, rising to 67,078 in 1955 and falling back to 62,224 in 1956. The net increase of sustained church attendance more than a year after the crusade was 5,721 people. The Baptist Union congregations' figures were 2,022 adults per Sunday in 1954, rising to 2,671 in 1955 and 2,240 in 1956, a net increase of 218 adults (10.8%). Membership in these churches also rose by 286 people, a 6.8% increase over two years.[70] The total national membership figures in Baptist Union congregations in Scotland rose from 18, 959 in 1954 to 19,658 in 1955 and to 20,340 in 1956. The assessments of the impact of this mission were measured. Edward Campbell, Convener of the Evangelism Committee stated wrote some months later: 'Saints have been refreshed and sinners converted. . . . Provided the gains to our Denomination are consolidated the coming years should witness extension and numerical growth.'[71] In the following year in his annual report the Union Secretary George Hardie remarked that the 'spectacular upsurge of last year' had been replaced by 'many moderate gains in membership, although these are balanced in some cases by considerable losses due in the main to rigorous roll revision.' He reported that overall seventy-eight churches had increased in membership, fifty-five churches had declined in membership and twenty-two were unchanged. At the time of writing his

---

[68] C.F. Geddes, *Love Lifted Me* (Glasgow; Gospel Tract Publications, 1986), pp. 113–124.

[69] Geddes, Love *Lifted Me*, pp. 113–124.

[70] Highet, 'The Churches', in Cunnison and Gilfillan (eds), *City of Glasgow: The Third Statistical Account of Scotland*, pp. 728–734.

[71] *Scottish Baptist Yearbook 1956*, p. 158.

report the total membership was 20,310, an overall increase of 177.[72] This level of membership in Baptist Union churches was broadly maintained for the rest of the 1950s before a steady small decline in total numbers would become the pattern in the 1960s. The impact of the 1955 mission was clearly significant in Scottish Baptist churches but it was a moderate rather than a dramatic success. It is much more likely that the relatively high membership figures in the later 1950s is due more to the effective Church Extension programme than any residual impact of the Graham mission.[73] It was the latter kind of work too that is much more effective in the longer-term as even supporters of the mission admitted in retrospect.[74]

## Church Extension

A new vision for outreach in the post-war years was not only evident in Baptist ranks, but was equally evident in the activities of other Christian Churches in Scotland. For example, John White, presenting the report of the Home Board on National Church Extension to the General Assembly of the Church of Scotland in 1944, sought their agreement to the establishment of a Special Fund of one million pounds for providing new church buildings for 'fifty per cent of the migrated population of Scotland'.[75] This would be a pressing need in the new housing areas of the country. Prof. John Riddell, at a Church of Scotland conference in Dunblane looking at the subject of National Church Extension, highlighted the success of this denomination in Church

---

[72] '87th Annual Report by 'The Secretary', *Scottish Baptist Yearbook 1957*, p. 127.

[73] This date fits with the perspective of those scholars who refer to a modest recovery of church attendance and membership figures in Scottish Churches between 1945 and 1960, rather than using terms like religious revival. One of the best accounts of the data is given in Clive D. Field, *Britain's Last Religious Revival?* (Basingstoke; Palgrave Macmillan, 2015), pp. 2–8.

[74] For example, D.P. Thomson, *Dr Billy Graham and The Pattern of Modern Evangelism* (Crieff: The Book Department St Ninians, 1966) and Francis Lyall & William Still, *The Gilcolmston Story 1868–1968* (Aberdeen: For the Church, 1967), p. 118. In England Robert Aitken, minister of Grenfell Baptist Church, Birmingham, came to the same conclusions. Ian Jones, *The Local Church and Generational Change in Birmingham 1945–2000* (Woodbridge: The Boydell Press, 2012), pp. 128–130. Others from very different theological perspectives such as George Macleod in Scotland and Sussex-based South African Reformed Baptist minister Erroll Hulse had even more fundamental concerns about the biblical and practical basis of this kind of evangelistic effort. See Ferguson, *George MacLeod*, pp. 270–274; and Erroll Hulse, *Billy Graham: The Pastor's Dilemma* (Hounslow: Maurice Allan, 1966).

[75] Rev. Tom Caldwell, 'The General Assembly of 1944' in *The Church of Scotland Yearbook 1945* (Edinburgh: The Church of Scotland Committee on Publications, 1945), p. 17.

Extension in the 1920s and 1930s in building some strong new churches whose congregations were now well placed to assist other communities in providing the funding for new causes to be launched not only in new housing areas on the edge of particular cities, but also in completely new towns like Glenrothes and East Kilbride. He urged creativity in how this work was to be undertaken, including the possibility of transporting entire congregations to housing areas without existing churches to launch new causes.[76] There was a genuine expectancy of the success of this new venture.

Scottish Baptists likewise sought to grasp the new opportunities. The vision for further advances of the Baptist witness in Scotland was in evidence in the creation of the Church Extension Committee in 1948. Its remit was to survey the new areas of population in Scotland with a view to ascertaining the potential for evangelistic work and the planting of new Baptist congregations. The churches at Ayr and New Cumnock had sought sites for new causes within their towns; the Paisley Baptist churches had secured a site in the Glenburn district; the Glasgow Association had similarly obtained sites at Househillwood and Cranhill. Fife Baptist Association had applied for one in Glenrothes[77] and the Baptist Union of Scotland likewise in the new town of East Kilbride.[78] In West Lothian, the new cause at Broxburn formed in 1940 erected its own premises in 1952, and another church-plant commenced in March 1951 at Bathgate that had seen more than fifteen baptism applications in its first year of operations.[79] The Baptist Home Mission brought in 'Work Camps' for young people in 1952 at Tobermory and Bunessan on Mull, that combined a holiday on an island with social action that enhanced the mission work of these two local congregations.[80] A few years later at the Baptist Union Assembly in 1951 a call was made for the raising of £50,000 for the new Church Extension Fund in the next five years to extend the work of this smaller network of churches. It was admitted that this was a big challenge at a time of rising costs for the churches, but the General Secretary George Hardie urged delegates to recommend the scheme to their churches in order to be

---

[76] Rev. Prof. J.G. Riddell, 'National Church Extension Review and Prospect', *The Church of Scotland Yearbook 1950* (Edinburgh: The Church of Scotland Committee on Publications, 1945), pp. 64–66.

[77] Details of the remarkable growth of this church are given in Neil E. Allison, *The Adventure of Faith: Glenrothes Baptist Church 1958–1993* (Glenrothes: Glenrothes Baptist Church, 2016).

[78] 'Church Extension', *Scottish Baptist Yearbook 1950*, p. 137.

[79] George Hardie, 'Church Extension in West Lothian', *SBM*, 78.8 (August 1952), p. 6.

[80] 'Annual Report of the Home Missionary Society', *Scottish Baptist Yearbook 1953*, p. 166.

ready for advancing the cause of Christ in new communities. In anticipation of funding being forthcoming new ventures in Pollok, Glasgow, East Kilbride, Bathgate and Glenrothes had commenced.[81] Over the next five years significant progress was made which ensured that the 1956 General Secretary's report on church extension work was upbeat. General giving from the churches was £21,460, a significant sum of money, though less than expected. By contrast the Women's Auxiliary who had set a target of £5,000 for their share of the target amount had surpassed it with £5,122 already collected. He was most encouraged by the numerical growth at Broxburn, East Kilbride, Granton, Edinburgh, and Pollok, Glasgow,[82] with 78, 86, 170 and 173 members respectively. In addition, the Baptist Union in partnership with Rattray Street Baptist Church, Dundee, had opened the Downfield Baptist Church, and twenty-four founding members committed to serve in Glenburn Baptist Church, Paisley.[83] The relatively healthy state of Scottish Baptist membership figures in this era was due more to its effective church extension programme than any other single contributory factor.

## East Kilbride Baptist Church

The church seen as the most successful of the new extension causes was undoubtedly the one in East Kilbride. However, its initial progress was exceedingly slow.[84] A committee was formed in March 1952 comprising representatives of the Rutherglen and Cambuslang Baptist Churches, the Baptist Union and the Lanarkshire Baptist Association. Their initial attempts to form a church attracted only two local residents. However, in June 1952 volunteers from neighbouring Baptist Churches in High Blantyre and Cathcart, Glasgow, conducted a house-to-house visitation programme to generate interest, but it was very disappointing. Undeterred it was decided to start Sunday evening services in the YMCA Hall in Kittoch Street, East Kilbride, with the first conducted by George Hardie, Secretary of the Baptist Union on 23 November 1952.[85] In its first year from 1 October 1952 to the

---

[81] Murray, *First Hundred Years*, pp. 131–132.

[82] *Pollok Baptist Church Silver Jubilee Year 1952–1977 25 Years of Christian Witness* booklet gives a summary of its work.

[83] '87th Annual Report by The Secretary', *Scottish Baptist Yearbook*, 1957, p. 128. He had expressed disappointment at the slow rate at which money had come in for Church Extension two years earlier. '85th Annual Report by The Secretary', *Scottish Baptist Yearbook*, 1955, p. 126.

[84] Fuller details are given by Peter Blackwood, 'East Kilbride', *SBM*. 85.5 (May 1959), pp. 7–8.

[85] *Souvenir Brochure to commemorate the Opening of East Kilbride Baptist Church 9th April 1960* (private publication: April 1960), p. 5.

summer of 1953 the total number of people involved was eight adults and six children. A Sunday School was started as late as Sunday 11 October 1953 with ten children. The official constitution of the church took place on 31 May 1954. It had an average of fifteen adults and eight children at the morning service and twenty adults and eight children at the evening one, with fifty children on the Sunday-School roll, a total that would reach over eighty by the end of the year. A Women's Auxiliary was started on 29 September 1954 and soon attracted seventeen members. Youth activities were encouraging as numbers were healthy with thirty members of the Junior Christian Endeavour by December 1954; at the same time the uniformed organisations prospered with twenty-two cadets and the same number in the junior and senior sections of the newly formed Girls' Life Brigade, together with seventeen members of the Life Boys Team. The small core of committed members persevered because they were convinced of the need for the church in that growing community. In the following year, 1953, after an outreach campaign other people started to join them. A next step was taken with the appointment of a student pastor James Graham, who for six months combined service alongside the twenty-four members with his studies at the Scottish Baptist College. The congregation had grown to thirty-six members by the time of Peter Barber's appointment as full-time pastor in June 1955. A hall was erected in 1958 with the church building opened in the East Mains area of East Kilbride in 1960.[86] Growth now became an established pattern with the membership total standing at 141 when the new premises were opened in 1960.[87] Scotland in the 1950s was not an easy time to plant new churches for Scottish Baptists. It is likely that other Christian Churches experienced the same challenges that could be overcome, but not without significant effort. This example illustrates the hard work and dedication required to accomplish this goal.

## Theological Education

The disagreements within the Union in 1932 over how to discipline Eric Roberts,[88] minister of Grantown-on-Spey Baptist Church, had seriously damaged relationships between some of the participants, most notably between John Shearer the Dundee Baptist minister and W. Holms Coats, Principal of the Baptist Theological College of Scotland. Prior to the 1940s

---

[86] Jim Hamilton, Ian Roberts & Peter Sampson, *East Kilbride Baptist Church Silver Jubilee 1954–1979* (East Kilbride: private publication, 1979), pp. 5–7, 19.

[87] *Souvenir Brochure to commemorate the Opening of East Kilbride Baptist Church 9th April 1960*, p. 11. See also D.R. Watts, 'Lanarkshire', in Bebbington (ed.), *Baptists in Scotland: A History*, pp. 193–194.

[88] See Chapter 5, pp. 142–145.

there had been cordial relations between the two because Shearer had been invited to speak at College events in 1921[89] and Coats had inducted Shearer into his Rattray Street pastorate in Dundee in the same year[90] and later preached for him at the Diamond Jubilee services in that congregation in 1938.[91] However, the trigger point for a new conflict over the theological soundness of the college came as a result of Coats's presidential address to the Baptist Union Assembly in October 1938.[92] Shearer would refer to that presentation as one which 'euologized the leaders of Modernist Infidelity and spoke of the Bible as an erroneous book.'[93] Looking back in the 1940s, Shearer, in reflection on the Roberts controversy, wrote: 'The whole tutorial staff of the College warmly supported him. . . . By its action at that time the College revealed its true character and from that hour it has been known throughout the whole land as a frankly Modernist institution.'[94] The years that followed would be ones of serious conflict over the training of candidates for pastoral ministry in Scottish Baptist ranks.

In 1944 the Jubilee year of the college Shearer issued a series of pamphlets attacking theological liberalism in that institution, in particular directing his aim at the Principal Dr Coats and lecturer Dr Miller. The pressure led to the College staff producing a 'Statement' of their theological convictions in June 1944, signed by W. Holms Coats and Alexander B. Miller and James Hair. After declaring their acceptance of the Declaration of Principle of the Baptist Union they highlighted five doctrines of particular importance to them, in response to recent criticism on these five doctrinal issues.[95] Firstly: 'The Inspiration of the Scriptures'; Secondly: 'The Fall of Man'; Thirdly: 'The Deity of Christ'; Fourth: 'The Doctrine of the Atonement'; Fifth: 'The Second Coming of Christ';[96] However, Shearer and his friends were not

---

[89] For example, Baptist Theological College of Scotland Report, *Scottish Baptist Yearbook 1922*, p. 6.

[90] *SBM*, 47.10 (October 1921), p. 119.

[91] Minutes, Rattray Street Baptist Church, Dundee, 1928–1945, GD/CH/B/2/1/3, June 14, 1938. The minutes are held in Dundee City Archives.

[92] W. Holms Coats, 'The Church's Task', *Scottish Baptist Yearbook 1939*, pp. 168–177.

[93] John Shearer, *The Menace of Modernism with Reply to Criticism* (n.p., 1944), p. 4, cited by Kenneth B.E. Roxburgh, 'The Fundamentalist Controversy Concerning the Baptist Theological College of Scotland', *Baptist History and Heritage*, Vol.36, Nos 1–2 (Winter/Spring 2001), p. 258. It is the standard account of this controversy.

[94] John Shearer, *Modernism: The Enemy of the Evangelical Faith* (n.p.: n.d.), p. 13.

[95] Shearer, *Modernism: The Enemy of the Evangelical Faith*, pp. 8–17.

[96] *The Baptist Theological College of Scotland Statement by Principal and Lecturers June 1944*, n.p.

convinced and formed the Evangelical Baptist Fellowship on 27 June 1944 and classes were begun for 'Evangelicals, men and women'. This led to a three-year training course, advertised as meeting two evenings a week in the Christian Institute, Bothwell Street, Glasgow, from January 1945, where John Shearer and T.J. Harvey lectured. In October 1946 the Evangelical Baptist Fellowship Bible College (EBFBC) moved to 153 West Regents Street, then in 1949 to Queens Drive, Glasgow, with Dr Henry Curr as Principal. Curr had been a Professor at McMaster University in Toronto and later Principal of All Nations College in Hertfordshire. It was ironic that during this time he worshipped in Queen's Park Baptist Church, Glasgow, in the same congregation as Dr Coats and his family. In later years, when the controversy had died down the former secretary and treasurer of the EBFBC, D.S.K. Mcleay and J.D. Taylor became members of the Baptist College Committee and served as Presidents of the Baptist Union in 1959 and 1965 respectively.[97] The new college failed to attract sufficient students and those graduating found it difficult to gain pastoral settlements in Scottish Baptist churches. It was a painful episode in Scottish Baptist life.

### Relationships with other Christian Churches
#### Partnership with Southern Baptists

A different approach to church-planting and evangelism in Scotland was launched at the end of the 1950s with the partnership agreement with the Foreign Mission Board of the Southern Baptist Convention (SBC). From 6–22 February 1959 fifteen Southern Baptist ministers came to conduct missions in Scottish Baptist congregations visiting nine association areas in Ayrshire, Borders, Edinburgh, Fife, Glasgow, Lanarkshire, Northern (and Shetland), Perthshire and Stirlingshire.[98] It appears that many of the churches received at least a single visit from one of the American team. Adelaide Place Baptist Church in Glasgow was the venue for a united mission in the city on the second week with meetings each evening. However, 'the numbers attending were not great, rising from 100 to 200 and 500 on the night of the monthly Baptist Youth Rally. There were 'four definite conversions ... and many rededications were made.' The best response appears to have been from the three-day mission in Peterhead where the aggregate attendance over five meetings was 1,050 with fifteen people coming forward for prayer including

---

[97] This information is given in Derek B. Murray, *Scottish Baptist College Centenary History*, p. 25 and Kenneth Roxburgh. 'Your Word is Truth: Theological Developments among Twentieth-Century Scottish Baptists', p. 142.

[98] The plan was explained for the mission in *SBM*, 84.10 (October 1958), p. 2; See also 'Evangelistic', *Scottish Baptist Yearbook 1959*, p. 161; *SBM*, 85.2 (February 1959), p. 4.

twelve individuals making a first profession of faith.[99] The Scottish team were part of a much larger group of Southern Baptists scattered across the country and even to the Channel Islands and France for their evangelistic work. The report they submitted to the various British Baptist bodies afterwards was very clear in its assessment of the current state of Christianity in the country and its prospects for the future. 'One thing is sure – poor, old, war-scarred, battered, disillusioned Britain is in desperate need of an awakening of evangelical, evangelistic New Testament faith.'[100] It was followed up the next year by twelve ministers and laymen conducting missions in Greenock, Motherwell, Dundee, Fraserburgh, Ayr, Glasgow and some other un-named places during which '84 decisions for Christ were made'.[101] It was the start of what was to become a significantly fruitful partnership between Southern Baptists and their Scottish colleagues over the remainder of the twentieth century.

### The Wider Baptist Family

Scottish Baptists were interested in the work of other branches of the Baptist family around the world, as well as that of the work of Christians of other theological traditions. It is only possible to give a few select examples from stories featured in the *Scottish Baptist Magazine* (*SBM*) Inevitably priority was given to Scottish Baptists serving overseas, such as the acknowledgement of W. Morrow Cook's induction as President of the Baptist Union of South Africa, noting that he had previously served as a minister of churches in Johnstone and Partick, Glasgow.[102] Likewise the *SBM* editor commended Professor Robert J. McCracken, now holding the chair of Systematic Theology at McMaster University, who had been elected as President of the Baptist Convention of Ontario and Quebec that same year.[103] Annual Greetings were printed from the President and Secretary of the Baptist World Alliance, alongside those of the President of the Baptist Union of Scotland.[104] BWA Sunday in February was always highlighted in the denominational periodical, promoting the work of colleagues overseas.[105] Baptist young people were encouraged to be outward looking in the practice of their faith. Joel

---

[99] 'Christian Venturers Campaign', *SBM*, 85.4 (April1959), p. 6.

[100] K. Owen White (First Church, Houston), 'Southern Baptists in Britain' *SBM*, 85.9 (September 1959), p. 12.

[101] 'Evangelistic', *Scottish Baptist Yearbook 1960*, p. 159;

[102] *SBM*, 71.2 (February 1945), p. 1.

[103] *SBM*, 71.9 (September 1945), p. 1.

[104] For example, *SBM*, 81.1 (January 1955), p. 4.

[105] *SBM*, 76.1 (January 1950), pp. 9–10.

Sorenson of Sweden, Youth Secretary of the Baptist World Alliance (BWA) was the guest speaker at the first West of Scotland Baptist youth conference in 1950.[106] A letter to young Baptists in Scotland from Sven Ohm, Secretary of the European Baptist Federation (EBF) Youth Committee was published both in its original German and in England translation in July 1960.[107] David Coats, secretary of the West of Scotland Baptist Youth Conference, from Queen's Park Baptist Church, Glasgow, who had been a delegate at the Baptist Youth Congress in Stockholm in 1949 and at the European Baptist Youth leader's conference in Holland in 1950, had the privilege also of being a delegate at the July 1950 BWA Congress in Cleveland, USA.[108] A full report from the Congress was featured in the September 1950 issue of this periodical.[109] The Jubilee Congress of 1955 in London naturally received the most prominence with a feature in the February 1955 *SBM* issue,[110] followed by an update on the number of delegates already booked to attend from around the world,[111] prior to the actual Congress features in September that year[112] and one on its new President Dr Theodore Adams in December 1955.[113] Information about the 1960 Rio de Janeiro BWA Congress in Brazil was very limited due to the 'prohibitive cost' of attending it. There were no Scottish Baptist delegates in attendance that year.[114] T. Kerr Speirs and Donald McCallum represented Scottish Baptists at the EBF Youth leaders' conference in summer 1960.[115] Anna Valberg Anderson, Baptist Youth Secretary in Denmark, through her contact with Donald McCallum provided an article outlining the nature and extent of Baptist youth work in her homeland.[116] Relationships between Scottish Baptists and members of the wider Baptist family were undoubtedly strengthened through attending these conferences or congresses in the years following World War Two.

---

[106] *SBM*, 76.6 (June 1950), p. 8.

[107] *SBM*, 86.7 (July 1960), p. 2.

[108] *SBM*, 76.6 (June 1950), p. 8.

[109] *SBM*, 76.9 (September 1950), pp. 3–4.

[110] *SBM*, 81.3 (March 1955), pp. 1–2.

[111] *SBM*, 81.5 (May 1955), p. 3.

[112] *SBM*, 81.9 (September 1955), pp. 3, 5–8.

[113] *SBM*, 81.12 (December 1955), pp. 4–5.

[114] *SBM*, 86.11 (November 1960), pp. 1–2. '91st Annual Report by The Secretary', *Scottish Baptist Yearbook 1961*, p. 132.

[115] *SBM*, 86.7 (July 1960), pp. 4–5.

[116] *SBM*, 86.8 (August 1960), pp. 4–5.

Reports on Baptist work in other countries was also a common feature in the *SBM* including Burma in July 1955[117], and Continental Europe, featuring Baptists in Yugoslavia, Romania, Bulgaria, Czechoslovakia, Austria and Belgium later the same year.[118] A feature article on a visit by overseas Baptists to their Russian co-religionists highlighted the conditions under which they operated in October 1955.[119] Scottish Baptists channelled aid to Continental colleagues through the British Baptist Continental Society. This work was carried out each year firstly, by raising funds for its regular annual commitments; secondly, by selecting particular projects to support, and thirdly, by assisting European Baptists who came to Britain for academic studies. In 1960, in the first category, an annual grant of £50 was given to the Finnish-speaking Finnish Baptist Union for work in Helsinki, together with £40 for youth work; the European Federation Women's Work, for which £25 per annum was granted, and £15 per annum towards the cost of mailing the Baptist Ministers' Fellowship Journal the 'Fraternal' to all Continental Baptist pastors. In the second category, $1,000 was awarded to the Polish Baptist Union towards the cost of their new seminary and denominational offices; 8,500 Swiss francs to Hungary towards the cost of a Ford Consul for their work there; £500 towards the cost of the erection of the John Smyth Memorial Church, soon to be erected in Amsterdam, together with £10 10/- towards the Bible Pavilion at the Brussels Exhibition. In the third category in 1960 the Revd Z. Pawlik of Poland was awarded the cost of his training at Westhill College in Birmingham; £50 was awarded to Paul Ferreira, a Portuguese Baptist towards his costs at Regents' Park College, Oxford, and an agreement to offer incidental expenses to assist any Russian students at Baptist Colleges in the United Kingdom.[120] Support in various forms for Baptist work in Continental Europe was a significant priority for British Baptists in the post-war years. Occasional articles covered Baptist work in Africa that included, for example, Nyasaland, in March 1960.[121] The evidence gained from issues of the *SBM* to 1960 suggested that the outward-looking approach taken by Scottish Baptists towards co-religionists in other countries in the pre-war years had been maintained in this era.

The BMS was also regularly featured in this periodical. The BMS Mobile Exhibition due to tour Scotland in autumn 1950 was commended to readers. They were informed that its features included models of BMS-run hospitals – Moorshead Memorial at Udayagiri in Orissa, India, and at Pimu in the

---

[117] *SBM*, 81.7 (July 1955), p. 3.

[118] *SBM*, 81.7 (July 1955), p. 9.

[119] *SBM*, 81.10 (October 1955), pp. 1–3.

[120] *SBM*, 86.1 (January 1960), p. 10.

[121] *SBM*, 86.3 (March 1960), pp. 3–6.

Congo Republic; the church at Kinshasa and the Mission station at Dacca as well as maps of the three Mission Fields in India, China and Africa, together with panels displaying Bible translation, printing, transport, orphanages and famine relief work carried out by BMS personnel.[122] The Glasgow Medical Mission Auxiliary of the BMS celebrated its jubilee in March 1955. An article was published that month highlighting the significant support it had provided to overseas mission through its fund-raising activities supporting BMS personnel. In 1954 £1,332 was raised for this cause. Post-World War Two it adopted in 1945 Nurse Maise Chaplin, Knightswood Baptist Church; in 1948 Dr Jack Gray from Kelso Baptist Church; in 1952 Nurse Mary Shearer, Rattray Street Baptist Church, Dundee; 1952 Nurse Jean McLellan, Harper Memorial Baptist Church, Glasgow; and in 1953 Dr Henderson Smith, Twerton Church, near Bath in England.[123] Regular updates on the changes of BMS personnel in various fields of service were also provided.[124] The centenary of the start of BMS work in China, 1860–1960, was also commemorated.[125] Scottish Baptist support for BMS remained consistently high in the post-war years.

Good practices or inspirational stories from other Christian traditions were highlighted. The testimony of Japanese Christian Muneharu Kitagaki, was known through him worshipping at St Andrews Baptist Church while studying at the University.[126] A feature on Bishop Eivind Berggrav, head of the Lutheran Church in Norway concerning his courageous defiance of the Nazis during World War Two was written by Baptist naval chaplain Douglas Robb.[127] Another article on the World Council of Churches highlighted its work in assisting sixty-two victims of Nazi persecution.[128] The Second General Assembly of the WCC at Evanston was reported on with details given of locations where presentations would be made on its activities.[129] A follow-up conference in Scotland exploring the themes promoted at Evanston was attended by two Scottish Baptists including the WA President Mrs Nisbet.[130] German Evangelical Churches were commended for the changes

---

[122] *SBM*, 76.9 (September 1950), p. 4.

[123] *SBM*, 81.3 (March 1955), pp. 5–6

[124] For example, *SBM*, 81.10 (October 1955), p. 6.

[125] *SBM*, 86.3 (March 1960), p. 8.

[126] *SBM*, 83.7 (July 1957), pp. 2–3.

[127] *SBM*, 71.12 (December 1945), pp. 4–5.

[128] *SBM*, 76.7 (July 1950), p. 5.

[129] *SBM*, 81.4 (April 1955), p. 8.

[130] *SBM*, 81.11 (November 1955), p. 21.

made in their practices in relation to the German Government. A more critical engagement with the authorities was viewed as a necessary corrective to previous subservience to the authoritarian state.[131] In 1955 the Scottish Churches Ecumenical Committee welcomed a delegation of the Russian Orthodox and Lutheran Churches. One of the host church leaders for the visit in Edinburgh was the Baptist Union of Scotland President, W.D. Macgregor, minister of Alloa Baptist Church. It was viewed as a good opportunity to engage with representatives of the Christian Church in a land where religious liberty was seriously restricted.[132] Many Scottish Baptists were comfortable in working with colleagues of other Christian traditions in these years, but only a smaller proportion of them were enthusiastic about the formal ecumenical ties developing between Protestant Churches in the post-war years.

The issue of religious liberty in other countries was a significant concern. In January 1945 there was a feature on attempts by the World Evangelical Alliance to draw attention to events in Spain where General Franco had brutally repressed all but Roman Catholic forms of worship, closing Protestant churches, with two-thirds of church members exiled, imprisoned, or executed for their faith.[133] There was delight that Romanian Baptists were now free from the persistent persecution they had experienced over the past twenty-five years. Russian troops occupying the country had insisted that the draconian law on which it was based should be repealed.[134] There was an encouraging 1958 report on the growing religious liberty for Evangelical Christians in Colombia, South America.[135] Another important issue in the years immediately following World War Two concerned the necessity of providing material assistance to the many refugees needing support. Contributions were channelled through interdenominational agencies. The forerunner body of the charity now known as Christian Aid was the main conduit for the funds raised by British Churches for this purpose. Scottish Baptists were keen to play their part in supporting this work.[136] They continued to share a real passion for Christian work outside their country,[137] conscious that the opportunities for witness and service needed to be grasped.

---

[131] *SBM*, 81.4 (April 1955), p. 3.

[132] *SBM*, 81.9 (September 1955), p. 9.

[133] *SBM*, 71.1 (January 1945), pp. 1–2.

[134] *SBM*, 71.4 (April 1945), p. 1.

[135] *SBM*, 84.8 (August 1958), pp. 4–5.

[136] *SBM*, 86.2 (February 1960), pp. 3–4.

[137] See Talbot, 'Baptists and Other Christian Churches in the First Half of the Twentieth Century', in Bebbington & Sutherland (eds), *Interfaces Baptists and Others*, pp. 171–172.

## World Council of Churches

The growth in inter-church co-operation in helping the refugees and displaced people in Europe after World War II, including the formation of Christian Aid, had led to renewed calls for the formation of a World Council of Churches (WCC).[138] This body was duly set up in Amsterdam in 1948. Alexander Clark, then minister of Motherwell Baptist Church, represented the interests of this small Scottish denomination. On his return a favourable report to the BUS Council[139] led these church leaders to recommend affiliation with the WCC and its corresponding agency in the United Kingdom the British Council of Churches, to the October annual Assembly.[140] A favourable decision was attained in 1948 by the smallest of majorities, eighty one votes to eighty, after an initially tied vote,[141] that would lead to regular calls for re-consideration of 'the official Baptist position' in the years to come, especially following the 1951 Assembly debate led by the delegates of Charlotte Baptist Chapel, Edinburgh, who had sought an immediate withdrawal from the WCC.[142] The motion to withdraw was defeated by 218 votes to 113, but it was raised again at the 1953 Dundee Assembly where a decision was taken by the office-bearers of the Union in collaboration with Charlotte Chapel delegates, and approved by the Assembly delegates, to create a formal committee of enquiry to investigate the activities of the WCC.[143] At the 1955 Assembly a sixteen page report was presented setting out the case for and against affiliation, a majority of the working group

---

[138] W. Holms Coats in commending the planning meetings for this new body, suggested that a WCC 'may nevertheless give a new impulse to world Christianity, foster Christian unity and indicate lines of advance in evangelism and practical Christian service specially relevant to our desperate situation.' *SBM*, 72.8 (August 1946), p. 1.

[139] *Scottish Baptist Yearbook 1949*, p. 124. The launch of the WCC was reported in the *SBM* in March 1948. The programme was commended in the *SBM*, 74.8 (August 1948), p. 4. Some details of its work were given in the September 1948 issue of the *SBM*, p. 4. The aims and objectives of the WCC were then commended to Scottish Baptists in the October issue of this periodical. *SBM*, 74.10 (October 1948), Editorial, p. 1, and p. 7.

[140] Baptist Union of Scotland Assembly, Tuesday 19 October 1948, *Scottish Baptist Yearbook 1949*, pp. 120–121. Murray, *First Hundred Years*, pp. 113–116.

[141] Baptist Union of Scotland Assembly, Wednesday 20 October 1948, *Scottish Baptist Yearbook 1949*, p. 124.

[142] Baptist Union of Scotland Assembly, Tuesday and Wednesday 23–24 October 1951, pp. 121–122. Balfour, 'Twentieth Century since 1914', p. 75.

[143] Baptist Union of Scotland Assembly, Tuesday 20 October 1953, *Scottish Baptist Yearbook 1954*, p. 116.

recommending affiliation for a seven year period. The two dissenters, elders of Charlotte Chapel, recommended immediate withdrawal.[144] The Union's largest congregation then circulated a critique of the WCC to all sister Baptist congregations and informed the Assembly of Charlotte Chapel's intention to withdraw from the Union. Assembly delegates undoubtedly influenced by this course of action voted by a majority of 197 to 176 to withdraw from the WCC for seven years 'in the hope that the basis of the WCC be brought nearer our own Faith and Order.'[145] It was unfortunate that it was followed so soon afterwards by a request from Charlotte Chapel to withdraw from the British Council of Churches and the Scottish Churches Ecumenical Committee. At the time the majority of delegates by 207 votes to 19 felt it was unfair to expect more changes so quickly and the proposal was rejected, it was inevitable from that assembly that Charlotte Chapel would resign from Union membership.[146] Wider ecumenical affairs that in the first half of the twentieth century had seen a greater convergence of opinions in Scottish Baptist ranks[147] now had developed into a source of serious tension for many Baptists in Scotland unpersuaded of the case for this new body, the WCC. In fact, the vast majority of sister Baptist Unions and Conventions did not join the WCC, though British Baptists in the Baptist Union of Great Britain and Ireland were strong advocates of and participants in the WCC.[148] Opinions were strongly expressed on both sides of this debate in Scotland, but it was surely unwise to affiliate when opinions were so polarised and evenly split within the denomination. It is extremely difficult with hindsight to see how the Union's leadership could have allowed this situation to develop. It was inevitable that future assemblies would be asked to reconsider this verdict.

*Social Action*

Temperance was still an important issue to Scottish Baptists though far less prominent in denominational pronouncements on social issues in the post-war

---

[144] 'Report of the Assembly Committee of the World Council of Churches for presentation to the Assembly 1955', *Scottish Baptist Yearbook 1956*, pp. 193–211.

[145] Baptist Union of Scotland Assembly, Tuesday 25 October 1955, *Scottish Baptist Yearbook 1956*, p. 123.

[146] Baptist Union of Scotland Assembly, Wednesday 26 October 1955, *Scottish Baptist Yearbook 1956*, p. 123.

[147] 'Report of the Assembly Committee of the World Council of Churches for presentation to the Assembly 1955', p. 195. See also Talbot, 'Baptists and other Christian Churches in the First Half of the Twentieth Century', in Bebbington & Sutherland (eds), *Interfaces, Baptists and Others*, pp. 156–176.

[148] Talbot, 'Baptists and other Christian Churches', pp. 174–175.

years. Concerns were raised and supported by delegates at the 1947 Assembly, at the ease with which alcohol was available for young men on active service. The Government and Armed Forces leaders were sent a communication to that effect.[149] The churches and individual members were committed to social care although not on the scale of the later nineteenth century. It is appropriate to highlight a few of the concerns of Scottish Baptists on social issues in these years. It must also be acknowledged that some individual church members gave years of excellent service in working in posts that addressed issues of social concern. John R.S Henderson of Rattray Street Baptist Church, Dundee, for example, succeeded his father as superintendent of the Dundee Working Boy's Home from 1936 to its closure in 1968. He was also Superintendent of the Curr Night Refuge for destitute people and welfare officer to the Dundee Discharged Prisoners' Aid Society, and after-care office for Borstal Services in Angus and Perthshire.[150] There was a growing concern amongst Scottish Baptists in the post-war years about the need for residential accommodation for elderly church members.[151] Rattray Street Baptist Church, Dundee, opened the Robertson Rest Home for members in 1947. Charlotte Chapel, Edinburgh, purchased a large villa for its members in 1955 in Newhaven Road, Edinburgh, a facility called Beulah Eventide Home that opened in 1958.[152] Gambling in its various forms was a concern for Baptists. The linkage of the pools with football was raised at the 1945 Baptist Assembly where delegates supported the Football Association in its proposal to ban football pools.[153] The scheme to introduce Premium Bonds in 1956 was opposed.[154] The Social Services Committee presented a clear statement on this subject. 'It is very disturbed by the proposal to issue Premium Bonds. This was regarded as a retrograde step and quite undignified. Gambling as a means of raising money for national requirements was condemned outright.'[155] The Report on the Royal Commission on Betting was also discussed by this committee with a report sent to the Secretary of State for Scotland in response. The other topics considered in 1951 were 'Sex Education', 'the

---

[149] BUS Assembly, 23 October, 1947 *Scottish Baptist Yearbook 1948*, p. 115.

[150] Murray, 'Be not Conformed but Transformed', p. 236.

[151] 'Social Services Report', Baptist Union Assembly, 21 October 1948, *Scottish Baptist Yearbook 1949*, p. 126. It continued to be discussed in succeeding years, for example, *Scottish Baptist Yearbook 1957*, p. 161; 1958, p. 167.

[152] *Scottish Baptist Yearbook 1946*, pp. 82–83; and Balfour, 'Twentieth Century since 1914', p. 79.

[153] *Scottish Baptist Yearbook 1946*, pp. 82–83; 1954, p. 152.

[154] *Scottish Baptist Yearbook 1957*, p. 161.

[155] Murray, 'Be not Conformed but Transformed', p. 244.

Christian doctrine of Work', and 'the Use of Sunday'.[156] An 8,000 signature petition against Sunday opening of businesses was sent to the Government in 1960 with the strong support of the Baptist Union Council.[157] There was a continuing concern for the needs of millions of refugees in Continental Europe after the war.[158] Scottish Baptists agreed to support an initiative led by the Society of Friends in sending large quantities of clothing to assist them.[159] Scottish Baptists at the 1955 Assembly supported a World Council of Churches statement condemning the South African Government's 1953 'Bantu Education Act' (later renamed the 'Black Education Act'), which implemented further aspects of the apartheid policies.[160] Significant numbers of Scottish Baptists were concerned about the proliferation of weapons of war, especially nuclear weapons.[161] John McKendrick, a well-known Baptist evangelist and minister, and declared pacifist, had protested at the 1951 Union assembly at the silence of his denomination over the arms race.[162] Later in his October 1958 Presidential Address to the assembly, he made this practical application of the gospel: 'I cannot, in view of the Cross of our Lord Jesus Christ, understand the Church of Jesus Christ countenancing modern warfare as a method of redemption, and particularly the use of nuclear warfare . . .

---

[156] 'Assembly Social Service Conference Discusses Sunday Labour', *SBM*, 83.12 (December 1957), pp. 4–5. *Scottish Baptist Yearbook 1952*, p. 154. 'Sunday Labour' was viewed as a growing problem, *Scottish Baptist Yearbook 1958*, p. 167; A comprehensive survey of its extent was sought from the churches, *Scottish Baptist Yearbook 1959*, p. 169.

[157] *Scottish Baptist Yearbook 1961*, p. 133.

[158] 'There Was No Room', *SBM*, 83.12 (December 1957), pp. 1–2.

[159] *Scottish Baptist Yearbook 1954*, p. 152. However, there was also a long-established inter-church organisation based in Glasgow collecting aid for the refugees in which Scottish Baptists were active supporters. Mary B. Hardie, 'For Our Women', *SBM*, 82.3 (March 1956), p. 6. European Baptists also had a Relief Committee based in Vienna, Austria. Scottish Baptists were connected to it through the European Baptist Federation, *SBM*, 83.1 (January 1957), p. 9.

[160] *Scottish Baptist Yearbook 1956*, p. 164. Concerns about racism was expressed by Scottish Baptists not only concerning South Africa but also in the USA, *SBM*, 84:10 (October 1958), p. 3;

[161] The British Council of Churches report: 'The End of Atomic Power', was discussed at a special meeting of the Social Services Committee in 1946, with a call to the churches to 'take a lead in responsible citizenship' on this subject. *Scottish Baptist Yearbook 1947*, p. 80. The Social Services Committee prepared a statement on this subject in 1959. James Taylor, 'The Christian Church and the Bomb', *SBM*, 85.6 (June 1959), pp. 2–3.

[162] Murray, 'Be not Conformed but Transformed', p. 242.

even in our own self-defence ....'¹⁶³ There were some longstanding concerns that were topics of consideration over a number of years and on which the Social Services Committee sought to provide guidance, most notably on the remarriage of divorcees and on the spread of communism.¹⁶⁴ Scottish Baptists were aware of their limited numbers and influence, but this did not hinder their desire to contribute to the national debates on these and other topics.

With the ending of World War Two there was a requirement to rise to the challenge of a changing world. Scottish Christians of the different networks of churches or denominations were confident that they could re-engage with Scots who had lost contact with the churches during the war years and plant new congregations in the growing number of new towns or additional housing estates on the edge of existing communities. Scottish Baptists, though relatively small in number were in step with this conviction. They were well aware of the growing proportion of their fellow citizens who had an increasingly tenuous link to any church, especially amongst younger adults and men in particular. The home evangelisation efforts in which they and other Scottish Christians were engaged were as significant as in any previous era of Scottish history and as a result there were a significant proportion of the population who reconnected with the churches in the late 1940s or early 1950s. At the height of that progress the nation was gripped with the remarkable All-Scotland Crusade with Billy Graham. There have been lengthy debates about its impact on the Scottish Churches, but for Scottish Baptists there was clear though modest sustained numerical growth in the remainder of that decade. Scottish Baptists, although unable to raise much financial support for church extension did plant a number of new congregations which gave them a foothold in new housing areas like Pollok in Glasgow and Granton, Edinburgh, and especially in new towns like East Kilbride and Glenrothes. A new chapter in church-planting began with the launch of a partnership with Southern Baptists that would flourish in future years. Connections with the wider Baptist family were strong in this era, as were ties with other Scottish Churches, but the decision to affiliate with the World Council of Churches by the smallest margin was very unwise and caused unnecessary division in their ranks. However, in 1960 Scottish Baptists were in reasonable heart having made significant progress in their work since 1945.

---

[163] *Scottish Baptist Yearbook 1959*, pp. 13–14.

[164] *Scottish Baptist Yearbook 1950*, pp. 143–144; 1951, p. 142. A submission was made to the Royal Commission on Marriage and Divorce in 1952 urging the retention of the current law on this subject. *Scottish Baptist Yearbook 1953*, p. 157. A proposal for an assembly seminar on this subject in 1954 was agreed. *Scottish Baptist Yearbook 1954*, p. 152.

CHAPTER 8

# Christian Witness in an Age of Religious Crisis[1]: The 1960s and 1970s

## An Overview of these Two Decade

The 1960s ushered in an era of extraordinary social transformation not only in Western Europe, but also in North America and Australasia. It is very clear that in the midst of huge social changes the Christian Churches struggled to adjust to the new circumstances with which they were faced in the 1960s and 1970s, but this must not be contrasted with exaggerated claims of modest numerical religious revival in the nation in the 1950s. The process of secularisation had already begun well before the 1960s.[2] It was not only Nonconformist clergy who struggled; this experience was shared by their Established Church colleagues as well.[3] Anthony Russell, Rector of Whitchurch, Shropshire, noted that clergymen even in small town locations like his own parish no longer occupied positions of prominence or centrality in the social, cultural, intellectual, political or any other aspect of national life. He noted that specialist caring roles formerly occupied by the clergy were now increasingly taken over by more specialist organisations like the Samaritans. The changes in youth culture had also made work amongst the young much more difficult.[4] There was a particular sense of betrayal felt by the new approach of the BBC which had previously been strongly supportive of the Christian Churches, but now its direction of travel was firmly in the opposite

---

[1] The language of 'religious crisis' in this era is commonly used in the scholarly literature on this subject. For example, Callum G. Brown, *Religion and Society in Twentieth-Century Britain* (Harlow: Pearson, 2006), pp. 224-225; and in the title of the standard work on this subject—Hugh McLeod, *The Religious Crisis of the 1960s* (Oxford: Oxford University Press, 2007).

[2] Clive Field, *Britain's Last Religious Revival: Quantifying Belonging, Behaving, and Believing in the Long 1950s*, p. 110.

[3] Stewart Ranson, Alan Bryman & Bob Hinings, *Clergy, Ministers & Priests* (London: Routledge & Kegan Paul, 1977), pp. 2–3, 169–170.

[4] Anthony Russell, *The Clerical Profession* (London: S.P.C.K., 1980), pp. 127–129, 262, 274–278.

direction.[5] In this context, for example, there was a fall of 19% in churchgoing in the Church of England in the 1960s,[6] with infant baptism numbers declining by 60% between 1956 and 1976.[7] The Methodist Church in Great Britain saw its membership figures decline by 14% in the 1960s and a further 24% in the 1970s.[8] In Scotland the two largest denominations the Church of Scotland and the Roman Catholic Church saw infant baptism statistics decline by 50% and almost 40% between 1967 and 1982.[9] In the light of what was happening in other British Churches during these two decades, it is appropriate to consider how Scottish Baptists adjusted to this changing social and religious environment.

In October 1959 in his report to the Annual Assembly the Union Secretary communicated his confidence in the Christian Church rising to the likely challenges of the new decade. He was not minimising the difficulties, but declared: 'Despite our concerns, it is mainly a hopeful world in which we live...'[10] In the summary of statistics from September 1959, including non-Union Baptist Churches, the membership total was 20,139, a slight fall from the 20,261 figure the previous year.[11] At the Centenary Assembly, a decade later in 1969, there was an inevitable focus on the growth of the present Baptist Union from 51 member churches in 1869 to 160 in 1969. When the comparative data for 1959 to 1969 is considered there is some encouragement for Scottish Baptists. First of all, the number of member churches had risen by five from 155–160. Secondly, the number of congregations reporting decreases in membership had fallen from eighty to sixty-five. Thirdly, there were District Associations whose membership totals had increased over the decade, for example, Lanarkshire and Stirling and Clackmannanshire, the former from 1,932 to 2,074 and the latter from 969 to 1,046. However, in line with other denominations there was an overall fall in membership figures from 20,139 to 17,547 and the admissions to membership by baptism down from 531 to 226.

---

[5] *Broadcasting, Society and the Church: Report of the Broadcasting Commission of the General Synod of the Church of England* (London: Church Information Office, 1973), p. 1. See also McLeod, *The Religious Crisis of the 1960s*, p. 195.

[6] P.A. Welsby, *A History of the Church of England 1945–1980* (Oxford; Oxford University Press, 1984), p. 104.

[7] Callum G. Brown, *The Death of Christian Britain* (Abingdon: Routledge, 2nd ed. 2009), p. 168.

[8] Clive Field, 'Joining and Leaving British Methodism since the 1960s', in Leslie J. Francis and Yaacov J. Katz (eds.), *Joining and Leaving Religion: Research Perspectives* (Leominster: Gracewing, 2000), p. 65.

[9] Brown, *Death of Christian Britain*, p. 168; Brown, *Religion and Society*, p. 237.

[10] '90th Annual Report by the Secretary', *Scottish Baptist Yearbook* 1960, p. 131.

[11] *Scottish Baptist Yearbook 1960*, p. 89.

There were only forty churches increasing in membership compared to sixty-five declining in numbers. Overall, there was no doubt that many churches found it harder to recruit new attendees and members in this decade, in particular finding it more difficult to attract or retain the interest of some younger people, but the proportionate decline was much smaller than in the larger denominations in Scotland.

At the end of the 1970s there had been further decline in Scottish Baptist ranks. The number of churches had reduced from 160 to 157 and the overall membership figures from 17,547 to 16,271. It appears that the majority of the decline in recorded District Association figures had been in the larger cities[12] such as Glasgow, down from 3,502 to 2,927 and Edinburgh and Lothians, down from 2,835 to 2,712; and other Central Belt areas like Renfrewshire down from 1,407 to 1,251, together with Stirling and Clackmannanshire down from 1,046 to 861. However, it was not a clear-cut picture of decline. There were District Associations where the membership figures had increased Argyllshire and the Isles up from 215 to 234; Ayrshire and Dumfriesshire up from 1,139 to 1,184; Dunbartonshire up from 409 to 433; Lanarkshire up from 2,075 to 2,155; and Northern up from 1,245 to 1,325. What is more one of the key indicators of success in evangelism, admission to membership by baptism had seen a significant rise from 226 to 656 by September 1979. There were now sixty-seven churches increasing in membership, a rise of twenty-seven, but also sixty-nine decreasing, compared to sixty-five a decade earlier.[13] These figures imply that a greater proportion of these churches had adjusted to the changing religious environment and were beginning to see encouragements in their evangelistic endeavours. By contrast, there were still many causes that were unsuccessful in this aspect of their work. In summary, dedicated outreach work in the 1970s was showing signs that there was the potential for an overall increase in membership in the next decade.

### New Churches and Church-Growth in the 1960s and 1970s

In Stirling and Clackmannanshire (SACBA) the growth in the 1960s was largely as a result of church-planting.[14] However, there were other factors that would enable growth. For example, in Stirling the growth in its population together, with the university presence from 1967, contributed significantly to the increased attendances in the Murray Place congregation. By contrast

---

[12] More detailed information confirming this point is given in Kenneth M. Stewart, *The Baptist Union of Scotland Towards 2000: a Statistical Look at Scottish Baptist Church Life in the Latter Half of the Twentieth Century* (Glasgow: Baptist Union of Scotland, n.d [1996]).

[13] *Scottish Baptist Yearbook 1970*, p. 100; and *1980*, p. 137.

[14] Talbot, *Brief History of Central Baptist Association*, pp. 25–26.

declining populations during the 1960s, in part due to reducing economic opportunities, led to reduced memberships in the Baptist Churches at Alva, Bo'ness and Tillicoultry.[15] The Stirling congregation also pioneered in summer 1960 a new initiative for evangelism amongst children. It hosted, at the request of the regional Baptist association, a first 'Holiday Bible School' which was a great success, but extremely hard work due to a lack of volunteers from neighbouring Baptist churches. However, innovative outreach methods like this in the summer months played a significant part in strengthening the work amongst young people in these SACBA congregations. The first of the two church-plants in this region of Scotland in the 1960s took place in Cumbernauld which grew from a tiny village to a New Town under the auspices of the Cumbernauld Development Corporation. This congregation was launched in 1961 and constituted a year later with Peter Bryan called as its first pastor in August 1963. Archibald McColl was his successor, inducted in 1967. The church grew steadily over its first decade, with a significant number of transfer memberships as the town grew in population. Its peak membership of 106 was achieved in 1975. One of the distinctive features of this church was the support it received from sister congregations through its regional association and the Baptist Union, together with the gift of £18,000 donated by the Women's Auxiliary of the Baptist Union towards the cost of the erection of its building in 1965. The Cumbernauld Church launched an outreach Sunday School in the Abronhill area of the town in May 1971 with eighty-three names on the roll by October of that year with an average attendance of fifty each Sunday, which compared well with the 150 children in the Carbrain Sunday School. Morning services were started in January 1975 and continued until June 1983. There were a number of members converted through this venture. However, the work struggled to attract more than a small core of local members and the Sunday School also closed in June 1987. Archibald McColl did explore with the Baptist Union the possibility of a new work in the Balloch-Eastfield area between 1974 and 1976, but a lack of personnel to commence this initiative ensured that no further action was taken at that time.[16] But there was clear evidence of the desire of this vibrant church to plant further congregations had resources been available. The other new Baptist work in this region at this time was the development on the Cornton estate in Stirling. Murray Place Baptist Church began a Sunday School work in this new location in 1959. It attracted over a hundred young people on its first Sunday. A women's meeting linked to the Women's Auxiliary of the mother church was begun in 1961. A crisis over facilities for meetings led to

---

[15] L.N. Cowan and F.C. Wright, 'Central', in Bebbington (ed.), *Baptists in Scotland*, pp. 210–211.

[16] Isobel Jarvie, *Cumbernauld Baptist Church* (Cumbernauld: For the Church, 2002), pp. 1–12. 25–26, 45–46.

the building of a church hall that was opened in 1966.[17] J.M. Weiland, a Baptist minister engaged in further studies was appointed as student pastor for two years, and other student pastors were appointed to succeed him[18] prior to the constitution of the church in 1978, a development which led in the following year to David Bowker bring called as the first full-time pastor of this congregation.[19] This regional association had demonstrated that numerical church growth was possible in the 1960s even if it was a modest increase.

The other Baptist Association that saw overall numerical growth in the 1960s was Lanarkshire. In 1960 there were fifteen Baptist congregations there with around 2,200 members and adherents.[20] The steady increase in membership of the Baptist work in East Kilbride was a key factor in the prosperity of Baptist witness in this region. However, a number of members came from Glasgow congregations, for example, in Cambuslang, that were weakened by their numerical losses.[21] The East Mains congregation with 170 members started a new cause in the Westwood district in 1964 and in 1966 these two congregations combined to launch a further congregation in the Calderwood area. By 1981 one quarter of Baptists in Lanarkshire were in these congregations that had a total of 470 members, together with many children and young people. There was a short-lived attempt to plant a fourth congregation in nearby Stonehouse in 1976, but these were abandoned when proposals to extend the New Town were dropped soon after.[22] Another encouraging development was the work in Hamilton. The Baptist congregation had seen its numbers diminish from the 1930s, but under the ministries of Gordon Heath (1969–1976) and Alistair Begg (1977–1983) it grew remarkably from a low point of 137 in 1952 to 326 members by 1979.[23] By contrast economic factors played a major part in the decline of the formerly strong Motherwell and Wishaw congregations as the Steel Industry reduced its production capacity and the steady closure of coal mines had a similar impact on the fortunes of the Shotts and Uddington congregations.[24] However, the remarkable consolidation of the church-planting work in East

---

[17] P. Catherine Coles, *"To God Be The Glory" Retelling the Story of The Cornton – "A Church Within A Community"* (Stirling: Private publication, 1974), pp. 9, 12, 17.

[18] Coles, *"To God Be The Glory"*, pp. 18–22.

[19] Cowan & Wright, 'Central', p. 205.

[20] D.R. Watts, 'Lanarkshire', in Bebbington (ed.), *Baptists in Scotland*. p. 193.

[21] I am grateful to Dr Derek Murray for this information.

[22] Watts, 'Lanarkshire', p. 194.

[23] *Scottish Baptist Yearbook 1953*, p. 84; 1980, p. 129.

[24] Watts, 'Lanarkshire', pp. 194–195.

Kilbride ensured that Lanarkshire Baptists had every reason to enter the 1970s with confidence.

In the 1970s modest numerical growth continued in Lanarkshire Baptist Association with a membership increase up from 2,075 to 2,155. It was joined by a number of the smaller regional bodies in registering increases in membership in this decade. In Argyllshire and the Isles there was an increase of nineteen members from 215 to 234. This was mainly shared out amongst its member churches with the majority having a very small increase of two to four members. The largest increases were in Dunoon from ninety-six to one hundred and seventeen members and in Lochgilphead from thirty-six to forty-four members. Ayrshire and Dumfriesshire Baptist churches also recorded increased membership figures in this decade up from 1,139 to 1,184; In Dumfries the Baptist cause had been under serious threat of closure in the 1960s as its congregation had shrunk to a handful of members at the start of the decade, but from 1962 onwards there was a steady increase in attendance as teachers and medical staff moved into the area and joined its ranks. It particularly flourished under the energetic ministry of Sandy Greig (1973–1985). In the 1970s the Girvan Baptist Church saw the need for a work in Wigtown when six of its members moved there. Despite the distance of thirty-seven miles the church provided a preacher each month, mostly their minister Ian Cameron. There was also some support from the Dumfries congregation and a further catalyst was a mission by a team from WEC. Its ministry was followed up by diligent visitation and the work became established and started to grow from that point onwards. It was formally constituted in 1983. Another community in which a Baptist church was planted was Dalbeattie. Work began with home visitation in 1976 and by 1981 when it was constituted the church had twenty-seven members and a regular congregation of between forty and fifty people. Another location in this region where a church-plant was launched in the 1970s was in Bourtreehill, Irvine. A site for a Baptist church had been purchased in 1968, but it was only in 1974 that R.H. Swanson commenced work in the area. The work prospered and from rented premises their own building was opened in 1978. The formal constitution of the church with thirty-five members and a regular congregation of around a hundred people took place the following year in 1979. The 1970s were a remarkable period of growth and new initiatives for Baptists in the South West of Scotland. Dunbartonshire Baptist Churches also grew at this time from 409 to 433 members. The most significant new development in this decade was the planting of the Bearsden Baptist Church in 1973 through some members of Adelaide Place and Hillhead Baptist Churches who started a work in a home in 1973 before moving to a converted community centre at Bearsden Cross. By 1975 under the leadership of their first pastor Gilbert Ritchie they also launched a branch Sunday School and a Sunday service in the western part of that town in an area of new housing estates. The Bearsden congregation had grown to 148 members by 1985.[25] There was also growth in the Northern Baptist Association (NBA); its affiliated churches had increased from 1,245 to 1,325 members. Under the encouragement of Union Secretary Andrew MacRae there was an emphasis on looking for opportunities for pioneering ministries. Linked to that development it was a recognized that the plentiful supply of ministers-in-training at the Scottish Baptist College provided an opportunity to establish some new churches. MacRae made a point of meeting the Association leaders around the country to ascertain what church-planting opportunities there might be in their particular setting. Alness Baptist Church was launched in 1975, through a partnership between the NBA and the Baptist Union of Scotland. MacRae eventually managed to persuade the Planning Director and Architect for Highland development to secure a rented property to serve as a manse for the pioneer minister Bill Clark and his family.[26] Decline was not inevitable. A clear and effective church-planting strategy could contribute significantly to further growth in the number of members and churches. However, alongside this approach a fresh focus on effective evangelistic initiatives was required if existing churches were to maintain or strengthen their presence in Scotland.

## Home Evangelism in the 1960s and 1970s

The drive to launch new evangelistic initiatives did not slow down in the 1960s. In 1963 the 'Call to Mission' was launched[27] followed by 'Evangelism in Depth', 'Think Again', and 'One Step Forward', with 1,000 Baptists from 115 churches attending a conference on evangelism in 1968.[28] It was no surprise that 1969 the centenary year of the Baptist Union was marked by some special outreach ventures. On that occasion around a hundred churches committed themselves to 'Simultaneous Evangelism', a three-year programme of preparation, proclamation and preservation.[29] This initiative was a success with at least 206 conversions, together with ninety-four applications for baptism and/or membership from the forty-seven churches that reported their

---

[25] D.R. Watts, 'Glasgow and Dunbartonshire', in Bebbington (ed.) *Baptists in Scotland*, p. 182.

[26] Andrew MacRae, Reflections on the Baptist Union of Scotland, 1966–1980, n.p., a copy is in the possession of the author of this book. See also Fisher, 'North-East', in Bebbington (ed.), *Baptists in Scotland*, p. 275.

[27] 'Evangelistic', *Scottish Baptist Yearbook 1963*, p. 166; *1964*, p. 166; *1965*, p. 169.

[28] 'Evangelistic Committee', *Scottish Baptist Yearbook 1969*, pp. 36–37.

[29] *Scottish Baptist Yearbook 1969*, p. 58; *1970*, p. 16.

statistics to the Baptist Union.³⁰ The blessings gained from this initiative gave a new sense of unity and purpose in Scottish Baptist ranks.³¹ It was no surprise that at a time when overall church attendances were falling rapidly in Scotland, in the late 1950s and 1960s, that Scottish Baptists managed to maintain or extend their work in a number of areas of Scotland.³² Although the decline in church-going must be put in a wider social context, there was an equally steep decline in numbers in cinema audiences, dance hall attendances and in spectators at football league matches as well as commitment to a variety of voluntary organisations.³³

Church Extension was increasingly the focus of Scottish Baptist outreach in the 1960s. The new causes at Bathgate; Broxburn; Downfield, Dundee; East Kilbride; Glenburn, Paisley; Glenrothes and Pollok, Glasgow, had become established with steady growth, though the East Kilbride church had seen remarkable growth to attain a membership of 242. The most recent church-plants in Cumbernauld, Drumchapel and Easterhouse in Glasgow had also seen very encouraging increases in the numbers committed to their cause.³⁴ The Home Mission work continued faithfully with an encouraging new work at Forfar supported by Dundee Baptists, though sadness on Mull at the closure of the Tobermory Church and the subsequent sale of its building. Twelve ministers were serving in Home Mission charges in 1964. Bunessan, Mull, was struggling to remain open with a monthly service for the faithful few led by the minister from Oban. Eday and Sanday Churches in Orkney held only occasional services. However, Dunrossness, Shetland, had been greatly encouraged by a mission in November 1964 in which numbers rose at services for a time from 60 to 200 with six young people professing faith in Christ. Another encouragement was Buckie Baptist Church which had continued to grow with over 200 children in the Sunday School. An innovative outreach amongst younger people in September 1964 led by thirteen Inter-Varsity Fellowship Students led them into cafes and dance halls in Buckie, including a significant time spent 'in interesting discussions with many teddy boys, of which only eternity will reveal the results'.³⁵ The momentum for Baptist home mission work in Scotland over the first hundred

---

³⁰ 'Evangelistic Committee', *Scottish Baptist Yearbook 1971*, p. 35.

³¹ *Scottish Baptist Yearbook 1971*, p. 15.

³² Central Baptist Association churches, for example, sustained steady growth in numbers from 840 members in 1952 to a peak of 1,053 members in 1970. Talbot, *Brief History of Central Baptist Association*, p. 22.

³³ Brown, *Religion and Society in Scotland*, pp. 166–169.

³⁴ 'Church Extension', *Scottish Baptist Yearbook 1965*, pp. 167–168.

³⁵ 'Annual Report of the Home Missionary Society', *Scottish Baptist Yearbook 1965*, pp. 182–189.

Christian Witness in an Age of Religious Crisis: The 1960s and 1970s    219

years of the Baptist Union had increasingly led to a greater concentration of resources on the larger more populated districts of central Scotland. It was in these locations that the most promising opportunities for effective evangelisation and church extension were to be found in the second half of the twentieth century.

The changing context for home mission in Scotland took a new form for Baptists with a decision to merge the Home Missionary Society with the Church Extension committee in 1971. Edward Campbell, in his 1971 Home Mission report, acknowledged that for the first 115 years of the society's work 'men and stations had a remoteness that no longer exists'. He also drew attention to the continuing depopulation of the more isolated rural communities as he recognised that greater attention was required to be focussed on more urban communities, although he urged that the small faithful Highland and Island churches should not be forgotten.[36] The newly formed 'Home Mission and Extension Committee' commenced its work in 1973 with encouraging reports from an evangelistic campaign amongst the Islay Baptist Churches and the emergence of the newly formed causes at Erskine and Bearsden, Glasgow.[37] In 1973 the Evangelism Committee sought to promote a lay evangelism programme called 'WIN Schools – Witness, Involvement, Now'. Andrew MacRae, General Secretary of the Baptist Union had taken part in a WIN School event in the USA in the summer of 1973. The approach to lay-witness was launched in Scotland in February 1973 at a conference in Granton Baptist Church, with a similar venture taking place in East Kilbride in November 1973.[38] After three WIN gatherings in the following year, interest in this form of training for evangelism peaked in 1975 with WIN Schools taking place in Arbroath, Carluke, Cumbernauld, Falkirk and Wishaw. New causes at Craigmillar in Edinburgh led by Harry Sprange; at Bishopbriggs, Glasgow, by David Black; Castlemilk, Glasgow by Ian Paterson; Bearsden by Gilbert Ritchie; and Alness near Inverness led by Bill Clark, all showed encouraging signs of progress in 1975. In 1977 as a result of participating in the WIN School initiative several congregations saw spectacular growth. The small church at Linwood had grown by 50% in a year; together with 35% growth in East Kilbride, 40% in Brechin; Bank Street, Irvine by 12%; Morningside, Edinburgh by 17%; Bearsden by 34% and the Bishopbriggs Church by 68%. A further twelve congregations had exceeded the target of 10% growth in one year.[39] Although some churches had

---

[36] 'Home Mission Committee', *Scottish Baptist Yearbook 1972*, pp. 35–36.

[37] 'Home Mission and Extension Committee', *Scottish Baptist Yearbook 1974*, p. 41.

[38] 'Evangelistic Committee, *Scottish Baptist Yearbook 1974*, p. 41. See also *1975*, p. 40;

[39] *Scottish Baptist Yearbook 1978*, p. 17.

a disappointing response there were enough churches with very significant progress to enable this outreach initiative to be described as a great success in Scottish Baptist ranks.

Andrew MacRae, though, was not satisfied with the amount of Church Extension activity taking place. He noted in his 'Home Mission and Extension Committee' report that: 'new trends in Baptist witness can now be clearly observed in some areas and that by far the biggest problem is the lack of committed people.'[40] As an attempt to make further progress he had initiated discussions with the leadership of the Foreign Mission Board of the Southern Baptist Convention. The October 1975 Annual Assembly had agreed to grant its blessing on a potential partnership with this body;[41] and subsequently MacRae met them at their headquarters in Richmond, Virginia in early 1977. It was agreed that a Southern Baptist minister would work with Scottish Baptists in the area of Church Planning and Church Growth with an option for another full-time minister to plant a cause in an 'oil-related area with considerable numbers of American personnel'. In addition, some Scottish ministers would be given the opportunity to visit the USA to study American Baptist approaches to a variety of subjects including Church Growth. Dr J.D. Hughey secretary for Europe and Board President Dr Baker Cauthen were invited as guests to the 1977 Annual Assembly in Scotland.[42] Twenty-nine Scottish Baptist ministers, for example, spent time in the USA with American colleagues for a month in March and April 1979, and Americans accepted pastorates in Brechin and the Cults area of Aberdeen, together with other mission personnel from the USA serving for short-terms with Scottish Baptist congregations.[43] The creative and energetic Andrew MacRae ensured that Scottish Baptists had little time for complacency during his term as General Secretary of the Baptist Union between 1966 and 1980. The involvement of American Southern Baptists with the Scottish Union was a great success and led to effective work in church-planting and evangelism in Scotland and was a source of significant encouragement to Scottish Baptists.

The new enthusiasm for working with American Baptists had not lessened the commitment to engagement in mission with other Scottish Churches. Andrew MacRae as chair of the Mission, Development and Unity Committee of the Scottish Churches Council, had persuaded that body in 1977 to promote a three-year scheme entitled the 'National Initiative in Evangelism'

---

[40] 'Home Mission and Extension Committee', *Scottish Baptist Yearbook 1976*, p. 41.

[41] 'Co-Operation with Southern Baptists', *Scottish Baptist* Yearbook *1976*, pp. 76–77.

[42] 'Home Mission and Extension Committee', *Scottish Baptist Yearbook 1977*, pp. 18–19.

[43] *Scottish Baptist Yearbook 1976*, p. 49; *1977*, p. 44; *1978*, pp. 18–19, 50; *1979*, p. 19; *1980*, pp. 16, 19, 69, 91.

for implementing effective forms of evangelism in the various Scottish Christian denominations by January 1978. The project began in the autumn of that year with 'Preparation including Re-appraisal and renewal'. The theme for the second year was Training 'not only in content but in the articulation of their faith verbally and through Christian lifestyle.' The culmination of these two years was to be followed by 'every possible kind of co-operative outreach' amongst churches in local, regional or national settings during 1980. This inter-church witness was a modest but encouraging development for these Churches.

## Work amongst Children and Young People

The collection and publication of data on Sunday Schools and other Children's and Youth work ceased during this decade. The last year the regular statistics were published was in the 1967 *Yearbook*. Although the layout of the data differs from the 1960 statistics it is possible to draw some comparisons between them. The 1960 *Yearbook* did give a wealth of data on the numbers of children and young people in the 160 Scottish Baptist congregations. In total there were 13,448 children attending a Sunday School. This was a decrease of 288 from the previous year, yet only half of these churches had a Bible class, attended by 1,230 young people. This statistic alone was a sobering acknowledgement that even before the social revolution in the 1960s that all was not well with respect to the attraction and retention of young people in the churches. John Dines, Convener of the Sunday School Committee, who wrote this report for the October 1959 Baptist Union Assembly provided these conclusions:

> Reports from Sunday Schools indicate that we still have cause for concern over the number of children who are attending regularly. While it may be that, in our situation, the drop over the past few years has not been as significant as in some denominations, we have no reason to sit back and be content. And this is particularly so as it concerns the older children in the schools and the members of our Junior Bible Classes.[44]

The drop over recent decades was quite alarming. In 1925 there were over 20,000 pupils in Baptist Sunday Schools, but this had dropped to just over 13,000 by 1960.[45] There was some encouragement in the larger numbers attending some of the Sunday Schools in the church-plant congregations in new housing areas, but by contrast there was disappointment that only the East Kilbride congregation had attempted to run a Holiday Bible School the

---

[44] *Scottish Baptist Yearbook 1960*, 'Summary of Statistics', p. 89 and John Dines, 'Sunday School', p 165.

[45] Andrew MacRae, 'Letter to the Editor', *SBM*, 87.6 (June 1962), p. 4.

previous summer. It had been a great success in attracting young people. Outside of Sunday worship activities there was a range of other organisations for young people affiliated to the churches. In terms of uniformed organisations the largest were the Life Boys and Boys' Brigade with thirty one and twenty-eight companies respectively affiliated to Scottish Baptist congregations; sixteen churches had troops of Cubs and Scouts; twenty-eight had Brownies and twenty-six Girl Guides; fourteen churches had Girls' Life Brigade and six Girls' Guildry groups. Although not specified, Dines' report referred to thirty-four different other named uniformed organisations under whose auspices at least one Scottish Baptist Church had an affiliated body. More commonly non-uniformed groups were reported. Christian Endeavour was prominent with Junior, Young People's and Senior Societies in sixty-one, twenty-three and forty-two congregations, alongside fifty-nine holding Youth Fellowships and eighty-two Young Worshiper Leagues. Fourteen congregations ran the temperance focussed Band of Hope.[46] Outside of Sunday activities there was a wide variety of work going on, but it did appear that there was no co-ordinated strategy between the churches. The variety of youth organisations reported is surprising for a relatively small denomination. What is clear is that morale was already low in this area of church life before the challenges of the 1960s began.

The last published statistics for children's and youth work was in September 1966. In that year 159 Scottish Baptist churches reported a total of 11,026 Sunday School pupils up to sixteen years old. This total was down 335 from the previous year. However, the tone of the report from Gilbert Ritchie, who directed this aspect of the Baptist Union's work, was significantly more upbeat. There was a clear sense that new ways of working with children and young people had to be found to ensure congregations engaged with them in a rapidly changing world. A new strategy to accomplish this goal was being promoted amongst the affiliated churches. The Baptist Union under the direction of its Secretary Andrew MacRae was reshaping its work under the influence of Southern Baptists in the USA and promoting All-Age Christian Education. Teacher-training courses were being run in the Abroath Baptist Centre and three summer camps for young people in Abroath had been a success with over twenty conversions reported. The twenty-five who had professed faith at the camps the previous year were now baptized and active participants in their local churches. Another Baptist facility that opened at this time was the Atholl Baptist Centre in Pitlochry. It would welcome a wide range of guests to use its facilities across the age ranges.[47] There were also significant changes in the numbers of midweek groups associated with the churches. The wide variety of uniformed youth organisations had ceased with

---

[46] *Scottish Baptist Yearbook 1960*, p. 166.

[47] *SBM*, 96.8 (August 1971), pp. 5–6.

only the more familiar names appearing. There were now twenty-two Boys' Brigade Companies operating and fourteen with Cubs and Scouts, together with twenty-nine with Brownies and Girl Guides and four companies of Campaigners. Of the non-uniformed organisations there were now only seven Bands of Hope, a fifty percent drop in six years. Christian Endeavour was still prominent with forty-seven Junior, twenty-four Young People's and seventeen Senior Societies, together with seventy-one Young Worshiper's Leagues.[48] A new feature was the launching of youth clubs. Twenty-eight congregations were running one with 810 regular attenders. Young Worshipper League meetings were still being held in seventy-one congregations down by eleven in six years. By contrast Youth Fellowships were a feature in seventy-six churches, up from fifty-nine at the start of the decade.[49] Unfortunately the data in this area of church work is not available for the rest of this decade and beyond it, but the trends are unmistakeable of a rapidly changing religious landscape. The process of secularisation was already a serious challenge to those Scottish Baptist leaders engaged in Children's and Young People's work in 1960, but it was a much bigger issue in the two decades that followed.

### The Influence of the Charismatic Movement[50]

The influence of the extraordinary events of the Lewis Revival 1949–1953[51] had caused a number of Scottish Christians to seek a greater empowerment of the Holy Spirit in the years that followed with the writings of advocates of a second blessing or a 'Baptism of the Holy Spirit' being read amongst students at the Bible Training Institution in Glasgow in 1960 as one example. David Black, a Baptist theological student, and Jim Graham, minister of Viewfield Baptist Church, Dunfermline, were amongst those influenced by these neo-Pentecostal emphases that predated charismatic renewal and were more

---

[48] *Scottish Baptist Yearbook 1967*, pp. 170–172.

[49] G.H. Ritchie, Director, 'Christian Education and Youth', *Scottish Baptist Yearbook 1967*, pp. 171–172.

[50] A standard text on this subject in Great Britain is Peter Hocken, *Streams of Renewal: The Origins and Early Development of the Charismatic Movement in Great Britain* (Exeter: Paternoster Press, 1986). The section on Scotland in this era is 'North of the Border', pp. 95–98.

[51] The details are given in Colin and Mary Peckham, *Sounds from Heaven: The Revival on the Isle of Lewis,1949–1952* (Tain: Christian Focus, 2004); and Alec Dunn, *The Hebrides Revival and Awakening 1949–1953 A Short History* (n.p.: private publication, 2009).

closely linked to the earlier Holiness movement.[52] A new development occurred in 1962 when it was reported that 'strange things were happening at Hermon Baptist Church. They were talking in tongues, frothing at the mouth, swinging on the chandeliers . . . .'[53] In the years that followed Jack Kelly of the Hermon Church regularly invited renewal advocates like Arthur Wallis and Campbell MacAlpine to address gatherings of Scottish Christians eager to receive more of the new experience of the Holy Spirit. In 1962 the modern charismatic movement began with the experience of Father Dennis Bennett, an Episcopal minister in California, whose story was told in the later book *Nine O' Clock in the Morning*. In 1965 Bennett was invited to Scotland to address an interdenominational group of ministers that included David Black of Springburn Baptist Church, Douglas Ross, Motherwell Baptist Church and Douglas McBain of Wishaw Baptist Church. This gathering was seen by some participants as the launch of the charismatic movement in Scotland. A new group was formed to promote this cause and it developed strong links with the Fountain Trust in England. In 1968 Douglas McBain moved to Streatham, London and set up Manna Ministries, a major source of renewal influences in the BUGBI.[54] Jim Graham also moved south to Goldhill Baptist Church in Buckinghamshire, to a church influenced in this direction under the previous pastor David Pawson. David Black briefly worked with a relief agency in South Korea where he studied movements of the Spirit in churches in that country, prior to becoming minister of Dennistoun Baptist Church in Glasgow. In September 1974 he was inducted as the first general secretary of Scottish Churches Renewal in Hillhead Baptist Church, participants in the service included Hillhead minister Kerr Speirs and Union Secretary Andrew MacRae, alongside a range of clergy and lay members of other Christian denominations in Scotland. Another figure of note in promoting renewal influences at that time was Ken McDougal who had come from a Methodist background to the pastorate of New Prestwick Baptist Church.[55] McDougal

---

[52] A discussion of the theological influences on David Black and some of the other pioneers of this movement is given in Jim Purves, *The Triune God and the Charismatic Movement* (Carlisle: Paternoster, 2004), pp. 1–9.

[53] The private memoir of David Black (2003) is a key source of developments. Details of this event and many other references to the charismatic movement in this section come from Black, through Alasdair Black, "Pour out your Spirit: Experiences of the Holy Spirit amongst Scottish Baptists in the Twentieth Century' in Talbot, *Distinctive People*, pp. 151–177.

[54] Douglas McBain, *Fire over the Waters: Renewal Among Baptists & Others from the 1960s to the 1990s* (London: Darton, Longman and Todd, 1997), pp. 27, 37–38.

[55] McBain, *Fire over the Waters*, p. 38.

wrote a series of articles in the *SBM* promoting this cause,[56] but some other Scottish Baptists were not as convinced of its merits.[57] The Baptist Union issued a positive 'Charismatic Renewal Statement' in the 1974 *Scottish Baptist Yearbook* with a fairly lengthy list of books for further study from different perspectives.[58] A further more detailed statement was published by the Doctrine and Inter-Church Relations committee (DICR) of the Union in 1978 'to take into account 'the new "shepherding" movement and to consider the relationship of water and spirit baptism'.[59] There appeared to be broad acceptance of these reports in this constituency and a cautious welcome to the positive enhancement of congregational life through the renewal movement.

In the early 1970s the Jesus movement in California[60] was an important renewal vehicle that had a significant influence on Christian churches under ministries of individuals like Arthur Blessitt,[61] who came to Scotland in 1972 and 1973. The younger people converted under this exuberant style of worship and ministry provided new opportunities for ministry and witness as well as challenges in integrating them into existing congregations. Amongst the new causes that emerged at this time and in which this charismatic influence was prominent included the Craigmillar Fellowship in Edinburgh under the leadership of Harry Sprange and the Bishopbriggs Baptist Church, Glasgow, formed from the converts of a Youth With A Mission (YWAM) outreach in Glasgow in 1974. This congregation, at the same time as the Brechin and Erskine churches, was accepted for affiliation to the Baptist Union at the September 1975 Baptist Union Council and welcomed into fellowship at the Assembly the following month.[62] The significance of that step was that in the 1960s and 1970s the charismatic movement in Scotland was focussed on transformation within historic denominations.[63] Developments in the

---

[56] For example, Ken McDougal, 'His deeper work', *SBM*, 96.8 (August 1971), pp. 12–13; 'The Charismatic Movement', 98.4 (April 1973), pp. 9–10.

[57] For example, E. David Cook, 'The Charismatic Movement', *SBM*, 98.3 (March 1973), pp. 10–11.

[58] *Scottish Baptist Yearbook 1974*, p. 93.

[59] *Scottish Baptist Yearbook 1979*, pp. 99–102.

[60] The standard work on them is Larry Eskridge, *God's Forever People: The Jesus People Movement in America* (New York: Oxford University Press, 2013). See also 'Hippies and Jesus', *SBM*, 96.7 (July 1971), pp. 6–7; and J.I.D. Hamilton' Frankly Speaking', *SBM*, 97.3 (March 1972), pp. 9–10.

[61] Arthur Blessitt with Walter Wagner, *Turned on to Jesus* ((London: Word Books, 1971), gives an account of his ministry up to 1971. See also Eskridge, *God's Forever People*, pp. 54–59.

[62] *Scottish Baptist Yearbook 1976*, pp. 59, 66.

[63] Balfour, 'Twentieth Century Since 1914', recorded similar conclusions, p. 77.

following decade for some would take a different direction. In summary, there were a considerable number of Scottish Baptists sympathetic to or participants in the renewal movement at that time.[64] A number of churches were revitalised in their worship practices and saw numerical growth during these years.

## The Atholl Centre

The founding of this denominational facility in Pitlochry was rightly viewed as a significant achievement of the visionary leadership of Watson Moyes, minister of Pitlochry Baptist Church from 1965 to 1983. The planning for such a centre began with conversations between Moyes and Gilbert Ritchie, the Baptist Union Youth Director, during the time the younger man was studying at the Baptist Theological College in Glasgow. Ritchie encouraged Moyes to consider applying for the vacant post in the church and then obtaining the support of that church for the erection of a training centre in the town. It was a big step of faith for the small church, but effective planning and good communication skills in the early years led to the adoption of the vision by Baptists across the country who raised funds in a variety of ways to cover the costs.[65] These included a National Sponsored Walk in autumn 1970, together with an 'Atholl Centre Shop' in Edinburgh during the Baptist Union Assembly week, 25–28 October, 1971. It sold a range of items all made and donated by Baptists in support of the Atholl Centre appeal.[66] The centre was opened in 1971 only two years after the Atholl Baptist Centre Ltd had been formed. It had a three-fold purpose as a youth centre, a training centre for the wider church and a resource centre for the disabled. In 1987 a new phase of development of the work was begun under the heading: 'A Christian training centre at the heart of Scotland'. There had been a conference in November 1986 to formulate a plan for the next ten years and agreement was reached to broaden the scope of its work to be 'a leader in international, interdenominational residential Christian training, exercising a ministry in key areas of social need'. In order to implement this vision a development fund of £10,000 needed to be raised from supporters.[67] The Atholl Centre has hosted many church-groups and was regularly used for a variety of training courses, including the Christians in Management courses run by David Cormack, together with Counselling courses run by Edith Cormack, Peter Bowes and

---

[64] Names of participant individuals and churches are given in Black, 'Pour out your Spirit', pp. 173–177.

[65] J. Quinn, 'Tayside', in Bebbington (ed.), *Baptists in Scotland*, pp. 254–255.

[66] 'Atholl Centre Shop', *SBM*, 96.8 (August 1971), pp. 5–6.

[67] David Sked, 'Atholl Centre', *Scottish Baptist Yearbook 1988*, pp. 63–64.

Chris Brown.[68] Despite significant financial challenges to ensure its ongoing viability, the Atholl Centre has been a success story, not only for Watson Moyes and Pitlochry Baptist Church in the early years of its work, but for the many volunteers and staff members who have continued to promote the vision and carry out the work at the centre in the years that followed.

## Inter-Church Relationships

### Relationships with Other Baptist Churches and Organisations

There had been a good relationship with the Baptist Union of Great Britain and Ireland over the first century of the Scottish Union. However, there was a determination to place a greater priority on strengthening the relationship with each other, together with the Welsh Baptists and BMS in the 1960s. In January 1963 all three of the Baptist Unions joined together in concerted prayer. They had also co-operated in the production of the new Baptist Hymnbook the previous year. There was a specifically Scottish edition of it that also contained the Psalms and Paraphrases.[69] This working arrangement between the BUS and the BUGBI was strengthened with discussion concerning the mutual recognition of ministers between the respective denominations. The agreement reached was accepted by the September 1973 BUS Council and subsequently by Assembly delegates in October that year.[70] From this date onwards ministers in the respective Unions could in principle have their names submitted to vacant churches in fellowship with the other body. A further step was taken in 1978 with the creation of the Joint Consultative Committee comprising of representatives of the BUS, BUGBI and Baptist Union of Wales (BUW) and the BMS, under the chairmanship of M.J. Williams from the BUW with W.R. Scott of the BUS as its minute secretary. Its purpose was to facilitate closer working relationships between these organisations. However, at this early stage the priority was to select an appropriate group of leaders who could work together effectively to implement a vision for better co-operation in their respectively ministries.[71] Relationships between the three Baptist Unions and the BMS had been harmonious during

---

[68] John R. Barclay, 'Atholl Centre', *Scottish Baptist Yearbook 1998*, pp. 132–33.

[69] '93rd Annual Report by the Secretary', *Scottish Baptist Yearbook 1963*, p. 137. See also Dr Hugh Martin, 'Our New Hymn Book' SBM, 88.9 (September 1963), pp. 4–6.

[70] 'Mutual Recognition', *Scottish Baptist Yearbook 1974*, pp. 58, 70. At the BUS Assembly in October 1972, a delegate asked about our relationship with the Federation of Independent Evangelical Churches (FIEC). The Union Secretary reported that there was no formal relationship with that body. *Scottish Baptist Yearbook 1973*, p. 70.

[71] 'Joint Consultative Committee', *Scottish Baptist Yearbook 1979*, p. 52.

these decades and there was a clear commitment to co-operate more closely in the years to come.

A European body to co-ordinate Baptist work and witness had been the vision of a group of individuals that had met in London from 13–17 August 1948. It had appointed a group of seven representative figures with a mandate to set up a European Baptist Federation.[72] It was duly constituted on 20 October 1950 in Lille, France.[73] In the first few years of the EBF British Baptists were represented solely by the BUGBI. Although the BUS had made annual donations to the work of the EBF it appears that the latter body had assumed it was from a subsidiary organisation within the larger British Baptist Union. EBF Secretary, Dr Erik Ruden, was invited to visit Scotland for a week in February 1964 to meet a wide range of Scottish Baptists[74] as well as to enter into negotiations with senior BUS leaders to ensure that Scottish Baptists gained by right membership of the EBF as a separate family of churches. The European Committee of the BUS had been promoting work in Continental Europe by sister churches over a number of years and was seeking to raise the circulation of *The European Baptist* periodical amongst the churches, as well as contributing to aid projects in Continental Europe, together with efforts to secure the freedom of worship for churches in sister Unions in this region.[75] The application for membership was accepted at the Amsterdam Council of the EBF with Dr Ernest Payne of the BUGBI the proposer of the motion. The visit of Dr Ruden to Scotland, together with the showing of a film about the life and work of Moscow Baptist Church, Russia, in various locations around Scotland during his visit stimulated greater interest in EBF work and led to a 50% increase in donations for the work of the EBF from Scotland. Another approach to encouraging relationship building with Continental Baptists was the planning of holidays in Europe organised by Youth Committee convener Donald McCallum, during which visits to local Baptist churches were part of the schedule.[76] Eleven Scottish Baptists were

---

[72] They came from Great Britain, Denmark, Germany, Italy, France Switzerland and Holland, Keith Jones, *The European Baptist Federation* (Milton Keynes: Paternoster, 2009), p. 32. There had been two congresses of European Baptists earlier in the century in 1908 (Berlin) and 1913 (Stockholm). World War One prevented the planning for a 1918 congress in Rome or St Petersburg. Not until post World War Two were serious steps taken to develop this vision further. Green, *Crossing the Boundaries: A History of the European Baptist Federation*, pp. 1–14.

[73] Green, *Crossing the Boundaries*, pp. 12–13.

[74] *SBM*, 89.2 (February 1964), p. 11.

[75] *SBM*, 88.3 (March 1963), p. 9; 'European Committee', *Scottish Baptist Yearbook 1964*, p. 165.

[76] Donald P. McCallum, 'Accent on Youth – Holland and Troon', *SBM*, 86.9 (September 1961), p. 7.

delegates at the Amsterdam Conference in August 1964, including some Scottish Baptist women who attended the European Baptist Women's Union meetings immediately preceding it. A German Baptist youth leader, Gerhard Claas, was invited to be one of the speakers at the BUS Assembly later that year.[77] Andrew MacRae who had served for a number of years on its Evangelism and Education Committee was the first Scottish Vice-President of the EBF.[78] He was then appointed as the EBF President for a two-year term in 1970 and 1971. A key feature of his presidential year was the arrangement of a special Pastor's Conference in Prague and preaching in some Czech churches. During that same year Stanislav Svec, a Czech Baptist pastor, made a short visit to Scotland to highlight Baptist work in his home country.[79] In late August to early September 1971 there was also the European Congress on Evangelism. Thirty-three attended from Scotland including Baptist ministers Peter Barber, Alex Hardie and James Taylor.[80] Scottish Baptists had demonstrated a commitment to supporting Baptist colleagues in Continental Europe throughout the history of their Baptist Union. However, it was in the time of Andrew MacRae's leadership as Union Secretary that this Union was recognised as an EBF member in its own right.

The *SBM* fairly frequently contained articles about Baptist work in other countries in Europe, for example, Czechoslovakia,[81] France,[82] Hungary,[83] Ireland,[84] Italy,[85] The Netherlands,[86] Poland,[87] Russia,[88] Spain,[89] West and

---

[77] 'European Committee', *Scottish Baptist Yearbook 1965*, pp. 168–169; 'The European Baptist Conference'. *SBM*, 89.10 (October 1964), p. 1, 3–4; Miss A.C. MacFarlane, 'European Baptist Women's Union', *SBM*, 89.10 (October 1964), pp. 3–4; Regular reports were given of the European Baptist Women's Union, for example, *SBM*, 92 .8 (August 1967), pp. 11, 13.

[78] Edward Burrows, 'Without a Vision the People Perish', in Talbot (ed.), *Distinctive People*, p.13.

[79] '101st Annual Report by The Secretary' and 'European Committee', *Scottish Baptist Yearbook 1971*, pp. 15–16, 34. Green, *Crossing the Boundaries*, p. 66. MacRae gave updates of his travels in Europe during those years. For example, 'News from Europe', *SBM*, 96.5 (May 1971), pp. 6–7;

[80] *SBM*, 96.10 (October 1971), Back Page and p. 15.

[81] *SBM*, 90.3 (March 1965), pp. 11–12; 96.7 (July 1971), p. 12.

[82] *SBM*, 87.10 (October 1962), p. 4; 89.8 (August 1964), pp. 7–9.

[83] *SBM*, 89.11 (November 1964), p. 13.

[84] *SBM*, 96.7 (July 1971), p. 12.

[85] *SBM*, 88.3 (March 1963), p. 8; 96.8 (August 1971), pp. 9–10.

[86] *SBM*, 89.9 (September 1964), pp. 7–8.

[87] *SBM*, 100.2 (February 1975), pp. 8–9.

East Germany,[90] Portugal,[91] Switzerland,[92] and Yugoslavia;[93] as well as features on more specific events such as the Baptist Women's conference in Sjorvik, Sweden, in June 1962.[94] An issue that particularly concerned Scottish Baptists was the restrictions on religious liberty of fellow believers. An example of their concerns was the article on Spiros Zodhiates, a Greek-American put on trial in Greece in 1971 for the unlawful act of 'translating and distributing the Bible without Orthodox permission'.[95] The *SBM* reported with sadness the demolition of large premises of Belgrade Baptist Church in Yugoslavia,[96] and the ongoing suffering of Russian Baptists and other Christians in the Soviet Union.[97] The distribution of copies of the Bible in the Communist-controlled countries of Eastern Europe was also important to them.[98] This focus on work in other countries was a clear sign that Scottish Baptists were outward looking and confident of the further advance of Baptist work in Europe.

Scottish Baptists were also committed supporters of the BWA in this era. The 1960s was the decade in which the BWA came of age as a World Communion holding its first congress outside Europe or North America in Rio de Janeiro in 1960, where record numbers attended including 150,000 at the final service in the Maracana Stadium. It also elected its first Latin American and first African Presidents in Brazilian Joao Filson Soren (1960–1965) and William Tolbert of Liberia (1965–1970) respectively, and expanded

---

[88] *SBM*, 86.2, (February 1961), p. 3; 87.2 (February 1962), p. 10; 87.8 August 1962, p. 7; 88.11 (November 1963), pp.8–9; 90.7 (July 1965), pp. 7–11; 96.2 (February 1971), p. 7.

[89] *SBM*, 86.5 (May 1961), p. 8; 86.10 (October 1961), p. 8; 90.2 February 1965), p. 7; 96.7 (July 1971), p. 13.

[90] *SBM*, 87.2 (February 1962), p. 6; 87.8 August 1962, p. 7; 96.7 (July 1971), p. 12.

[91] *SBM*, 87.8 (August 1962), p. 7.

[92] *SBM*, 87.8 (August 1962), p. 4.

[93] *SBM*, 90.4 (April 1965), p. 12; 91.2 (February 1966), pp. 11–13; 92.9 (September 1967), pp. 6–7.

[94] A.C. Macfarlane, 'Baptist Women of Europe', *SBM*, 87.8 (August 1962), p. 6.

[95] 'Outlook- Spiros Zodhiates', *SBM* 96.2 (February 1971), p. 2.

[96] *SBM*, 100.5 (May 1975), p. 13.

[97] *SBM*, 100.2 (February 1975), p. 5.

[98] *SBM*, 96.6 (June 1971), pp. 6–7.

the Executive Committee to include delegates from each member body.[99] Andrew MacRae was an enthusiastic participant in the activities of the Baptist World Alliance; while minister of Ward Road Baptist Church, Dundee (1961–1966), he had been one of the speakers at the BWA Congress in Miami Beach, Florida, in 1965 delivering an address on 'Baptist Churches Around the World Teaching the Word'.[100] The Beirut 1963 BWA Youth Congress had been advertised in the *SBM*.[101] It is unclear, though, if any Scots attended that event. However, there was a delegation of young people from Scotland participating in the BWA Youth Congress in Berne, Switzerland in 1968.[102] The Annual Assembly in the Union Centenary year in 1969 had welcomed BWA President William Tolbert from Liberia as a guest speaker. Scottish Baptists had been strongly supportive of Baptist World Aid providing relief and development support in projects around the world. MacRae himself had served under BWA auspices as an Evangelist in East Pakistan, Thailand, Malaysia and Indonesia and also had the privilege of preaching in Japan around the time of the BWA Congress in Tokyo, Japan, in 1970. At the Congress MacRae spoke on 'The Divine Imperative of the Teaching Ministry'.[103] In 1980 at the Toronto, Canada, Congress, MacRae served both as the secretary of the Long Range Planning Committee of BWA and presented its report following the death of the committee chairperson Theodore F. Adams, who had been for many years Pastor of First Baptist Church, Richmond, Virginia and former BWA President, 1955–1960.[104] The *SBM* actively promoted attendance at BWA Congresses[105] and reported on

---

[99] James Leo Garrett, Jr, 'The Internationalisation of the Alliance,1960–1970', in Richard V. Pierard (ed.), *Baptists Together in Christ 1905–2005* (Falls Church, VA: Baptist World Alliance, 2005), pp. 128–164

[100] Josef Nordenhaug (ed.), *The Truth That Makes Men Free: Official Report of the Eleventh Congress, Baptist World Alliance, Miami Beach, Florida* (Nashville: Tennessee: Broadman Press, 1966), pp. 340–343, 531.

[101] *SBM*, 87.3 (March 1962), p. 9.

[102] Cyril E. Bryant (ed.), *One World, One Lord, One Witness: Official Report of the Seventh Baptist Youth World Congress, Berne Switzerland* (Waco, TX: Word Books, 1969), p. 161.

[103] Cyril E. Bryant (ed.), *Reconciliation Through Christ: Official Report of the Twelfth Congress Baptist World Alliance Tokyo, Japan* (Valley Forge, PA: Judson Press, 1971), pp. 423, 438.

[104] Cyril E. Bryant & Ruby Burke (eds), *Celebrating Christ's Presence Through the Spirit: Official Report of the Fourteenth Congress Baptist World Alliance, Toronto, Canada* (Nashville, Tennessee: Broadman Press, 1981), pp. 148–154, 157.

[105] 'Baptist World Wide Fellowship', an article promoting the Eleventh BWA Congress in Miami Beach Florida, *SBM*, 90.4 (April 1965), p. 11

their proceedings.[106] There was usually a small representative group from Scotland present at these events. These decades, but especially the 1960s, were a time of major social change in the Western world. It was in some respects a time of religious crisis, but Scottish Baptists also viewed this era as a time of new opportunities and advances, 'with much to encourage in the Christian scene in Scotland'.[107]

Interest in the wider Baptist family, and other Christian Churches outside of Europe, was also evident in the pages of the denominational periodical. There were a number of general articles taken and reused from the BWA periodical *The Baptist World*, in which very short summaries of information from a range of countries on Baptist work was summarised.[108] Amongst the many references to Baptist church life in America,[109] there was concern for African–American churches in the USA, in particular the congregations whose premises were burnt down by racists. The work of the interdenominational Committee of Concern in Mississippi in assisting with the rebuilding or repairing of church buildings, largely a venture of Baptists and Methodists in that American State, was commended.[110] A Baptist regional gathering in Southern Mexico was also featured,[111] as well as an update on the work of Cuban Baptists.[112] David Kyles reported on the varieties of Baptists in Canada following a visit to that country[113] and Andrew McKie of Queen's Park Baptist Church, Glasgow, presented primarily but not exclusively a more focussed update on the life and work of a single American Baptist church during his exchange of pulpits with Dr James Young, pastor of University Baptist Church, Baton Rouge, Louisiana, in 1965.[114] Attention was drawn with approval to the World Congress on Evangelism due to be held in

---

[106] *SBM*, 90.9 (September 1965), pp. 2–3.

[107] 'Outlook', *SBM*, 97.12 (December 1972), p. 1.

[108] For example, 'New Day for Baptist Witness', *SBM*, 92.2 (February 1967), pp. 12–13; and 'A Visit with Russian Baptists', which included visits to Baptists in Latvia and Estonia, *SBM*, 92.4 (April1967), pp. 5–7.

[109] For example, Jim McLeod's 'Letter from America', *SBM*, 96.1 (January 1971), back page; 96.2 (February 1971, back page; 96.3 (March 1971), pp. 2–3.

[110] *SBM*, 90.4 (April 1965), facing page, prior to page 1.

[111] *SBM*, 90.6 (June 1965), p. 5.

[112] *SBM*, 91.7 (July 1966), pp. 5–6.

[113] *SBM*, 90.8 (August 1965), pp. 2–3.

[114] *SBM*, 90.9 (September 1965), pp. 8–9; other pulpit exchanges with American Baptist Churches were also described in articles in this periodical, for example, G.B. Hossack, 'Impressions of the American Pulpit Exchange', *SBM*, 90.10 (October 1965), pp. 6–7.

Berlin in 1966.[115] The baptism of three young Chinese ladies in Morningside Baptist Church, Edinburgh, reported in the February 1971 issue of the *SBM*, led to an article on the wider development of Chinese Christian Fellowships in Britain in a subsequent issue of this periodical.[116] Another event involving Baptists oversea was the formation of the Church of North India. There were three networks of churches that held to believers' baptism that chose to affiliate with that body.[117] The martyrdom of relatively new Christians in West New Guinea, for example, ensured interest in a less familiar place.[118] Other locations, especially where BMS workers were or had been based, attracted the greatest interest. In Africa there were, for example, a number of reports from Angola,[119] Congo,[120] and Nigeria[121] and in Asia from China,[122] Japan,[123] and Thailand.[124] It was clear that during these two decades regular readers of the *SBM* would be kept up to date not only with news of events in Europe but from an impressively wide range of other countries overseas as well.

### *Relationships with Other Christian Churches*[125]

The decision to affiliate with the WCC by the most slender of margins in 1948 had been a cause of increasing tension amongst Scottish Baptists and had led to the withdrawal from its ranks in 1955 by the largest congregation, Charlotte Baptist Chapel, Edinburgh, despite the Union agreeing to leave the

---

[115] *SBM*, 90.3 (March 1965), p. 13.

[116] *SBM*, 96.2 (February 1971), p. 6; 96.4 (April 1971), p. 14.

[117] *SBM*, 96.4 April 1971, back page, and p. 16.

[118] *SBM*, 87.12 (December 1962), pp. 9, 12.

[119] *SBM*, 86.5 (May 1961), p. 8; 86.6 (June 1961), p. 7; 86.8 (August 1961), pp 5, 7–8.

[120] *SBM*, 88.2 (February 1963), p. 1; 88.3 (March 1963), p. 7; 89.9 (September 1964), p. 10; 96.4 (April 1971), pp. 12–13.

[121] *SBM*, 87.2 (February 1962), p. 11; March 1962, p. 10.

[122] *SBM* 88.3 (March 1963), p. 2.

[123] *SBM*, 88.8 (August 1983), p. 2.

[124] *SBM*. 87.2 (February 1962), p. 11.

[125] More detailed discussions on ecumenical relationships in this era is given in Murray, *First Hundred Years*, pp. 113–120; and from a very personal pro-ecumenical perspective in T. Watson Moyes, *Our Place Among the Churches* (N.P.: Scottish Baptist History Project, 2013), pp. 33–38.

WCC at its Annual Assembly in October 1955.[126] An agreed seven year period of reflection on relations with this ecumenical body led to a working group being appointed to consider whether there had been sufficient movement within the WCC towards a more evangelical theological position, which Scottish Baptists held, and was the essential requirement if re-affiliation with the WCC was to be considered.[127] However, the small group appointed to bring a recommendation could not come to one mind in time for the BUS Assembly in October 1962 so a further year was granted to present their recommendations. It was a wise decision. The report they submitted a year later won the unanimous approval of the BUS Council and recommended 'continuing in disaffiliation' with respect to the WCC.[128] The working group acknowledged that the New Delhi Assembly of the WCC had added the phrase 'according to the Scriptures' to its basis of faith, but this step was viewed as insufficient for them to recommend Scottish Baptists re-joining this ecumenical body. The motion to 'continue in disaffiliation' was passed by a convincing 85% majority, 284 votes to 50.[129] It was recognised by affiliated churches and their delegates that this vote was decisive.[130] However, this result was not the end of conflict over ecumenical relationships. Scottish Baptists were still affiliated with the British Council of Churches (BCC) and the Scottish ecumenical agencies. In 1964 the latter groups were amalgamated in a new SCC.[131] A decision was then required from member churches whether to renew their affiliation the following year. The series of votes on 26 October 1965 were in favour of continuing membership of these British ecumenical bodies. The final vote on continuing affiliation was won by 197 votes to 108, a

---

[126] Apparently, Charlotte Chapel took the decision to leave the Union prior to the Assembly vote, but that was not communicated clearly either inside or outside the congregation at that time. Balfour, *Revival in Rose Street*, pp. 302–305, for more details.

[127] See the report by the Union Secretary at the BUS Council, 18 September 1962, *Scottish Baptist Yearbook 1963*, p. 121.

[128] Appendix, 'World Council of Churches', *Scottish Baptist Yearbook 1964*, pp. 179–182.

[129] Baptist Union Assembly, 22 October, 1963, *Scottish Baptist Yearbook 1964*, pp. 132–133.

[130] Watson Moyes, 'There is one body: Scottish Baptist Ecumenical Relations in the Twentieth Century', in Talbot (ed), *Distinctive People*, p. 108. A small group of younger ministers committed to ecumenical involvement, in response, formed a group 'The Lower Fifth' that provided a forum for discussing topics of mutual interest. An unpublished paper on 'The Lower Fifth' group was given by Robert Armstrong, one of the ministers involved in the group at the Scottish Baptist History Project on 19 April 2008.

[131] Moyes, 'There is one body', p. 108.

65% majority.[132] Sadly the disagreements over inter-church co-operation continued in the next few years with five churches choosing to leave the Union over its continued affiliation to these ecumenical bodies and a further eleven dissociating themselves from the decision while retaining their Union membership.[133] It was a time of painful disagreements in the Union.

By contrast, this decision allowed a number of Scottish Baptists to hold office in the BCC and SCC. In the former organisation James Taylor was appointed to the Executive, Andrew MacRae to the department of Mission and Unity and Donald McCallum to the committee on Evangelism in 1971[134]; Taylor also served as the Vice-Chairman of the SCC as did Derek Murray.[135] Three Scottish Baptist ministers served as Chairman of one of the SCC committees in the years that followed with Andrew MacRae, Donald McCallum and Derek Murray chairing the Mission, Development and Unity, Evangelism and Christian Aid committees respectively.[136] In addition, J.W. McLeod was appointed as Warden of the Scottish Churches House, under the auspices of the SCC in 1974 and Peter Clark became the Assistant General Secretary of the National Bible Society in the same year.[137] However, a new approach to inter-church relations was adopted at the 1967 Union Assembly. The Baptist Union Council had requested that the Inter-Church Relations Committee draw up a statement around which Baptists could unite, articulating our positive understanding of Christian unity and the theological basis for that position. The catalyst for this decision was a common concern that the call by the 1964 Nottingham Faith and Order Conference of the BCC for organic church unity by 1980[138] was not in line with a biblical understanding of Christian unity.[139] Instead of simply rejecting this proposal,

---

[132] Baptist Union Assembly, 26 October, 1965, *Scottish Baptist Yearbook 1966*, pp. 130–131.

[133] Harper Memorial, Glasgow, *Scottish Baptist Yearbook 1967*, p. 126. The churches that left the Union were Inverness, Hermon, Glasgow, Old Cumnock, and New Cumnock. The dissociating churches were Bowhill, Buckie, Cathcart, Falkirk, Girvan, Gourock, Hopeman, Musselburgh, Rattray Street, Dundee, Wick and Wishaw; *Scottish Baptist Yearbook* 1971, p. 36.

[134] 'Inter-Church Relations Committee', *Scottish Baptist Yearbook 1972*, p. 36.

[135] Moyes, 'There is one body', p. 109.

[136] *Scottish Baptist Yearbook 1971*, pp. 30, 59; *1972*, p. 36; *1973*, pp. 35. 43; *1975*, pp. 38–39; *1976*, pp. 38–39.

[137] *Scottish Baptist Yearbook 1975*, p. 14; *1976*, pp. 38–39.

[138] 'Outlook –Visible Union By 1980', *SBM*, 89.11 (November 1964), pp. 1, 8–9.

[139] Balfour, 'Twentieth Century Since 1914', in Bebbington (ed.), *Baptists in Scotland*, p. 76.

a decision was taken to articulate a more constructive approach to this subject. The work put in to producing this considered statement was appreciated by Baptists across the spectrum of opinions on the ecumenical debate.[140] This document was warmly received by the churches and highlighted that for Baptists Christian unity is based not on organic unity but on shared theological convictions concerning the person of Jesus Christ, a biblical doctrine of the Church, Christian Baptism and a commitment to the evangelisation of the world. The adoption of this document allowed the churches to begin to refocus their energies on more constructive engagements with other Churches in Scotland.[141] It was a significant step forward in a positive affirmation of Scottish Baptist convictions. The October 1976 Assembly heard a report on conversations with the Roman Catholic Church and a summary of Roman Catholic convictions discussed was presented to the delegates. It was reported that the representatives of their conversation partner viewed the document as fairly articulating their views. Although a few delegates were unhappy that the conversations had taken place, the report was accepted by an 'overwhelming majority' of those present.[142] On Wednesday 26 October 1977 in an Assembly debate on the Doctrine and Inter-Church Relations committee report, delegates heard from the Union Secretary Andrew MacRae some details of conversations with the Church of Scotland concerning believers' baptism requests from persons in membership with the National Church. A joint statement on Baptismal practice was prepared by the two denominations. After a time of discussion it was unanimously adopted by Assembly delegates. Divisions of opinion amongst Scottish Baptists on Inter-Church Relations still existed, but the heated conflicts on this subject had begun to subside and more constructive engagement with theological differences were in evidence in the later years of the 1970s.

## Women in the Ministry

It was inevitable in an era of significant changes that some acknowledgement of the changing perceptions of the ministry of women in society and in churches should arise, although there were no significant developments in Scottish Baptist ranks at this time. Throughout the Union's history, lay people both men and women had utilised their gifts in service in local Baptist

---

[140] 'Statement on Christian Unity' adopted by an 'overwhelming vote' 24 October 1967, Baptist Union Assembly, *Scottish Baptist Yearbook 1968*, p. 139

[141] 'Christian Unity', *Scottish Baptist Yearbook 1968*, pp. 148–151; see also Murray, *First Hundred Years*, pp. 118–120.

[142] 'Doctrine and Inter-Church Relations Committee' report, BUS Assembly, 21 October 1976, *Scottish Baptist Yearbook 1977*, pp. 79–80; 'Roman Catholic/Baptist Conversations', *Scottish Baptist Yearbook 1977*, pp. 85–86.

churches. The Scottish Baptist Lay Preachers' Association (SBLPA) had been formed in May 1925 at a meeting in Charlotte Baptist Chapel, Edinburgh. It had been resolved 'to proceed with the preparation of a list of men suitably qualified for Lay Ministry'. A letter to this effect was published in the June 1925 edition of the *SBM* and it had resulted in a list of twenty four recognised lay preachers being recognised.[143] It has been stated that when lay preachers had been 'recognised' in 1927, women had been listed on the same terms as men.[144] However, the first lady named as passing the examination and qualifying as a recognised lay preacher was Miss Nellie Allan of Dundee in 1939.[145] The official minute of this milestone is given in the minutes of the 28 May 1941 SBLPA committee meeting. The entry on Miss Allan included these words: 'It was noted that Miss Allan was the first woman Lay Preacher to be admitted to this list in Scotland.'[146] There were no further changes in perspective in the next few decades. In 1964 Mary Causton wrote a thoughtful article in the *SBM* on the increasing number of roles being undertaken by women in Scottish Baptist Churches. She noted that there are 'many churches where women can be found doing everything except preaching and administering the sacraments.' However, she expressed concern about the increasing reluctance of men to attend church or take on leadership roles and wondered how this situation could be addressed effectively. Had church life become too feminine making it hard for men to feel at home in our congregations? Causton acknowledged that some Baptists were advocating 'women in the ministry', but she cautioned against the inevitable acceptance of such a step, calling instead for a humble acknowledgement that a much deeper rethinking of our calling as Christians was required so that men and women –

---

[143] 'Baptist Lay Preachers', *SBM*, 51.6 (June 1925), p. 84; Philip H. Staley, *The Scottish Baptist Lay Preachers' Association: A Historical Review* (N.P.: Scottish Baptist History Project & The Scottish Baptist Lay Preachers' Association, 1993), p. 2. 'Lay Preachers Association' First Annual Report, Baptist Union Assembly, 28 October 1926, *Scottish Baptist Yearbook 1927*, p. 117.

[144] Balfour, 'Twentieth Century Since 1914', p. 85 stated that 'women were listed on the same terms as men'. This is likely to be incorrect. Those individuals recognised in October 1925 were all men. 'Lay Preachers' Association of the Baptist Union', Minute Book 1, 12 May 1925 to 26 May 1937, p. 4; In the minutes for 20 October 1930 on p. 58 of this minute book, for example, it states: 'The annual report and the revision of the List of Recognised Men were remitted to the Convener and Supply Secretary'.

[145] Staley, *Scottish Baptist Lay Preachers' Association*, p. 5. Miss Allan's obituary was published in the *SBM*, 114.7 (9 July 1989), p. 12.

[146] 'Minutes of Meeting of Committee held on 28 May, 1941, in Charlotte Chapel, Edinburgh', 'Lay Preachers Association of the Baptist Union', Minute Book 2, 15 September 1937 to 24 November 1953, p. 31.

people of all ages – would play their full part in local congregational life.[147] These were important questions to ask about the respective roles of men and women in Scottish Baptist congregations.

The decision by the Church of Scotland to appoint women elders at their General Assembly in May 1966 was noted in an article in the *SBM* that was previously printed in a BUGBI publication. The unknown English author made plain his own sympathies for ordaining women and expressed concern that so few General Assembly delegates had considered the matter to be of much importance. He turned to reflect on attitudes in the British Baptist Unions and concluded that: 'especially in Scotland, we have been slow to give women a place in the courts of the church.'[148] An anonymous article on 'Deaconesses' later that year highlighted the good work they did and ended with a cryptic comment about looking forward to see 'where the exploration of "New Paths" will lead in the days to come'.[149] The Scottish Baptist College had previously had a woman student in 1930, Miss Florence Stewart, as part of her training for overseas service. It was not until 1976 that another woman, Janice Sneddon from Motherwell Baptist Church applied and was accepted to study for the London Diploma of Theology with a view to teaching Religious Education. In the following year a second woman Muriel McNair was accepted to study for the London B.D. She gained that award in 1980.[150] A brief article in September 1972 noted the appointment of Margaret Jarman as minister of Dalston and Salters Hall Baptist Church in London.[151] In addition, the BUS Council did produce this affirmative statement on the place of women at its 9 September 1975 meeting: 'The time is right to recognise that God has given gifts of Christian leadership to women as well as to men, and believes that this should be borne in mind in the life of the local church and the Denomination at large.'[152] However, no serious changes of practice were under consideration amongst Scottish Baptists at that time.

---

[147] Mary Causton, 'The Ministry of Women'. *SBM*, 89.4 (April 1964), p. 5.

[148] 'Mainly For Women Elders!', *SBM*, 91.8 (August 1966), p. 5.

[149] Anon, 'Deaconesses . . . Men and Women!', *SBM*, 91.10 (October 1966), p. 5.

[150] Murray, *Scottish Baptist College Centenary History*, p. 72.

[151] 'A Woman in a Man's World', *SBM*, 97.9 (September 1972), p. 15.

[152] *Scottish Baptist Yearbook 1976*, p. 59.

## Scottish Baptists and Social Action[153]

In the 1960s there appears to have been a greater emphasis on the social application of the gospel to daily life, with a higher profile in the pages of the *SBM* accorded to the work of the charity that later became known as Christian Aid. Baptists in Scotland, alongside the other Protestant Churches in the country, had been supporters of 'Christian Reconstruction in Europe', a charitable body formed in 1945 by British and Irish Churches to aid refuges and the rebuilding of communities required after World War Two. This body had been renamed the 'Inter-Church Aid and Refugee Service' in 1948. A 'Christian Aid' fundraising week was pioneered from the 1950s, an event promoted in the *SBM* in the 1960s. It included a variety of innovative ways to raise funds.[154] This charity became known as 'Christian Aid' in 1964 when the threat of hunger and potential famine made agricultural development a greater priority in some of the world's poorest communities. It was also under the auspices of this cause in 1969 that Action for World Development was formed raising awareness of the need for sustainable development alongside global trading arrangements.[155] Annual reports on the work of Christian Aid were published in the *Scottish Baptist Yearbook*.[156] However, in 1968, at a time when some Scottish Baptists were concerned that the traditionally supported aid agencies, like Christian Aid were beginning to forget the importance of evangelistic efforts that the Evangelical Alliance formed its own aid agency Tearfund. Jim Taylor, editor of the *SBM*, echoed the views of many of the SBM's readers with respect to these two aid agencies.

> Those fully committed to offering the Gospel to men are beginning to rediscover the biblical emphasis that faith without works is dead and that bread must be offered too. It is hoped that those deeply committed to offering bread will also discover their evangelistic obligations.[157]

Support for Christian Aid was maintained by the majority of these congregations, though a small but increasing number of Baptist Churches felt more comfortable channelling their funds for aid and development work

---

[153] A fuller treatment of this subject is given in Murray, 'Be Not Conformed but Transformed, in Talbot (ed.), *Distinctive People*, pp. 228–247.

[154] For example, *SBM*, 86.5 (May 1961), pp. 4, 8; 86.8 (August 1961), p. 8; 91.2 (February 1966,p. 1; details of supported projects were reported also – see, for example, 87.3 (March 1962), p. 7; 90.9 (September 1965), pp. 5, 10–11; 91.4 (April 1966), pp. 9–10;

[155] www.christianaid.org.uk/about-us/our-history accessed 12 February 2019.

[156] For example, 'Scottish Churches Committee on Christian Aid', *Scottish Baptist Yearbook 1979*, pp. 60–61.

[157] 'Outlook', *SBM*, 93.6 (June 1968), p. 1.

through this more overtly Evangelical agency in the 1970s. However, the principle of supporting aid and development work as part of Christian ministry by Scottish Baptists was in line with the wider recovery of a more balanced social vision by Evangelicals[158] that would receive formal acknowledgement at the Lausanne Conference on World Evangelisation in 1974.[159]

There was also a growing awareness of practical needs at home with Scottish Baptists being asked to give generously to a new charity called 'Shelter' that was formed to address the needs of homeless people in the United Kingdom.[160] It was a natural development at this time also to be aware of the growing need for accommodation for elderly people. As early as 1956 the Social Services Committee of the Baptist Union had indicated its awareness of this problem.[161] In time a number of facilities were established by Scottish Baptists including the Robertson Rest Home in Newport, Fife, just across the Tay Bridge from Dundee. It had been previously used as a Baptist holiday home.[162] In April 1971 the *SBM* had a report of progress on 'The Tor', a home for elderly people set up under the auspices of the Edinburgh and Lothians Baptist Association, with Peter Clark, minister of Bristo Baptist Church, Edinburgh, the driving force behind it.[163] There was also growing awareness of the need to care for people with mental health issues. A number of articles on this subject appeared in the *SBM*.[164] Peter Bowes, minister of Morningside Baptist Church, Edinburgh, inspired by the work of the L'Arche Community in France set up the Ark Housing Association, first in Edinburgh and then in other parts of Scotland, to care for people with mental health

---

[158] See Tim Chester, *Awakening to a World of Need: The Recovery of Evangelical Social Concern* (Leicester: IVP, 1993), for more details of this change.

[159] See Jacob Thomas, *From Lausanne to Manila: Evangelical Social Though: Models of Missions and the Social Relevance of the Gospel* (Delhi: ISPCK, 2003), pp. 52–65. A wider assessment of the significance of Lausanne is found in Margunn Serigstad Dahle, Lars Dahle and Knud Jorgensen (eds), *The Lausanne Movement: A Range of Perspectives* (Regnum Edinburgh Centenary Series Volume 22; Oxford: Regnum, 2014).

[160] *SBM*, 92.12 (December 1967), pp. 3–4.

[161] *Scottish Baptist Yearbook 1957*, p. 161.

[162] D. Eric Watson, 'Robertson Rest Home', *SBM*, 96.5 (May 1971) p. 12.

[163] See Murray, 'Be Not Conformed but Transformed', p. 239; and Maurice Oates, 'The ELBA Housing Society', *SBM*, 96.4 (April 1971), p. 4; 96.10 (October 1971), p.16;

[164] For example, *SBM*, 92.2 (February 1967), pp. 8–9; 92.3 (March 1967), pp. 6–7.

issues.¹⁶⁵ Scottish Baptists had consistent and repeated concerns about drug and alcohol consumption because of the social consequences associated with these activities.¹⁶⁶ They also, for example, opened hostels for alcoholics at St Vincent Street and Argyle Street in Glasgow, and Adelaide Place Baptist Church in that city opened a hostel for homeless girls, The Elpis Centre in Buccleuch Street.¹⁶⁷ The best known Scottish Baptist response to the problem of homelessness was the launch of Bethany Christian Trust in Edinburgh. Alan Berry, minister of South Leith Baptist Church, launched a venture that has been a remarkable success, both in Edinburgh and further afield in Scotland.¹⁶⁸ Scottish Baptist words were matched by effected action on the ground in addressing some of these social problems.

This Christian constituency also offered a measured response to proposed amendments to the laws relating to marriage and divorce.¹⁶⁹ David Steel's 'Medical Termination of Pregnancy' bill in 1967 received little coverage, but it is clear from James Taylor's editorial comment in the May 1967 *SBM* that he viewed its passage with deep regret.¹⁷⁰ Scottish Baptists like many other Christians were troubled by the increasing quantity of programmes on television and in theatre and cinema productions and published literature that promoted moral stances at variance with Christian moral convictions.¹⁷¹ There was strong support for work of Mary Whitehouse and the National Viewers and Listeners Association and the Festival of Light movement that led to the formation of CARE, the Christian Action, Research and Education agency to

---

[165] Peter Bowes, 'The launching of the ark', *SBM*, 104.1 (January 1979), pp. 4–5; Murray. 'Be Not Conformed', p. 240.

[166] For example, William H. Fleming, 'The Christian & Social Problems', *SBM*, 90.6 (June 1965), pp. 6–8;

[167] 'Christian Citizenship Committee report, *Scottish Baptist Yearbook 1978*, p. 41.

[168] The best source of information on its work is Anne E. Berry, *Giving Hope and A Future* (Tain: Christian Focus, 2009).

[169] Michael J. Walker, 'Outlook Divorce', *SBM*, 91.9 (September 1966)

[170] "What's In A Name?", *SBM*, 92.5 (May 1967), front facing page.

[171] Pressure from the BBC in London for a more diverse range of Sunday broadcast programmes on Scottish television was in evidence as early as 1957. However, the key leaders of Scottish television led by Melville Dinwiddie resisted the proposed changes at that time. There were also battles with the BBC in London during the 'Swinging Sixties' over what standards of conduct should be enforced over broadcast material. See the controversy over the broadcast in Scotland in 1964 of a short clip of a film version of Buchan's *The Thirty Nine Steps* that was about to open in London's West End. Walker, BBC IN SCOTLAND, pp. 217–218, 241–242.

promote traditional moral convictions.[172] The large crowd of over 4,500 people that gathered in George Square, Glasgow, for the Scottish Festival of Light in January 1972, was a source of encouragement and quiet confidence that this event was a symbol of Christians around the country beginning to take more seriously their engagement with social and moral issues at that time.[173] Scottish Baptists alongside other Christians in the early 1970s were displaying a quiet confidence that they had something to contribute to debates on these issues in the public square.

It was not only issues of personal morality that engaged their attention at that time. There were contributions raised on a range of wider topics of which the ones chosen here are examples. Concern was expressed for the wellbeing of 'Travelling People' in a report from the Christian Citizenship Committee to the Annual Assembly in 1978. Members had foreseen that the proposed Government housing legislation could make it very difficult for members of this community to find sufficient legal sites for their caravans in future.[174] Industrial relations problems in the wider society were also an increasing concern in these decades especially the growing problem of unofficial strikes. A motion passed at the October 1974 Baptist Union Assembly stated: 'The Assembly expresses its concern about the incidence of unofficial strikes and the acquisitiveness which threatened to paralyse industry and disrupt our economy…It is our conviction that men and women should seek higher standards for their lives rather than higher standards of living.'[175] This call for sustainable social and economic progress was a more progressive measure than might have been recognised at the time in the light of more recent concerns about climate change and sustainable development of the earth's natural resources.

Issues around Race Relations were understood as an ongoing concern in the United Kingdom,[176] but this issue was seen as a particular problem overseas in both South Africa and the United States. At the 1963 Assembly the convener of the Christian Citizenship committee proposed a clear motion on this topic.

---

[172] Examples of articles from the SBM include: Ben Davis, 'Clean Up Television', *SBM*, 96.6 (June 1971), p. 8; 96.8 (August 1971), Back page; Ben Davis, 'Schools Broadcasting Investigation', *SBM*, 96.9 (September 1971), p. 13; James Taylor, 'Outlook – Questions from a Festival', *SBM*, 96.12 (December 1971), p. 1.

[173] James Taylor, 'Outlook – Reflections of a Festival', *SBM*, (February 1972), p. 1.

[174] Christian Citizenship Committee report, *Scottish Baptist Yearbook 1979*, pp. 41–42.

[175] Baptist Union of Scotland Annual Assembly, 24 October 1974, *Scottish Baptist Yearbook 1975*, p. 70.

[176] 'The new Black presence in Britain', *Scottish Baptist Yearbook 1978*, p. 40.

> The Baptist Union of Scotland, met in Assembly, expresses its deep concerns at racial antagonism in various parts of the world, especially in South Africa and the United States of America, although in this country we are not immune from its expression with tragic consequences. The Assembly condemns all racial discrimination, whatever form it takes and wherever practised and asserts equal rights for all men.[177]

It was a clear and unequivocal declaration of the equality of persons.[178] A more sophisticated statement on Human Rights, composed by the BWA, was adopted by the October 1978 Assembly and affirmed liberty for all people, advocating for the freedom of conscience, religion, belief and speech and called for the release of persons imprisoned purely for their political or religious beliefs. At the same time there was a clear condemnation of all forms of physical or psychological torture of prisoners in state custody. Another motion passed at the same assembly called on the United States and the Soviet Union to conclude treaties on Strategic Arms Limitation.[179] Concerns about nuclear radiation and the potential damage caused by nuclear proliferation had also been raised on a number of occasions over these decades.[180] Others in Scottish Baptist ranks went further and questioned whether in a nuclear age it was possible to advocate the old familiar 'Just War' approach.[181] In summary, Scottish Baptists in the 1960s and 1970s showed a clear commitment to social action in a variety of forms in practice, as well as the retention of a strong conviction about the priority of personal evangelism and the public proclamation of the Christian Gospel. A holistic approach to ministry in the wider community was normative for many in their ranks.

The 1960s and 1970s has been viewed as an age of religious crisis for the Christian Church in the Western world. There was no doubt that many Scottish Baptists struggled to adjust to some of the changes taking place in the wider society in these years. However, under the bold and dynamic leadership of Union Secretary Andrew MacRae Scottish Baptists saw new churches planted, innovative forms of evangelistic endeavours carried out, and in particular a growing partnership with Southern Baptists that contained the

---

[177] BUS Assembly, 24 October 1963, *Scottish Baptist Yearbook 1964*, p. 136.

[178] White rule in Rhodesia and South Africa was viewed as simply wrong, *SBM*, 92.4 (April 1967), p. 1.

[179] 'Baptist World Alliance Resolutions', *Scottish Baptist Yearbook 1979*, pp. 86, 106–107.

[180] For example, Dr Douglas G. Neilson, 'Scientific Facts About Radiation and Fall-Out', *SBM*, 89.3 (March 1964), pp. 10–12; 'Citizenship Report', BUS Assembly 26 October 1977, *Scottish Baptist Yearbook 1978*, p. 83.

[181] Robert Armstrong, 'Is War Ever Justified?', *SBM*, 89.2 (February 1964), pp. 7–8.

promise of further successes in the coming years. There were real difficulties in gaining and retaining the allegiance of many older children and young people which have to be acknowledged, though the influence of the renewal movement provided a significant engagement with some younger adults that led to some growing churches at that time. Scottish Baptists developed closer ties with other British Baptists in these years and made a valued contribution to the work of the EBF and BWA. There were painful disagreements in their ranks over relations with other Christian Churches, especially on the world stage, but by 1980 a more coherent vision of appropriate ecumenical engagement had been reached. Discussions about the role of women continued with an acknowledgement that further steps were likely to be taken in recognising their contributions in Christian ministry in the coming years. In the field of social action small but significant contributions were made by notable individuals. Overall, despite acknowledging the difficulties for Christian witness in these decades Scottish Baptists seized some of the opportunities for developing their work at this time and entered the 1980s with real confidence that further progress could be made.

CHAPTER 9

# Shoots of Recovery:
# The Baptist Union of Scotland, 1980–1994

In 1980 there were significant signs of optimism in Scottish Baptist ranks concerning their prospects for the decade to come. Andrew MacRae the retiring General Secretary had written the following in his final report before handing over to his successor Peter Barber. 'Prospects for Scottish Baptists in the future are quite enormous. Signs of God's blessings abound, giving us every encouragement to know we have His blessing. But He is demanding more of us in terms of the stewardship of our lives and resources.'[1] Later in the same report he declared:

> 'The days before us are full of possibilities. I have never felt more excited or expectant about Scottish Baptist life. The dreams and the possibilities of tomorrow crowd my mind.... As Caleb said to the hesitant and fearful as well as to the expectant as he viewed the land of God's promise, 'Let us go up at once and possess it, for we are well able to occupy it.'[2]

How realistic was this perspective on Scottish Baptist church life and how did it compare with the situation in other Scottish Churches at that time? The 1984 Census of Scottish Church attendances[3] was broadly welcomed by the participant bodies, because although there were some underlying challenges there was also some encouraging news from its results.[4] Overall 17% of the

---

[1] 'Prospects for the Future', *Scottish Baptist Yearbook 1980*, p. 17.

[2] 'Expectancy', *Scottish Baptist Yearbook 1980*, pp. 19–20.

[3] The data given in this paragraph comes from John Highet, 'Trends in Attendance and membership', in Peter Brierley and Fergus MacDonald (eds), *Prospects for Scotland From a Census of the Churches in 1984* (Bromley: MARC Europe & The National Bible Society of Scotland, 1985), pp. 9–10.

[4] It is important to note that the low level of returns from the churches has had an impact on the data given in this particular survey. Baptist churches, for example, not reporting their statistics were given the average figures for other sister congregations. This resulted in lower figures for Baptist churches in the Central Region because the largest Baptist church in the area, Stirling Baptist Church, had not submitted its figures. I am grateful to David Bebbington for providing this information.

adult population of Scotland attended church each week compared to 9% in England and 13% in Wales. There were more churches whose attendance was growing compared to those that were in decline. In addition, 45% of all Protestant churchgoers belonged to churches which had grown significantly over the four-year period 1980–1984. Most encouragingly there were more children attending church in 1984 than in 1980 as well. It was disappointing that Protestant church attendance overall had declined by 2% over the past four years, but it was evident that the level of decline had slowed down.[5] In terms of specific churches' results there was also some good as well as some disappointing news that emerged from this Census. The Roman Catholic Church whose attendance figures had stood up remarkably well compared to those of the Church of Scotland in previous surveys, now also exhibited significant decline. For example, from 1959 when 63% of Roman Catholic members attended weekly mass, it was down to 35% in 1984. By comparison 34% of Church of Scotland members were counted at Sunday worship in 1959 and 29% in 1984. The narrowing of the gap highlighted in particular the weakening of the commitment to Sunday worship attendance by Scottish Roman Catholics. The data relating to Scottish Baptists, by contrast, showed a 4% rise in church membership between 1980 and 1984, though a fall of 4% in attendances. However, the latter was largely attributed to the numerical falls in attendances at Independent or Grace or Reformed Baptist congregations, rather than in the Baptist Union causes. In fact, proportionate to membership, attendances at Baptist Union of Scotland congregations was actually greater in 1984 than 1959.[6] The Congregation Union also saw attendances rise by 3% though church membership fell by 7% over these four years. In the same time period the Scottish Episcopal Church and 'Other Churches', showed a 9% and a 1% increase in attendances respectively, with the former body having comparable attendances at its congregations in 1984 as it had done previously in 1959. The more conservative Presbyterian bodies, the Free Church of Scotland and the Free Presbyterian Church of Scotland, had declined by around 10% in attendances. The Methodist Church recorded a 9% fall in membership and a 5% fall in attendances over this short time period. In summary, for the Church of Scotland congregations there was some evidence that the rate of decline in attendances was slowing, though the opposite was true for the Roman Catholic Church. By contrast, some of the

---

[5] Fergus MacDonald, 'Introduction', in Brierley & MacDonald (eds), *Prospects for Scotland*, pp. 5–6.

[6] It is interesting that in the 1980s English Baptists also saw significant growth in numbers. Growth in membership in Baptist Union of Great Britain affiliated causes was the largest for sixty years. Two of the contributory factors for growth were the success of Mission England 1984, the Billy Graham campaign of that year and involvement in the charismatic renewal movement. See Randall, *English Baptists of the Twentieth Century*, pp. 417–418.

smaller denominations like Baptists and Congregationalists registered an actual increase in the number of people attending Sunday worship services. As a result the latter bodies were optimistic about their future prospects in the early 1980s.

The upbeat tone in Scottish Baptist ranks was exemplified in the October 1979 Presidential Address from Gilbert Ritchie, descendant of the well-known Christian missionary Hudson Taylor, and given the middle name Hudson after him. Ritchie was minister of Bearsden Baptist Church. It was entitled 'The audacity of faith' and was inspired by the visionary missionary service of Hudson Taylor in China. Ritchie challenged his fellow Scottish Baptists not to become risk averse in their planning for the future, instead to be bold and courageous. 'Forward planning calls for vision ... and faith – courageous, persevering faith which will stir us to work to bring our visions to fulfilment.'[7] The call for action was matched on the ground by some deeds reported in the Union Secretary's Annual Report. The second church-plant in Livingston in the Dedridge area had commenced with Alastair Brown appointed as an assistant to the Ladywell minister William Slack.[8] New fellowships had begun in Kinross, Beith, Bridge of Don and Inverurie. The most remarkable statistic was the 34% increase in believers' baptisms compared with the previous year, a figure that was 23% higher than any total attained in the previous decade. In addition, the number of young adults attending Baptist Churches was significantly up on previous years and new members added on profession of faith was 50% above the average in the last ten years. There had been a concerted campaign during the year to encourage adherents to become members of their local churches and these statistical increases were in part a measure of the success of that initiative. Andrew MacRae was convinced that the deliberate setting of goals for growth each year by local churches led to members taking greater responsibility to ensure that these targets were accomplished or at least achieved greater success than would have been attained without this kind of goal-setting. MacRae ideally hoped that congregations would aim annually for baptising new converts at a number equivalent to 10% of the church membership figure. In the increasingly secular climate in Scotland this was a remarkably ambitious target to propose, but it was clear that at least a proportion of Scottish Baptists were endeavouring to attain it.[9]

The commitment levels in a typical Baptist church were a significant contributory factor to the achievements highlighted in this network of

---

[7] Gilbert H. Ritchie, 'The Audacity of Faith', *Scottish Baptist Yearbook 1980*, pp. 7–14.

[8] 'And Now there are two', *SBM*, 105.1 (January 1980), p. 3.

[9] Andrew MacRae, '110th Annual Report by the General Secretary', *Scottish Baptist Yearbook 1980*, pp. 15–20.

churches. Dr Campbell Murdoch, in an interesting study of denominational statistics from 1965 to 1980 found that the numerical growth in Scottish Baptist life was more likely to be found in a number of the smaller churches, alongside some of the recent church-plant congregations, with the largest decreases being found in some of the largest congregations. He highlighted that Scottish Baptists had been good at attracting new members during these years, but the downside was that a slightly larger number left our ranks. If the churches had a better track record of retaining its members, Murdock suggested, there could be further significant rises in total attendance at and membership of Baptist Union of Scotland congregations.[10] In the 1984 Census Scottish Baptists recorded the highest rate of church attendance per membership (107%) and 41% of its members attended twice on a Sunday compared to a national average of 13%. In addition, 38% of its churches were growing in size compared to the average figure of 26% and a smaller percentage of declining churches (10%) compared to a 22% average for the Churches as a whole in Scotland.[11] However, it was not a success story in all the churches because on the ground there were also ministers and congregations struggling to make progress in evangelising their communities. In addition, there was concern over the number of ministers who were resigning from pastoral ministry suffering from 'disillusionment, despair or disenchantment', for a variety of reasons that included the inflexibility of churches to make changes in areas like evangelism or disagreements over worship styles or conflicts with other church leaders, together with serious struggles for many manse families to make ends meet on the low stipends.[12] When these challenges are taken into account and the decline in most other sets of denominational statistics at that time are duly acknowledged, the relatively modest increase in numbers in their ranks must be viewed as a significant success.

## Home Evangelism

The 1980s had been a period of growth for Scottish Baptists, a unique phenomenon amongst the major Christian traditions in Scotland, as no other denomination that had experienced membership decline in the twentieth century had been able to reverse that trend. It was suggested that standing firm on orthodox doctrine, modernising forms of worship under the influence

---

[10] Dr Campbell Murdock, 'Small is Beautiful and Productive', *SBM*, 107.8 (August 1982), pp. 8–9.

[11] Peter H. Barber, 'Baptist Churches', in Brierley & MacDonald (eds), *Prospects for Scotland*, p. 45. See also his comments on the 1984 Census Report in the *Scottish Baptist Yearbook* 1986, p. 28.

[12] 'Ministers–Deacons–Elders', *Scottish Baptist Yearbook 1980*, pp. 98–102.

of the charismatic renewal movement and engaging in outreach to younger people had been the key factors for the Baptist successes.[13] Another small, but not insignificant factor was the increasing number of attendees coming from other ethnic backgrounds. This was not particular to Baptist causes as other denominations also gained adherents and members as well. One congregation that gained a much higher proportion of worshippers from other countries was Adelaide Place Baptist Church, Glasgow, under the inspirational leadership of Donald McCallum. It saw a remarkable level of ethnic diversity for a Scottish Baptist congregation in the 1980s. On Sunday 4 May 1980, the service was led by Pan Chi-Khen, the first member of the Glasgow Chinese Christian Fellowship to be baptised in Adelaide Place, and now a full-time worker amongst Chinese-speaking residents of Glasgow, with guest-preacher Daniel Cheung, pastor of Kowloon Baptist Church, Hong Kong, with a congregation comprising of people from nineteen different countries. A Sunday afternoon service in Cantonese filled the sanctuary and, in the evening, a newly formed African and Caribbean Christian Fellowship took the service, resulting in over twenty-five nations represented that Sunday.[14] This particular congregation was exceptional in its ethnic diversity, but increasingly the numbers of attendees from other countries though small was rising from this time onwards in many urban Scottish Christian churches, including Baptist causes.

In 1980 steps forward were seen with the constitution of the Bourtreehill Baptist Church in Irvine and the Alness cause in the Highlands, together with a replanted congregation established under Brian Jago in Bo'ness. Noel Kirkman was leading a growing new church in Dalbeattie, near Dumfries and one of the pioneer ministries being planned was for the Whitfield estate in Dundee.[15] On Sunday 7 March 1982 over 100 people gathered in Capelrigg House for a family worship service to launch the new Newton Mearns Baptist Fellowship.[16] It was noteworthy also that in a number of areas in Scotland Baptist Churches were partnering together in outreach and church-planting ventures, that included the south-west of Scotland, the new causes in Aberdeen and in Caithness.[17] Other churches utilised evangelistic teams from

---

[13] Brown, *Religion and Society in Scotland since 1707*, pp. 158–161.

[14] Donald McCallum, 'Twenty-five nations represented at service', *SBM* 105.6 (June 1980), p. 2. See also 'Vietnamese 'boat people' baptised' [in Adelaide Place], *SBM*, 105.7 (July 1980), p. 2.

[15] Muriel McNair, 'Contacts made in Unusual Ways', *SBM*. 107.4 (April 1982), p. 12; *Scottish Baptist Yearbook* 1980, pp. 16,18.

[16] Newton Mearns New Birth', *SBM*, 107.4 (April 1982), p. 15.

[17] Peter H. Barber, 'Scene Around', *SBM*, 107.8 (August 1982), p. 12. For more details see Stewart, *Baptist Union Towards 2000; A Statistical Look at Scottish Baptist Life in the Latter Half of the 20$^{th}$ Century*, p. 44; Fisher, 'North-East', in Bebbington

sister churches in other parts of the country, for example in April 1985 the Islay congregations hosted a mission team from Motherwell led by Laurie Dennison that greatly encouraged the small groups of local believers,[18] and in August the same year a team from Ayr Baptist Church led by its associate minister John Robb attracted a significant proportion of the local population to its meetings. Its success raised hopes for the third partnership mission week scheduled that year when an American Baptist team came to Islay.[19] In his October 1984 'Department of Mission' report Peter Barber drew attention to a wide range of new initiatives that showed encouraging progress. The new cause at Wigtown led by Robert and Marsha Ford had purchased a house in an ideal location for holding group meetings and had already attracted interest from a growing number of contacts in that rural location. The Stenhouse-Gorgie Church in Edinburgh had purchased a hall from the Episcopal Church in Colinton Mains which after refurbishment had now been brought into use for its work. The new work in Stranraer led by Ian Cameron was building up contacts in the town. Planning permission had finally been granted for new premises to be erected for International Baptist Church in Cults and the neighbouring Aberdeen congregation in Bridge of Don had purchased a manse and were also in negotiations for the erection of a church building. Loren and Cherry Turnage had launched another church-plant in nearby Ellon. The Montrose Church had given an offer for a site in a different part of their community with a view to erecting a new church building as well as selling the old premises. St Andrews Baptist Church had begun a witness in Langlands and the Castlehill Fellowship in Bearsden, a few months previously, had appointed John Hay as pastor. He had previously served there as a student pastor. The church in Thurso was now established after two excellent years of service by the McPhees, a Canadian Baptist couple, who had subsequently returned to their homeland after this assignment. In Fife, the Granary, a building gifted to the Collydean Church by the Glenrothes Development Corporation, after two years of building alterations by the congregation, was opened officially as the premises of Collydean Baptist Church.[20] All these developments were a sign of the real potential for further growth in Baptist witness in different parts of the country.

Three years later in 1987 there was a request to affiliate with the Baptist Union from three churches, the newly formed Ellon Baptist Church and

---

(ed.), *Baptists in Scotland*, pp. 275–76; and J.A. Andrew, 'Ayrshire, Dumfries and Galloway', in Bebbington (ed.), *Baptists in* Scotland, pp. 142–144.

[18] 'Island Mission', *SBM*, 110.6 (June 1985), p. 16.

[19] *SBM* 110.10 (October 1985), p. 15.

[20] Peter H. Barber, 'Church Extension', *Scottish Baptist Yearbook 1985*, pp. 49–50. On the earlier work in Collydean see James Thomson, 'Collydean Granary awaiting harvest', *SBM* 106.7 (July 1981), pp. 6–7.

likewise from Central Baptist Church, Dundee, after the merger of the former Ward Road and Rattray Street congregations in the city, together with Carlisle Baptist Church, which became the first congregation in England to become a member of the Baptist Union of Scotland. Of the newer congregations there was good news concerning the building projects of the Montrose and Bridge of Don churches. In Newton Mearns increasing attendances required a third move to larger school premises to accommodate the number wishing to be present at Sunday services. The new work in Stonehaven was seeing encouraging attendances at their Sunday service as was the St Ninians witness under the auspices of Stirling Baptist Church. In addition, the Falkirk congregation had launched a new work in Polmont, the Morningside Edinburgh church in Burdiehouse and Charlotte Chapel had seen the successful birth of a new church in the Barnton district of Edinburgh.[21] It was clear that the momentum for church growth was in evidence in the ranks of Scottish Baptists throughout the 1980s.

The most influential factor for this renewal of Baptist churches was the adoption of a three-year Simultaneous Evangelism Crusade, known as the 'Scotreach' programme, in 1983, in which 144 Baptist congregations joined in three years of preparation, mobilisation and consolidation. This figure is substantially higher than the 100 churches that participated in the 1969 Simultaneous Evangelism Crusade.[22] In fact, the ownership of this mission by Scottish Baptists was greater than any previous mission since the Graham Crusade of 1955. The comprehensiveness of the planning for this initiative was crucial. There were prayer triplet schemes set up; thirty-three ministers were trained to lead church day conferences in Worship, Fellowship and Stewardship; a Scotreach newspaper produced that sold over 135,000 copies; regional rallies to promote the vision during the time of the programme; a range of publicity materials from car stickers to tee-shirts, sweatshirts, calendars, stickers and posters; local churches were required to have evangelism committees that had the task of keeping the Scotreach vision before each congregation. The range of outreach events varied from big rallies to house meetings, the use of films to partnership missions with American Baptist teams and friendship evangelism over meals for invited guests. Falkirk Baptist Church, for example, featured as the lead story in their local newspaper, during the time they, in partnership with some other local churches in the autumn of 1985, were showing the Jesus Film at their local cinema. Much to the surprise of the cinema owners more people wanted to see

---

[21] Peter H. Barber, 'Growth Points', *Scottish Baptist Yearbook 1988*, p. 33.

[22] It was the model for the 'Advance 87' evangelistic programme in the Yorkshire Baptist Association. Peter Barber gave some assistance with visits to Yorkshire at that time. I am grateful to Keith Jones, then Association Secretary for providing this information.

it than the Rambo film which led to the memorable headline: 'Jesus ousts Rambo'. In total, 3,645 people turned up over the fortnight to view the film. It was followed up by a series of monthly celebration events in the local Technical College which attracted a number of unchurched people who had been impressed with the film.[23] The recorded conversions at Scotreach-related events took place overwhelmingly in local church settings rather than at large rallies, which indicated that the effectiveness of the large-scale Crusades was being called into question.[24] When the statistics for the 1980s are compared with previous years in the Baptist Union's history it is clear that this programme was more effective than any other Scottish Baptist initiative since the early years of the twentieth century. For a healthy church to maintain its position and to replace members who died or left for a variety of reasons there is a requirement for a minimum reproduction rate of 4% of the membership total. Scottish Baptists exceeded this percentage for baptisms throughout the 1980s until 1991 with the highest figures recorded in 1986 and 1987, 5.68% and 5.59% respectively, as a result of Scotreach.[25] These impressive results were not exclusively down to the impact of Scotreach as there was a measurably significant impact on Scottish Baptist churches by the 1981 Luis Palau Glasgow Crusade[26], the satellite-linked Shetland involvement in the Billy Graham Sheffield mission of June 1985, the 1989 Billy Graham Livelink Mission and his three-city 1991 Mission Scotland.[27] There was also a Dick Saunders Crusade in Edinburgh in 1981.[28] However, the length of impact of Scotreach was greater even than the 1955 Graham Crusade and it provided great encouragement for Scottish Baptists as they entered the last decade of the twentieth century because not since the 1920s had there been such a consistent advance of the cause.[29]

---

[23] Ian M. Reed, 'Jesus Ousts Rambo', *SBM*, 110.12 (December 1985), p. 5.

[24] *Scottish Baptist Yearbook 1983*, pp. 28, 49, 94; *1984*, pp. 65–67; *1985*, pp. 55–56; *1986*, pp. 54–55; *1987*, pp. 58–59.

[25] Hunt, 'Figure 16 Membership and Reproduction Rate', *Reflecting on Our Past*, pp. 32, Appendix 2, n.p.

[26] Articles in the *SBM* on this Crusade include 106.3 (March 1981), pp. 7, 9; 106.5 (May 1981), p. 1, 3, 7; 106.6 (June 1981), p. 1; 106.7 (July 1981), p. 2.

[27] Hunt, *Reflecting on Our Past*, pp. 18, 34; Peter Barber, 'Mission Shetland', *SBM*, 110.6 (June 1985), p. 10; 'Satellite Takers Hit Century', *SBM* 114.1 (January 1989), p. 12; 'Mission 89'. Editorial, *SBM*, 114.4 (April 1989), p. 1; 'Scottish Livelink', SBM, 114.8 9August 1989), p. 11.

[28] *SBM*, 106.5 (May 1981), p. 1.

[29] Hunt, 'Figure 16: Membership and Reproduction Rate', *Reflecting on Our Past*, p. 32.

The partnership in mission and church-planting with the Foreign Mission Board of the Southern Baptist Convention flourished in this era. To get an idea of the scale of commitment provided to Baptist Union of Scotland it is helpful to give an example of the numbers and variety of input given in support of this initiative. In October 1983, for example, Maurice and Kitty Anderson came to serve while established missionaries Loren and Cherry Turnage had a sabbatical year. Robert and Marsha Ford came to Wigtown to engage in outreach in the south-west peninsula. Kathy White was engaged in music and youth ministries in Ayr, the Ayrshire and Dumfriesshire Association as well as with the Baptist Union. Wanda Tallman returned home at that time after working alongside the Morningside Baptist Church in Edinburgh. Further requests for American personnel were made on behalf of the following churches: International and Bridge of Don in Aberdeen, Peterhead and Morningside Churches. An American youth team was expected in summer 1994 and the Masterlife Workshop was to be led in Glasgow in November 1983 by Dr Bill Wagner. Ron Barker who had delivered his seminar on the Continuous Witness Training Scheme for Personal Evangelism in September 1982, in Glasgow, was planning on developing this scheme in other parts of Scotland. In addition, there were placement opportunities for students in the USA, sabbatical study, pulpit exchanges and partnership team missions all being experienced by Scots in America or in Baptist congregations here in Scotland.[30] To give one example in the first week of October 1989, for example, there were eight evangelistic teams from the USA engaged in Partnership Missions in Scottish Baptist churches.[31] It could not be doubted that this was a significant investment of Southern Baptist personnel in Scotland and it was also clear that it brought real encouragement to Scottish Baptists as they gained a fresh confidence in outreach ministries through working alongside ministry colleagues from overseas.

At the end of the 1980s there had been further encouraging developments in many churches such as the new Wigtown Church being able to call its first Scottish Baptist pastor and the Tiree cause its first full-time pastor for several years, although the closure of the Largo Church was a reminder that other congregations were struggling to maintain a witness in their communities. New initiatives at Kinmylies and Nairn near Inverness were making good progress. The Castlehill church-plant in Bearsden was constituted as an autonomous church. The Montrose Baptist Church had now completed its new building in the Borrowfield area of the town. Peebles Baptist Church was investigating a site for a building to be erected and the Perth Church had

---

[30] 'United States Links', *Scottish Baptist Yearbook 1984*, p. 39.

[31] 'Partnership Missions Positive Reports', *SBM*, 114.11 (November 1989), p. 3.

made a start on its new church building.³² In 1993 the Arbroath Baptist Church began worshipping in their new Inverbrothock premises, a former Church of Scotland building. In Glasgow the Partick Baptist Church renovated its premises to be more effective in mission and the Queen's Park congregation purchased the nearby Camphill Church of Scotland premises to alleviate overcrowding on its current site. An even more ambitious redevelopment project was undertaken by the Adelaide Place congregation to turn their large premises into a multi-purpose centre that would include a nursery, hotel and restaurant, in addition to the retention of some existing facilities for its ongoing church work. A smaller number of church-plants were launched in the early 1990s. These ventures included Annan Baptist Fellowship, led by a pioneer minister that was jointly sponsored by the local congregation, Dumfries Baptist Church, the Baptist Union and the Southern Baptist Foreign Mission Board and the new witness in the Doonfoot area of the town established by Ayr Baptist Church at the same time as it launched its new community-care ministry.³³ It was evident that Scottish Baptists were working hard to adjust to the changing social context, but it was noticeable that the gains made in the early 1990s were much smaller than in the previous decade.

A determination to maintain this momentum was seen in the planning for participation in a number of conferences in the next few years including a denominational conference 'Toward 2000 – Scottish Baptists renewed for mission' that was held in June 1990 in Stirling University.³⁴ In addition, 'There is Hope', an Edinburgh based interdenominational outreach initiative was taken up by churches, including Baptist ones in a number of towns in Scotland during this decade. In 1989, for example, 149 churches of different denominations participated in 'There is Hope' campaigns, 30% of the churches were Church of Scotland, 19% Baptist, 14% Episcopal or Anglican, and the remainder were drawn from a smaller number of Christian congregations from other networks of churches.³⁵ A local example of a BUS Church participating in 'There is Hope' was Viewfield Baptist Church, Dunfermline that joined with other local churches in the town in distributing literature to homes in Crossford. It was responsible for the visitation to 2,000 homes in March 1989.³⁶ In 1990 ten Baptist churches shared in Partnership missions with visiting teams of Southern Baptists from the USA. The Baptist

---

³² Peter H. Barber, 'Among the Churches', *Scottish Baptist Yearbook 1990*, p. 97.

³³ Peter H. Barber, 'Growth Points', *Scottish Baptist Yearbook 1994*, pp. 105–106.

³⁴ 'Things to Come', *Scottish Baptist Yearbook 1990*, p. 98.

³⁵ 'There is Hope is Christians Praying Together for Revival', *SBM*, 114.9 (September 1989), p. 5.

³⁶ 'There is Hope', *SBM*, 114.4 (April 1989), p. 16.

Union mission fieldworker David Neil along with other Baptist ministers was exploring new ways of engaging in urban mission. He also began conversations with Operation Mobilisation and Youth with a Mission, two Christian parachurch organisations to explore the possibility of working together in evangelism in Scotland.[37] However, the momentum of the previous decade had gone by the mid-1990s. Interest in Partnership missions had diminished significantly.[38] The 'Minus to Plus' campaign of Reinhard Bonke in 1994 had produced hardly any conversions, despite the inflated expectations of its promoter and there was little interest shown by Scottish Baptists in the 'Disciple a Whole Nation (DAWN) 2000' interdenominational church-planting initiative that same year.[39] Remarkably, there had been some significant shoots of recovery with a reversal of the decline in the church membership figures of causes affiliated to the Baptist Union, as a result of vigorous evangelistic initiatives and effective church-planting strategies with growth in numbers effectively from the low-point of 15,791 members in 1976 up to a high point of 16,632 members in 1986. Between 1986 and 1995 there were decreases in membership some years and slight increases in other years, but after 1995 there would be a slow steady decline in the annual statistics.[40] Overall, though, under the visionary leadership of Andrew MacRae and Peter Barber the Baptist Union of Scotland had experienced significant success in its work of home evangelisation during these years.

## New Scottish Baptist History

John Stewart of Glasgow wrote a letter to the *SBM* editor in June 1980 to encourage the proper recording, preservation and storage of church records. He also asked the question: 'Who will write this new history?'[41] It was only a short time later on 4 October 1980 that the Scottish Baptist History Project was formed under the leadership of David Bebbington and Derek Murray.[42] A series of day conferences were organised twice yearly to look at aspects of Scottish Baptist history that would prepare the way for a new one volume

---

[37] 'Department of Mission', *Scottish Baptist Yearbook 1991*, pp. 118–119; *1992*, p. 122; *1993*, p. 142.

[38] 'Mission Department', *Scottish Baptist Yearbook 1992*, p. 122.

[39] 'Evangelism and Church Extension Committee' *Scottish Baptist Yearbook 1995*, pp. 147–149.

[40] Hunt, *Reflecting on Our Past*, Appendix 2, n.p..

[41] 'Letters', John Stewart, *SBM*, 105.6 (June 1980), p. 4.

[42] David W. Bebbington, 'Interest in History', *SBM*, 105.8 (August 1980), p. 11

history of Baptists in Scotland.⁴³ There were twenty contributors to the book. After a number of overview chapters covering earlier centuries, the others had a regional focus revealing that Baptists had established a presence in most parts of Scotland. This book provided a more detailed and scholarly analysis of the growth or decline of Baptist witness in Scotland compared with the earlier 1926 history of the denomination, edited by George Yuille.⁴⁴ It was a significant achievement that was warmly welcomed in the detailed review by James Taylor in the *SBM*.⁴⁵ This account in particular of the majority of the twentieth century provided a helpful focus for Scottish Baptists entering the last decade of the century.

## Wider Baptist Links

### Baptists in Britain

The ties with other Britain Baptists remained strong with regular settlement of ministers moving between Scotland and other parts of the United Kingdom. Peter Barber, himself, had come to his current post after serving as the minister of Upton Vale Baptist Church in Torquay. He was keen to maintain ties with colleagues in BUGBI and one particular opportunity was presented through attendance at the new Mainstream Conference held at Swanwick in Derbyshire. Mainstream was formed by Dr Raymond Brown, Principal of Spurgeon's College, Paul Beasley-Murray, senior minister of Altrincham Baptist Church and Rev. Douglas McBain of Streatham, formerly of Wishaw Baptist Church, to bring together charismatic and non-charismatic Baptists who shared a common desire for the further renewal of spiritual life in the churches.⁴⁶ This new venture, that was strongly commended by Barber, quickly became a regular fixture for a number of key leaders amongst English Baptists.⁴⁷ By contrast to this development south of the border, Alex Russell,

---

⁴³ For example, 'Baptists in the Highland and Islands', 6 November 1982, *SBM*, 107.10 (October 1982), p. 13.

⁴⁴ 'A Contemporary Mission Guide: Report on newly published history of Scottish Baptists', *SBM*, 113.8 (August 1988), p. 12.

⁴⁵ *SBM*, 103.9 (September 1988), p. 21.

⁴⁶ For a detailed analysis of the contribution of Mainstream see Derek Tidball, 'Mainstream:' 'far greater ambitions' – An Evaluation of Mainstream's Contribution to the Renewal of Denominational Life, 1979–1994', in Pieter Lalleman, Peter J. Morden and Anthony R. Cross (eds), (eds), *Grounded in Grace: Essays to Honour Ian M. Randall* (Didcot: Baptist Historical Society, 2013), pp. 202–222; and McBain, *Fire Over the Waters: Renewal Among Baptists & Others From the 1960s to the 1990s*, pp. 82–85.

⁴⁷ Peter Barber, 'Scene Around – Impressions of MAINSTREAM Conference', *SBM*, 107.3 (March 1982), p. 12.

in a July 1982 *SBM* article on charismatic renewal pointedly noted how few Scottish Baptists attended Scottish renewal conferences.[48] Barber also attended the annual Assemblies of other Baptist bodies to build ties of friendship, such as the English Assembly of the Welsh Baptist Union in July 1985 and followed that up with a detailed article in the *SBM* that gave some insights into the joys and challenges facing Welsh Baptists at that time.[49] In its bicentenary year BMS took a strategic decision to amend its constitution to open up the possibility of work inside the United Kingdom, alongside its existing commitments overseas, under the leadership of Reg Harvey. At the same time the Joint Consultative Committee (JCC) of the British Baptist Unions was discussing in detail more closer working between them and the BMS. In addition to providing information on respective ministries and co-operating in planning for visits by international guests or tours together to events overseas, it was clear that the time was right to extend co-operation to include planning for mission in Europe and encouraging joint meetings of those from the four bodies who shared common tasks such as youth-workers or mission advisers. The catalyst for this development had been the shared planning of the BMS bi-centenary celebrations in 1992, but it was made clear that though it was hoped stronger ties of fellowship would emerge between British Baptists none favoured the setting up of a federation with a further tier of organisation and administration. The autonomy of each member body must be retained.[50] On 1 January 1995 the JCC was renamed the 'Fellowship of British Baptists' (FBB). Its main purpose was to 'co-operate in mission in the United Kingdom and to consult more frequently on various areas such as publications, communications, promotion, fund-raising, youth work and other appropriate activities.'[51] A milestone was reached with the retirement of Eric Watson as Superintendent of the Baptist Union of Scotland. He has been the first holder of that post and in this context was the longest serving member of the JCC representing the Scottish Baptist Union. At the time of the signing of the covenant when the FBB was constituted Eric Watson continued to be present but in the capacity of President of the BMS. It was a remarkable acknowledgement of the high esteem in which his colleagues held him that this Londoner by birth was so prominent in the collective witness of British Baptists, serving on the FCC from its launch in 1971 until it became the FBB in 1994. The representatives on the JCC had worked together towards the

---

[48] Alex Russell, 'What is Charismatic Renewal all about?', *SBM*, 107.7 (July 1982), pp.3–4.

[49] Peter H. Barber, 'Scene Around', *SBM*, 110.8 (August 1985), pp. 10–11.

[50] 'British Baptists in Fellowship', in the '124th Annual Report by the General Secretary', *Scottish Baptist Yearbook 1994*, p. 109.

[51] Ian Mundie, Joint Consultative Committee Report, *Scottish Baptist Yearbook 1995*, pp. 150–151, 184.

acceptance of one another's pension schemes and parity in the setting of stipends and other allowances, together with greater mutual acceptance of ministers.[52] The British Baptist Unions and the BMS were now working together more closely than in past years and were committed to a trajectory of further co-operation in Christian service.

*Baptist Work in Europe*

The extraordinary energy put into home mission under the leadership of Andrew MacRae and Peter Barber was never at the expense of interest in or commitment to work outside of Scotland.[53] On the contrary, in these years Scottish Baptists would play an increasing part in work taking place in Continental Europe and also further afield becoming established participants in EBF activities. A second strand of involvement was through BMS's work in Europe. In the later 1980s it had accepted an invitation from the French Baptist Federation to partner in mission there.[54] They also joined with Baptist colleagues from other countries in the region in annual relief projects. In 1980, for example, projects in Hungary, Italy, Spain and West Germany were featured and supported.[55] An appeal was made through the pages of the *SBM* in April 1981 for assistance for Italian Baptists in Napoli affected by an earthquake. One hundred and thirty Italian towns, villages and four Baptist Churches were severely damaged by it. The aim was to raise sufficient funds through the EBF to erect between ten and twenty prefabricated new homes in a number of communities, under the oversight of the Federation of Evangelical Churches in Italy. EBF's aid workers were amongst the first relief agencies to arrive at the scene of the devastation. It was a demonstrable proof of the close ties of Baptists in Europe and their ability to work effectively together in addressing this kind of need.[56] Another project in which Scottish Baptists were wholeheartedly involved was their support for Croatian Baptists from the early 1990s, through support for the Baptist Response Europe fund, a means whereby food, medicine and other goods in short supply were

---

[52] Edward Burrows, 'Douglas Eric Watson', in 'Without a Vision the People Perish: The Distinctive Contribution to Scottish Baptist Life by Key Leaders of the Baptist Union', Talbot, *Distinctive People*, pp. 19–21.

[53] There was some unfair criticism that MacRae spent too much time focussing on work in other countries. See the review of his ministry by Gilbert Ritchie, 'Breathtaking in its scope', *SBM*. 105.6 (June 1980), p. 1.

[54] Ron Armstrong, 'BMS now in Europe', *SBM* 114.2 (February 1989), p. 3.

[55] 'Help for Europe', *SBM*, 105.1 (January 1980), p. 5.

[56] Letter from Knud Wumpelmann (EBF), *SBM* 106.4 (April 1981), p. 3. See also Peter Barber, 'Relief Work', *SBM*, 107.1 (January 1982), p. 8.

provided in the East by Western European colleagues. An increasing number of citizens of the former Yugoslavia lost their homes and were dependent on aid supplies in the brutal civil war, 1991–1995.[57] The Church that took the lead in this work was Viewfield Baptist Church, Dunfermline. Initial support for a Leeds-based charity in seeking to bring refugees temporarily to the UK in 1992 was unsuccessful due to a tightening of admission procedures by the British Government. As a result, a decision was taken to organise aid deliveries by truck from Dunfermline and work in partnership with the Croatian Baptist aid organisation Moz Blizni (My Neighbour) under the name Dunfermline Eurosave. As early as January 1994, their fourteenth truckload of aid in as many months was delivered to the warehouses run by the charity based in Rijeka Baptist Church. Moz Blizni had the responsibility for caring for in excess of 68,000 refugees in the district. It was a remarkable work run by local volunteers who made a point of seeking to build bridges between refugees from the different ethnic and religious communities in the former Yugoslavia.[58] From small beginnings a valuable partnership was established that would continue for more than a decade until 2005 when the refugee camps in Croatia were finally closed with the displaced persons settled in new homes.[59] The wider Scottish Baptist Union became committed to this cause in 1994 with the decision to support as their overseas project the aid work being carried out in the town of Karlovac in Croatia on the front line of this conflict.[60] Baptists in Scotland valued the opportunity to support fellow Baptists in Europe. Aid work was a significant part of their contribution in the 1980s and early 1990s.

Another venture they were committed to was the work of Eurolit. This scheme was jointly run by the BUS and the BUGBI, together with the United Society for Christian Literature, to provide theological literature for students and ministers in Eastern Europe, in particular in association with the Summer Institute for Theological Education (SITE) programme at the Ruschlikon Seminary in Zurich.[61] It consisted of a month's intensive study on site, followed by a correspondence course and provided each student on the completion of their studies with a mini-library which the individual was able to take home with them. In addition, more specialist literature would be

---

[57] 'Baptist Response Europe', *Scottish Baptist Yearbook 1993*, p.166.

[58] 'Ladies First', *SBM*. 119.3 (March 1994), p. 5.

[59] Dr David Hicks report at the BUS Annual Assembly, 29 October 1993, *Scottish Baptist Yearbook 1994*, p. 217.

[60] BUS Assembly, 27 October 1994, *Scottish Baptist Yearbook 1995*, p. 194.

[61] A report on the June 1980 SITE School was given in *SBM*, 105.10 (October 1980), p. 9.

provided for the libraries of theological institutions in a number of countries.[62] In summer 1981 there were forty students from twelve countries who participated in the SITE programme at Ruschlikon and afterwards each Eastern European attendee went home with a mini-library of sixty books.[63] Eurolit also placed students at other academic facilities, including nine Eastern Europeans, of whom four were Baptists, who spent a week studying at Oxford University in 1985.[64] Dr Vasile Talpos, President of the Baptist Theological Seminary in Bucharest visited Scotland for six days in January 1989 as part of a UK-wide tour to promote the importance of the Eurolit programme. He highlighted that simple things like the printing of Bibles in Romania had received permission from the Government, but there was no paper available to carry out this task. It has been provided through Eurolit and printed on the presses of the Orthodox Church in Romania.[65] Scottish Baptists also supported the National Bible Society of Scotland's work with sister agencies in the region, for example, in Poland where there was a high demand for Bibles and permission to print them, but a severe shortage of paper hindered its work in producing Bibles since the new Bible translation in Polish had appeared in 1975.[66] At the October 1981 EBF Council European Baptists were able to celebrate the production of a modern version of the Gospel of Mark in Russian braille as a contribution to 'The Year of the Handicapped'. This initiative was a joint venture between the BWA, the United Bible Societies and some other agencies. The Russian delegates at this gathering were thrilled at the valuable book they could hold in their hands. It was a symbol of the fruit of international co-operation.[67] Scottish Baptists, in line with other Christian denominations in their native land, placed a high priority on ensuring fellow believers had access to the Bible, They also valued the provision of theological education for the training of Christian workers and were willing participants in the Eurolit initiative.

There were also regular features in the denominational periodical *SBM* on the life of particular Baptist Unions in other European countries, for example in Czechoslovakia,[68] Denmark,[69] Latvia,[70] Poland,[71] and Russia.[72] The *SBM*

---

[62] 'Eurolit', *SBM*, 105.7 (July 1980), p. 3.

[63] Peter Barber, 'Less Privileged', *SBM*, 107.1 (January 1982), p. 8.

[64] Ron Marr, 'Library Building through Eurolit', *SBM*, 110.6 (June 1985), p. 11.

[65] 'Welcome for European President' *SBM*, 114.2 (February 1989), pp. 7, 10.

[66] George Hossack, 'Hunger for the Word in Poland', *SBM*, 105.10 (October 1980), p. 2.

[67] Peter Barber, 'Priceless Treasure', *SBM*, 107.1 (January 1982), p. 8.

[68] 'Czech Baptist D.I.Y.', *SBM*, 110.10 (October 1985), p. 16.

[69] R. Armstrong, 'Not Roman Candles', *SBM*, 106.3 (March 1981), p. 8.

also reprinted information on Christian work in China by Sven Ohm that was originally published by him as the editor in the Swedish Baptist magazine *Veckoposten*.[73] Individual Baptists on their own initiative had also made contacts with colleagues. For example, Peter Clark, minister of Bristo Baptist Church, Edinburgh, visited Hungarian Baptist Churches while on sabbatical leave.[74] Others made new friendships during summer holidays and reported their travels in Europe in the *SBM*, for example, Bob Younger from Leslie Baptist Church on his contacts with Polish Baptists,[75] and Delores Dickson from Keiss Baptist Church with Russian Baptists.[76] It must be said very clearly that a significant number of Scottish Baptists were interested in the work of brothers and sisters overseas. The two Union Secretaries of this era led from the front in support of work outside of the United Kingdom, but it is clear that many other colleagues shared that wider vision. The level of input in the *SBM* reflected that broader vision that had been maintained over the twentieth century in Scottish Baptist ranks.

The General Secretaries of the BUS, Andrew MacRae and Peter Barber had been active participants at the regular EBF Council meetings since the first EBF Council meeting in Scotland, in Glasgow in September 1970. Peter Barber, towards the end of his Union Presidential Year, had given the welcome address to the assembled delegates in the week that MacRae had taken up the EBF Presidency.[77] His speech revealed a detailed interest in EBF work, something he maintained throughout his life.[78] In an article published in the *SBM* in February 1986, Barber explained the purpose behind his investment in relationships with Baptists outside the United Kingdom. He wanted Scottish Baptists not to see themselves as a declining influence in Scottish Society, but as members of a 'truly international family –and a rapidly

---

[70] Gerhard Class, 'He is our peace', *SBM*, 106.4 (April 1981), p.7.

[71] 'Wage cut for new college' *SBM* 110.12 (December 1985), p. 3.

[72] 'Going for Glasnost', *SBM* 114.1 (January 1989), p. 10.

[73] Sven Ohm, 'Christ at work in China', *SBM*, 106.5 (May 1981), p. 8.

[74] Peter Clark, 'Building for God in Hungary', SBM, 107.2 (February 1982), pp. 4–5.

[75] 'Readers Letters', *SBM*. 106.9 (September 1981), p. 2.

[76] Delores C. Dickson, 'Moscow visit', *SBM*, 110.7 (July 1985), p. 2.

[77] 'Address of Welcome to the EBF Council', Notes in his BUS Centenary Presidency file, 17 September 1970, cited in Edward W. Burrows, *'To Me To Live is Christ': A Biography of Peter H. Barber* (Milton Keynes: Paternoster, 2005), p. 190.

[78] For fuller details of his commitment see 'European Baptist Statesman', chapter 17 of Burrows, *'To Me To Live is Christ'*, pp. 190–205.

growing one at that.'[79] History was made in 1980 with the EBF gathering in Bucharest being the first official Christian conference held in Romania since the Second World War. The invitation to hold the event in that country had come from the host churches, but it had required government permission which had been granted. In addition, conference delegates had been free to visit and preach in churches across that country for a few days following their meetings. Andrew MacRae at his final EBF Council as BUS General Secretary found the occasion profoundly inspiring.[80] Other Scottish Baptists represented their home country at other EBF events. Lynn Pollock from Thomas Coats Memorial Baptist Church, Paisley and Kate Young from Rattray Street Baptist Church, Dundee, for example, were participants in the Fifth European Baptist Youth Conference in Eisenach, East Germany, in July 1985. The 140 delegates came from fourteen different countries.[81] A larger number of Scottish Baptists chose to attend the EBF Congress in Budapest in July 1989. This party included the twenty-five member Inverclyde Christian Brass Band, half of whose members attended Orangefield Baptist Church, Greenock, who took part in a number of fringe events at the congress. Three Scottish Baptists, Vicki Shaver, Jim Clarke, and Jim Gordon were amongst the seminar leaders chosen for this four day event. A major highlight for Scottish Baptists was the induction of Peter Barber as the new EBF President, a post he would hold for a two-year term of office.[82] The Congress was reported on in detail in the pages of the *SBM*.[83] He was thrilled with the diversity within EBF ranks. 'No other Regional Fellowship of the Baptist World Alliance includes within its area such a diversity of cultures, languages and political systems.'[84] What is more the extent of its breadth was in part due to his advocacy for Middle Eastern Baptists to be included in EBF. Jordanian Baptists joined Israeli Baptists in membership at the EBF Council at Zwolle, Netherlands, in September 1990.[85] The 1980s, according to the December 1989 *SBM* editorial article was a decade of 'widening the horizons of our

---

[79] *SBM*, 111.2 (February 1986), p. 10.

[80] Andrew MacRae, 'Historic Meetings in Romania', *SBM*, 105.5 (May 1980), pp. 6–7.

[81] Lynn Pollock, 'Experience of a lifetime for young Baptists', *SBM*, 110.9 (September 1985), p. 4.

[82] Alex Russell, 'Band for Budapest', *SBM*, 114.4 (April 1989), p. 15; 114.7 (July 1989), p. 9; 114.8 (August 1989), pp. 1, 10–11.

[83] For example, *SBM*, 114.9 (September 1989), pp. 9–16.

[84] Peter Barber, 'Scene Around', *SBM*, 114.9 (September 1989), p. 18.

[85] Karl Heinz Walter, *Reflections* (a private communication with Edward Burrows, 22 May 2002); Burrows, *'To Me To Live is Christ'*, p. 197.

Baptist fellowships'.[86] This verdict was an accurate description of Scottish Baptist involvement with other European Baptists since 1980. In no previous decade had they been more involved with Continental Baptists in the structures and organisation of the EBF than in the 1980s.

### Baptist World Alliance (BWA)

Stanislav Svec, secretary of the Baptist Union of Czechoslovakia and vice-president of the European Baptist Federation highlighted the growth and importance of the BWA as an opportunity for Baptists around the world to pray for one another and be informed about respective ministries together with collaboration in various aid projects. This world communion had grown significantly from its small beginnings in 1905. Then there were approximately six million Baptists in twenty-three countries, but by 1980, Svec reported, the numbers had grown to 116,000 churches in 115 member bodies, that is around thirty-four million members in 140 nations with a growth rate of 2% per annum.[87] The *SBM* editor gave opportunities to the BWA General Secretary Dr Gerhard Claas and President Duke K. McCall to communicate with Scottish Baptists by reporting some of their messages, including the addresses they gave at the Toronto 1980 Baptist World Congress. Claas was particular struck by the evangelistic zeal of Baptists in the Philippines who had seen a growth rate of 16% in church membership in the previous year and seen 111 new churches welcomed into their union with a further 143 causes in the process of application for membership.[88] The Baptist world family was becoming increasingly ethnically diverse as it spread around the globe.

It was inevitable that conflicts between governments could make the choice of locations for international gatherings difficult. One example to illustrate this point was the conflict between the United Kingdom and Argentina over the Falkland Isles between April and June 1982. Sam Henry, in a July 1982 *SBM* article entitled 'Nothing new under the sun', wanted to challenge Scottish Baptists to re-examine our attitudes to war and to work more strenuously for peace. He asked: 'Can war of any kind be justified at all?'[89] This conflict caused the Baptist World youth conference due to be held in July1983 in the Argentine capital Buenos Aires, to be rescheduled for the

---

[86] 'The Eighties in Retrospect', Editorial, *SBM*, 114.10 (December 1989), p. 1.

[87] Stanislac Svec, 'Worldwide Expansion of Baptist Family', *SBM*, 105.1 (January 1980), pp. 6–7.

[88] *SBM* 106.1 (January 1981), pp. 6–7. Gilbert Ritchie gave a report on the congress, 'Toronto 1980', SBM, 105.9 (September 1980), pp. 2–3

[89] Sam Henry, 'Nothing new under the sun', *SBM*, 107.7 (July 1982), p. 10.

following year to allow time for some of the tensions of the war to dissipate.[90] Gerhard Claas reminded Scottish Baptists that it is not always easy to make judgements about what is happening in other countries. He illustrated his point by looking at understandings of religious freedom in different parts of Europe and demonstrated the complexity of choices faced in particular social contexts. In the Cold War era this reminder that genuine Christians can come to very different conclusions in addressing issues relating to religious freedom was insightful.[91] The one reason the BBC in its new bulletins gave any reference to the 1985 BWA Congress in Los Angeles was due to an anti-Communist protestor seeking to pull down the Russian flag from the array of flags of attending delegates from 134 different countries. However, it was most noteworthy for the warm greetings to the Russian delegates from their American hosts. Another special feature was the presence of two representatives of the Christian Church in China. This was the first time since the Communist Revolution that church representatives had been allowed to attend an outside denominational gathering. In his Presidential address, Duke McCall reminded delegates that for the first time in a thousand years, white people were a minority in the Christian Church. The growth in world Christianity was overwhelmingly outside its European and North American regions. In addition, in terms of the languages in which Christians engaged in worship, there were now 208 million Spanish-speaking believers, 196 million English-speakers and 128 million Portuguese first-language speakers. Baptist World Aid had also received record donations of $21,486,709 from the world Baptist family for its relief and development work.[92] In a rapidly changing world this international Christian communion was in good heart with high expectations of further growth in its work and witness.

### *BWA Youth Conference Glasgow 1988*

The Baptist Union of Scotland Council in May 1985 voted to apply to host the 1988 World Youth Congress in Glasgow.[93] Peter Barber had asked two men to take responsibility for this venture. Douglas Inglis, a chartered surveyor and member of the Newton Mearns Baptist Church, and Rodney Beaumont, a partner in a firm of landscape architects, which had been involved in the overall design of the Liverpool Garden Festival held between May and October 1984 and had acted as advisors for the more recent Glasgow

---

[90] 'Baptist youth to meet in Argentina', *SBM*, 107.9 (September 1982), p. 11.

[91] Gerhard Claas, 'East and West speak different languages on freedom', *SBM* 107.9 (September 1982), pp. 8–9.

[92] Peter H. Barber, 'Scene Around', *SBM* (110.9 (September 1985), pp. 10–12.

[93] 'World Youth Congress likely for Scotland', *SBM*, 110.6 (June 1985), p. 3.

Garden Festival that took place from April to September 1988. These two men agreed to be co-chairmen of the Committee on Local Arrangements and presented their case to Gerhard Claas and Denton Lotz (then BWA Executive Secretary with responsibility for youth and evangelism) in May 1985. The proposal was welcomed and taken forward for further consideration with other expressions of interest from the Netherlands and West Germany.[94] Peter Barber took the application to deliver in person at the Baptist World Congress in Los Angeles in July 1985. The application was warmly received and accepted by the Council of the BWA.[95] It was held in the Scottish Exhibition and Conference Centre, Glasgow, from 27–31 July 1988. The organisers were hoping for 10,000 delegates after initial levels of interest in attendance were high. Generous donors provided over £100,000 to subsidise attendance at this event, the largest total ever achieved for this purpose in BWA ranks, with a remarkable £58,000 donated by Baptists in the host nation, to offer scholarships to young people from Eastern Europe and Third World countries.[96] The young people at Newton Mearns Baptist Church alone raised £1,000 for this fund with a variety of entrepreneurial schemes, the most successful of which was a car valet business that raised £400.[97] However, eighty-two countries were represented by the 6,748 delegates, at what was the largest BWA youth conference to date. There were, for example, one hundred who came from Nagaland, north-east India; a twenty-five-member youth choir came from Russia; twenty-five from East Germany alongside 300 from West Germany and ninety-five from Portugal. The booking forms for the Baptists from Israel, Jordan, Lebanon and Cyprus came together which was a remarkable symbol of unity. African Baptist delegates included representatives from Angola, Egypt, Liberia, Malawi, Mozambique, Rwanda, Sierra Leone, Zaire, Zambia and Zimbabwe. Asian Baptists included small groups from Japan, Hong Kong and Macau. There were 990 Scottish Baptists registered for this event.[98] However, there were also 450 volunteers from the host country working behind the scenes to ensure all the planned meetings and

---

[94] Burrows, *'To Me To Live is Christ'*, p. 209.

[95] 'Baptists of the World', *SBM*, 110.7 (July 1985), pp. 10–11; 'Scottish Baptists give for new BWA office', 110.8 (August 1985), p. 4; 'A Baptist voice at world level', *SBM*, 110.9 (September 1985), p.11.

[96] 'Global Effect of Conference', *SBM*, 113.8 (August 1988), p. 1; 113.9 (September 1988), p. 19.

[97] *Conference News: 11th Baptist Youth World Conference, 27–31 July 1988, Glasgow*, Issue 3, February 1988, pp. 1, 3, 7.

[98] *SBM*, 113.3 (March 1988), p. 10; 113.6 (June 1988), p. 10; 113.7 (July 1988), p. 9; 113.8 (August 1988), p. 1.

activities were able to run so smoothly.⁹⁹ It was a remarkably successful event that would ensure that Glasgow 1988 would be remembered with pleasure for delegates of this event.

## Christian Service Overseas

Scottish Baptists had consistently over the years been committed supporters of the BMS. However, there was an increasing trend to supplement support for the denominational mission agency with partnerships with other missionary societies. Significant coverage of work in other countries was featured in the pages of the *SBM*. In the August 1985 issue, for example, the lead story in the editorial, together with the main story on page two, focussed on BMS missionaries Joan Sargent and Joan Smith being forced to end their terms of service in India because residential permits were no longer being issued as in previous years due to the growing rise of Hindu nationalism. It was no accident that it was in areas where the Christian Church was increasing in number that these permits were being declined.¹⁰⁰ By contrast, doors of opportunity were still available in many places in Africa. Ron Armstrong, the BMS representative in Scotland, together with his wife Rita, visited their daughter and her husband serving with that society in Kinshasa, Zaire. He also took the time to visit other BMS workers in that country and reported on his tour in some detail.¹⁰¹ Overall, BMS was greatly encouraged because record numbers of candidates were coming forward to serve overseas, though it did highlight struggling to recruit candidates to serve in different ministries in Angola.¹⁰² There was also a feature on the work of the Missionary Aviation Fellowship (MAF) in Africa in a time of famine in Ethiopia, Chad and Sudan. It explained the complexity of famine relief work and its cost and highlighted the partnership of this agency with Tearfund and Oxfam in transporting much needed supplies to their geographically isolated destinations. Another story featured the link between Leith Baptist Church and Sidang Injil Borneo (The Evangelical Church of Borneo) in Sabah, North Borneo, in Malaysia. Dr Judson Tagal, a member of the Sabah congregation, had visited Leith some years earlier to see for himself the place from which Bibles had been printed for his homeland. While in Edinburgh he had worshipped in Leith Baptist Church. An invitation was issued by his home

---

⁹⁹ 'Partnership', 113.9 (September 1988), p. 19.

¹⁰⁰ 'Missionary's forced return' and 'Scots nurse forced to leave India', *SBM*, 110.8 (August 1985), pp. 1–2.

¹⁰¹ Ron Armstrong, 'Memorable visit to Zaire', *SBM*, 110.8 (August 1985), pp. 5, 12.

¹⁰² David Pountain, 'BMS wants to keep its promise to Angola', *SBM*, 110.8 (August 1985), p. 12.

church to the minister, William Cowie, to bring a mission team from Scotland to engage in evangelistic outreach for a period of six to seven weeks that would involve visiting forty local churches in Borneo, many in remote areas. They would follow in the footsteps of some of the first Christian missionaries in that part of Borneo who had set out from Leith many years earlier to share the Christian gospel.[103] Even the obituary notices featured distinguished records of service for former BMS personnel Dr Ronald Still of St Andrews, who had served in China from 1935–1946, together with Miss Alison McGregor who was a missionary nurse in Zaire (then Congo) from 1946–1956.[104] It is remarkable how many overseas mission projects were being supported by churches from this relatively small denomination. The examples chosen here were all contained in one monthly issue of the *SBM* to illustrate the priority placed on supporting work outside of Scotland. Christian service overseas has been something that Scottish Baptists have consistently supported generously with their finances and disproportionately high too, compared to their numbers, have been the many men and women who have volunteered to carry out this work.

## Theological Education

Gordon Martin had been appointed as the Principal of the Scottish Baptist College on the resignation of R.E.O. White from that post in 1979.[105] Martin had been a tutor in the college for many years prior to that appointment and focussed on Church History and Systematic Theology. He was joined that year by Edward Burrows[106] who had previously taught at Serampore College, India, under the auspices of the BMS. He was a gifted New Testament scholar who also took responsibility for administering the college library. This era was a time of expansion for the college with three additional tutors appointed to serve. T. Deans Buchanan, of Knightswood Baptist Church, Glasgow, taught Reformation History; Ian H. Thomson of Mosspark Baptist Church, Glasgow, taught Early Church History, and William Wright, Secretary for the Department of Church Life in the Baptist Union, became the Director of Practical Theology. When Wright moved to St Andrews Baptist Church in 1981 Deans Buchanan took over his responsibilities in this area of college life[107] until Bill Clark, minister of Dedridge Baptist Church,

---

[103] 'Christians involved in relief air lift' and 'Edinburgh Baptists off to Borneo' *SBM*, 110.8 (August 1985), p. 7. A second trip to Borneo took place in 1989, and a full report was given in the *SBM*, 114.2 (February 1989), pp. 12–13.

[104] 'In Memoriam', *SBM*, 110.8 (August 1985), p. 14.

[105] 'Report by the College Committee, 1979', *Scottish Baptist Yearbook 1980*, p. 192.

[106] 'College appointment', *SBM*, 104.4 (April 1979), p. 2.

[107] 'Report by the College Committee, 1980', *Scottish Baptist Yearbook 1981*, p. 151.

Livingston, succeeded him in 1988. These appointments were part of a process of significant change in the life of the college, especially after its removal from Oakfield Avenue in the University area of Glasgow in 1981.[108] Another innovation was the opportunity for students at the Scottish Baptist College to study for a B.D. through Rüschlikon Seminary in Switzerland. This opportunity resulted in participating students spending two years at the seminary in Zurich.[109] In addition, specialist lecturers were increasingly invited to contribute from their areas of expertise. From outside the denomination, the lecturers included Dr Geoffrey Scobie, an Anglican minister who taught Psychology from 1982–1990,[110] and Dr Eric McKay, a retired General Practitioner, and member of the Free Church of Scotland, who taught Pastoral Studies (Clinical) in the 1990s. Other Scottish Baptist contributors included Dr John Drane and Dr George Mitchell teaching Old Testament Studies and Dr David Hicks, who after his retirement from teaching Systematic Theology at Aberdeen University taught Ethics and the Philosophy of Religion. In 1980 a new course of study leading to the award of a Diploma in Practical Theology was introduced which the Joint Ministerial Board of the Baptist Union required ministerial candidates to complete.[111] The Christian Service Certificate was introduced in September 1986 to enable lay-people to obtain training to help them work more effectively in their local congregations. This course was modelled on existing ones in some English Baptist Colleges.[112] Gordon Martin in the later years of his time at the college was also looking at models of distance learning and the use of training videos in spreading the benefits of a theological education. He had also been noted for his detailed pastoral care of the students.[113] It had been a decade of significant changes in the life of the college.

In 1988 Martin moved to take up a pastorate in Durham in the north-east of England. He was replaced by Dr Ivor Oakley, who came from the Irish Baptist College in Belfast.[114] There in addition to teaching New Testament, he had also taught Church History and Theology, Baptist History and Principles and Homiletics since his first appointment at that institution in

---

[108] 'Report by the College Committee, 1979', pp. 192–193; Murray, *Scottish Baptist College Centenary History 1894–1994*, pp. 38–39.

[109] 'Report by the College Committee, 1984', *Scottish Baptist Yearbook 1985*, p. 165.

[110] 'Report by the College Committee, 1982', *Scottish Baptist Yearbook 1983*, p. 161.

[111] 'Report by the College Committee, 1980', *Scottish Baptist Yearbook 1981*, p. 151.

[112] 'Report by the College Committee, 1985', *Scottish Baptist Yearbook 1986*, p. 173; Murray, *Scottish Baptist College Centenary History 1894–1994*, p. 53.

[113] Peter Barber, 'A matter of principle', *SBM*, 114.4 (April 1989), p. 10.

[114] 'Report by the College Committee, 1988', *Scottish Baptist Yearbook 1989*, p. 183.

1964.[115] He had been greatly in demand as a preacher in Ireland and had done so in most if not all the Irish Baptist congregations.[116] He had a track record of producing well-qualified preachers. Oakley continued this practice in his time at the Scottish Baptist College, ministering in over 90 congregations in his six years at the College, and as in Ireland this direct contact with local congregations strengthened the bond with supporting churches. His passionate advocacy of the college significantly increased the number of ministerial students attending in the early 1990s. He moved to a retirement pastorate in Guisborough, Cleveland in April 1994,[117] during the college's centenary year.[118]

## Women in Ministry

There was a further attempt to raise this subject at the May 1983 Baptist Union Council. A report was produced by the Joint Ministerial Board and the Executive entitled: 'Women in the Ministry' and presented to the Council. Following discussion introduced by Dr Gordon Martin, this motion was put to the Council: 'That Women should be accepted for training for the Baptist Ministry and in due course be placed on the Accredited List on the same terms as men.' It was agreed that unless the motion received the support of at least two-thirds of Council members it would not proceed to the Annual Assembly. An insufficient number of those present supported it. However, it was agreed that a copy of the report on this matter should be sent to each Baptist Church in Scotland.[119] The January 1985 Baptist Union Council was informed that Hillhead Baptist Church was planning to bring a motion with the same wording as presented to the Council in 1983 to the 1985 Baptist Union Assembly; their right to do so was affirmed by the Council and in addition, it was decided that each affiliated congregation should receive advance notification of it.[120] At the start of the debate on 24 October 1985 the General Secretary explained the background to this debate. An application for the ministry had been received from a woman.[121] As there had been no

---

[115] 'College appoints new principal', *SBM*, 114.5 (May 1988), p. 2; 114.9 (September 1988), p. 1.

[116] Joshua Thomson, 'College Principal with concern for smaller Churches', *SBM*, 114.9 (September 1988), p. 6.

[117] Murray, *Scottish Baptist College Centenary History 1894–1994*, p. 53.

[118] 'Into a New Century. *SBM*, 119.4 (April 1994), p. 11.

[119] Baptist Union Council, 17 May 1983, *Scottish Baptist Yearbook 1984*, p. 93.

[120] Baptist Union Council, 15 January 1985, *Scottish Baptist Yearbook 1986*, p. 88.

[121] This person wishes to remain anonymous in this history. However, she has had an effective and influential ministry in the BUGB.

previous case of a woman on the accredited list of ministers, the Joint Ministerial Board set up a sub-committee to consider what response to give. A majority were in favour of the request though a minority favoured something similar to a deaconess order. The council vote in 1983 had only been 56% in favour so the motion did not go forward to Assembly. However, Hillhead Baptist Church had given notice of motion of revisiting this issue at the 1984 Assembly. Peter Barber reminded delegates that the decision whether to call a woman or not to a local church pastorate was a matter for that individual congregation. The choice before them was whether a woman could be placed on the accredited list and thus be eligible to serve in an aided church. 466 votes were cast in the ballot with 231 in favour of the Hillhead motion and 235 against, thus falling eighty votes short of the required majority.[122] There was, though, the election of the first woman Vice-President of the Union at the 1989 Assembly. Marjorie McInnes from the Adelaide Place Baptist Church, Glasgow, had previously served as a Senior Social Work Adviser in the Scottish Office. Her appointment was warmly welcomed by the assembly delegates that year.[123] She was installed as President at the 1990 Assembly and addressed the delegates on the theme: 'Called to Care'. Those present were challenged to consider what a Christian caring ministry would involve in the wider community. While welcoming specialist homes for the elderly and hostels for other specialist needs –she asked whether 'we have lost sight of the call to mission?' Could ministers be released to serve more in the wider community as chaplains, she asked? In addition, she called on doctors, social workers and other caring professionals to exercise greater willingness to recognise the contribution that ministers could bring to the provision of care in the wider community.[124] It was a fresh and innovative call for integrated social care provision that included catering for the spiritual needs of each person.

Her appeal for more Baptists to take up chaplaincy appointments began to be realised in the appointment of Ian Livingstone as the first Accredited Baptist Minister for many years to be appointed as a Chaplain in the Royal Navy.[125] However, it was at times very difficult as the solitary Baptist working alongside Paedo-baptist colleagues from larger denominations. Livingstone stated that 'ecumenism was not really present in the Church of Scotland and

---

[122] Women in the Ministry Debate' 24 October 1985, Baptist Union Annual Assembly, *Scottish Baptist Yearbook* 1986, pp. 102–105.

[123] 'Historic Election', Editorial, *SBM*, 115.9 (November 1989), p. 1 and 'First Woman President', p. 9.

[124] 'Caring is Not An Optional Extra', Presidential Assembly Address, *SBM*, November 1990, p. 8. The full address is printed in the *Scottish Baptist Yearbook* 1991, pp. 88–94.

[125] 'Chaplain RN', Superintendent's Report, *Scottish Baptist Yearbook 1992*, p. 134.

Free Churches branch of the RN' (the United Board). Other Baptist chaplains serving in the Armed Forces at that time also noted a complete ignorance of Baptist convictions from those amongst whom they served – even when they had a better experience of ecumenical relationships with colleagues.[126] In the October 1985 issue of the *SBM* a brief report was given on the remarkable ministry of a South Korean Baptist Army Chaplain, Chong Shik Kim, who in his eleven years of service from 1974 to 1985 had baptised 2,658 service personnel during active military service. His goal, apparently, had been to reach a total of 3,000 baptisms prior to his retirement at the end of 1985![127] New ground was broken with respect to healthcare chaplaincy with the appointment of Marjorie Taylor as a full-time Hospital Chaplain at Hairmyres Hospital in East Kilbride. In previous years full-time hospital chaplaincy posts had usually been the preserve of Church of Scotland ministers, but in a changing environment a Scottish Baptist woman was ordained to serve in this form of chaplaincy ministry.[128] The door of opportunity in chaplaincy ministries in Scotland became increasingly open in these years; however, the time had not been seen as right to accredit women to local church pastoral ministry within the Baptist Union of Scotland.

### Inter-Church Process

The issue over which Scottish Baptists struggled most to come to a common mind in the twentieth century was over inter-church relations. The debates that culminated at the 1989 Annual Assembly would mark a decisive moment in the collective understanding of ecumenical relations in this Scottish family of churches. Scottish Baptists had been comfortable in commenting on major ecumenical documents such as the 1982 *Baptism, Eucharist and Ministry* Report from the World Council of Churches. Peter Barber, the General Secretary had asked the DICR committee of the Union to submit a response to it, because of its significance. The submitted response, though, was largely

---

[126] Ian Livingstone, 'Questionnaire, 1998', in Neil E. Allison. *The Age of Conflicts 1950–2014: The Official History of the United Board Volume Three* (N.P.: United Navy, Army and Air Force Board, 2018), p. 22. For the views of English Baptist chaplains on this subject, see pp. 20–23,

[127] 'Baptism Goals', SBM, 111.10 (October 1985), p. 16.

[128] 'Annual Report' Scottish Baptist College, *Scottish Baptist Yearbook 1992*, p. 197. Alan Stoddard was Assistant Chaplain at Aberdeen Hospitals from 1991 and several ministers served as part-time Hospital Chaplains alongside their work in the churches, For example Harry Telfer, at City Hospital while at Duncan Street Baptist Church, Edinburgh, and Robert Armstrong at Hawkhead Hospital Paisley during his ministry at Thomas Coats Memorial Baptist Church, Paisley. Murray, 'Be Not Conformed but Transformed', p. 241.

critical because of the understanding of baptism in that document.[129] It was, though, straightforward to offer a critique of documents and statements without having any formal ties to the body that issued them. In the 1980s in Scotland there was considerable ecumenical activity, in particular the Multilateral Church Conversation amongst the main denominations. The basis of these conversations was a call by the Church of Scotland to the other churches to begin to work towards the unity of the Christian Church in Scotland. Scottish Baptists had participated in these conversations as full members until the decision was taken for the denominations to work towards structural union in 1983. At that point they reverted to observer status.[130] It was a vision that contrasted sharply with that held by the vast majority of Baptists.

Scottish Baptists were represented by Peter Barber, at the BCC gathering of thirty-two denominational leaders at Lambeth Palace, London, in May 1985, to discuss the *Not Strangers but Pilgrims* document produced by a working party of the BCC. A series of responses to this document was forthcoming from a wide range of Christian bodies including the Evangelical Alliance, 'House Churches' and a range of parachurch organisations. In Scotland, it was in April 1987 that the equivalent gathering to the Lambeth Palace discussions to consider this document took place. Scottish Baptists were represented by Peter Barber, Muriel McNair, BUS Director of the Department of Church Life 1981–1985, James Gordon, minister of Crown Terrace Baptist Church, Aberdeen, Brian Muir, a layman from Hillhead Baptist Church who was prominent in Christian radio ministry, and Watson Moyes, minister of Viewfield Baptist Church, Dunfermline. The report produced by this conference received some criticisms from the DICR, but no objections were made to participation in this process. The culmination of these conversations around the country was a final United Kingdom gathering at Swanwick in Derbyshire from 31 August to 4 September 1987. There were over 330 representatives of thirty-four Christian bodies ranging from the Christian Brethren and the Salvation Army to the Anglican and Roman Catholic Churches. Watson Moyes and Peter Barber held the status of 'Observers' at this event.[131] Peter Barber gave an upbeat summary of events at Swanwick in the October 1987 issue of the *SBM*.[132] Watson Moyes and Brian Muir were tasked with explaining what ACTS, the new *Churches Together* ecumenical body for Scotland stood for at the 1988 Annual Assembly. This

---

[129] The response was submitted in the name of the DICR. DICR Minutes, 3 May 1983, cited by Moyes, 'There is one body', in Talbot (ed.), *Distinctive People*, p. 111.

[130] Moyes, 'There is one body', pp. 113–114.

[131] Moyes, 'There is one body', pp. 114–117.

[132] Peter H. Barber, 'Scene Around', *SBM*, 113.10 (October 1987), pp. 10–11.

was followed over the next twelve months by area consultations prior to a formal vote at the 1989 Annual Assembly. There was a decidedly mixed response at these regional gatherings. Although some present were in favour of the new ecumenical initiative, it appeared that a larger number held to an opposing view. It was a clear pointer to events at the forthcoming assembly, as was the letter that appeared in the June 1989 *SBM*, subscribed by the names of thirty-five accredited ministers.[133] There was strong opposition to further participation in ecumenical bodies in Scottish Baptist ranks on the threshold of the 1989 Annual Assembly.

The debates took place in the Methodist Central Hall in Edinburgh on Thursday 26 October 1989. Delegates were informed that there were a number of motions being presented to them for decision from full membership, associate membership, observer status or non-participation altogether in ACTS. The first vote on full membership was rejected by 345 (69%) votes to 152 (31%), The second vote on associate membership was rejected by 261 (54%) against and only 222 (46%) for the motion. The third vote on observer status had the greatest support with 287 (60%) for and only 192 (40%) against it, but it fell short of the two-thirds threshold. The final vote on no-participation in ACTS gained 234 (52%) votes for and 217 (48%) against the motion.[134] As a result, the Assembly was left with no decision, but in practice it was a decisive step to change course regarding formal participation in the major ecumenical organisation in Scotland. This decision must not be viewed as unwillingness on the part of the majority of Scottish Baptists to work with other Christian Churches, but it was a clear statement that in future years decisions about ecumenical engagement would be taken in local churches and with respect to their particular context. At a national level, though, it was clear that a majority of Scottish Baptists had sought a change of direction with respect to inter-church co-operation,

## Social Action

Scottish Baptists were involved in a variety of social ministries and took an interest in a growing number of wider community causes. It is clear that the

---

[133] 'Ministers voice concern about Inter-Church process', *SBM*, 115.6 (June 1989), p. 2. There was, however, confusion over exactly how many of the thirty-five had actually agreed to their names being attached to the letter. See SBM, 115.7 (July 1989), pp. 1–3. but it was abundantly clear that there was strong opposition in Scottish Baptist ranks

[134] 'No to ACTS', Editorial, *SBM*, 115.11 (November 1989), p. 1. For details of the votes see 'Assembly says No to ACTS', *SBM*, 115.12 (December 1989), pp. 11, 18; and Baptist Union Assembly, 26 October 1989, *Scottish Baptist Yearbook 1990*, pp. 172–179. For a very detailed account of a participant strongly in favour of joining ACTS, see Moyes, *Our Place Among the Churches*, pp. 90–122.

vast majority were committed to applying their faith to daily life. A few individuals made a particular contribution to social ministries of which two brief examples will be given with respect to end-of-life care and addressing the needs of homeless people. The Hospice Movement in the United Kingdom began when Dame Cicely Saunders opened St Christopher's Hospice in London in 1967. It gradually spread out through the country. In Scotland, several Baptist ministers and laypeople served in various voluntary or paid capacities in the work of their local hospice. James Taylor, minister of Stirling Baptist Church, and Dr Harold Lyon from the same congregation, were active participants in the formation of the Strathcarron Hospice near Denny. Dr Lyon became the first Medical Director of the facility.[135] In Paisley, Accord Hospice appointed Kenneth Jackson of Central Baptist Church as a Volunteer Co-ordinator and the Prince and Princess of Wales Hospice in Glasgow had three successive Baptist ministers as its full-time Chaplains. Two of whom served there in the twentieth century – Alan Donald and Stuart Webster. St Columba's Hospice in Edinburgh opened in 1977 with Dr Derek Murray, minister of Dublin Street Baptist Church as its part-time chaplain from 1977 to 1987 then on a full-time basis from 1987 to 2001. Many other Baptist laypeople served on a voluntary basis in hospices.[136]

Another area of need to which some Baptists responded was the work amongst homeless people. Bethany Christian Trust was founded by Alan and Anne Berry in partnership with other Christians in Edinburgh who shared their vision of providing residential care for individuals who had no home of their own. The vision had been shared with South Leith Baptist Church in 1979 and the search for suitable affordable premises had begun. It was not until 4 April 1983 that Bethany Christian Centre opened in a former Burns Club building across the road from their church premises. At the official opening of the centre there were present in support of this project: the officials of the Edinburgh and Lothians Baptist Association, a local minister, the general secretary of Edinburgh City Mission, members of the South Leith Baptist Church, together with friends of Alan from other parts of the country, as well as the first residents of the facility.[137] In January 1985 an adjacent property was purchased, the disused licensed Caley Club. It required a huge amount of work to render it usable. Paid workers and volunteers with skills to offer worked hard together to complete this task.[138] It became apparent within the first couple of years that many Bethany residents faced other issues besides

---

[135] 'Strathcarron Hospice open', *SBM*, 107.5 (May 1981), p. 1.

[136] Murray, 'Be Not Conformed but Transformed', pp. 240–241.

[137] Anne E. Berry, *Giving Hope And A Future: Bethany Christian Trust The First 25 Years* (Fearn: Christian Focus, 2009), pp. 11–16.

[138] Berry, *Giving Hope And A Future*, pp. 18–19.

a lack of suitable accommodation so the first tentative steps were taken in assisting with informal rehabilitation. Numbers of residents in Bethany accommodation continued to grow, reaching full capacity of twenty-seven individuals by December 1988.[139] The growth of the work required more a more formal legal structure to its activities. On 22 February Bethany was registered with the Government as a care unit for people who were homeless and had special needs. This development led to a more professional approach with respect to staffing, accommodation for residents and the care package offered.[140] By the early 1990s the 'Seven Levels of Care' programme for which Bethany is now well-known came into being, taking people in need off the streets and working with them to rehabilitate and restructure their lives within a supportive community setting.[141]

By the 1980s, although not a new development, Scottish Baptists were more willing to address economic issues. In 1984 the General Secretary proposed a motion on behalf of assembled delegates that: 'we are deeply concerned at the continuing deadlock in the mining industry and at the dissention, hardship and violence this dispute is producing; we urge both restraint from violence and respect for law on the part of all concerned; . . . we appeal to . . . all caught up in this strike to seek the way of peace and reconciliation . . . .' There was a lively debate on the motion. Those who spoke in the debate were in broad agreement that they were not claiming competence to speak on economic, industrial or political matters, instead having a concern for the suffering of people involved in the dispute. The motion was overwhelmingly carried with only fifteen voting against it.[142] At the 1985 Assembly there was a motion expressing concern at the possible closure of the Gartcosh Cold Strip Mill and the nearby Steel-making plant at Ravenscraig, Motherwell. Delegates were concerned at the implications for shipyards and Grangemouth docks. There was overwhelming support for the motion.[143] There were still regular concerns in the 1980s over the rising levels of unemployment[144] as well as about moral and family issues, including, for

---

[139] Berry, *Giving Hope And A Future*, p. 37.

[140] Berry, *Giving Hope And A Future*, p. 42.

[141] Berry, *Giving Hope And A Future*, pp. 45–46.

[142] Baptist Union Annual Assembly, 25 October 1984, *Scottish Baptist Yearbook 1985*, pp. 96–97. See also 'Resolution: The Miners' Strike', *SBM*, 110.11 (November 1984), p. 1.

[143] Baptist Union Assembly, 24 October 1985, *Scottish Baptist Yearbook 1986*, p. 106.

[144] For example, Andrew White, 'Unemployment – towards a Christian response', *SBM*, 106.3 (March 1980), pp. 6–7; Andrew White, 'Personal effect of redundancy', *SBM*, 106.4 (April 1980), pp. 6–7;

example, a statement from the Department of Mission in the Baptist Union in 1982 on total abstinence from alcohol,[145], but equally newer issues were addressed like supporting bereavement counselling through Cruse[146] and raising the growing issue of AIDS,[147] that attracted their attention as well.

The 1980s in particular was a decade in which Scottish Baptists were quietly confident of seeing further growth in the work of their churches and the effectiveness of their mission strategy. However, by the early 1990s there was less evidence of this on the ground. This chapter has explained why that expectation was reasonable and in a number of locations around the country there were some significant advances. A key factor that was an essential component of this growth was the collaborative efforts in in-house programmes like the Scotreach initiative in the mid-1980s and partnerships with other Christian denominations in support of outreach ventures led by evangelists from outside Scotland like Billy Graham and Luis Palau, together with the ongoing fruitful work that resulted from working with American SBC workers. Ties in this era with other Baptists in the United Kingdom, Europe and further afield were strong and growing, with the successful BWA Youth Conference of 1988 a particular highlight. Missionary service overseas had always been a priority for Scottish Baptists, but the agencies supported by this time were increasingly diverse with many inter and non-denominational bodies soliciting support. The ease of travel now made it much easier for individual congregations to take mission trips abroad as seen in the visits by Edinburgh Baptists to Borneo. The Scottish Baptist College had begun to diversify not only in the courses offered but in the number of qualified staff being appointed to teach courses to its students. Good foundations had been laid under the principalship of Gordon Martin which flourished with the highest number of ministerial students and widest support from the churches during the time of his successor Ivor Oakley. Discussions and assembly debates over women in ministry and the inter-church process again featured in this era. The former although not progressing as some would have wished, saw Marjorie McInnes elected as the first female President of the Baptist Union. In the latter there was a clear statement at the 1989 assembly that participation in ACTS did not command the majority support of delegates, but no other vision for inter-church co-operation gained the necessary majority either. Scottish Baptists were engaged in a wide variety of social projects at that time as well as bringing resolutions and raising issues on new as well as familiar topics. Overall, they had good grounds for believing that the

---

[145] 'Commendation of case for total abstinence', *SBM*, 108.1 (January 1982), p. 11.

[146] Mary Barnes, 'Organisation Built on Generosity', *SBM*, 108.3 (March 1982), p. 14.

[147] 'AIDS Report Launched', *SBM*, 115.1 (January 1989), p. 3.

shoots of recovery for their work in the later part of the twentieth century had been seen in both evangelistic and social action initiatives at that time.

CHAPTER 10

# Changing Times: An Era of Transition, 1994–2009

## Introduction

There is no doubt that the 1990s was a time of significant change in Scotland. Scottish Baptists could point to the untimely death in office of the General Secretary of the Baptist Union, Peter Barber in September 1994, but it was not the only unexpected passing at that time. The death of John Smith, MP for Monkland East and leader of the Labour Party in the United Kingdom on 12 May that same year, removed from the political scene a figure of integrity widely respected across political party lines. In the wider world the implications of the genocide in Rwanda where more than 800,000 ethnic Tutsis were murdered by Hutus between April and July 1994 and the ongoing civil war in former Yugoslavia raised questions about international law and morality that were not easy to answer. However, the 27 April 1994 democratic election in South Africa which resulted in the African National Congress winning 62% of the vote and Nelson Mandela becoming President was a triumph for former President F.W. De Clerk and new President Mandela who had done a magnificent job in handling the transition process. It was a major symbol of hope at a time of great uncertainty.[1] Following the decisive vote on 11 September, 1997 by the Scottish people for a devolved Parliament, the parliamentary draftsmen coined a memorable opening clause for the resultant Scotland Bill. 'There will be a Scottish Parliament . . . .'[2] The majority of Scots were delighted at this turn of events. A new chapter in Scottish political history was soon to begin.

Scottish Baptists were also facing a time of major change in their ranks. In his final report for Assembly, written before his early passing, Peter Barber drew attention to other changes taking place around that time. He acknowledged that his own medical diagnosis received in April 1994 was bleak, and stated that he and his wife Isobel had to live life one day at a time. Ian Mundie, assistant General Secretary and Douglas Hutcheon, the new

---

[1] These particular examples were highlighted by Peter Barber, '125th Annual Report by the General Secretary', *Baptist Union of Scotland Assembly Papers*, Glasgow October 1994, p. 32

[2] 'Gordon Murray, 'The Scottish Parliament and **You**', *SBM*, 123.3 (March 1999), p. 11.

Superintendent Minister had willingly taken over many Union duties to ensure continuity in the work. Eric Watson, after distinguished service as the first Superintendent Minister, was concluding his office-holding as BMS President in April 1995. David Neil, the mission adviser had provided six excellent years of dedicated service to Scottish Baptist Churches prior to his retirement, moving south to Crook in County Durham. At the same time the retirement of Ivor Oakley as Scottish Baptist College Principal, also after six very successful years ensured that a new era was beginning in that area of denominational life as well. At a national level in Scotland Barber expressed real concerns for the future of the Church of Scotland highlighting the controversial moderatorial statement on the Virgin Birth and another pronouncement on human sexuality that only served 'to disaffect some and confuse many'. But by contrast, he welcomed the formation of an Evangelical Alliance in Scotland and hoped it would help bridge the gaps in fellowship amongst Scottish Evangelicals.[3] At a national level the next year was a transitional one with Ian Mundie appointed as the Acting General Secretary until a new General Secretary was appointed and the Mission Coordinator post left unfilled for the time being.[4] It was the passing of an era and new leaders were required to pick up the baton in the closing years of the twentieth century.

Overall it was clear that the influence of the Scottish Churches on the wider society had diminished significantly in the last quarter of the twentieth century. The Scottish Church Census of 2002 revealed that there were 120,000 fewer churchgoers in Scotland on Census Sunday compared with the equivalent day in 1994, two-thirds of those who had left were women. Half of that number was aged between twenty and forty-four. Attendance by women in this age-group at churches has been significant for attracting and retaining children and also increasing links with other younger families in the community. Focus Groups were held to try and explain why such a high proportion of those no longer in church fitted this demographic. The explanations given were primarily economic not religious. More women were working full-time and had less time for other activities and crucially with the passing of the Sunday Trading Bill of 1994 in England and Wales, which also had a big impact in Scotland, as many larger companies with shops in Scotland had their headquarters in England and increasingly over the next decade more women were in jobs that required Sunday work. The question for churches was whether they could or would provide opportunities for worship at other times or risk losing contact with a significant number of individuals

---

[3] Peter Barber, '125th Annual Report by the General Secretary', pp. 32–39.

[4] '126th Annual Report by the General Secretary & Associate General Secretary', *Baptist Union of Scotland Assembly Papers*, Inverness, October 1995, p. 31.

who would wish under other circumstances to attend church.[5] It is true that Christian influence on the wider society was contracting further at this time,[6] but it was untrue to state a simple decline in religiosity as the explanation. A more accurate explanation of the data presents a more complicated picture.

On Census Sunday, 12 May 2002, there were 570,130 people in church in Scotland, 11.2% of the population. It was an 18% reduction on the numbers attending in 1994 when a total of 691,120 people attended church. These headline figures were similar a decade earlier when the 1994 total was compared with the previous survey in 1984. In 1984 853,700 individuals had attended church on Census Sunday. This was a 19% decline over the decade to 1994. However, 11.2% is significantly higher than the 7.5% figure for the 1988 Religious Census in England. An additional factor to take into account is to add in the numbers of people attending midweek meetings or activities in churches. There were 250,000 people attending a midweek activity at a church in Scotland compared to 570,000 on a Sunday. However, what is crucial to note is that 200,000 of the midweek attenders only go midweek. This increases the total involvement figure for Scottish Churches to 15.1% and 10% for their English counterparts. This figure is reached from recording attendances at pre-school age activity groups, mid-week services to older peoples' meetings and youth clubs. There were 47% of the churches running youth clubs that attracted 102,000 young people, of which only 14% attend church on a Sunday. Boys' Brigade and Girls' Brigade Companies were especially popular at that time.[7] In 2002 75% of worshippers attended either the Church of Scotland or the Roman Catholic Church, but their proportion of the church-going population had declined from 83% in 1984. Journalist Harry Reid was commissioned by the Church of Scotland to write a report on the Kirk which came out in 2002. His conclusion was that the quality of Sunday worship services was generally high with a few excellent examples, However, he outlined that the big challenge for the Church of Scotland, and by implication for other denominations as well, was how to persuade non-churchgoers to be willing to attend a worship service in an age where an increasing proportion of the population has no interest in attending any

---

[5] Quadrant: Special Edition: Scottish Churches Census, *Religious Trends* No. 4 (July 2003), pp. 1–2. It is in the light of this trend that the first Messy Church was formed at St Wilfred's Church of England in Cowplain near Portsmouth in 2004. www.messychurch.org.uk/story-messy-church, accessed 30 April 2019.

[6] Callum G. Brown, *Religion and Society in Twentieth-Century Britain* (Harlow: Pearson Educational Ltd, 2006), pp. 278–280.

[7] Quadrant: Special Edition: Scottish Churches Census, *Religious Trends* No 4 (July 2003), p. 2.

church on a Sunday.[8] In the period 1984–1994 the newer independent congregations, smaller denominations and the Scottish Episcopal Church all grew, though they all declined between 1994 and 2002, The exception amongst the larger mainstream churches was the Scottish Baptists. Although overall numbers attending Baptist Churches had declined in 1994 to 24,530 from 29,240 on Census Sunday in 1984, it had increased by 1% between 1994 and 2002 to 24,830.[9] There was also growth in attendance amongst the Christian Brethren, the Church of the Nazarene, the Fellowship of Independent Evangelical Churches, Pentecostal Churches, Orthodox Churches and the Salvation Army.[10] The overall headline figures were discouraging for Scottish Churches as a whole. This fact cannot be avoided. However, it was not a uniform picture of decline as there were other churches that were growing in numbers, not least amongst the smaller networks of churches. It is also significant to note the much greater connections of Scottish Churches to their communities for weekday activities. It is definitely easier to contemplate attending a church for a worship service when you are already participating in other activities on the premises and may already know some people who will be there.

It is important to consider from the 2002 Scottish Church Census what factors led to church growth over the previous eight years. In the case of the Christian Brethren, they had a relatively small number of congregations but some significantly larger than the average in Scotland. Larger churches can offer a wider range of ministries and thus often attract a greater number of worshippers at Sunday and other services. The growth in numbers in the Churches of the Nazarene congregations appears to be linked to greater investment and training of leaders. It had doubled its ministerial numbers over two decades to 2002. The Pentecostal and Independent Charismatic Churches also grew most significantly in larger Independent and ethnic congregations.[11] In 1994 there had been 203 Baptist churches in Scotland, a figure that includes Independent and Grace Baptist causes. By 2002 it had increased to 204. Baptist churches had an average congregation of 122, up

---

[8] Harry Reid, *Outside Verdict: An Old Kirk in a New Scotland* (Edinburgh: St Andrews Press, 2002), pp. 39–40.

[9] Peter Brierley, *Turning the Tide The Challenge Ahead: Report of the 2002 Scottish Church Census* (London: Christian Research, 2003), pp. 15–16. The average attendance in Scottish Baptist churches at Sunday worship had dropped by 3,000 from 21,000 to 18,000 between 1984 and 1994 according to Brierley & Macdonald, *Prospects for Scotland 2000: Trends and Tables from the 1994 Scottish Church Census*, p. 17.

[10] Quadrant: Special Edition: Scottish Churches Census, *Religious Trends* No 4 (July 2003), pp. 1–2.

[11] Brierley, *Turning the Tide The Challenge Ahead*, pp. 19–23.

from 121 in 1994. It is also significant that there was expectancy for growth in Baptist Churches. 86% of Baptist churches were expecting their congregations to grow larger by 2010. This feature was also evident in other denominations where growth had been experienced. It may tentatively be suggested that where congregations have expectations of numerical success in their work there is significant encouragement to work towards the accomplishment of their goals. It could, though, be argued that these responses to that question in the Census were realistic based on past evidence of growth or decline in particular denominations. However, 57% of all churches had expectations of at least modest growth, which was remarkably optimistic, although at the other end of the scale the percentage of 'Other Presbyterians' expecting their churches to decline or close was more gloomy than the reality on the ground.[12] The churches that had grown between 1994 and 2002 were mainly the less institutional causes.

The most serious challenge for all the Churches related to the loss of children and young people from their ranks. There were 142,000 children aged 0–9 years in 1984; of these individuals ten years later in 1994 when aged 10–19 years, there were only 76,000 of them still attending a local church. By 2002 when they were aged between 20 and 29 only 37,000 were left. A drop-out rate of 74% over eighteen years is incredibly serious and the most serious challenge for churches to address quickly in the twenty-first century.[13] There was no room for complacency in any of the churches in addressing this issue, but equally no need for despair as long as the challenges were faced up to and changes made to address them.

At the Baptist Union Council on 17 January, 1995, William (Bill) G. Slack, minister of International Baptist Church, Aberdeen, was appointed General Secretary[14] of the Baptist Union of Scotland. He had trained for pastoral ministry at the Scottish Baptist College, prior to serving at two churches, first the Ladywell Baptist Church in Livingston, in 1974. Then from 1982 he was appointed to the International congregation in Aberdeen, a congregation constituted as recently as 1978. It was noted that he had a warm engaging personality, a passion for evangelism combined with a strong commitment to pastoral care. Slack had served on a variety of Baptist Union Committees including the Ministerial Recognition Committee and the Joint Ministerial Board, in addition to membership on the Baptist Union Council and Executive. This depth of experience prior to his commencement of service in April 1995 ensured he was very familiar with the ongoing work of the

---

[12] Brierley, *Turning the Tide The Challenge Ahead*, pp. 22–27.

[13] Brierley, *Turning the Tide The Challenge Ahead*, pp. 27–28.

[14] The post title became 'General Director' at the January 2003 Baptist Union Council, *Scottish Baptist Yearbook 2004*, p. 109.

Baptist Union.[15] He was joined by Andrew Rollinson who was appointed as the Ministry Advisor in May 2003 to succeed Douglas Hutcheon who retired in July that year.[16] The new ministry advisor complemented the General Director as they took forward together the new national structure of the Baptist Union, following the completion of the 'Challenge to Change' process, after the one day Assembly in Hamilton in March 2002. The Baptist Union had deliberated over the implications of the 'Challenge to Change' initiative over a period of three years. Various groups had fed into this process including at the 2001 Annual Assembly with the presentation of the final report of the Think Tank entitled: 'Together in Christ – Together in Mission' together with the 'Heart, Mind and Mission' submission of The Theology of Mission group. In essence, it was discerned that a simpler structure for the Union was more suitable to the needs of the present day. A new approach to national leadership was required which allowed those appointed to these offices to be given effective remits to allow them to engage personally and in a pro-active manner with pastors and local churches. It led to the structural changes which resulted in the creation of the roles of General Director, Ministry Advisor, Mission Advisor and a lay Convenor who would chair various denominational gatherings to reduce the administrative and management responsibilities of the General Director. The third major change was a call to find new ways of associating between the churches as it was believed that the traditional regional Associations were no longer effective and a decision was taken that they should cease to exist by 2002.[17] However, hopes for new forms of associating did not materialise which led to a weakening of ties between the churches.[18] It was also felt by many that the *SBM* was no longer effective as a means of reaching particularly younger people in the churches as electronic means of communication were the future.[19] In the early years of the twenty-first century these were significant structural changes to

---

[15] 'Appointment of General Secretary', *Scottish Baptist Yearbook 1995*, p. 3.

[16] 'Other Staff Changes', *Scottish Baptist Yearbook*, 2004, p. 109, '134th Annual Report Compiled by the General Director, *Scottish Baptist Yearbook 2004*, pp. 118–119.

[17] The details of this process are given in *"Challenge to Change" Fulfilling the Vision*, the papers for the Baptist Union of Scotland One-Day Assembly, in Hamilton on 2 March, 2002.

[18] This was acknowledged by Bill Slack in his '138th Annual Report', *Scottish Baptist Yearbook 2008*, p. 90.

[19] A significant minority of Scotland's Baptists doubted the wisdom of closing the regional associations and the *SBM*. The hopes for new forms of associating were not achieved and the sense of fellowship and knowledge of sister churches gained through reading the *SBM* was not adequately replaced by the new means of communication.

collective Baptist life. But it was only the next steps in a process of change that would require further restructuring of Union life in the following decade.

## A Fresh Focus on the Highlands and Islands of Scotland

One of the key tasks to address during Slack's term of office was the problem of decline in the smaller churches, particularly in the Highlands and Islands of Scotland. The Mission Strategy Group reconstituted in 1998 sought to refocus on more targeted strategies for effective evangelism to address these concerns.[20] The new General Secretary was convinced that too great a priority had been placed on urban church-planting or renewal at the expense of the old island churches in areas of depopulation and poor employment. He was convinced that either these causes had to be viewed as 'lost causes' or alternatively Scottish Baptists tried to find new ways at reinvigorating their witness in these locations. A Mission Strategy Group was set up under the convenorship of Ken Stewart, with three sub-groups for Urban Strategy, Small Towns and Rural Strategy and Highlands and Islands Strategy. One of the key decisions of the latter group was the part-time appointment of Peter Williams, minister of Tiree Baptist Church, as the Highlands and Islands Co-ordinator. The area covered by Williams contained thirty-one Baptist churches. His wide remit included improving communications between these congregations and the Baptist Union; to stimulate the churches with appropriate support and fellowship; to facilitate new partnerships, structures or groupings designed by the churches and to explore locations without a Baptist witness to see if a viable opening could be found to initiate a new congregation in that area.[21] Slack recalled that: 'Williams travelled extensively around the area exploring options for possibilities of new congregations and consulting with existing churches about how best the Union could help strengthen their witness.'[22] One example of a new approach with historic congregations was the union of Port Ellen and Bowmore Baptist Churches into Islay Baptist Church. Another decision as one of the Millennium Projects was to place a full-time worker in Bunessan on Mull in 1996[23] to see if there

---

[20] Donald E. Meek (Specialist Advisor, Highlands and Islands Strategy Group), ' A Vision for the Highlands and Islands', in *Catch the Vision*, the Baptist Union of Scotland newspaper, Autumn 1998, p. 3; See also 'Mission Strategy Group', BUS Assembly report, 30 October 1998, *Scottish Baptist Yearbook 1999*, pp. 218–219.

[21] Ken Stewart, 'Mission Strategy Group', *Scottish Baptist Yearbook 1995*, pp. 179–181.

[22] Bill Slack, 'Some Reflections on my Ministry within the Baptist Union', a document written to assist the author in writing this chapter, p. 3. Peter Williams resigned from this post in August 2003, *Scottish Baptist Yearbook 2004*, p. 117.

[23] *Scottish Baptist Yearbook 1998*, p. 123.

could be a renewal of the work there and the retrieval of a work where a previous congregation had closed in Tobermory. Jim Miller, an experienced pastor was the first full-time Baptist pastor in Bunessan for almost half a century. A weekly children's club was established with around twenty participants. The church premises hosted a local nursery and playgroup. From the families associated with these activities ties have strengthened with the church community. However, young people from Mull boarded in Oban during the week while they were at school, so there were limited opportunities for contact during the week. A particular disappointment for the new pastor was the number of supportive young families who took the decision to move from the island to the mainland. This depopulation from the area led to the Children's club attendance halving to ten regulars and the youth fellowship from twelve to eight participants. The typical Sunday attendance was seven adults, though following the summer holiday club for children, led by Gary Smith forty people attended the family service. This was the same number as was present at the main Christmas service in 1998.[24] The hard work of the Millers and the local congregation had attracted some new younger people to the church, but the continuing depopulation of the area through young families moving to the mainland greatly hindered any prospects for serious numerical growth.

A new cause formed on 10 January 2004 was Arran Baptist Fellowship. Twenty-seven people attended its first service in Brodick Free Church premises.[25] Tiree Baptist Church was strengthened in its witness in a variety of ways at this time, for example, through visiting teams like the Youth-With-A-Mission team from West Kilbride who engaged in an eleven day mission in February 1998 and innovative approaches to prayer meetings and Sunday evening services held in a variety of different venues on the island.[26] The small congregation at Colonsay was encouraged by this support to continue in its work. The early stages of church-planting work were commencing on Skye, led by Frances and Harry Godden, and supported from time to time by the Tiree minister. This was another of the BUS Millennium Projects. Earlier hopes for a new work in Kyle of Lochalsh were not realised.[27] A new venture did begin in Stromness in Orkney, but it began independently of the General Secretary's initiative in rural mission. Eleanor McNeill, the secretary of the Colonsay Church, on his retirement from the post of General Director, wrote

---

[24] 'Mull', in 'Millennium Projects', *SBM,* 123.3 (March 1999), p. 20.

[25] 'Launch of Arran Baptist Fellowship' *Scottish Baptist Yearbook 2004*, p. 109.

[26] Peter Williams, 'YWAM takes Tiree by storm' and 'Island Retreat', in in *Catch the Vision*, the Baptist Union of Scotland newspaper, Spring 1998, p. 7.

[27] 'Skye', in 'Millennium Projects', *SBM,* 123.3 (March 1999), p. 21. 'Skye and Kyle', in '129th Annual Report by the General Secretary', *Scottish Baptist Yearbook 1999*, p. 117.

a letter expressing her gratitude that Bill Slack had not 'despised the day of small things'.[28] A decision was taken to appoint a church-planter at Brae in Shetland in 1997 as one of the BUS Millennium Projects.[29] Vincent McDougall, a former BMS Missionary in Brazil with his wife Sadie, began his ministry there in one of Scotland's most northerly communities in August 1998. The Brae Baptist Fellowship held its services in the local Community Centre with eighteen in regular attendance that increased to thirty-one for the special Christmas service that year. In January 1999 a BMS Youth Action Team came to work with them for three weeks. These three young people from Jamaica, Germany and Guernsey respectively were very talented in music and drama and were very popular in the local school.[30] The Grantown-on-Spey congregation saw significant numerical growth under the four year ministry of Mark and Rozanne Baker, SBC church-planters, and after their departure from the area in 2001 the church was in a sufficiently strong position to move forward in a new partnership with the Baptist Union of Scotland.[31] Other encouraging developments in the Highlands included the Kinmylies Baptist Church in Inverness seeking to raise funds for a building project in 2001 on a site they purchased some years previously, the same year in which a newly founded congregation, The Lighthouse Church in Forres, joined the Baptist Union.[32] In depopulated rural areas it was much harder to plant and build a new congregation or to build up an existing one, but no-one could fault the BUS for its efforts in these areas at this time. The greatest potential opportunities were in areas of new housing, but these were limited in number.

### Outreach Initiatives and Church Growth in Other Areas of Scotland

It was not only in Highland and Island locations that the Baptist Union Millennium projects were based. The earliest exploration of a potential pioneering ministry in East Lothian had begun in 1998.[33] There were moves to investigate the possibility of a new church in the south-east of Edinburgh in the Prestonpans/Port Seton/Tranent area in the vicinity of the new Royal

---

[28] Slack, 'Some Reflections on my Ministry', pp. 3–4.

[29] '128th Annual Report by the General Secretary, *Scottish Baptist Yearbook* 1998, p. 123. 'Millennium Projects', *SBM*, 123.3 (March 1999), p. 20.

[30] 'Brae', in 'Millennium Projects', *SBM*, 123.3 (March 1999), p. 20.

[31] *Scottish Baptist Yearbook 2002*, pp. 158–159.

[32] *Scottish Baptist Yearbook 2002*, pp. 119, 158; 2003, p. 33.

[33] Slack, 'Some Reflections on my Ministry', pp. 3–4.

Edinburgh Hospital.[34] Representatives of the Baptist Union and others from the Edinburgh and Lothians Baptist Association (ELBA) met with the Midlothian Council to express an interest in developing a Baptist witness in this area of new housing. Another potential opportunity under consideration in 1999 was the employment of an Asian Christian worker from Pakistan to engage in outreach work amongst the large Punjabi community on the south side of Glasgow. The Baptist Union and Queen's Park Baptist Church planned to make a joint appointment of someone to lead this new venture with an intended start date of the year 2000.[35] Mahboob Masih was commissioned for his new work on 3 September 2000.[36] He had an early opportunity to develop links with newly arrived asylum-seekers at the new Drop-In Centre opened up in the Queens Park Baptist Church premises the following year. It averaged around sixty to seventy people per week. Out of this group an Iranian church had been established that attracted around 100 people each Sunday with sixty baptisms in 2003, together with an Iranian Alpha course that proved an excellent tool to assist in sharing the Christian faith.[37] Another congregation assisting with asylum-seekers was Castlemilk Baptist Church. Three Iranians who came to faith through their witness were baptised in 2001.[38] Sheddocksley Baptist Church, Aberdeen, began as an outreach from Gerrard Street Baptist Church in November 1990 under the dynamic leadership of Jim Pirie a former Gerrard Street elder and a primary-school head-teacher who became the lay-pastor and Brian Stewart, a former youth-leader at Gerrard Street. After an extensive door-to-door visitation programme the church commenced Sunday services in September 1991. Both mother and daughter churches grew between 1991–1994, a combined membership growth of 28% and in the daughter church 150% growth with fifty-seven conversions, followed by fifty-two baptisms and a congregation of 120 people at the end of these three years. It prioritised strong community links and during the pastorate of Stephen Hibbard, with Baptist Union support, appointed Carol Hutchison as a full-time children's worker in 2006

---

[34] Details are given in the 'Secretary's Report' to and the Minutes of the Edinburgh and Lothians Baptist Association General Meeting, held in Dalkeith Baptist Church, 28 April, 1998.

[35] BUS Assembly, 5 May 1997, *Scottish Baptist Yearbook*, 1998, p. 207; '128th Annual Report by the General Secretary, *Scottish Baptist Yearbook 1998*, p. 123; Edinburgh's South-East Wedge' and 'Asian Outreach Worker for Glasgow', in 'Millennium Projects', *SBM*, 123.3 (March 1999), p. 21. *Scottish Baptist Yearbook 1999*, p. 117.

[36] 'Focus on Asian Community Work', *Scottish Baptist Yearbook 2001*, p. 239.

[37] *Scottish Baptist Yearbook 2004*, p. 109.

[38] *Scottish Baptist Yearbook 2002*, p. 119.

and during those years welcomed from the local area people of more than twenty nationalities, in particular from Africa and Eastern Europe. The Fine Piece Community Café, formed in 2008, quickly became a key gathering place in that part of the city of Aberdeen. Over the seven years from 2004 the church witnessed forty-seven baptisms and a Sunday congregation rising from less than one hundred adults to 170 regularly attending services. In 2011 Simon Dennis was taken on as Assistant Pastor to help consolidate this development in particularly to strengthen Community Groups and support a varied range of ministries in the congregation.[39] Cumbernauld Baptist Church had been aware of the new housing estates being built on the other side of the A80 dual carriageway and in September 1996 Brian Talbot, the minister met with David Moensch, an American Baptist working with the SBC in Scotland to discuss a potential church-plant in the Broadwood area. Consultation with the Kirkintilloch and Cumbernauld congregations led to times of prayer and the establishment of a home Bible study group in the area. In January 2001 Danny and Carolyn McVay, SBC church-planters in San Sebastian, Spain, were called to lead this new work. Sunday services were launched in May 2003 and the church constituted as an autonomous congregation in September 2005.[40] Stirling Baptist Church in 2003 had purchased 'The Rock' centre for children's and youth work, a counselling service and a gym.[41] St Ninian's Baptist Church in Stirling had renovated their new Community Outreach Centre that was to be used for a variety of community based ministries.[42] Another new venture launched in 2001 was the Bathgate church-plant led by Colin Baker.[43] The work focussed on marginalised young people and saw eighteen professions of faith in its first year. By 2002 around twenty-five people met on Sunday mornings for worship in Bathgate.[44] In the Borders Selkirk Baptist Church had reached a critical point in its more than a century of witness in 1983 when only a faithful few were in attendance, but remarkable growth through conversions followed by believers' baptism together with increasing numbers at the Sunday School and Bible class has led

---

[39] Stephen Hibbard, 'History of Sheddocksley Baptist Church', a presentation given at the Scottish History Project Day Conference in Crown Terrace Baptist Church Aberdeen in November 2011.

[40] 'The Origins of Broadwood Baptist Church', a copy of this document is in the possession of the author.

[41] Details on activities taking place in 'The Rock' facilities are given in Talbot, *Standing on the Rock: A History of Stirling Baptist Church*, pp. 175–176.

[42] Digest of Council Minutes' 13 January 2004, *Scottish Baptist Yearbook 2005*, p. 111.

[43] *Scottish Baptist Yearbook 2002*, p. 120.

[44] *Scottish Baptist Yearbook 2003*, pp. 116–117.

to average attendances on Sunday mornings of around 100 people in 1998 with consideration being given to employing a youth worker in addition to the minister.[45] The neighbouring congregation in Peebles had taken a big step in June 1997 calling Alex Russell as the full-time pastor after a four-year vacancy. It led to growth in Sunday School attendance with over twenty children each week and a fresh commitment to outreach in the wider community and engagement with the Masterlife discipleship course within the congregation. The special guest services held monthly by the church attracted a significant number of men, who had been under-represented at a typical Sunday morning service. The financial support from the Scottish Baptist fund had helped make these initiatives possible.[46] It was clear that the commitment to evangelism was strong in many churches and some found fresh and innovative ways to impact their communities in these years.

## Home Evangelisation, 1994–2009

The appointment of a Director of Mission and Evangelism was a priority and the September 1995 Baptist Union Council was informed that Robert Breustedt, minister of Carluke Baptist Church, had accepted this position.[47] The new director was fortunate to have a Mission Strategy Group, ably chaired by Noel McCullins, the senior pastor at Ayr Baptist Church together with the growing Step-Out youth mission initiative that had been co-ordinated effectively by Cindy Mackenzie. She stepped down from this post in 1996 in order to play a more active role in women's work in Scottish Baptist churches. This area of national work was later strengthened by the decision of the Union, in partnership with Partick Baptist Church, to employ Gary Smith in 1997 as a part-time National Youth Worker and part-time Youth Worker at Partick Baptist Church, Glasgow. He was well-known amongst Scottish Baptists through his previous involvement in a number of their congregations, though immediately prior to this appointment he had been serving as Youth Minister in North Cheam Baptist Church in England.[48] The Baptist Union had also sought to utilise the gifts of some of its younger members through

---

[45] George Mackenzie, 'Encouraging news from Selkirk: Church Growth Is Possible', in *Catch the Vision*, the Baptist Union of Scotland newspaper, spring 1998, p. 2.

[46] Alex Russell, 'Dedicated giving by Baptists in Scotland helps one small church to flourish', in *Catch the Vision*, the Baptist Union of Scotland newspaper, spring 1998, pp. 2–3.

[47] 'Director of Mission and Evangelism', 12 September 1995, BUS Council, *Scottish Baptist Yearbook 1996*, pp. 186–187.

[48] 'Changing Times in the Youth Scene', *Scottish Baptist Yearbook 1998*, pp. 123–124, 220; *1999*, pp. 220–221;

these Step-Out Missions and Operation Gideon, another form of outreach work.[49] Team members on the later scheme took a year out to serve in a particular local congregation. The first year it operated in partnership with Youth for Christ was at Leven Baptist Church in Fife where Claire McFarlane and David Ramsay were the volunteer workers.[50] In 1998–1999 'Katy and Nicola' served through Dalkeith Baptist Church 'opening up opportunities into a local high school and developing a drop-in café'; and in 1999–2000 'Katy for a second year and Neil' were seconded to St Andrews Baptist Church.[51] In the years of its operation the numbers for Operation Gideon were relatively small, but the principle of a year-in-training in a local church setting was a welcome new venture.

By contrast, the shorter and more targeted weeks of youth and children's mission attracted more workers and opportunities for service. A very large proportion, though, of the young people who joined Step-Out teams were female. In 1998, for example, there were only two Scottish young men on the teams, Stuart Gilmour and Neil Pearson from Cumbernauld Baptist Church. The team members who were appointed were very talented and enthusiastic, but Breustedt in 1998 admitted that he was disappointed how hard it was to recruit sufficient volunteers to make up teams for the churches that requested them.[52] However, in 1996, for example, there were still Step-Out missions in six Baptist churches, at Buckhaven, Cambuslang, Cowdenbeath, Montrose, Springburn, Glasgow and Cornton, Stirling.[53] There was still the same number of teams a couple of years later in 1998. That year their missions took place in Ladywell Baptist Church, Livingston, Southside, Ayr and Buckie followed by weeks in Wick, Gourock and Carluke Baptist Churches.[54] Although hard work Step Out missions were a good opportunity for Scottish Baptist churches to raise their profile in their local communities.

Breustedt and Smith worked together in training younger leaders in effective forms of mission activities, together with providing opportunities for fellowship and fun for the younger people in the churches through a series of Mega Youth Weekends. For example, the 1999 one at Newton Mearns Baptist Church, led by Robert Breustedt and Gary Smith that involved a mix of Bible teaching on topics such as 'Can we trust the Bible?', 'Science versus

---

[49] 'Changing Times in Baptist Mission', *Scottish Baptist Yearbook 1998*, p. 123.

[50] 'Operation Gideon', *Scottish Baptist Yearbook 1999*, p. 151.

[51] 'Operation Gideon', *Scottish Baptist Yearbook 2000*, p. 178.

[52] 'Mission and Evangelism' Report, *Scottish Baptist Yearbook 1999*, p. 151.

[53] 'Step-Out Missions', Mission and Evangelism Report, *Scottish Baptist Yearbook 1997*, p. 149.

[54] 'Step Out Teams', Mission and Evangelism Report, *Scottish Baptist Yearbook 1999*, p. 151.

Scripture' and 'The Genesis Flood', as well as a couple of sessions on "life issues', followed by practical training on preparing epilogues and producing and performing drama sketches. The Saturday evening of these weekends was taken up with the performances of these dramatic presentations. Similar events took place all over the country, including as far north as Shetland in March 1999. A year later in March 2000 the Newton Means and Shetland venues offered similar events, together with an additional weekend at International Baptist Church in Aberdeen. This scheme of equipping young people and building ties of friendship led to a small but steady increase in the numbers of young people giving up at least a week of their summer breaks on Step-Out teams. In fact, the majority of the forty-one team members in summer 2000 signed up for two or three weeks of service. Four of the team members were Baptists from other European countries. One young woman from Berlin, Germany came for the entire duration of the missions that summer. Three others from Finland, France and Mallorca joined teams after finding out about these mission opportunities the previous year when the Director of Mission and Evangelism had been a guest speaker at an EBF youth camp. That year saw some of the largest Step-Out teams with twenty-one in the Alness team and twenty-two visiting Wick Baptist Church.[55] The total numbers may not have been high but those who participated in these schemes were trained effectively and gained significant confidence in serving in a local church context. It was a noteworthy contribution to the equipping of younger Scottish Baptists to share their faith and engage in different forms of ministry in an increasingly secular society, prior to Breustedt stepping down from this effective ministry after five years of service in the year 2000.[56]

The new mission advisor David Gordon, former minister of Broadway Baptist Church, Isle of Man, commenced his work in July 2001.[57] In 2002, he promoted a 'Seize the Day' Prayer initiative and indicated that one of his key priorities was assisting struggling congregations in urban priority areas. Another in 2003 was the appointment of part-time Mission Networkers in the nine regions of the country with a view to forming an effective team of colleagues to assist the churches across Scotland.[58] By January 2004 funding was in place for Jacqueline Primrose to work six days per month with the Central Association, Neil Young was appointed to start working in Glasgow from Easter 2004, Richard Higginbottom, half-time in Fife and Tayside, Bob

---

[55] 'Mission and Evangelism', *Scottish Baptist Yearbook 2000*, pp. 176–177.

[56] Bill Slack, '131st Annual Report by the General Secretary', *Scottish Baptist Yearbook 2001*, p. 128.

[57] *Scottish Baptist Yearbook 2002*, p. 118. He stayed in post until 2007 when he moved back into pastoral ministry at Kirkintilloch Baptist Church. Andy Scarcliffe was appointed his successor in March 2007, *Scottish Baptist Yearbook 2008*, pp. 43, 93.

[58] *Scottish Baptist Yearbook 2003*, p. 116.

Baxter working six days per month in the Lothians and the Borders, Noel McCullins was appointed half-time in the South-West, Olive Drane was working in Aberdeen and Shetland and work was ongoing to make appointments in the other regional areas.[59] By November 2007 when a review of this initiative took place under the direction of Andy Scarcliffe, the recently appointed Mission Adviser, there were nine post-holders in place. In addition to those mentioned above, Bill Cairney worked half-time in Lanarkshire; Kate Maclennon served in the West Central area six days a month. Harry Sprange covered the North-West Highlands and Islands one long weekend a month, with a broader remit that included investigating communities with no Baptist witness to see if there was the potential for planting a new church and establishing relationships with emerging baptistic fellowships.[60] Some examples of the kind of work to which they gave some input included: in Aberdeen and in Glasgow, interdenominational 'Street Pastors' ministries were launched; Ayr and Southside churches launched 'Broken Chains' to assist needy people; Kilmarnock Baptist Church, with other local congregations formed the Kilmarnock Youth Project; and two fresh expressions formed under the guidance of Richard Higginbottom were formed at Tulloch in Perth called TullochNET and 'The Haven' in the Blairgowrie-Coupar Angus area.[61] There were thirty churches that worked with mission networkers on consultations, mostly evaluating their mission strategies or in preparing a community audit, together with a smaller number of exciting new initiatives such as the church-plant in Girvan.[62] That small group in Girvan was growing and seeing people come to faith in Christ. They had met on a Tuesday evening for their activities, but by the autumn of 2007 was considering a regular weekend event 'along the lines of a fresh expression of Church'.[63] The mission networker initiative worked particularly well in the South-West because the Baptist churches in the region were fully behind and committed to working with Noel McCullins. The initial funding of £100,000 from the Baptist Union for this initiative was used up by the end of 2007 and the

---

[59] 'The Mission Adviser', 'Digest of Council Minutes', 13 January 2004, *Scottish Baptist Yearbook 2005*, p. 113.

[60] 'Mission Networker Review November 2007', pp. 1–13; a copy of this document is in the possession of the author. Harry Sprange, 'Associate Mission Networker: North-west Highlands & Islands', *Scottish Baptist Yearbook 2009*, p. 161.

[61] Mission Networkers' reports in *Scottish Baptist Yearbook 2009*, pp. 154–161.

[62] 'Mission Networker Review November 2007', pp. 1–13.

[63] Mission Networkers Reports: 'South-West', by Noel McCullins, *Scottish Baptist Yearbook 2008*, pp. 103–104

majority of the networkers concluded their service in this ministry around that time.[64]

Another feature of the mission advisor's work was a concern for a greater focus on church-planting especially in urban areas. Under Gordon's leadership in 2006, the Baptist Union of Scotland partnered with the Church of Scotland and International Christian College in Glasgow to form Urban Expression, an initiative driven from the grassroots by urban church-panting teams and led by Paul and Esther Ede. In addition, a church-planting conference was organised in May 2007 in Edinburgh at which Stuart Murray of Urban Expression and Martyn Atkins, the Principal of Cliff College in Derbyshire were the invited speakers. Following on from these developments in partnership with the Mission Resource Team the Baptist Union agreed to provide significant funding for up to ten new initiatives over the following three years, including up to 50% of a stipend and this funding would be available both for personnel and projects.[65] The Baptist Union was supportive of the development of BIG (Business in Glasgow) in 2007 through Adelaide Place Baptist Church and Renfield St Stephens Church of Scotland under which Jack Quinn, minister of the Adelaide Place congregation would be released part-time to seek to plant a new expression of church meeting the needs of the business community in Glasgow. Another example of a new expression of a church launched at that time was the Garioch Church. A group of members covenanted together, under the auspices of Bridge of Don Baptist Church, Aberdeen, to start this new work in the Inverurie area.[66] In a time when smaller churches were struggling to maintain their witness and some were closing new forms of church and approaches to mission were required. In this time of significant change it was clear many congregations were struggling to adapt to the changing context in which they sought to bear witness to their faith.

Chaplaincy work was an area of mission and ministry that flourished for Scottish Baptists in these years. Various Baptists had previously served as educational chaplains as part of a team in Scottish Universities, but hospital chaplaincy had not been open to Scottish Baptists prior to the 1990s. Marjorie Taylor was the first Scottish Baptist hospital chaplain to be appointed in 1991. The Church of Scotland had up to that point handled all appointments to NHS chaplaincy posts on behalf of the health service, and candidates seeking such posts from other denominations would have found it difficult to

---

[64] 'Mission Networker Review November 2007', p. 7.

[65] David Gordon, 'Church-Planting-three year initiative', Mission Advisor Report, *Scottish Baptist Yearbook 2007*, pp. 127–130. Reports from the regional Mission Networkers appear on pp. 131–140.

[66] '138th Annual Report' by the General Director, *Scottish Baptist Yearbook 2008*, p. 91.

access information about them. She was invited to take up the vacant part-time post at Hairmyres Hospital in East Kilbride. Taylor also gained the distinction in 2003, alongside Beth Dunlop, Associate pastor in Dumfries Baptist Church, of being the first women to be fully accredited as ministers in the Baptist Union of Scotland.[67] In 2003 three Scottish Baptists were serving as hospital chaplains. Marjory Taylor in Hairmyres; Patricia McDonald who had served at Glasgow Royal Infirmary for the past eight years, and who would later serve also in the Princess Royal Maternity in Glasgow, together with Muriel Knox at Woodend Hospital and Royal Cornhill Hospital, Aberdeen; Knox was appointed to the full-time post in the latter hospital that year.[68] As the first decade of the twenty-first century progressed a greater number of Baptists were appointed to some of these posts. Carol Campbell was appointed to the Royal Hospital for Sick Children and Queen Mother's Hospital, Glasgow, in 2006.[69] Anne Dougall, who had previously served from 2003 to 2007 as a hospital chaplain in Newcastle, was called in the latter year to a post at Gartnavel General Hospital in Glasgow,[70] and Stuart Webster was appointed as chaplain of the Prince and Princess of Wales Hospice, Glasgow, in 2007.[71] Military chaplaincy opportunities also began to increase from the late 1990s into the present century. Neil Allison, former minister of Glenrothes Baptist Church was a pioneer of peace-time Army Chaplaincy since his appointment to that position in 1998,[72] and Alasdair Nicol, likewise, was the first Scottish Baptist appointed to RAF Chaplaincy when he took up that role in 2003, following service at Anstruther Baptist Church.[73] There were also other chaplaincy posts filled by Baptists at this time, including Howard Drysdale as the Port Chaplain in Aberdeen from 2001, through the British International Sailors' Society.[74] Douglas Wright who was based at the

---

[67] More details are found in Lumsden, 'Her Children Arise and Call her Blessed: The Place of Women in Scottish Baptist life, in Talbot, *Distinctive People*, pp. 77–78.

[68] 'Chaplaincies', reports in the *Scottish Baptist Yearbook 2004*, pp. 141–143.

[69] Carol Campbell, 'Royal Hospital for Sick Children and Queen Mother's Hospital, Glasgow', in 'Chaplaincies', report in the *Scottish Baptist Yearbook 2007*, pp. 179–180.

[70] Anne Dougall, Gartnavel General Hospital, Glasgow, in *Scottish Baptist Yearbook 2009*, pp. 64, 189.

[71] Stuart Webster, 'Prince and Princess of Wales Hospice, Glasgow, *Scottish Baptist Yearbook 2008*, pp. 134–135.

[72] Neil E. Allison CF, 'Army Chaplaincy', *Scottish Baptist Yearbook 2004*, pp. 53, 140.

[73] Alasdair Nicol, 'RAF Chaplaincy', *Scottish Baptist Yearbook 2007*, pp. 178–179.

[74] 'Howard Drysdale, 'B.I.S.S. Port Chaplain, Aberdeen', in 'Chaplaincy Reports', *Scottish Baptist Yearbook 2008*, pp. 65, 130–132.

Rock Community Centre of Stirling Baptist Church served as the Stirling City Centre Chaplain from 2006,[75] and Graham Bell was appointed as the full-time prison chaplain at H.M. Prison Glenochil in Tullibody, near Stirling.[76] Scottish Baptists were now making a notable contribution in chaplaincy work with a growing number of opportunities now available and an increasing number of their ministers appointed to posts.

The relationship with the Foreign Missions Board of the SBC continued to be strong in this era with, for example, four partnership missions taking place in October 1998 at Baptist Union-affiliated congregations in Grantown-on-Spey, Johnstone, Ladywell, Livingston and Nairn.[77] However, there was a major reorganisation of its structure as well as a change of name to the International Mission Board (IMB) in the late 1990s. It is possible only to give a snapshot of its range of ministries in this era with a particular focus as an example, on those serving in 1998. Approximately twenty-one years after the first Southern Baptist workers arrived in Scotland, the new pattern of working now consisted of two teams with distinctive ministries. The 'Scotland Team' had a vision for developing evangelistic work. The new team-leader would be Scott McIntosh who with his wife D'Lisa would move to the Central Belt to undertake this role and consequently would relinquish his post as pastor of Nairn Baptist Church. Mark and Rozanne Baker arrived in 1998 to undertake pastoral duties at Grantown Baptist Church and lead outreach work in the Spey valley. Peggy DuCharme arrived as a specialist children's worker and would work alongside the Denny, Larbert and St Ninian's (Stirling) Baptist Churches. John Moore was appointing as a church planting intern to work under Scott's direction in Forres, evaluating the situation and beginning evangelistic work in that town of 8,000 people. Gena Wilson who had already served two years in Cathcart Baptist Church and in the IMB Office in Kirkintilloch was appointed for a further two years to continue that work, but with a view to moving into a full-time church position at Cathcart. David and Laura Moench who had carried out an effective ministry amongst young people in Dundee would also adapt to new responsibilities in Western Europe, but based in Scotland. David had been asked to serve as a consultant and trainer with all of the new IMB team leaders, Cluster Co-ordinators and our Regional Leadership Team to ensure the new structures worked effectively. The second team in Scotland focussed on work amongst college and university students. Karl and Marilyn Nyquist who had already spent five

---

[75] 'The Rock Community Project: Stirling City Centre Chaplaincy', *Scottish Baptist Yearbook 2009*, pp 176–177.

[76] Graham Bell, 'H.M. Prison Glenochil', in 'Chaplaincy Reports', *Scottish Baptist Yearbook 2009*, p. 190.

[77] 'Partnering Churches', in 'Mission and Evangelism' report, *Scottish Baptist Yearbook 1999*, p. 152.

years developing 'Student Impact' alongside Adelaide Place Baptist Church in Glasgow, had seen that work grow to the extent that two Scottish staff members were added to their team after raising the funds for their salaries from supporters of their work. Preparations were being made in 1998 to launch a similar ministry in St Andrews, led by Steve and Laura Van Buren.[78] It was clear that though a major re-organisation of its structures had taken place the IMB was still firmly committed to its partnership with Scottish Baptists. It was demonstrated by the number of individuals and projects that were supported by the IMB in the fulfilment of this mission.

## Relations with Other Churches

### Other Churches in Scotland

At the 1989 Annual Assembly Scottish Baptists had expressed very clearly what they did not approve of in terms of inter-church relations, but there was a lack of clarity going forward as to how we ought to relate to other churches. Bill Slack had been shaped by his first experience of a Baptist Assembly as a teenage delegate from Hamilton Baptist Church at the Centenary Assembly in 1969. He had a vivid memory of churches resigning from the Union because they disagreed with the decision taken with reference to the Scottish Council of Churches.[79] In 1989, two decades later, a very different conclusion had been reached to discussions on the same topic, but the underlying strength of feelings expressed by Baptists with different views on this topic had not changed. One of his key aims as the new General Secretary of the Baptist Union was to help this family of churches rediscover its confidence and security in its identity in a constructive manner. He intentionally used the phrase 'Our family of Baptist Churches' with regularity with a view to helping colleagues accept the legitimate diversity of opinions within our ranks, while at the same time recognising that the things Scottish Baptists had in common was far greater than the issues over which there were some differences of opinion.[80] Slack placed a great importance on having good relationships with other Scottish Christians and wanted other Church leaders in Scotland to know that the decision over ACTS did not mean Scottish Baptists were unwilling to work with other Churches where or when that was appropriate.

---

[78] David Moench, 'International Mission Board', *Scottish Baptist Yearbook*, 1999, pp. 143–145. Another major change in structure of the IMB was reflected in its working arrangements in Scotland from 2003 onwards – see "International Mission Board', *Scottish Baptist Yearbook 2004*, pp. 149–150.

[79] Slack, 'Some Reflections on my Ministry', p. 1. This story also featured in his '130th Annual Report by the General Secretary', *Scottish Baptist Yearbook 2000*, p. 124.

[80] Edward Burrows, 'William George Slack'. in his chapter, 'Without a Vision the People Perish', in Talbot (ed.), *Distinctive People*, p. 17.

His offer of friendship was reciprocated and 'leaders of other churches afforded me a warm welcome to some groups in which I could participate without compromising our Assembly decision.'[81] A Joint Study Group was established with the Church of Scotland in the 1990s that looked at a Mutual Recognition of Ministry. This was agreed at the end of the conversations, but it must not be 'confused with Mutual Eligibility of Ministry', this was not under discussion.[82] A message was clearly communicated to other Scottish Churches in this era that although formal involvement in ecumenical bodies like ACTS was not being pursued that good relations with other Christian bodies in the country was still an important priority for Scottish Baptists. This was clearly demonstrated at a local level as individual congregations worked well with other churches in their communities.[83] Slack's bridge-building efforts were effective and welcomed.

At the start of his tenure as General Secretary Baptists in Scotland had no formal ties to any inter-church body outside of Baptist ranks. Both he and many other colleagues in the Union regarded this state of affairs as less than satisfactory. In particular, it was time to see if a closer relationship could be developed with other Evangelical Churches in Scotland. Slack, together with his predecessor as General Secretary, Peter Barber, had a longstanding connection with the Evangelical Alliance (EA) in Scotland and Slack had served on their Executive. Other Scottish Baptists had also served on the Council and Executive of the Alliance in Scotland in the 1990s.[84] It was during Slack's time in office at the Baptist Union that conversations were held with Alliance leaders to explore the possibility of this family of churches joining the Alliance. The General Secretary reminded the 1997 Assembly delegates, in the course of the discussions on EA membership that reports on discussions on this subject had been made at two previous annual assemblies.[85] They were informed that EA was prepared to accept the Baptist Union of Scotland as a member on the basis of its Declaration of Principle. He explained that the EA was able to equip Christians to be effective in their service to society. They also brought Christians from a wide denominational spectrum to celebrate their oneness in Christ Jesus. BMS had already become

---

[81] Slack, 'Some Reflections on my Ministry', p. 5.

[82] Douglas Hutcheon, 'Reflections on Baptist Union Life 1993–2003', p. 1. This was a document provided for the author to assist with the writing of this chapter.

[83] Hutcheon, 'Reflections on Baptist Union Life, p. 3.

[84] 'Evangelical Alliance Membership', Baptist Union Annual Assembly, 3 May 1997, *Scottish Baptist Yearbook 1998*, pp. 206–207.

[85] 'Baptist Union of Scotland and the Evangelical Alliance', September 1996, a paper printed in 'Welcome to Kingdom Living 1997: Baptist Union Assembly Handbook', pp. 20–21.

a member of the Evangelical Missionary Alliance. He argued that the Union could have an effective role in this body and benefit from its insights and resources. On a motion proposed by Slack and seconded by Brian Talbot, minister of Cumbernauld Baptist Church, assembly approved the motion to become members of EA.[86] This decision was a powerful positive statement of the mind of Scottish Baptists on a form of inter-church engagement with which the vast majority could agree. After half a century of serious disagreements in their ranks on this subject there was now an expression of ecumenical identity with which the overwhelming majority of Scottish Baptists could wholeheartedly support.

Bill Slack was not content to restrict his endeavours to Union membership of the EA, but sought also to build bridges with other Evangelical Christians. Slack was aware of the struggles many Evangelical Presbyterians were having within the Church of Scotland over its changing stance on human sexuality and he made contact with some of their leaders to see if there was any way Scottish Baptists could support them in their defence of historical Christian convictions on this matter. He received no response from them. A more likely opportunity for bridge-building appeared to come from growing relationships with the progressive wing of the Brethren in Evangelical Churches. Slack had been encouraged through his EBF contacts in finding out how Baptists and Brethren had supported each other during the Hitler era in Germany in the 'Gemeinde', ties of fellowship that continued after the close of World War Two. He had conversations with Regina Claas, the German Baptist General Secretary and with another 'Gemeinde' leader whose roots were in the Brethren tradition and was encouraged to consider that closer co-operation might be possible in Scotland as well. In addition, Slack knew personally some Open Brethren leaders in Scotland and had been invited to preach on a number of occasions at Allander Evangelical Church in Milngavie and Strathaven Evangelical Church. Slack convened a number of meetings over meals between pastors and leaders of the two networks at the Baptist Union offices. However, his earlier high expectations of progress were not realised as 'A sense of independency with Evangelical Churches and a deep seated concern about Baptist principles within Baptist Churches proved too difficult for us to overcome at that time.'[87] Although the substantial efforts at building closer ties with other Evangelical Churches, most notably with the more progressive Christian Brethren congregations, had been less successful than he had hoped, membership of the Evangelical Alliance had sent out a clear message that Scottish Baptists did wish to work with other families of Churches with whom they shared common convictions

---

[86] Evangelical Alliance Membership', p. 206.

[87] Slack, 'Some Reflections on my Ministry', p. 6. Some details of these conversations are given in 'Developing our Relationships with Evangelical Churches' *Scottish Baptist Yearbook 2005*, p. 119; *2006*, p. 124.

## Other Baptist Churches

### BRITISH BAPTIST CHURCHES

There were good relationships with the other Baptist bodies that built on the closer ties established in the previous decade. The Fellowship of British Baptists (FBB) was constituted formally at the beginning of Bill Slack's term of service and confirmed that the Baptist Unions in the United Kingdom would have more active and intentional fellowship and co-operation.[88] These developments included more closely aligned lists of accredited ministers to ease settlements in churches affiliated with another member body and the joint assemblies in Scotland in partnership with the BMS that began with the October 2006 Assembly in Aberdeen and which have proved to be a great success.[89] Subsequently a group of Northern Irish Baptists, who were unhappy at their Union remaining outside the new arrangements, formed themselves into the Irish Baptist network which was in time accommodated within the new structural arrangements.[90] The new FBB structure worked well during these years, although reading minutes of the meetings gives a clear impression that there was some disappointment that more co-operative working had been hoped for but not realised at that time.

### EUROPEAN BAPTIST FEDERATION

Slack was acutely aware that his predecessor in office, Peter Barber, had played a very significant and high-profile role within EBF at a critical time in Europe's political turmoil. He had been the EBF President when the Berlin Wall had come down and pressure for change within various Communist regimes in Central and Eastern Europe had led to new political structures being formed. The new post-holder was aware that some Scottish Baptists had felt that the new General Secretary needed to place a much greater priority on the growing spiritual and practical needs at home. This feedback to him came out of regional meetings entitled: 'Meet the General Secretary' he had arranged at the start of his time as leader in this denomination. In practice, this meant that although he was deeply involved in the work of the EBF, he twice turned down invitations to become Vice President and subsequently President of EBF. The timing was not right for him as it was necessary to focus on the 'Challenge to Change' initiative within the Scottish

---

[88] 'Fellowship of British Baptists' in the Joint Consultative Committee report, *Scottish Baptist Yearbook 1995*, pp. 150–151. A fuller account of the changes is given in Ian Mundie, 'Fellowship of British Baptists' report, *Scottish Baptist Yearbook 1996*, pp. 144–146; See also *Scottish Baptist Yearbook 1997*, pp. 138–141; *1998*, pp. 150–152; *2000*, pp. 163–165; *2004*, pp. 123–124.

[89] 'Fellowship of British Baptists' report, *Scottish Baptist Yearbook 2007*, pp. 185–186.

[90] Slack, 'Some Reflections on my Ministry', p. 2.

Union that would enable it to become to a greater degree fit for purpose at the start of the twenty-first century.[91] Scottish Baptists would make a major contribution to supporting colleagues in Continental Europe, but it was primarily outside the formal structures of EBF.

In November 1995 Boschidar Igoff, the General Secretary of the Baptist Union of Bulgaria, met with Baptists in different parts of Scotland to highlight the difficulties faced by fellow Christians in Bulgaria. In particular, he highlighted the fact the Sophia City Council had withdrawn permission for the Sophia Baptist Church to build a school and orphanage, in addition to a church on a site they owned in the city. In response to appeals from Baptists all over Europe the decision was revisited by the Council and this time permission was granted to erect the school and orphanage but not the church premises. Another EBF-related project promoted in Scotland was the national appeal to assist the Baptist Church in Karlovac, Croatia, to erect a new building. The sum of £7,000 was raised in 1995 largely through the work of the World Mission & International Affairs Committee, and in particular, Watson Moyes, minister of Viewfield Baptist Church Dunfermline. The four-year war in the former Yugoslavia, 1991–1995, had delayed the erection of this building. In August 1997 Bill Slack visited Croatia with a vision of developing a partnership with them as well as taking the opportunity of visiting some of the sites where their humanitarian aid agency, Moj Blizni (My Neighbour), was operating. He informed the 1996 Assembly that he has been encouraged by attending the EBF Council and looked forward to participating in the work of the BWA as well.[92] Viewfield Baptist Church, Dunfermline, in summer 1998 sent a group of twenty-six people to Fuzine to spend two weeks building and renovating the Hope Centre, a facility used for the work with refugees.[93] The Baptist Union denominational appeals in 1999 and 2000 were both for Croatia. A range of fundraising activities were launched in aid of this appeal. Café Croatia, for example, in 1999 was one of the significant contributors to this project. Gary Smith encouraged young people in various Baptist churches in Scotland to hold lunches and coffee mornings to raise funds for this cause.[94] In the year 2000 the Women's

---

[91] Slack, 'Some Reflections on my Ministry', p. 2.

[92] '127th Annual Report by the General Secretary, *Scottish Baptist Yearbook 1997*, p. 103.

[93] 'Holiday with a difference in Croatia', in *Catch the Vision*, the Baptist Union of Scotland newspaper, Autumn 1998, p. 5.

[94] 'Café Croatia – The Baptist Union of Scotland's Christmas Project 1999' and 'Christmas Family Boxes Christmas 1999: To help meet the urgent needs of refugees in the Balkans' – copies of these promotional leaflets are in the possession of the author. See also 'Christmas Appeal and Café Croatia' in John Barclay, 'Croatia Partnership Report', *Scottish Baptist Yearbook 2001*, p. 152.

Auxiliary of the Baptist Union, together with the BUS provided financial support for the work of Maria Bujadzic, a counsellor based in Karlovac Baptist Church. Her efforts in supporting those traumatised by things that happened during the war were greatly appreciated.[95] In 2003 the Baptist Union gifted one month's salary from their Response Fund to help support the salary of Srecko Illisinovic's work with refugees through the Moj Blizni agency. The rest of his salary came from two sources, Dunfermline Eurosave, the charity administered through Viewfield Baptist Church, Dunfermline, and a Baptist Church in Wales. In the same year the Baptist Union sent a gift to help refurbish a house near Plitvice in Croatia that was used to resettle a refugee family from the ROS Refugee centre. The Christmas Box appeal in 2003 for Croatia was very well supported by forty Baptist Churches with the goods collected delivered by lorries in three trips in December 2003 and January 2004.[96] In 2005 the Baptist Union sent financial gifts towards the building projects in Rijeka and Duga Resa and towards the running costs of the Children's and Youth Camps run by the Baptist Union of Croatia on the island of Ugljan.[97] These examples of support for Croatian Baptists demonstrate the depth of the commitment to this partnership

Alan Donald, then minister of Denny Baptist Church helped organise Partnership Links between the respective countries. Ayr Baptist Church, linked with the Karlovac congregation, took out a building and erected it for one of the church-plants of the Karlovac church. Morningside Baptist Church, Edinburgh, sent out a ministry team to assist their link church, Zagreb Baptist Church. This team visited two villages where the Zagreb congregation has been carrying out evangelistic work with a view to supporting these endeavours.[98] Cathcart Baptist Church, Glasgow, also established a partnership with Zadar Baptist Church in Croatia in 2003,[99] and Tiree Baptist Church with Pula Baptist Church.[100] Cumbernauld Baptist

---

[95] 'Marija Bujadzic', in Barclay, 'Croatia Partnership Report', *Scottish Baptist Yearbook 2001*, pp. 152–153.

[96] 'Partnership with Croatian Baptists' *Scottish Baptist Yearbook 2004*, pp. 122–123; 2005, p. 120.

[97] 'Partnership with the Baptist Union of Croatia', *Scottish Baptist Yearbook 2006*, p. 126.

[98] 'Partnership Links', in Barclay, 'Croatia Partnership Report', *Scottish Baptist Yearbook 2001*, p. 152.

[99] 'Partnership with Croatian Baptists' *Scottish Baptist Yearbook 2004*, pp. 122–123.

[100] *Scottish Baptist Yearbook 2006*, p. 126.

Church was linked with Pakrac Baptist Church in eastern Croatia.[101] In addition to visits to the church with trucks containing aid of various kinds between 2001 and 2005, contacts were made between schools in North Lanarkshire and Croatian schools and English textbooks were donated as a gift to Croatian schools from their Scottish counterparts at that time.[102] In another area of European Baptist work seven younger Baptists attended the EBF Youth Camp at Parnu in Estonia. Five of them were funded by their respective churches and two others from a new fund, The Peter Barber Memorial Fund, created to allow Scottish Baptist younger people to attend this annual event and also serve as a reminder of the former General Secretary's commitment to colleagues in the EBF.[103] Ties with Croatian Baptists in particular were strong in these years.

One feature of EBF life that Slack promoted amongst Scottish Baptists was the Indigenous Missions Church-planting work led by Polish Baptist Daniel Trusiewicz. Despite a good amount of publicity only a few congregations got involved in the decade following their initial support in Scotland from 2005. Broughty Ferry Baptist Church, Dundee supported a new Serbian Baptist congregation in the town of Ruma; Hamilton Baptist Church committed to a similar venture in Lithuania and King's Park Baptist Church, Glasgow, supported a work in Armenia. There was also a financial gift to this ministry from Ardbeg Baptist Church in Rothesay, and also some support was given to Samsun Baptist Church in Turkey.[104] The total number of supported projects was small, but this must not be interpreted as a lack of interest in working with colleagues in Europe, because Scottish Baptists had a strong track record in support of Christian and other Baptist work overseas.

An example of this commitment was the partnership with Baptist colleagues in Belarus, following the Chernobyl nuclear tragedy of 1986.[105] Scott McHaney, minister of Crieff Baptist Church, informed the 1993 Baptist Assembly in Edinburgh of a plan to bring children over to Scotland from Belarus for a holiday to help build their immunity against the high

---

[101] Isobel Jarvie, secretary of Cumbernauld Baptist Church, 'Croatia Partnership', in *Catch the Vision*, the Baptist Union of Scotland newspaper, spring 1998, p. 8, gives information on the link with the Pakrac Church.

[102] The author was minister of the Cumbernauld Church at that time and participated in a number of the visits to Pakrac and other communities in Croatia.

[103] '126th Annual Report by the General Secretary and the Associate General Secretary', *Scottish Baptist Yearbook 1996*, pp. 104–105.

[104] Daniel Trusiewicz to Brian Talbot, email dated 2 May 2019.

[105] Information in the next two paragraphs unless otherwise indicated comes from a communication with the author from Colin Mackenzie, 'Kids Aloft and Beyond', 14 May 2019.

radiation levels in their native country at that time. The project named 'Kids Aloft' did not commence until summer 1995 when seventy-five children and their interpreters came to spend three weeks with various churches in Scotland. The following year Colin Mackenzie, minister of Montrose Baptist Church, spent three weeks of his sabbatical in Belarus visiting some of the families who had visited Montrose the previous summer. This visit led to a friendship with Pavel Rudoi, pastor of Grodno Baptist Church, and in turn a long-term relationship with the Baptist Union of Belarus. In 1997 Colin and his wife Cindy were asked to form a team of people to engage in some building work at a sanatorium on the outskirts of Minsk. During the summer of 1997 another group of seventy children and five adult helpers had come to Scotland and thirty-three Scottish Baptists went to work in Minsk, not only on construction projects, but also including dental surgery, English lessons and running a children's club.[106] In the year 2000 ninety-six children and ten adults were brought to twelve host churches in Scotland and a further 100 children and ten adults were provided with a two-week holiday at the Mayaki camp besides the Black Sea. It was an expensive project in 2000 costing approximately £40,000 that the organisers had struggled to raise.[107] The Kids Aloft work ceased in 2000, but it had been a most successful initiative with wider community support for the hosting churches in evidence as they welcomed these children to Scotland.

A new chapter in this work was the formation of the charity Servants Aloft Ministries (SAM) in Spring 1998 by Colin and Cindy Mackenzie and Ronnie Cartwright from Ayr in partnership with other supporters.[108] In the years that followed further children from Belarus visited Scotland and teams of Scots engaged in construction or pastoral visits and in some cases, for example Bill Slack had preaching opportunities at Christian conferences in Baptist congregations in Belarus.[109] Colin Mackenzie had the privilege of performing two weddings. The largest project SAM supported by raising funds and sending construction teams was assistance in building the new church premises for Grodno Baptist Church.[110] Pastor Pavel was particularly

---

[106] 'Kids Aloft' and 'Servants Aloft' 1997, Digest of Council Minutes, 2 September 1997, *Scottish Baptist Yearbook 1998*, p. 192.

[107] Ronnie Cartwright, Chairman (of SAM), in *Servants Aloft Ministries Prayer & Information*, April 2000, pp. 1–3.

[108] 'Servants Aloft Ministries' the leading article in *Catch the Vision*, the Baptist Union of Scotland newspaper, Spring 1998, p. 1.

[109] 'Visit to Baptists in Belarus', '136th Annual Report of the Baptist Union of Scotland', *Scottish Baptist Yearbook 2006*, p. 125.

[110] The details of the work carried out by the 1999 SAM Project team in Grodno and Minsk is given in *Servants Aloft Ministries Prayer and Information*, September 1999.

concerned to erect a facility to provide for the needs of children with disabilities, as there was no social care for them in that country. In 1999, for example, Renfrew Baptist Church paid for one year's salary for Maxime, the Belarussian interpreter for Scots traveling to Grodno and was engaged in fund-raising efforts to raise the £5,000 required to equip the four medical rooms in the new church centre.[111] Grodno Hope Centre caters for the needs of 100 disabled children every week and has served as a model for two other facilities built by churches in Belarus. The SAM charity closed its work in 2013 but the ties of friendship between those involved in this work continued. This charitable work was an excellent example of the generosity of Scots in assisting these children in need

BAPTIST WORLD ALLIANCE

The world Baptist family has in line with other Christian denominations grown significantly in numbers over the last century since the Baptist World Alliance was founded in 1905. At that time there were believed to be around six million Baptists.[112] By 1960 the total had risen to at least thirty-six million, rising to sixty-seven million in 1995.[113] In 2010 there were estimated to be 58,205,000 members in approximately 177,000 congregations,[114] with approximately 80 million in total that year.[115] The most recent 2019 figures record a further increase to 59,600,000 members and a total figure of approximately 84,200,000.[116] Membership of the BWA affiliated Unions and Conventions had reached 34,624,167 in 2005[117] and 47,500,324 in 2019,[118]

---

[111] *Servants Aloft Ministries Prayer and Information*, May 1999, p. 3.

[112] This figure comes from John Howard Shakespeare who stated it at the first BWA Congress in London in 1905. In addition to members, he claimed that if children, adherents and others who were regularly associated with the Baptist cause were added a total of twenty million people worldwide was a credible figure. John H.Y. Briggs, 'From 1905 to the End of the First World War', in Richard V. Pierard (ed.), *Baptists Together in Christ 1905–2005: A Hundred Year History of the Baptist World Alliance* (Falls Church, Virginia: BWA, 2005), pp. 24–25.

[113] 'The Baptist Churches', in Peter Brierley, *Future Church: A Global Analysis of the Christian Community to the Year 2010* (Crowborough: Monarch Books, 1998), pp. 140–147.

[114] Todd M. Johnson & Kenneth R. Ross (eds), *Atlas of Global Christianity 1910–2010* (Edinburgh: Edinburgh University Press, 2010), p. 70.

[115] Brierley, *Future Church*, pp. 140–147.

[116] Todd M. Johnson and Gina A. Zurlo (eds), *World Christian Database* (Leiden/Boston: Brill, accessed May 2019). I am grateful to Todd Johnson for providing these figures for me on 27 May 2019.

[117] *Jesus Christ Living Water Baptist World Centenary Congress, Birmingham, England, July 27–31, 2005* (Falls Church, Virginia: BWA, 2006), p. 245.

despite the withdrawal from BWA membership of the sixteen-million-member Southern Baptist Convention in 2004; Denton Lotz, General Secretary of BWA, told delegates at the Birmingham, England, 2005 BWA Congress of some of the changes that had occurred within the Baptist family over the last one hundred years. In 1905 65% of Baptists lived in Europe and North America, but in 2005 65% lived in the Third World.[119] Over 12,000 Baptists had gathered for the Centenary Congress in Birmingham in July 2005 with over one hundred attending from Scotland.[120] The Baptist Union of Scotland sponsored the attendance of the Baptist Union of Croatia General Secretary Zeljko Mraz and his wife and welcomed them to Scotland after the congress and Central Baptist Association sponsored Timothy and Ivan Spicak from Pakrac Baptist Church.[121] In 2005 Bill Slack was reappointed to serve on the BWA Church Health and Effectiveness Workgroup, Heritage and Identity Commission and Vice-chair of the Evangelism and Education Executive Committee. Brian Talbot was also appointed to serve on the Heritage and Identity Commission.[122] Financial limitations restricted the level of involvement in BWA activities outside the Centenary Congress, but the two denominational representatives sought to convey the interest in and support of Scottish Baptists for the world-wide Baptist family through the work of the BWA.

## Women in Ministry

Attempts in the previous decade to accredit women in ministry on the same basis as men had been unsuccessful. A new attempt to address this issue began at the May 1996 Baptist Union Council, following the receipt of a letter from a Council member requesting fresh consideration of this subject. It was agreed to ask the Doctrine and Inter-Church Relations Committee for their input and the Ministry Study Review Group to look again at 'the role of women in the church' and report back after further reflection and consideration. At the same time the Joint Ministerial Board was asked to review 'what we are

---

[118] Current figure taken from the BWA website on 21 May, 2019.

[119] Taken from an extract of his speech noted in the *Scottish Baptist Yearbook 2006*, p. 129.

[120] There were 11,669 registered delegates with 14,612 in attendance on site including day visitors. *Jesus Christ Living Water Baptist World Centenary Congress, Birmingham, England, July 27–31*, pp. 201–202.

[121] *Scottish Baptist Yearbook 2006*, p. 125.

[122] *2005 Yearbook of the Baptist World Alliance* (Washington Falls: BWA, 2005), pp. 83, 88.

selecting and training men for' that year.[123] Two contrasting presentations on this topic were planned for the May 1997 Assembly in Glenrothes by Rosemary Dowsett and Jim Graham with a view to a decision being taken at a 'one day' Assembly in Glasgow on 1 November 1997.[124] It quickly became apparent that significant differences remained amongst Scottish Baptists over whether women should be appointed to serve in accredited pastoral ministry in this family of churches.[125] This was reflected in the discussions at the May and September 1997 Baptist Union Council meetings. At the former meeting a majority were minded to adopt the following motion: 'That the Christian ministry accredited by the Baptist Union of Scotland be open to women on the same basis and procedures as for men' and require a two-thirds majority of assembly delegates to vote in favour for it to be adopted.[126] However, the Baptist Union Office-bearers and Executive asked for a reconsideration of how this matter would be addressed at the September 1997 Council. A paper on this topic setting out the reasoning for this change was prepared by the Executive in advance of the September Council.[127] A fresh approach to this topic was agreed at the start of the 2 September 1997 Council. It was noted that in the Declaration of Principle 'that each church has liberty under the guidance of the Holy Spirit to interpret and administer (Christ's) laws'. This implies each local church has the freedom to decide whether or not to call any man or woman to the pastoral office. In the light of this insight, the following motion was agreed:

This Assembly agrees to adjust its procedures: –

---

[123] *A Report on the Nature of Ministry* was produced by the Joint Ministerial Board in September 1998 and distributed at Annual Assembly that year.

[124] 'Digest of Baptist Union Council Minutes', 14 May 1996 & 3 September 1996, *Scottish Baptist Yearbook 1997*, pp. 176–178; see also Douglas J. Hutcheon, 'Superintendent's Report', *Scottish Baptist Yearbook 1997*, p. 121. See also 'Welcome to Kingdom Living 1997: Baptist Union Assembly Handbook', p.4. Summaries of the two papers by Rosemary Dowsett and Jim Graham are given in 'Minutes of Assembly Business Sessions', 3May 1997, *Scottish Baptist Yearbook 1998*, pp. 197–206.

[125] Bill Slack, 'Getting to Grips with our Differences', in the 127th Annual Report by the General Secretary, *Scottish Baptist Yearbook 1997*, p. 103.

[126] 'Digest of Baptist Union Council Minutes', 20 May 1997, *Scottish Baptist Yearbook 1998*, p. 190–191.

[127] 'The Baptist Union of Scotland Background Paper on Women in The Ministry', accepted by the Baptist Union Executive Council on 22 April 1997 and used as the basis for the motion adopted at the September 1997 Baptist Union Council and printed in 'Baptist Union of Scotland Assembly Papers Glasgow 1997', p. 100.

(a) So that any persons who feel a call to pastoral ministry may present themselves for recognition and for any subsequent required training and may be brought before the Ministerial Recognition Committee.
(b) So that any persons called by local Scottish Baptist churches to pastoral ministry shall be eligible to apply for accreditation by the Baptist Union of Scotland.

The Assembly notes that acceptance of this Motion in no way implies a decision by Assembly on the validity of the call of women to the pastoral office which decision properly lies with the local church.'[128]

In the light of the change of direction on this motion the necessity for a two-thirds majority vote was also withdrawn, but it was reinstated at the 1 November 1997 Assembly in Glasgow. There were 260 who voted for the motion and 171 against it, twenty-eight votes short of the required majority. The motion fell. It was an unexpected result for many of those present, but the late change of motion less than two months previously probably contributed to this decision being made. Had this motion been 'on the table' prior to the Glenrothes Assembly earlier that year it is possible that there might have been a different outcome.[129]

A full discussion on this topic took place at the 13 January 1998 Council because a number of churches had written to the Union enquiring if the 1997 Assembly decision on 'Women in the Ministry' had been in conflict with the Declaration of Principle. It was agreed to carry out further work on this topic prior to bringing another motion to the 1999 Assembly.[130] At the 12 January 1999 Council meeting the redrafted assembly motion was agreed and a decision taken for members of Executive Council to hold meetings in each Association with local church representatives to explain the motion and clarify any misunderstandings and to reassure all concerned that if the motion passed in due course that applicants for all national offices in the Baptist Union in the future would equally be eligible regardless of their opinions on this matter.[131] At the 16 October 1999 Assembly the General Secretary carefully outlined the meaning of the motion before delegates, prior to the wider debate and vote.

---

[128] 'Women in the Ministry', Digest of Council Minutes', 2 September 1997, *Scottish Baptist Yearbook 1998*, pp. 194–195.

[129] 'Issue for Debate: Women in the Ministry', *Scottish Baptist Yearbook 1998*, pp. 222–231.

[130] 'Digest of Council Minutes', 13 January 1998, *Scottish Baptist Yearbook 1999*, pp. 196–197.

[131] 'Recognition and Accreditation Procedures', 'Digest of Council Minutes', 12 January, 1999, and 18 May, 1999, in Baptist Union of Scotland Assembly Papers, Hamilton, 1999, pp. 21, 22; Motion II 'The Union's Recognition and Accreditation procedures (with reference to women and Baptist ministry), pp. 117–118.

The motion this time passed with 247 votes in favour and 113 against, a majority of 68.6%.[132] It was a significant milestone for Scottish Baptists. It was a big step to trust one another to honour this decision in the future life of the Union. It must be noted that this new position was one of neutrality for the Union equally respecting the differing views within its ranks. This was distinct from the BUGB position, as that body actively promotes an egalitarian position at a national level.[133] Twenty years later there have been no further motions on this subject at Assemblies as proponents of both perspectives have sought to honour this decision in each area of Baptist Union life. A milestone had been reached as Scottish Baptists had now agreed a common position for this family of churches on the two major issues that had divided them in recent decades, this topic and that of inter-church relations. They were able to go forward as a more united body into the new century.

### Overseas Mission

Scottish Baptists at the end of the twentieth and first decade of the twenty-first centuries were as committed to world mission as they had been a century earlier. However, the diversity of mission agencies had multiplied over these years. In the nineteenth-century it was only in the later decades that significant support began to be given by Baptist churches to non-denominational agencies.[134] At the time of George Yuille's survey in 1925 BMS was the most prominent society supported, with the China Inland Mission also a common choice, but Scottish Baptist churches were also contributing to the work of at least thirty-one other mission agencies with which their members were serving at that time.[135] In 1995 the World Missions and International Affairs Committee of the Baptist Union of Scotland carried out a survey of its affiliated churches to ascertain the breadth

---

[132] 'Recognition and Accreditation Procedures', Baptist Union Assembly, 16 October 1999, *Scottish Baptist Yearbook 2000*, pp. 236–241, 244. See also the report in the *Baptist Times* 21 October 1999, pp. 1–2.

[133] This difference can be seen in the exchange of letters in the *Baptist Times* in April 2010 between Derek Tidball on Friday 9 April, 2010 and the response from Graham Sparkes from the Faith and Unity Department of BUGB on Friday 16 April, 2010.

[134] See chapter 3 pp. 71–74.

[135] For details see Brian R. Talbot, 'Spreading the Good News from Scotland: Scottish Baptists and Overseas Mission in the First Three Decades of the Twentieth Century', in Anthony R. Cross, Peter J. Morden and Ian M. Randall (eds), *Pathways and Patterns in History: Essays on Baptists, Evangelicals and the Modern World in Honour of David Bebbington* (London: Spurgeon's College & the Baptist Historical Society, 2015), pp. 145–171; also chapter 5, pp. 137–140.

of overseas mission agencies supported. The response rate was 40% so it is not a full picture; however, this survey revealed that over 110 mission societies or agencies were being supported by finance and/or prayerful interest at that time. The vast majority of the bodies named are supported only by one congregation, with nineteen other societies named by seven or more churches. There are two missionary societies with significant levels of support. Top of the list was BMS to which over 72% gave financial donations in 1995 and approximately 30% that supported the Worldwide Evangelization Crusade (WEC). The two countries in which there was the strongest missionary interest are Brazil where BMS had a strong presence and Nepal. In the latter country there are various societies who co-operate through the United Mission to Nepal and the International Nepal Fellowship. In total, seventy overseas countries were referenced as places where Scottish Baptists were supporting mission work.[136] In summary, it is evident that this survey demonstrates a continuing interest in and support for overseas mission.

## Scottish Baptists and Social Action

The provision of retirement accommodation had been a significant concern amongst Scottish Baptists in the later twentieth century.[137] It was expressed as a priority both at local, association and national levels. For example, at a national level the Baptist Union had set up a Retirement Property Scheme in 1991 to ensure sufficient adequate accommodation was available for ministers and their spouses when they reached retirement age. Donations of properties and finance towards the costs of the scheme had been encouraging in the first decade of its operations.[138] Regional Associations also supported this kind of work. The Tor Christian Nursing Home in Edinburgh operated under the auspices of the ELBA Housing Agency. In April 1999 the chair of this body Geoff Hibbard reported to an Association meeting that the nursing home's work was going well, although their plans to extend the capacity of the premises to fifty beds together with the erection of some extra sheltered housing on the site had been rejected twice by the city planning officials. It was agreed to return for a further meeting to overcome the objections to this development.[139] There had also been initiatives by local churches in the

---

[136] 'Missions Survey', *SBM*, 119.7/8 (July/August 1995), p. 14; the detailed results obtained from this survey are found in the BUS Archive in Glasgow.

[137] More details are given in Murray, 'Be Not Conformed but Transformed', pp. 238–239.

[138] 'Do you own the key . . . to someone's future?' in in *Catch the Vision*, the Baptist Union of Scotland newspaper, Autumn 1998, p. 6.

[139] Geoff Hibbard, 'ELBA Housing Society Annual Report' to the Edinburgh & Lothian Baptist Association, April 1999. Unfortunately, this difficulty was never

provision of residential accommodation for the elderly. Ayr Baptist Church, for example, had opened Airlie House as a Residential Home in Victoria Park, Ayr. It was a quiet street in a well-known residential area of the town in 1988. This facility was extended and nursing care added to the residential care in the upgraded facilities that were opened in October 1997. The Health Board had agreed in March 1998 to allow the number of residents to be extended from seventeen to twenty-four. It was the fulfilment of the vision of the church to provide a care home for the benefit both of the church and the wider community.[140] Scottish Baptists were committed to a holistic gospel and the provision of suitable accommodation in the later years of life was a priority for many Scottish Baptists.

There were a wide range of issues on which Scottish Baptists sought to make a contribution to public debates. At the 2000 Assembly, for example, there were seminars on medical ethics with Annette Morrison, particularly surrounding the new possibilities for the initiation of life and end of life issues when doctors had to decide whether sustaining life was simply prolonging death; on human rights with Jeremy Balfour which addressed some of the challenges in a global context that included when the rights of society and that of the individual were in conflict; and on Religious Freedom with Theo Angelov, General Secretary of the European Baptist Federation. Delegates voted on resolutions that addressed concerns about religious freedom in Turkey, France, Austria and Italy, together with the ongoing conflict between Israelis and Palestinians.[141] The Social Action Committee reported on the plans for the sixth 'Love Your Neighbour' Conference being held in Stirling in November 2000. Its major focus for action was on the issues of drugs and alcohol abuse. Delegates were informed that thirteen congregations affiliated to the Union had some level of involvement in agencies seeking to address these issues. Several others had expressed an interest in providing some assistance for work in these fields. It was reported that two Scottish Baptists as representatives of the Baptist Union were appointed to the Scottish Christian Drugs Forum run by the Evangelical Alliance, an agency that sought to facilitate cooperation and networking amongst Christians working in this field as well as relating to those responsible for political decision-making. The

---

resolved and planning permission continued to be refused. Tor Christian Nursing Home closed in November 2016 with residents and staff transferring to a new purpose built care home nearby called Manor Grange. I am grateful to Ian Balfour for providing this information on 30 May 2019.

[140] Tom Barrie, 'Airlie House in Ayr', in *Catch the Vision*, the Baptist Union of Scotland newspaper, Spring 1998, p. 7.

[141] Baptist Union Assembly, 1 November 2000, Public Issues Seminars on Medical Ethics, Human Rights and Religious Freedom, *Scottish Baptist Yearbook 2001*, pp. 234–237.

other prominent issue this committee was working on at that time was homelessness. Its convener Kathleen Arton represented the Baptist Union on the Board of the Scottish Churches Housing Agency. She reported to assembly that inter-church projects established on this issue included the 'Glasgow Starter Packs' project and appealed for a volunteer willing to serve as the link between this project and the Baptist churches in Glasgow.[142] In addition, the Public Issues advisory group reported on issues in Parliament related to the laws surrounding Section 28 (2A in Scotland) on human sexuality; the rights of Christian groups to apply for broadcasting licenses and attempts to ban the physical punishment of children.[143] Scottish Baptists increasingly sought to work together with other Scottish Christians to address issues of common interest in the wider society. There was recognition that their contribution was relatively small in these national debates. However, this insight did not lesson their attempts to raise a distinctive voice in partnership with others on subjects of particular concern.

The last decade of the twentieth century and the first one in the twenty-first were a time of significant changes both within the wider society and in Scottish Baptist life. In the wider nation the major change was undoubtedly the decision to create a devolved Parliament in Scotland. For Scottish Baptists at a national level it is possible that the changes that came about through the 'Challenge to Change' process restructuring the Union for a new century had the biggest impact on relationships between the churches as well as in the reshaped national posts that emerged from that process. Scottish Baptists like other Christians in Scotland were well aware of the continuing decline in overall numbers attending churches at this time, in particular the alarmingly high loss of children and teenagers. However, between 1994 and the Churches' census in 2002 there had been a very small increase in the number of Baptist churches in Scotland and a very modest increase in the size of the average Baptist congregation at that time. New General Secretary Bill Slack had created strategy groups to bring about more effective evangelistic work that included a fresh focus on the Highlands and Islands. New works began at this time, for example, on the island of Arran, Brae in Shetland and The Lighthouse Church in Forres and a strengthened witness in Grantown-on-Spey. In other parts of the country the appointment of a worker in the Asian Community in Glasgow was particularly effective in reaching Iranians in the city. Gerrard Street Baptist Church and its daughter church at Sheddocksley saw significant growth through conversions and baptisms. Church-planter Colin Baker launched a new work in Bathgate that was particularly effective at

---

[142] Kathleen Arton, 'Social Action Committee', *Scottish Baptist Yearbook 2001*, pp. 193–194.

[143] Baptist Union Assembly, 2 November 2000, Public Issues Advisory Group report, *Scottish Baptist Yearbook 2001*, pp. 237–238.

engaging with young adults and in the Borders the renewal of spiritual life in the Selkirk congregation also saw many people come to faith and a church that had been critically small in the early 1980s had by 1998 around 100 people regularly at its Sunday worship services. The appointment of Mission networkers had given a fresh focus to community engagement as opportunities for mission were sought by a number of churches. There were few major successes through this initiative though the planting and establishment of the Girvan congregation was one particular highlight. The work amongst young people led by national leaders Robert Breustedt and Gary Smith was formative for a good number of younger leaders and the Step-Out children's and youth missions were a great encouragement in many smaller congregations. In the midst of challenges there were also many other signs of new life and strengthened witness amongst the churches at that time.

In relation to other churches, ties with the Evangelical Alliance were deepened and a good partnership developed on a range of issues of common interest. Despite his best efforts to build or maintain good ties with other networks of churches, it was disappointing for Bill Slack that events in the USA had led to the demise of the partnership with the IMB. Attempts to build closer ties with some of the other Evangelical Churches did not develop as he had hoped though cordial relations were maintained with the other Christian Churches in Scotland. The new Fellowship of British Baptists worked well and welcomed the Irish Baptist Network into its partnership. Work in Europe through the EBF and in direct partnerships with particular sister Unions was especially strong. The ties with Croatian Baptists and with the Baptist Union of Belarus were especially fruitful enabling many Baptists and some other Scots as well to assist with significant humanitarian projects. The contribution to the BWA was maintained but was less prominent than in the 1980s. Overseas mission work was another significant strength in these years, though it was a concern that limited resources were being stretched to support an increasing number of mission agencies. Another success in these years was the willingness of Scottish Baptists to come to an agreed resolution for handling their differences over the issue of women in pastoral ministry. Overall, despite many issues to address in these changing times there were also plenty of encouragements for Scottish Baptists as well.

CHAPTER 11

# An Invitation to a Journey, 2009–2019

## Introduction

The last decade in Scotland has been a remarkably eventful time in the life of the nation. It is likely that the majority of citizens will recall the two referendums on Scottish Independence and leaving the European Union as the major defining moments,[1] yet despite the result of the popular votes, calls for both referendums to be rerun have added greatly to the uncertainty about the way forward for the country, and for the United Kingdom of Great Britain and Northern Ireland as a whole. It was, though, not only Governments that struggled to chart their course through these years; the Christian Church in Scotland has also endured some challenging times. It was an era in which the Christian Churches recognised more clearly the changing social context in which they sought to present the good news of Jesus to the wider society.[2] There were a number of significant inter-related social issues in the twenty-first century over which Scottish society was divided, from the battle over the repeal of 'Section 28', the prohibition on the promotion of homosexuality in Schools,[3] to the appointment of clergy in same-sex relationships to posts in the Church of Scotland,[4] together with the later decision of the Scottish and

---

[1] *The Herald* Thursday 18 September, 2014 in its front page headline described it as 'Scotland's Day of Reckoning'. *The Times* newspaper had the headline: 'Brexit Earthquake' the day after the European Referendum result was known; *The Times*, 25 June, 2016, p. 1.

[2] The editorial by David Robertson, in *The Record*, the periodical of the Free Church of Scotland, in October 2010, had the headline: 'Church of Scotland 1560–2033-RIP?' pp. 4–5. The article itself was a broader challenge to all Presbyterian Churches in Scotland to harness their energy and commitment 'for the good of the Gospel – rather than for the protection of our own wee domains'. Robertson highlighted that the date '2033' came from a Church of Scotland document that indicated that if present rates of decline continued that the Church of Scotland itself would cease to exist by 2033.

[3] [Section 2A in Scotland] For example, the letters to the Editor of *The Scotsman* on 27 January, 2000, p. 21, illustrated the division in the country on this subject.

[4] The appointment in 2009 of Scott Rennie as minister of Queen's Cross Church, Aberdeen, triggered the controversy in the National Church. However, it was the handling of the matter by that Church that caused just as much controversy in the

Westminster parliaments to legalise gay marriage that came into force in 2014.[5] There were fears by some in the Church of Scotland that an exodus by clergy and members holding traditional Christian views on same-sex relationships would trigger a financial crisis but others were convinced any losses would be minimal.[6] It could not be denied that the churches as well as many other sectors of society were struggling to keep up with the pace of change in contemporary society.

It was not just Scotland, but throughout the United Kingdom that there were declining statistics for the majority of the Christian Churches. In 2011 the latest UK church statistics revealed that the growth of fresh expressions of church and other forms of outreach activities, together with the overall increasing numbers in Pentecostal and Orthodox Churches did not compensate for the larger decline in more traditional denominations such as the Methodist Church. UK Baptist numerical decline though less than most other denominations had not been halted by 2011.[7] Another sign of changing times can be seen in the impact of the papal visit by Pope Benedict in September 2010, compared to the response to his predecessor's visit. It was deemed a success by the majority of religious and political commentators of the day,[8] but expectations for what could be accomplished through it were so

---

years that followed. See for example, Andy Collier, 'Crisis of Faith', *Daily Mail*, 28 May, 2001, pp. 16–17.

[5] 'MSPS back Gay Marriage', *The Scotsman*, 21 November, 2013, pp. 4–5; The lack of adequate safeguards being promised by the Scottish Government left opponents of that decision unconvinced. For example, see John Mason MSP, 'Intolerant, ill-conceived and opposed by the public', *Daily Mail*, 5 February, 2014, p. 14. The editorial in that paper on the same page noted that 67% of submissions to the Scottish Parliament on the subject prior to the vote had advised against a change in the law on this subject.

[6] 'Financial Fears over Kirk exodus', *The Times*, 13 June, 2013, p. 7, citing the views of David Fergusson, head of New College School of Divinity, Edinburgh University. This was not a new situation as the annual financial loss reported by the Church of Scotland in 2011 alone was £5.2 million. See Craig Brown, 'Kirk in Crisis', *The Scotsman*, 27 May, 2001. Article viewed on *The Scotsman* website on 27 May, 2011. By contrast, Finlay Macdonald, a former Moderator of the General Assembly was less concerned by any losses. Finlay Macdonald, *From Reform to Renewal: Scotland's Kirk Century by Century* (Edinburgh: St Andrews Press, 2017), p. 213.

[7] 'Hope amid church decline' the headline of *The Baptist Times*, 1 July, 2011, p. 1, citing Peter Brierley, *UK Church Statistics 2005–2015*, that was published in 2011.

[8] 'Papal visit judged success', *The Baptist Times*, 24 September, 2010, pp. 1, 7–9. The front page carried quotations from mainstream church leaders recognising the visit had been a success. See also *The Times*, 20 September, 2010, pp. 6–8, that included the commendation of the Prime Minister David Cameron; and *The Scotsman*,

modest that no-one could deny the huge contrast with the triumphal scenes in Bellahouston Park in June 1982 when his predecessor Pope John Paul II was welcomed to Scotland during his visit to the United Kingdom that year, the first by a reigning pope since the sixteenth-century Protestant Reformation. Free Church of Scotland commentator and journalist John MacLeod agreed with Pope Benedict's central claim on the tour that not only Christianity but religion in general was under threat from aggressive secularism and being pushed increasingly to the margins of British society.[9] By contrast, former general secretary of the Conference of European Churches Dr Keith Clements concluded that he was more concerned about: 'the quiet, slow, widening seepage of credibility' of the Christian Churches.[10] What was abundantly clear was that Scotland had become a more secular country since the 1980s. The Christian Church although retaining its core message had to learn to communicate it more effectively in an environment where many younger people had no prior connection to any form of Christian Church.

The General Director of the Baptist Union of Scotland, Alan Donaldson in an April 2019 article in the *Future First* bulletin entitled his contribution: 'Am I serving a Dying Church?' It was a thoughtful article pointing out that there are no quick or easy solutions to reversing numerical decline in church attendance across the nation. However, in his conclusions, he reported: 'there are many early signs of fruitfulness in the Scottish churches'. He also stated: 'I see "growth amidst decline".'[11] In 2016 Peter Brierley published the results of the second Scottish Church Census of the twenty-first century using the same words for the title of his published account of the census data. What were the key findings for the Scottish Churches and in particular the Baptist churches in Scotland?[12] The 2016 Census was the fourth of its kind recording attendances at Christian Churches in Scotland since 1984. In 2016 there were 390,000 people who regularly attended church, 7.2% of the Scottish population, down from 17% in 1984. The only major Christian tradition to

---

17 September, 2010, pp.1–7, 29 and *Special Pictorial Souvenir* supplement issued that same day.

[9] John MacLeod, 'Keeping the Faith', *Daily Mail*, 18 September, 2010, pp. 14–15. Interestingly, some secular journalists agreed with this thesis. For example, Australian journalist Amanda Platell, 'Twisted values of the noisy bigots', *Daily Mail*, 18 September, 2010, p. 17.

[10] Keith Clements, 'Gearing up for change?' *The Baptist Times*, No. 8330, 24 September, 2010, p. 9.

[11] Alan Donaldson, 'Am I Serving a Dying Church?' in *Future First,* No. 62, (April 2019), pp. 1, 4.

[12] Information in the rest of this paragraph comes from Peter Brierley, *Growth Amidst Decline: What the 2016 Scottish Church Census Reveals* (Tonbridge: ADBC Publishers, 2017), pp. 15–16.

increase in numbers in 2016 was the Pentecostals whose attendance has almost doubled since the third census of 2002, reaching 19,000, approximately 5% of all churchgoers. There were some encouraging features to highlight from the 2016 census. These include many new congregations started by people born outside the United Kingdom, together with a growing number of Messy Church services. There are 12,000 people worshiping in 300 congregations founded since the 2002 census. There were 500 churches that recorded significant growth, an additional 6,000 new worshippers in church each Sunday. Roman Catholic attendance figures increased particularly in Aberdeenshire as a result of Polish immigration by workers in the oil industry. Although the overall decline reported in the previous censuses is continuing, the rate of decline has slowed. However, a greater number of new churches will need to be planted in future years to offset the inevitable closure of others, if the decline is to be halted completely.

Some interesting features in twenty-first century church life revealed in this census[13] were the increasing number of people who attended mid-week events. Three-fifths of churches, 60%, held some form of week-day worship; this was a distinctive feature of Baptist, Pentecostal and Roman Catholic congregations. The average attendance at a service was thirty-four, up from twenty-seven in the 2002 Census. However, 89% also attended Sunday worship. Half of the churches held mid-week youth events with an average attendance of forty-one, down from fifty-nine in 2002. This was the only event patronised by 42% of these young people. Nearly half the churches also had other meetings held during the week with an average attendance of fifty-one, the majority of whom did not attend on Sundays. It appears that these gatherings were social or likely to be non-religious in character. However, in total 235,000 Scots attended a mid-week activity in one of the churches, and when combined with Sunday attendance figures there were approximately 10% of the population present at a church service or activity on a weekly basis in 2016. Outreach to the local community included 48% of congregations citing neighbourhood visitation, 35% had used 'Alpha' courses in recent years with 17% doing so in 2015, the last full year for statistical purposes, and 10% used 'Christianity Explored' courses that year. Amongst Scottish Baptist Churches 65% had run 'Alpha' courses, a higher proportion than in any other network of Scottish Churches and 23% used 'Christianity Explored' materials. Only the Presbyterian Churches outside the Church of Scotland had a higher take up of this evangelistic resource with 39% of them using 'Christianity Explored' courses.[14] The two charities that figured most prominently amongst the 77% of congregations that supported them included 61% naming Christian Aid

---

[13] Information in this paragraph comes from Brierley, *Growth Amidst Decline*, pp. 17–19, unless otherwise indicated.

[14] Brierley, *Growth Amidst Decline*, p. 161.

week and 34% Tearfund. It is evident that Scottish Churches although declining in overall numerical attendance figures for Sunday worship still have significant connections with a large proportion of their local communities. The challenge moving forward will be how many of these congregations are sufficiently able to adapt their worship services and wider ministries to attract a much greater proportion of the people sympathetic to their aims and objectives, but who currently chose to retain looser ties to particular congregations.

In terms of more specific findings for Baptists,[15] 23% of their congregations attended church twice on a Sunday and 63% weekly with the remainder less frequently present.[16] Out of 185 Baptist congregations in Scotland three reported Sunday congregations over 500, twenty-three between 201 and 500; three 151 to 200; twenty-four 101 to 150; forty-nine fifty-one to 100; forty-eight between twenty-six and fifty worshippers; twenty-five reported ten to twenty-five in attendance and ten congregations reported less than ten people present on a Sunday.[17] In total 17,810 people were present on Census Sunday 2016 in a Scottish Baptist Church. This was a significant drop from the 24,830 in 2002. Overall, 92% of Baptist congregations in Scotland belong to the Baptist Union. Interestingly attendance figures in specifically Baptist Union churches for the last full year prior to the Census in 2015, was 16,500, a total very similar to their proportion of the Baptist Census data the following year.[18] There had been a relatively high number of Baptist church closures reported, but these were almost entirely Independent Baptist churches with no connection to the Baptist Union of Scotland.[19] By contrast five new Baptist congregations had opened since the previous Census in 2002, alongside 305 other newly-planted congregations in other denominations.[20] In terms of size of congregations 20% of Baptist causes reported significant increases in attendance; 13% a modest increase; 24% reported no change in numbers; 33% reported a slight decrease and 10% a significant decrease in congregational size. This pattern presented a very mixed picture of growth and decline. A more prominent feature in Baptist churches in this Census was the proportion employing a full or part-time youth worker. It had risen to 23%, twice the overall average of Scottish Churches. It will be of interest if the next

---

[15] Baptist data included other Baptists in Scotland including Grace Baptists and Independent Baptists as well as the majority of churches that were Baptist Union affiliated congregations.

[16] Brierley, *Growth Amidst Decline*, p. 181.

[17] Brierley, *Growth Amidst Decline*, p. 183.

[18] Brierley, *Growth Amidst Decline*, p. 40.

[19] Brierley, *Growth Amidst Decline*, p. 49.

[20] Brierley, *Growth Amidst Decline*, pp. 50, 55.

Census asks about the employment of Children and Families Workers, as this is a small but growing trend amongst mainstream Evangelical Churches that prioritised work across the full range of ages in their ranks.[21] The Churches in Scotland that had grown had usually been the most committed to outreach work and the networks that had succeeded in planting the most new congregations were rewarded with higher overall growth in numerical statistics.[22] It could fairly be reported for Scottish Baptists, in line with a majority of other Evangelical Churches, that there was growth amidst decline in their ranks in the second decade of the twenty-first century.

## An Overview of Denominational Life and Witness

Scottish Baptists have often struggled in local churches to live and work together effectively.[23] Differences over theological convictions, worship styles and approaches to ministry and mission have too often been highlighted more prominently that the far greater number of things we have in common. It was clear in the first decade of the twenty-first century that this difficulty was having a detrimental, in some cases terminal, effect of the witness of too many congregations. In 2007 under the leadership of Bill Slack there was a focus on 'Growing Healthy Churches' and with it good leaders and good followers in our midst. The 2007 denominational assembly highlighted this theme with a series of regional days in 2008 planned to help congregations to facilitate the necessary changes so that they might have more healthy relationships within the local community of faith and between our family of churches. It was clear that the decision to end the regional associations in 2002 had not helped ties between churches; on the contrary there was increasingly little contact between the churches in many regions of Scotland, with the exception of those in more remote and rural settings, for example in Shetland. It was, though, easier to highlight the problems than to provide a workable solution to these difficulties. The general Director, Bill Slack, also highlighted that it was not a uniquely Baptist problem. He highlighted the failure of the Evangelical Churches in Scotland even to support an Evangelical Media office as a sign of unwillingness to take the necessary steps to co-operate on issues of common interest and importance in the nation. Slack was not convinced sufficient Christians grasped the challenge of effectively communicating the good news of the gospel in an increasingly secular and diverse society. Naturally, it was appropriate for him to ask fellow Baptists about their relationship with other Christian Churches in Scotland. With respect to inter-

---

[21] Brierley, *Growth Amidst Decline*, p. 131.

[22] Brierley, *Growth Amidst Decline*, pp. 50–51.

[23] The information in this paragraph comes from Bill Slack, General Director, '138th Annual Report', *Scottish Baptist Yearbook 2008*, pp. 89–93.

church relations, it was insufficient to know what we were against in terms of relationships, there had to be more consideration concerning what we were in favour of in the light of a rapidly changing society where other religions, particularly Islam, were gaining a much greater influence. In summary, the General Director challenged Scottish Baptists to acknowledge that in too many churches old ways of operating were no longer working with declining numbers and the consequent decline in the necessary resources to sustain full-time pastoral ministry, even apart from what was required to fund additional ministry posts. He challenged Baptist congregations to consider sharing resources to allow new forms of ministry to be launched or to flourish. There were no simple solutions to resolve the underlying challenges both within congregations and in finding effective ways to communicate the Christian gospel effectively to the unchurched in local communities. It was a clear but also effective message about the necessity both for further structural changes within the wider Union, and within local Baptist congregations.

## That Journey Called Ministry

The appointment of John Greenshields as Ministry Development Co-ordinator in 2007 was an important step forward in implementing the new approach to ministry in Scottish Baptist ranks in the twenty-first century. He had the remit of overseeing an integrated scheme of Continuous Professional Development (CPD) for ministers,[24] something that had been seen as desirable for a number of years. There was a particular concern at the difficulties many ministers had in adjusting to the demands of their calling in the early years of pastoral ministry. He was tasked with overseeing the care of probationer ministers, overseeing the CPD for accredited ministers and organising the *Next Stage of Ministry* conferences in addition to his contribution to the Board of Ministry.[25] The phase of changes begun at that time was essential as the number of candidates applying for interviews to test their calling to Baptist pastoral ministry had declined significantly. In 2007, James Clarke, chair of the Board of Ministry, had reported: 'What a disappointing year', because only three individuals applied for consideration and two out of the three possible Board of Ministry gatherings had been cancelled due to no individuals coming forward for interview. On top of this concern, Clarke reminded fellow Baptists that twenty-six churches were actively seeking a new pastor, a few more would shortly be vacant due to their pastors retiring and only six ministers were seeking settlement. 'We have a

---

[24] The settled name was Continuing Ministry Development (CMD), although CPD was used at first for this scheme.

[25] Andrew Rollinson, 'Ministry Advisor's Report', *Scottish Baptist Yearbook 2008*, pp. 94–95.

problem' was his conclusion.[26] Greenshields co-authored with Andrew Rollinson the important Baptist Union resource *That Journey Called Ministry* in 2008. This document set out the framework for future Baptist ministry in this family of churches. There was a clear vision for ministry with a call to continual growth and excellence; a commitment to life-long learning and a covenant to journey together. The broad acceptance of these principles in the ranks of not only pre-accredited ministers, but also more experienced pastors brought a greater sense of unity and co-operation amongst serving ministers in the Union.[27] Acceptance of the principles behind this new vision and the practical outworking of it in congregational life as well as in the wider denominational structure set in place a foundation for the further changes that would follow in the next decade.[28]

The immediate change in the ranks of the ministers was a growing acceptance of the importance of accredited ministry. The vision articulated in *That Journey Called Ministry* had been owned by those set apart to pastoral ministry. There had been a significant development in 2009 with the adoption of a clearly stated agreement for accredited ministers. Candidates for accredited ministry, where approved of by the Board of Ministry, were required to sign an agreement to abide by the terms of the Ministry Agreement. This agreement included both a commitment to an ethical code and also to a path of continuing ministry development. At that time candidates seeking to enter accredited ministry were commonly doing so after having engaged in other careers and many had also already undertaken some theological study prior to coming before the Board of Ministry.[29] It is notable that there was from this time onwards a sustained increase in the numbers of individuals willing to explore the possibility of a call to this vocation through engagement with the Board of Ministry. For example, John Greenshields informed the October 2011 Baptist Union Assembly that most of the Board

---

[26] James R. Clarke, 'Board of Ministry Report', *Scottish Baptist Yearbook 2008*, pp. 128–129. By contrast after the changes in ministry preparation and CMD had begun, the situation changed quite dramatically. In 2011 eight churches were actively looking for a new minister and nineteen individuals were looking for a post in which to serve in pastoral ministry, 17–18 May, 2011, BUS Council, in *Assembly Handbook Outrageous Generosity Dunfermline, 27–29 October 2011*, p. 11.

[27] This was recognised and welcomed by Andrew Rollinson in his 'Ministry Advisor' Report, *Scottish Baptist Yearbook 2010*, pp. 106–107.

[28] Andrew Rollinson & John Greenshields, *That Journey Called Ministry* (Glasgow: Baptist Union of Scotland, 2008), pp. 1–22. It was clear that the success of the newer structures for Baptist ministry in the larger BUGB had in a number of ways influenced this fresh approach in Scotland, see for example, p. 18, section (i).

[29] I am grateful to Rev Dr Jim Purves for information on the Board of Ministry – 'BOM procedural changes' in an email dated 18 June 2019.

of Ministry meetings in 2012 were already fully booked with people applying for ministry. In addition, there were a significant number of new Board members appointed to serve. The new challenge would be finding enough places for those offering to serve as ministers in the Scottish Baptist Churches.[30] These changes were a sign of real encouragement for this family of churches for the future.

A further development in 2009 was the exploration of the place for and recognition of those engaged in new forms of ministry. It led to the publication of a further Baptist Union document *Enabling Structures for Emerging Ministries*. It was also that year that Catriona Gorton was appointed as the minister of Hillhead Baptist Church, the first female pastor in a sole pastoral charge since the 1920s, and the first to do so as an accredited minister.[31] By February 2010, the date of the Next Stage of Ministry conference that year, sixty percent of serving ministers in Union affiliated congregations had participated in one of these annual events within the first three years. The Continuing Ministry Development programme (CMD) was rolled out with the issuing of personal folders to all ministers in 2009 with guidelines offered as to how best to use them. In the years that followed various materials would be issued offering options for resources for an individual CMD programme. Each minister was entrusted with the responsibility for their ongoing growth and development. A further initiative launched in autumn 2009 was the guided self-appraisal scheme. This lengthy questionnaire was intended to be filled in by Baptist ministers and its contents reflected on in the company of a chosen guide –who was also an accredited colleague.[32] The pre-accredited ministers, which are those in pastoral posts in their first three years of service, were invited to the first annual residential conference in 2009. This opportunity to meet for an intensive time of reflection with experienced colleagues, combined with the time spent with a Union-appointed ministry mentor in the pre-accredited years was both largely welcomed and appreciated by individuals engaged in the formative early years of ministry. John Greenshields and Andrew Rollinson also invested a significant amount of time in 2008 and 2009 in visits to individual ministers

---

[30] John Greenshields, 'Ministry Report', Minutes of the Baptist Assembly in Scotland 2011, in *Come Home Again*, Assembly Handbook for 2012, p. 15.

[31] Andrew Rollinson, 'Ministry Advisor' report, *Scottish Baptist Yearbook 2010*, pp. 106–108. Jane Henderson had served as pastor at Lossiemouth Baptist Church, 1918–1921 and Mary Flora McArthur as pastor of Tobermory Baptist Church, Mull, 1938–1941 and Colonsay Baptist Church from 1945 to 1947. See Lumsden, 'Her Children Arise and Call her Blessed', in Talbot, *Distinctive People*, p. 71 for fuller details.

[32] Eight ministers volunteered for the pilot scheme. 'The Guided Self-Appraisal Pilot Scheme', in 'Digest of Council Minutes', 12 January 2010, *Assembly Handbook Communities of Conviction 28–30 October 2010*, p. 11

and others in groups to ensure that the vision for CMD was both understood and appreciated.[33] By the end of the first decade of the twenty-first century the new system for supporting pre-accredited ministers and the CMD programme for accredited colleagues was firmly established in Scottish Baptist ranks.

In 2015 John Greenshields noted that a remarkable 45% of serving ministers had come into their pastoral calling since 2007.[34] It was a remarkable turnaround in less than a decade from a time when so few individuals were coming forward to consider a call to pastoral ministry. In 2018 when the Union was about to enter its 150th year there were thirty-six pre-accredited ministers and a further ten people accepted for entry into pre-accredited ministry that year. Congregations were also increasingly training and calling their own members to pastoral positions which contributed significantly to the fact that from 2015 to 2018 two-thirds of candidates accepted by the Board of Ministry had already been called to a Ministry role by a local church.[35] Another positive sign for the future was the emergence of a greater number of gifted younger leaders in some Scottish Baptist churches. For example, in 2018 nearly one-third of the nearly 400 delegates at Deep Impact, the training conference for youth and children's workers, came from within our Union of churches.[36] These were clearly signs of spiritual vitality in Scottish Baptist ranks that laid some good foundations for future ministry.

## Mission Networkers

2009 was a year of transition for the team of Mission Networkers who served in partnership with Andy Scarcliffe the Mission Advisor.[37] Neil Young who worked with the Glasgow churches had died. Jacqueline Primrose in the Central Region had become Convenor of the Baptist Union and Richard Higginbottom in Fife and Tayside had moved to take responsibility for a

---

[33] The majority of information in this paragraph comes from John G. Greenshields, 'Ministry Development Coordinator' report, *Scottish Baptist Yearbook 2010*, pp. 109–111.

[34] John Greenshields, 'A New Generation', Ministry Development Coordinator report, 2015, in *Mind the Gap: Baptist Assembly in Scotland, 29–30 October 2015*, Motherwell, p. 13.

[35] Martin Hodson, 'Ministry Development Coordinator' report, in *Fearless: Baptist Assembly in Scotland, 25–26 October 2018*, Motherwell, p. 12.

[36] Ali Laing, 'Next Generation Development Co-0rdinator (Youth and Young Leader)' report, in *Fearless: Baptist Assembly in Scotland, 25–26 October 2018*, p. 13.

[37] The information in this paragraph comes from Andy Scarclife, 'Mission Advisor' report, *Scottish Baptist Yearbook 2010*, pp. 111–114; or the regional Mission Networker reports in the same 2010 *Yearbook*, pp. 115–121.

church plant initiative in Perth. Later that year Harry Sprange, Associate Mission Networker in the North-West Highlands and Islands, Bob Baxter in Edinburgh, Lothian and the Borders, Olive Drane in Aberdeenshire and Noel McCullins in the South-West of Scotland concluded their terms of service. The initial financial support from Baptist Union funds had been intended to stimulate churches to provide matched funding for these posts around the country. However, it was a mixed picture with strong support in some regions but very limited in others and even within regions a few churches gained significantly from Mission Networker input while others chose not to utilise them. The formal end of the scheme was the 2010 Baptist Union Assembly.[38] In Aberdeenshire, for example, Olive Drane highlighted her work with Sheddocksley Baptist Church in supporting a number of mission ventures including the launch of one of the first parish nursing ministry projects in Scotland, following a retreat with a group of women from that congregation to look at creative initiatives in mission.[39] Harry Sprange despite extensive visits to churches and meetings with individuals was unable to see much progress. His final report to the Baptist Union Core Leaders: 'Prospects for the Highlands and Islands in the 21$^{st}$ Century' raised the key question of how effective evangelistic work could be carried out in the underpopulated 40% of the land mass of Scotland. He also asked them to consider how the smaller churches in the region might be supported by their family of churches in the coming years.[40] Despite much hard work in some areas there was far less accomplished on the ground than had been hoped for.

One of the most effective mission partnerships took place in the South-West region. In addition to the Union-affiliated churches, three other Baptist causes in Cumnock, New Cumnock and Stranraer were committed to this initiative. Noel McCullins and those who worked with him produced a regular news sheet to encourage churches to pray for one another and held praise and prayer evenings as a basis for churches worshipping and praying together for the work in their respective congregations. Over his five years in post an annual pastors-and-spouses meal encouraged both fellowship and creative thinking about possible new mission initiatives in their own areas; there was a range of very different projects that were a source of encouragement. For example, the small Bourtreehill congregation in Irvine ran the Oasis café which served as a springboard for many of their activities. These included the monthly Breakfast Church where many more adults and children attended services than would be found at regular Sunday worship.

---

[38] 'Mission', Baptist Union Assembly Minutes, 30 October 2010, *Assembly Handbook* 2010, p. 19.

[39] Olive Drane, 'Aberdeenshire', 2010 *Yearbook*, pp. 116–118.

[40] Harry Sprange, 'Associate Mission Networker North-West Highlands and Islands', pp. 120–121.

*The Ark* in Ayr attracted many unchurched young people not only at weekends, but at lunchtimes and after school during the week, where they were able to enjoy themselves taking part in a variety of activities in an alcohol and drug free environment. Christian young people were also able in that setting to speak about their faith to their peers. Kilmarnock Baptist Church along with other churches in that town set up a similar venture called the Kilmarnock Youth Project. Using sport as a mission tool, Southside, Ayr, ran the Southside Soccer and Golf Outreach in partnership with volunteers from a number of churches during the school summer holidays. Another collaborative venture between churches in Ayr for young adults was the *Touch the World Ministries* where they were trained, equipped and sent to various locations for mission in places as far apart as Orkney, Lisburn, London, Bulgaria and Portugal. Members of the Ayr, Southside and New Prestwick congregations formed a new centre for reaching people with a wide spectrum of needs called 'Broken Chains'. They offered counselling, and other forms of practical assistance together with a meal and a church service at each gathering. Noel McCullins led a number of workshops on topics such as 'Restructuring for Mission'; 'Thinking outside the Box'; 'Leadership and Child Protection'; 'Vision Casting' and 'Discovering Your Gifts'. It was a remarkably fruitful partnership between the churches of the South-West; and the planting of the new cause in Girvan a particular highlight.[41] This collaborative effort demonstrated that partnership between churches in mission was able to accomplish significantly more than might have been attained individually.

## New Steps Forward

The Baptist Union of Scotland appointed a Union structure review group in 2009 to consider the role of the General Director and the appointment of Core Leaders. It was a crucial time in the life of this family of churches as there was a vacancy for the post of General Director, due to the previous office holder returning to local church ministry in 2009. In January 2010 the Baptist Union Council appointed Alan Donaldson, minister of Dumfries Baptist Church, to this post.[42] The Baptist Union funds were found to be in a precarious place in April 2010 when it was established that there was a £100,000 budget deficit and very limited reserves. If there had been no improvement in this situation it was feared that the Scottish Baptist Fund (SBF) would have had a negative bank balance by July that year. The

---

[41] Noel McCullins, 'South West', pp. 118–120.

[42] 'Digest of Council Minutes' 12 January 2010', p. 11. Alan Donaldson provided some helpful notes to the author on his time in office as General Director by email on 13 May 2019. They have been particularly helpful in confirming information from those years and especially in this section of this chapter of the book.

international financial crisis that began in 2007 and led to the collapse of a number of banks, most spectacularly Lehman Brothers Bank in the USA in September 2008, had led to a huge fall in investment interest rates. This problem was highlighted with respect to the SBF by the Finance Director Norman McNeish. Anticipated investment income had been reduced, and the shortfall in SBF giving had been expected to be around £50,000, but a number of late gifts and a larger one-off donation reduced this estimated figure to a small actual deficit of £4,834 in the SBF in the financial year to March 2009 and small reduction in the Union's financial reserves.[43] A further structure review group was appointed in April 2010 to identify a model for the Union that could ensure a financially sustainable future. The new General Director was convinced that residential Councils would help deepen relationships between Council members and allow them to take more time over major decisions. The first residential council was held in Gartmore House near Stirling 18–19 May 2010.[44] The October 2010 Baptist Union Assembly delegates were informed that following the reception of the report of the structure review group, the Baptist Union Council had taken some key decisions. In order to address the financial challenges facing the Union it was necessary to sell the larger premises in Aytoun Road in Glasgow and purchase smaller fit-for-purpose offices. The Speirs Wharf premises in Glasgow were purchased in July 2011 and opened in November that year.[45] It was inevitable that staffing levels could not be maintained. The Mission and Ministry Advisor posts were to be merged with Jim Purves, minister of Bristo Baptist Church, Edinburgh, appointed to this position in 2012. BMS had agreed with the Union jointly to fund a post in Scotland that both promoted BMS work and mission development.[46] Judy White, who had previously served in Stirling Baptist Church, was appointed to serve in that capacity from 2012 to 2014. There was to be a reduction in the number of admin staff employed by the Union. Norman McNeish the Finance Director had decided to take early retirement, first by reducing his hours from five to three days and then being replaced by a new post holder working one and a half days for the Union. Between March and May 2011 Mary McKay, Gillian Ferguson and Norman

---

[43] Norman McNeish, 'Finance Director' report, *Scottish Baptist Yearbook 2010*, pp. 104–105; Baptist Union of Scotland, Financial Statement Year Ended 31 March 2009, p. 21, this separate report was printed and included in the *Scottish Baptist Yearbook 2010*.

[44] 'Union Vision', Digest of Council Minutes, 12 January, 2010, p. 11.

[45] Minutes of BUS Assembly 2011, Thursday 27 October 2011, p. 15; and BUS Council report, 31 January, 2012, in *Come Home Again*, Assembly Handbook for 2012, p. 9.

[46] 'BMS Scottish Coordinator', report in *Assembly Handbook Outrageous Generosity Dunfermline, 27–29 October 2011*, p. 16.

McNeish completed their service in the employment of the Union. Andy Scarcliff the mission advisor accepted a call to Portobello Baptist Church in June that year and Andrew Rollinson a call to St Andrews Baptist Church in August 2011. Mo Murray came into post as Youth Development Coordinator and Peter Dick as Finance Director.[47] Roberta Hope who served the Baptist Union for a remarkable thirty years died after a long battle with cancer in 2015. Her knowledge of and enthusiasm for the people and work of the Baptist Union were irreplaceable. Lynn Scott was appointed to take her place.[48] It was a major change of staffing in a short period of time. There was also a hope that when finances permitted that the employment of a children's specialist and the launch of an intern programme for young adults might be possible.[49] The agreed staffing changes and attaining financial stability enabled this family of churches to focus on the shared future they sought and to reflect on the common convictions that motivated them to engage in Christian service in their respective congregations.

At the 2010 Baptist Union Assembly Alan Donaldson highlighted the increasing loss of relationships within the Scottish Baptist family. The factual basis of this statement was clear from the 'Better Together' tour of meetings with local church leaderships.[50] There was a real need to regain the commitment to being 'intentionally relational'. This meant that collectively a common vision needed to be discovered, articulated and owned. In line with historic Baptist practice, it needed to be based on our understanding of union with Christ and on his commission to go to the world with the gospel. There was a requirement for building missional relationships. Delegates were asked to consider in small groups what Scottish Baptists needed to do in order to be a radical movement? Four key responses reaffirmed convictions historically owned within this family of churches with respect to the lordship of Jesus Christ, historic Baptist distinctives, connecting churches with their communities and relating intentionally with one another.[51] An important document published at the 2011 Assembly was *An Invitation to a Journey*, in various draft forms it had been considered in a number of Baptist forums over

---

[47] 'Staff changes', in '142nd Annual Report submitted by the General Director', *Assembly Handbook, 2011*, p. 19.

[48] Alan Donaldson. '146th Annual Report', in *Mind the Gap: Baptist Assembly in Scotland, 29–30 October 2015*, Motherwell, p. 6.

[49] Alan Donaldson, 'Interim Report of the Structure Review Group', section entitled: 'Proposed new Structure', Assembly Minutes: 2010, in *Assembly Handbook Outrageous Generosity Dunfermline 2011*, p. 16.

[50] Andrew Rollinson, 'Better Together': Synopsis of Findings from the Tour of Church Leadership Teams, Appendix E, *Assembly Handbook* 2010, pp. 99–100.

[51] Alan Donaldson, notes, pp. 1–2.

nearly two years. It set out the framework of three key values that would unite the collective witness of Scottish Baptists throughout the second decade of the twenty-first century, 'Intentionally Relational', 'Unashamedly Missional' and 'Creatively Rooted'. The adoption of these values by this Christian constituency called them in response to adopt six further convictions. Firstly, to live authentically as a Believers' Church; this involves communal discipleship, building missional relationships, communal discernment of the voice of God, inter-church resourcing, together with prophetic and dissident political engagement.[52] This was the vision for radical Christian discipleship around which Scottish Baptists united.

Ties within Scottish Baptist ranks were strengthened by the appointment of a Regional Pastors Network in 2011 to share the responsibility of caring for ministers and their families in the region.[53] At the same time a Conflict Resolution Team, later renamed the Peaceful Transition Team, was established with trained individuals to assist churches struggling with interpersonal relations or seeking resources to strengthen their abilities to handle times of change.[54] Another new development occurred when the Baptist Union Council made a point of changing its language in relation to ownership of the Union in 2012. It sought to avoid referencing the Union as a 'third party' and instead sought to refer to 'our Union' in a consistent attempt to remove the 'them and us' type of thinking between national leaders and local congregations. Alan Donaldson made a point of addressing this issue at the Annual Assembly in Dundee in October 2012.[55] Following the sale of 14 Aytoun Road and the move to the much smaller Speirs Wharf offices in Glasgow, the Baptist Union was able to allocate £200,000 to a mission initiative fund in 2012 in order to support pioneering projects and new mission initiatives taking place in and from local churches. The initiative allowed the Union to have a greater prominence in some of the member bodies with its support for their innovative outreach activities. BMS was also going through a process of change in its ministries at that time and had strengthened its relationship with Benjamin Francis, the director of Big Life

---

[52] *An invitation to a journey* (Glasgow: Baptist Union of Scotland, 2011).

[53] John Greenshields, 'Ministry Department' report, Minutes of the Baptist Assembly in Scotland 2011, 27 October, 2019, in *Come Home Again*, Assembly Handbook for 2012, p. 15.

[54] 'Conflict Resolution', 6 September 2011, BUS Council report, *Assembly Handbook Outrageous Generosity Dunfermline, 27–29 October 2011*, p. 12. 'Conflict Resolution', in Jim Purves, 'Mission and Ministry Advisor's Annual Report', in *Come Home Again*, Assembly Handbook for 2012, pp. 26–27.

[55] Alan Donaldson, 'Introduction to the Annual Reports – 'Our Union', in the 'Minutes of the Baptist Assembly in Scotland 2012, in Dundee, Thursday 25 October, in *Forging the Future*, Assembly Handbook 2013, p. 8.

Ministries, a remarkably successful church-planting ministry in India.[56] Nine Scottish Baptist women visited Kolkata under BMS auspices in 2014, under the leadership of Judy White, in order to experience for themselves some of the innovative projects run by Indian Baptists.[57] In the middle of this decade there was a further transition in the national leadership team of the Union with the retirement of John Greenshields in 2015. He was replaced by Martin Hodson, who had served previously at Bridge of Don Baptist Church in Aberdeen, prior to a very fruitful ministry at St Peter's Baptist Church in Worcester over the previous eleven years.[58] Jacqueline Primrose also stepped down from the Convenor's post after seven years in 2016 to be replaced by Frances Bloomfield.[59] This was a time of constant but necessary changes in the life of the Union, though it was marked with a good spirit of cooperation between the different congregations and the wider Baptist family in Scotland.

There were two further ministry initiatives launched in the second decade of the twenty-first century. The first, 'Theology to Go' that began in 2016 was provided as an opportunity for ministers serving in areas of urban deprivation to meet together and reflect theologically on their particular social context.[60] The second in 2017 was 'Lead Academy', a programme to equip church leadership teams to develop their skills in working together.[61] Another national team-member was added with the appointment of Ali Laing as the Next Generation Development Coordinator in 2017.[62] It has been noted that Baptists and other Evangelical Churches had been able to retain teenagers within their ranks more effectively in the twenty-first century than in the later years of the previous century, but there was a particular challenge to face in addressing the serious under representation of eighteen to thirty year-olds in

---

[56] BMS had provided funding for a new boat to assist Benjamin Francis and his team travel to remote communities inaccessible by road. Mark Craig, 'BMS Report', in Assembly Handbook Outrageous Generosity Dunfermline, 27–29 October 2011, p. 11.

[57] 'Judy White, 'Women's Insight Trip to Kolkata', and 'Report on trip to Nepal and Kolkata', Residential Council, 22–23 May 2013, in *Forging the Future*, Assembly Handbook 2013, pp. 6–7, 16.

[58] 'Ministry Development Coordinator', Residential Council 21–22 March, 2015, in *Mind the Gap: Baptist Assembly in Scotland, 29–30 October 2015*, Motherwell, p. 6.

[59] Minutes of the Baptist Assembly in Scotland 2016, Glenrothes, in *Messages of Hope: Assembly Papers 2017, 26–27 October 2017*, Motherwell, p. 9.

[60] 'Theology to Go', Minutes of the Baptist Assembly in Scotland 2015', *Gazing on God's Glory: Assembly Papers 2016, 27–28 October 2016*, Motherwell, p. 11.

[61] 'LEAD Academy Learning Community', *Connect*, March 2017, p. 4.

[62] 'Appointment of Ali Laing as Next Generation Development Coordinator', *Connect*, April 2017, p. 4.

Scottish churches. One contribution made by the Baptist Union was the launching of a small pilot internship scheme in 2018. Five young people were committed to spending a year on this scheme. Alpha Arakaza and David Spencer working with Ali Laing in the BUSYounger team in Speirs Wharf, Glasgow; Elidh Fordyce and Laura Moir alongside Andy Craig and Mark Fyfe at Kirkintilloch Baptist Church and Shaun Craig with Rob Fraser-Binns at Stirling Baptist Church.[63] It was hoped that local churches would take up this initiative in future years providing gap year opportunities for ministry for some of their younger leaders. The hope of forming a future intern programme agreed at the 2011 Annual Assembly had now begun. The 150th anniversary year, 2019 saw the high profile 'Give me Springs of Water' initiative led by Alan Donaldson the General Director. It was an attempt to bring Scottish Baptists together to celebrate the past, but equally and more importantly to pledge to work together to accomplish fresh goals in the years to come. His announcement early in that year of concluding his term of service later in 2019 brought to a close a decade of both significant changes and a fresh sense of optimism in the ranks about the future prospects for Baptist Churches in Scotland. It was, though, an invitation to continue a journey of faith not to arrive at a particular destination. Scottish Baptists were acutely aware of the rapidly changing social context in their country, but sought to continue their work with a renewed optimism for future progress in sharing the good news of the Christian Gospel with their fellow citizens.

## Signs of Hope in Local Church Life

It is easy to highlight the challenges facing many churches in Scotland, but there are also other indications of church growth as well as decline. It is only possible to give some limited examples of encouraging progress in local congregations. Firstly, there are some examples from two regions of Scotland, followed by selected examples from other parts of Scotland. They are used to illustrate some of the encouraging developments from around the country. In the Tayside region, for example, there have been new churches planted under the auspices of Central Baptist Church, Dundee, beginning in Carnoustie in March 2011 and more recently in 2014 in Lochee, through an agreement with *Twenty Schemes* church-planting initiative.[64] Forfar Community Church was launched in February 2012 under the leadership of the founding minister Oliver Vellacott and now has its own premises on the site of the former

---

[63] 'A warm welcome to our interns!', *Connect*, October 2018, pp. 4–5.

[64] Jim Turrent and Paul, Hammond, 'Central Baptist Church Dundee – Planted in the Word', in *Forging the Future: Our Place in the Nation* (Glasgow: Baptist Union of Scotland, 2014), pp. 45–47. See also, 'Carnoustie Community Church', in Resource Grant Update Reports', in *Forging the Future: Our Place in the Nation* pp. 17–18.

Wellbrae school in Forfar.⁶⁵ Its work continues under its current minister Brian Mulraine, who was appointed to his post in that church in 2015. Perth Baptist Church had erected new premises in 1990, with a sports hall added in 1999, but as a result of further growth required a substantial increase in the size of the main hall in 2009. The church has a wide range of ministries including an innovative approach to working with senior citizens in the community with their 'holiday at home' scheme that has been held each summer since 2015, in which they organised a week of creative activities for seniors based on their church premises, in partnership with Social Services, to provide a break for people in the local area who might not have had any holidays. Messy Church, a monthly Sunday afternoon outreach event, has attracted around ninety people per month over the last five years with between thirty and fifty volunteers from the church participating in each service. 'Footwise' was a new programme that was launched in 2018 to help provide basic foot care services for local people in their community, and in June 2019, in partnership with other churches in the city, they have started a Christians Against Poverty Centre in Perth.⁶⁶ St Mary's Community Church, Dundee, extended and refurbished its premises in April 2016 to provide more appropriate facilities for its range of ministries that included a community café and a foodbank in partnership with other local congregations.⁶⁷ Pitlochry Baptist Church called David Barry as its minister in October 2007. He had previously worked as the Youth Pastor in Stirling Baptist Church. In line with the wider community, the church had a high proportion of older members but over the last decade the focus on utilising the gifts and ministries of all ages in church life has seen a growing number of younger families. With a growing children and youth work a decision was taken to employ a youth worker, Ken Naquin, to help further develop this expanding ministry. As a result of numerical growth the church premises are increasingly too small for its work.⁶⁸ Another congregation, Broughty Ferry Baptist Church has seen significant growth in its attendance and work since the 1990s. This small congregation grew significantly under the ministry of Kenneth Jefferson between 1999 and 2005 and struggled with inadequate accommodation for its growing Sunday

---

⁶⁵ *Forfar Community Church: The Gutter Kirkie and The Braeheidie Schule: A Short History of the Baptist Church in Forfar*, a leaflet produced by the church at the time of its launch in 2012. See also BUS Council report, 31 January 2012, in *Come Home Again*, Assembly Handbook for 2012, p. 9.

⁶⁶ I am grateful to Gillian Ferguson, Anne McCully and Dr Ken Russell for providing this information on 26 and 27 June 2019.

⁶⁷ St Mary's Community Church celebrates new era after £400,000 refurbishment', *The Courier*, 23 April 2016, article accessed on *The Courier* website, 15 June 2019.

⁶⁸ David Barrie, 'Pitlochry Baptist Church- Family', in *Forging the Future: Our Place in the Nation*, pp. 13–17.

School and youth work that reached a record high of forty-five children in 2011.[69] In addition to the current minister Brian Talbot, appointed in 2007, Gary Torbet was taken on as a part-time Youth Worker (later as Youth Pastor) and Claire McNutt as Children and Families worker in 2014. The community work with young children and their families grew steadily and provided the basis on which Messy Church was launched on 4 April 2015.[70] By 2019 around forty unchurched families were regular attenders at its monthly services in its recently extended premises in Panmurefield area of Broughty Ferry.[71] In a region of Scotland more familiar with churches declining and closing, here was evidence in the twenty-first century of encouraging signs of spiritual life and new church growth.

In Fife the Collydean Granary Baptist Church was relaunched in 2007 with a grant from the Baptist Union that allowed John MacSporran to serve as the part-time minister of the church. As a result, this small congregation by 2009 grew to a membership of thirty with forty worshippers on a Sunday with a growing Sunday School. A particular highlight of the year in 2009 was the first baptismal service held in the church for thirteen years. Several people made first-time professions of faith on that occasion.[72] Over the next decade the church further strengthened its witness under the leadership of a new minister David Purves, and is now engaging in a wider range of ministries; more it recently appointed Liam Morton as first a Youth and Children's intern in December 2015, then as Youth and Children's worker in November 2016. Another small congregation, Buckhaven Baptist Church, over the last four years, since 2015, has seen great encouragements through its community café through which good relationships have been built with people outside the congregation. It has seen former church-goers return to church, professions of faith and baptisms and a rise over that time in regular Sunday attendance from less than twenty people to sometimes above fifty people, and the membership total up from nineteen to twenty-nine, with existing members gaining a fresh confidence in evangelistic work.[73] A good example of investment in its church

---

[69] 'Broughty Ferry Baptist Church', a feature article in the Dundee for Christ periodical *Broadcast* (Spring/Summer 2011), Issue 10, pp. 16–17.

[70] I am grateful to Claire McNutt, Children and Families' Worker at Broughty Ferry Baptist Church for confirming this date. 'Broughty Ferry Baptist Church', Resource Grant Update Reports', in *Mind the Gap: Baptist Assembly in Scotland, 29–30 October 2015*, Motherwell, p. 15. See also 'Broughty Ferry', *Connect*, January 2017, p. 3.

[71] The premises and site of the church in Panmurefield were generously gifted to Broughty Ferry Baptist Church by Panmurefield Village Church in 2014.

[72] 'Collydean Granary Baptist Church', *Scottish Baptist Yearbook 2010*, p. 157.

[73] Information about Buckhaven Baptist Church came by email from the minister Rob Jones, 23 May 2019.

buildings is witnessed at Viewfield Baptist Church in Dunfermline. It has carried out a major refurbishment of its premises from 2015 to 2016 that will allow better access to its premises for people with disabilities as well as greater flexibility in its ministry activities with the local community.[74] Glenrothes Baptist Church has had a consistently effective ministry since its foundation in 1957. In March 2011 Jacob Brothers was appointed as the pastor. The church experienced further growth in its work, with its existing premises that were already in need of significant improvements becoming too small for its needs. In 2016 a large office block in the town centre of Glenrothes became available for rent. After extensive renovations the church moved into the new premises at the end of June 2017. Building work continued over the next two years with an office and conference suite with various youth rooms completed on the top floor and refurbishment on the ground floor in order to establish a café and community outreach centre on the ground floor. Funds from the sale of the previous premises, together with financial gifts from outside agencies and generous giving by the congregation, ensured that the £800,000 relocation costs have been paid. The church appointed Matthew Marshall as Assistant Pastor of Mission in 2015 and Gavin Thomson as a part-time Children & Youth Pastor in September 2018. Growth in attendances at services in the new premises has been accompanied by a steady increase in church membership from 120 in 2011 to the current figure of 150 in 2019.[75] These examples of church growth in Fife are particularly encouraging because two of the examples were quite small causes that have seen new life and growth. The larger church at Glenrothes has been able to develop a wider range of ministries in the new more suitable premises and at the same time welcome a larger number of people across the age ranges to its Sunday services.

It is impossible to reference all the good news stories taking place across the country, but some examples include: in the far north the planting of a new church at Stromness in Orkney. On Sunday 29 September 2002, Stromness Baptist Church held its inaugural service with twenty-four people present. Its numbers grew to a peak of seventy in the next decade, though they have declined in recent years to around forty-five, due to some older couples moving off the island and fifteen younger people leaving to go to university. In 2018 they called Ally Heath, a pre-accredited minister, to serve with this congregation.[76] Thurso Baptist Church took a big step of faith to purchase

---

[74] 'Viewfield Baptist Church, Dunfermline', *Connect*, June 2016, pp. 1, 4, 5.

[75] Information about Glenrothes Baptist Church in this paragraph came from Colin Roworth by email on 15 June 2019. Matthew Marshall was subsequently elected as Associate Pastor in May 2019.

[76] I am grateful to Bill Gilmour of Stromness Baptist Church for providing this information.

more suitable premises which opened in June 2018.[77] Culloden-Balloch Baptist Church opened their first permanent church building in 2016.[78]

In the Western Highlands and Islands Tiree Baptist Church opened their refurbished premises in February 2016.[79] Islay Baptist Church has built increasingly strong ties with local children through an annual summer beach mission that began in 2012 with twelve children and now regularly attracts sixty, with a peak one year of 100 attending. 'A Sunday School has restarted on the island with children from the mission going along, and some of the young people helping.'[80] Oban Baptist Church had seen attendances fall to quite low numbers at worship services prior to the appointment of Ian McFarlane as minister in 2012. During his more than five-year ministry the congregation grew to the point where their premises were filled to capacity on Sunday mornings. It was a remarkably encouraging story. Fort William Baptist Church, a former United Free Church congregation, had seen significant numerical growth and completed an extension to their premises in 2013.[81] In the North-East of Scotland encouraging progress in the work of Hillview Community Church, formerly known as International Baptist Church in Aberdeen until 2011, has led to growth in its witness including the launch of a church-plant congregation in Kintore in 2017. This congregation, originally planted to reach international workers in the oil industry around Aberdeen, mainly Americans, felt that in a city that had changed so much in recent years it too needed to change its vision and identity. The decision to embrace a new name and experience staff changes together with a new understanding of membership and leadership was a significant faith step for 'the few dozen members of IBC'. The new vision of the church is 'to be a church that plants churches'.[82] Aberdeen Christian Fellowship, based in Union Grove, Aberdeen, started a church-plant congregation in Portlethen in October 2017.[83] Another new church-plant in Aberdeen, Bridge Community Church, began under the ministry of Glen Innes in 2014, but despite seeing

---

[77] 'A Leap of Faith', *Connect*, November 2018, p. 8.

[78] Allan J. Donaldson, '147th Annual Report', in *Gazing on God's Glory: Assembly Papers 2016, 27–28 October 2016*, Motherwell, p. 12.

[79] 'Renovated premises at Baugh', *Connect*, March 2016, p. 2.

[80] Sue MacFarlane, 'Your mission should you choose to accept it', *@SU Creating Communities* (July 2019), pp. 4–5.

[81] *Forging the Future*, BUS Magazine, issued for the 2013 Baptist Union Annual Assembly, p. 5.

[82] Information provided by Martin Clarke, minister of Hillview Community Church by email on 31 May 2019. See also 'Hillview Community Church', *Connect*, April 2018, p. 3.

[83] I am grateful to Douglas Hutcheon for this information on 27 June 2019.

people coming to faith and others reconnecting with church, a loss of key leaders saw the work cease in August 2018.[84] Meanwhile Ellon Baptist Church, a congregation that has seen significant growth in recent years, obtained its first permanent premises in December 2018 after thirty-one years in a variety of locations.[85] In times of economic challenges and population fluctuations it has been encouraging to see new life in Highland and island settings. and in Aberdeen at a time when the oil industry has seen some adverse times there is still a sense of optimism of further growth in development through the witness of the city churches, of which the above congregations are good examples.

Christian witness in the wider community has taken on varied and creative forms. Scottish Baptists have played their part alongside other Christian Churches in serving their communities with a diverse range of mission and ministry activities. In the Central Belt, Kirkintilloch Baptist Church was one of a number of Baptist Churches that has opened a Christians against Poverty Centre. It has also partnered with The Message Trust to put an Eden team into the socially disadvantaged Hillhead area of the town. Drumchapel Baptist Church also started a similar partnership with Eden in 2017.[86] Portobello Baptist Church, Edinburgh, a congregation that grew significantly since 2011 through creative outreach events during the ministry of Andy Scarcliffe, saw, for example, a remarkable 250 people attend its 'Carols by Candlelight' on Portobello Beach in December 2018.[87] Scottish Baptists in a variety of urban communities have had members who have participated in Street Pastor teams.[88] The most high profile Baptist participant in this work was Andy Burns of Central Baptist Church in Dundee who founded the Rock Street

---

[84] The work began in the Bridge of Dee with the support of other Baptist Churches in Aberdeen. 'Church Planting', in Judy White, 'Mission Development Co-ordinator Scotland' report, in *Forging The Future: Our Place in the Nation? Baptist Assembly in Scotland 30 October to 2 November, 2014*, Motherwell, p. 16. See also, Glen Innes, 'The Bridge Church, Aberdeen', Resource Grant Update Reports, in *Gazing on God's Glory: Assembly Papers 2016, 27–28 October 2016*, Motherwell, p. 17. Glenn Innes, 'The Bridge Community Church Aberdeen', Resource Grant Update Reports, in *Fearless: Baptist Assembly in Scotland, 25–26 October 2018*, p. 14.

[85] 'A Place to call home!', *Connect*, February 2019, pp. 3–4.

[86] Eden: Hillhead, Kirkintilloch, *Connect*, January 2018, p. 3. 'Eden in Drumchapel', *Connect*, August 2017, p. 3. See also for a more general explanation of The Message Trust's aims for these projects in the Glasgow area www.message.org.uk/2015/04/16/exploring-eden-glasgow accessed 27 June 2019.

[87] 'Carols by candlelight . . . on the beach!', *Connect*, February 2019, p. 5.

[88] 'Stuart Crawford, 'Ten years of being salt and light on the streets of Glasgow', *Connect*, June 2019, p. 4. This was a short article on the work of Street Pastors in Glasgow, a work that began in January 2009.

Chaplains team there in 2000[89] and subsequently helped others to establish teams in other parts of North-East Scotland and more recently in Northern Ireland. He was awarded the British Empire medal for this work in Dundee City Hall on 26 April 2019. A few Baptists have served as football chaplains. David Barrie, minister of Pitlochry Baptist Church, has served as club chaplain for St Johnstone FC in Perth for more than six years and prior to that for a decade at Stirling Albion FC. Football chaplaincy posts are usually honorary positions but are an opportunity to build relationships with a fairly large number of people with limited or no church connections.[90] Workplace Chaplaincy initiatives were participated in by Baptist churches in Stirling, Aberdeen and Adelaide Place Baptist Church in Glasgow.[91] Although Scotland has become an increasingly secular country in recent years there are still plenty of opportunities open for Christian individuals and churches to participate in various forms of social engagement.

It is also encouraging to see congregations being planted or replanted in communities where Baptist Churches have struggled to launch or maintain a witness in past years. Stirling Baptist Church has provided pastoral support to a group of Christians in Callander through the appointment of Brian Gooding as Regional Pastor for Callander in February 2015. Meetings for prayer were arranged followed by a home group in August that year. This group of Christians was then recognised as a new congregation under the auspices of that church in October 2016.[92] In Glasgow that same year, Queen's Park Baptist Church launched a West End Campus congregation in the former Partick Baptist Church premises and there are encouraging developments taking place in the replanted Dennistoun Baptist Church.[93] The new Crookston congregation that met in Ross Hall Academy was welcomed

---

[89] 'A Rock for those in need', *The Courier and Advertiser*, 27 March, 2010, p. 5.

[90] Graeme Macpherson, 'What it feels like to be a chaplain for St Johnstone FC', *The Herald*, 27 April 2019, story accessed on *The Herald* website, 26 June, 2019.

[91] Alan Donaldson,'143rd Annual Report submitted by the General Director', August 2012, in *Come Home Again*, Assembly Handbook for 2012, pp. 20–21. See also Karen Murdarasi, 'Adelaide Place Baptist Church' report, in in *Forging the Future*, Assembly Handbook 2013, p. 16.

[92] I am grateful to Alasdair Black and Brian Gooding, ministers at Stirling and Callander for this information on 23 June 2019. See also David Gooding, 'Callander: A Regional Expression of Stirling Baptist Church', in *Mind the Gap: Baptist Assembly in Scotland, 29–30 October 2015*, Motherwell, p. 16; 'Stirling Baptist @ Callander', *Connect*, March 2017, p. 3.

[93] Alan J. Donaldson, '147th Annual Report', and Mark Morris, 'Dennistoun Baptist Church', Resource Grant Update Reports', in *Gazing on God's Glory: Assembly Papers 2016, 27–28 October 2016*, Motherwell, pp. 12, 17. See also, 'Messy Church comes to Partick', *Connect*, December 2017, p. 3.

into membership of the Baptist Union in 2012,[94] together with Milestone Christian Fellowship in Girvan. This new congregation had a membership of thirty-five and welcomed between twenty-five and fifty people at its main worship service on Tuesday evenings. This Girvan congregation opened their first permanent church building in 2016.[95] On a Monday to Friday basis it offers breakfast and lunches to those who are in need of support. It operates a foodbank from the premises and also offers a weekly nutritious cooked evening meal enjoyed by about thirty diners each week. It also offers a fortnightly cinema club that enables initial connections with local families with no prior church connection. It also operates an after-school club for older primary children and jointly with Girvan North Parish Church runs a Scripture Union group in Girvan Primary School. A church that began with seven people in 2005 has seen a good number of people come to faith in Jesus Christ and has experienced steady growth in its weekly worshipping community.[96] Other examples of the newer congregations welcomed into the Union in recent years at the Annual Assembly are Carnoustie Community Church, later called Carnoustie Baptist Church in 2012,[97] and Campbeltown Community Church in 2013.[98] Good news stories in the south of Scotland include a church-plant in nearby Tweedbank launched by thirty-three people from Selkirk Baptist Church in October 2013[99] and the decision by Peebles Baptist Church in 2019, after many years in rented premises, to explore an opportunity to build its own premises.[100] The congregation in Peebles in the years without owning any premises had used various approaches to building relationships with their local community including running a café and a foodbank and using Café Church and Messy Church services as part of their

---

[94] 'Crookston Baptist Church', BUS Council report, 31 January, 2012, in *Come Home Again*, Assembly Handbook for 2012, p. 9.

[95] 'Milestone', BUS Council Report, 22–23, May 2012 and 4 September, 2012, in *Come Home Again*, Assembly Handbook for 2012, pp. 12–13. Alan J. Donaldson, '147th Annual Report', in *Gazing on God's Glory: Assembly Papers 2016, 27–28 October 2016*, Motherwell, p. 12.

[96] Adam Oellermann, 'A Brief History of Milestone Christian Fellowship', a document provided for the author on 27 June 2019.

[97] 'Application for membership', BUS Council report, 4 September, 2012, in *Come Home Again*, Assembly Handbook for 2012, p. 14.

[98] 'Campbeltown Community Church Application for Membership', Residential Council, 22–23 May, 2013, in *Forging the Future*, Assembly Handbook 2013, p. 6.

[99] I am grateful to Brian Talbot, minister of Selkirk Baptist Church for this information on 27 June 2019.

[100] I am grateful to Ian Gray the minister of Peebles Baptist Church for sharing this information with the author in June 2019.

evangelistic outreach in the town. The King's Meadow Community Garden, created on part of a plot of land owned by the church, has led to many interesting conversations and some developing relationships in the community.[101] Signs of new life are very promising in these communities.

Two Scottish Baptist Churches have embarked on major redevelopment projects in recent years. Dumfries Baptist Church has benefitted from the courageous decision of a former generation of believers in the town to continue a witness when it might have been easier to close the doors of the church in the late 1960s. It has experienced remarkable and sustained growth in recent decades from a very low base in the late 1960s to the large congregation of around 350 on a Sunday in 2019. It had a vision for new church facilities purpose built for the twenty-first century. The 2,000 square meters community facility was erected at a cost of £4.7 million. The church had outgrown the facilities they had worshipped at in Newall Terrace, Dumfries since 1873, and prior to entry into the new facilities had hired Dumfries High School for Sunday morning services. The new premises include a 500-seater main hall, a café, sports hall with changing facilities and specialist youth facilities.[102] The other example comes from East Kilbride where East Mains Baptist Church opened its innovative new facilities called 'The Village Centre'. Regularly 155 community groups use the buildings, with an average weekly attendance of around 3,000 people. These include more than forty counsellors assisting troubled people. In addition to community groups, there is an out of School Care club running five days a week giving breakfast to children, taking them to school and looking after them at the end of the school day. There is a Physiotherapist Company located on the site. The Centre itself runs a Scottish Vocational Qualifications (SQV) programme in partnership with a company called MGT who provide all of their services free of charge, so the training is free to clients, together with the provision of training, work experience and support to people with additional needs. It employs ten full-time staff and twenty regular volunteer staff. From a vision to create 'The Village Centre' twenty years ago, the church committed itself to making the necessary changes to bring the vision into reality. The £1 million cost, of which £800,000 paid for new buildings and £200,000 was incurred in staffing costs, was raised through a variety of grant funders as well as from

---

[101] Christine Drummond, 'Peebles Baptist Church' report and 'Grant Aided Church Report- Peebles Baptist Church'. BUS Council, 22 January 2013, in *Forging the Future: Baptist Assembly in Scotland, Motherwell, 31 October to 2 November, 2013*, pp. 5, 18.

[102] 'Dumfries Baptist Church', in *Dumfries & Galloway Standard*, 19 January, 2018, article viewed on McLean Architects website, www.mcleanarchitects.co.uk/news/2018/1/15/dumfries-baptist-church-in-the-dumfires-galloway-standard, accessed on 15 June 2019. See also 'Obedience Rooted in Faith in Dumfries!', *Connect*, June 2018, pp. 2–3.

members of the congregation. Over the twelve years the Centre has been open hundreds of people have been cared for, many have come to Christian faith and the church has experienced numerical growth.[103] These are two remarkable stories of vision and church growth which may not be typical of Scottish Baptist churches, but they are a solid reminder of the vitality of a good number of Christian churches in contemporary Scotland.

## Theological Education

The Scottish Baptist College has continued to play a prominent part in the training and equipping of men and women for a range of ministries in partnership with the BUS in the twenty-first century. This institution is celebrating its own 125th anniversary in 2019. It concluded a Memorandum of Understanding with the BUS at the time of the incorporation of these two bodies as Charitable Companies limited by Guarantee in 2018 and 2019 respectively. Each body recognised its commitment to and support for the other in a common goal of training and equipping ministers 'for preaching and leadership in BUS churches and the college affirmed that its principal purpose remains to service these churches, with the Union as its primary vocational partner.'[104] The college and the BUS undertook to assess annually 'the progress of pre-accredited ministers in training at the college and to ensure that students are developing in knowledge and practice of ministry to the standards sought by the Union and in particular, by their Board of Ministry.'[105] Both bodies expressed their commitment in the agreement to developing 'relevant forms of discipleship training across Scotland. To this end the Union affirmed that it would seek to consult with College staff when developing plans in the area of training and discipleship formation.'[106] The Scottish Baptist College and some of the churches of the Baptist Union have not always had the most harmonious of relationships over the previous century,[107] but in more recent years the BUS and the College have developed a good understanding and common purpose which stands them in good stead in their collaborative efforts in the coming years.

---

[103] Jim McGillivray, 'The Village Centre', pp. 1–6; I am very grateful to Jim McGillivray putting this information together in June 2019 so it would be available for use in this book.

[104] This quotation comes from the 'Memorandum of Understanding between The Baptist Union of Scotland Ltd. And The Scottish Baptist College', 2019.

[105] This quotation comes from the 'Memorandum of Understanding . . .', 2019.

[106] This quotation come from the 'Memorandum of Understanding . . .', 2019.

[107] See for example, chapter five, pp. 99–101. See also Murray, *Scottish Baptist College*, pp. 24–27.

In the twenty-first century the Scottish Baptist College is serving an increasingly diverse constituency with students not only from Baptist churches, but also from congregations in the Church of the Nazarene, the Church of Scotland and the Salvation Army.[108] In 2019 there are forty-six registered students, twenty full-time and twenty-six part-time, of which thirteen are training for Baptist ministry. Students from this College also prepare to work in various forms of chaplaincy or prior to training with a view to teaching religious education in schools. More recently appointed members of staff include John Drane teaching on 'Creative Mission in a Changing Culture'; Martin Hodson teaching on 'Pastoral Care'; Marion Carson teaching on biblical studies and Stephen Younger on 'Creative Preaching'. In 2020 Alasdair Black will introduce a completely new module: 'The Scottish Church in Context: Past, Present and Future'. A number of other new steps have been taken in 2019. Firstly, an agreement has been reached with the University of the West of Scotland to offer a PhD track by research which is expected to commence in the 2019–2020 year.[109] Then, secondly, an agreement was reached with the Baptist Union of Scotland, and advertised on 22 May 2019, that would enable the college to expand its provision of education to a wider audience in the Scottish Baptist Constituency. As a first step in this process, Professor Andrew Clarke has been appointed to operate from this Northern Hub from September 2019. Under his supervision it aims to deliver training and education as an extension of the College, and facilitate flexible learning opportunities for church members. His work includes initiating conversations with churches about training and education; advising ministers about courses delivered by the College that will enhance their work and offer opportunities for CMD. He will also support students, individually or in small groups who are undertaking College modules on a blended learning or distance-learning basis.[110] At a time of increasingly fragility in the field of theological education this institution has not only survived, but continued to prosper and faces the future with a renewed confidence of a place for its services in support of Scottish Christians and Churches, and in particular amongst the Scottish Baptist constituency.

---

[108] Ian Birch, 'Principal's Report', Scottish Baptist College AGM Tuesday 6 March, 2018,

[109] Ian Birch, 'Scottish Baptist College Report', in BUS Council Papers, 5–6 March 2019, Pitlochry.

[110] 'Widening Access to the Scottish Baptist College', a press-release issued by the SBC on 22 May 2019.

## Social Issues

Scottish Baptists continued to be deeply interested in and engaged with a wide range of social issues that included for example, 'Human Fertilisation and Embryology', 'HIV /AIDS' and 'Nuclear Weapons in 2008'[111] 'Land Reform', 'EU Referendum' and 'Child Poverty' in 2015,[112] together with issues of Freedom, of Religion and Belief, with a particular focus on the issue of anti-Semitism in 2018.[113] However, the subject of marriage and attempts to redefine it in Western societies was of particular concern to many Scottish Baptists. The Convener Jacqueline Primrose and General Director Alan Donaldson presented the EBF resolution on marriage to the 2011 Baptist Union Assembly. Their aim was for Scottish Baptists to show solidarity with other European voices in the wider Baptist family on this subject. The full text presented was a longer document that included these statements:

> . . . Gives thanks to God for creating man and woman in his image and seeks to follow the witness and teaching of scripture for an expression of human sexuality. Urges Baptists to model value and teach that marriage is the creational and biblical setting of any sexual relationship between a man and a woman, as expressed in Genesis 2:24 . . . .

The content of the motion presented was warmly welcomed by the assembled delegates. However, there was also an amendment presented by Derek Hutchison, minister of Hamilton Baptist Church, seconded by John McKinnon, minister of Calderwood Baptist Church, East Kilbride, to sharpen the motion in the current context of debate over same-sex marriage in the Church of Scotland and the Scottish Government's consultation on that same issue. The amendment called on the Scottish Government to delay introducing legislation on same-sex marriage until further conversation had been held with Christians in Scotland, because of serious concerns over what they were proposing. It also asked delegates at the assembly to: 'Affirm the authority and beauty of Scripture as it points towards true and wholesome human sexuality, expressed in the words of Genesis 2:24.' The fairly lengthy debate that followed the raising of the amendment was conducted with real grace and pastoral sensitivity towards individuals who self-identified as gay. It was a sign of the quality of relationships between Scottish Baptists in the twenty-first century that complex issues over human sexuality could be

---

[111] Eileen Baxendale, 'Public Issues Advisory Group' report and 'Appendix B-Nuclear Weapons', in *DNA of Discipleship Assembly Handbook 2008*, pp. 97, 108–110.

[112] Brian Muir, 'Public Issues and Social Action Group' report, in *Mind the Gap: Baptist Assembly in Scotland, 29–30 October 2015*, Motherwell, p. 24.

[113] Norman R. Graham, 'Public Theology Group' report, in *Fearless: Assembly Papers 2018*, p. 23.

discussed with a real spirit of respect as different perspectives were articulated in debate. The motion on marriage together with its amendment was overwhelmingly accepted by delegates and was in line with the 1998 statement of the Board of Ministry, on one aspect of this subject, with respect to applicants for pastoral ministry within the Baptist Union of Scotland.[114] The principle point about marriage was understood and accepted and not a focus in the debate. The majority of concerns raised were pastoral as delegates sought to be sensitive as to how the resolution was understood and received by individuals who did not share their convictions. However, they were very clear in reaffirming a commitment to the traditional and historically Christian understanding of marriage.

### Inter-Church Relations

#### *Other Churches in Scotland*

The General Director Bill Slack raised the topic of inter-church relations in Scotland at the January 2008 Baptist Union Council, with particular reference to the question of whether it was now time to join ACTS. He acknowledged that in 1989 there had been a stalemate on the different votes because no one option of the four proposed had received the required number of votes.[115] However, he believed that ACTS had changed significantly from the vision articulated in 1989, but acknowledged that it was a particularly sensitive topic to raise. He proposed the setting up of a task group made up of a representative group of Scottish Baptists to explore the issues involved with a view to an eventual recommendation to Assembly for a final vote – if their collective mind was in favour of Slack's proposal. The majority of Council members were favourable to this review of the current position and they were unanimous as to the proposed format by which it would be conducted.[116] The Inter Church Relations Task Group (ICRTG) met six times between April 2008 and August 2009. It reviewed previous discussion and decisions on this subject in the Baptist Union prior to considering if any new issues were

---

[114] 'Resolution on Marriage', Baptist Union Assembly 29 October 2011, *Assembly Handbook*, 2012, pp. 17–19. The Board of Ministry guidance document was drawn up by Douglas Hutcheon, Ken Roxburgh and Andrew Rollinson on 3 September 1998. It included the following statement: 'Homosexual orientation is not of itself a reason for exclusion from ministry, but homosexual genital practice is to be regarded as unacceptable in their pastoral office. Ministers are expected not to advocate homosexual or lesbian genital relationships as acceptable alternatives to male/female partnership in marriage.'

[115] See Chapter nine, pp. 271–273.

[116] Bill Slack, 'Addressing Isolation', Digest of Council Minutes, January 2008, *Scottish Baptist Yearbook*, 2009, pp. 89–90.

contributing to the current debate, together with reflection on the possible reasons and benefits for joining ACTS at that time. One of the most helpful meetings in that process took place in November 2008 when Brother Stephen Smyth, General Secretary of ACTS, met with the ICRTG and explained the aims, structure, activities and aspirations of ACTS. He invited those present to explain what reasons they had in mind for joining this inter-church agency. The main point raised from the working group was to seek a stronger national voice in Scotland, especially in relation to the Government. However, though both this major aim and others raised in favour of joining this body, for example, demonstrating in public a greater sense of unity with other Scottish Churches, were laudable aims, Smyth explained that joining ACTS was unlikely to have any major impact on the wider community in an increasingly secular Scotland. At their final meeting the ICRTG concluded, with respect to ACTS, that they were 'unconvinced that progressing towards membership would be effective stewardship of the Union's energies and resources.'[117] Twenty years after the decision not to join the newly-formed ACTS, the position of the Baptist Union to stay outside the membership of this body was confirmed following a discussion at the Baptist Union Assembly on 29 October 2009.[118] However, it was noteworthy that the gracious and respectful tone of the debate on this topic as different points of view were expounded was a significant advance on some of the earlier debates in Scottish Baptist ranks. In the twenty-first century the greater sense of unity amongst the churches represented at assemblies has been seen in the more mature way in which controversial issues were handled.

*Other Baptist Churches and Organisations*

The priority given to relationships with the wider Baptist family often do depend on the connections of individual leaders within the Baptist Union of Scotland, but there is no doubt that Scottish Baptists are firmly committed to maintaining and where possible strengthening these relationships.[119] The Union sent out to its member churches a document expressing its commitment to the wider Baptist bodies in 2014 setting out the extent of its partnership arrangements. Some of these arrangements include: First of all, the Convenor, General Director and the Mission and Ministry Advisor meeting twice yearly with their counterparts in the Fellowship of Baptists in

---

[117] Rebeca Morison & Andrew Rollinson, on behalf of the working group, 'Inter-Church Relations Task Group', *Scottish Baptist Yearbook 2010*, pp. 199–200. The author of this book was a member of the ICRTG.

[118] 'Assembly Minutes: 2009', 29 October 2010, *Assembly Handbook 2010*, p. 17.

[119] The majority of information in this paragraph comes from the BUS document 'Commitment to Wider Baptist Engagement (May 2014)'.

Britain and Ireland. This change of name for the Fellowship of British Baptists in 2011 into the Fellowship of Baptists in Britain and Ireland (FBBI) came about because of the addition of the Irish Baptist Networks to its ranks. Secondly, under the auspices of the FBBI a body called the Mission Community meets twice yearly with twenty-four mission portfolio personnel from the member bodies. From the BUS there are three participants, the General Director, the Mission Development Coordinator and the Mission Initiative Group Chairperson. The other task-group under FBBI auspices launched in 2011 was the Mission Forum, a body that brought together representatives of the member bodies of the FBBI, the Baptist colleges and BUGB Associations, to share existing resources and creatively explore new ones. Also, the Union has continued a long-standing arrangement of having representatives on the BMS Council of Reference. It currently has five members on this body.[120] In Europe the General Director and one other delegate, currently Mark Morris, minister of Dennistoun Baptist Church, Glasgow, attend the annual European Baptist Federation Council and the BUS has committed to an annual gift of £6,400 to its work. Marion Carson is the secretary of the EBF Anti-trafficking Working Group and in 2014 Margaret Brown was secretary of the European Baptist Women's Union. A number of Scottish Baptists have had ties with the Arab Baptist Theological Seminary (ABTS) in Beirut. Jim Purves, Mission and Ministry Advisor, for example, has had opportunities to teach classes in the seminary.[121] The March 2019 BUS Council heard a report on possible closer ties with ABTS in the future, and the General Director Alan Donaldson visited ABTS in June 2019 with a view to giving further consideration to this matter.[122] The International Baptist Seminary formerly in Prague, now in Amsterdam, has also received small financial gifts and the participation of a number of Scottish Baptist scholars as tutors to post-graduate students. Derek Murray, Jim Purves and Marion Carson have served in this capacity. The Baptist World Alliance is the international body of the world Baptist family. The General Director has been committed to attending at least the five-yearly annual congress where he has been accompanied by his spouse. The Youth development Coordinator has also attended the five-yearly Youth Congress. The Baptist Union gives an annual gift of £4,000 to BWA. In the last decade a number of Scottish Baptists have served on BWA bodies, in addition to the Union General Director. Brian Talbot has served on the Religious Freedom Commission and the Heritage and Identity Commission and is the chair of this body for the

---

[120] Jacqueline Primrose, 'Convener Report', *Assembly Handbook*, 2011, p. 20. See also the BUS Council Report, 31 January, 2012, in *Come Home Again: Participating in the mission of God, Baptist Assembly in Scotland, 24–27 October 2012*, Dundee, p. 9.

[121] Jim Purves, 'Resurrection', *Connect*, April 2018, p. 2.

[122] Baptist Union of Scotland, Council Digest, 5–6 March, 2019, p. 2.

current quinquennium to 2020. Marion Carson serves on the Commission on Social and Economic Justice; Jim Purves was appointed as Vice Chair of the Commission on Ministry and Stephen Holmes as a correspondent to the Commission on Doctrine and Christian Unity.[123] The commitment to relations with the wider Baptist family is strong and in the 150th anniversary year of the Union, it is fitting that in September 2019 the EBF Council will meet in Cumbernauld, Scotland, and Baptist leaders from a variety of countries will preach in Scottish Baptist churches during their time in the country.

Scottish Baptists have served in recent years with an increasingly wide range of mission agencies as was indicated in the previous chapter. It is both recognition of the diversity of the world Church, together with an acknowledgement of the growing number of partnerships between Churches and individual mission workers from an increasing number of countries. This diversity was clearly in evidence at the 2 to 6 June 2019 Edinburgh 2010 World Mission Conference where it is probable that to date it was the most diverse and representative gathering of Christians held in one location.[124] The largest of the four 2010 mission conferences building on its 1910 predecessor, was The Third Lausanne Congress on World Evangelisation held in Cape Town, South Africa. There more than 4,000 participants from 198 countries participated in its proceedings.[125] The Baptist Union Council welcomed the decision to hold a centenary conference in Edinburgh during 2010 to celebrate the impact of the 1910 gathering in that same city.[126] Due to the world financial crisis at that time the size of the event and number of delegates was greatly reduced. In the end there were almost 300 delegates, from more than

---

[123] Ruth Donaldson, 'Baptist World Alliance', *Mind the Gap: Baptist Assembly in Scotland, 29–30 October 2015*, Motherwell, p. 18.

[124] As stated at this event by Vinoth Ramachandra, a Sri Lankan leader of the International Fellowship of Evangelical Students, recorded in Brian Talbot, 'Edinburgh 2010 Reflections on the Conference', a paper prepared for SCOT following the conference. The context for this conference is given in David A. Kerr & Kenneth R. Ross (eds), *Edinburgh 2010 Mission Then and Now* (Oxford: Regnum Books, 2009). The major papers prepared for the conference are found in Daryl Balia & Kirsteen Kim (eds), *Edinburgh 2010 Volume II Witnessing to Christ Today* (Oxford: Regnum Books, 2010).

[125] The proceedings of this conference are given in J.E.M. Cameron (ed.), *Christ Our Reconciler Gospel/Church/World* (Nottingham: IVP, 2012). The document prepared for churches following its meetings is Rose Dowsett (ed.), *The Cape Town Commitment: A Confession of Faith and A Call to Action* (Peabody, Massachusetts: Hendrickson Publishers, 2012).

[126] 'Edinburgh 2010', Digest of Council Minutes, January 2008, *Scottish Baptist Yearbook 2009*, p. 90.

sixty countries and over eighty churches or denominations. Delegates came from all the big families of churches: Anglican, Baptist, Roman Catholic, Evangelical, Lutheran, Orthodox, Pentecostal, Presbyterian, Reformed and from new churches in Asia, Africa and South America. Support in Scotland came from the Churches affiliated to ACTS, the Evangelical Alliance, the Free Church of Scotland and the BUS.[127] In addition to BMS representation, there were seventeen other Baptist participants that included from other European countries Christoph Haus from Germany, Malkhaz Songulashvili from the Republic of Georgia and Darrell Jackson from BUGB; and from Scotland, Brian Stanley, Professor of World Christianity at Edinburgh University who was one of the conference leaders and Brian Talbot, as a member of the SCOT working group.[128] It was remarkable to see the ethnic and geographical diversity represented in 2010 compared to its predecessor conference in 1910.[129] From a Christian perspective the growth of the truly world Church between 1910 and 2010 was remarkably encouraging.

The primary mission agency that continues to receive the highest level of support from Scottish Baptists is the BMS. An exciting new development in 2008 was the conclusion of negotiations with the Chinese Government that resulted in the decision to recommence work in that country. These talks had begun at the invitation of the Chinese Government. BMS viewed this approach as a right time to reconsider work opportunities in that country, the first time since previous efforts had been closed down in 1952. In terms of their wider work: BMS have four key mission centres around the world in Kolkata, India, Pretoria, South Africa, Guayaquil, Ecuador and Sao Paulo in Brazil. New developments in technology had allowed this mission agency's website in 2008 to include new channels for communication with supporting churches on many aspects of BMS work. Another new development that year was the launch of the Graduate intern programme. The significance of this step was seen in the fact that one third of people serving overseas on mission teams were graduates who wanted to gain experience of working abroad in a mission context.[130] Another aspect of the changing mission scene is the

---

[127] Stephen Smyth, 'Report to ACTS, SCOT and the National Ecumenical Instruments', June 2010.

[128] Brian Talbot, minister of Broughty Ferry Baptist Church, was deputising for the General Director of the Baptist Union Bill Slack on the SCOT working group, a body of nine people representing the Scottish Churches supporting the conference, who worked with the Edinburgh 2010 staff in preparing for and organising this event. See Bill Slack 'Edinburgh 2010' report in *DNA of Discipleship: Assembly Handbook 2008*, 31 October to 1 November 2008, Glasgow, pp. 92–93.

[129] The official history of the 1910 conference is Brian Stanley, *The World Missionary Conference, Edinburgh 1910* (Grand Rapids: Eerdmans, 2009).

[130] Derek Clark, BMS Report', *DNA of Discipleship: Assembly Handbook 2008*, 31 October to 1 November 2008, Glasgow, p. 14.

increasing depths of partnerships with indigenous Christians in areas of the world where BMS is working, making the work on the ground less reliant on international workers. The best known of these initiatives is with Benjamin Francis and his remarkable team of church-planters in India. In 2018, 45,000 people professed faith in Christ through their work, of which 8,000 went on to attend training sessions on how to spread the Christian faith. Despite intimidation, persecution and even the murder of some mission workers, the work has continued in Indian states like Odisha (formerly called Orissa), where more than forty church-planters have taken the gospel to over 1,600 villages in the last few years.[131] However, there are still many British Baptists serving at home and overseas under the auspices of this mission agency in the twenty-first century. Scottish Baptists contribute a significant proportion of the total BMS staff. In the UK office in 2009, for example, Alastair Clunie was the Marketing manager; Mark Craig, the Director for Communications; Malcolm Currie, intern designer; Gordon McBain Regional Secretary for the Middle East and North Africa; David McLellan, Manager for Mission Partnerships and acting Director for Mission and Lynne Weir Production Co-ordinator. In terms of the overseas personnel that year – Lynne Brown and Fiona Welsh were serving in Angola; Chris and Debbie in Afghanistan; Philip and Rosemary Halliday in France; Grant and Geraldine in Tunisia; David and Ann Macfarlane in Italy; Graham and Mhairi McBain and Jill Morrow in Albania; Graeme and Jenny Riddell in Uganda; Steve and Jane Williams in Cyprus; Eileen McNeill was in training that autumn at the BMS International Mission Centre in Birmingham; Shelly Stewart was a member of the Sao Paulo Action Team in Brazil and Louise Edwards on the Action Team in Delhi, India. The continuing commitment of Scottish Baptists to BMS in the twenty-first century remains strong.

The decade 2009 to 2019 has been a remarkable period of considerable change both in the Baptist Union of Scotland and the wider life of the nation in Scotland. It has undoubtedly been a time of serious challenges for many Scottish churches facing financial shortfalls and numerical decline, as well as increasing divergence in doctrinal convictions and agreed moral convictions over issues such as marriage. Scottish Baptists have maintained their conservative theological doctrinal standards as well as a clear commitment to historic Christian lifestyle choices. There is no doubt that some smaller churches struggled to cope with the necessity of change to minister effectively in the twentieth-first century and took a decision to close. However, other congregations have flourished and a number of new churches have been planted in this decade. A final unexpected change in its ranks came at the extra BUS Council meeting in Perth on Thursday 9 May 2019 when Alan Donaldson the General Director gave notice of concluding his term of office

---

[131] David Dunham. 'The Power of Your Own Story: Helping people in India come to faith . . .', *Engage: The Magazine of BMS World Mission* (Issue 44, 2019), pp. 14–15.

later in the year. This decision resulted in a search committee being appointed to find a successor for this post.[132] On Thursday 27 June 2019 this small group unanimously presented to Council a candidate for consideration for this post, Martin Hodson, the current Ministry Development Coordinator for the Baptist Union. Council members unanimously elected Martin Hodson to serve as the next General Director.[133] In the autumn of 2019 a new chapter in the Union's history will begin with a new national leader in post as the journey of faith continues for this family of churches in Scotland.

---

[132] Minutes of the 'Extra Council Meeting – Thursday 9 May, 2019'.

[133] 'Baptist Union of Scotland General Director Appointed', press release issued by the Baptist Union of Scotland, 27 June 2019.

CHAPTER 12

# Conclusions

The formation of the Baptist Union of Scotland in October 1869 was the fourth attempt at founding a national body to enable Scottish Baptists to worship, work and witness together in Scotland. It was not a forgone conclusion that this Union would succeed when the previous three bodies had failed to attract and retain a sufficient proportion of Baptist congregations in Scotland to their ranks. The first attempts to unite Scottish Baptists in 1827 had appeared to be very successful with the merger of the three home mission agencies to form the Baptist Home Missionary Society for Scotland and the formation of the first Baptist Union of Scotland with the affiliation of many of Scottish Baptist churches at that time. However, unwillingness to compromise over differences in some theological convictions and church practices ensured that by the 1850s there had been greater disharmony between the churches than in the 1820s. It took the careful and strategic relationship building skills of key Baptist leaders in the 1850s and 1860s to persuade their colleagues that they had so much more in common than the smaller number of issues that divided them. Their determined efforts paid off with the commitment of fifty-one out of 101 churches to launch the current Baptist Union of Scotland in 1869.

The new Baptist Union was committed to retaining a conservative Evangelical doctrinal foundation, but it was primarily task-orientated, focussing on a commitment to home evangelisation and church planting; to build ties of friendship between Scottish Baptists; to theological education, in particular the training of young men for pastoral ministry in their churches and to support the smaller congregations. It also had a model to follow in the London Baptist Association, founded in 1865, that had overcome similar challenges in its ranks. It is very clear that this time around Scottish Baptists were convinced of the case for uniting to work together to attain common objectives. Within three years, the number of affiliated causes had risen to sixty, and by 1879 eighty-three out of the then ninety-two congregations, 90% of the total, were supportive of the Baptist Union.[1] There was a major focus on urban evangelism at a time of rapid growth in population in many areas of

---

[1] 'Appendix 4.2 'The Proportion of Churches Affiliated to the Scottish Baptist Association or the Baptist Union of Scotland, 1827–1879', in Talbot, *Search for a Common Identity*, p. 357.

central Scotland. Four new congregations began in the early 1870s as a result of these efforts. In 1874, for example, the shoots of new life that were springing up all over the country had resulted in net growth that year of an average of eleven new members per congregation, in excess of 780 baptized believers and five newly affiliated churches to the Union. In addition, to their cottage and home meetings, the sixty-eight member churches had an additional 130 preaching stations. Sunday Schools previously run by only twenty-eight congregations had risen to sixty-eight and Bible classes were also reported in forty-seven churches. Within a decade of committing to work together, the level of increased activity in affiliated causes has led to a flourishing of their work in many areas of Scotland. However, that was not the whole story because twenty-three congregations, primarily due to difficult economic circumstances, were declining in numbers. Local circumstances were highly significant in the prosperity or adversity experienced by congregations. It was, though, a remarkably successful first decade of collaborative efforts.

In the second decade of Union life to 1889 it was a picture overall of further advancement with an increase of eight more congregations in fellowship with the Baptist Union of Scotland, up to eighty-nine in 1889. Baptismal statistics also remained high with 795 baptisms in affiliated causes that year. Over these ten years an additional 3,034 members were added to the churches and 3,058 more children regularly attended their Sunday Schools. There were now eighty Sunday Schools and fifty-five Bible classes operating under their auspices. Yet despite the level of overall growth, thirty-one congregations affiliated to the Baptist Union saw a decline in numbers attending in the 1880s. However, there were a remarkable thirty-eight additional churches in fellowship with the Union within the first twenty years of its commencement, of which thirty-one had been planted under the auspices of its member bodies. The intense efforts at home did not lead to a diminution of support for evangelistic efforts overseas. In line with other Scottish Protestant Churches at that time, missionary efforts were also flourishing with high expectations of further growth in the last decade of the nineteenth century. There was also a marked increase in social concern at that time with a number of Scottish Baptists prominent in work to alleviate the suffering of men, women and children, particularly in the larger cities of Scotland. The Temperance cause was also attracting significant support in Scottish Churches and as in the previous forty years, there were people affiliated to Baptist congregations that were prominent in advocating its concerns. It was clear that the years 1869 to 1889 were a time to advance for Scottish Baptists.

Over the next two decades to the First World War the overall outlook was very encouraging, though as before not all the churches were seeing numerical increases and an expansion of their work. However, the headline figures were showing significant growth. At the October 1913 Annual Assembly it was reported that the number of affiliated churches had gone up from ninety-two in 1890 to 137 in 1913. Total membership in the churches had risen from 11,846 to 20,527 and admissions by baptism that year as high as 1,073, a rise from 908 in 1890. Yet a surprisingly high number of congregations had declined in numbers, fifty-six, compared to fifty-eight that had seen increases in 1913. Sunday Schools had also increased from 152 in 1908 to 160 in 1913 and Bible classes increase from seventy-four to eighty-seven. Once again economic factors had made a significant contribution in determining whether the churches were apparently prospering or struggling to endure times of adversity. However, the overall picture painted in this era appeared to be one of further growth with expectations that it would continue in future years.

A key factor in consolidating growth and assisting with expansion of the work of Baptist churches in Scotland at this time was the formation of regional associations. Their formation brought churches in particular regions of the country closer together and enabled better use of their resources to engage in evangelistic efforts or look to plant new congregations. Times of economic adversity in some places enabled churches that had been opposed to joining a regional association recognise their need for assistance and enabled them to recast their vision about co-operative work amongst Baptist churches. It was also an era that experienced growth in women's work under the inspiring leadership of Jessie Yuille, wife of the General Secretary of the Union George Yuille. In its first year of operations the WA formed eighteen local branches, with twenty-eight affiliated groups by October 1912 and sixty by 1920. The WA workers engaged in home visitation and literature drops for their local churches and obtained the funding to erect 'the Pearl Hut' at Lerwick, in order to assist Miss Jane Henderson, the Deaconess in Stirling Baptist Church, in her work amongst the Fisher Girls. The WA was also prominent in raising funds in response to the appeal for financial assistance for the newly created Settlement and Sustentation Fund of the Union in 1914. They had raised £12,500 out of the £52,000 given for this project by 1920. It was clear that the profile of women in the Baptist Union had been significantly enhanced by these efforts in the decades leading up to 1914.

There had also been significant encouragement in children's and youth work in Scottish Baptist churches at that time. In 1889 eighty-two of the ninety-two churches in the Union had Sunday Schools. However, by 1914 there were 162 Sunday Schools operated by affiliated churches with 2,778 teachers and 19,838 enrolled children. But there was a pattern emerging in the early years of the twentieth century of churches struggling to retain the interest of young adults of fifteen years and older. It was a common feature in many congregations across the Christian Churches in Scotland in the later nineteenth and early twentieth centuries. As a result a range of new organisations were formed during these years. Some Baptist Churches formed Young Worshipper Leagues, an organisation that aimed to attract mainly existing church attenders and strengthen the ties between them as well as helping them grow in their faith. The best-known Christian youth organisation focussed on discipleship training was Christian Endeavour (CE). Many Scottish Baptist congregations joined other Protestant Evangelicals in forming branches of CE. The first continuing branch of CE was formed at Crown Terrace Baptist Church in Aberdeen in 1891. A number of churches reported significantly higher retention rates of their senior young people as a result of CE activity in their local congregation. By autumn 1905 sixty-four Baptist churches operated CE societies comprising 3,630 individuals in sixty-three senior and twenty-two junior branches. Young people very committed to CE were also highly likely to consider becoming church members. However, the problem was that a greater number of young people associated with the churches did not want to commit to joining a CE group. One of the national figures who sought to address this issue was William Smith, the founder of Boys' Brigade. His remit was specifically to engage with older working-class boys in Sunday Schools. He envisaged an organisation with 'Drill and Discipline', but combined with games, gymnastics and other sports as well as hymns and prayers. A key centre for this work was Glasgow where, by 1885, twelve of the first fifteen Boys' Brigade Companies were formed. The other three were located in Edinburgh. A number of Baptist congregations had Boys' Brigade Companies, but others were suspicious of 'the warlike spirit' it appeared to promote. As a result, in proportion to numbers, Scottish Baptists were less enthusiastic than their English counterparts in hosting Boys' Brigade organisations. Yet it was clear that Scottish Baptists, like other Scottish Christians were committed to finding innovative ways of promoting their faith to children in the years leading up to World War One.

Temperance work had been strong in many Baptist congregations in the second half of the nineteenth century, especially towards the end of that century and as a result the vast majority of Baptist churches in Scotland had changed the wine served at communion to a non-alcoholic product and most ministers in Scottish Baptist affiliated churches had declared themselves teetotal. As a result of the apparent success of this work, there was a discernible shift by 1870 to focus primarily on educating the young people in newly formed organisations like Bands of Hope. A Scottish Baptist Total Abstinence Society was formed in 1881, at a time when there were only a small number of Bands of Hope in existence in Scotland. However, there were 700 branches across the Scottish Churches by 1908, with seventy-five Baptist congregations hosting one. The catalyst for this work amongst many of the churches was seeing the devastation in family homes caused by excessive alcohol consumption by a parent or the parents. Addressing the underlying causes of poverty became a much greater priority for Scottish Churches towards the end of the nineteenth century, alongside other measures, Temperance work contributed significantly to improving the lives of many impoverished families at that time.

Another major step forward in Scottish Baptist ranks in the decades prior to World War one was in theological education. There had been a significant lack of consistency in the quality of theological education provided for ministerial students by the Baptist Union, but it had been very difficult to reach a consensus about how to address this issue. A group of prominent Scottish Baptist individuals decided that too much time had been spent trying to resolve differences over theological education and committed themselves to funding a new theological institution, the Baptist Theological College of Scotland, which was formed in 1894. There was a great deal of discussion over who should be appointed as tutors and it is clear with hindsight that some unwise decisions were taken by the college founders, which allowed negative feelings about its work to be retained in some churches and led to future conflicts in the twentieth century. However, it is also important to note that some of the individuals who were critical of the college could also have been more conciliatory in their contribution to this debate. It is ironic, though, that after half a century of seeking the formation of a Baptist College that there were two in operation during these years. The second one was located in Dunoon and founded by the minister of that church, Duncan Macgregor in 1893. It closed after his death in 1915. There is no doubt that at the start of the twentieth century that theological education was a much greater priority for many Scottish Baptists leaders than it had been in earlier years.

Scottish Baptists, like counterparts in other Churches in Scotland, had a growing sense of unity with fellow believers of the same theological convictions and through literature and by ministers emigrating to work in other countries built increasingly close ties with one another. For the Baptist Union of Scotland this was seen first in greater engagement with fellow British and Irish Baptists, then with colleagues in countries in the wider British Empire and in Europe; and then in 1905 through the formation of the Baptist World Alliance with the wider Baptist family in other parts of the world. There were also closer ties with other Churches, especially for mission work and conferences like the World Missionary Conference in Edinburgh in 1910. It must be acknowledged that better communications and easier transport links had made possible this greater engagement with the wider Baptist bodies and other branches of the World Christian family. Scottish Baptists had been branching out with confidence in the later years of the nineteenth century and in the earlier years of the next one. It may have been overshadowed latterly by the growing threat of a major European war, but Scottish Baptists retained their focus and priorities and reaped the rewards of that dedication.

There is no doubt that World War One cast a shadow over Europe in the second decade of the twentieth century and changed forever the social context in which the churches sought to proclaim the Christian faith to their fellow citizens. In line with other Christian Churches in Scotland, Baptists spoke in measured tones about the possibility of war and with sincere regret about its inevitability at the time it was declared. There was, in fact, more concern amongst the Churches about possible troubles in the north of Ireland in July

2014 than events in Continental Europe. Scottish church leaders had very close ties with German counterparts in the early twentieth century and had real difficulties in contemplating that their respective countries might soon be at war. In time, there was a reluctant acceptance that German actions, especially in Belgium, had required a military response, but it was with a heavy heart, far from the triumphalism of a minority in the various European countries. Many people were well aware that this conflict would exact a heavy price before any possible resolution was possible.

Once the war began, Christian in Scotland gave the war effort their full support with a remarkably high proportion of 'sons of the manse' in Presbyterian Churches volunteering to serve in the early years. Scottish Baptists also, in proportion to their smaller numbers, signed up in significant numbers, although Baptists across the United Kingdom expressed deep disappointment at the necessity of conscription when it was introduced in 1916. They were naturally concerned about the potential implications for conscientious objectors, although on this occasion few could see why others might take issue with this particular war. With hindsight, it is clear to see that the era of the distinctive 'Nonconformist Conscience' in British society had passed as Baptists along with other Nonconformists now wished to play a greater role in the wider society, including serving as chaplains in the Armed Forces. The presence of some of their own members at the highest ranks of the Government during the war made this an easier transition than might otherwise have been the case. There were many ministers, like Walter Mursell of Thomas Coats Memorial Church, Paisley, who by their public sermons and private instruction tried to make sense of the war for their congregations, but it was a difficult task. It is abundantly clear that the traumas experienced at The Front both for active service personnel and for the many volunteers working for support agencies like the YMCA would impact their lives for many years to come. Scotland, and indeed the whole United Kingdom, had been deeply affected by the traumatic events of World War One. It was not only Governments with social reforms that needed to take account of the sacrifices of ordinary men and women, but the Churches too had to acknowledge that its mission in coming years must take into account what had been experienced through the war. Some aspects of the necessary changes in society were easier to accept than others, such as a greater acknowledgement of the rights of women and the welfare of children and the need for a better quality of social housing. However, for Scottish Baptists and the other Churches in the country, proclaiming the unchanging Christian gospel and providing a welcoming place in their midst for former service personnel who had endured so much during the war would be a sufficient challenge to address in the post-war years.

The collective work of the churches through the Baptist Union had enabled congregations that had been particularly hard-hit by the war to receive financial grants to aid their continuing witness. In November 1918, for example, there were twenty-five congregations receiving this support. R.E Glendening, in his Presidential address in October 1918, drew attention to the changes in British society that had to be acknowledged, but also highlighted the support of Empire countries for the war effort and declared that a new relationship with these nations would have to be negotiated in the future. Their sacrifices too had to be acknowledged. He challenged Baptists alongside other Scottish Christians to live consistently in the light of our convictions. There was an unspoken recognition that too often the Churches had focussed on the concerns of the middle classes and allowed secular socialist political organisations to fill the gap in articulating the concerns of the working classes. William Adamson, a member of Dunfermline West Baptist Church, later the first Labour Secretary of State for Scotland, challenged the 1919 Annual Assembly that labour was no longer content to acquiesce in the system by which industry is conducted for the benefit of the few and which involved the servitude and exploitation of the mass of the people. It was a prophetic warning about the social and political changes that would inevitably take place in the 1920s onwards. Although, with relatively small numbers Scottish Baptists had only limited influence on the wider society, but they were aware of and willing to adjust to some of these changes, more so than some of the larger Presbyterian denominations in the 1920s. The latter bodies understandably had given a significant amount of their time to the union efforts amongst Presbyterians that concluded in the reunion of the majority of Presbyterians in the reformed Church of Scotland in 1929.

At the Jubilee Assembly in October 1919 there was quiet satisfaction at the progress of Scottish Baptists over the first fifty years of Union life. In 1869 there had been fifty-one churches with 3,688 members. Now there were 140 churches with 21,346 members. There were no grounds for complacency because although fifty churches had increased their membership that year, sixty-four others had seen numerical decline. Sunday School numbers had held up well over the war years, unlike Bible class attendances which had seen a significant decline, although there was a modest upturn after the war. George Yuille, the retiring General Secretary of the Baptist Union, was pleased to announce the formation of the Ministers' Provident Fund to provide for ministers and their spouses in retirement in 1919. He also took great satisfaction in noting that the struggles between 'the ideal and the practical' in ministerial education in Scottish Baptist ranks had been concluded, with clarity on the way forward. It has been most encouraging to note that through the work of the Evangelistic and Church-Extension Committee of the Union twenty new causes had been planted over the previous fifty years and sixty others through other Scottish Baptist initiatives. Sunday Schools in that time had increased from only seventy-eight in 1869 to 156 in 1919 and from 8,000 to over 18,000 children in attendance. In addition, ninety-six church building has been erected in only half a century. Interest in and support for overseas mission had also increased during these years. After thirty-nine years as Union Secretary, and ably supported by his wife Jessie for the last twenty-five years, it was a well-earned retirement for George Yuille.

The most significant growth over these years for Scottish Baptists had taken place in Glasgow and the West of Scotland where the fourteen churches in 1869 had become fifty-three. In the city of Glasgow alone, by the start of World War One, twenty-seven churches had been constituted, establishing a presence in most areas of the city, together with five missions operating in the poorest working-class neighbourhoods. Unfortunately, the loss of so many gifted younger people during the war did slow down advances in the post war years. However, as well as further growth through evangelistic work in some existing congregations, other causes were planted in the new suburban areas like Cathcart and Mosspark. Home Mission efforts also continued effectively in the 1920s. Baptist Union Evangelistic Thomas McQuiston had noted that 1926 was one of the most fruitful years in the history of our evangelistic enterprise. In addition, at a time of significant growth, and not decline, the Union and the Home Mission agency entered negotiations to discuss their future partnership in mission in Scotland. The reason for this proposal being discussed was the changing nature of outreach work in Scotland. There were now, for example, many more churches established with settled pastors. The long summer tours traditionally carried out by the Home Mission workers had ceased. Transport and communication links had improved enormously in recent decades. It was rightly seen that the time was right for a new strategy for future Scottish Baptist evangelistic work. A merger between the BHMS and the evangelistic committee of the Union took place in October 1931.

There were high expectations for future outreach work in Scotland in the inter-war years. There was, though, another factor that brought encouragement to Christians on the East coast of Scotland, notably the remarkable revival that began in Lowestoft in Suffolk under the ministry of Douglas Brown, the Minister of London Road Baptist Church, Lowestoft. There in 1921 thousands of young Scots were working in the fishing industry and who travelled with the fleet around the eastern side of the country gutting, pickling and barrel packing herring. Economic conditions in this industry were extremely difficult at that time, but it is important to note that this was not a primary catalyst on this occasion. A much more significant factor was the presence of different preachers, like Jock Troop, in East coast communities who had knowledge of past religious revivals together with expectancy for future awakenings in the communities they served. In places like Hopeman, Wick, Fraserburgh, Peterhead, Anstruther and Pittenweem there were many professions of faith during the revivals and Baptist churches were amongst those that grew numerically as a result. There were some inland churches that also were touched by this awakening in the 1920s, but it was primarily contained within communities linked to the fishing industry.

However, the churches that were impacted during this revival were greatly strengthened in their witness.

In the Inter-War years there was significant rebuilding work after the interruptions in 1914 to 1918. Ties with other European Baptists were strengthened as were those on the overseas mission fields. However, major social and political changes in the two main mission fields in China and India resulted in the reduction of activities of many Christian mission organisations, in part due to rising financial costs, but also as a result of rising nationalist influences in those countries, which ensured that after the 1920s British mission agencies would significantly reduce the numbers of serving staff overseas. BMS, for example had employed 311 workers overseas in 1900 to 1901. Numbers rose to 515 in 1921 to 1922, but were reduced to 397 by 1932 to 1933. It was also clear that the diversification of mission efforts in the late nineteenth century had multiplied further in the next century, with an even greater number of faith missions seeking the support of the Christian Churches in Scotland. In 1925 it is probable that there were in excess of 260 Scottish Baptists serving as missionaries overseas with eighty-nine serving with either BMS or the China Inland Mission, the two most popular agencies, together with a further 119 identified individuals serving with a large number of smaller missions. The surviving data on overseas missionary service is extremely limited so it is not impossible that the figures given here may need to be revised upwards again in the future.

Inter-Church relations in these decades were stronger than they had been in the previous half-century with Scottish Baptists willing to join the Scottish Churches Council formed in 1924. Ecumenical relations, often linked with support for overseas mission work, were harmonious in the Inter-War years. Scottish Baptists were fully supportive of the Temperance referendum campaigns in the post-war years and were disappointed by their failure to make greater progress towards prohibition in the 1920s. It is noteworthy that the levels of support they attained were as high as some Governments have won at General Elections in the twentieth century, but a combination of opposition from the Upper classes and the poorer working classes, together with substantial funding for campaigning from the Drinks industry, ensured that they faced an almost impossible task at the outset. Scottish Baptists, overall, had navigated confidently through the Inter-War years, but the increasing shadow of another European war in the late 1930s dampened their spirits like those of the rest of their fellow citizens.

Scottish Baptists, in line with other Christian Churches, took a very cautious line in support of the war effort in 1939. They recognised that every possible step had been taken to avoid this becoming a reality, but acknowledged that the ultimate sacrifice needed to be paid to free Europe from a tyrannical regime. In the 1930s there were a number of Scottish Baptists who joined other British Baptists in the Baptist Pacifist Fellowship, and that organisation's numbers had continued to rise up to the end of 1942, though the detailed statistics were not released during the war years. However, it is known that in 1937 there were up to 448 Baptist ministers and lay-people formally associated with the Pacifist Fellowship. The majority of Scottish Baptists, though, consistently supported the war effort against the Nazi regime, emphasising in their sermons that the battle was not ordinary British citizens against the German people. The mistake of bearing ill-will towards all German people in the later years of the First World War, they said, must not be repeated. However, even the measured tones expressed by ministers did not please all of their congregations, with a few individuals leaving the churches because of their opposition to any apparent political statements from the pulpits. The vast majority of the Scottish people consistently recognised the rightness of this war effort and the Churches' message during those years largely resonated with similar voices in the wider community.

Evangelistic campaigns run by Scottish Baptists during the war years promoted a clear message that individuals needed to turn to God as well as overcome evil. There was a determination to seize all the opportunities available to promote the Christian faith in non-religious settings as well as in church services. There were noticeably more 'youth services' and 'women's services' as well as an increased number of evening services in some locations. In others, attendances at church prayer meetings notably increased during the early 1940s. Open air meetings were a common sight at that time, though as the war progressed and some members were conscripted for service overseas, together with the requisitioning of buildings and the transfer of other members to work in England it became more difficult to continue this work. Good relations between Scottish Churches were a greater priority in the 1940s and it is clear that Scottish Baptists felt very secure in their place amongst the Churches in the middle of the twentieth century. There were common calls for further social and political changes required in Scottish society in the post-war years and recognition that there was a growing proportion of the population that had no connection with any of the Churches. There was a struggle for spiritual values taking place and the various Churches all acknowledged that building ties with those unconnected with the faith would be increasingly difficult in the second half of the century.

It was a relief when the war-time restrictions were lifted, but it would take some time before regular patterns of church life were established and returning members reintegrated into their local communities. There were also some welcome changes taking place at that time. The BBC launched a new Scottish home service and Melville Dinwiddie, the BBC's Scottish regional director stated that a weekly Christian service would be one of the highlights of the new schedule. It was evident to Baptists and other Scottish Christians that it would be much harder work either retaining or establishing connections with an increasing proportion of the Scottish population in the post war years. There had also been a decline in the number of candidates offering to train for Baptist ministry and overall membership figures had begun to diminish. From a highpoint of 21,310 affiliated church members in 1935 it had sunk to 21,121 in 1945. It was no surprise to see this trend because the fall in the number of baptisms conducted had fallen sharply from 1,444 in 1922 to 570 per annum in 1939 and only 519 in 1945. The extent of the challenge facing Scottish Baptists could not be underestimated, but they together with other Scottish Christians in the post-war years faced up to it with great enthusiasm and commitment.

There were a series of new ventures launched to overcome the lack of younger adults in the churches. There was a greater emphasis on youth fellowships being run for the benefit of those already within the church families. Another initiative that happened in many major urban centres in Scotland was the formation of 'Open Doors' youth project launched by the Church of Scotland Presbytery of Glasgow in the winter of 1945–1946. Attendances at the chosen venue exceeded over 1,000 per night in the 1946–1947 year with hundreds turned away for lack of space to accommodate them. By the autumn of 1947 this initiative spread across the country, although financial challenges led to the cessation of this venture in November 1948. In Scottish Baptist ranks youth rallies became a major feature of the lives of many of its younger members. They began at Adelaide Place Baptist Church in Glasgow as a follow-up to the All Scotland Billy Graham Crusade in the city. Glasgow Baptist Association ran the first two events in 1955, and a special committee was formed to take over for future events. Donald McCallum who became Convenor of the Young People's Committee of the Baptist Union in 1959 organised rallies in Stirling and then in other parts of the country that were a great success.

It must be acknowledged, though, that the growing absence of young people from churches, especially teenage boys had been a significant issue since the 1940s. The total numbers attending Sunday Schools in Scotland had fallen from 51% of children in 1911 to 30.8% in 1945, a fall of over 121,000 between 1938 and 1941 alone. Concerted efforts to turn this around by the churches in the 1950s did have some success as a new highpoint of 35% attendance, 325,000 children, was attained in 1956. It has been commonly understood that church and Sunday School attendances had continued relatively high to the 1950s and then started to fall dramatically from 1960 onwards. This would not be a fair reflection of the evidence. In the decade from 1949 to 1959, for example, attendances at Christian youth organisations like Christian Endeavour or Boys' Brigade had fallen significantly, although undoubtedly these organisations did allow churches to keep in touch with some families who had either stopped or never begun to attend Sunday worship services. It is also likely that the failure of the larger Presbyterian Churches to prune their membership rolls of non-attending members in the 1950s made the dramatic reductions of the 1960s seem much greater than they were in practice. Scottish Baptists although seeing some decline had more carefully pruned their rolls and so were a much better guide to what was actually happening on the ground in those years.

Home evangelistic efforts were as vigorous in the 1950s as in any previous decade in the twentieth century. Major interdenominational agencies like the Faith Mission and the Scottish branch of the Worldwide Evangelism Crusade had record numbers of people in training or engaged in other forms of evangelism. The Scottish Evangelistic Council and the Scottish Colportage Society focussed on door-to-door outreach visiting over 40,000 homes in 1958 alone and between 1930 and 1960 had visited over one million homes in Scotland. However, the majority of outreach activities were run by the different networks of Churches. Walter Main, chair of the Baptist Union Evangelism Committee, was a key leader in Baptist outreach ventures, but there was also great creativity used in the planning and execution of various initiatives by local churches. The *Tell Scotland* movement, led by Tom Allan and D.P. Thomson, two Church of Scotland ministers, was the most prominent outreach agency in the post-war years. It sought to build on the BBC Scotland Radio Missions of 1950 and 1952 and engaged in varied forms of local mission in communities across the land. Many of the meetings they organised took place in secular venues like cinemas or schools and hospitals, together with others in various leisure facilities that included greyhound tracks, though *Tell Scotland* was best known for inviting Billy Graham to come to Scotland for his 1955 Crusade. It was a remarkable series of meetings over three months with over two million people attending one of the meetings and over thirty million listening to his Good Friday sermon broadcast live on the BBC – the first live service broadcast on national television. There is an ongoing debate as to how successful these services were over the longer term, but in the short term the Christian Church was centre-stage in national life

It is probable, though, that church-extension initiatives on the ground had a greater long-term impact. Scottish Baptists made a real effort to start new congregations in new towns like Glenrothes and East Kilbride and were rewarded with a number of new congregations being planted in those years. In 1959 the first partnership missions with Southern Baptists from the United States began, that would be very fruitful in later years in promoting the Christian faith in Scotland. The post war years with increasing ease of travel led to greater contacts with the wider Baptist family around the world and especially in Europe following the establishment of the European Baptist Federation in 1948. But ties with other Churches through the World Council of Churches were increasingly questioned in the 1950s. Overall, Scottish Baptists were in reasonable heart in 1960 having made significant progress in their work since the ending of the war in 1945.

The 1960s ushered in an era of extraordinary social transformation not only in Western Europe but also in North America and Australasia. There is no doubt that Christian Churches struggled to adjust to these changes in the 1960s and 1970s. Baptismal statistics, whether of infant baptisms or believers' baptism, together with attendance figures and church membership totals all fell quite dramatically in these years. It is with this backdrop that Scottish Baptist witness must be evaluated. In October 1959 while acknowledging the challenges faced, the Union Secretary in his Annual Assembly address expressed real hope for their prospects in the coming decade. The membership total in 1959 was 20,139, a slight fall from the previous year. At the Centenary Assembly in 1969 it was natural to compare the progress made with the comparative year a century earlier. However, over the 1960s there were grounds for encouragement. The total number of churches in fellowship with the Union had risen from 155 to 160. The number of congregations reporting decreases in membership had fallen from eighty to sixty-five in ten years. There were also District Associations whose membership totals had risen, for example, in Lanarkshire and Stirling and Clackmannanshire. It was true that the overall membership total had fallen from 20,139 to 17,547, but there were forty congregations that had experienced growth in attendance and membership figures in 1969. The rate of decline was also smaller than in the larger denominations in Scotland. In the 1970s, the numbers of churches declined from 160 to 157 and overall membership figures from 17,547 to 16,271. The decline was greatest in Glasgow and Edinburgh and some other Central-belt locations. Yet it was not all doom and gloom as membership figures were up in a number of District Association areas, Argyllshire and the Isles, Ayrshire and Dumfriesshire, Dunbartonshire, Lanarkshire, and Northern. At the end of the 1970s there were now sixty-seven churches increasing in membership, a rise of twenty-seven, though sixty-nine were decreasing, compared to sixty-five a decade earlier. These figures indicate that more churches were able to promote their mission work with greater effect than had previously been the case.

Why were there signs of hope in a time referred to by scholars as an age of Religious Crisis? The key for Scottish Baptists was a determination to seize opportunities for new church plants. In the Stirling and Clackmannanshire area, for example, new causes were formed in the new town of Cumbernauld and at Cornton in Stirling. In Lanarkshire, the remarkably successful new work in East Kilbride that began with East Mains led to further church-plants in the districts of Westwood in 1964 and Calderwood in 1966. Hamilton Baptist Church saw significant growth under the ministries of Gordon Heath and Alistair Begg. The growth in these churches compensated for the decline in other Lanarkshire Baptist churches as a result of the closure of coal mines or a reduction in the production capacity in the Steel Industry. In the South-West of the country further growth in Dumfries Baptist Church and new works at Dalbeattie and Wigtown and at Bourtreehill in Irvine were grounds for further encouragement. There were also new churches planted at Bearsden in Dunbartonshire and Alness in the north of Scotland and these and other outreach initiatives demonstrated that decline was not inevitable.

There was a strong focus on training in evangelism in the WIN schools, a methodology brought over from the USA by General Secretary Andrew MacRae. It peaked in intensity in 1975 with courses held that year in Arbroath, Carluke, Cumbernauld, Falkirk and Wishaw. It led to some remarkable growth statistics in participating congregations with nineteen congregations attaining numerical increases of 10% or greater as a result. Unfortunately, the decline in the numbers of children and teenagers attending on Sundays or midweek organisations continued to decline in these decades. The influence of the charismatic renewal movement also helped retain or recruit some younger adults in the new Craigmillar Fellowship in Edinburgh and especially in the Bishopbriggs congregation in Glasgow. It is likely that other churches were revitalised through this renewal movement and in some cases this helped to retain or attract young people.

Relationships with other Baptist bodies in the United Kingdom had been good, but there had been a lower priority placed on meeting with each other in the decades prior to the 1960s. In January 1963 representatives of the three Baptist Unions met together for prayer, following their collaborative efforts in the production of a new hymnbook that had been published the previous year. In 1978 a Joint Consultative Committee was formed of the three British Baptist Unions and the BMS demonstrating a determination to work together more closely in the years that followed. Scottish Baptists had always been committed to the EBF, but had been represented on the governance structures of that body by the larger BUGBI. In 1964 Scottish Baptists were determined to have membership in their own name and succeeded in this endeavour. Andrew MacRae had been determined to give the Scottish Union a higher profile in the EBF and it was clear that he had succeeded. There was also increased though lesser commitment to the work of the BWA with MacRae again an enthusiastic participant and speaker at BWA events. If Baptist ties were greatly strengthened in these decades the same could not be said for ecumenical relations with other churches. Scottish Baptists took increasingly polarised positions for and against membership of both the Scottish Council of Churches and the wider World Council of Churches. Withdrawal from the WCC in 1963 did not change the atmosphere as attention simply turned to affiliation to other ecumenical bodies at home. It was the most disappointing aspect of the collective witness of Scottish Baptists in this era that so much time was taken up with heated debates on this issue.

The question regarding the ministry roles that could be held by women had been an issue over which there had been some differences of opinion. Two women in the early twentieth century had held pastorates, but they had been an exception to the general pattern of exclusively men being considered for local church pastoral ministry. Miss Nellie Allan of Dundee was the first woman to be admitted to the list of accredited Baptist lay-preachers, apparently in 1939, though the minute book of the lay-preachers association only recorded this fact on 28 May 1941. There were some discussions about whether women might be considered eligible for pastoral ministry in the 1960s and 1970s but no changes were considered at that time.

There was a noticeable increase in attention given to the social application of the gospel from the 1960s onwards. In terms of overseas work, Scottish Baptists had been very active in support of Christian Aid, but there were concerns that it and some other well-established aid organisations were beginning to forget the importance of evangelistic efforts alongside their relief and development work. As a result, they increasingly turned to support the more overtly Evangelical Tearfund agency after its formation in 1968. At home there was a growing interest in the needs of the homeless and the work of Shelter was warmly welcomed in the pages of the SBM. However, Scottish Baptists also created their own agencies, the Elpis Centre in Glasgow and Bethany in Edinburgh to address particular needs in their local communities. Residential homes for the elderly and the founding of the Ark Housing Association in Edinburgh to support people with mental health issues were amongst the important new initiatives begun at this time. There were many other social concerns that engaged the attentions of Scottish Baptists in these decades. It was fair to say that this network of churches was increasingly promoting a holistic gospel message in the 1960s and especially by the 1970s. Overall Scottish Baptists saw these years as a time of fresh opportunities for both evangelism and social action. Not all their efforts succeeded as they had hoped, but it was certainly not an era of religious crisis as far as they were concerned.

The 1980s began with a real sense of expectancy for Scottish Baptists and especially for their General Secretary Andrew MacRae. He had high expectations of turning the tide of numerical decline and instead finding significant shoots of recovery and spiritual vitality across Scotland. In part, some of his hopes were realised. In proportion to membership, attendance at Scottish Baptist Churches in 1984 was actually greater than in 1959. Overall, between 1980 and 1984 45% of all Protestant churchgoers belonged to churches that had grown significantly during these years. There were new church-plant congregations begun in the Dedridge area of Livingston, together with others in Kinross, Beith, Bridge of Don and Inverurie. Also in 1984, 38% of Scottish Baptist churches were increasing in size with only 10% in decline at that time. In 1980 the constitution of the new church at Bourtreehill in Irvine and the re-founding of the cause in Bo-ness were followed two years later by the launch of a new work in the Newton Mearns area on the outskirts of Glasgow. New causes were planted in Stranraer, Thurso, the Castlehill area of Bearsden, Barnton in Edinburgh and in Ellon, north of Aberdeen, which together with new or refurbished premises in other places presents a picture of important signs of spiritual growth in Scotland.

One of the most significant factors for the church-growth in the 1980s was the adoption of the three-year Simultaneous Evangelism Crusade, known as the 'Scotreach' programme in 1983. There were 144 congregations that participated fully in this programme. Ownership of this initiative by Scottish Baptists was greater than any other venture since the 1955 All Scotland Crusade led by Billy Graham. What is more, this initiative was locally driven and led to a significant number of professions of faith followed by baptism, a pattern of growth that continued up to 1991. It was the most effective mission strategy carried out by Scottish Baptist Churches since the early twentieth century. Not since the 1920s had there been such a consistent advance of the cause. There were other crusades taking place during the 1980s and the partnership with Southern Baptist church-planters had also been remarkably fruitful during the years. However, by the early 1990s there was a decline in the intensity of these mission efforts and from 1995 a slow decline in the annual statistics of Scottish Baptists.

Under the leadership of Andrew MacRae and then Peter Barber, Scottish Baptists had made significant progress in their outreach work in Scotland. They were also strongly engaged in their collaborative work with other Baptist bodies both in the United Kingdom and further afield. There was growing cooperation in different aspects of their respective ministries with fellow British Baptists and the BMS, and to reflect this the Joint Consultative Committee (JCC) was renamed the Fellowship of British Baptists (FBB). Eric Watson, by birth a Londoner, had represented Scottish Baptists at these collaborative meetings from 1971 to 1995, and the longest serving member from any member Union. In his final year of service, having stepped down from his position as Superintendent of the Baptist Union, BMS appointed him as their President and in this capacity he signed the covenant on their behalf when the FBB was launched in January 1995. Under the auspices of the JCC the various representatives had worked towards the acceptance of one another's pension schemes and parity in the setting of stipends and other allowances, together with the greater mutual acceptance of ministers.

Scottish Baptists played an increasing role in EBF life during these years. During and after the Yugoslav war of 1991 to 1995, Scottish Baptists led by Watson Moyes and Viewfield Baptist Church, Dunfermline, delivered numerous aid convoys under the auspices of the charity Dunfermline Eurosave, created for that purpose, in aid of the Croatian Christian humanitarian aid organisation Moz Blizni (My Neighbour). They also supported the Ruschlikon Theological Seminary in Zurich. A small number of Baptist theological students from Scotland carried out some of their studies in Switzerland. Both MacRae and Barber took turns as EBF Presidents and were also committed to regular attendance at its Council meetings. However, one of the highlights of this era was the hosting of the BWA Youth Congress in 1988. Eighty-two countries were represented by the nearly 7,000 delegates and Scottish Baptist young people were greatly inspired by their time spent with colleagues from all over the world. It was one of the most successful conferences hosted in the Scottish Exhibition and Conference Centre in Glasgow.

The running debate over whether Scottish Baptists should be members of ecumenical bodies in Scotland led to a change of practice in 1989 when delegates at the Annual Assembly in Edinburgh decided not to join the newly formed ACTS ecumenical body. Another area of discussion was over the propriety of women serving as pastors in Scottish Baptist churches. At the 1985 Assembly an insufficient number of delegates supported a proposal to allow women to serve in this capacity, though there was a notable first with the appointment of Marjorie McInness as the first woman vice-President of the Union in 1989. She duly served as President from the 1990 Assembly. Overall, in the 1980s and into the 1990s Scottish Baptists had good grounds for believing that the shoots of recovery for their work had been seen in both the evangelistic and social action initiatives of those years.

The 1990s was a time of significant change in Scotland. The untimely death of John Smith MP leader of the Labour Party and Peter Barber as General Secretary of the Baptist Union had both come across as a real shock in their respective spheres of service. In the wider world the failure to stop the genocide of Tutsis in Rwanda raised serious questions about international law and morality that were not easy to answer, though, by contrast, the end of apartheid in South Africa and the installation of Nelson Mandela as President had inspired many young people to believe that change for the better was possible.

Overall, in Scotland the 2002 Religious Census revealed that there had been an 18% drop in church attendance since the previous census in 1984. The period of church growth between 1984 and 1994 had been followed by years of numerical decline between 1994 and 2002. However, one encouraging statistic for Scottish Baptists was that though membership figures had continued a slow decline, attendances at Sunday worship services had increased between 1994 and 2002. A similar or even more encouraging set of statistics regarding attendance figures were recorded by some of the smaller networks of churches including the Church of the Nazarene, Pentecostals, Independent Charismatic fellowships and the newer ethnic churches. However, there was little encouragement regarding the attendance statistics by children and teenagers. A drop-out rate of 74% over eighteen years was incredibly serious and required urgent attention by all the Scottish Churches.

Bill Slack as the new General Secretary, General Director after 2003, led the Baptist Union through a period of significant change. There was a sincere attempt to overhaul all aspects of the collective witness of Scottish Baptists with a view to rebuilding afresh a more effective way of working together more suited for the twenty-first century. These structural changes included closing the regional Associations and hoping that the churches would work together more effectively in smaller cluster groups and moving towards more internet-based methods of communication and ending the production of the *SBM* in 2000. Another key task needing attention was how to address the problem of decline in the smaller churches, particularly in the Highlands and

Islands of Scotland. It was acknowledged that a great deal of energy was put into the task groups that were established and the resources spent to make progress in reversing the decline in these communities. In addition, new works began on the island of Arran and at Brae in Shetland and the reception into membership of the recently formed Lighthouse Church in Forres showed some encouraging signs of progress. In more central areas new works were also started at Sheddocksley in Aberdeen and Broadwood in Cumbernauld. An innovative new work amongst marginalised young people saw a very different kind of church launched in Bathgate and in the Borders there was encouragement with the fresh growth in the work in Selkirk and Peebles. In these times of major changes there were inevitably some disappointments over a lack of progress in some areas of Baptist witness, but there were other congregations whose ministries appeared to be more fruitful.

Under the leadership of Robert Breustedt and Gary Smith, the Step-Our Mission teams were both an encouragement to a number of local congregations and also a most effective leadership training scheme for younger leaders. David Gordon, appointed as Mission Advisor in the year 2,000, introduced a 'Seize the Day' Prayer initiative and saw a key objective of his time in office being to aid struggling churches in urban priority areas. Another important initiative he brought in during 2003 was the regional mission networkers who were appointed to assist local churches become more effective in their work. It is fair to say that less was accomplished than had been hoped for in some areas of the country despite the best efforts of the networkers, although some did accomplish a great deal, especially where the churches were all committed to engaging with the worker. In the South-West in particular both Union and non-Union churches united to work with Noel McCullins and one of the fruits of those collaborative efforts was the founding of Milestone Christian Fellowship in Girvan. Another new cause started at this time was the Garioch Church in rural Aberdeenshire. At a time when many churches were struggling to maintain let alone strengthen their witness, it was right to attempt new approaches with the recognition that not all will be successful.

Scottish Baptists until the 1990s had often struggled to gain access to the range of chaplaincy ministry positions in Scotland, which had often been almost the exclusive preserve of the Church of Scotland. However, in the last decade of the twentieth century the situation was completely transformed. Marjorie Taylor was the first Baptist hospital chaplain appointed in that century when she secured a part-time post at Hairmyres Hospital in East Kilbride in 1991. Taylor also gained the distinction in 2003, alongside Beth Dunlop, Associate pastor in Dumfries Baptist Church, of being the first women to be fully accredited as ministers in the Baptist Union of Scotland. In the next two decades an increasing number of Scottish Baptist men and women served in hospital or hospice chaplaincy posts. Military Chaplaincy posts were also accessible at this time. Neil Allison was a pioneer of so-called 'peacetime' Army Chaplaincy exercising a distinguished career over sixteen years which included frontline service in places like Bosnia and Kosovo, Iraq and Afghanistan and led to a growing number of other colleagues having similar opportunities in the twenty-first century. Alasdair Nicol was the first Baptist appointed to RAF chaplaincy and Howard Drysdale served as a Port Chaplain in Aberdeen. Workplace chaplaincy opportunities were taken in Glasgow, Stirling and Aberdeen by Scottish Baptists and Graham Bell became the full-time chaplain at H.M. Prison Glenochil in Tullibody near Stirling. This was undoubtedly a flourishing form of ministry for a growing number of Scottish Baptists in the twenty-first century

Bill Slack as General Secretary placed a high priority on good relations with other Scottish Churches. Although Scottish Baptists remained outside the ACTS network there were plenty of other opportunities to work collaboratively with Christians from other networks of Churches. One of the new steps in his time in office was the decision to join the Evangelical Alliance (EA). A number of Scottish Baptist Ministers had been associated with EA. or even served on its Executive in previous years. The decision to associate had the support of the vast majority of Scottish Baptists and communicated a clear statement that Scottish Baptists could make a positive contribution in ecumenical engagement after previous assembly debates in this area that had failed to bring agreement over the way forward in this family of churches. Slack also made a big effort to strengthen ties with European Baptists, although he declined formal appointment to offices in EBF due to the extent of his commitments at home. The work of Dunfermline Eurosave and the partnership with Croatian Baptists was particularly important in assisting with the support of refuges until they could return to their own homes or gain new ones. In addition, a number of Scottish churches twinned with Croatian counterparts that led to exchange visits and the support of various projects in Croatia. Another venture that obtained generous support from Scottish Baptists was the Kid's Aloft and Servants Aloft Ministries working with children, churches and communities affected by the Chernobyl nuclear tragedy in 1986. Scott McHaney, Minister of Crieff Baptist Church and then Colin and Cindy Mackenzie in the Montrose Baptist Church with Ronnie Cartwright from Ayr Baptist Church led this valuable work for many years until it closed in 2013. Scottish Baptists have been very cautious about commitment to formal ecumenical bodies over the years, but their willingness to work with other Christians in various forms of evangelism or social action ministries was unquestioned.

In an era of significant change, a further examination of the issue of Women in Baptist pastoral ministry was considered at the October 1999 Annual Assembly. There had been very thorough preparation of the motion to be presented and its implications for future ministry in the years leading up to this assembly. It was a big step of trust to agree to the proposal on the table that was different to the approach taken by the BUGB, and commits the

Baptist Union leaders to a position of neutrality regarding the different theological positions held by member churches and invited each local congregation to acknowledge the position taken by sister churches. For churches who held to egalitarian convictions they were now not only able to call a woman to the pastoral office as had previously been possible, but she was able to enter the accredited ministry process on the same basis as men in future years. The conclusion of debates on the two major theological issues that had divided Scottish Baptists in recent decades ensured that the churches were able to go forward into the twenty-first century as a more united body.

The last decade in Scotland has been remarkably eventful in national life with two referendums conducted on our relations with the rest of the United Kingdom and with the European Union. There have also been significant changes over the understanding of marriage and same-sex relationships. Scottish Baptists made a clear statement on their commitment to historic Christian teaching in this area in the major debate in this decade in its ranks. The process of change in the Baptist Union that had begun under the leadership of Bill Slack continued with the 2007 focus on 'Growing Healthy Churches' and with it good leaders and good followers. His colleagues on the national team also contributed to this process. *That Journey called Ministry* was a particularly influential document produced by John Greenshields and Andrew Rollinson that set a framework for future Baptist ministry within this family of churches. It was a call to continual growth and excellence, a commitment to life-long learning and a covenant to journey together. The broad acceptance of these principles laid the foundation for future changes in ministerial practices. It had led to a 2009 agreement about best practice for accredited ministers. There was from this time onwards a sustained increase in candidates applying to the Board of Ministry for acceptance into the pre-accredited ministry. For those already serving but not accredited there was now also an opportunity to receive recognition of their existing calling and of the exercise of good practice in previous years of ministry. The individual Continuing Ministry Development programme that began that year has been firmly established and welcomed within the Baptist Union. It is notable that in excess of 45% of serving ministers have entered into their pastoral calling since this transformation of ministry practice began.

A new phase of this process began with the appointment of Alan Donaldson as General Director in January 2010. He was immediately faced with a serious financial challenge as a significant potential budget deficit in the Scottish Baptist Fund that year had to be addressed. A structure review group was appointed to create a model that would ensure a financially sustainable future. This work was successful and in more recent years giving to the SBF has been very healthy, close to the figures planned for in the budgets. However, in order to make the necessary changes to create a workable structure for the Union going forward, the larger premises in Aytoun Road, Pollockshields, were sold and more modest accommodation purchased in

Speirs Wharf, Glasgow. There was also a reduction in the number of staff employed by the Baptist Union. It was a difficult time for Union staff to handle, but the new structures created have worked well over the last decade.

At the 2010 Annual Assembly Alan Donaldson expressed his real concerns that there had been an increasing loss of relationships within the Scottish Baptist family. He shared of his desire to reinstate some shared values that he hoped would be owned by the churches. An important document *An Invitation to a Journey* was published in 2011 after various drafts had been debated and reflected on in various forums. Scottish Baptists were called to be 'Intentionally Relational', 'Unashamedly Missional' and 'Creatively Rooted'. Fellowship ties were strengthened by the creation of a team of regional pastors. A Conflict Resolution Team, later named the Peaceful Transformation Team, was trained and made available to help churches work through times of change or of internal difficulties. These were some of the small building blocks put in place to maintain and strengthen healthy relationships between Scottish Baptists.

It has to be acknowledged that many churches have struggled to maintain their witness in recent years, but there are also plenty of signs of hope of new shoots of growth in other places. There have been new church-plants launched in Callander, Kintore, Partick in Glasgow, and Portlethen and other congregations constituted in Carnoustie, Crookston in Glasgow and Forfar. There are congregations that have seen significant growth in numbers such as East Mains in East Kilbride and Adelaide Place Baptist Church in Glasgow, and quite a few major building developments as churches adapted existing premises or built new ones, for example, in Dumfries, for more effective ministry in the twenty-first century. The Scottish Baptist College has also made significant changes to its programme of training for students on its Paisley campus and recently announced the creation of a northern hub to ensure its resources are more easily accessible to Baptists in northern Scotland. It has also welcomed students from a growing number of denominational backgrounds and recently announced the introduction of a PhD track by research from the 2019–2020 year. All the above examples point to encouraging preparation for future years of fruitful service

Scottish Baptists, although choosing to remain outside ACTS, have intentionally sought to have good relations with other Scottish Churches working in partnership with others where that has been possible. Examples of this include assisting in the preparations for and participating in the Edinburgh 2010 World Mission Conference. Partnership with the wider Baptist family has continued with a number of Scottish Baptist men and women playing a part in its work. It is fitting that the EBF Council will meet in Scotland in September 2019 as part of the 150th anniversary celebrations of the Baptist Union of Scotland. A new chapter of its history has begun with the appointment of Martin Hodson as the new General Director elect in June 2019. Scottish Baptists have been building on a common foundation since they agreed to work together as a family of churches in October 1869. Although they have faced many challenges there have also been many notable successes and accomplishments. It is a history of attainments that provide encouragement for believing that further steps of progress in the advance of God's kingdom can take place under their auspices, in partnership with other Scottish Christian Churches, in the years to come.

# Bibliography

## Annuals

*Baptist Handbook* (London: Various Publishers, 1873–1926).
*Baptist Union of Scotland Annual Assembly Handbook,* 1968–to the present day.
Baptist Union Council Minutes or Digest, 1869–to the present day.
*Baptist Union of Scotland Annual Reports* (Edinburgh: John Lindsay, 1869–1875) and (Glasgow: The Baptist Union of Scotland, 1876–1897).
*Northern Baptist Educational Society Reports* (*NBES*), 1806–1806 to 1842–1843.
*The Principal Acts of the General Assembly of the Free Church of Scotland,* 1901–1926.
*Report of the Baptist Home Missionary Society for Scotland chiefly for The Highlands and Islands* (Edinburgh: Various Publishers, 1829–1868) (except 1847, 1851, 1865 and 1867).
*Reports to the General Assembly of the United Free Church of Scotland* (Edinburgh: T. & A. Constable, 1901–1915).
*Report of the Schemes of the Church of Scotland for the Year 1900* (Edinburgh: William Blackwood and Sons, 1900–1925).
*Scottish Baptist Yearbook,* (Glasgow: Various Publishers, 1899–2015).
*The Church of Scotland Yearbook,* 1940–1950.
*The Scottish Temperance Annual,* 1901.

## Unprinted Primary Sources[1]

Baptist Union of Scotland Minute Book, 1869–1880.
Baptist Union of Scotland Minute Book, 1880–1885.
Baptist Union of Scotland Minute Book, 1885–1896.
Baptist Union of Scotland Minute Book, 1896–1906.
Baptist Union of Scotland Minute Book, 1906–1915.
Baptist Union of Scotland Minute Book, 1915–1926.
Baptist Union of Scotland Minute Book, 1926–1931.
Baptist Union of Scotland Minute Book, 1935–1939.
Baptist Union of Scotland Minute Book, 1939–1942.
Baptist Union of Scotland Minute Book, 1942–1945.
Baptist Union of Scotland Minute Book, 1945–1950.
'Lay Preachers' Association of the Baptist Union', Minute Book 1, 12 May, 1925 to 26 May, 1937.

---

[1] Items held in the BUS Archive in Speirs Wharf, Glasgow, unless otherwise specified.

'Lay Preachers Association of the Baptist Union', Minute Book 2, 15 September, 1937 to 24 November, 1953.
Rattray Street Baptist Church, Dundee, Minutes 1928–1945, GD/CH/B/2/1/3. The minutes are held in Dundee City Archives.
Stirling Baptist Church, Deacons' Meeting Minute Book, 5 February, 1883 to 24 November, 1902, held in Stirling City Archive.
Stirling Baptist Church, Deacons' Minute Book, 2 June, 1937 to 9 September, 1947, held in Stirling City Archive.
Stirling and Clackmannanshire Baptist Association Minute Book, May, 1909 to August, 1963.
The Baptist Pacifist Fellowship, Minute Book 1933 to 9 September 1946, held at the Angus Library, Regent's Park College, Oxford.
Minute Book of the Congregation of Baptists meeting in the Thomas Coats Memorial Church, Paisley, Volume III, 14 July, 1913–28 March, 1948.
Thomas Coats Memorial Church, Minute Book Volume IV, 14 July, 1948 to 29 March, 1973.
Thomas Coats Memorial Church (Baptist), Paisley, Deacons' Minute-Book, January, 1947 to July, 1955.

### Newspapers and Printed Journals

*@SU*, the periodical of Scripture Union Scotland, July, 2019.
*Broadcast* (Spring/Summer 2011), Issue 10, the periodical of Dundee for Christ.
*Catch the Vision*, 1988 issues of the Baptist Union of Scotland newspaper.
*Christian World* 51, no. 2,636 (10 October, 1907).
*Connect*, Scottish Baptist print and online periodical, 2000–the present day.
*Daily Mail*, 18 September, 2010, and 5 February, 2014.
*Engage*, a magazine produced by BMS World Mission.
*Free Church Magazine,* January to December, 1845, Vol. 2 (Edinburgh: John Johnstone, 1845).
*Future First*, No. 62 (April 2019).
*Life and Work*, the monthly periodical of the Church of Scotland, 1879–1948.
*Northern Baptist Education Society Reports*, 1805–1805 to 1837–1838.
*Reports of the Baptist Union of Scotland*, 1869–1899.
*Scottish Baptist Magazine* (*SBM*), 1875–2000.
*Stirling Journal*, 1853–1969.
*Stirling Observer*, 1850–2005.
*Strathspey Herald*, 6 May, 1932.
*The Baptist Times*, a periodical of the Baptist Union of Great Britain, 1925–2011.
*The Baptist Times and Freeman*, 1899–1925.
*The Courier*, Tayside and Fife regional newspaper, 23 April, 2016.
*The Freeman*, 1855–1899.

*The Herald*, Thursday 18 September, 2014.
*The Monthly Record of the Free Church of Scotland*, 1914–1918.
*The National*, 12 April, 2016.
*The Primitive Church Magazine*, n.s. 6.3 (March 1849).
*The Record of the Home and Foreign Mission Work of the United Free Church of Scotland*, 1914–1919.
*The Scotsman*, 27 January, 2000, 27 May, 2001, 17 September, 2010, and 21 November, 2013.
*The Times*, 20 September, 2010, 13 June, 2013, and 25 June, 2016.

### Contemporary Printed Material

Allan, Tom. *The Face of My Parish* (London: SCM, 1953).
—— (ed.). *Crusade in Scotland* (Glasgow: Pickering and Inglis, 1955).
*A Survey and A Call: The Report of the Foreign Mission Committee to the General Assembly of 1935* (Edinburgh: Wm Blackwood & Sons, 1935).
*Adelaide Place Baptist Church 1829–1929* (Glasgow: Adelaide Place Baptist Church, 1929).
Allan, Charles. 'VI 'Where God comes in', in Charles Allan, *The Beautiful Thing That Has Happened To Our Boys And Other Messages In War Time* (Greenock: James McKelvie & Sons, 1915).
Anon, *An invitation to a journey* (Glasgow: Baptist Union of Scotland, 2011).
Anon, *Forging the Future: Our Place in the Nation* (Glasgow: Baptist Union of Scotland, 2014).
Armstrong, R.M. *A Brief History of Alva Baptist Church 1882–1982* (private publication, 1982).
Balfour, Ian L.S. *Revival in Rose Street: Charlotte Baptist Chapel Edinburgh, 1808–2008* (Edinburgh: Rutherford House, 2008).
*Baptist Theological College of Scotland Jubilee 1894–1944* (Glasgow: Baptist Theological College of Scotland, 1944).
*Baptist Union of Scotland Temperance Committee Special Jubilee Number 1881–1931* (Glasgow: Baptist Union of Scotland, 1931).
Barclay, R.A. *The Story of Alva Baptist Church 1882–1952* (private publication, 1952).
Berry, Anne E. *Giving Hope and A Future* (Tain: Christian Focus, 2009).
Blessitt, Arthur, with Walter Wagner. *Turned on to Jesus* (London: Word Books, 1971).
*Broadcasting, Society and the Church: Report of the Broadcasting Commission of the General Synod of the Church of England* (London: Church Information Office, 1973).
*Broughty Ferry Baptist Church Jubilee Souvenir 1876–1927* (privately printed for the church, 1927).
*Conference News: 11th Baptist Youth World Conference, 27–31 July 1988, Glasgow*, Issue 3 (February 1988).

Bryant, Cyril E. (ed.). *One World, One Lord, One Witness: Official Report of the Seventh Baptist Youth World Congress, Berne Switzerland* (Waco, TX: Word Books, 1969).
——— (ed.). *Reconciliation Through Christ: Official Report of the Twelfth Congress Baptist World Alliance Tokyo, Japan* (Valley Forge, Pennsylvania: Judson Press, 1971).
———, and Ruby Burke (eds). *Celebrating Christ's Presence Through the Spirit: Official Report of the Fourteenth Congress Baptist World Alliance, Toronto, Canada* (Nashville, TN: Broadman Press, 1981).
Buchman, Frank N.D. *Remaking the World: The Speeches of Frank N.D. Buchman* (London: Blandford Press, 1947).
Burnham, George. *Billy Graham: A Mission Accomplished* (London: Marshall, Morgan and Scott, 1955).
Burrows, Edward W. *Change at Springburn: A Centenary History of Springburn Baptist Church 1892–1992* (Glasgow: Campsie Litho Ltd, 1992).
———. *'To Me To Live is Christ': A Biography of Peter H. Barber* (Milton Keynes: Paternoster, 2005).
Byford, Charles T. *Peasants and Prophets: Baptist Pioneers in Russia and South Eastern Europe* (London: The Kingsgate Press, 1911).
Chaplin, W. Knight. *Francis E. Clark* (London: The British Christian Endeavour Union, 1920).
W. Knight Chaplin and M. Jennie Street. *Fifty Years of Christian Endeavour 1881–1931* (London: The British Christian Endeavour Union, 1938).
——— (eds). *"Advance Endeavour!" Souvenir Report of the World's Convention of Christian Endeavour, London 1900* (Wilmore, KY: First Fruits Press, 2016 [1900]).
*'Christ Our Life' Addresses given and Resolutions passed at the Second Young Baptist International Congress, Zurich 1937* (London: Youth Committee of the Baptist World Alliance, 1937).
Coats, Olive Mary. *'After Twenty–One Years': Women's Auxiliary To The Baptist Union of Scotland 1909–1930* (private printing, 1930).
Coles, P. Catherine. *"To God Be The Glory": Retelling the Story of The Cornton – "A Church Within A Community"* (Stirling: private publication, 1974).
Colquhoun, Frank. *Harringay Story: A Detailed account of the Greater London Crusade 1954* (London: Hodder & Stoughton, 1955).
Crabb, Stewart. *A History of Mosspark Baptist Church* (Glasgow: private printing, 1974).
Denney, James. *War and the Fear of God* (London: Hodder & Stoughton, 1916).
*Denny Baptist Church 1891–1991* (Denny: For the Church, 1991).
Dinwiddie, Melville. *Religion by Radio* (London: George Allen & Unwin, 1968).
Dunn, Alec. *The Hebrides Revival and Awakening 1949–1953: A Short History* (s.l.: private publication, 2009).

Everson, J. 'The Scotch Baptist Churches', *The Christian Advocate and Scotch Baptist Repository*, 1.1 (March, 1849), page 1.
*Jesus Christ Living Water Baptist World Centenary Congress, Birmingham, England, July 27–31, 2005* (Falls Church, VA: BWA, 2006).
Johnston, F. *An Inquiry into the means of advancing the Baptist Denomination in Scotland* (Cupar: G.S.Tullis, 1843).
Falconer, Ronald H.W. *Message Media Mission The Baird Lectures 1975* (Edinburgh: Saint Andrews Press, 1977).
Anon, *Success and Failure of a RADIO MISSION* (London: SCM, 1951).
*Forfar Community Church: The Gutter Kirkie and The Braeheidie Schule: A Short History of the Baptist Church in Forfar* (Forfar: Forfar Community Church, 2012).
*Forging the Future: Our Place in the Nation* (Glasgow: Baptist Union of Scotland, 2014).
*Free Church of Scotland Missionary Enterprise South Africa, India, Peru 1900–1949* (Edinburgh: Free Church of Scotland, 1949).
Gammie, Alexander. *A Romance of Faith: The Story of the Orphan Homes of Scotland and The Founder* (Glasgow: Pickering and Inglis, 1937).
Geddes, C.F. *Love Lifted Me* (Glasgow: Gospel Tract Publications, 1986).
Gillies, A.D. *Pastor William Wright* (Denny: private publication, 1927).
Hamilton, Jim, Ian Roberts and Peter Sampson, *East Kilbride Baptist Church Silver Jubilee 1954–1979* (East Kilbride: private publication, 1979).
Howie, Robert. *The Churches and the Churchless in Scotland* (Glasgow: David Bryce & Son, 1893).
Hulse, Erroll. *Billy Graham: The Pastor's Dilemma* (Hounslow: Maurice Allan, 1966).
*Into All the World: A Statement on Evangelism by the Church of Scotland* (Glasgow: For the denomination, 1946).
Jarvie, Isobel. *Cumbernauld Baptist Church* (Cumbernauld: For the Church, 2002).
Jones, William. 'A Compendious Account of the Principles and Practices of the Scottish Baptists', *The Theological Repository*, 4.23 (April, 1808), 199–200.
Laing, D. (ed.). *The Letters and Journals of Robert Baillie A.M.* (3 Vols; Edinburgh: Robert Ogle, 1842).
—— (ed.). *The Works of John Knox* (Edinburgh: Printed for the Bannatyne Club, 1855).
Landels, T.D. *William Landels D.D.* (London: Cassel, 1900).
*Letters of Principal James Denney to W. Robertson Nicoll 1893–1917* (London: Hodder and Stoughton, 1920).
Lyall, Francis, and William Still, *The Gilcolmston Story 1868–1968* (Aberdeen: For the Church, 1967).
McBain, Douglas. *Fire over the Waters: Renewal Among Baptists & Others from the 1960s to the 1990s* (London: Darton, Longman and Todd, 1997).

McQuiston, T.A. *Church Evangelism* (London: Kingsgate Press, 1926).
McLean, Archibald. *The Promise that all Nations shall be brought into Subjection to Christ* (Edinburgh: J. Guthrie, 1796).
McNeish, Kenneth. *A History of Helensburgh Baptist Church 1881–1998* (Helensburgh: For the church, 1998).
Makey, W. *The Church of the Covenants 1637–1651* (Edinburgh: John Donald, 2003).
Morrison, J.H. *The Scottish Churches' Work Abroad* (Edinburgh: T. & T. Clark, 1927).
Moyes, T. Watson. *Our Place Among the Churches* (s.l.: Scottish Baptist History Project, 2013).
Muir, Augustus. *John White* (London: Hodder & Stoughton, 1958).
Murray, Derek B. *The First Hundred Years: The Baptist Union of Scotland* (Glasgow: Baptist Union of Scotland, 1969).
Murray, William W. *Queen's Park Baptist Church 1878–1978* (Glasgow: Queen's Park Baptist Church, 1978).
Mursell, Walter A. *Afterthoughts* (Paisley: Alexander Gardner, 1914).
———. *The Bruising of Belgium and other sermons during war time* (Paisley: Alexander Gardner, 1915).
———. *Echoes of Strife* (Paisley: J. and R. Parlane, 1919).
———. *Ports In The Storm* (Paisley: Alexander Gardner, 1919).
———. *The Waggon and the Star* (Paisley: Alexander Gardner, 1903).
Nordenhaug, Josef (ed.). *The Truth That Makes Men Free: Official Report of the Eleventh Congress, Baptist World Alliance, Miami Beach, Florida* (Nashville: TN: Broadman Press, 1966).
Novotny, J. *The Baptist Romance in the Heart of Europe: The Life and Times of Henry Novotny* (East Orange, NJ: Czechoslovak Baptist Convention in America and Canada, 1939).
Peckham, Colin and Mary Peckham. *Sounds from Heaven: The Revival on the Isle of Lewis, 1949–1952* (Tain: Christian Focus, 2004).
Pitcairn, T. (ed.). *Acts of the General Assembly of the Church of Scotland 1638–1842* (Edinburgh: The Edinburgh Printing and Publishing, 1843).
*Pollok Baptist Church Silver Jubilee Year 1952–1977: 25 Years of Christian Witness* (Glasgow: For the church, 1977).
*Principal Acts of the General Assembly of the Free Church of Scotland 1901* (Edinburgh: William Nimmo, 1901).
Quarrier, William. *A Narrative of Facts relative to Work done for Christ in connection with the Orphan and Destitute Children's Emigration Homes, Glasgow* (Glasgow: George Gallie, 1872).
Reith, George M. *Reminiscences of the United Free Church General Assembly 1900–1929* (Edinburgh: The Moray Press, 1929).
'Report of the Committee on Presbyterian Chaplains in the Army and the Navy', in *Report to the General Assembly of the United Free Church of Scotland*, Report 22 (Edinburgh: T. & A. Constable, 1915).

'Report of Committee on Statistics', in *Report to the General Assembly of the United Free Church of Scotland 1901*, Report 30 (Edinburgh: T. & A. Constable, 1901).

*Report of the Schemes of the Church of Scotland* (Edinburgh: William Blackwood, 1900).

Reynolds, Isobel. *Changed Days in Montrose: The Recollections of members and friends of Montrose Old Kirk 1900–1999* (Montrose: The Open Door Committee of the Church, 2000).

Rippon, John (ed.). *The Baptist Annual Register*. Volume 2 (London: Dilly, Button & Thomas, 1795).

Rollinson, Andrew, and John Greenshields, *That Journey Called Ministry* (Glasgow: Baptist Union of Scotland, 2008).

Rushbrooke, J.H. (ed.). *First European Baptist Congress* (London: Baptist Union Publications Department, 1908).

────── (ed.). *Sixth Baptist World Congress, Atlanta, Georgia, USA July 22–28, 1939* (Atlanta, GA: Baptist World Alliance, 1939).

*Scots Confession 1560 and Negative Confession 1581* (Edinburgh: Church of Scotland, 1937).

Semple, Anne. *Hillhead Baptist Church 1883–1983* (Glasgow: Hillhead Baptist Church 1983).

Shearer, John. *Modernism: The Enemy of the Evangelical Faith* (s.l.: s.n., n.d.)

──────. *The Menace of Modernism with Reply to Criticism* (s.l.: s.n., 1944).

Simpson, Alex. R. 'The Enemy', part two of three sections of a larger article 'The Church, The Nation, and the War', *The Record of the Home and Foreign Mission Work of the United Free Church of Scotland*, 15.7 (July 1915), 286–288.

Small, Ramsay G. *Broughty Ferry Baptist Church: The First Hundred Years* (privately printed for the church, 1976).

Smith, Frederic (ed.). *The Jubilee of the Band of Hope Movement* (London: United Kingdom Band of Hope Union, 1897).

*Souvenir Brochure to commemorate the Opening of East Kilbride Baptist Church 9th April 1960* (private publication, 1960).

Spear, Hilda D. *Remembering We Forget: A Background Study to the Poetry of the First World War* (London: Davis Pointer, 1979).

Spurr, F.C. *Some Chaplains in Khaki* (London: Baptist Union of Great Britain and Ireland, 1916).

Staley, Philip H. *The Scottish Baptist Lay Preachers' Association: A Historical Review* (s.l.: Scottish Baptist History Project and The Scottish Baptist Lay Preachers' Association, 1993).

Stewart, John. *Adelaide Place Baptist Church During World War II* (Glasgow: Adelaide Place Baptist Church, 1983).

Stewart, Kenneth M. *The Baptist Union of Scotland Towards 2000: A Statistical Look at Scottish Baptist Church Life in the Latter Half of the Twentieth Century* (Glasgow: Baptist Union of Scotland, n.d [1996]).

Studdert Kennedy, G.A. *Lies* (London: Hodder and Stoughton, 1919).

———. *Rough Rhymes Of A Padre* (London: Forgotten Books, 2015 [1918]).

Temple, William. *Christianity and Social Order* (London: Penguin Books, 1942).

*The Baptist Theological College of Scotland Jubilee 1894–1944* (Glasgow: private publishing, 1944).

*The Baptist Theological College of Scotland Statement By Principal and Lecturers June 1944* (Glasgow: for the College, 1944.

*The Baptist World Congress, London July 11–19, 1905* (London: Baptist Union Publication Department, 1905).

*The Church At Work* (Edinburgh: Church of Scotland, 1948).

The Church of Scotland Committee on Education. *Centenary of Education (Scotland) Act, 1872* (Edinburgh: William Blackwood & Sons, 1972).

*Tillicoultry Baptist Church: Centenary 1893–1992* (Tillicoultry: Clackmannan District Libraries, 1993).

Thomson, D.P. *Dr Billy Graham and the Pattern of Modern Evangelism* (Crieff: The Book Department St Ninians, 1966).

———. *Harnessing The Lay Forces of the Church* (Glasgow: private publication, 1955).

——— (ed.). *We Saw the Church in Action: The Press and the BBC Report on those Visitation Campaigns 1947 to 1954* (Crieff: D.P. Thomson, 1954).

Toynbee, Arnold J. *The German Terror in Belgium* (London: Hodder & Stoughty, 1917).

Urquhart, J. *The Inspiration and Accuracy of Holy Scripture* (Glasgow: Pickering and Inglis, n.d.).

———. *The Life Story of William Quarrier* (London: S.W. Partridge, n.d. [c.1901]).

Wilson, Patrick. *The Origins and Progress of the Scotch Baptist Churches from their rise in 1765 to 1834* (Edinburgh: A. Fullarton, 1844).

Winskill, P.T. *The Temperance Movement and its Workers* (4 Vols; Glasgow: Blackie & Son, 1893).

*Wishaw Baptist Church: Rooted and Built up in Christ Jesus 1871–1971* (privately printed for the church, 1971).

Yuille, George (ed.). *History of the Baptists in Scotland* (Glasgow: Baptist Union of Scotland, 1926).

## Secondary Sources
### Books

Allison, Neil E. *The Adventure of Faith: Glenrothes Baptist Church 1958–1993* (Glenrothes: Glenrothes Baptist Church, 2016).

Neil E. Allison, *The Clash of Empires 1914–1939. The Official History of the United Board Revised. Volume One* (Norfolk: The United Navy, Army and Air Force Board, 2014).

———. *The Clash of Ideologies 1939–1950: The Official History of the United Board Revised. Volume Two* (Norfolk: The United Navy, Army and Air Force Board, 2015).

———. *The Age of Conflicts 1950–2014: The Official History of the United Board. Volume Three* (Norfolk: The United Navy, Army and Air Force Board, 2018).

———. *The Scottish Thistle: Rev. Dr William (Bill) Speirs* (Dereham: private publication, 2013).

———. *'The Spirit of Cromwell': Nonconformist Chaplain's War Ministry and Experience (1914–1918)* (The Congregational Lecture 2013. London: The Congregational Memorial Hall Trust, 1978).

Allison, Neil E., and Nicola A Sherhod. *Bunyan History Padre W.J. Coates Letters from the Front* (Bedford: Bunyan Meeting, John Bunyan Museum, and the United Navy, Army and Air Force Board History Project, 2015).

Armitstead, David. *The Army of Alba: A History of the Salvation Army in Scotland, 1879–2004* (London: The Salvation Army, n.d. [2017]).

Balia, Daryl, and Kirsteen Kim (eds). *Edinburgh 2010: Volume II. Witnessing to Christ Today* (Oxford: Regnum Books, 2010).

Bardgett, Frank D. *Devoted Service Rendered* (Edinburgh: St Andrews Press, 2002).

———. *Scotland's Evangelist D.P. Thomson* (Haddington: The Handsel Press, 2010).

Bateman, Charles T. *John Clifford Free Church Leader and Preacher* (London: National Council of the Evangelical Free Churches, 1904).

Batty, Margaret. *Scotland's Methodists 1750–2000* (Edinburgh: John Donald, 2010).

Bebbington, David W. *The Nonconformist Conscience* (London: George Allen & Unwin, 1982),

——— (ed.). *The Baptists in Scotland: A History* (Glasgow: Baptist Union of Scotland, 1988).

——— (ed.). *The Dominance of Evangelicalism* (Leicester: IVP, 2005).

———, and Martin Sutherland (eds), *Interfaces: Baptists and Others* (Milton Keynes: Paternoster, 2013).

Begg, Hugh M., Chris Davey and Nancy Davey. *The Memory of Broughty Ferry* (Dundee: The Authors, 2013).

Binfield, Clyde. *George Williams and the Y.M.C.A.: A Study in Victorian social attitudes* (London: Heinemann, 1973).

Bingham, Matthew. *Orthodox Radicals* (Oxford: Oxford University Press, 2019).

Bisset, Peter. *The Kirk And Her Scotland* (Edinburgh: The Handsel Press, n.d.).

Black, C. Stewart. *The Scottish Church* (Glasgow: William Maclellan, 1952).

Bonsall, H. Edgar, and Edwin H. Robertson. *The Dream of an Ideal City Westbourne Park 1877–1977* (York: The Ebor Press, 1978).

Breitenbach, E. *Empire and Scottish Society: The Impact of Foreign Missions at Home c.1790– c.1914* (Edinburgh: Edinburgh University Press, 2009).

Brierley, Peter. *Future Church: A Global Analysis of the Christian Community to the Year 2010* (Crowborough: Monarch Books, 1998.

———. *Growth Amidst Decline: What the 2016 Scottish Church Census Reveals* (Tonbridge: ADBC Publishers, 2017).

———. *Turning the Tide: The Challenge Ahead: Report of the 2002 Scottish Church Census* (London: Christian Research, 2003).

Brierley, Peter, and Fergus MacDonald (eds). *Prospects for Scotland from a Census of the Churches in 1984* (Bromley: MARC Europe and The National Bible Society of Scotland, 1985).

——— (eds). *Prospects for Scotland 2000* (Edinburgh: National Bible Society of Scotland and London: Christian Research, 1995).

Briggs, John H.Y. *The English Baptists of the Nineteenth Century* (Didcot: Baptist Historical Society, 1994).

——— (ed.). *A Dictionary of European Baptist Life and Thought* (Milton Keynes: Paternoster, 2009).

———, and Anthony R. Cross (eds). *Baptists and the World: Renewing the Vision* (Oxford: Centre for Baptist History and Heritage Studies, Regent's Park College, 2011).

Brown, Callum. *The Death of Christian Britain: Understanding Secularisation 1800–2000* (Abingdon: Routledge, 2nd ed., 2009).

———. *Religion and Society in Scotland since 1707* (Edinburgh: Edinburgh University Press, 1997).

———. *Religion and Society in Twentieth-Century Britain* (Harlow: Pearson Educational, 2006).

Brown, Stewart J. *Providence and Empire 1815–1914* (Harlow: Pearson, 2008).

———, and George Newlands (eds). *Scottish Christianity in the Modern World* (Edinburgh: T. & T. Clark, 2000).

Buchan, John. *The Kirk in Scotland* (Dunbar: Labarum Publications, 1985).

Burleigh, J.H.S. *A Church History of Scotland* (London: Oxford University Press, 1960).

Byrne, Georgina. *Modern Spiritualism and the Church of England, 1850–1939* (Woodbridge: Boydell Press, 2010).

Cameron, J.E.M. (ed.). *Christ Our Reconciler Gospel/Church/World* (Nottingham: IVP, 2012).

Cameron, N.M de S. (ed.). *Scottish Church History & Theology* (Edinburgh: T.&T. Clark, 1993).

Carey, Hilary M. *God's Empire: Religion and Colonialism in the British World, c.1801–1908* (Cambridge: Cambridge University Press, 2011).

Ceadel, Martin. *Pacifism in Britain 1914–1945: The Defining of a Faith* (Oxford: Clarendon Press, 1980).

Anon. [Chambers, Franklin]. *Oswald Chambers His Life and Work* (London: Marshall, Morgan and Scott, 1959).

Checkland, Olive. *Philanthropy in Victorian Scotland* (Edinburgh: John Donald, 1980).
Checkland, Sydney and Olive. *Industry and Ethos: Scotland 1832–1914* (London: Edward Arnold, 1984).
Chester, Tim. *Awakening to a World of Need: The Recovery of Evangelical Social Concern* (Leicester: IVP, 1993).
Cheyne, A.C. *The Transforming of the Kirk* (Edinburgh: St Andrews Press, 1983).
Clarke, Peter. *Hope and Glory: Britain 1900–2000* (London: Penguin Books, rev. ed. 2004).
Clement, A.S. (ed.). *Great Baptist Women* (London: Carey Kingsgate Press, 1955).
Clements, K.W. *Faith on the Frontier A Life of J.H. Oldham* (Edinburgh: T. & T. Clark, 1999).
Cooper, R.E. *From Stepney to St Giles: The Story of Regent's Park College 1810–1960* (London: Carey Kingsgate Press, 1960).
Cowan, I.B. *The Scottish Reformation* (London: Weidenfeld and Nicolson, 1982).
Anthony R. Cross. (ed.). *Ecumenism and History: Studies in Honour of John H.Y. Briggs* (Carlisle: Paternoster Press, 2002).
———, and John H.Y. Briggs (ed.). *Freedom and the Powers: Perspectives from Baptist History* (Didcot: Baptist Historical Society, 2014).
———, Peter J. Morden, and Ian M. Randall (eds). *Pathways and Patterns in History: Essays on Baptists, Evangelicals, and the Modern World in Honour of David Bebbington* (London: Spurgeon's College and the Baptist Historical Society, 2015).
Cross, F.L., and E.A. Livingstone (eds). *The Oxford Dictionary of the Christian Church* (London: Oxford University Press, 2$^{nd}$ ed., 1974).
Cunnison, J., and J.B.S Gilfillan (eds). *The City of Glasgow: The Third Statistical Account of Scotland* (Glasgow: Collins, 1958).
Dahle, Margunn Serigstad, Lars Dahle and Knud Jorgensen (eds). *The Lausanne Movement: A Range of Perspectives* (Edinburgh Centenary Series, 22. Oxford: Regnum, 2014).
Davey, Nancy, and John Perkins, *Broughty Ferry Village to Suburb* (Dundee: Dundee City Council, 1976).
Davies, Rupert E., A. Raymond George and Gordon Rupp (eds). *A History of the Methodist Church in Great Britain:* Volume 3 (London: Epworth Press, 1983).
Devine, T.M. *The Scottish Nation 1700–2000* (London: Penguin, 1999).
Dickson, A., and J.H. Treble (eds). *People and Society in Scotland:* Volume 3. *1914–2000* (Edinburgh: John Donald, 1992).
Dickson, Neil T.R. *Brethren in Scotland 1838–2000* (Carlisle: Paternoster Press, 2002).

Dickson, Tony (ed.). *Scottish Capitalism: Class, State and Nation from before the Union to the Present* (London: Lawrence & Wishart, 1980).
Donaldson, G. *The Scottish Reformation* (Cambridge: Cambridge University Press, 1960).
Dowsett, Rose (ed.). *The Cape Town Commitment: A Confession of Faith and A Call to Action* (Peabody, Massachusetts: Hendrickson, 2012).
Drummond, Andrew L., and James Bulloch. *The Church in Late Victorian Scotland, 1874–1900* (Edinburgh: St Andrew Press, 1978).
Eskridge, Larry. *God's Forever People: The Jesus People Movement in America* (New York: Oxford University Press, 2013).
Etherington, N. (ed.). *Missions and Empire* (Oxford: Oxford University Press, 2005).
Ferguson, Ronald. *George MacLeod Founder of the Iona Community* (London: Collins, 1990).
Ferguson, William. *Scotland 1689 to the Present* (Edinburgh: Mercat Press, 1965).
Field, Clive D. *Britain's Last Religious Revival?* (Basingstoke: Palgrave Macmillan, 2015).
Findlay, Jr, James F. *Dwight L. Moody: American Evangelist 1837–1899* (Chicago, IL: University of Chicago Press, 1969).
Finlay, Richard. *Modern Scotland 1914–2000* (London: Profile Books, 2004).
Finstuen, Andrew, Anne Blue and Grant Wacker (eds). *Billy Graham American Pilgrim* (New York: Oxford University Press, 2017).
Fleming, J.R. *The Story of Church Union in Scotland*, (London: James Clarke, 1929).
Fraser, W. Hamish, and R.J. Morris (eds). *People and Society in Scotland: Volume 2. 1830–1914* (Edinburgh: John Donald, 1990).
Forsyth, Alexander. *Mission by the People: Re–Discovering the Dynamic Missiology of Tom Allan and His Scottish Contemporaries* (Eugene, OR: Pickwick Publications, 2017).
Francis, Leslie J., and Yaacov J. Katz (ed.). *Joining and Leaving Religion: Research Perspectives* (Leominster: Gracewing, 2000).
Gibbon, F.P. *William A. Smith of The Boys' Brigade* (Glasgow: Collins, 1934).
Gilbert, Martin. *A History of the Twentieth Century:* Volume 1. *1900–1933* (London: Harper Collins, 1997).
Goodhew, David (ed.). *Church Growth in Britain 1980 to the Present* (Farnham: Ashgate, 2012).
Gordon, James M. *James Denney (1856–1917): An Intellectual and Contextual Biography* (Carlisle: Paternoster, 2006).
Graham, C. (ed.). *Crown Him Lord of All: Essays on the Life and Witness of The Free Church of Scotland* (Edinburgh: The Knox Press, 1993).
Gray, Ernest. *A Short History of the Baptist Industrial Mission of Scotland in Nyasaland, 1895–1930* (Cambridge: Churches of Christ Historical Society, 1987).

Green, Bernard. *Crossing the Boundaries: A History of the European Baptist Federation*, (Didcot: Baptist Historical Society, 1999).
———. *Tomorrow's Man A Biography of John Henry Rushbrooke* (Didcot: Baptist Historical Society, 1997).
Griffin, Stanley C. *A Forgotten Revival East Anglia and NE Scotland, 1921* (Bromley: Day One, 1992).
Gundry, Stanley N. *Love Them In: The Life and Theology of D.L. Moody* (Grand Rapids: Baker, 1976).
Haldane, Alexander. *Robert and James Alexander Haldane* (Edinburgh: Banner of Truth Trust, 1990 [1853]).
Harvie, Christopher. *No Gods and Precious Few Heroes* (Edinburgh: Edinburgh University Press, 1993).
Hastings, Max. *Catastrophe: Europe goes to war 1914* (London: William Collins, 2013).
Heasman, Kathleen. *Evangelicals in Actions: An Appraisal of their Social Work* (London: Geoffrey Bles, 1962).
Highet, John. *The Churches in Scotland To–Day* (Glasgow: Jackson Son, 1950).
———. *The Scottish Churches: A Review of Their State 400 years after the Reformation* (London: Skeffington, 1960).
Himmelfarb, Gertrude. *Poverty and Compassion: The Moral Imagination of Late Victorians* (New York: Vintage Books, 1991).
Hocken, Peter. *Streams of Renewal: The Origins and Early Development of the Charismatic Movement in Great Britain* (Exeter: Paternoster Press, 1986).
Holland, James. *The War in the West A New History:* Volume 1. *Germany Ascendant 1939–1941* (London: Bantam Press, 2015).
Holsti, Kalevi J. *Peace and war: armed conflicts and international order 1648–1989* (Cambridge: Cambridge University Press, 1991).
Hoover, A.J. *God, Germany and Britain in the Great War* (New York: Praeger, 1989).
———. *God, Britain and Hitler in World War II: The View of the British Clergy, 1939–1945* (Westport: Praeger, 1999).
Hopkins, Mark. *Nonconformity's Romantic Generation: Evangelical and Liberal Theologies in Victorian England* (Milton Keynes: Paternoster, 2004).
Hunt, David *Reflections on Our Past: A Statistical Look at Baptists in Scotland 1892–1997* (Hamilton: Hamilton Baptist Church, 1997).
Ives, Keith A. *Voice of Nonconformity: William Robertson Nicoll and the British Weekly* (Cambridge: The Lutterworth Press, 2011).
James, Judith (ed.), and Kenneth Dix. *'Amid This Gigantic Sorrow:' The First World War and the Strict Baptist Communities* (Didcot: The Baptist Historical Society, 2018).
Johnson, W. Charles. *Encounter in London: The Story of the London Baptist Association, 1865–1965* (London: Carey Kingsgate Press, 1965).
Johnson, Todd M., and Kenneth R. Ross (eds). *Atlas of Global Christianity 1910–2010* (Edinburgh: Edinburgh University Press, 2010).

Jones, Ian. *The Local Church and Generational Change in Birmingham 1945–2000* (Woodbridge: The Boydell Press, 2012).
Jones, Keith G. *The European Baptist Federation* (Milton Keynes: Paternoster, 2009).
Jones, Rufus M. (ed.). *The Church, the Gospel and War* (London: Harper Brothers, 1948).
Jordan, E.K.H. *Free Church Unity: History of the Free Church Council Movement 1896–1941* (London: Lutterworth Press, 1956).
Kerr, David A., and Kenneth R. Ross (eds). *Edinburgh 2010 Mission Then and Now* (Oxford: Regnum Books, 2009).
Kidd, R. (ed.). *Something to Declare: A Study of the Declaration of Principle of the Baptist Union of Great Britain* (Oxford: Whitley Publications, 1996).
King, E. *Scotland Sober and Free: The Temperance Movement, 1829–1979* (Glasgow: Glasgow Museums and Art Galleries, 1979).
Koss, Stephen. *Nonconformity in Modern British Politics* (London: B.T. Batsford, 1975).
Kramer, Ann. *Conscientious Objectors of the Second World War* (Barnsley: Pen & Sword Publishers, 2013).
Krebs, Paula M. *Gender, Race, and the Writing of Empire: Public Discourse and the Boer War* (Cambridge: Cambridge University Press, 1999).
Kreitzer, Larry J. (ed.). *'Step into Your Place:' The First World War and Baptist Life & Thought* (Centre for Baptist History and Heritage Studies, 9. Oxford: Regent's Park College, 2014).
Kruppa, Patricia Stallings. *C.H. Spurgeon: A Preachers Progress* (Abingdon: Routledge, 2017 [1982]).
Kyd, James Gray (ed.). *Scottish Population Statistics* (Edinburgh: Scottish Academic Press, 1975).
Lalleman, Pieter, Peter J. Morden and Anthony R. Cross (eds). *Grounded in Grace: Essays to Honour Ian M. Randall* (Didcot: Baptist Historical Society, 2013).
Lennie, Tom. *Glory in the Glen: A History of Evangelical Revivals in Scotland 1880–1940* (Fearn: Christian Focus, 2009).
Lord, F.T. *Baptist World Fellowship: A Short History of the Baptist World Alliance* (London: Carey Kingsgate Press, 1955).
Lowry, D. (ed.). *The South African War reappraised* (Manchester: Manchester University Press, 2000).
Lumsden, Christine. *A Century of Association: 100 Years of Baptists in Edinburgh and Lothians* (Edinburgh: Strathfleet, 1995).
———. *A Rich Inheritance: Sir William Sinclair and Keiss Baptist Church* (Didcot: Baptist Historical Society, 2013).
Michael Lynch, *Scotland A New History* (London: Pimlico, 1992).
——— (ed.). *Oxford Companion to Scottish History* (Oxford: Oxford University Press, 2007).

McCasland, D. *Oswald Chambers Abandoned to God* (Grand Rapids: Discovery House Publishers, 1993).
Macdonald, Catriona M.M. *Whaur Extremes Meet Scotland's Twentieth Century* (Edinburgh: John Donald, 2009).
———, and E.W. McFarland (eds). *Scotland and the Great War* (East Linton: Tuckwell Press, 1999).
Macdonald, Finlay. *From Reform to Renewal: Scotland's Kirk Century by Century* (Edinburgh: St Andrews Press, 2017).
McFarlan, Donald M. *First For Boys: The Story of the Boys' Brigade 1883–1983* (Glasgow: Collins, 1983).
McNaughton, W.D. *Early Congregational Independency in the Highlands and Islands and North–East of Scotland* (Tiree: Trustees of Ruaig Congregational Church, 2003).
Macpherson, John M. *At the Roots of a Nation: The Story of San Andres School in Lima, Peru* (Edinburgh: Knox Press, 1993).
McMeekin, Sean. *July 1914: Countdown to War* (London: Icon Books, 2013).
Hugh McLeod, *The Religious Crisis of the 1960s* (Oxford: Oxford University Press, 2007).
——— (ed). *The Cambridge History of Christianity: World Christianities c.1914–2000* (Cambridge: Cambridge University Press, 2006).
MacLeod, J.L. *The Second Disruption* (East Linton: Tuckwell Press, 2000).
MacPherson, John. *Revival and Revival–Work: A Record of the Labours of D.L. Moody & Ira D. Sankey* (London: Morgan and Scott, n.d. [c.1876]).
Mackenzie, Agnes Mure. *Scotland in Modern Times 1720–1939* (London: W.R. Chambers, 1941).
McVicar, M. *A Great Adventure Scotland and the BMS* (Glasgow: Baptist Union of Scotland, 1992).
Magnusson, A. *The Village A History of Quarrier's* (Bridge of Weir: Quarrier's Homes, 1984).
Marwick, Arthur. *The Deluge: British Society and the First World War* (London: Macmillan, 1965).
Mason, R.A. (ed.). *John Knox and the British Reformations* (Aldershot: Ashgate, 1998).
Mechie, Stewart. *The Church and Scottish Social Development 1780–1870* (Oxford: Oxford University Press, 1960).
Mitchel, George. *Revival Man: The Jock Troup Story* (Fearn: Christian Focus, 2002).
Moody, W.R. *The Life of Dwight L. Moody* (London: Morgan & Scott, n.d. [1904]).
Morgan, Sue, and Jacqueline de Vries (eds). *Women, Gender and Religious Cultures in Britain, 1800–1940* (Abingdon: Routledge, 2010).
Morton, Andrew R. (ed.). *God's Will in a Time of Crisis: A Colloquium Celebrating the 50th Anniversary of The Baillie Commission* (Edinburgh:

Centre for Theology and Public Issues, The University of Edinburgh, 1994).
Murray, Derek B. *The First Hundred Years: The Baptist Union of Scotland* (Glasgow: Baptist Union of Scotland, 1969).
———. *The Scottish Baptist College Centenary History 1894–1994* (Glasgow: Scottish Baptist College, 1994).
Murray, Douglas M. *Rebuilding the Kirk: Presbyterian Reunion in Scotland 1909–1929* (Edinburgh: Scottish Academic Press, 2000).
Myers, J.B. (ed.). *The Centenary Celebrations of the Baptist Missionary Society 1892–1893* (London: The Baptist Missionary Society, 1893).
Orchard, Stephen, and John H.Y. Briggs (eds). *The Sunday School Movement* (Milton Keynes: Paternoster, 2007).
Ernest A. Payne, *The Baptist Union A Short History* (London: Carey Kingsgate Press, 1959).
———. *James Henry Rushbrooke 1870–1947: A Baptist Greatheart* (London: Carey Kingsgate Press, 1954).
Pennell, C. *A Kingdom United: Popular Responses to the Outbreak of the First World War in Britain and Ireland* (Oxford: Oxford University Press, 2012).
Phillips, David. *The Hungry Thirties: Dundee Between the Wars* (Dundee: David Winter & Son, 1981).
Pierard, Richard V. (ed.). *Baptists Together in Christ 1905–2005* (Falls Church, VA: Baptist World Alliance, 2005).
Pitts, W. (ed.). *Baptists and Revival* (Macon, GA: Mercer University Press, 2018).
Purves, Jim. *The Triune God and the Charismatic Movement: A Critical Appraisal of Trinitarian Theology and Charismatic Experience from a Scottish Perspective* (Carlisle: Paternoster, 2004).
Randall, Ian M. *The English Baptists of the Twentieth Century* (Didcot: Baptist Historical Society, 2005).
Ranson, Stewart, Alan Bryman and Bob Hinings. *Clergy, Ministers & Priests* (London: Routledge & Kegan Paul, 1977).
*The Baptist Theological College of Scotland Statement By Principal and Lecturers June 1944* (Glasgow: For the college, 1944).
Reader, W.J. *At Duty's Call: A Study in Obsolete Patriotism* (Manchester: Manchester University Press, 1988).
Reid, Harry. *Outside Verdict; An Old Kirk in a New Scotland* (Edinburgh: St Andrews Press, 2002).
Reith, George M. *Reminiscences of the United Free Church General Assembly (1900–1929)* (Edinburgh: Moray Press, 1933).
Reynolds, David. *The Long Shadow: The Great War and the Twentieth Century* (London: Simon & Schuster, 2013).
Ritchie, Jackie. *Floods upon the dry ground: God working among fisherfolk* (Peterhead: Peterhead Offset, 1983).

Roberts, Andrew. *A History of the English–speaking Peoples since 1900* (London: Weidenfeld and Nicolson, 2006).

———. *The Storm of War: A New History of the Second World War* (London: Allen Lane, 2009).

Roberts, Colin A. *These Christian Commando Campaigns* (London: The Epworth Press, 1945).

Roberts, Dyfed Wyn (ed.). *Revival, Renewal and the Holy Spirit* (Milton Keynes: Paternoster, 2009).

Roberts, J.M. *Twentieth Century: The History of the World 1901–2000* (London: Viking, 1999).

Keith Robbins, *The Abolition of War: The Peace Movement in Britain 1914–1919* (Cardiff: University of Wales Press, 1976).

———. *England, Ireland, Scotland, Wales: The Christian Church 1900–2000* (Oxford: Oxford University Press, 2008).

———. *History, Religion and Identity in Modern Britain* (London: The Hambledon Press, 1993).

Ross, Kenneth R. (ed.). *Roots and Fruits Retrieving Scotland's Missionary Story* (Oxford: Regnum Books, 2014).

Roy, Kenneth. *The Broken Journey: A Life of Scotland 1976–1999* (Edinburgh: Birlinn, 2016).

———. *The Invisible Spirit: A Life of Post–War Scotland 1945–75* (Edinburgh: Birlinn, 2nd ed., 2014).

Royle, Trevor. *A Time of Tyrants: Scotland and the Second World War* (Edinburgh: Birlinn, 2011).

Russell, Anthony. *The Clerical Profession* (London: S.P.C.K., 1980).

Ryrie, A. *The Origins of the Scottish Reformation* (Manchester: Manchester University Press, 2006).

Sell, Alan P.F., and Anthony R. Cross (eds). *Protestant Nonconformity in the Twentieth Century* (Carlisle: Paternoster Press, 2003).

Shepherd, P. *The Making of a Modern Denomination: John Howard Shakespeare and the English Baptists 1898–1924*, (Carlisle: Paternoster, 2001).

Shiels, W.J., and Diana Wood (eds). *Voluntary Religion* (Oxford: Basil Blackwell, 1986).

Sittser, Gerald L. *A Cautious Patriotism: The American Churches and the Second World War* Chapel Hill: The University of North Carolina Press, 1997.

Sjolinder, Rolf. *Presbyterian Reunion in Scotland 1907–1921: It's Background and Development* (Stockholm: Almquist & Wiksell, 1962).

Smith, Donald C. *Passive Obedience and Prophetic Protest: Social Criticism in the Scottish Church 1830–1945* (Bern: Peter Lang, 1987).

Smith, Mark (ed.). *British Evangelical Identities Past and Present:* Volume 1. (Milton Keynes: Paternoster, 2008).

Smout, T.C. *A Century of the Scottish People, 1830–1950* (London: Fontana, 1987).

Snape, M. *God and the British Soldier: Religion and the British Army in the First and Second World Wars* (Abington: Routledge, 2005).

Snell, K.D.M., and Paul S. Ell. *Rival Jerusalems: The Geography of Victorian Religion* (Cambridge: Cambridge University Press, 2000).

Springhall, John. *Sure and Steadfast: A History of the Boys' Brigade 1883–1983* (Glasgow: Collins, 1983).

Spurlock, Scott. *Cromwell and Scotland: Conquest and Religion 1650–1660* (Edinburgh, John Donald, 2007).

Stanley, Brian. *The History of the Baptist Missionary Society* (Edinburgh: T. & T. Clark, 1992).

———. *The World Missionary Conference, Edinburgh 1910* (Grand Rapids: Eerdmans, 2009).

Storkey, Alan. *War or Peace?* (Cambridge: Christian Studies Press, 2015).

Sutherland, John. *Godly Upbringing: A Survey of Sunday Schools and Bible Classes in the Church of Scotland* (Edinburgh: Church of Scotland Youth Committee, 1960).

Talbot, Brian R. *A Brief History of Central Baptist Association 1909–2002* (Glasgow: Baptist Union of Scotland, 2002).

———. *Search for a Common Identity: The Origins of the Baptist Union of Scotland 1800–1870* (Carlisle: Paternoster, 2003).

———. *Standing on the Rock: A History of Stirling Baptist Church 1805–2005* (Stirling: Stirling Baptist Church, 2005).

———. *The 'Fellowship of Trial': Religious Rhetoric in World War One: The Sermons and Poetry of Revd Walter Mursell* (J.H. Shakespeare Memorial Paper 1917. Helensburgh: United Board History Project, 2017).

——— (ed.). *A Distinctive People: A Thematic Study of Aspects of the Witness of Baptists in Scotland in the Twentieth Century* (Milton Keynes: Paternoster, 2014).

Thomas, Jacob. *From Lausanne to Manila: Evangelical Social Though: Models of Missions and the Social Relevance of the Gospel* (Delhi: ISPCK, 2003).

Urquhart, Anne M. *Near India's Heart* (Edinburgh: Knox Press, 1990).

Walker, David Pat. *THE BBC IN SCOTLAND: The First Fifty Years* (Edinburgh: Luath Press, 2011).

Wardin, A.W. *Baptists Around The World: A Comprehensive Handbook* (Nashville: Broadman and Holman, 1995).

Watts, Michael R. *The Dissenters from the Reformation to the French Revolution* (Oxford: Clarendon Press, 1978).

Welsby, P.A. *A History of the Church of England 1945–1980* (Oxford: Oxford University Press, 1984).

Wilkinson, Alan. *Dissent or Conform? War, Peace and the English Churches 1900–1945* (London: SCM Press, 1986).

Winter, Jay. *Sites of Memory, Sites of Mourning* (Cambridge: Cambridge University Press, 2014).

*Wishaw Baptist Church: Rooted and Built up in Christ Jesus 1871–1971* (privately printed for the church, 1971).
Wolffe, John. *God and Greater Britain: Religion and National Life in Britain and Ireland 1843–1945* (London: Routledge, 1994).
—— (ed.). *Evangelical Faith and Public Zeal: Evangelicals and Society in Britain 1780–1980* (London: SPCK, 1995).
*World Missionary Conference, 1910:* Volume 9. *The History and Records of the Conference* (edinburgh and London, n.d.).
Wormald, Jenny (ed.). *Scotland: A History* (Oxford: Oxford University Press, 2005).

## Journal Articles and Book Chapters

Allison, Neil E. 'Fighting the Good Fight: Changing Attitudes to War', in Talbot (ed.) *Distinctive People*, pp. 178–202.
——. 'Shakespeare's Man at the Front The Rev. William Cramb Charteris O.B.E., MC.,' *Baptist Quarterly*, 41.4 (October 2005), pp. 224–235.
——. 'The Spirit of Cromwell: Nonconformist Chaplains War Ministry and Experience (1914–1918)', *International Congregational Journal* 13.1 (Summer 2014), pp. 89–120.
Andrew, J.A. 'Ayrshire, Dumfries and Galloway', in Bebbington (ed.), *Baptists in Scotland*, pp. 132–145.
Anon. 'Scotland Back in the Day: Spirited Souls led the fight to defeat the demon drink', *The National*, 12 April 2016, p. 12.
Bardgett, Frank. 'The *Tell Scotland* Movement: failure and success', *Scottish Church History Society Records* 38 (2008), pp. 105–150.
Balfour, I.L.S. 'The Twentieth Century since 1914', in Bebbington (ed.). *Baptists in Scotland*, pp. 67–90.
Barclay, J.R. 'Edinburgh and Lothians', Bebbington (ed.) *Baptists in Scotland*, pp. 91–116.
Barrie, Tom. 'Airlie House in Ayr', in *Catch the Vision*, Spring 1998, n.p.
Bebbington, D.W. 'Baptist Members of Parliament in the Twentieth Century', *Baptist Quarterly* 31.6 (April 1986), pp. 252–287.
——. 'The Oxford Group Movement Between the Wars', in Shiels and Wood (eds), *Voluntary Religion*, pp. 495–507.
Black, Alasdair. 'Pour out your Spirit: Experiences of the Holy Spirit amongst Scottish Baptists in the Twentieth Century', in Talbot, *Distinctive People*, pp. 151–177.
Bone, John S. 'The Scottish Baptist Total Abstinence Society', in *The Scottish Temperance Annual*, 1901, pp. 64–67.
Briggs, John H.Y. 'From 1905 to the End of the First World War', in Pierard (ed.). *Baptists Together in Christ 1905–2005*, pp. 20–46.

Brown, Callum G. 'Religion and Secularisation', in A. Dickson and J.H. Treble (ed.). *People and Society in Scotland:* Volume 3. *1914–2000* (Edinburgh: John Donald, 1992), pp. 48–79.

Brown, Stewart J. 'Reform, Reconstruction, Reaction: The Social Vision of Scottish Presbyterianism c.1830–c.1930', *Scottish Journal of Theology* 44 (1991), pp. 489–517.

———. 'The Social Ideal of the Church of Scotland During the 1930s', in Andrew R. Morton (ed.). *God's Will in a Time of Crisis: A Colloquium Celebrating the 50th Anniversary of The Baillie Commission* (Edinburgh: Centre for Theology and Public Issues, University of Edinburgh, 1994), pp. 14–31.

———. '"A Solemn Purification by Fire": Responses to the Great War in the Scottish Presbyterian Churches 1914–1919', *Journal of Ecclesiastical History* 45.1 (January 1994), pp. 82–104.

Brown, W. Rounsfell. 'Report of the Foreign Missions Committee', *Principal Acts of the General Assembly of the Free Church of Scotland 1901* (Edinburgh: William Nimmo, 1901), p. 371.

Burrows, Edward. 'Without a vision the people perish: The distinctive contribution to Scottish Baptist life by key leaders of the Baptist Union', in Talbot (ed.). *Distinctive People*, pp. 1–23.

Campbell, R.H., and T.M. Devine. 'The Rural Experience', in W. Hamish Fraser and R.J. Morris (eds), *People and Society in Scotland:* Volume 2. *1830–1914* (Edinburgh: John Donald, 1990), pp. 46–72.

Chandler, Andrew. 'Catholicism and Protestantism in the Second World War in Europe', in Hugh Macleod (ed.). *Christianity: World Christianities c.1914–c.2000* (Cambridge: Cambridge University Press, 2006), pp. 262–284.

Clements, Keith W. 'Baptists and the Outbreak of the First World War', *Baptist Quarterly* 36.2 (April 1975), pp. 74–92.

Coats, Olive Mary. 'Elizabeth Sale: A Pioneer Among Women', in A.S. Clement (ed.). *Great Baptist Women* (London: Carey Kingsgate Press, 1955), pp. 56–63.

Cowan, L.N., and F.C. Wright. 'Central', in Bebbington (ed.). *Baptists in Scotland*, pp. 198–213.

Cross, Anthony R. '"Christ Jesus ... exalted ... farre aboue all principalities and powers": Baptist Attitudes to Monarchy, Country, and Magistracy, 1609–1644', in Cross and Briggs (ed.). *Freedom and the Powers*, pp. 3–22.

Cuthbertson, G. '"Pricking the nonconformist conscience": religion against the South African War', in D. Lowry (ed.). *The South African War reappraised* (Manchester: Manchester University Press, 2000), pp. 169–187.

Davey, Nancy. 'Broughty Ferry before 1913', in Hugh M. Begg, Chris Davey and Nancy Davey, *The Memory of Broughty Ferry* (Dundee: The Authors, 2013), pp. 1–19.

*Bibliography* 391

———. 'The Churches of Broughty Ferry', in Begg, Davey and Davey, *Memory of Broughty Ferry*, pp. 21–28.
Denney, James. 'War and the Fear of God', January 21 1915, in James Denney, *War and the Fear of God* (London: Hodder & Stoughton, 1916), pp. 27–28.
Denny, N.D. 'Temperance and the Scottish Churches, 1870–1914', *Records of the Scottish Church History Society*, 23.2, 1988, pp. 217–239.
Dickey, Brian. '"Going about and doing good": Evangelicals and Poverty c.1815–1870', in Wolffe (ed.). *Evangelical Faith and Public Zeal*, pp. 38–58.
Donaldson, Alan. 'Am I Serving a Dying Church?' in *Future First* 62 (April 2019), n.p.
Field, Clive. 'Joining and Leaving British Methodism since the 1960s', in Leslie J. Francis and Yaacov J. Katz (ed.). *Joining and Leaving Religion: Research Perspectives* (Leominster: Gracewing, 2000), pp. 57–85.
Finlay, Richard. 'Missions Overseas', in M. Lynch (ed.). *Oxford Companion to Scottish History* (Oxford: Oxford University Press, 2007), pp. 424–425.
Finlay, Richard. 'The Turbulent Century: Scotland since 1900', in Jenny Wormald (ed.). *Scotland: A History* (Oxford: Oxford University Press, 2005), pp. 241–271.
Fisher, J.S 'The North East', in Bebbington (ed.). *Baptists in Scotland*, pp. 258–279.
Garrett Jr, James Leo. 'The Internationalisation of the Alliance, 1960–1970', in Pierard (ed.). *Baptists Together in Christ 1905–2005*, pp. 128–168.
Gordon, J.M. 'The Later Nineteenth Century', in Bebbington (ed.). *Baptists in Scotland*, pp. 48–66.
Graham, W.D. 'Beyond the Borders of Scotland: The Church's Missionary Enterprise', in C. Graham (ed.). *Crown Him Lord of All: Essays on the Life and Witness of The Free Church of Scotland* (Edinburgh: The Knox Press, 1993), pp. 91–105.
Hastings, Adrian. 'British Churches in the War and Post-War Reconstruction', in Morton (ed.). *God's Will in a Time of Crisis*, 1994, pp. 4–13.
Henry, S.D. 'Scottish Baptists and the First World War', *Baptist Quarterly*, 21.2 (April 1985), pp. 52–65.
Highet, John. 'The Glasgow Churches' Campaign, 1950', in J. Cunnison and J.B.S Gilfillan (eds), *The City of Glasgow: The Third Statistical Account of Scotland* (Glasgow: Collins, 1958), 738.
———. 'Trends in Attendance and membership', in Peter Brierley and Fergus MacDonald (eds), *Prospects for Scotland From a Census of the Churches in 1984* (Bromley: MARC Europe and The National Bible Society of Scotland, 1985), pp. 8–13.
Jarvie, Isobel. 'Croatia Partnership', in *Catch the Vision* (Spring 1998), n.p.

Kernohan, R.D. 'Postscript: The Kirk since 1929', in John Buchan (ed.). *The Kirk in Scotland* (Dunbar: Labarum Publications Ltd, 1985), pp. 138–167.

Latourette, Kenneth Scott. 'Christianity and the Peace Movement', in Rufus M. Jones (ed.). *The Church, the Gospel and War* (London: Harper Brothers, 1948), pp. 93–110.

Lumsden, C. 'Her Children Arise and Call Her Blessed: The place of women in Scottish Baptist Life', in Talbot (ed.). *Distinctive People,* pp. 47–79.

Lynch, M. 'John Knox, Minister of Edinburgh and Commissioner of the Kirk', in R.A. Mason (ed.). *John Knox and the British Reformations* (Aldershot: Ashgate, 1998), pp. 242–267.

Macdonald, Catriona M.M. 'May 1915: Race, Riot and Representations of War', in Catriona M.M. Macdonald and E.W. McFarland (ed.). *Scotland and the Great War* (East Linton: Tuckwell Press, 1999), pp. 145–171.

Mackenzie, George 'Encouraging news from Selkirk: Church Growth Is Possible', in *Catch the Vision* (Spring 1998), n.p.

Macleod, James Lachlan, 'Greater Love Hath No Man Than This: Scotland's Conflicting Religious Responses to Deaths in the Great War', *The Scottish Historical Review* 81.1 (April 2002), pp. 70–96.

McLeod, Hugh. 'Sport and the English Sunday School, 1869–1939', in Stephen Orchard and John H.Y. Briggs (ed.). *The Sunday School Movement* (Milton Keynes: Paternoster, 2007), pp. 109–123.

Matheson, Peter C. 'Scottish War Sermons 1914–1919', *Records of the Scottish Church History Society* 17 (1972), pp. 203–213.

Meek Donald E. 'A Vision for the Highlands and Islands', in *Catch the Vision* (Autumn 1998), n.p.

———. 'Fishers of Men: The 1921 Religious Revival—Its Causes, Context and Transmission', *Scottish Bulletin of Evangelical Theology* 17.1 (Spring 1999), pp. 40–54.

Donald E. Meek, 'The Highlands', in Bebbington (ed.). *Baptists in Scotland*, pp. 280–308.

Morris, R.J. 'Urbanisation and Scotland', in Fraser and Morris (ed.). *People and Society in Scotland:* Volume 2. *1830–1914*, pp. 73–102.

Moyes, T. Watson. 'There is one body: Scottish Baptist Ecumenical Relations in the Twentieth Century', in Talbot (ed.). *Distinctive People*, pp. 99–127.

———. 'Scottish Baptist Reactions with the Church of Scotland in the Twentieth Century', *Baptist Quarterly*, 33.4 (October 1989), pp. 174–185.

Mumm, Susan. 'Women and philanthropic cultures', in Sue Morgan and Jacqueline de Vries (ed.). *Women, Gender and Religious Cultures in Britain, 1800–1940* (Abingdon: Routledge, 2010), pp. 54–71.

Murray, Derek B. 'Be Not Conformed but Transformed: Scottish Baptists and Social Action', in Talbot (ed.). *Distinctive People,* pp. 228–247.

———. 'The Scotch Baptist Tradition in Great Britain', *Baptist Quarterly* 33.4 (October 1989), pp. 186–198.

Murray, Jocelyn. 'Gender Attitudes and the Contribution of Women', in John Wolffe (ed.). *Evangelical Faith and Public Zeal*, pp. 97–116.

Mursell, Walter A. 'The Spirit of Discernment' [sermon in] Walter A. Mursell, *The Waggon and the Star* (Paisley: Alexander Gardner, 1903), pp. 149–162.

Newlands, George. 'John Baillie and Friends, in Germany and at War', in Stewart J. Brown and George Newlands (ed.). *Scottish Christianity in the Modern World* (Edinburgh: T. & T. Clark, 2000), pp. 133–152.

Quinn, Jack. 'Tayside', in Bebbington (ed.) *Baptists in Scotland*, pp. 236–257.

Quadrant: Special Edition: Scottish Churches Census, *Religious Trends* No. 4 (July 2003).

Porter, Andrew. 'An Overview, 1700–1914', in N. Etherington (ed.). *Missions and Empire* (Oxford: Oxford University Press, 2005), pp. 40–63.

Randall, Ian M. 'Baptists and the First World War: The Place of Pacifism', in Larry J. Kreitzer (ed.). *Step into Your Place: The First World War and Baptist Life & Thought* (Centre for Baptist History and Heritage Studies, 9; Oxford: Regent's Park Baptist College, 2014), pp. 23–39.

Richardson, A.T. 'The Later Advance: 1850–1925', in G. Yuille (ed.). *History of the Baptists in Scotland* (Glasgow: Baptist Union Publications Committee, 1926), pp. 76–88.

Riesen, R.A. 'Smith, George Adam (1856–1942)', in N.M de S.Cameron (ed.). *Scottish Church History & Theology* (Edinburgh: T.T. Clark, 1993), pp. 780–781.

Roberts, Alasdair. 'Coll MacColl (1787–1842): Son of the manse and Highland priest', *West Highland Notes & Queries*, 3.26 (October 2014), pp. 13–23.

Ross, Andrew C. 'Scottish missionary concern 1874–1914', *Scottish Historical Review* 51.151 (April 1972), pp. 52–72.

Roxburgh, Kenneth B.E. 'Eric Roberts and Orthodoxy among Scottish Baptists', *Baptist Quarterly* 39.2 (April 2001), pp. 80–95.

———. 'The Fundamentalist Controversy Concerning the Baptist Theological College of Scotland', *Baptist History and Heritage* 36.1-2 (Winter/Spring 2001), pp. 251–272.

———. 'Your Word is Truth: Theological Developments among Twentieth-Century Scottish Baptists', in Talbot (ed.). *A Distinctive People*, pp. 128–150.

Russell, Alex. 'Dedicated giving by Baptists in Scotland helps one small church to flourish', in *Catch the Vision* (Spring 1998), n.p.

Ruston, Alan. 'Protestant Nonconformist Attitudes towards the First World War', in Sell and Cross (ed.). *Protestant Nonconformity in the Twentieth Century*, pp. 240–263.

Scottish Catholic Archives, Oban Letters 1/25/6. Rev. Coll MacColl, Morar, to Bishop Andrew Scott, Greenock, 10 July 1838.

Smith, Sydney. 'Indian Missions', *Edinburgh Review* 12 April 1808 (Edinburgh: Archibald Constable, 1808), pp. 151–181.

Snape, M. 'The Great War', in McLeod (ed.). *The Cambridge History of Christianity: World Christianities c.1914–2000*, pp. 131–150.

Spitzer, Lee B. 'The Nazi Persecution of the Jews and Scottish Baptist Indignation', *Baptist Theologies* 9.2 (2017), pp. 68–84.

Stanley, Brian. 'Edinburgh 1910 and the Oikumene', in Cross (ed.). *Ecumenism and History*, pp. 89–105.

Storrar, William F. 'Liberating the Kirk: The Enduring Legacy of the Baillie Commission', in Morton (ed.). *God's Will in a Time of Crisis*, pp. 60–72.

Stowe, David. 'Rethinking 10/West Yorks at Fricourt', *Standto! The Journal of the Western Front Association* (August/September 2008), pp. 39–47.

Talbot, Brian R. 'Baptists and Other Christian Churches in the First Half of the Twentieth Century', in David W. Bebbington and Martin Sutherland (ed.). *Interfaces: Baptists and Others* (Milton Keynes: Paternoster, 2013), pp. 156–176.

———. 'Blest be the Tie that Binds: Scottish Baptists and their Relationships with Other Churches 1900–1945', in Talbot (ed.). *Distinctive People*, 80–98.

———. 'A Clear and Certain Sound: The Ministry of John Shearer, 1913–1921', in Talbot (ed.). *Standing on the Rock*, pp. 70–89.

———. 'Competing Voices: Contrasting Approaches to the Development of a Distinctive Evangelical Identity amongst Baptists in Nineteenth-Century Scotland', in Mark Smith (ed.). *British Evangelical Identities Past and Present:* Volume 1 (Milton Keynes: Paternoster, 2008), pp. 61–73.

———. '"Confronting the Powers": Baptists in Scotland prior to 1765', in Anthony R. Cross and John H.Y. Briggs (ed.). *Freedom and the Powers: Perspectives from Baptist History* (Didcot: The Baptist Historical Society, 2014), pp. 35–64.

———. 'Endure hardness as a good soldier of Jesus Christ: The Ministry of William C. Charteris O.B.E. M.C. 1921-39', in Talbot, *Standing on the Rock*, pp. 90–108.

———. 'Fellowship in the Gospel: Scottish Baptists and their Relationships with other Christian Churches', *Evangelical Quarterly* 78.4 (October 2006), pp. 341–360.

———. 'First in Jerusalem: Scottish Baptist Home Mission work in Twentieth Century Scotland', in Talbot (ed.). *Distinctive People*, pp. 203–227.

———. '"A larger outpouring of the Spirit of God": British Baptists and the "1859 Revival", with a particular focus on Scotland', in W. Pitts (ed.). *Baptists and Revival* (Macon, GA: Mercer University Press, 2018), pp. 227–241.

———. '"Preserved from Erroneous Views?": The Contribution of Francis Johnston as a Baptist Voice in the Scottish Evangelical Debate, in the mid–Nineteenth Century, on the Work of the Holy Spirit', in Dyfed Wyn Roberts (ed.). *Revival, Renewal and the Holy Spirit* (Milton Keynes: Paternoster, 2009), pp. 95–106.

———. '"Rousing the Attention of Christians": Scottish Baptists and the Baptist Missionary Society prior to the Twentieth Century', in John H.Y Briggs and Anthony R. Cross (ed.). *Baptists and the World: Renewing the Vision* (Oxford: Centre for Baptist History and Heritage Studies, 8; Oxford: Regent's Park College, 2011), pp. 51–69.

———. 'Scottish Baptists and the First World War', in Kreitzer (ed.). *'Step Into Your Place*, pp. 40–69.

———. 'Spreading the Good News from Scotland: Scottish Baptists and Overseas Mission in the first three decades of the Twentieth Century', in Cross, Morden and Randall (ed.). *Pathways and Patterns in History*, pp. 145–171.

———. 'The Struggle for spiritual values: Scottish Baptists and the Second World War', *Perichoresis* 16.4 (2018), pp. 73–94.

———. 'William Quarrier: Philanthropist and Social Reformer', *Records of the Scottish Church History Society* 39 (2009), pp. 89–129.

Tidball, Derek. 'Mainstream: "far greater ambitions"—An Evaluation of Mainstream's Contribution to the Renewal of Denominational Life, 1979–1994', in Lalleman, Morden and Cross (ed.). *Grounded in Grace*, pp. 202–222.

Watts, D.R. 'Glasgow and Dunbartonshire', in Bebbington (ed.). *Baptists in Scotland*, pp. 162–184.

———. 'Lanarkshire', in Bebbington (ed.). *Baptists in Scotland*, pp. 185–197.

Wishart, John. 'History of Fife Baptist Association', in *Fife Baptist Association: "75 Years Old"* (Anstruther: C.S. Russell & Sons, 1970), n.p.

Yi, Liu. 'From Christian Aliens to Chinese Citizens: The National Identity of Chinese Christians in the Twentieth Century, *Studies in World Christianity* 16.2 (2010), pp. 145–168.

## Unpublished Theses, Lectures and Essays

Balfour, Ian. 'Congregational Life in Twelve Central Belt Baptist Churches, 1918 to 1939', paper presented at the Scottish Baptist History Project, Stirling, 27 April 2019.

Coulter, Kenneth. 'The context of the Baptist Industrial Mission of Scotland to Nyasaland', MTh thesis, University of Aberdeen, 1989.

Hibbard, Stephen. 'History of Sheddocksley Baptist Church', presentation given at the Scottish History Project Day Conference in Crown Terrace Baptist Church Aberdeen in November 2011.

MacRae, Andrew. 'Reflections on the Baptist Union of Scotland, 1966–1980', unpublished and undated manuscript.

Rodger, Alex, Donald Stewart and Ruth Witherow, *Broughty Ferry Baptist Church 1876–1976: "These Tremendous Years"*, unpublished manuscript, 1976.

Roxburgh, Kenneth B.E. 'The Great War and the Protestant Churches of Scotland', an unpublished and undated paper.

Roxburgh, Kenneth B.E. 'The Mission of the Church in Scotland 1940–1960', an unpublished and undated paper.

Talbot, Brian R. 'Alva Baptist Church 126th Anniversary Celebrations: The Witness of Alva Baptist Church in its Community and as part of the wider Baptist witness in Central Scotland', unpublished historical lecture, 18 September 2009.

# General Index[1]

Aberdeen Baptist Churches:
   Aberdeen Christian
      Fellowship 333
   Bridge of Don BC 247, 250,
      253, 293, 328
   Bridge Community Church
      333
   Crown Terrace BC 61, 70,
      272, 351
   International BC / Hillview
      Community Church 250,
      253, 282, 291, 333
   Sheddocksley BC 287–288,
      311, 323, 365
Aberdeen, Banff, Moray and
   Inverness BA 53
ABTS, Beirut 343
Abortion 241
ACTS 272–273, 296–297, 341–
   342, 364–368
Adams, Theodore 202, 231
Adamson, William 119, 354
Advent Testimony League 131
Airdrie BC 158
Aitken, R.W. 155
All Scotland Crusade, 16, 183,
   192–195, 358, 363
Allan, Nellie 237, 361
Allan, Tom 191, 359
Allander Evangelical Church 298
Allen, William 80
Allison, Neil E. 294, 365–366
Alloa BC 205
Alness BC 217, 219, 249, 291,
   360
Alpha 287, 316
Altrincham BC 256
Alva BC 55–56, 214

*An Invitation to a Journey* 368
Anabaptists 2–4
Anderson, Anna Valberg 202
Anderson, Christopher 7–8, 38
Anderson, Hugh 38
Anderson, John 38
Anderson, Maurice and Kitty 253
Anderson, Robert 27
Andrews, Stanley 158
Angelov, Theo 310
Angola Mission 74
Angus, Joseph 57
Angus and Perthshire BA 54,
   163, 208
Annan Baptist Fellowship 254
Anstruther BC 108, 133, 294, 355
Arbroath BC 25, 33–34, 80, 254
Arakaza, Alpha 329
Argyllshire and the Isles BA 213,
   216
Ark Housing Association 240–
   241, 362
Armed Forces Chaplains 106,
   117, 171–173, 271, 353
Arton, Kathleen 311
Atholl Baptist Centre, Pitlochry
   222
Atkins, Martyn 293
Aubrey, M.E. 143
Auden, W.H. 157–158
Austin, H.W. (Bunny) 154
Ayr auxiliary of Orissa Baptist
   Mission 41–42
Ayr Baptist Churches:
   Ayr BC 52, 148, 167, 187,
      201, 250, 253–254, 289–
      292, 301–303, 310, 324,
      366

---

[1] BC stands for Baptist Church; BA stands for Baptist Association. For all other abbreviations, see "Abbreviations."

Southside BC 290, 292
Ayrshire and Dumfriesshire BA 213, 216, 253, 360

Baillie, Donald 93
Baillie John 93, 175
Baillie, Robert 2–3
Baillie Commission 175
Baker, Colin 288, 311–312
Baker, Mark and Roxanne 286, 295
Balfour, Jeremy 310
Band of Hope 66–67, 124
Banton BC 54–56
*Baptism, Eucharist and Ministry* 271–272
Baptist Academical Society 36
Baptist Advance Campaign 189–190
Baptist Industrial Mission of Scotland 74
Baptist Pacifist Fellowship 155, 356
Baptist Pioneer Mission 74
Baptist Students Association 183
*Baptist Times* 92, 95, 105, 107, 156
Baptist Union of All Russia 135
Baptist Union of Belarus 312
Baptist Union of Croatia 259, 300–302, 305
Baptist Union of Ireland 77
Baptist Union of South Africa 77, 201
Baptist Zenana Mission 42, 58, 72
Barber, Peter 17, 198, 229, 245–279, 297
Barclay, George 7, 48
Barker, Ron 253
Barr, Alex 194
Barry, David 330, 335
Bathgate BC 196–197, 288, 311, 365

Baxter, Bob 291–292, 323
Baxter, Sidlow 145, 159
BBC Scotland Radio Missions 190, 359
BCC 234–235, 27
Bean, Albert 80
Beasley–Murray, Paul 256
Beaumont, Rodney 264
Bebbington, David 11, 255
Begg, Alistair 215, 360
Begg, James 45
Belgrade BC, Serbia 230
Bell, Graham 295, 366
Bellshill BC, 52
Bennett, Dennis 224
Berggrav, Eivind 204
Berry, Alan 260, 274–275
Berry, Anne 274–275
Bethany Christian Trust 241, 274–275, 362
*Beveridge Report* 175–176
BHMS 8–9, 15, 30–34, 124–131, 355
Bible Training Institution 71, 223
BIG (Business in Glasgow) 293
Black, Alasdair 339
Black, Alex 70
Black, David 219, 223–234
Black, Robert 158
Blaikie, William 45
Blair Atholl BC 31
Blairgowrie BC 31–34
Blessitt, Arthur 225
Bloomfield, Frances 328
BMS 4, 6, 14, 40–44, 71–74, 80–83, 138–140, 203–204, 227, 233, 257–258, 266–267, 279, 286, 297–299, 308–309, 325–328, 343, 345–346, 356, 361, 363
BMS Youth Action Team 286
Bo'ness BC 54, 214, 249
Bohemian Baptist Mission 43
Bone, John 65

*General Index* 399

Bonke, Reinhard 255
Bowes, Peter 226–227, 240
Bowhill BC 54
Bowker, David 215
Bowser, Howard 39, 42, 67
Boys' Brigade 62–63, 186, 222–223, 280, 351, 358
Branderburgh / Lossiemouth BC 31
Bratton BC, Wiltshire 38
Brechin BC 220, 225
Bremner, Alexander 145
Breustedt, Robert 290–291, 312, 365
Brierley, Peter 315
Bristol Baptist College 36
Broadway BC, Isle of Man 291
Brock, William 10
Brodie, Charles 79
Brothers, Jacob 332
Brown, Alastair 247
Brown, Charles 38, 91
Brown, Chris 227
Brown, Douglas 131–133, 355
Brown, Lynne 346
Brown, Margaret 343
Brown, Raymond 256
Brown, W. Roundsfell 41
Brownies 222–223
Broxburn BC 196–197, 218
Bryan, Peter 214
BTCS /Scottish Baptist College 38, 68, 98, 130, 144–145, 198, 200, 217, 238, 267–269, 276, 279, 282, 338–339, 352, 368
Buchannan, Deans 267
Buckhaven BC 54, 331
BUGB/BUGBI 75–76, 162, 227–228, 238, 256, 308
Bujadic, Maria 301
Burns Andy, 334
Burns, Joseph 97
Burrows, Edward 267
BUW 77, 227

BWA 81, 135–136, 201–202, 230–232, 243, 260–264, 304–305, 312, 343, 361,
BWA Congress London 1905 81,
BWA Congress, Birmingham, England 2005 305
BWA Congress, Los Angeles 1985 264
BWA Congress, Miami Beach, Florida 1965 231
BWA Congress, Rio de Janeiro 1960 202
BWA Congress, Tokyo, 1970 231
BWA Congress, Toronto, 1980 231
BWA Jubilee Congress London 1955 202
BWA Youth Conference, Glasgow, 1988 18, 264–266, 363
BWA Youth Congress Zurich, 1937 134
BWA Youth Congress, Beirut 1963 231
BWA Youth Congress, Berne 1968 231
BWA Youth Congress, Stockholm, 1949 202

Callander BC 335, 368
Cameron, Ian 216, 250
Campbell, Carol 294
Campbell, Edward 190–191, 194, 219
Campbell, J. Munro 31
Campbell, Peter 87
Campbell, R.J. 101
*Canadian Baptist* 79
Canadian North–West Mission 74
CARE 241
Carey, William 40

Carlisle BC 251
Carluke BC 219, 289–290
Carnoustie BC / Community Church 329, 336
Carson, Marion 339, 343–344
Cartwright, Ronnie 303, 366
Causton, Mary 237
Cauthen, Baker 220
Cavell, Edith 104
CE 61, 194, 198, 222–223, 351, 358
Central Africa Mission 74
Ceylon and India General Mission 74
Chamberlain, Neville 152–159
Chambers, Clarence 70
Chambers, Oswald 70
Chaplin, Nurse Maise 204
Charismatic Movement 223–226
Charteris, William C. 155
Cheung, Daniel 249
Chinese Christian Fellowship 233, 249
Christian Aid 205, 235, 239, 316–317
Christian Brethren 13, 131, 272, 281, 298
*Christian World Pulpit* 158
Christianity Explored 316
Christians Against Poverty 330, 334
Christie, J. Robertson 128
Church of England 2, 63, 212
Church of Scotland 3, 16, 41, 45, 63, 73, 82, 102, 105, 106, 118, 127, 137–142, 146, 162, 165, 170, 175, 178, 181, 188–196, 236, 246
Church of the Nazarene 188, 281
Churchill, Winston 88, 146
CIM 74, 81, 140, 247, 261, 264, 308, 356
Claas, Gerhard and Regina 229, 298

Clapham Bible Training Institution 70–71
Clark, Alexander 164, 166, 170,
Clark, Bill 217, 267
Clark, Francis 61
Clements, Keith 315
Cliff College, Derbyshire 293
Clifford, John 92–93, 101
Climie, John 59
Clunie, Alastair 346
Clydebank BC 148
CMD 321–322, 339
Coats, David 202
Coats, Jervis 68, 98, 115–116
Coats, Joseph 67
Coats, Thomas (1809–1883) 67
Coats, Thomas 176
Coats, W. Holms 155, 165–166, 174, 198
Colan, Archbishop 135
College Free Church, Glasgow 62
Colonsay BC 29, 31, 285
Conference of European Churches 315
Conflict Resolution Team 327, 368
Congregational Churches / Union 7, 26, 127, 132, 137, 142, 169–173, 188, 247
Conway, R.F. 180
Conway, Samuel 133
Cook, W. Morrow 201
Cormack, David and Edith 226
Cowdenbeath BC 290
Cowie, Peter 158
Cowie, William 267
Cox, Kenneth 182
Craig, Andy 329
Craig, Mark 346
Craig, Shaun 329
Crieff BC 31, 34–35, 51, 155, 302
Crouch J. 24
Crozier, William 70

*General Index* 401

Crusade of Visitation Evangelism 190
Crusaders 66
Cubs 222–223
Culloden–Ballock BC 333
Culross, James ix, 37
Cumbernauld Baptist Churches:
    Broadwood BC 288, 365
    Cumbernauld BC 214, 218, 288, 298, 302
Cummings, Miss Elizabeth 27
Cupar BC 24, 48, 68, 158–159
Curr, Henry 200
Currie, Malcolm 346

Dalbeattie BC 216, 249, 360
Davies, Gwilym 157
De Clerk, F.W. 278
Declaration of Principle 57, 143, 199, 297, 306–307
Deep Impact 322
Denney, James 93, 103, 105,
Dennis, Simon 288
Dennison, Laurie 250
Denny BC 55, 295, 301
Denovan, Joshua 44
Dewar, A 138
Dick, Peter 326
Dickson, Delores 261
Dines, John 221
Dinwiddie, Melville 180–182, 357
Distinctive Principles of the Baptists 56–58, 144
Donald, Alan 274, 301
Donald, Charles 46
Donaldson, Alan 315, 324, 326–327, 329, 340, 343, 346, 367–368
Dougall, Anne 294
Douglas, James 38
Dovey, Campbell 155
Dowsett, Rosemary 306
Drane, John 268, 339
Drane, Olive 292, 323

Drysdale, Howard 294, 366
DuCharme, Peggy 295
Dumfries BC 52, 216, 254, 294, 324, 337, 360, 365, 368
Dunbartonshire BA 24, 213, 216, 360
Dunblane BC 55
Dundee Baptist Churches:
    Bell St / Long Wynd / Ward Road 27, 49, 90, 231, 251
    Broughty Ferry BC 26–27, 33, 51, 148, 180, 187, 302, 330–331
    Central BC 251, 329, 334
    Downfield BC 197,
    Lochee BC 27, 329
    Maxwelltown BC 147
    Rattray St BC 144, 197, 199, 204, 208, 251, 262
    St Mary's Community Church 330
Dunfermline Baptist Churches:
    Dunfermline West BC 354
    Viewfield BC 160, 223, 254, 259, 272, 300–302, 332, 357, 360, 363
Dunfermline Eurosave 301, 363, 366
Dunlop, Beth 294, 365
Dunnet, William 38
Dunoon Baptist College 13, 69–71
Dunoon BC 35, 37, 69–71, 125, 167, 216
Durno, George 38

East Kilbride Baptist Churches: 197–198, 210, 215, 218, 221–222, 359
    Calderwood BC 215, 340, 360
    East Mains BC 198, 215, 337, 360, 368
    Westwood BC 215, 360

EBF 17–18, 202, 228–229, 244, 258, 260–263, 291, 298–302, 312, 340, 343–344, 361
European Baptist Congress 78, 87, 91–92
Edinburgh and Lothians BA 54, 240, 274, 287
Edinburgh 1910 Conference 81–82
Edinburgh 2010 Conference 344–345, 368
Edinburgh Baptist Churches:
  Abbeyhill BC 54
  Barnton BC 251, 362
  Bristo BC 34, 82, 144, 153, 183, 240, 325
  Burdiehouse BC 251
  Rose Street / Charlotte Chapel 8, 19, 25, 38, 133, 145, 147, 159, 206–208, 233, 237, 251
  Craigmillar BC 219, 225, 361
  Dalkeith BC 35, 290
  Dublin Street BC 20, 25, 42, 65, 80, 274
  Duncan Street BC 70, 80
  Gorgie BC 54
  Granton BC 197
  Leith BC 24, 34, 266–267
  Marshall Street BC 68, 163
  Morningside BC 54, 219, 233, 240, 251, 253, 301
  Portobello BC 54, 130, 164, 167, 326, 334
  South Leith BC 70, 158, 241, 274
  Stenhouse–Gorgie BC 250
Edinburgh Churches Campaign 187
*Edinburgh Review* 4
Edwards, Louise 346
Ellon BC 250, 334
Elpis Centre, 250, 334, 362
'English' Particular Baptists 6–7

Erskine BC 219, 225
Eurolit 259–260
European Referendum 313
Evangelical Alliance 8, 205, 239, 272, 279, 297–298, 310, 312, 345, 366
Evangelical Baptist Fellowship Bible College 145, 200
Eyemouth Baptist Church 34

Faith Mission 127, 186, 359
Falconer, Ronnie 190
Falkirk BC 24, 251–252
FBB / FBBI 257, 299, 343, 363
Ferdinand, Archduke Franz 96
Ferguson, Gillian 325
Ferreira, Paul 203
FIEC 227
Fife and Clackmannanshire BA 54
Fife BA 53–54, 196, 291, 322
Fleming, Peter 70, 80
Flett, Oliver 37, 39
Flinders Street BC, Adelaide 80
FMB / IMB 200, 220, 253–254, 295–296,
Football chaplains 335
Forbes Mackenzie Act 65
Forbes, J.T. 87
Ford, Robert and Marsha 253
Fordyce, Elidh 329
Forfar BC /Community Church 25, 61, 218, 329–330, 368
Forgan, J.R 170
Forres BC and Lighthouse Church 31–32, 286, 295, 311, 365
Fort William BC 333
Francis, Benjamin 327, 346
Fraser–Binns, Rob 329
Fraserburgh BC 28, 108, 132, 201, 355
Fraserburgh Congregational Church 132

*General Index*

Free Church National Council 101
Free Church of Scotland 32, 41, 43, 63–64, 82, 87, 94, 103, 138, 178, 246, 268, 315, 345
Free Church *Record* 104–105
Free Presbyterian Church of Scotland 246, 260
Freemantle BC Western Australia 80
Fyfe, Mark 329

Gambling 222
Garioch Church, Aberdeenshire 379
German Baptist Mission 74
Gibb, A. Grant 91, 95
Gibson, John 26–27
Gilmour, Stuart 266
Girls' Brigade 257
Girls' Guides / Guildry 222–223
Girls' Life Brigade 222
Girvan BC / Milestone Christian Fellowship 158, 216, 292, 312, 324, 336, 365
Girvan North Parish Church 336
Glasgow BA 121–124, 183, 358
Glasgow Baptist Churches:
    Bearsden BC 216–217, 219, 247, 360
        Castlehill BC, Bearsden 253,
    Bishopbriggs BC 219, 225, 361
    Bridgeton BC 122
    Cambridge Street BC 129, 133, 167
    Cambuslang BC 133, 141, 147, 197
    Canning Street, Calton BC 34
    Castlemilk BC 219, 287
    Cathcart BC 123, 158, 197, 295, 301, 355
    Crookston BC 335–336, 368

    Dennistoun BC 224, 335, 343
    Drumchapel BC 218, 334
    Easterhouse BC 218
    Govan BC 33, 68
    Paisley Road BC / Harper Memorial BC 123, 148, 204
    Hermon BC 122, 125, 224
    Hillhead BC 63, 105, 108, 121, 123, 216, 224, 269–270, 272, 321
    Hope Street / Adelaide Place BC 10, 24, 37, 42, 48, 56–57, 63, 68, 82, 158, 163, 183, 189–190, 200, 216, 241, 249, 254, 270, 293, 296, 335, 358, 368
    St Clair Street Mission 63
    John Street BC 130
    John Knox Street BC 69, 160
    Kelvinside BC 80
    King's Park BC 302
    Knightswood BC 154, 204, 267
    Mosspark BC 123–124, 267, 355
    Newton Mearns BC 249, 251, 264–265, 290, 362
    Partick BC 123, 148, 201, 254, 289, 335, 368
    Pollok BC 197, 210
    Queen's Park BC 147, 186, 188, 200, 202, 232, 254, 287, 335
    Rutherglen BC 197
    Springburn BC 122, 224
    Victoria Place BC 63, 130, 133
    Whiteinch BC 122
Glasgow Churches Campaign (Commandos Campaign) 187–188
Glendening R.E. 99, 117, 119 354

Glenlyon BC 31
Glenrothes Baptist Churches:
　Collydean Granary BC 250, 331
　　Glenrothes BC 196–197, 210, 218, 294, 332, 359
Godden Frances and Harry 285
Goldhill BC, Buckinghamshire 224
*Good Words* 59
Gooding, Brian 335
Gordon, David 291, 293, 365
Gordon, James (Jim) 262, 272
Gore, Charles 81
Gorton, Catriona 321
Gourock BC 125, 290
Graham, Billy 16, 183, 192–195, 210, 252, 276, 358–359, 363
Graham, James (Jim) 198, 223–224, 306
Grand Ligne Mission, Quebec 44, 74
Grant Donald 38
Grant, Alexander 38
Grant, William 49, 82,
Grantown-on-Spey BC 36, 80, 142–144, 198
Gray, Jack 204
Greenock Baptist Churches:
　George Square BC 125
　Orangefield BC 125, 262
Greenshields, John 319–322, 328, 367
Greig, Sandy 216
Grey, Sir Edward 87–88
Grodno BC, Belarus 303

Haig, James 37
Hair, James 136, 153,199
Haldane, James Alexander 7–9, 36
Haldane, Robert 7–9, 29, 36
Halliday, Philip and Rosemary 346

Hamilton BC 51, 215, 296, 302, 340, 360
Hamilton, Grant and Geraldine 346
Hannen R.B. 158–159
Hardie, Alex 229
Hardie, George 194, 196–197
Harvey, Reg 257
Harvey, T.J. 200
Haus, Christoph 345
Hawick BC 24,134
Hay, William 80
Heath Gordon 215, 360
Heath, Ally 332
Helensburgh BC 51, 125, 147–148
Help for Brazil 74
Henderson, Jane 59, 350
Henderson, John R.S. 208
Henry, Sam 263
Hibbard, Geoff 309
Hibbard, Stephen 287
Hicks, David 160
Higginbottom, Richard 291
High Blantyre BC 197
Hitler, Adolph 152–160, 174, 298
HIV / AIDS 340
Hodson, Martin 328, 339, 347
Holmes, Stephen 344
Hope, Roberta 326
Hopeman BC 133, 355
Horsley J.W. 64
Horton Baptist College, Bradford 36
Hospice Movement 91, 274, 294, 365
Hospital Chaplains 38, 271, 293–294, 365
Hughey, J.D. 220
Human Fertilisation / Embryology 340
Hutcheon, Douglas, 278–279, 283,
Hutchison, Carol 287

*General Index*

Hutchison, Derek 340

ICRTG 341–342
Igoff, Boschidar 300
Illisinovic, Srecko 301
Independent Charismatic
    Churches 281, 361, 364
Indigenous Missions Project 302
Inglis, Douglas 264
Ings, James 81
International Christian College
    293
International Nepal Fellowship
    309
Inverclyde Christian Brass Band
    262
Inverkeithing BC 54
Inverness Baptist Churches:
    Castle Street BC 166
    Kinmylies BC 253, 286
Inverurie BC 247, 362
Iona Missions 191,
Irish Baptist Network 299, 312
Irvine Baptist Churches:
    Bank Street BC 28, 33, 37, 48,
        52, 70, 129, 219
    Bourtreehill BC 216, 249,
        323, 360, 362
Islay BC 219, 250, 284, 333
    Bowmore BC 31, 284
    Port Ellen BC 284

Jackson, Darrell 345
Jackson, Kenneth 274
Jago, Brian 249
Jarman, Margaret 238
JCC 257, 363
Jedburgh BC 120
Jefferson, Kenneth 330–331
Jellico, Admiral 88
Johnston, Francis 9, 19–20, 24,
    36–37, 56
Johnston, J. Bell 95
Johnston, Sir Archibald 3

Johnstone BC 201
Jones, Henry 143
Jones, Thomas 70
Jones, William 6

Karlovac BC, Croatia 259
Keiss BC 5, 31, 148, 261
Kelly, Jack 224
Kelso BC 28, 61, 71, 204
Kemp, Joseph 71
Kettle, Robert 48
Kids Aloft 302– 303
Kirkintilloch BC 155, 288, 329,
    334
Kitagaki, Muneharu 204
Knox, John 1–2,
Knox, Muriel 294
Kowloon Baptist Church, Hong
    Kong 249
Kyles, David 232

Laing, Ali 328–329
Laing, D.W. 55
Lanarkshire BA 197, 212–216,
    302, 360
Landels W.K. 43
Landels, John 43
Landels, William 39, 43, 48
Larbert BC 54, 295
Largo BC 52, 61, 253
Larkhall BC 120
Law, Alexander 158
Lead Academy 328
League of Prayer 70
Lennie, Robert 24
Leslie BC 28, 34, 53, 147, 261,
Leven BC 290
Lewis Revival 223
Lewis, Marianne 58
*Life and Work* 102–105, 162
Linwood BC 219
Lionel Fletcher Mission 121
Lismore BC 31
Lister, Thomas Whitson 28

Livingston Baptist Churches:
    Dedridge BC 247, 267, 362
    Ladywell BC 247, 282, 290
Livingstone, Ian 270–271
Lloyd–George, David 64,101
Lochgelly BC 54
Lochgilphead BC 31, 42, 216
London BA 10, 56, 348
Lotz, Denton 265
Lowestoft, London Road BC
    131–132, 355
Lutheran Churches 204–205

MacColl, Coll 4
Macdiarmid, Mrs Allan 42
MacFarlane, David and Ann 346
Macgregor, Duncan 69, 352
Macgregor, W.D. 184
MacKay, James 71
Mackenzie, Hugh 122
Mackintosh, Hugh R. 164
Mackintosh, Lachlan 36
Maclennon, Kate 292
MacLeod, George 191–192
MacLeod, John 315
MacRae, Andrew 17, 211–247,
    255, 258–262
MacSporran, John 331
MAF 266
Main, Walter 187
Mainstream 256
Mandela, Nelson 278, 364
Marshall, Matthew 332
Martin, Gordon 267–269, 276
Martin, Thomas H. 42, 57, 68,
    82, 95–96
Masih, Mahboob 287
Maxton, James 152
McCallum, Donald 183–184,
    202, 228, 235, 358
McCallum, Sir John Mills 66
McColl, Archibald 214
McConachie, W.M. 102

McCullins, Noel 289, 292, 323–
    324, 365
McDonald, Patrica 294
McDougal, Ken 224
McDougall, Vince and Sadie 286
McFarlane, Claire 290
McFarlane, Ian 333
McGregor, A.Y. 53
McGregor, Alison 267
McGuinness, J. 158
McHaney, Scott 302–303, 366
McInnes, Marjorie 270, 276
McInnes, William 175
McIntosh, Scott and D'Lisa 295
McKay, Eric 268
McKay, Mary 325
McKendrick, John 182
McKenzie, Cindy 289, 303–304,
    366
Mckenzie, Colin 303–304, 366
Mckie, Andrew 232
McKinnon, John 340
McLean, Archibald 40
Mclean, Ebenezer 24
Mcleay, D.S.K. 200
McLellan, David 346
McLellan, John 24, 68–69
McLeod, Elizabeth 138
McLeod, J.W. 235
McNair, Muriel 238
McNeill, Duncan 122
McNeill, Eileen 346
McNeill, Eleanor 285
McNeish, Norman 325–326
McNutt, Claire 331
McPhee, Mr and Mrs 250
McPherson, Lachlan 38
McQuiston, Thomas 70, 125,
    129, 170, 355
McVay, Danny and Carolyn 2
McVicar, Marjorie 140
*Medical Missionary* 71–72
Menzies, George 80

*General Index* 407

Messy Church 280, 316, 330–331, 336–337
Methodist Church 13, 50, 127, 172, 212, 224, 232, 246, 273, 314
Metrustry, T.S. 70
Mid–Century Campaign, Paisley 189
Mildmay Jewish Mission 74
Miller, Alexander B. 199
Miller, Jim 285
Miller, John 55
Miller, Stanley 112
Millport BC 125
Ministerial Association of Perthshire, Stirlingshire and Fifeshire 53
Ministerial Recognition Scheme 77
Mission Networkers 291–292
Mission to Fisher Girls 59
Mission to Lepers 74
Missionary Congress of Scottish Churches 140–141
*Missionary Herald* 71
Mitchell, George 268
Moensch, David and Laura 288, 295
Moir, Laura 329
Montgomery, H.H 81
Montrose BC 250–251, 253, 303, 366
Moody, D.L. 25, 71, 132,
Moore, John 295
Moral Rearmament 153–155
Morris, Mark 343
Morrison, Annette 310
Morrow, Jill 346
Morton, Liam 331
Motherwell BC 51–52, 97, 201, 206, 215, 224, 238, 250
Mount Morgan BC Queensland 80

Moyes, Watson 226–227, 272, 300, 363
Moz Blizni (My Neighbour) 259, 363
Mraz, Zeljko 305
Muir, Brian 272
Mull Baptist Churches:
  Bunessan BC, Mull 31, 284–285
  Tobermory BC 31
Mulraine, Brian 330
Mundie, Ian 278–279
Murdock, Campbell 248
Murray, Derek 11, 235, 274, 343
Murray, Mo 326
Murray, Mr and Mrs William 27
Murray, Stuart 293
Mursell, James 80
Mursell, Walter 14, 93–94, 99–100, 109–114, 353

Nairn BC 253, 295
Naquin, Ken 330
National Bible Society 235, 260
Neil, David 254–255
New Cumnock BC 196, 323
New Prestwick BC 148, 224, 324
Newington Free Church, Edinburgh 45
Newman, John Henry 87
Next Stage of Ministry 319
Nicol, Alasdair 294, 366
Nicoll, William Robertson 101
Nicolson, William 82
Nimmo, Adam 77
Nisbet, Mrs WA President 204
Noble, John 166
Nonconformist Conscience 107
North Africa Mission 74
North Cheam BC, Surrey 289
Northern BA 53, 166, 200, 213, 217,
Novotny, Henry 43–44,
Novotny, Joseph 43–44

Nuclear Weapons 340
Nyquist, Karl and Marilyn 295

Oakley, Ivor 268–269, 276
Oban BC 71, 333
Ohm, Sven 202, 261
Old Cumnock BC 70, 323
Oldrieve, W.T. 97
Oncken, Gerhard 129
One Step Forward 217–218
Open Doors youth project 182–183, 358
Operation Gideon 290
Operation Mobilisation 255
Original Secession Church 142
Orkney Baptist Churches:
  Burray BC 25, 31
  Eday BC 31, 218
  Kirkwall BC 31
  Sanday BC 218
  Stroma BC 29
  Stromness BC 285, 332
Orthodox Churches 81, 134, 205, 230, 314, 345
Overseas Mission 6, 40–44, 71–74, 120–121, 137–140, 203–204, 267, 308–309, 312, 354, 356
Oxford Group Movement 130

Paisley Baptist Churches:
  George Street BC 70, 147
  Glenburn BC 196–197, 218
  Victoria Place BC 24, 177, 274
  Storie Street / Thomas Coats Memorial Church 14, 37, 66, 93, 108, 147, 262, 353
Palau, Luis 276
Paraguay Mission 74
Parsons, W., Harold 163
Paterson, Ian 219
Paterson, James 37, 48, 56, 69
Pavloff, P.V. 135

Pavloff, W.G. 135
Pawlik, Z. 203
Pawson, David 224
Payne, Ernest 228
Peace Pledge Union 160
Pearl Hut, Lerwick 59
Pearson, Neil 290
Peebles BC 253, 289, 336, 365
Pentecostal Churches 281, 314, 316
Perth BC 24, 253–254, 330,
Peterhead BC 29, 51, 53, 132–133, 200, 253
Peters, Claus 90
Pilgrim Preachers 131
Pilrig Free Church, Edinburgh 45
Pirie, Jim 87
Pitlochry BC 29, 51, 222, 226–227, 330, 335
Pittenweem BC 54, 133, 355
Pollock, Lynn 262
Poona and India Village Mission 74
Pope Benedict 314
Pope John Paul II 315
Port Glasgow BC 53
Potter, Mr and Mrs 55
Primrose, Jacqueline 291, 322, 328, 340
Pula BC, Croatia 301
Purves, David 331
Purves, Jim 325, 343–344

Quarrier, William 13, 45–48, 66, 111
*Quarterly for General Readers* 71
*Quarterly for Juvenile Readers* 71
Queen of the Netherlands 154
Quinn, Jack 293

Race–Relations 96, 150, 242
Ramsay, David 290
Ramsay, Frank 136
Recall to Religion Mission 121

*General Index*

Rees, Abel 185–186
Regent's Park Baptist College, Oxford 57
Regional Associations 53–56
Regions Beyond Missionary Union 74
Reid, James 129
Reith, John 181–182
Renfrew BC 175, 304
Renfrewshire BA 213
Residential Homes for the Elderly 309–310, 362
Revival in NE Scotland 131–133
Richards, Walter 97–98
Riddell, Graeme and Jenny 346
Riddell, John 195
Ritchie, Gilbert 216–217, 219, 222, 226, 247
Robb, Douglas 204
Robb, John 250
Roberts, Eric 142–145, 151,
Rollinson, Andrew 283, 320–322, 326, 367
Rollo, P.J. 69
Roman Catholic Church 4, 81, 87, 182, 186, 205, 212, 236, 246, 272, 280, 316
Rose Mrs C.S. 58–59
Rose, Mrs Alexander 42
Rose, Mrs Hugh 42
Ross, Douglas 224
Rothesay, Ardbeg BC 34, 302
Ruden, Eric 228
Rudoi, Pavel 303
Ruma BC, Serbia 302
Rüschlikon Theological Seminary, Zurich 259–260, 268, 363
Rushbrooke, John Henry 92, 101, 135
Russel, Alex 256–257, 289
Russell, Anthony 211

Sacred Songs and Solos 25
Sale, Elizabeth 58
Salvation Army 13, 50, 132, 272, 281, 339
SAM 303–304
Same–sex relationships 313–314, 340, 367
San Pedro Mission 74
Sankey, Ira D. 25, 71, 132
Sargent, Joan 266
Saunders, Dame Cicely 274
Saunders, Dick 252
Sawyers Miss 123
Sawyers Mrs 123
SBA 9
SBLPA 237,
SBTAS 64–66
Scarcliffe, Andy 322
SCC 142, 169, 234–235,
Scobie, Geoff 268
Scofield, F.R. 158
Scotch Baptists 6–7, 76
Scott, Bishop Andrew 4
Scott, James [BUS secretary] 168
Scott, James 31–32
Scott, Lynn 326
Scott, W.R. 227
Scottish Baptist Individual Cup Association 147–148
Scottish Churches Ecumenical Committee 205
Scottish Colportage Society 187
Scottish Episcopal Church 83, 142, 188, 246, 250, 254, 281
Scottish Evangelistic Council 187
Scouts 63, 223
Scroggie, Graham 133
Scrymgeour, Edward 146
Selkirk BC 288, 312, 336, 365
Shakespeare, John Howard 58
Shanks, Jervis 38
Shaver, Vicki 262
Shearer, John 144–145, 198–200
Shearer, Nurse Mary 204
Shelter 362
Shetland BA 53, 292

Shetland Baptist Churches:
    Brae BC 286, 311, 365
    Burra BC 30
    Dunrossness BC 30
    Sandsting BC 30
    Semblester BC 30
    Spiggie BC 30
Simpson, James 26
Simpson, Sir Alex 102
Simultaneous Evangelism 251, 362–363
Sinclair, William 5
SITE programme 259–260
Skye BC 285
    Uig BC, Skye 31
Slack, Bill 247, 278–312, 318, 341, 364–367
Smith, Gary 285, 289–291, 300, 312
Smith, George Adam 56–57
Smith, Henderson 204
Smith, Joan 266
Smith, John 364
Smith, Sydney 4
Smith, William 62–63
Smithson, R.J. 162
Smyth, Stephen 342
Sneddon, Janice 238
Society for the Propagation of the Gospel at Home 7
Songulashvilli, Malkhaz 345
Soren, Joao Filson 230
Sorenson, Joel 201–202
South Africa General Mission 74
Southern Baptist Convention 200–201, 220, 253, 305
Southern Morocco Mission 74
Speirs, T. Kerr 202, 224
Speirs, William 161, 172–173
Spencer, David 329
Spezzia Mission 74
Spicak, Timothy and Ivana 305
Sprange, Harry 225, 292, 323
Spurgeon, Charles 10

Spurgeon's College, London 256
Squires, Cyril 188
St Andrews BC 61, 204, 250, 267, 290, 32
Stanley, Brian 345
Stark, J.T. 177
Step–Out Missions 290–291, 312
Stewart, Brian 287
Stewart, Douglas 150
Stewart, Florence 238
Stewart, John 255
Stewart, Shelly 346
Stewart, Thomas 123
Still, Ronald 267
Stirling and Clackmannanshire BA 54–56, 212–213, 360
Stirling Baptist Churches:
    Cornton BC 214, 290, 360
    Murray Place BC 10, 37, 55, 58–59, 133, 155, 182, 189, 213–214, 251, 274, 288, 295, 325, 329–330, 335, 350
    St Ninians BC 251
Stobo, Edward 79
Stranraer BC 250, 323, 362
Strathaven Evangelical Church 298
*Strathspey Herald* 143
Street Chaplains / Pastors 292, 334
Sunday Schools 28–29, 35, 52, 60–63, 126, 167, 184, 221, 349–351, 354, 358
Svec, Stanislav 229, 263
Swanson, R.H. 216

Tagal, Judson 266
Talbot, Brian R. 12, 288, 298, 305, 331, 343, 345
Talbot, Edward 81
Tallman, Wanda 253
Talpos, Vasile 260
Tattersall, T.N. 163

Taylor, Hudson 247
Taylor, J.D. 200
Taylor, James (Jim) 235, 239, 256,
Taylor, Marjorie 271, 293–294, 365
Tearfund 266, 362
Tell Scotland Movement 16, 190–192, 359
Temperance 13, 48–49, 64–67, 83, 114, 145–148, 151, 207, 222, 349, 351, 356
Temple, Archbishop William 175–176
Tennant, J.N. 134
*That Journey Called Ministry* 319–321, 367
*The Baptist Argus / The Baptist World* 78
*The British Weekly* 101
*The Chapel Record* 145
*The Christian World* 143
*The Christian World Pulpit* 158
*The Monthly Messenger* 59
*The Record* 104
*The Scotsman* 154–155
*The Scottish Review* 48
*The Scottish Temperance Review* 48
*The Times* 154
Theological Education 7, 9–10, 21, 36–40, 67–71, 83, 142–145, 198–200, 259–260, 267–269, 338–339, 348, 351–352
Theology to Go 328
There is Hope 254
Think Again 217
Third Lausanne Congress, Cape Town 344
Thomson, D. P. 190–191
Thomson, Gavin 33
Thomson, Ian H. 267
Thomson, P.T. 119
Thurso BC 250, 332–333
Tillicoultry BC 55, 214
Timoshenko, M. 135

Tiree BC 253, 284–285, 301, 333
Tolbert, William 230
Torbet, Gary 331
Travelling People 242
Troop, Jock 132, 355
Trusiewicz, Daniel 302
Tullibody BC 31
Tulloch, William 105
Tulloch, William 25–27, 33, 39
Tulloch, William Jr 27
TullochNET 292
Tullymet BC 31
Tunnicliffe, Jabez 66
Turnage, Loren and Cherry 250, 253
Turner, Henry 160
Twenty Schemes 329
Twerton BC, Bath 204

Uddingston BC 158, 188
Unitarians 142
United Army and Navy Board 172
United Free Church of Scotland 41, 56, 73, 93, 102, 105–106, 118, 137, 170, 333
United Mission to Nepal 309
United Presbyterian Church 41, 64, 82
University Baptist Church, Baton Rouge 232
Upton Vale Baptist Church, Torquay 256
Urban Expression 293
Urquhart, John 57
Urquhart, W.M. 136

Vale of Leven BC 52
Van Buren, Steve and Laura 296
Vellacott, Oliver 329–330
Vining, A.J. 79

WA 58–60, 177, 197–198, 214
Waddelow, Reginald 163

Wagner, Bill 253
Walcott, Mrs 42
Waldensian Mission 74
Walker, A.T. 90
Walker, D. Merrick 52
Wallis, Arthur 224
Watson, D. Eric 257, 363
Watson, Jonathan 7, 20
Watt, George 38
Waugh, Percival 34, 144
WCC 101, 171, 204–207, 209–210, 271, 359, 361
Webster, Stuart 294
WEC 187, 309, 359
Weiland J.M. 215
Weir, Lynne 346
Welsh, Fiona 346
Wesleyan Missionary Society 81
West Coast Mission 127
Westbourne Park BC, London 101
Westminster Assembly 2–3
White, John 195
White, Judy 325
White, Kathy 253
White, R.E.O. 267
White, Robert 70
Whyte, William 164, 167
Wick BC 132, 291
Wick Salvation Army 132
Wigtown BC 216, 250, 253, 360
Williams, M.J. 227
Williams, Peter 284
Williams, Stephen and Jane 346
Wills, J.O. 24
Wilson, A.A. 134
Wilson, Gena 295
WIN School 219
Wishaw BC 24, 33, 129, 215, 224, 256
Women in Ministry 18, 269–271, 276, 305–308

*Wonderlands* 71
Woods, E.B. 59
World Evangelical Alliance 205
World War One 85–116
World War Two 152–179
Wright, Douglas 294
Wright, J. Allan 154
Wright, William (Denny) 55
Wright, William 267
Wrigley, John 182
Wylie, Alexander 64, 68, 136

YMCA 62, 71, 112, 117, 197, 353
Young Worshippers League 61, 124, 223, 350
Young, Alexander 38
Young, David 32–33
Young, George 189–190
Young, James 232
Young, Kate 262
Young, Neil 291
Younger, Bob 261
Younger, Stephen 339
Youth and Children's work 60–64, 67, 168, 177, 182–186, 198, 200, 202, 210, 221–223, 225–226, 228–229, 231, 253, 255, 257, 262, 280, 285–286, 288–292, 301–302, 312, 316–317, 322, 326, 330–331, 337, 343, 350, 357–358, 363
Youth for Christ 225, 290
Youth With A Mission 225, 255
Yuille, George 11–12, 15, 37, 55, 120, 136
Yuille, Jessie 13, 58–60

Zadar BC, Croatia 301
Zagreb BC, Croatia 301
*Zenana Magazine* 71
Zodhiates, Spiros 230

www.ingramcontent.com/pod-product-compliance
Lightning Source LLC
Chambersburg PA
CBHW071227290426
44108CB00013B/1320